Human Sexuality

Human Sexuality

Louis H. Janda   **Karin E. Klenke-Hamel**

Old Dominion University

D. Van Nostrand Company
New York   Cincinnati   Toronto   London   Melbourne

Cover photo by Martin S. Halpert

D. Van Nostrand Company Regional Offices:
New York   Cincinnati

D. Van Nostrand Company International Offices:
London   Toronto   Melbourne

Copyright © 1980 by Litton Educational Publishing, Inc.

Library of Congress Catalog Card Number: 79-64470
ISBN: 0-442-25737-6

Published by D. Van Nostrand Company
135 West 50th Street, New York, N.Y. 10020

10 9 8 7 6 5 4 3 2 1

To our spouses
Meredith and Willi

Preface

Exploring the field of human sexuality can be extremely rewarding, both personally and intellectually. On a personal level, sexuality exercises a vital influence over our emotions, motivations, and interpersonal relations. In our sexual lives we express not only our basic relations to others but also the entire spectrum of our personality.

Intellectually, the study of human sexuality has become a uniquely challenging topic. Many people have contributed to the establishment of scientific foundations for investigations of sexual behavior. Prompted in part by the Kinsey reports, researchers and scholars have been responsible for an outpouring of information about sexuality over the last three decades. Sexual behavior has been studied and researched from many perspectives and by many disciplines and has gained academic respectability. In addition, "how to" books about sex have become bestsellers, and advice to readers on sexual matters has become a daily feature in many newspapers. Nevertheless, the understanding of human sexuality is still obscured by contradictions and misconceptions.

Human Sexuality is a comprehensive text with much up to date information incorporating current research. We wrote *Human Sexuality* in order to present a wide spectrum of sexual issues in an honest, nonjudgmental way. Where possible, we discuss relevant topics with reference to empirical evidence. Recognizing that certain topics, such as the biological foundations of sexuality, techniques of sexual stimulation, and types of sexual dysfunctions, need to be covered, we have included a number of nontraditional chapters dealing with the dynamics of interpersonal attraction, sex guilt, and historical and crosscultural comparisons of sexual behavior. Many topics currently under discussion—including stereotypes of sexual behavior as perpetuated by our society, nontraditional life styles, controversies over contraception, abortion, rape, and futuristic means of reproduction—are covered. The selection of topics represents our attempt to provide a new integration of the growing body of research in the area of human sexuality.

The materials are grouped around three major themes. In Part One, "Foundations," we discuss the major foundations of human sexuality from a historical, theoretical, biological, and sociocultural perspective. Part Two, "Sexual Behavior and Relationships," is devoted to the exploration of various sexual and intimate relationships, including dating, traditional marriage, emerging variant sexual styles, and sexuality in later life. Part Three, "Topics in Human Sexuality," which covers topical issues such as sex differences and sex roles, sexual guilt, and sexual decision making, reflects in part our own research interests and endeavors.

A summary and a list of references appear at the end of each chapter. A Glossary of main terms and an annotated list of Further Readings, which includes material of interest to students, are at the end of the book. An Instructor's Manual including short answer and discussion questions for each chapter and a chapter by chapter list of additional readings, is available from the publisher.

The book is intended for undergraduate courses in human sexuality taught in departments of psychology, sociology, health education, or wherever the intention is to offer a basic survey course in human sexuality.

Many people have contributed their time, suggestions, and support as we worked on this book. Joseph LoPiccolo, State University of New York at Stony Brook read a large part of the manuscript and made many sensitive and helpful suggestions. Other reviewers read selected chapters, and their suggestions and criticism were invaluable in the preparation of the manuscript. Their names and affiliations are acknowledged on a separate page.

We also appreciate the understanding of our chairman, Peter J. Mikulka, who encouraged us to carry out the project while we were also fulfilling our teaching and research duties. Our colleagues were always willing to offer their help and advice, for which we are thankful. Marsha Keilty and Beverly Stanley deserve our special thanks for typing the drafts of the manuscript. They never lost interest or enthusiasm in this task.

Several people at D. Van Nostrand Company deserve special thanks. Judith Joseph guided us throughout the development of this book and offered many valuable suggestions. Her assistant, Andrea Shefler, was always willing to help when we needed it. Harriet Serenkin helped us through the process of turning our initial drafts into a final manuscript. Two of our students, Carole Dwyer and August Zinkl, and the staff photographer for the Old Dominion University News, Don Freedman, spent many hours taking pictures, for which we are grateful.

We also wish to thank our families, to whom we owe a great deal. Meredith and Willi, our spouses, were always willing to offer their support and encouragement. Our children, Christopher, Michael, Katja, and Max were daily reminders of one aspect of the joy that can result from sexuality.

Our position in the development of this book has been that knowledge can facilitate appropriate, responsible, and gratifying sexual behavior. We hope that this book will not only add to the knowledge of readers but also help them in their understanding of men and women as sexual beings.

Critical Reviewers

Robert Athanasiou   *Albany Medical College*
Ruth H. Bleier   *University of Wisconsin, Madison*
Vera Borosage   *Michigan State University*
Ellen S. Berscheid   *University of Minnesota*
Kay Deaux   *Purdue University*
Joan DiGiovanni   *Western New England College*
Richard Kaye   *Kingsborough Community College*
Marjorie H. Klein   *University of Wisconsin, Madison*
Judith W. Leavitt   *University of Wisconsin, Madison*
Abraham Lavender   *University of Miami*
Joseph LoPiccolo   *State University of New York at Stony Brook*
William McManus   *Mercy College*
Gary Nelson   *University of Colorado*
Barry Singer   *California State University at Long Beach*
E. W. Wickersham   *Penn State University*
Steve Worchel   *University of Virginia*

Contents

Human Sexuality

Part One

Foundations

Chapter 1

The Study of Human Sexuality:
A Scientific Enterprise

Human sexuality is unique in many ways; probably no other activity plays such a large role in the lives of so many people. Our interest in sex begins in early childhood when we become interested in body parts, the differences between boys and girls, and how children are conceived or born. When we reach adolescence, we expend a great deal of energy attempting to be attractive and to attract others in romantic and sexual relationships. Our early adulthood years may be a time of experimentation, or decision making in an attempt to sort out our feelings about what type of sexual relationship suits us best. Our interest in sex is likely to continue in our later years. Many elderly people are faced with conflicts regarding their sexual needs and society's expectations of senior citizens.

The importance of sex in our lives is not limited to the direct and explicit expression of our sexuality. It can serve as a motivating force for many behaviors that, on the surface, bear little relation to sex. The advertising industry certainly believes that sex is a powerful force. Advertisements for beer, cigarettes, soap, deodorants, cars, and countless other products, hint, however subtly, that our sexuality will be enhanced if we just buy the right brand. Social scientists have speculated that sex serves as a motivating force for many other behaviors. Our desire to be successful, to earn a lot of money, or to achieve power may be influenced by our sexual natures. Henry Kissinger recognized the connection between politics and sex when he reportedly said that power is the ultimate aphrodisiac. It had also been suggested that the accomplishments that led George Washington to being known as the father of his country may be derived, in part, from his need to compensate for feelings of inadequacy about being sterile and unable to father children of his own (Colton, 1972). While various theorists disagree about the extent of its influence, it is recognized that

Figure 1.1
Sex is often used in business to get people to spend their money.
(Dwyer and Zinkl)

sexuality, to some degree, influences many aspects of our lives.

A second aspect of sex is the tremendous diversity of attitudes within our society regarding what is considered to be appropriate or inappropriate sexual behavior. At one extreme are those who contend that the only legitimate reason to have sexual intercourse is to conceive children, and even then it should not be enjoyed too much. Another point of view is that any form of sexual behavior is acceptable as long as it involves consenting adults. A bewildering variety of attitudes fall between these extremes, attitudes about premarital sexual intercourse, open marriage, bisexuality, abortion, sex education in the schools, test-tube babies— the list seems almost endless. For each issue it is not difficult to find substantial numbers of people with contradictory views.

Debates about sexual issues are likely to be intense. Typically, most individuals or groups will not engage in a calm, rational exchange of views when they attempt to resolve sexual issues. In debating the issues mentioned above it is common for some individuals to resort to name calling and even violence. To mention one example in the past decade, a group of adults at a public meeting screamed hysterically, "Kill him, kill him" about a young man who was attempting to defend the use of a four-letter word used in a local high school play (Colton, 1972). While this incident is an extreme example, it does remind us how intensely people react to sexual matters. It is hard to believe that one might have to endure threats on his or her life for using sexual words openly.

When emotional reactions are intense, it is safe to assume that such reactions signify inner conflict. This is certainly the case with regard to sex. Estimates from physicians suggest that from 10 to 15 percent of their patients have sex-related problems. This figure would probably be substantially higher if people felt freer to discuss sexual matters.

Masters and Johnson (1970) have estimated that fully one-half of all marriages experience some form of sexual difficulty. The popularity of sex manuals such as *The Sensuous Man, The Sensuous Woman, The Joy of Sex, More Joy,* and so on, would seem to indicate that large numbers of people feel either somewhat dissatisfied with their sex lives or would enjoy sex even more if they only knew what to do.

The fact that so many people find sex a source of frustration rather than a source of pleasure is disturbing because most experts believe that this need not be the case. If we were able to view sex as the natural human activity that it is, we would not feel compelled to create so many sanctions regarding the expression of our sexuality. Also, we would not be so reluctant to discuss sexual topics and provide sexual knowledge to our children. It is these taboos that can contribute to the feelings of frustration, dissatisfaction, and even fear that so many people have regarding their sexuality.

One defense against these repressive forces is knowledge. At the most basic level we must be prepared to provide our children with accurate information about sex. And we must be prepared to provide them with information that is relevant to their lives. The sex educator Sol Gordon (1976) has commented that when sex education is offered in the schools it tends to be of a highly technical nature involving endless discussions of Fallopian tubes and the like. Gordon finds this distressing; after answering thousands of handwritten anonymous questions submitted by teenagers, he has yet to encounter a single question about Fallopian tubes.

In order to provide accurate information about sex, we have to have such knowledge to begin with. This means that human sexuality must be considered a legitimate area for scientific study. Remarkably, it has only been in recent years that scientists have felt free to pursue this knowledge. Freud was labeled a pervert and a moral degenerate by his colleagues for presenting his ideas on infantile sexuality. Kinsey was threatened with loss of financial support in the 1950s after publishing his landmark research. The president of Princeton University compared Kinsey's work to "toilet-wall inscriptions." As recently as 1966, sociologist Ira Reiss commented on the low status and relative rarity of scholarly research studies on sex. He claimed that the number of objective studies of sex could be counted "on one's fingers and toes." It is, of course, impossible to disseminate accurate information about sex if such knowledge does not even exist.

Fortunately, times are changing. The study of sex is rapidly approaching scientific and academic respectability. Assistant professors in most colleges and universities no longer have to weigh tenure considerations when choosing sex as a topic of study. Not only have Masters and Johnson remained "respectable" after studying sexual intercourse in their laboratory, but countless graduate students feel free to study human sexuality for doctoral dissertations. This increase in freedom to pursue the scientific study of sex has led to tremendous increases in our knowledge during the past decade. There is still much to be learned, however, and sex will provide much excitement (intellectual and otherwise) for years to come.

The Development of Scientific Knowledge of Human Sexuality

The accumulation of scientific evidence is not immune to social and cultural influences. However much scientists try to be objective, they, too, are human and have feelings, values, and attitudes that result from the same psychosocial forces that influence everyone. Thus, while scientific knowledge may shape public attitudes about sex, the converse occurs as well. There appears to be a complex relationship between public atti-

tudes and scientific knowledge, with each having its influence on the other. Let us briefly review the history of scientific knowledge of human sexuality.

The Nineteenth Century

Although sex has only recently achieved academic and scientific respectability, a few brave physicians and scientists began to publish books and articles about sexual behavior in the latter part of the nineteenth century. The culture in which these writers lived was strongly antisexual (see Chapter 2) and their writings were an attempt to foster acceptance of the sexual nature of men and women. These early sexologists, however, were not completely free from the antisex sentiment of the times. Havelock Ellis, for example, known for his seven-volume work, *Studies of the Psychology of Sex* (1899-1928), considered himself a sexual radical. He is reported to have said, "What others have driven out of consciousness as being improper or obscene, I have maintained or even held in honor" (Colles, 1959). In spite of his attitudes, which were extremely liberal for the time, Ellis believed masturbation to be psychologically and medically dangerous. He suggested that excessive masturbation could, among other things, lead to epilepsy, acne, deafness, asthma, criminality, insanity, and feeblemindedness. The warnings of popular writers were even more forboding. Masturbation was viewed as responsible for everything from bad breath to convulsive death. These early researchers believed masturbation to be dangerous for physiological reasons. One writer suggested that the loss of one drop of semen was equivalent to the loss of sixty drops of blood (MacFadden, 1900).

Although these physicians and scientists were considered radicals at the time, their views seem extremely restrictive and conservative to us today. They argued that sexual intercourse was not sinful as long as it occurred in moderation and within the confines of a marriage. The pleasure derived from moderate marital intercourse was considered a natural component of the reproductive process and of the spiritual love between man and woman. Yet it could be overdone. An early sexologist wrote *The Virile Powers of Superb Manhood* (MacFadden, 1900) to combat ". . .that horrible curse of prudishness and the ignorance of sex it entails." This work warned about the dangers of couples giving ". . .themselves up to the embrace daily." Frequent intercourse was said to result in "the most desperate cases of paralysis and epilepsy."

These early writers perpetuated the view of women as asexual creatures. While they argued that it was normal for men to derive moderate pleasure from intercourse, "good" women derived no pleasure from sex and were interested in it only as a means of having children. This view was reflected in a marriage manual written in the late nineteenth century. It offered the following advice to husbands about the frequency of sexual intercourse: "Woman is the final umpire as to its frequency—A husband who tenderly loves a delicate wife will find no difficulty in being continent, because he loves her too well to subject her to what would be injurious" (Fowler, 1875).

It has been suggested that although these early experts were attempting to increase acceptance of sexuality, they may actually have had just the opposite effect (LoPiccolo and Heiman, 1977). They succeeded in making moderate marital sexual intercourse more acceptable, but, in effect, they prohibited many forms of sexual behavior that are considered normal and harmless today. They merely substituted one set of sanctions—the physiological and psychological—for another—that of sex as sin. Thus a person who masturbated, engaged in oral sex or any number of other activities was not necessarily sinful, but was bound to become insane or

Figure 1.2
In the Victorian era, women were thought to have little interest in sex. (Bettman Archives Inc.)

epileptic. This early "scientific" knowledge may have increased people's anxiety about sex rather than reduced it.

The Influence of Freud

In the first part of the twentieth century, scientific knowledge of sex was strongly influenced by psychoanalytic theory. Sigmund Freud's theories made a significant contribution, if for no other reason than that he emphasized the importance of sex in one's total personality. Sex was no longer viewed as a relatively discrete area of human functioning; sexual motives came to be viewed as being interwoven with virtually all aspects of personality.

Like the scientists and physicians that preceded him, Freud was influenced by his culture. Psychoanalytic theory reflects, to some degree, the antisexual nature of the times in which it was developed and, to a larger degree, prevailing antifemale attitudes.

Freud believed that heterosexual intercourse was completely normal, harmless, and, in fact, indicative of psychological maturity. However, he continued the tradition of defining "normal" sexuality in an extremely narrow fashion. Activities such as masturbation and oral sex were no longer viewed as physically dangerous but were considered symptoms of immaturity. In general, Freud viewed sexual pleasure as a potentially dangerous force. He believed that it was crucial for society to tame this energy and channel it into work or monogamous relationships.

The psychoanalytic view of women was unflattering. Freud believed that "anatomy is destiny", and the female anatomy was viewed as inferior to the male anatomy. This thesis holds many implications. To mention just one, Freud's views left women with few "psychologically healthy" ways of expressing their sexuality. Sex drive was thought to be a masculine trait, so the woman with a strong interest in sex was, at best, masculine and, at worst, perverse.

As LoPiccolo and Heiman (1977) have pointed out, the effect of Freudian theory on people who sought counseling on sexual matters was potentially devastating. Men who masturbated or engaged in sexual behavior other than coitus were told that they were immature or abnormal. It was virtually impossible for women to be reassured: both the woman unable to reach orgasm and the highly orgasmic woman might be viewed as suffering from arrested psychological development. At least one writer has suggested that the science of psychoanalysis was as harmful as nonscientific moralizing. De Beauvoir (1952) wrote: "Replacing value with authority, choice with drive, psychoanalysis offers an *Ersatz*, a substitute for morality— the concept of normality" (p. 45).

Up to this point one could reasonably argue that science had done as much to harm as to enhance human sexuality. In the first part of the nineteenth century, people worried only about the morality of their sexual behavior. With the advent of the early "experts", they had the additional concern of possible adverse physiological effects. In the early 1900s, with the rise of psychoanalysis, the question of normality of sexual behavior became a concern. In all cases the message was almost the same: sexual behavior should be limited to circumscribed types of activities; furthermore only moderate pleasure should be derived from these activites.

The Modern Era

The beginning of the modern era of science and sex is closely associated with the publication of Alfred Kinsey's two volumes, *Sexual Behavior in the Human Male* (1948) and *Sexual Behavior in the Human Female* (1953). For the first time it was possible to obtain some idea about how common various sexual behaviors were. Kinsey's findings that substantial numbers of both men and women masturbated, had premarital intercourse and extramarital affairs invalidated some earlier contentions about physical health and normality. The effect of the Kinsey data "was to normalize the sexual activities that were a part of people's sexual repertoires in spite of religion, laws and Freud" (LoPiccolo and Heiman, 1977, p. 175).

While quashing many old "scientific truths" regarding sex, the Kinsey data helped generate a few new ones. For example, although Kinsey did much to further the understanding of female sexuality, in many ways he also reinforced myths about male-female differences. His data indicating that males begin sexual activity at an earlier age, masturbate in greater numbers, and are more orgasmic than women implied that these differences are biological in origin. That is, men have the greater libido. Kinsey did not emphasize, nor did other "experts" at that time point out, that these differences could, and to a large extent probably did, reflect cultural expectations of men and women. Women had to overcome a heritage that taught them that "good" women are not interested in sex.

Another myth that originated from the Kinsey data concerned the finding that males have their highest rate of orgasm around the age of nineteen, while females have their highest rate around the age of twenty-nine. Again, this difference was interpreted as reflecting a difference in biology rather than a difference in societal expectations of men and women. That is, it is likely that the average woman reaches the peak of her interest in sex at age twenty-nine because she has to spend a number of years in a sexual relationship to overcome the antisexual attitudes learned while growing up. Yet many "experts" accepted the biological interpretation and counseled couples about how they might deal with this "innate" difference.

A second milestone of the modern era is the research of Masters and Johnson, culminating in the publication of *Human Sexual Response* (1966) and *Human Sexual Inadequacy* (1970). That these researchers were able to observe acts of sexual intercourse in the laboratory without losing their credibility attests to the cultural changes that have occurred during the past century.

Of the many contributions to the understanding of sexuality made by Masters and Johnson two are of special importance. First, the two researchers raised the sexual status of women to equivalency with that of men. They showed that during the sexual response cycle there are more similarities than differences between men and women. Orgasmic contractions of men and women occur at about the same intervals. Women were found to be able to masturbate to orgasm in about the same amount of time as men. And, perhaps most important, women were found to have a much greater capacity for multiple orgasms than men.

A second important contribution of Masters and Johnson was their emphasis on sexual pleasure. For centuries sexual pleasure was relegated to the areas of immorality, perversion, sin, and abnormality. Masters and Johnson found it necessary to *teach* the giving and receiving of pleasure in therapy. Not only did they suggest that pleasure was an acceptable goal but challenged the notion that sexual problems reflect a deep-seated psychological problem, as Freud had maintained. That is, sexual behavior is a learned skill; with accurate information about foreplay, technique, and the like, one can acquire the ability to derive and afford pleasure from sex.

Although the research of Masters and Johnson is a remarkable scientific contribution and has done much to enhance the sexuality of countless people, it, too, has been at least partially responsible for generating new fears and anxieties. This certainly is not the fault of Masters and Johnson but, rather, of the media and many self-proclaimed experts who have distorted the findings of Masters and Johnson. Their message, that it is acceptable and desirable to derive pleasure from sex, has, in many cases, been translated as "you *must* receive pleasure from sex and you *must* provide your partner with pleasure, and something is wrong with you if you don't." Popular books such as *The Sensuous Man* and *The Sensuous Woman* communicate the message to men that they are responsible for their partners' orgasms, and women are subtly—and sometimes not so subtly—informed that something is wrong with them if they do not have an orgasm (or multiple orgasms) during every act of coitus. Thus the cultural acceptance of Masters and Johnson has, in many cases, led to an increase in anxiety regarding sexual performance. This is ironic and unfortunate, because a specific goal of Masters and Johnson was to reduce such anxiety.

The Status of Current Experts

One might suppose that since the scientific study of sex has achieved respectability, it would be relatively easy to obtain good, sound information about sexual matters. Unfortunately, while such information is available, it is not always easy for the lay person to obtain; there seems to be a generous supply of inaccurate, distorted, and even harmful information. Much of this inadequate information comes from people whom society views as experts. For example, a psychiatrist who wrote a best selling book in the late 1960s that promised to tell people everything they might want to know about sex, asserted that a husband's impotence is a sure sign that he does not love his wife. Not only is such a conclusion totally without merit; it is potentially destructive. Couples with a sexual dysfunction are probably already experiencing a strain in their relationship and do not need an "expert" to tell them that their problem is proof that no love exists.

A major problem is that many people who are considered experts in human sexuality simply do not have sufficient training in the field. Patrick McGrady (1972) has written about the sometimes incredible ignorance about sex that exists within the medical profession. As recently as 1959, a survey indicated that half of graduating medical school students believed that masturbation resulted in mental illness. This ignorance is inexcusable, since many people consult their physician about sexual matters. Fortunately, the medical profession has recognized the problem and has begun to deal with it. In the past decade or two, many medical schools have initiated courses in human sexuality.

The lack of guidelines for qualifications is a major problem in the field of sex therapy. LoPiccolo (1978), in a review of this issue, pointed out that in most states anyone can legally advertise and practice as a "sex therapist" with no training whatsoever. Furthermore, several organizations offer "training" that is minimal in sex therapy. In some organizations it is possible to receive an impressive-looking diploma, for example, certifying one's status as a trained sex thera-

pist after attending a one-day workshop with perhaps a hundred other people.

Another problem is that many experts seem to be unable to separate their own values from the counsel they provide clients. One example, provided by the American Medical Association, concerned a woman who asked her physician what fellatio meant. The physician defined it (mouth contact with the penis) and asserted that only homosexuals and perverts did that. The woman, who had been enjoying this practice with her husband, eventually saw a psychiatrist for feelings of guilt and shame about her "perversion" (Myers, 1976).

We do not mean to paint an overly pessimistic picture. There are many highly qualified psychologists and psychiatrists who are prepared to deal with sexual issues in a thoroughly competent manner. There are also books written for the general public that provide accurate, scientifically sound information. However, the problem of finding the best available advice does exist. Potential consumers of sex therapy or sex information must be prepared to evaluate critically what they are getting.

Needed: A Multidisciplinary Approach to Human Sexuality

Part of the intellectual appeal associated with sex is that it requires a very broad perspective. No single scientific discipline can encompass this subject. To illustrate this consider the following case history of an average married couple.

Case 1.1
The Case of Mr. and Mrs. Smith

Mr. and Mrs. Smith met when they were both juniors at a state university. They were both history majors and had taken several courses together before Mr. Smith asked his future wife for a date. Their relationship progressed quickly. Within a few months they decided that they loved each other and began to discuss the possibility of marriage.

During their courtship Mr. Smith made many tentative sexual advances, but Mrs. Smith insisted that premarital sex was wrong and that she would have intercourse only with her husband. She did acquiesce, however, after Mr. Smith proposed and they set a wedding date for shortly after their college graduation. Mrs. Smith did not particularly enjoy their sexual encounters and experienced some guilt over them, but decided that it was acceptable since they were engaged.

Upon graduation they did marry, and both obtained jobs teaching. After several months Mrs. Smith began to find their sexual relationship more rewarding and started to take a more active role in their encounters. This caused some concern in Mr. Smith, who had grown up believing that "nice" girls have little interest in sex and shouldn't enjoy it too much. Eventually he discussed his concerns with a friend who had done some graduate work in psychology and was assured that it was pefectly normal for his wife to have sexual feelings and desires. After reading several books that had been recommended to him, Mr. Smith began to realize that his sex life could become even more rewarding because his wife was becoming an eager and active participant.

After two years of marriage Mrs. Smith gave birth to their first child. Both parents were excited about the addition to the family, and Mrs. Smith resigned from her teaching position to become a fulltime mother and homemaker. The birth of the child marked an abrupt change in Mr. and Mrs. Smith's sex life. Mrs. Smith lost all interest in sex and was quite resistant to her husband's advances. Mr. Smith was hurt by his wife's rejection but was willing to give her time to adjust. Their relationship in general began to show signs of strain over the next year, but gradually began

to improve. Mrs. Smith's interest in sex was rekindled, and within a few months their sex life was better than ever.

After they had been married for six years Mr. Smith began to experience some feelings of dissatisfaction with their sex life. Although there were no apparent problems, he missed the sense of excitement and eager anticipation he had felt during the early years of their marriage. Once again he read a few recently published books about sexual techniques and realized that he and his wife had been unnecessarily restricting the range of their sexual activities. He discussed with his wife the possibility of enlarging their sexual repertory by trying oral sex, more exotic sexual positions, and by enacting some of their fantasies. Mrs. Smith was concerned about the morality of some of these activities. However, after discussing her feelings with her gynecologist, who was well informed and understanding, she agreed to give it a try. The results were gratifying, and both Mr. and Mrs. Smith were pleased with the renewed excitement in their sex lives.

Their marriage and sex life went smoothly for a number of years until, after nineteen years of marriage, Mr. Smith began to develop a sexual problem. He held an administrative position that required him to attend many business lunches and cocktail parties. One night, after a three-martini lunch, a cocktail party at which he had several drinks, and dinner with his wife during which he consumed most of a bottle of wine, he was unable to obtain an erection when he attempted to have intercourse. Mr. Smith was extremely concerned since nothing like this had happened before. Also, having recently celebrated his fortieth birthday, he believed that his failure was a sign of things to come now that he was middle-aged.

Mr. Smith's problem became a recurring one and placed a great strain on the marriage. Mr. Smith was becoming convinced that his sex life was over, and Mrs. Smith concluded that either her husband no longer loved her or that he no longer found her attractive. Their relationship gradually deteriorated until Mrs. Smith discussed their problem with her gynecologist. She referred Mr. and Mrs. Smith to a therapist experienced in such problems. With much trepidation, they made an appointment, and were relieved to discover that their problem was not unusual; the chances were excellent that they could be helped.

After a relatively brief course of therapy Mr. and Mrs. Smith were able to resume their sexual relationship. Therapy provided an added benefit by teaching them the importance of communication. During the years after therapy their sexual life was generally rewarding, but when problems arose, they were able to talk about the issues and to achieve satisfactory resolutions.

While there is nothing unusual about the case of Mr. and Mrs. Smith, the curious student of human sexuality is likely to have several questions about this couple. The answers would have to draw upon a variety of disciplines. Let us speculate about what questions might be asked and where one would go to find the answers.

1. This couple seems pretty typical. Is there really anything unusual about them?

The couple indeed seems typical but only within the perspective of the times and society in which we are living. Historians have provided us with valuable information about the evolution of male-female relationships (see Chapters 2 and 3). From this body of knowledge we can gain an appreciation of the forces that shaped Mr. and Mrs. Smith's attitudes toward marriage and family structure. Cultural anthropologists would also be able to provide insight into the role that societal norms play in shaping behavior and attitudes (see Chapter 9). Some societies would pity Mr. and Mrs. Smith because of their inhibitions, while others would be shocked by their libertine ways.

2. What about their sexual behavior? How typical is that for our society?

Sociologists have collected data about people's sexual behavior and the factors associated with such behavior (see Chapter 8). For example, sociological surveys tell us that, considering Mr. and Mrs. Smith's age and educational level, their premarital and marital sexual behavior are indeed fairly typical. Sociological literature would also elucidate the relationship between sexual behavior and numerous other factors, such as religion, socioeconomic status, ethnic background, and so on.

3. What happened after the birth of their first child to cause Mrs. Smith to lose interest temporarily in sex?

Several disciplines would be concerned with this question. Medical scientists and physiological psychologists might suspect that the hormonal changes associated with pregnancy and childbirth might be responsible for Mrs. Smith's loss of interest (see Chapter 7). Clinical psychologists might focus on the psychological impact of the birth of a child. Perhaps Mrs. Smith was simply too tired to have sex after caring for an infant all day. In many instances, several factors act and interact with each other to determine sexual behavior.

4. Why did Mrs. Smith have reservations about trying out new sexual techniques when her husband suggested it?

Clinical psychologists and psychiatrists believe that, along with historical and cultural forces, personality variables influence attitudes about sexuality. Mrs. Smith may have had feelings of guilt about sexual matters that made it difficult for her to engage in activities she suspected were immoral (see Chapter 18).

5. Do many men have problems such as the one Mr. Smith developed? Can they usually be successfully treated?

A variety of mental health professionals, including clinical psychologists and psychiatrists, have studied and treated sexual problems. Such problems are indeed relatively common, and in a majority of cases can be successfully treated (see Chapter 14).

These are just a few questions that one might ask about this couple. Numerous others readily come to mind. For example, what attracted Mr. and Mrs. Smith to each other in the first place? How did they develop their attitudes about what is proper sexual behavior? What accounts for the fact that it took several months before Mrs. Smith began to enjoy sex? What can they expect from their sex life as they grow older? These are but a few of the questions that might be asked. The point we wish to make is that the knowledge derived from any single discipline alone will provide us with only a partial understanding of human sexuality. The rapid growth of knowledge in recent years has come from integrating the work of specialists such as biologists, cultural anthropologists, sociologists, physicians, and psychologists. These specialists hold the hope that as knowledge increases and is communicated to the public, society may be able to create conditions in which people find their sexuality a source of reward and pleasure rather than a source of guilt, frustration, and conflict.

Summary

Human beings are sexual creatures. Not only is much of our time and energy devoted to sex and sexual relationships, but much of our nonsexual behavior may be motivated by sexual needs. Although sexuality is potentially a rich source of pleasure, unfortunately many people find it to be a source of guilt, frustration, and conflict.

If this situation is to be reversed, sound scientific knowledge of human sexuality must be available. In the past, however, "scientific" knowledge was strongly influenced by the antisexual attitudes of society. For example, many "experts" in the late nineteenth century believed that masturbation caused a variety of physical disabilities. In the early twentieth century Freud led many people to believe that their sexual behavior was a symptom of psychological immaturity. Even modern scientists, while making many invaluable contributions, have promulgated inaccurate information or interpretations of sexual behavior. The scientific study of sex and society's attitudes toward sex have a mutual influence. As society begins to view sexuality in more positive ways, researchers are able to conduct more objective research. This research in turn will contribute to alleviating the sexual problems that many people have.

The scientific study of sex requires a multidisciplinary approach. The historian, biologist, sociologist, cultural anthropologist, psychologist, and philosopher all have important contributions to make in furthering our understanding of human sexuality. It is hoped that sound, accurate information about sexuality will enable society to create conditions that serve to enhance the sexuality of all people.

References

Colles, J.S. *An artist of life*. London: Casall, 1959.

Colton, H. *Sex after the sexual revolution*. New York: Association Press, 1972.

de Beauvoir, S. *The second sex.* New York: Bantam, 1952.

Ellis, H. *Studies in the psychology of sex* (7 vols.). Philadelphia: F.A. Davis, 1899-1928.

Fowler, O.S. *Amativeness, or evils and remedies of excessive and perverted sexuality including warnings and advice to the married and the single.* London: G. Vickers, 1875.

Gordon, S. "Freedom for sex education and sexual expression." In S. Gordon and R.W. Libby (eds.), *Sexuality today and tomorrow.* North Scituate, Mass.: Duxbury, 1976.

Kinsey, A., Pomeroy, W.B. and Martin, C.E. *Sexual behavior in the human male.* Philadelphia: W.B. Saunders, 1948.

Kinsey, A., Pomeroy, W.B., Martin, C.E. and Gebhard, P.H. *Sexual behavior in the human female.* Philadelphia: W.B. Saunders, 1953.

LoPiccolo, J. "The professionalization of sex therapy: Issues and problems." In J. LoPiccolo and L. LoPiccolo (eds.), *Handbook of sex therapy.* New York: Plenum, 1978.

LoPiccolo, J. and Heiman, J. "Cultural values and the therapeutic definition of sexual function and dysfunction." *Journal of Social Issues,* 1977, 33, 166-183.

Masters, W. and Johnson, V. *Human sexual response.* Boston: Little, Brown, 1966.

Masters, W. and Johnson, V. *Human sexual inadequacy.* Boston: Little, Brown, 1970.

McGrady, P.M. *The love doctors.* New York: Macmillan, 1972.

Myers, L. "The high cost of MDeity's prudery." In S. Gordon and R.W. Libby (eds.), *Sexuality today and tomorrow.* North Scituate, Mass.: Duxbury, 1976.

Chapter 2

Human Sexuality in Historical Perspective

Present patterns of human sexual behavior can be traced back to the dawn of recorded history. Although there have been vast changes in sexual expressions and norms governing sexual conduct and mores, some universal patterns of sexual behavior have remained relatively constant throughout the ages. Sexuality has been glorified or condemned. Attitudes toward sex have fluctuated between prohibitive restriction and unadulterated inhibition. Specific forms of sexual activities, such as homosexuality and sacred prostitution, respectively, which were accepted at times or associated with religious ceremonies, are no longer tolerated within a religious context. Heterosexual intercourse apparently transcended time and civilizations as one of the most prevalent sexual activities of men and women in all societies, past and present.

In order to gain a better understanding of the diversities and complexities of human sexuality in today's world, an examination of past behavior patterns illustrating the changes, continuity, and universal acceptance of certain expressions of human sexuality can be informative. This chapter, then, is concerned with historical variations of sex from prehistoric times to the beginning of the twentieth century. Time periods during which unique, unusual, or no longer existing patterns of sexual conduct occurred will be highlighted.

Since much of our knowledge of past sexual behaviors comes from art and literature, the study of human sexuality throughout history is dependent upon remaining tangible evidence, much of which is obscure or hidden, especially as far as unrecorded history is concerned. Most of the documentation—whether in the form of visual representations, decorative or other creative art—is rather sparse. In addition, much of the remaining evidence has been damaged or is difficult to decipher, since not all ancient people have left sexual art.

Finally, few cultures have maintained written records. As a result, our present reconstruction of the sexuality of past civilizations is based upon evidence that may not be totally representative of the range of sexual activities of the time. Therefore, it has to be recognized that most accounts of the sexual lives of ancient people are open to speculative interpretations. Nevertheless, an examination of past societal attitudes toward sex is instrumental in providing insight and understanding of sexual attitudes and behavior today.

Before Recorded History

People have inhabited the earth for approximately two million years. Homo sapiens, the first representative of modern man, appeared about 70,000 years ago. Continuous discoveries of new fossil remains and technologically sophisticated dating techniques tend to push back constantly the date of the arrival of the first humans. From prehistoric times on, perhaps some 20,000 years ago, suggestive evidence from rock art reflects human sexual awareness and involvement in sexual activities. Some of the earliest archaeological artifacts portraying the sex life of prehistoric people have been discovered in the Stone Age cave art of France and Spain. Paintings, finger tracings, engravings, and sculptures tell the story of men and women as hunters and food gatherers who were dependent for their existence on the pursuit of wild animals, birds, and fish as well as on the collection of fruits, berries, and nuts. In terms of major functions and responsibilities, men and women did not differ sharply in the hunting and gathering societies. Both sexes were equally dependent upon each other in procuring basic survival resources. As a result, male-female relationships were rather equalitarian in nature. Since the male-female status distinction characteristic of industrial societies did not exist, an important source of power difference between men and women was absent in hunting and gathering societies (Yorburg, 1975).

Gradually, prehistoric societies evolved into matriarchal social structures. Old Stone Age man began to worship womanhood and looked upon the female sex as the intermediary between man's and nature's history. Typical representations of female figures of this period show women with large breasts, prominent hips, and exaggerated sex organs. Prehistoric cave art was, by and large, female in its sexual imagery. It has been suggested that this emphasis on female sexuality as functionally expressed in portrayals of pregnancy and birth reflects the fact that man during this age was not aware of his physical role in the procreation process (Rawson, 1973); that is, impregnation was recognized as an exclusively female activity. Presumably, the sexual imagery symbolized fertility in reproduction and was used in some rites to promote fruitfulness among animals upon which Old Stone Age societies depended (Roebuck, 1966). During this period, menstruation, pregnancy, and care of children were essentially incompatible with the hunting style of life that had become an essentially male occupation. As a result, a division of labor developed, leaving the women in charge of food gathering, and requiring economic cooperation between the sexes. This cooperation between males and females, in turn, made it imperative that sexual rivalry between males remain at a minimum.

Gradually, the early prehistoric cultures became more complex, and specialized social structures, such as art, technology, and mastery over the environment, became more sophisticated. The revolutionary change in the human way of life which marked the beginning of the New Stone Age began in the Middle East and may have taken place as early as 8,000 B.C. The major element of change was that people gradually ceased to be hunters and food gatherers and became food producers. About 10,000 years ago, the technique of plant cultivation was discovered. People learned how to raise crops and domesticate animals. Plant cultivation rapidly changed the social life of prehistoric cultures because it provided a more dependable food supply. For the first time, economic surplus was produced. Consequently, people could afford to become stationary, and extended families became prevalent.

Initially, during the early phase of the New Stone Age, the characteristic form of social organization was predominantly matriarchal, with women carrying out the essential work of tilling the soil and planting roots. As during the Old Stone Age, the mysterious menstrual cycle, pregnancy, and birth of a new life out of a woman's womb formed the basis of the fertility rites and cults. The sexual act and pregnancy were still disconnected in the mind of New Stone Age people. However, consistent with the horticultural life style, the fetus was thought of as a seed placed into the woman's womb through contact between her and some animal, sacred object, or magic.

There has been speculation that under these circumstances women did not suffer from Freudian *penis envy.* Freud (1931) presented a theory of female psychosexual development suggesting that little girls in their preteens were destined to make a "momentous discovery." They would notice the penis of a brother or playmate and feel inferior because of their own internal sex organs. The exacerbated desire to have a penis on the part of the female was assumed to be an expression of a feeling of biological inferiority. Instead, it has been suggested that early man was haunted by uterus envy, protesting against the exclusively female power in creating new life (De Riencourt, 1974). One psychiatrist, the late Karen Horney (1967), suggested that this male envy of procreativity served and still serves as the major driving force in setting up cultural values. According to Horney, the male is painfully aware of the small part he plays in the procreation of new life and therefore overcompensates through achievement.

Toward the latter part of the New Stone Age, when technological advances such as the practice of metallurgy and the use of the plough were introduced, some noteworthy changes occurred that, in turn, affected human sexual behavior. For the first time, representation of ceremonial sexual orgies with manifestations of superhuman sexual powers are found. More important, though, images of masculine sexual potency gradually began to appear, adding a new male sexual element to the formerly prevailing female image. From Spain to China, the sexual power and prowess of the male was universally represented by the penis. *Phallic* symbols were found in the form of amulets, stylized emblems, or naturalistic appendages of the male body. They were shaped like single, double, or multiple penises or grossly enlarged male *genitals.*

The emergence of agriculture and the new mode of life revolving around farming greatly facilitated the development of phallic imagery and phallus cults by associating the male sex organ with essential components of land cultivation. Identifying the penis with the plough and the *semen* with seed became one of the most widespread metaphors of male sexuality. The penis was typically represented as an axe, dagger, or sword, while the semen was symbolized as rain, snake, or bird. Although it is beyond the scope of this chapter to discuss the full nature and significance of phallic symbolism, a few examples taken from early civilizations may suffice to demonstrate the universality and richness of phallic symbolism.

Phallic Symbolism

The phallic cult originated in the idea of fertility and was in the past, and still is, intimately connected with procreation. Intense reverence for male ancestors and an equally intense desire for male offspring have imbued the phallus with a creative force that guarantees the continuity of mankind.

In ancient Egyptian rites in honor of the gods Isis and Osiris, for instance, enormous phallus symbols were carried during the ceremonial processions. Frequently, Isis herself was portrayed holding an emblem of the *vulva* awaiting penile penetration. In face of the overwhelming sexual imagery of the cult, men and women participating in the ritual ceremonies engaged in numerous orgiastic behaviors.

Similarly, phallic symbolism was found extensively among Greek civilizations where *pederasty*—the relationship between an older man and an early-adolescent boy—was an integral part of Greek upbringing. Through his phallus, the older man was assumed to transfer to the boy the essence of his finest qualities. As a result of the phallic act, the adolescent became a man with the strength, sense of duty, eloquence, generosity, ingenuity, and all the other virtues possessed by the older man (Vanggard, 1972).

In Roman culture, during the festival of Venus, a gigantic phallus was brought to the temple where it was presented to the sexual parts of the image of the goddess. Another Roman phallus cult involved young girls and brides who would sit astride the phallus of a temple image of Jupiter to break their *hymen* (Rawson, 1973).

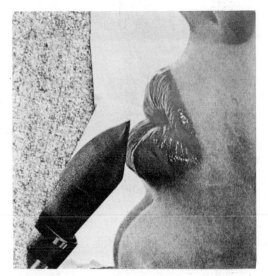

Figure 2.1
Phallic symbolism is as prominent in today's media as it was in the art of the past. (Dwyer and Zinkl)

Returning to prehistoric man, who introduced phallic symbolism to de-emphasize female sexuality, we find that societies underwent radical social reorganizations. With the invention of agriculture, the division of labor became more rigid. As a result, sex typing became more pronounced: the double standard sanctioning certain sexual activities for males but condemning them for females came into existence. Rigid sex typing had been difficult to maintain among the isolated nuclear families of the Old Stone Age, but the prevalence of extended families in horticultural and agricultural societies encouraged greater sex differences and sex typing.

As part of this process, most female rites and sex symbols were reinterpreted to accommodate the by now full-fledged masculine phallic cult. Gradually, the fertility rites of the big-breasted, wide-hipped mother goddesses disappeared. Instead, the sun was worshipped as the major masculine divinity, symbolically represented by phallic sunbeams striking down on Mother Earth. From Greece to India, the prehistoric sun god stood for sexual prowess, masculinity, and male supremacy. With the introduction of the all-powerful, all-domineering male principle, the time was now ripe for a patriarchal revolution, which indeed swept the ancient civilizations some 3,500 years ago. The period of fundamental reorientation of the male's social and sexual status was followed by the invention of writing, which in turn ushered in the era of recorded history.

Ancient Near East

Most of the early civilizations of the ancient Near East, particularly the Mesopotamians and Egyptians, displayed little modesty about sex. Since most of the cultures of this period developed written language and sizable bureaucracies, the reconstruction of their sexual lives becomes less speculative. For example, among the Sumerians, one of the earliest people of the ancient Near East, aspects of male and female sexuality were simplified as drawings of male and female sex organs. A married couple was typically depicted as the juxtaposition of man and woman engaged in *coitus*. Sex was accepted among most civilizations of the ancient Near East as a fact of life, without need for disguise.

Temple Prostitution

One particular pattern of sexual behavior stood out as common to and characteristic of most ancient cultures of the Near East. This was the practice of temple prostitution. In Mesopotamia, for instance, the sexual act was performed by a priest and priestess in the temple as a means of securing fertility for the entire community (Bullough, 1976). According to the ancient historian Herodotus, all women were required to serve in the temple at least once in their lives for a short period of time. They were expected to sit in the temple until some man claimed the right to have intercourse with them. In the case of young girls, this act symbolized the sacrifice of their virginity to the divine principle represented by a priest, pilgrim, or total stranger. The fee paid by the visitor constituted an offering to the goddess presiding over the temple.

At the dawn of civilization, prostitution was nearly always associated with religion. Prostitutes were referred to as "daughters of the temple," priestess, or by other euphemized terms. Women prostituting themselves in the name of a divinity served at the temple personifying the dual female principle of fertility and eroticism. They entered into spontaneous sexual relations with all male visitors at the shrine. Their services at the temple were available at all times and particularly to total strangers.

Sacred or temple prostitution elevated sex to a sacrament that symbolized the sexual encounter as holy communion with the divinity. The prostitute typically regarded herself as married to the divine entity governing the temple; intercourse was a pious act performed in the name and honor of the divine personage. Sacred prostitution was an integral part of many official religious cults.

Sexual Mores of the Ancient Egyptians

In ancient Egypt, too, sex was a source of pleasure; there is little or no evidence of taboos associated with certain sexual practices. Temple paintings as well as hieroglyphic writings reflect acceptance of the sexual nature of man. For example, the hieroglyphic symbol for heterosexual intercourse simply combined the symbol for pudendum (external female sex organs) with that for penis. Similarly, the gods are depicted in various sexual acts in the illustrations in tombs and temples.

One Egyptian custom not widely adopted by other societies of the ancient Near East was the so-called woman-superior position as the proper form of intercourse. This particular coital position coincided with a reversal of the positions of the gods. Unlike most other peoples of the time, the Egyptians held that the earth was a male deity and the sky a female one, and the earth god Geb is usually pictured lying beneath his spouse Nut, the sky goddess (Brandon, 1963).

A second Egyptian deviation from the sexual mores of surrounding peoples concerned the sanction of incestuous marriages, particularly between brothers and sisters. The example for this custom was set by the gods when Isis married her brother Osiris. Since the pharaoh, the Egyptian king, was a reincarnation of the deity on earth, he was expected to follow the incestuous custom.

In summary, then, most civilizations of the ancient Near East enjoyed and tolerated a wide variety of sexual activities. Illustrations of sex acts ranging from bestiality to anal intercourse to oral-genital contacts are portrayed reflecting a rather unrestricted acceptance of human sexuality. Some of the universal sexual practices included sacred or temple prostitution, phallic symbolism, and a considerable degree of sexual permissiveness. The attitudes of these early societies shaped those of surrounding and later peoples and ultimately affected contemporary sexual behavior.

Ancient Jews: A Sex-Negative Society

Although part of the Near Eastern civilizations, the sexual attitudes of ancient Jews deserve separate consideration because of the Judaic interpretation of sexuality. Sexual restrictions set forth in the Judaic code were influential in forming traditional Western attitudes toward sex and sexual behavior. For many centuries Judaism prescribed the direction of social control, expressing negative evaluation and condemning attitudes of most forms of sexual behavior outside of marital intercourse, and had a pervasive influence on Western Christianity.

The case of *masturbation* may illustrate the intense impact of the Judaic tradition. Traditionally, masturbation has been equated with the term *onanism* in Biblical writings. The word onanism derives from Onan's "spilling his seed upon the barren ground" (Genesis XXXVIII:9). For the ancient Jews the intentional depositing of the semen anywhere else than in the female vagina was considered sinful and immoral. It was a violation of the divine command of the first commandment to "be fruitful and multiply." Even to this day, contemporary Orthodox Jews maintain this position.

Following the Judaic mandate against diverting the male seed, the history of many pre-Christian and Christian societies has become replete with rules against masturbation. The original Judaic prohibitions were later reinforced by the medical teachings of the eighteenth and nineteenth centuries, when much was written on disturbances—particularly mental and emotional—that were thought to have been caused by masturbation. Even today, though many contemporary religious groups are re-examining their attitudes toward masturbation, some of the traditional beliefs remain strong. Parents still punish their children for genital self-stimulation. The common belief that masturbation leads to mental disorders, skin disorders, and possibly impotence or sterility is still perpetuated by professionals, even by physicians and nurses (Johnson, 1976).

Early Jewish traditions recognized prostitution. Both male and female prostitutes were at times attached to the temple in Jerusalem, as well as to local shrines. Although sacred prostitution was generally not approved by the majority of Jewish tribes, it was actually sanctioned by some communities. In spite of this early liberal outlook, standards of sexual morality eventually changed radically and drastically to an extremely strict code that negated most sexual expression (Epstein, 1948). The term "compulsive sexuality" has been coined (Ellis and Abarnabel, 1961) to imply that the divine command to be "fruitful and multiply" was the determining force that directed and shaped the sex life of the early Jews.

In accord with the divine command, procreation became the only justification for sex. The purpose of sexual intercourse was to propagate the species. Consequently, failure to produce children resulted in divorce and exclusion from the religious and social activities of the community. Consistent with the strictly procreational view of sex, Jewish teachings strongly forbade nonprocreative sexual activities such as masturbation or *homosexuality*. Both of these practices, according to Levitical law, could be punishable by death. Similarly, adultery, rape, or other forcible sexual relationships were equally serious transgressions.

Contrary to the uninhibited sexuality that characterized the majority of the earliest societies, the sexual morality and norms of the early Jews were governed by rigidity and numerous prohibitions. Sexual intercourse between a man and a wife was encouraged, provided that children were the nominal purpose of the sex act. The historical impact of the restricted and uncreative sex propagated by ancient Judaism had profound and long-lasting ethical consequences for centuries to come. The ancient Hebrews emerged as the first culture with a predominantly negative outlook toward sex. However, the Jewish influence on Western sexual attitudes was only one part of the tradition passed down through the centuries. Equally important, and perhaps even more so, was the contribution of the ancient Greeks, who were the first people who attempted to arrive at a scientific or at least naturalistic explanation of human sexuality.

Ancient Greece: A Sex-Positive Society

The societies of ancient Greece provided the first clear, well-documented picture of human sexuality in Western society. None of the sexual activities typically associated with ancient Greece, i.e., pederasty, prostitution as a social hierarchy of courtesans, or attitudes toward homosexuality, may have truly originated with the Greeks. However, the unique contribution of the Greeks involved the superbly refined sensuality and heightened sensitivity that was added to existing expressions of human sexuality. The Greeks introduced an appreciation of frank and open eroticism, nudity, and intellectual excellence in conjunction with sexuality. At all times, the Greeks were very sensitive to physical beauty and enjoyed the sight of the naked human body. The physical qualities of a healthy body were emphasized to indicate that a good body is a necessary correlate of a good soul. Consequently, the training of the body became the training of the soul, glorified in the Olympic games and in the surviving remnants of Greek sculpture representing gracious nudes in harmonious motion.

The Greeks not only valued physical excellence but also recognized human dependence on the world of the senses. Sex and sexual activities were accepted as an important source of pleasure, delighting all sensory modalities. For the ancient Greeks, sex life ceased to be dichotomized in a male-female, heterosexual-homosexual, all-or-none dimension. In turn, sexual relations were not a matter of either/or but occurred along a continuum. The continuum ranged from exclusive responsiveness toward members of the opposite sex to erotic arousal by persons of both sexes to exclusive interest and involvement with a member of the same sex. As a result, a wide spectrum of sexual activities was acceptable, allowing individuals to engage in bisexual, heterosexual, or homosexual activities.

Minoan Sensuality

The new sexual outlook and expression of sexuality is reflected in the frescoes and decorative art found in the royal palaces of the Minoan societies on the island of Crete. Ancient Crete shared the goddess-worshipping cults of Egypt and Mesopotamia, which exalted certain female characteristics. However, privilege and prestige were more equally distributed among Minoan women than in the high civilizations of the ancient Near East. For example, the typical attributes of low-status women such as seclusion, veiling, and female-to-male deference patterns do not appear in artistic representations of the Minoans (Yorburg, 1975). As a matter of fact, a totally different type of woman had emerged. Contrary to earlier civilizations which emphasized big breasts and wide hips, implying childbirth as the major female function, the Minoans introduced the sensuous woman sparkling with liveliness, sophistication, and careless elegance. Instead of references to pregnancy and fertility, sexual provocation and aesthetic harmony took precedence.

Clearly, Minoan women had much freedom and shared a status of equality with men. The separation of the sexes was minimal in the major areas of sexual and social responsibilities. Some of the frescoes show girls dancing before men while other women were trained to take part in the dangerous bull sport. Although no direct representations of sexual activities have been uncovered among the wealth of decorative Minoan art, the scholar gains the impression of a sexually permissive, uninhibited culture, whose people for the first time in history enjoyed sex for pleasurable and recreational purposes.

Sex was not only a pleasure for mortals but was equally enjoyed by the promiscuous and lascivious gods of the Olympic Pantheon. Especially Zeus, the most powerful god among the Olympians, was known to succumb frequently to the desires for sexual gratification. His numerous affairs included the abduction of Ganymede, a handsome youth who became the cup bearer of the gods because Zeus was overwhelmed with lust for him. Similarly, Apollo, the patron of art and music, had sexual relationships with many young people of both sexes. Finally, Heracles, better known as Hercules, had an insatiable appetite for women and copulated frequently with humans, according to Greek mythology.

Pederasty

At the height of the Greek civilization (500 B.C.), three specific sexual behavior patterns emerged that characterized the sex life of the classical Greeks. The first of these sexual activities, introduced and uniquely shaped by the Greek way of life, was the practice of *pederasty*. The word literally means the love of boys and refers to the relationship between an older man and a boy. Contrary to contemporary society, which reserves some of its harshest judgments for homosexual acts between a man and a boy, this type of sexual behavior was accepted in classical Athens and elsewhere in Greece. Many vases of high artistic value portray the pederastic encounter in the typical and most direct way: a man approaching or sexually interacting with a boy. Usually, the man's stature is powerful with a muscular body contrasted by that of the smaller slender boy. The two male figures are further distinguished by the fact that the man is shown with a full beard and an erect penis, while the boy is typically beardless and without genitals. A few vases of the fifth and sixth century depict the young boy with a penis. However, when depicted it is always immature and never erect.

Figure 2.2
Classical Greek vase showing an older man offering a lyre and a ball to a youth. (Metropolitan Museum of Art, Rogers Fund, 1941)

In ancient Greece, pederasty was more than a physical relationship between an older and a younger man. It was regarded as an institution providing an essential part of the young boy's emotional and mental growth. Since sex was not an inevitable component of pederasty, the pederastic relationship served important pedagogic functions, because the older man was immensely concerned with the development of the character of his pupil. Pederasty was to the Greeks the most influential way of bringing up male youths. It was not incompatible with marriage since the mature man in most instances was fully potent with women and the younger partner was expected to later develop the same dual attitude.

Typically, the age of the beloved boy was between fifteen and twenty. Similarly, as a rule, the lover in these relationships was usually a mature man, less than forty years of age. In most cases, the pederastic relationship was terminated when the youth showed the first growth of beard signaling the advent of puberty.

Pederasty as an educational institution was under legal control, since sexual intercourse with prepubertal boys was considered a punishable offense. Most of the time an entire body of law existed in Athens for the purpose of restraining the indiscriminate spread of pederasty and to prevent the older pederast from searching for adolescent boys in schools and exercising arenas (Flaceliere, 1962). Pederasty was cultivated and practiced by heterosexually normal males and cannot be equated with modern homosexuality. On the contrary, the primary aim of the older partner was to pass on masculine traits to an adolescent boy who was developing gender identity. Some of the greatest literary figures of classical Greece, including Sophocles and Aeschylus, were active pederasts. In addition, the philosophical ideal of pederasty involved many prominent philosophers and politicians, among them the philosophers Socrates and Plato, and the politician Alcibiades.

Homosexuality

A related aspect of Greek sexuality concerns the attitude of the ancient Hellenes toward homosexuality. Since the Greeks recognized and accepted the bisexual nature of men and women, encompassing both homosexual and heterosexual elements, the widespread prevalence of sexual intimacy among men is not surprising. In Greece, homosexuality arose from the depreciation of women in an exclusively male-oriented society. Women were typically held in very low status in democratic Athens, where Greek wives were presumably illiterate, uninteresting, and uninspiring. Consequently, the Greek male harbored considerable contempt for his wife and was inclined to seek alternate sexual outlets.

Compared with contemporary attitudes toward homosexual behaviors, maladaptive implications were largely absent in classical Greece. The homosexual was not motivated or characterized by his inability to respond appropriately to the opposite sex. Rather, he was conscious of both homosexual and heterosexual inclinations and was free to express them in sexual activities without coming into conflict with himself or his environment. Most homosexuals of ancient Greece were married and fulfilled their procreative duties.

Homosexuality was particularly widespread during times of war. Many homosexual bonds were formed through the Greek military ideal stressing the importance of close male friendships. Sexual intimacy among men became an essential element in some military formations, where pairs of lovers formed the basic tactical unit fighting side by side. In such situations, homosexual bonds proved to be of immense military value. For instance, the Sacred Band of Thebes, the backbone of the Theban army and presumably the finest fighting force in the Hellenic world, was made up entirely of homosexuals. This unusual battlefield force remained unconquered for more than forty years; when it was finally overcome, all were killed. Pairs of lovers were found lying side by side on the battlefield.

Female homosexuality received less attention in the literary and artistic accounts of Greek sexual life. In theory, the Greeks were as tolerant of female homosexuality as they were of the male variety. One of the few samples of female homosexuality or *lesbianism* was intimately linked with the poetess Sappho who lived on the island of Lesbos, hence the term. Sappho's life and work were filled with love for her own sex. Her boarding school for young girls, famous in antiquity, was dedicated to the love goddess Aphrodite and overseen by the poetess, providing an idyllic setting for Lesbian encounters.

Homosexuality in both men and women was not treated as a perversion, a sign of emotional disturbance, or immaturity in ancient Greece. Rather, homosexual behaviors were tolerated or accepted as widespread social and psychological expressions of human sexuality and were considered as substitutes for or supplements of heterosexual relationships.

Prostitution

Finally, *prostitution* as the third expression of sexuality takes on a typical flavor in ancient Greece. Although sacred as well as secular prostitution had been practiced by numerous societies prior to the Greeks, it never existed in the form of the elaborate social hierarchies of mistresses characteristic of ancient Greece. For the Greeks there were two types of women, the wife and mother on the one hand and the courtesan on the other. The famous Greek orator, Demosthenes, summed up the situation with the saying: "We have wives for childbearing, *hetaerae* or pleasure girls and concubines for our daily needs." Greek men of high social status frequently turned to courtesans for intellectual and sexual gratification and stimulation.

The Greek language reflects the many social levels of prostitution by the wide repertory of terms describing prostitutes, ranging from sophisticated companions (hetaerae) to a category comparable to the modern streetwalkers. The lowest rank of the social strata of pleasure girls was occupied by concubines who were usually slaves. These girls were typically expected to engage in sexual relations with their masters. Very often they served not only the sexual passions of their masters but also the caprices of their mistresses. One of the privileges accorded to the upper class Athenian included the right to exploit slaves and servants sexually.

Next in the social hierarchy were the common prostitutes who lived in brothels. Their quarters were unmistakably identified by a wooden or painted phallus near the door (Hunt, 1959). A little higher on the social scale were the female flute players who were usually foreign-born. These girls were hired out by their teachers or masters as an accompaniment to an Athenian banquet. At the end of the meal, the flute player was given a signal to play and dance. Often she would spend the night with one of the dinner guests.

Finally, at the top of the social hierarchy, prostitution was quite different. The hetaera must not be confused with the common prostitute. Hetaerae were carefully trained to be sexually exciting, mentally stimulating, and capable of infatuating intellectual men. Their education, charm, and social graces allowed them to fascinate the most distinguished personalities of their time—statesmen, generals, artists, philosophers, and poets.

In addition to the various forms of secular prostitution, temple prostitution was also practiced. Certain religious cults not only tolerated but protected and even organized prostitution. This was particularly true at the shrine of the love goddess Aphrodite in the city of Corinth, which, at one time, had more than a thousand prostitutes in the service of the deity. The girls appointed to the temple offered their sexual services for money that was either put into the temple treasury or used as a dowry.

The contribution of the Greeks considerably influenced sexual morality and attitudes of many later Western traditions. Among the first societies to adopt the sexual attitudes and morality of the Greeks was ancient Rome.

Ancient Rome: Sexual Extremes

Although the Romans shared many of the sexual activities and customs practiced by the Greeks, Roman sexuality was clearly distinct from the Greeks' sexual outlook. Some of the basic differences between the two ancient civilizations involved a greater reluctance on the part of the Romans to accept homosexuality or to approve of public nudity. The family as an institution played an important role in the Roman social order. Considerable legislation was passed to safeguard the family, and premiums were placed on marriage and the birth of children in wedlock. But the Romans also introduced sadistic tendencies and orgiastic extremes that rarely occurred in Greek sexuality.

As in Greece, the social organization of the early Roman Republic as well as the later Empire was essentially male-oriented and male-dominated. Since women were essentially regarded as property of the male head of the household, their legal rights were very limited. Nevertheless, women had a different status in Rome than in Greece, with the Roman woman enjoying considerably more freedom and prestige than her Athenian counterpart. Wealthier women in Rome were educated, at least at an elementary level, and allowed to share in the social lives of their husbands. Especially high-born women often enjoyed roles of social and political prominence. Women were also publicly accepted as spectators at the gladiatorial shows in the arena. According to Finley (1968), the Roman woman vicariously relished the cruelty and brutality of the circus games and identified with the gladiators.

Like the Greeks, the Romans were familiar with and enjoyed a variety of sexual activities. The Latin vocabulary testifies to the diversity of Roman sex practices. Terms such as masturbation, prostitution, *cunnilingus* (oral stimulation of female genitalia) were introduced by the Romans and are still in use. Roman sexuality, in general, expressed itself in cruder and coarser ways than in Greece. Typically, the Romans were less concerned with aesthetic ideals and consequently ap-

proached sexuality from a less sublimated and more matter-of-fact point of view. The Roman poet Ovid, for instance, in his major works *Love* and *The Art of Love* demonstrates the concreteness of the Roman sexual outlook when he gives detailed technical advice on how to make love. The emotional component of the sexual relationship was played down and replaced by elaborate strategies of seduction.

During the first centuries of the Republic, homoerotic activities were rather uncommon. Unlike the Greeks, Roman soldiers undergoing military training did not tend to form homosexual relationships. Apparently, factors such as camaraderie among men at arms and the physical proximity of men in military camps did not contribute significantly to the later development and eventual pervasiveness of homosexuality.

Sexual Behavior of the Roman Emperors

As the Romans came to power, many of the simple and austere ways of life were discarded. By the time of the first Caesars, many of the old virtues and patriotic ideals had disappeared. The names of several Caesars and emperors were associated with bisexual and homosexual practices. For example, Julius Caesar was known to his contemporaries as "every woman's man and every man's woman." His numerous homosexual affairs made for much of the gossip among his contemporaries. In addition, many of Caesar's immediate associates were reportedly known for their homosexual tendencies. Even Octavian, who after Caesar's murder became the Emperor Augustus, presumably had prostituted himself to Caesar.

Among the emperors who openly practiced homosexuality, Hadrian's (A.D. 117-138) love for Antinous is perhaps the most famous homoerotic relationship in Roman history. Antinous was a handsome Greek boy to whom Hadrian was attached by erotic idealism. Their relationship represented an elaborate and conscious effort to idealize homosexuality in the glorified Greek tradition. According to Ellis and Abarnabel (1961), Elagabalus (A.D. 218) was the most homosexual of all emperors. Described as a particularly beautiful boy, he succeeded to the throne at the age of fourteen. Not only did Elagabalus prefer male lovers but also dressed as a woman and appeared to have been a true invert of the feminine type.

It should be noted, however, that homosexuality in Rome cannot be compared either in character or in influence on later traditions with the sophisticated and romanticized pederasty of ancient Greece. Unlike the mature Greek who chose an adolescent of equal social status as the recipient of his love, the Romans usually chose a slave as their homosexual love object. Roman attitudes toward homosexuality clearly lacked the subtleties, sophistication, and philosophy typically associated with the Greek treatment of homosexuality.

Roman Prostitutes

As in Greece, the ubiquity of Roman prostitution was attested to by a socially organized, well-defined system. The lowest group, street prostitutes, entertained their customers in the archways and underneath public buildings such as theaters or circus arenas. As a matter of fact, the area below the stadium was frequented so much for these purposes that the Latin word for a series of arches under the stadium, "fornices," eventually gave rise to the verb "to fornicate" (to engage in intercourse). These street prostitutes had ample opportunities to offer and exercise their erotic skills, especially among the theater- or circusgoers. Many plays and games were sexually arousing. When visitors emerged from the theater, they could translate their sexual arousal or fantasies into immediate activities by following the luring prostitutes. Similarly, spectators of the circus games frequently left the arena in a state of sexual arousal, since a variety of sexual acts were performed in conjunction with the gladiatorial show. For example, couples were forced to engage in sexual activities in front of the visiting crowd, or women were tied down spread-eagled for sexual contact with animals. Prostitutes waiting for the return of the visitors from the arena provided a ready outlet for their aroused senses.

At the upper end of the spectrum, prostitutes were actresses, artists, or flute players. They lived in comfortable villas, carefully chosen by their lovers, and their needs were provided for rather than payment of an outright fee for their services. However, even the high-class Roman courtesan never attained the degree of sexual sophistication, intellectual excellence, or social grace typical of her Athenian sister, the hetaera.

Roman sexual behavior revealed many sadistic tendencies, which became most evident in the latter stages of the Empire. This period was marked by an overall atmosphere of moral decadence with a widespread breakdown of traditions and loss of respect for authority. The fading glory of the last days of Rome was intimately linked with sexual crudeness and sadism. Historians have implied that the corrupt personal lives of the Roman ruling class were among the major causes for the decay and decline of the Empire. Prostitution became one of the most flourishing, and best-organized, of Roman industries. Contrary to the austerity of the Roman Republic, homosexuality and sodomy were practiced on a grand scale. Some historians (Cantor, 1963) interpret the increase of homoerotic activities as symptomatic of some deep-rooted malfunctioning of the social and moral order. Whether or not the deterioration of sexual mores was a factor contributing to the imperial decline is difficult to ascertain retrospectively. However, it has been documented that the scandalous sexual conduct of the ruling elite had a debilitating effect on the functioning of the aristocratic families, the institution that had contributed so powerfully to the operation of the old Republic.

Early Christianity Through the Middle Ages: Beginnings of Sexual Repression

With the fall of the Roman Empire in the West, Europe entered a period of history known as the Middle Ages. The era spans a time period of almost 1,000 years, from the collapse of Rome in A.D. 476 to the beginning of the age of the Renaissance in the fourteenth century.

The decline of the Roman world and the rise and triumph of Christianity were concurrent historical developments. Toward the end of the Empire masses of people, suffering from the despotism of the emperors, eagerly grasped the ideas of the new religion. Large numbers of the population, particularly the huge urban proletariat, lived precariously from day to day, because life in the later Empire was hard and miserable. Since the government could not offer salvation from the pains of the world, many people, but especially the lower classes, readily accepted the Christian ideology. Eventually, however, even educated and wealthy citizens turned to the new faith and by the third century A.D. Christianity had become a perceptible social force.

Sexuality Controlled by Religious Doctrines

Christian codes of sexual morality contrasted sharply with the pagan outlook of the declining Roman Empire. The greatest upheaval brought about by the triumph of Christianity was an almost complete redefinition of sexual values. The sexual ethics advocated by early Christianity included a definite emphasis on the value of virginity, a quest for the abolition of polygamy, promiscuity, and prostitution. According to early Christian thinking, human sexual behavior was no longer considered an integral part of human nature. Sex and sin became closely linked. Sex was essentially a distraction from the spiritual life, which represented the Christian ideal.

With the rise of the Christian Empire and the shaping of the Catholic Church, the sexual behavior of medieval people became more and more controlled by religious doctrines. According to the teachings of the early Church the fulfillment of sexual desire for itself only was a sin and a consequence of human depravity. For example, St. Jerome postulated that a man should not love his wife with passion but with a judgment guided by control and restraint. Even in marriage, sexual intercourse was considered to be unhealthy and wicked. Although the Church sanctified marriage because of strong sanctions in the Old and New Testament, the enjoyment of sexual pleasure was not condoned, even between husband and wife. The philosophy of the time is best expressed by St. Gregory: "When not the love of producing offspring but pleasure dominates the act of intercourse, married persons have something to mourn over in the intercourse."

However, several of the Church Fathers who strongly condemned sex had experienced the pleasure of sexual fulfillment. St. Augustine, for instance, believed that his youth "boiled over in fornication." It has therefore been suggested that the writings of the early Church Fathers, at least in part, reflect the struggle between their gonads and their guilt (Murstein, 1974).

Eventually, the ascetic antisexual outlook advocated by the Church was transformed into doctrine as the Church became obsessed with the control of human sexuality.

Sexual abstinence and celibacy were idealized. The Church even attempted to regulate the sexual behavior of husband and wife during intercourse. The missionary position was advocated as the only proper copulatory position for those joined in holy wedlock (Sadock, Kaplan, and Freedman, 1976). Divorce was forbidden, since a marriage, once it was consummated, could not be terminated.

Most of the nonprocreative sexual practices tolerated or even encouraged by pagan societies became sexual taboos during the Middle Ages. Homosexuality, for instance, was judged to be more sinful than intercourse. Presumably, people with homoerotic tendencies jeopardized humanity by deflecting their sex organs from their primary reproductive purpose (Bullough, 1976). Similarly, there were various types of penalties for nongenital male-female sexual contacts. People engaging in oral-genital contacts were subjected to a four-year penance to atone for their perverse acts. Bestiality, incest, and adultery were all punishable offenses. To withstand the struggle with sexual desires, the Church recommended the denial of sexual impulses and emphasized the value of renouncing the physical body.

As might be expected, contemporary literature stressed the superiority of the virgin state as the ideal for men and women. Consequently, the Fathers of the Church taught that virginity was preferable to marriage and attempted to popularize celibacy by dwelling on the vices of women. It was argued that the Mother of God was a virgin, that the Church was the virginal bride of Christ and that, therefore, the ideal state was to refrain from sexual intercourse.

The wave of antisexuality that characterized the medieval period is uniquely represented by the introduction of the chastity belt, which appeared in Europe during the twelfth century. The chastity belt was intended as a means of securing the virginity of young women as well as guaranteeing the fidelity of wives. Typical medieval chastity belts were made out of metal and locked around the waist of the woman. The front and back of the belt consisted of a band of metal that tightly covered the vagina. A small opening, too little to allow a finger to penetrate it, was left for functions of elimination. Quite frequently, the apertures over the vagina were fortified with sharp teeth. Some chastity belts also guarded the rectal opening to prevent anal intercourse. The invention of chastity belts reinforced the notion that medieval wives were the property of husbands who felt compelled to lock them up in the literal sense of the word to safekeep them.

Status of Women

During the Middle Ages, the general status of women declined considerably relative to Imperial Rome. The male was viewed as the superior of the two sexes, while women existed merely as possessions of their husbands. According to Thomas Aquinas (1225-1274), women were inferior because of their emotional nature and their lesser capacity to reason. The female sex was characterized as having a feeble intellect and being emotionally labile. In many medieval writings women are portrayed as evil, greedy, and incapable of loving any man in their hearts. Because of the nature of their sex, all women were tarnished with sin and vice. It was not until the end of the twelfth century that medieval attitudes toward women changed. At that time, European medievalism introduced something new in the concept of love, namely courtly love.

Courtly Love

The pattern of *courtly love*, that is, the romantic and chivalrous love in the man-woman relationship, arose during the twelfth

Figure 2.3
Courtly love in the middle ages.

century among the upper classes in Europe. Courtly love was an erotic ideology that idealized the aristocratic lady by putting her on a pedestal. Romantic elevation and adoration of feminine qualities became the essence of troubadour poetry, which singing minstrels carried all over Europe during the thirteenth and fourteenth centuries.

Romantic or courtly love applied only to nonmarital relationships. Marital love was impossible because it was believed that true love thrives on freedom of choice and is spontaneous. Love between husband and wife, on the other hand, represented the fulfillment of a contract, the legal permanence of which was incompatible with burning passion. In theory, romantic relationships were not consummated sexually because of the notion that true love is unattainable.

The most elaborate theory of romantic love was presented by Andreas Capellanus (Parry, 1969) who wrote *The Art of Courtly Love* toward the end of the twelfth and the beginning of the thirteenth centuries. Love was defined as an inborn suffering derived from the sight of and excessive meditation upon the beauty of the admired lady. Love between the noble lady and her knight was said to increase if the lovers rarely saw each other and then only under difficult conditions. Rewards for the knight's unrestrained admiration might have included intimate favors such as a smile, kiss, or an embrace. However, the presence or absence of physical intimacies presumably did not affect the love itself.

Ennobling powers were ascribed to courtly love. The lover became a better man, braver, more courageous and generous. Murstein (1974) suggested that courtly love served as a projective technique for eliciting the fantasies, wishes, and desires of the knight. Romantic love presumably embodied a wish for freedom of action in heterosexual relations and a revolt against the rigid constraints placed upon male-female relationships by the domineering medieval Church.

Renaissance to the Nineteenth Century: A Re-evaluation of Sex

Although some aspects of medieval sexuality continued well into the nineteenth century, Europe was about to enter upon a period of social, political, economic, and intellectual change, marked by the steady decay of medieval institutions and medieval culture. Men and women of the fourteenth and fifteenth centuries started to question the concepts of the Middle Ages regarding sexuality and began to rebel against the attempts of the Church to regulate sexual behavior. The spiritual reputation of the Church declined. The period of the Renaissance witnessed a renewed interest in the classical past and an apparent rebirth of the Graeco-Roman spirit.

Inevitably, the revival of Greek and Roman ideas had its effect on attitudes toward sexual behavior. Most generally, the sexual life of men and women during the Renaissance gradually patterned itself on a revised paganism without the restraints of the Church. The idea that pleasure was associated with evil weakened and was eventually replaced by a wave of sexual activities. According to de Riencourt (1974), the frenzy with which men and women threw themselves into sexual enjoyment displayed a form of moral freedom and ethical blindness that was a direct response to the hostility toward sex expressed by the Church.

A number of revolutionary developments contributed to the change in the social matrix. The growth of universities, the rise of a new middle class, and the thriving of commerce and industry set the stage for the breakdown of traditional Christian morality and ethics. Furthermore, with the invention of printing, the large-scale dissemination of information became possible, whereas previously only a few had had access to written materials.

Revival of Sensuality and Sexual Freedom

The period of the Renaissance saw one of the greatest outpourings of artistic creativity in history. The art of the time is characterized by sensuality and a frank openness about sexual matters. Several of the most creative men of the period presumably practiced various forms of unconventional sex activities. The Italian painter Leonardo da Vinci, for instance, was accused of engaging in unusual sexual behavior and charged with sodomy. Freud (1964), however, suggested that Leonardo was motivated more by his passionate devotion to the scientific investigation of the human body rather than being driven by homoerotic tendencies.

Witchcraft

A particular phenomenon of the time involved the development and spread of witchcraft, which became closely linked with forbidden sexuality and sexual deviance. Witch-hunting was a historical phenomenon that reached epidemic proportions during the sixteenth and seventeenth centuries when a wave of hysterical witch craze swept over Europe. By 1650, witchcraft had become a stigmatized delusion of monstrous proportions (Henningsen, 1973). For the next two centuries, the collective obsession of witch persecution accounted for the deaths of thousands of women who were tortured and executed throughout Europe.

The sexual activity most often reported

Figure 2.4
Nudes representing the Renaissance ideal of beauty. Pintoricchio's *Judgment of Paris*. (Metropolitan Museum of Art, Rogers Fund, 1914)

was intercourse with a demon, either incubus, that is, a manifestation of a male demon, or succubus, the manifestation of a female demon. The witch presumably had entered into a pact with the Devil. This contract with Satan was primarily sexual and the witch was bound to the Devil's services in a magical way. While intercourse was an integral part of the contract, the demons also forced witches to engage in a number of variant sexual activities such as bestiality and *necrophilia*, the latter meaning literally "love of death and decay." In addition, sexual offenses of almost every conceivable kind were found in the witch lore—rape, defloration, incest, and the profanation of the sacred. Most likely, the sexual activities associated with witchcraft were either heterosexual or autoerotic and only occasionally homosexual (Russell, 1972).

Intercourse with demons was said to be painful as well as repulsive. Frequently the penis of the demon was described as being made of horn, or was half flesh and half iron. Some witches reported that the demon's sex organ was covered with scales. Once penile penetration had been effected, the scales would open out like barbs so that the withdrawal movement was excruciatingly painful (Masters, 1972). The penis of the demon was also described as freezing cold or burning hot. Finally, witches claimed that the demon's penis was forked like the tongue of a serpent, which permitted simultaneous copulation and anal intercourse.

During the fifteenth century, the papacy became involved in the struggle against witchcraft. Pope Innocent III (1485-1495) issued a papal bull that forbade any resort to witches and put the Inquisition in charge of official witch-hunting. The papal bull, in turn, became the justification for a handbook for witch-hunters, the *Malleus Maleficarum* or *Witches' Hammer*, written by Heinrich Kramer and Jacob Sprenger. The *Malleus* became inseparable from the bull because it

gave force to the papal mandate by legalizing the persecution of witches. In view of the authors of the *Malleus Maleficarum*, the witch was the natural agent through which Satan contaminated the world. Consequently, women involved in demonology had to be executed.

As the obsession with witches increased in scope and intensity, witchcraft was held responsible for causing numerous sex-related malfunctions. For instance, failure of the male to achieve an erection, impotence, and on the part of women, frigidity, infertility, and stillbirth were all attributed to the magical powers of the witch.

The witch craze, which reached its height around 1650, continued until the end of the eighteenth century. Labeled as witches, thousands of women became victims of a distorted ideology, a corrupt judicial system, and superstitious beliefs. The last legal execution occurred in Switzerland in 1793. Since none of the contemporary records is complete, it is impossible to estimate the number of witches burned at the stake, hanged, beheaded, or whipped to death during the period of the witchcraft persecutions. At the final collapse of the witch craze the witch laws were repealed, almost without debate (Trevor-Roper, 1969).

Meanwhile, a new trend started during the sixteenth century when different religious sects were formed, which later came to be known as Protestant. Under the auspices of Martin Luther, the Reformation led to a break with the Church of Rome and destroyed the traditional division of power between the Church and the state.

Luther himself made many revolutionary statements relative to sexual behavior. His own life best illustrated his thinking and ideas. Initially a monk, Luther denounced his vows and married a nun. Although his attitude toward sexuality reflected the male point of view, he openly recognized the existence of sexual needs and desires in women. How-

Figure 2.5
Witches' sabbath. (Bettman Archive Inc.)

ever, sex was to be confined to marriage, and intercourse between husband and wife twice a week was approved. Sexual frigidity and impotence were grounds for divorce. Luther also firmly believed that vows of lifelong celibacy created problems by enforcing abstinence and thereby frustrating sexual needs.

If Italy was the center of the Renaissance in the fifteenth century and Germany the center of the Reformation in the sixteenth century, the center of attention shifted to France during the eighteenth century. French cultural supremacy was recognized all over Europe, with many countries imitating French court life. The French royal families set the standards for the sexual behavior of the time. Since the majority of the French kings maintained numerous mistresses, either simultaneously or successively, royal affairs and scandals were mimicked by members of all social classes, from noblemen to peasants. Prostitution—there were houses for homosexual prostitution as well as non-commercial liaisons—flourished at all levels.

Although there was still a fear of sexual deviance throughout much of the eighteenth century, variant sexual activities were likely to be tolerated especially when practiced in a discreet manner.

The Victorian Era of the Nineteenth Century

The development of an urban middle class toward the end of the eighteenth century significantly modified the sexual character of society. The Victorian era was in part the result of the industrial revolution. More specifically, the main roots of the purity movement that characterized Victorianism were found in the lower middle classes. As a result of the wave of moral seriousness that swept through society, the social tone and temper of the time became more and more austere (Trudgill, 1976). The early pre-Victorian moral stiffness was particularly strengthened when, in 1837, the virginal young queen, Victoria, succeeded to the English throne. Her insistence on spotless moral character, coupled with the virginal modesty of her demeanor, set official standards for appropriate behavior for the remainder of the nineteenth century.

Some of the most obvious changes of the period occurred in the sex roles assigned to men and women. Based on increased economic and social differentiation, sex typing and sex labeling of male and female characteristics became more and more pronounced. Typically, men were expected to be calculating, aggressive, and sexual, while women were thought to be emotional, passive, and asexual. In an age that required a vast investment of human energy in the creation of capital and industry, men presumably concentrated on the "really important masculine things" like work, making money, building factories, and the like (Reiss, 1966), while women belonged in the home.

The official view of sexuality during the Victorian period was determined by the ethic of purity, discretion, and prudery. It was a time of both rigid sexual repression and vigorous rebellion, since official codes of sexually appropriate behaviors worshipped the inherent "purity" of women while accommodating the inherent "evil" of men (Pearson, 1972). Victorians have been described as approaching sexuality like a dog would a hot piece of meat—too hot to touch, yet too desirable to turn away from (Murstein, 1974). The final product of the contradictory attitudes toward sex and the elaborate system of double standards was the creation of the stereotype of the sexless woman and pious hypocritical man who preached sexual abstinence while entertaining sexual thoughts of women. Clearly, then, there was a great deal of hypocritical fastidiousness in the Victorian repression of sex. Apparently, the Victorian era, instead of remaining aloof from sex, was obsessed with sexuality, as other periods of sexual repression have been.

The subject of sex in any form was hidden by a veil of silence (Chesser, 1960). Actions or objects even remotely associated with sexuality were not named but referred to only in euphemisms. For instance, words such as whore or fornication became completely taboo. To be pregnant was to be "in an interesting condition" or was alluded to as "being with child" or "in the family way." Any mention of sex-related matters in public, especially before unmarried girls, or in mixed company, was considered improper.

The dominant note of nineteenth-century orthodoxy was sexual restraint (Walters, 1974). Frequent sex relations in marriage were believed to be dangerous and harmful to health. Many Victorians, therefore, became obsessed with guilt over sexual actions or urges. This obsession was reinforced by authorities predicting physical and divine punishment for sexual activities. The reward for sexual abstinence, moral respectability, and control of erotic desires was the elevation of the human spirit, widely promoted by the prevailing views of the time. Sexual activities such as masturbation were viewed with horror. As a matter of fact, the word masturbation itself became a catchword for all "unnatural" sex from use of contraceptives to homosexuality. Consequently, it is not surprising that the Victorians carried their prudery to fantastic extremes to prevent the occurrence of forbidden sexual acts. One example was the invention of an urethral ring intended to protect men from nocturnal emissions (Trudgill, 1976). The ring was designed as a leather band with four metal points and was strapped around the penis at night. When the man had an erection, he was awakened by the pains caused by the metal prongs. The prescription was to remove the ring and bathe the genitals in cold water until the erection had subsided. Before the man returned to bed, the ring was to be placed over the penis again.

One aspect of Victorian sexuality, closely

linked to the progress of industrialization, was the encouragement of males to convert their erotic impulses into economic productivity. Sexuality was sublimated into a passion for work. The parallel between sexual orthodoxy and the economic dogma of the nineteenth century is best illustrated by the fact that metaphors of business and sex could be easily interchanged. Thus "to spend" became a common slang term for ejaculation.

The concept of women during the Victorian period was closely modeled on the sexual and moral code of the time. Good women were not supposed to have any sexual desires. The English physician, William Acton, noted that the majority of women, happily for society, were not much troubled with sexual feelings of any kind (Marcus, 1967). As a matter of fact, most Victorian authorities viewed sexuality in women with fear and disgust. Although sex for ladies was completely taboo, not only in terms of enjoyment but also in terms of having any knowledge or recognition of it, the Victorian wife was expected to provide sexual services; at the same time, she was supposed to regard sensuality with disgust and reproduction as a necessary evil.

The Victorian conceptualization of the female sex idealized women as sexless creatures. They were expected to be fragile and to blush at the slightest provocation. Women's general status essentially regressed to the medieval level. However, unlike the masculine view of the Middle Ages, which considered the female sex as a source of sin, the Victorians viewed female sexuality as degrading and disgusting.

Women's submissive role during the Victorian era was clearly reflected in the clothing of the time, which denoted the role of each sex. Men's clothes reflected their seriousness, activity, strength, and aggression; women's expressed inactivity, delicacy, and submission. Victorian clothing symbolized by the corset, reinforced women's and men's beliefs that submissiveness and pain were related and that they were women's lot. In addition, Victorian women's clothing actually influenced female behavior by restricting activity and creating health dangers (Roberts, 1977).

With the evolution of sexual prudery for women there emerged a cult of domesticity that glorified the Victorian family. The home became the guardian of sexual morality. Frank discussions on matters of sexuality were avoided, partly because of the parents' own embarrassment over and repugnance for the subject matter. In addition, parental reticence and prudishness tended to make the topic of sex seem repulsive for their children.

In spite of the multitude of rules and regulations that controlled sexual behavior during the nineteenth century, the Victorians manifested a strong interest in sex. Victorian prostitution flourished to such a degree that in the 1880s there were some 40,000 prostitutes on the streets of London. The prostitute was, of course, the antithesis of sexual purity and the symbol of immorality. One reason for the importance of prostitution was probably sheer sexual frustration since many husbands rarely experienced sexual gratification with their wives.

Like prostitution, pornography also exposed the Victorians to charges of sexual hypocrisy. The latter part of the nineteenth century produced pornographic literature and art of unprecedented volume, reflecting the Victorian obsession with sex. Marcus (1967) has stated that the view of human sexuality represented in Victorian pornography and the view of sexuality held by the official culture were reversals or mirror images. It seemed that for every warning against masturbation issued by official authorities, another work of pornography was circulated. Similarly, for every cautionary statement against the harmful effects of excessive sexual activities issued by physicians or parents, pornographic works showed copulation

Figure 2.6
Sexual subculture in a sexually restricted era.
Victorian house of prostitution. (Bettmann
Archive Inc.)

between the official account of sexuality and
the various manifestations of the sexual subculture. Similar mechanisms operated in both
sets of attitudes, with both cultures expressing somewhat obsessive ideas in relation to
sexual matters.

Summary

At the end of the nineteenth century Western sexual attitudes were not fundamentally
different from what they had been in ancient
times. Prehistoric cultures had advanced
from nonliterate hunting and gathering societies with equalitarian distribution of sexual,
economic, and caring responsibilities to
agricultural societies with elaborate patterns
of sex typing. The ancient civilizations of the
Mediterranean shared a relatively uninhibited
sexual outlook and expanded the scope of
sexual activities. The Greeks in particular
recognized the bisexual and promiscuous
tendencies of men and women and tolerated
most sexual activities, as long as they did not
threaten the survival of the family. The Romans, too, practiced a variety of sexual activities. However, in spite of the open display of
sexual extremes and orgiastic excesses, the
Roman moral code did not officially condone
deviant forms of sexual behavior. Roman sexuality, in general, was characterized by a
touch of crudeness and sadism that were particularly prevalent during the latter period of
the Empire.

The basis of Western hostility to sex that
dominated the culture for at least 500 years
originated in the medieval code of sexuality,
which in turn was reinterpreted by different
societies to meet their specific needs until the
nineteenth century. Both the Middle Ages
and the Victorian era were, by and large, sex-
negative cultures determined largely to
repress the entire subject of sexuality. Human sexuality during the Middle Ages was

in endless orgies. Finally, for every effort
made by the official voices to minimize and
belittle the importance of sex, pornography
emphasized that sex was the only thing in the
world that had any importance at all.

Hidden behind the façade of sexual and
moral prudery was an extensive sexual underworld, the so-called sexual subculture
(Sadock, Kaplan, and Freedman, 1976). Elements of this subculture included not only
prostitution and pornography but also led to
a sharp rise of extramarital sex. The upsurge
of sexual activities outside matrimony was at
least in part a result of the unrealistic roles
prescribed for husband and wife. In addition,
venereal disease had become rampant, and
contraception, although officially taboo, was
unofficially becoming widespread in respectable marriages. Obviously, the members of
the sex culture adhered to codes of sexual
morality significantly different from the official Victorian ethic. Yet there is a connection

controlled by medieval Catholic thinking, which was characterized by an ascetic, anti-sexual outlook. Rather than accepting that human nature could be fulfilled in sexual love, the Church taught that human nature reaches its culmination by denying the physical body. Therefore, the recommendation was for men and women to refrain from sexual activities. In spite of this restricted medieval doctrine, many contradictions existed. Church officials advocated the notion that sex was sinful and evil and advised men and women to concentrate on the spiritual. At the same time, the concept of courtly love introduced an erotic ideology praising the joys of a sensuous life. Women were condemned by the Church and glorified by the troubadours. Essentially, the gulf between the concept of sexuality as put forth by the Church and the sexual activities engaged in by medieval people was unbridgeable.

During the era of the Renaissance, Europeans began to question the traditional concepts of sexuality, which were strongly influenced by Christian morality. With the growth of secularism, many people turned away from organized religion, and the Church gradually ceased to be the major force in the control of sexual behavior. The era of the Renaissance, followed by the Reformation, marks the stages of society's emancipation from medieval restraints. While Europe stood on the threshold of the modern age, one extraordinary episode in history, namely the witch persecutions, appeared to be more in line with medieval thinking than with the intellectual and social changes taking place during the age of the Renaissance and the Reformation.

The emergence of industrialized societies during the nineteenth century led to a shift in sexual attitudes and behaviors. Officially sanctioned were purity, prudery, and discretion. "Victorian" became a synonym for repressive. In spite of the officially sanctioned code of procreative sex, the myth of the sexually passionate yet restrained Victorian gentleman and the ideal of the pure asexual woman dissipated toward the end of the era. Instead, widespread prostitution, a voluminous traffic in pornographic materials, venereal disease, and extramarital activities dominated the Victorian sexual subculture.

Historical surveys reveal that most current forms of sexual behavior have been recorded in the past. Almost every society defined some type of sexual activity as deviant behavior. However, ideas of what constituted deviance showed a good deal of variation from culture to culture and era to era. Historical periods that held punitive attitudes toward sexuality usually failed to ban sexual activities completely from the behavioral repertories of men and women. The extreme denial of sex resulted not so much in the disappearance of sexual behaviors as their submergence in underground subcultures. Somehow, people have always been able to express themselves sexually, even during periods of restriction.

At the end of the nineteenth century, then, historical forces had not only shaped the sexual behavior of men and women but also called for a new conceptualization of sex.

References

Brandon, S. *Creation legends of the ancient near east.* London: Hodder & Stoughton, 1963.

Bullough, V. *Sexual variance in society and history.* New York: John Wiley & Sons, 1976.

Cantor, N. *Medieval history: The life and death of a civilization.* New York: Macmillan, 1963.

Capellanus, A. *The art of courtly love.* Translated by J. Parry, New York: W. W. Norton, 1969.

Chesser, E. *Is chastity outmoded?* Toronto: W. Heineman, 1960.

De Riencourt, A. *Sex and power in history.* New York: David McKay, 1974.

Ellis, A., and Abarnabel, A. *The encyclopedia of sexual behavior.* New York: Hawthorn Books, 1961.

Epstein, L. *Sex laws and customs in Judaism.* New York: Bloch, 1948.

Finley, M. *Aspects of antiquity.* New York: Viking Press, 1968.

Flaceliere, R. *Love in ancient Greece.* New York: Crown, 1962.

Freud, S. *Leonardo da Vinci: A memory of his childhood.* New York: W. W. Norton, 1964.

Freud, S. "Female sexuality" (1931). In Strouse, J. (ed.). *Women and analysis.* New York: Grossman, 1974.

Henningsen, G. *The European witch persecution.* Danish Folklore Archives, Copenhagen, 1973.

Horney, K. *Feminine psychology.* New York: W. W. Norton, 1967.

Hunt, M. *The natural history of love.* New York: Alfred Knopf, 1959.

Johnson, W. *Masturbation.* Sex Information and Education Council of the U.S., 1976.

Marcus, S. *The other Victorians.* New York: Bantam, 1967.

Masters, R. *Eros and witchcraft.* Baltimore: Penguin Books, 1972.

Murstein, B. *Love, sex, and marriage through the ages.* New York: Springer, 1974.

Pearson, M. *The five-pound virgins.* New York: Saturday Review Press, 1972.

Rawson, P. *Primitive erotic art.* London: Weidenfeld and Nicolson, 1973.

Reiss, I. "The sexual renaissance in America." *Journal of Social Issues,* 1966, 22, 2, 1-140.

Roberts, H. "The exquisite slave: The role of clothes in the making of the Victorian woman." *Journal of Women in Culture and Society,* 1977, 2, 3, 554-569.

Roebuck, C. *The world of ancient times.* New York: Charles Scribner's Sons, 1966.

Russell, J. *Witchcraft in the middle ages.* Ithaca, N.Y.: Cornell University Press, 1972.

Sadock, B., Kaplan, H., and Freedman, A. *The sexual experience.* Baltimore: Williams and Wilkins, 1976.

Trevor-Roper, H. *The European witchcraze of the sixteenth and seventeenth century.* Middlesex, England: Penguin Books, 1969.

Trudgill, E. *Madonnas and magdalens: The origins and development of Victorian sexual attitudes.* New York: Holmes and Meier, 1976.

Vanggard, T. *Phallos: A symbol and its history in the male world.* New York: International University Press, 1972.

Walters, R. *Primers for prudery: Sexual advice to Victorian America.* Englewood Cliffs, N.J.: Prentice-Hall, 1974.

Yorburg, B. *Sexual identity.* New York: John Wiley & Sons, 1975.

Chapter 3

The Sexual Revolution

We saw in the last chapter that the main foundations of the sexual repressiveness that characterized nineteenth-century attitudes toward sexuality were a product of the Victorian period. By the end of the century, Victorianism had become a shorthand term for the dominant sexual tradition and morality. It stood for an antisexual period during which sex was taboo and not to be talked about. Social standards governing the sexual conduct of the Victorians were rigidly antisex-oriented without allowances for exceptions. Officially, almost every expression of sexuality met with hostility or condemnation. At the turn of the century, however, it had become evident that the hypocritical Victorian sexual ethos would not suit the sociocultural climate of the twentieth century.

Many people associate the sexual revolution with a complete liberation of social and moral constraints, as if the new sexuality were all a matter of group sex and orgies, with men and women engaging in sexual activities that could only be imagined before. Behind the sexual revolution, which is much more than a revolt against the restricted Victorian codes of sexual behavior, lies the recognition and conviction that all forms of sexuality—heterosexual, homosexual, premarital, extramarital, adolescent—are a reflection of the sexual drives and preferences of people who seek satisfying sexual experience. At a deeper level, the sexual revolution may not only be regarded as a reaction against Victorianism but also as a protest against the sexual ideology portrayed by the Judeo-Christian ideal, which restricts sexual activities to those who are "joined in holy wedlock."

At the eve of the sexual revolution at least three important goals were considered crucial and needed to be achieved in order to justify the term sexual revolution (Rinzema, 1976). The first goal involved the removal of taboos surrounding sexuality. One such taboo, masturbation, was thought to lead to mental disturbances. Similarly, sexual "excess" was generally believed to result in physical debilitation. Women were required "to submit" to their husbands' sexual demands. If a woman initiated a sexual encounter she was easily labeled a nymphomaniac. Even at the beginning of the twentieth century many people supported the old morals out of fear and anxiety, assuming that a breakdown of sexual taboos would lead to a complete breakdown of the traditional morality.

The second goal of the sexual revolution was the fight for equal sexual rights for women. The old norms not only gave men the prerogative of initiating sexual relations, but also implied that women had a less powerful sex drive than men. Consequently, it was believed that women had a lesser need for sex than men.

Ideally, sexual equality for women would eliminate the so-called double standard, which prescribes different sexual prerogatives for men and women. Essentially, the double standard implies the notion of sexual inferiority of women, which is, of course, incompatible with equal sexual rights and privileges for both sexes. During the first decades of the twentieth century social pressures forced drastic revisions of the Victorian pattern of male-female relationships—a pattern according to which men had the right to enjoy sexual activities but women had to endure them. The quest for equal sexual rights for women is not over, although the myth of sexual inferiority of women has been almost completely discredited.

Finally, the third major aspect of the sexual revolution concerned a change in moral standards to accommodate the new attitudes toward sex. With the easing up of sexual constraints, many of which were founded on ignorance and prejudice, people required greater personal freedom to choose and change in sexual relationships. For example, traditional morality accepted only one form of sexual partnership—that of one man and one woman joined in marriage. This traditional code provided no solutions for the unmarried or people with unconventional sexual preferences. Moreover, it failed to recognize that sexuality has a value of its own, apart from any relationship to marriage. Proponents of the sexual revolution therefore argued vehemently for a separation of heterosexual relations and reproduction as part of the new morality.

After the antisex syndrome of the Victorian period it was not surprising to see revolutionary ideas and goals swinging in the direction of "sex is everything." However, as happens often in many reactionary periods, the changes in sexual behavior and attitudes that were ultimately brought about were not as extreme or radical as one might have expected at the onset of the revolution. The changes that have occurred emerged gradually and were closely linked to sociocultural changes. In this chapter we will examine some of these social changes responsible for a redefinition of nineteenth-century sexuality and pay tribute to the men and women whose work was instrumental in producing the changes we have witnessed during this century.

Sex Out of the Closet

Changes in sexual standards are intimately associated with the social changes that have occurred over the last seven decades. From the turn of the century to the 1920s, many Western societies evidenced a transition from the industrial to the postindustrial era, from an age of production to an age of consumption (Lipton, 1965). Whereas the majority of men and women were preoccupied with survival before and during the industrial period, people of the postindustrial age are afforded the luxury of leisure time. Sex, of course, thrives on prosperity and

leisure. What work meant for the old era, play was to the new. The shift into the postindustrial age also provided increased social and economic freedom for women. In less than two decades the sexual ideology of the nineteenth century became obsolete.

American society entered a period of enormous changes during the 1920s, a decade ushering in automobiles and contraceptives. Men and women of the "Roaring Twenties" suddenly experienced freedoms heretofore unknown. The automobile not only offered young people the opportunity to escape from supervision temporarily but also provided sheltered privacy for sexual experimentation. By 1919, Americans were interested in or practicing birth control. In addition to providing control over one's fertility, contraceptive devices allow a couple to separate procreative from nonprocreative or recreational sex. With the link between sexual intercourse and reproduction broken, the connection of intercourse with marriage lost much of its validity.

The use of contraceptives also led to a decline in birth rates. Reformers in the 1920s suggested that family size should be limited. With the goal of zero population growth, this trend is even stronger today. The suburban matron who produces her eighth child, obligating the community to provide additional educational and recreational facilities, may provoke negative sanctions from neighbors or friends (Bernard, 1966).

The prewar changes had been largely limited to the upper class, which became very preoccupied with sex. After World War I other social classes began to model their sexual behavior after the upper class. Taboos about sex discussion were lifted and men and women talked freely about sexual preferences, inhibitions, and "sex starvations" (O'Neill, 1972). The beginnings of greater sexual freedom were also reflected in the fashions of the period. Numerous undergarments disappeared and loose, low-cut

Figure 3.1
Men and women experienced greater sexual freedom with the advent of
the automobile. (Bettman Archive Inc.)

dresses became fashionable, underscoring women's increased activities and recognition of their sexuality.

At the same time, Freud's theory of human sexuality (see Chapter 4) had a profound and inevitable influence on the revolution of sexual morals. Not only did Freud reject many of the restrictions of Victorian sexuality, but he also expressed his conviction that sex is a major aspect in our life from infancy to old age. Freud's theory implied that unless we freely express our sexual desires, and provide outlets for our sexual energies, we could jeopardize our mental health. This notion was the antithesis of the rigid, hypocritical Victorian ethic. In spite of his revolutionary ideas, Freud had an extremely conservative view of sex; he saw it as a powerful, even "chaotic force" that required taming.

The Roaring Twenties

The decade of the 1920s, which brought pronounced changes in sexual attitudes, has often been compared to our own recent decade of the 1960s (Steinman and Fox, 1974). The flapper and Joe College were probably no less puzzling and threatening to parents in the 1920s than hippies were to parents of the 1960s; alcohol, under Prohibition, was probably no less inviting than marijuana was forty years later; petting and free love in automobiles no less tempting than group sex became.

As a result of the changes of the 1920s, many Americans became preoccupied with self-analysis and self-evaluation of their sexual behavior during the following decade. It was a period in which satisfaction and climax became the most important considerations in sexual encounters. This was reflected in the proliferation of marriage manuals emphasizing sexual satisfaction for women and making the responsibility for producing it a male concern. One of the most popular marriage manuals was Theodore van de Velde's (1873-1937) *Ideal Marriage*, which went through forty-two printings between acceptable to a generation severely inhibited by the Victorian tradition (Brecher, 1969).

Economic Depression

The national economic depression of the 1930s prematurely terminated the evolution of further changes and put a lid on the gains of sexual freedom. Large numbers of women were forced to seek employment for minimal pay. The traditional definitions of masculinity and femininity began to blur. A man was no longer masculine because he worked or made love. To be feminine traditionally meant to be passive, obedient, and, if possible, pretty. Seldom was a woman considered apart from her husband and family. While this conceptualization of the female role may have been satisfactory or functional for nineteenth-century women, it certainly clashed with the values and ideals of the period immediately preceding World War II, when women were on the verge of consciousness of their own economic potential.

Beginnings of Birth Control

Nationwide polls in 1936 reported a majority of 70 percent of men and women in favor of teaching or practicing birth control. Condoms, once concealed by censorship, were distributed in gasoline stations, tobacco stores, and poolrooms. The automobile and amusement parks continued to permit or facilitate more open expressions of sexuality.

World War II

War has always had an interesting and intimate relationship with sex, because the sexual behavior of men and women during times of war represents a distinct, highly visible departure from the prevailing norms of proper sexual conduct. Many times in history, wars have given fighting men a license to seek uncensored release of their passions.

Figure 3.2
The flapper of the 1920's. (Bettman Archive Inc.)

1926 and 1932 in Germany alone, and forty-three printings in the English translation. In this manual the author stressed the importance of variety in intercourse to avoid monotony in marital sex. Ten positions were described in detail, six in which male and female are face to face and four with the male behind the female. In addition, van de Velde recommended the use of various types of foreplay including, daringly for that time, oral genital stimulation. One of van de Velde's main concerns was how a married couple could learn to achieve ideal communication and simultaneous orgasm. Perhaps his greatest contribution was that van de Velde found a way to make at least some of the joys of human sexuality aesthetically and ethically

This was true during World War II. Thousands of virgins offered themselves as nurses or aides and followed the troops to the front. Many women who were detained desired passionately to make some sacrifice by offering sexual services in order to be able to participate in the mass delirium.

The period of World War II witnessed a transient but profound breakdown of the traditional sexual morality. In the spirit of feverish abandon, the population swelled with war brides, war prostitutes, and war babies. And even though involvement in war meant that freedom from sexual constraints was temporary, it was unthinkable that women would adhere again to the old traditions that categorically separated good women from bad women, the moral from the immoral.

Sexuality during the Postwar Era

The postwar period saw a renewed agitation for improved status of women.

Many forces contributed to provide a new impetus for the movement, among them the quest for economic independence and increased educational opportunities. Gradually, expanding roles for women outside the home emerged, mainly as a result of greater economic and geographical mobility. Since the 1950s there has been a steady movement from the small town to the big city and from the big cities to the suburbs. As a result of increased job mobility, family ties have loosened and women have been forced to consider alternatives to fulltime home-making.

By the 1950s sexual standards and mores had become significantly different from the Victorian ideal. Many Western cultures had become societies of abundance rather than scarcity. The economic change was also reflected in the sexual sphere. Sexual abundance became an important commodity; heterosexual, gay, bisexual, swinging, autoerotic, married, and single sex became acceptable practices. All sorts of sexual

Figure 3.3
Kissing orgy. Soldiers and sailors celebrate the reunion with their wives. (Bettman Archive Inc.)

Figure 3.4
Sex-appealing ads advertise many different products. (Dwyer and Zinkl)

relationships, ranging from the most refined expression of human emotions to the release of primitive urges, became feasible.

In a society characterized by a drive for consumption, sexual pleasure became a prominent consumer commodity. This is most clearly reflected by the media, which has increasingly applied sex as a selling device, playing on sexual fantasies and anxieties. Sensuous-looking women appear on the hoods of the latest car models or behind a tube of toothpaste. The nude female breast, formerly portrayed only in pornographic magazines, has become an everyday sight in the advertisements of many products. Cigarette ads feature rugged men engaged in outdoor activities while beer consumers are alerted to the new, slim beer can designed for the woman buyer. Many times, as Packard (1957) has pointed out, the merits of the product are irrelevant; instead, the advertisement caters to the images of masculinity and femininity.

Increased sexual freedom not only became visible in the media, but was further perpetuated by the first report of successful inhibition of ovulation by oral contraceptives in 1956. Within a few years millions of women were taking the "pill." With the fear of unwanted pregnancy removed, many restrictions formerly imposed on sexual activities disappeared. At least theoretically, the scientific advances in contraception promised to make involuntary reproduction a phenomenon of the past.

Women's Liberation Movement

The introduction of oral contraceptives provided a new impetus for a continued reevaluation and redefinition of female sexuality. According to the traditional conceptualization of male and female sex roles, male sexuality was associated with economic power and dominance over dependent women. The women's liberation movement which began during the latter part of the nineteenth century set out to destroy the image of the yielding, responsive, and

Figure 3.5
The women's liberation movement in the early days (1907). (Bettman Archive Inc.)

appreciative woman and replace it by a new conceptualization of femininity, according to which women do not submit sexually to men but claim sex as a right.

Changing Roles of Women

A number of social changes occurring during the late 1950s and 1960s facilitated the redefinition of the feminine role. Oral contraception, a plethora of labor-saving household appliances, and increased participation of women in competitive employment produced social changes calling for a restructuring of the role of women in virtually all aspects of daily life.

In the 1960s an old theory reappeared: sexual equality. With the publication of Kate Millet's *Sexual Politics,* (1969) and Germaine Greer's *The Female Eunuch* (1971), a new wave of the women's liberation movement began. Again, the major goal was to change stereotypical ideas about what women are

capable of doing and how they should behave to fulfill their potential as individuals with personal talents and particular sexual needs.

Moderate feminists argued for egalitarian status of women within the traditional family structure, while the more radical proponents of the movement advocated the abolishment of the patriarchal family. Hand in hand with the social manifestations of the feminist movement went demands for sexual reforms. The discovery of the pill resulted in a generation of women who took complete control over and responsibility for their reproductive functions, independent of, and without need for, male cooperation. Extremists such as Shere Hite (1976) went even further, urging women to secure sexual gratification independent of men. One women's liberationist declared, "It is wonderful that women have discovered masturbation because it will enable them to keep apart from men as long as necessary." (Frankl, 1974). At a more conservative level, women were encouraged to take the responsibility of understanding their sexual responses rather than aim for abstract standards such as multiple orgasms or the expectations of their partners.

Many feminists—moderate as well as radical—feel that women's sexual liberation, the freedom to please and to be pleased, the freedom to make choices and to enjoy their sexuality, can take place only if women achieve economic independence and equality. Numerous investigators (Broverman, Vogel, Broverman, Clarkson, and Rosenkrantz, 1972, Lunneborg, 1970) have noted that sex-role stereotypes are still widely held. Despite the apparent flexibility of sex-role definitions in our contemporary society, contrasted with previous decades, sex-role stereotypes are pervasive and persistent. These stereotypes ascribe characteristics to men that entail competence, rationality, and assertion, traits highly relevant to professional or occupational success. Women, on the other hand, are perceived as relatively less competent, less independent, less objective, with feminine traits forming a cluster that reflect warmth and expressiveness. In the eyes of many, the existence of sex-role stereotypes is a major barrier to economic independence of women (see Chapter 17).

The women's liberation movement has had a considerable influence on the attitudes of many people, but particularly of women. Travis and Jayaratne (1973) reported that two out of three women favored the women's liberation movement. Among single women, this proportion increased to almost eight out of ten. Furthermore, about one-half of the women admitted that the feminist movement had changed their thinking. Fewer than 2 percent of women indicated that most women can best develop their potential by being good wives and mothers. Traditional women, as well as proponents of the feminist movement, share a strong belief in the equality of women. Since a greater number of women are leaving the traditional realm of the home to enter the world of work, we can expect a strengthening commitment to the principle of equality of the sexes.

Critiques of the Feminist Movement

The feminist movement has not been accepted uncritically but has had its opponents. People of both sexes have expressed the fear that women's sexual liberation means neglected child rearing or no marriage. Men in particular have viewed the feminist movement as a threat, since it encourages women to compete for money, jobs, and power.

As an ideology, the women's liberation movement presently reflects a considerable degree of ambiguity about female sexuality. Some feminists have called for less sex because women are viewed as sex objects or sexual playmates rather than whole persons.

As women have increasingly attacked and withdrawn from the traditional male-centered sexual behavior, they seem to be abandoning both men and sex itself (Coyner, 1976). On the other hand, there are those feminist voices demanding more sex and wanting to maximize female pleasure. Armed with the findings of Masters and Johnson (1966) attesting to women's capacity for multiple orgasms, the advocates of "more sex for women" encourage nontraditional behaviors such as masturbation and bisexuality. And, finally, there are those feminists generally identified with NOW (National Organization for Women) who are not primarily concerned with issues of sexuality or intimacy. As a group, these women are more interested in the social problems facing contemporary women, especially the limitations imposed on women by traditional sex roles and stereotypes and the discriminations that keep women from exploring other life options. Equalizing educational and occupational opportunities remains a major priority for this group.

Sex on Campus

Just as the feminist movement has been viewed as making significant contributions to the sexual revolution, some people have alleged that we are undergoing a sexual revolution because many college students are engaging in intercourse prior to marriage. Sharing room, board, and bed has become an acceptable housing alternative for many students at coeducational schools.

How much change has there been in sexual attitudes and behaviors among university students? Recent surveys suggest that important changes in students' attitudes are reflected in "cohabitation on campus," which has become widespread and open. The significant number of unmarried couples living together across the country represents

Figure 3.6
The sex liberators: H. Ellis (Bettman Archive Inc.), W. H. Masters and Virginia E. Johnson (Masters and Johnson Institute, St. Louis, Missouri), Alfred C. Kinsey (William Dellenback, Institute for Sex Research), S. Hite (United Press International, Inc.)

an important contemporary living pattern of the college scene.

Based on available research, estimates of the number of college students living together range from less than 10 percent to more than 33 percent, depending on a variety of factors, among them housing and parietal regulations, the geographic location of the university, and the male-female student ratio. The effects of housing and parietal regulations and their enforcement are of particular importance. Some universities offer twenty-four hour visitation privileges or off-campus housing. Although, from the students' viewpoint, parietal rules are designed more for curbing rather than condoning sexual experiences, cohabitation is more frequent at institutions with liberal housing and visitation arrangements. On the other hand, colleges that do not permit off-campus housing and place restrictions on opposite-sex visitors or even enforce a separation of male and female students, can be expected to have a lower number of students living together. At these colleges the motel room frequently becomes the principle off-campus facility for sexual experiences. And, finally, there are many universities located in sexually conservative regions or with very strict regulations, where

cohabitation is still an exception, likely to have negative social consequences.

Cohabitation Statistics

Table 3.1 presents some statistics that were summarized from cohabitation surveys

Table 3.1

Survey of Students Living Together

School	Definition of Cohabitation	Housing Policy	Rate of Cohabitation		Sample Size*
			Current	Ever	
1. City College City University of New York	Living together relationship with a member of the opposite sex.	Commuter.	20% (23% M*) (17% F)	—	900 UG
2. Small liberal arts college in Midwest†	Share bedroom and bed with someone of the opposite sex to whom not married for four or more nights a week for three or more months.	All but 10% on campus; 24-hour visitation.	—	17% (18% M) (15% F)	200 UG
3. Small liberal arts college in Midwest†	Same	On-campus, noncoed dorms; no 24-hour visitation (except one senior dorm).	—	9%	175 UG
4. Arizona State University	Two unrelated persons of the opposite sex living together without being legally married.	Majority off-campus; 24-hour visitation.	—	29% M 18% F	350 UG
5. California State University	Two persons of the opposite sex living together in a relatively permanent manner similar in many respects to marriage but without legal or religious sanctions.	Majority off-campus.	10% M 9% F	25% (30% M) (21% F)	557 UG/G
6. Cornell University	Same as 2 and 3.	Off-campus options, 24-hour visitation.	10% M 9% F	31% (20% M) (21% F)	400 UG
7. Pennsylvania University	Are now or have ever lived with someone of the opposite sex.	Off-campus options, 24-hour visitation.	—	33% (33% M) (32% F)	2,500 UG
8. Univ. of Texas Austin	Are now living with a person of the opposite sex.	Off-campus options, 34-hour visitation.	—	36%	431 UG/G

* UG—undergraduate; G—graduate; M—male; F—female.
† These two schools requested anonymity.

Source: E. Macklin, University of Maryland, Personal Communication, 1979.

on college campuses across the country. The table also points to the vagueness and ambiguity found in definitions of cohabitation. Definitions have ranged anywhere from academic terms such as "consensual" cohabitation to more popular terms such as "living together," to rather pejorative labels such as "shacking up."

In the early 1970s psychologist Eleanor Macklin conducted a study of college students living together at Cornell University, a large coeducational school in upstate New York, that shed some light on the dynamics of cohabitation (Macklin, 1974). Probably the most important finding of the study was that there were no significant differences in academic performance between student couples living together and those who choose not to. Despite the fears of many parents, cohabitation does not interfere with academic success nor does it lead to reduced attention to schoolwork. The second important finding concerned the reasons given for living together. About 70 percent of the students of the Cornell sample indicated that they were emotionally attached to one another. This finding is consistent with earlier results reported by Reiss (1966), indicating that young people, although less sexually inhibited than past generations, display a tolerance strongly linked with affection. Other reasons for living together included security, companionship, the loneliness of a large university, and the superficiality of the dating game.

The Cornell study, as well as those conducted at other schools, clearly revealed that students viewed living together not as a preparation for marriage but as an end in itself; however, most considered marriage as a viable alternative and intended to marry eventually.

Patterns of Cohabitation

The most common pattern of cohabitation is for the female student to move in with her boyfriend. A smaller percentage of students share a dormitory room, and still fewer live alone as a couple in an off-campus setting. In most instances, students living together officially maintain separate residences, which often serve as mail-drops only. Although the majority of students spend seven nights a week together, some prefer to return to their own rooms to have some time alone or to be with their roommates and friends. Most student couples share the household chores and costs for food and entertainment, but few go so far as to pool their financial resources completely.

Cohabitation has emerged as an acceptable living pattern on many campuses. The available data seem to suggest that college students living together are primarily concerned with the total quality of the relationship and that the sexual aspects of this relationship—often unduly overemphasized—are an integral part of the ongoing involvement with and commitment to each other. Whether or not the relationship will grow into a permanent partnership depends on a number of factors, among them the depth of commitment in the relationship and the cohabitation experience itself. In the meantime, however, living together represents an experience to be enjoyed as an end in itself.

The Liberators

In addition to the social changes that have taken place over the last fifty years there have been a number of men and women whose research, thinking, or theorizing contributed a great deal to our present attitudes toward sex and the sexual freedom we are enjoying. Since it is impossible to include the work of all sex researchers who have helped to bring sex out of the closet, we will limit our discussion to the most influential ones.

Early Sex Research

Most of the early sex studies were either rather unscientific or based on inadequate samples. Nevertheless, much could be learned from them, and many early investigations revealed startling bits of information. Women, for example, who had made love in the missionary position for so long, were surprised to learn that they were capable of orgasms. Homosexuality, another example, was first identified as separate from transvestism by Magnus Hirschfeld as late as 1910. As a matter of fact, Hirschfeld was probably one of the most progressive sex researchers of his time. During the latter years of the 1920s he organized the "World League for Sexual Reform" to implement the following program (Reich, 1974):

1. Political, economic, and sexual equality for women.
2. Liberation of marriage, particularly divorce, from all domination by church or state.
3. Protection of unwed mothers and their children.
4. Accurate evaluation of nonconventional sexual behaviors, especially as applied to homosexual men and women.
5. Prevention of prostitution and venereal diseases.
6. Planned sex education.

In spite of Hirschfeld's deliberate efforts, sex research did not become systematic until the Kinsey studies.

Nevertheless, some of the early sex researchers were men of science whose work put sex on the map as a proper scientific discipline and gave rise to a new intellectual type, the sexologist. Major contributions were made by Havelock Ellis, Alfred Kinsey, William Masters and Virginia Johnson. These sex researchers undermined the assumptions of Victorian thinking about sexuality

and repudiated many of the sexual doctrines of the past. As Robinson (1976) has pointed out, their repudiations have grown more emphatic as the twentieth century progresses. From Ellis to Kinsey to Masters and Johnson, the absurdities of Victorian prohibition are denounced with increasing vehemence.

Havelock Ellis (1859-1939)

A central figure in the emergence of modern attitudes toward sexuality was Havelock Ellis, who studied the sex lives of his Victorian contemporaries. He recorded his findings in a monumental series of volumes, *Studies in the Psychology of Sex,* published and periodically revised between 1896 and 1928. The books contained in this series describe the physical aspects of sexual functions, together with elements little appreciated at the time, such as the significance of touch, smell, or sight in sexual encounters.

Ellis knew that he lived in the middle of a pathologically modest society. He refuted the notion that women lacked sexual feelings and suggested that women were at least equal to men in their sexual needs. Ellis did, however, maintain that female sexuality was essentially passive. Although Ellis voiced a strong plea for the sexual rights of women, he was not successful in eliminating the masculine bias of the Victorian sexual ethic.

Ellis's studies covered almost all of the generally recognized variations—male and female homosexuality, masochism, sadism, incest, and transvestism, to name only a few. In his writings Ellis expressed empathy and understanding for even those sexual variations, which his contemporaries found repelling and disgusting.

In regard to heterosexuality, Ellis was a romantic who believed that the proper context for sexual relations is the complex emotional state we call love. In his private life

Ellis lived out his beliefs. He and his wife Edith decided not to have children and agreed to end sexual relations with each other while accepting each other's extramarital relationships; Edith's were all with women. Ellis took both the enduring relationships of his wife with a series of young women, as well as her more casual mistresses, in stride. He himself engaged in a number of extramarital affairs. In addition, he was known to enjoy sexual arousal at the fantasy or the observation of a woman urinating, preferably in a standing position.

In his sixties, after the death of his wife, Ellis formed the first really satisfying sexual union in his life: he fell in love with a woman thirty-six years younger than he, and they lived together, without getting married, for the remaining twenty years of his life.

Ellis not only paved the way for the more tolerant sexual standards of our own day but also anticipated the findings of Kinsey, Masters and Johnson, and other recent sex researchers. For instance, Ellis maintained that orgasm is remarkably similar for men and women, an observation confirmed later by Masters and Johnson. Similarly, he suggested that homosexuality and heterosexuality are not absolutes like black and white, but are present in men and women in varying degrees, reflecting expressions of sexuality along the same continuum. Finally, Ellis recognized male impotence and female frigidity as psychological rather than physiological phenomena.

Ellis was also an active crusader who campaigned all his life for early sex education for children, birth control, an end to the concept of illegitimacy, experimental unions for couples without marriage, and for the repeal of criminal laws against homosexual acts between consenting adults. Perhaps Ellis's most significant contribution to the liberation of sex lies in the pervasive attitudes of tolerance and enthusiasm with which he approached all forms of human sexuality.

Alfred Kinsey (1894-1956)

"How do I love thee? Let me count the ways," Elizabeth Barrett Browning had written in the Victorian era. Alfred Kinsey took her literally and counted who does what sexually, when and with whom. The resulting figures and reports Kinsey published startled the majority of the population because they played havoc with the archaic sexual standards of the time. Even today, Kinsey's figures are still widely cited, since there are no others of comparable scope to contradict them.

Before embarking on the monumental task of collecting statistics concerning the frequencies of sexual behaviors of thousands of men and women, Dr. Kinsey was a respected zoologist, teacher, collector of wasps, and author of a widely used biology text. When he was appointed in 1938 to coordinate a new course in marriage at Indiana University, he realized that he could not answer many of the frank questions about sex raised by his students. "Knowing a good deal about gall wasps but little about human sexual behavior," Dr. Pomeroy, his close associate of many years notes, Kinsey went to the library to learn more (Pomeroy, 1972). He soon learned that apparently no one else knew very much either. As a matter of fact, there were few scientific or quantitative answers to be found. Most of Kinsey's predecessors, including van de Velde and Freud, knew little about statistics. Some of their most serious errors resulted directly from the failure to use at least some rudimentary or crude statistics to support their observations. For example, early in his writings Freud concluded that intercourse with a condom leads to anxiety neurosis. In order for this conclusion to be valid, however, statistics should demonstrate that anxiety neurosis is more frequent among couples when the man wears a condom than among other couples who resemble condom users in other relevant respects but practice a different type of birth control. In Kinsey's opinion the type of research badly needed to test the theories and observations of earlier sex researchers would be based on statistics. Kinsey pioneered to collect and analyze statistical information about sexual behavior.

In the absence of any reliable data regarding the various sexual habits and practices of his contemporaries, Kinsey turned the tables on his students. Since he could not tell them what other people did sexually, he could at least ask his students what they did. Within a short period of less than a year, Kinsey had secured some 350 sexual histories of his students—which provided the foundation for his later collection of data.

The centerpiece of Kinsey's research was the personal interview. The goal was to collect, through interviews, 100,000 sexual histories, which for Kinsey represented a method of investigation that could break through barriers of modesty and prejudice. The interviewers, all of them male, were carefully screened. Kinsey demanded that they must be happily married, be able to travel about half of the time and possess a doctoral degree. Only six interviewers were used in the male study and four in the female study. Kinsey worked primarily with formal and informal groups and made ingenious use of social pressures (Hyman and Barmack, 1954). He described some group contacts that required a year or two of cultivation before group members would consent to be interviewed.

The interview itself covered between 300 and 500 items and required about two hours for completion. Kinsey did not use a conventional questionnaire. Although the items to be covered and the definitions of each item were standard, the interviewer had the freedom to vary the wording, as well as the sequence of particular questions, in the most meaningful way for the respondent.

Each interview began with a series of nonsexual, neutral questions, such as asking the respondent's age and education. Questioning then gradually led into sexual but emotionally neutral topics, for example, establishing the age of onset of puberty. Typically, the more provocative questions, the frequency of intercourse or homosexual acts, for instance, were reserved for the latter part of the interview.

Altogether, 5,300 males and 5,940 females were interviewed. Kinsey reported his findings in two volumes, *Sexual Behavior in the Human Male* (1948) and *Sexual Behavior in the Human Female* (1953). Upon publication, many people were highly disturbed by Kinsey's concept of sexual "outlets" such as pre- and extramarital intercourse, homosexual relations, or animal contacts. A major finding of the reports was the high frequency of both sanctioned and unsanctioned forms of sexual behaviors. For example, Kinsey reported that over 96 percent of men masturbated, as did 85 percent of all women. Kinsey must be counted among the foremost defenders of masturbation. He was convinced that *auto-eroticism* was harmless, no matter how often one indulged in it. He also argued that masturbation, especially in the case of women, can help a person achieve satisfactory adjustment in marriage.

When Kinsey laid to rest the part of the double standard that maintained that women got no pleasure at all from sex, many people believed that a new sexual revolution was afoot. Equally shocking to some people were Kinsey figures indicating that 37 percent of males had or will have at least one homosexual experience to the point of orgasm. The corresponding figures concerning the incidence of female homosexuality were somewhat lower for women. Twenty-eight percent of female respondents reported that they had had one or more lesbian experiences by the age of forty-five. At an age when the official version of normal sexual behavior was defined within narrow puritanical limits, holdovers of nineteenth-century Victorianism, Kinsey's statistics aroused considerable alarm and disbelief.

Kinsey's report on multiple female orgasm caused as much consternation as his statistics giving the incidence of male and female homosexuality. Some people simply dismissed the idea of multiple orgasm as fantastic tales told to the interviewers by female volunteers.

Another major revelation was Kinsey's discovery that a person's sexual behavior is significantly influenced by his or her social-class membership. Kinsey's data showed that people from middle and upper classes differed considerably from those of lower socioeconomic levels in their sexual behaviors and attitudes. As a matter of fact, Kinsey concluded that the differences in sexual styles between lower and upper classes were as great as those between separate national cultures. The Kinsey reports characterized the sexual life of the poor as determined by a single-minded commitment to genital relations, above all heterosexual intercourse. Members of the middle or upper classes, in contrast, are more likely to engage in a variety of sexual behaviors, including nongenital activities, reflecting a more differentiated and sophisticated style of sexual behaviors. Kinsey's discovery of the existence of two distinct class patterns of sexual behavior has been supported by the subsequent research, some of which we shall be discussing in Chapter 8.

Although the Kinsey reports extended people's knowledge of sexuality in a spectacular way, his findings were not received without criticism. While the Kinsey studies have been attacked on a number of counts, most criticisms have been directed at the sampling procedures employed. It has been rightly claimed that the sample in both the male and female study did not represent a true cross-section of the American people. The male sample was weighted toward un-educated men, whereas the female sample was biased in the opposite direction, that is, it contained too many educated women. Since the male and female samples were biased in opposite directions, interpretations of male-female differences found in the data are difficult to make, and remain inconclusive. In addition, both samples were geographically restricted.

A second criticism related to the composition of the sample concerns the validity of volunteer samples. Many people are suspicious that the men and women who volunteered for the project were among the less inhibited members of society who enjoyed disclosing intimate details about their sex lives. Respondents who agreed to be interviewed may also have engaged in more varied types of sexual activities and may have done so more frequently. Bergler (1969), for instance, suspected that the sample contained many homosexuals who gladly used the opportunity to show by volunteering that "everybody" has homosexual tendencies, thus diminishing their own guilt.

Finally, some people criticized Kinsey for his mechanical study of sex. In the first volume, virtually no direct data were collected on the psychological processes underlying the reported overt male sexual behavior. In the female study, Kinsey was more accurately aware of this need and collected some attitudinal and psychological data. Nevertheless, in both studies there is little emphasis on the quality of interpersonal relationships between men and women and their perception of sex. The primary focus appears to be on "outlets" and the number of orgasms achieved through the various sources. Pomeroy (1972) defends Kinsey's ideology by reminding us that Kinsey was first and last a taxonomist—a namer, describer, and classifier of behavior. He used the modern taxonomic approach that he had helped to develop by studying gall wasps and applied it to a field as controversial as human sexuality.

Whatever their shortcomings, the Kinsey data today remain the most complete and most reliable sampling of human sexual behavior. Kinsey's research not only dispelled many superstitions that could have delayed the "revolution," but also established a tradition that led to the Masters and Johnson studies and the setting up of sex clinics. Apart from their intrinsic value, Kinsey's reports have helped considerably to establish sex research as a legitimate and important field of research.

William Masters and Virginia Johnson

At about the same time that Kinsey died in 1956, Dr. William Masters and his assistant Virginia Johnson commenced their work at Washington University, St. Louis. Their laboratory work investigating the physiology of the human sexual response (see Chapter 5) was built upon Kinsey's work and was helped by changes in public opinion that the Kinsey reports had provoked. Where Kinsey had asked people only how they behaved sexually, Masters and Johnson brought sex into the lab, observing people directly. Whereas Kinsey's focal commitment was to research, Masters and Johnson are primarily concerned with sex therapy (see Chapter 14 for a detailed discussion of Masters and Johnson's sex therapy program).

Dr. Masters launched his sex studies in 1964, starting off with prostitutes who contributed their sexual and professional histories to his project. Almost immediately, however, he realized that prostitutes had some atypical characteristics that set them apart from the average American in whom Masters was primarily interested. For example, many prostitutes exhibited a chronic congestion of the pelvic region as a result of frequent sexual stimulation without orgasmic release. Masters concluded that observations of prostitutes would probably be of little

value in establishing sexual response patterns in average women.

Setting out to find "respectable" volunteers, Masters decided to hire a woman to help him interview and screen them. He found Ms. Johnson, who was looking for a job when Masters advertised for an assistant. Their association became one of the great twentieth-century research partnerships, and nearly twenty years after the beginning of the project they married.

Recruiting volunteers turned out to be a relatively simple task after Masters announced to the university community that private funding had enabled him to establish the Reproductive Biology Research Foundation to study the human sexual response based on laboratory observations. Of the 1,273 men and women who volunteered, 694 were accepted to become participants of the project. Included in the 694 individuals were 276 married couples and 106 women and 36 men not married. The unmarried participants mainly took part in those units of the project not requiring sexual intercourse, such as studies of male patterns of ejaculation or the effects of contraceptives on the female sexual response.

Each participant was questioned about his or her personal and sexual history by a team composed of a male and female interviewer. This interview format is based on the assumption that some people talk more freely with someone of the same sex whereas others feel more comfortable and less inhibited with a person of the opposite sex. In addition, variations in the account that a person gives to a male vs. a female interviewer may reveal some clinically interesting differences. The two-sex interview team and, later, a male-female therapist team became standard features of Masters and Johnson's research and therapy.

The actual laboratory procedures, initiated after the participants felt secure in the surroundings and became accustomed to the presence of the investigators as well as the highly specialized equipment, involved basic types of sexual stimulation: masturbation, artificial intercourse (by means of vibrators), and natural intercourse. Under each condition, physiological recordings of bodily changes were measured, behavioral observations were recorded, and participants had the opportunity to describe their subjective experiences before, during, and after sexual stimulation. It has been conservatively estimated that 10,000 complete cycles of sexual response were studied in the first decade of the research program (Masters and Johnson, 1966).

The report of the work, published under the title *Human Sexual Response*, not only confirmed some of the controversial findings of the Kinsey reports, but established a valid physiological basis of human sexuality on which psychological theories can be built. The work of Masters and Johnson is the first scientifically valid description of how the human body responds to sexual stimulation. Responses of the penis, testes, vagina, breasts, and other parts of the body are presented and explained. In addition to providing a viable biological and physiological basis of sexuality, the work of Masters and Johnson helped to dispel superstitions and myths. For example, their laboratory studies showed that a man's sexual performance is in no way related to the size of his penis. They also proved Freud's legacy of two types of orgasms—vaginal vs. clitoral—to be a pure speculation without physiological evidence. While Kinsey took women's words that they do not necessarily need rest after an orgasm, as most men do, Masters and Johnson objectively demonstrated that women are capable of multiple orgasms.

By 1969 Masters and Johnson were ready to apply their observations to couples with sexual dysfunctions. In sex-therapy clinics they concentrated on the treatment of impotence and frigidity. The report of Masters and Johnson's work in the area of sex therapy, entitled *Human Sexual Inadequacy*, appeared in 1970. It has become a standard work for sex therapists and has stimulated the development of new treatment methods for people suffering from sexual distress or dysfunction.

Some of the criticisms launched against Kinsey's research have also been advanced against the work of Masters and Johnson. Again, we encounter the problem of inadequate representation of the overall American population in the sample. All the participants had above average levels of education, were sexually responsive, and motivated by a genuine desire to contribute to scientific and clinical progress. Like Kinsey, Masters and Johnson were criticized for focusing on the physiological components of the sexual act, thereby creating a view of human sexuality that is narrowly biological. However, Masters and Johnson do recognize that "sexuality is a dimension and an expression of personality."

And, finally, some critics have concerned themselves with the ethical questions raised by the observation of sexual activities under laboratory conditions. For some people, sex is simply the ultimate area of privacy and hence not appropriate for evaluation by observation. In their opinion, men and women masturbating and performing other sexual acts under the eyes of impartial investigators are violating basic ethical standards.

Prior to the research of Masters and Johnson, many aspects of the human sexual response, normal or dysfunctional, were pure matters of speculation. In the absence of established physiological facts, a number of psychological and sociological theories regarding the sexual response had been postulated and turned out to be fallacies rather than viable constructs. The work of Masters and Johnson is a hallmark in the history of the sexual revolution, providing us with the first scientific and objective account of the orgasmic response.

Recent Sex Research

Since the pioneering studies of Kinsey and Masters and Johnson, a number of large-scale sex surveys have been conducted. Recently, two studies, one dealing with female and the other with male sexuality, have received some attention. Shere Hite, a doctoral student in history at Columbia University, developed a questionnaire to assess contemporary female sexual behavior. For four years Hite made the questionnaire available through a variety of sources, including chapters of the National Organization for Women, church newsletters, abortion-right groups, and university women's centers. Hite supports the assumption that even in the midst of the sexual revolution female sexuality is essentially seen as a response to male sexuality. In sex, as elsewhere, she claims, women are still waiting for men "to mete out the goodies."

The Hite Report (Hite, 1976) describes the responses of 3,000 women, narrating in great detail what they have experienced during sex and how they feel about it. Perhaps the most surprising finding is the relatively low percentage of women who reported that they reached orgasm regularly during intercourse. Hite's data indicated that only 30 percent of the respondents experienced orgasm during intercourse, while the majority could easily reach climax by masturbation, and did so, but rarely without feelings of guilt.

However, in view of Hite's position, these results are not totally astonishing. Arguing that a woman should not have to depend on a man "to give" her orgasms, Hite advocates that women "take charge" of getting them, either by asking for stimulation or by masturbation. Masturbation, according to Hite, is an important means for women to obtain sexual independence.

So far reactions to *The Hite Report* have been mixed. Since its publication, *The Hite Report* has been alternately praised and con-demned, praised as the first real book about female sexuality and condemned as a misinterpretation of research in the guise of a well-conducted advertising campaign (Heiman, 1978). Dr. Marty Calderone, president of the Sex Information and Education Council of the U.S. (SIECUS), has only praise for the report, stating that the book lets men and women in "on a great and good thing." Women who read the report are likely to be assured by how many women share their own attitudes and sexual experiences, and men should be pleased to have so much specific information about what women really want. Others, Dr. W. Pomeroy, for example, commend the book for paving the way for greater sexual independence. At the same time, he has expressed strong reservations about the author's strong feminist bias, with a sample drawn largely from militant ranks of women's organizations, and its effect on the interpretation of the data. And, finally, there are those who regard *The Hite Report* as a lesbian polemic in which the author perpetuates her own prohomosexual views.

Regardless of the evaluation of *The Hite Report*, the survey raised the question of whether or not women's basic sexual outlook has changed as a result of the women's liberation movement, which reached a new momentum in the 1970s. It is conceivable that marked changes in attitudes of women could have had a significant effect on their sexual behavior in a relatively short time period. Further research will be necessary to test for changes in sexual behavior as a result of the feminist movement.

Shortly after the publication of *The Hite Report*, the corresponding male survey, *Beyond the Male Myth*, was published (Pietropinto and Simenauer, 1977). It is the first large-scale look at the sexual behavior of the American male since Kinsey studied it in 1948. This nationwide survey, based on a sample of more than 4,000 men, failed to disclose any revolutionary changes. However, some of the male responses did reflect some new trends that are part of the sexual liberation. Most men of the 1977 survey, for instance, indicated that they welcome sexually competent women, women who sometimes initiate sexual activities and who are open to the idea of adding a variety of techniques to their lovemaking. Contrary to the prevalent belief that a woman who takes the initiative in sexual relations is creating a serious challenge to her partner's masculinity, and that men are threatened by sexually aggressive or even assertive women, these men did not want passive sexual partners. They preferred women who display an interest in and enjoyment of sexual activities and who are active participants during intercourse.

Behavioral Effects of the Sexual Revolution

If we assume that the changes in male and female sex roles, the Kinsey reports, the work of Masters and Johnson, and the recent nationwide sex surveys are part of a sexual revolution, we must look for behavioral evidence to indicate that people actually behave differently than they did, let us say, forty years ago. If sexual changes are dealing only with attitudes but not behaviors, if people are only paying lip service to a "new" sexuality, the sexual revolution has fallen short of its goals.

Changes in Sexual Behavior

Over the last generation or two there have been some indications that men and women are becoming sexually more sophisticated. Knowledge about sexuality is becoming increasingly available. Many high schools and colleges offer courses in human sexuality.

Hundreds of sex manuals provide interested couples with explicit instructions about how to refine their lovemaking techniques. Nude encounter groups afford more direct experiences by teaching married couples and single people, in groups, to explore each other's bodies, touching, feeling, smelling. In some of the more progressive "sexual development groups," surrogate partners are provided for sexual intercourse for those who need to enhance their sexual skills.

As a result of the easier access to sexual information, the repertory of sexual activities enjoyed by men and women seems to have broadened considerably since Kinsey's time. Many younger couples have adopted, or at least experimented with, a variety of positions during intercourse. For example, two-thirds of the married couples interviewed by Kinsey indicated that they always used the missionary position, while the remaining one-third reported that they also had intercourse with the woman on top. At the time, the male superior position, considered to be the proper one by both sexes, symbolized the domination of the masculine role. Two decades later, however, three-fourths of the couples interviewed by Hunt (1974) said that they use the woman superior position. In addition, more than half of Hunt's respondents had enjoyed intercourse lying side by side compared to only one-fourth of Kinsey's couples.

Oral-genital sex has also become more widely accepted. In the 1940s, for instance, only four out of ten of Kinsey's married males had engaged in oral-genital sex. In contrast, as can be seen in Table 3.2, 63 percent of the males in Hunt's sample had done so. Similarly, among the women in the Kinsey study, 52 percent had experimented with oral sex, whereas 91 percent of the twenty-to-thirty-nine-year-old women in a recent *Redbook* magazine study (Levin and Levin, 1975) had experienced this form of sexual activity and 41 percent practiced it regularly.

Table 3.2

Oral–Genital Sex: A comparison of Kinsey's and Hunt's sample

	Percent of marriages in which fellatio was used		Percent of marriages in which cunnilingus was used	
	1938-1946 (Kinsey)	1972 (Hunt)	1938-1946 (Kinsey)	1972 (Hunt)
High school males	15	54	15	56
College males	43	61	45	66
	1953 (Kinsey)	1972 (Hunt)	1953 (Kinsey)	1972 (Hunt)
High school females	46	52	50	58
College females	52	72	58	72

Sources: Kinsey, A., Pomeroy, W., Martin, C. Sexual behavior in the human male. Philadelphia: W. B. Saunders Co., 1948. Hunt, M. Sexual behavior in the 1970's. Chicago: Playboy Press, 1974.

Premarital Sex

There has been a major change in the attitudes toward premarital intercourse, especially among women. Twenty to twenty-five years ago it was a disgrace for an unmarried girl not to be a virgin. In the 1970s virginity has become a questionable virtue. Even the use of the word has lost its traditional support, since the risk of unwanted pregnancy has been greatly reduced by the development of effective contraceptive methods and effective treatment methods for venereal diseases have become available. Even social condemnation of premarital intercourse is no longer as strong as several decades ago.

Since the Kinsey studies, when about 23 percent of all females had some premarital experience by age twenty-five, while for males the figures ranged from 68 percent for the college-educated to 98 percent for those with a grade school education, the highest increase in premarital intercourse occurred among college girls (Croake and James, 1973). Yet in both studies one-half of the women with premarital experience had intercourse with their fiancés or steady boyfriends. Reiss (1967) suggested that young Americans believe in what he called "permissiveness with affection" which means that sex will be respectable when there is mutual affection. However, Reiss also cautioned that permissiveness with affection leads to the adoption of a standard midway between the traditional double standard and a single standard, according to which premarital sex is acceptable for both sexes. Presently, the notion prevails that it is all right for a man to sleep with anyone, whereas a woman should be in love or at least emotionally involved with her partner.

In spite of the apparent increase in premarital sex, the question remains whether the data actually reflect an increase in sexual activity or merely a willingness to respond more honestly. For many college women of past generations, sex was not a topic openly discussed and "indiscretions" were shared only with close friends.

Homosexuality

Homosexuals are probably the major sexual minority that has become more and more visible in recent times. Presently, more than 600 homosexual organizations and publications exist in this country, and gays are represented on most college campuses. During the last few years we have witnessed events that would have been inconceivable a decade ago: thousands of homosexual men and women marching in parades and demonstrations, homosexual representatives appearing on national TV to argue for their cause, gays filing court suits in an effort to establish the legality of homosexual marriages. As in the case of premarital sex, however, the emergence of homosexuals from the closet is more a reflection of coming out and being open than an increase in the incidence of homosexuality.

Implications of the Sexual Revolution

At this stage of our sexual history we have reached a point where we are free to engage in many forms of sexual behavior not sanctioned one or two generations ago. Social license and sexual freedom, however, do not mean throwing away all constraints, as if to say, "If the family does not work, let's abolish it; if heterosexual relations are not satisfying let's try homosexuality; if you don't like what sex you are, try the opposite." Some people have expressed the fear that more sexual freedom will depersonalize and dehumanize sex. They point out that in a society such as

Sexual Myths: Past and Present	Past Myths	Present Myths
	1. Masturbation causes mental disturbances	1. Masturbation is more fulfilling than intercourse (Hite, 1976).
	2. A man with a large penis can satisfy a woman better than a man with a small penis.	2. Penis size is completely irrelevant.
	3. Rape victims basically want to be raped.	3. Women enjoy rape because they fantasize about it.
	4. Women have a lesser sex drive than men.	4. The women's liberation movement has made women so sexually aggressive that they threaten men.
	5. Young men and women must abstain from premarital sexual experiences.	5. Young men and women are sexually promiscuous.
	6. Virginity is the greatest gift a woman can bring into marriage.	6. Virginity is totally obsolete.
	7. Vaginal orgasms are superior to clitoral orgasms.	7. There is no difference between vaginal and clitoral orgasms.
	8. For ultimate sexual gratification a couple should experience simultaneous orgasms.	8. Achieving orgasms sequentially is the ultimate sexual experience.
	9. Love and sex go together, one is not right without the other.	9. Love is not essential for satisfying sexual relations. Sex can be just fun.
	10. People of the lower classes experience a less inhibited sex life and are sexually more active.	10. It takes the sophistication and financial prestige of an upper-class person to experience an extraordinary sex life.

ours, driven by competition, we are now told to compete for sexual satisfaction. In a world already dominated by a drive for consumption, sexual pleasure has become nothing but another consumer commodity. It has also been stated (Slater, 1973) that our obsession with achievement pervades our sexual lives. Instead of enjoying the pleasures of leisurely love, we strive to perfect the "product": orgasm in multiple and simultaneous forms. Greer (1971) shared these fears when she said, "Sex for many has become a sorry business, a mechanical release, involving neither discovery nor triumph, stressing human isolation more dishearteningly than before."

While many attitudes toward sexuality became more liberal in the course of the sexual revolution and different sexual lifestyles became acceptable, actual sexual behaviors have not changed much since Kinsey's time. As in the past, sexuality is still surrounded by a host of myths. Some of the old misconceptions have been replaced by new ones that reflect changes in sexual attitudes and morality.

Rather than viewing the consequences of being sexually liberated in such a dim, pessimistic light, we believe that for the majority of young Americans sexual liberation means the right to enjoy all parts of the body, the right to explore different expressions of sexuality, the right to be sensuous—all within the framework of meaningful relationships. Sexuality is basically involved with our fundamental values, our personality, as well as our conception of who we are, and who we want to be. Sex, for many men and women, including the liberated, continues to express loving feelings, or to engender them, or both. Our choices in the sexual sphere reflect our personality.

Summary

In this chapter we have explored some of the revolutionary changes in sexual attitudes and behaviors that have taken place during the twentieth century. If we accept the idea of a sexual revolution, we can view the changes after World War I as a series of explosions that destroyed the restricted, hypocritical sexual code of the Victorian period. Changes occurring during the 1920s and 1930s, such as the practice of birth control or the acceptance of sex as a means of emotional fulfillment and pleasure, have become dominant attitudes in the 1970s. Interrupted by World War II, the social changes and gains in sexual freedom were slowly consolidated during the 1940s and early 1950s. The renewed sexual emphasis of the late 1950s owed much of its impetus to the discovery of oral contraceptives, as well as to the publication of the Kinsey reports.

The decades of the 1960s and 1970s evidenced many changes with far-reaching implications that are unlikely to be reversed. The 1973 decision of the Supreme Court to legalize abortion and the rejection of the long-held belief by the American Psychiatric Association that homosexuality is associated with mental illness are only two examples.

Sex has been more openly discussed during the last decade than in the past. Graphic depiction of sexual acts in movies and theaters, the availability of effective contraception and safe abortions, accessibility to sex information and education have contributed to an unraveling of sexual mysteries as well as fallacies.

One of the major influences for a new awareness has been the change in women's attitudes brought about, at least in part, by the fight for equal sexual rights by the women's liberation movement. Especially during the past decade, women's sexual potential has become increasingly accepted. One of the most noticeable aspects of the sexual revolution has been the decrease of male-female differences in sexual behavior. Current data regarding pre- and extramarital sex support the notion that women's sexual behavior is becoming more and more similar to that of men. The final outcome of the feminist movement will probably have a powerful influence on our pattern of sexual behavior.

Particularly prominent among the many men and women who contributed to the sexual revolution by broadening our scientific knowledge in the area of human sexuality are Havelock Ellis, Alfred Kinsey, and William Masters and Virginia Johnson. After Ellis's frank and extensive studies of the sex life of his contemporaries, concern about changing attitudes toward sexual behavior emerged again when Kinsey's studies served notice that traditional beliefs were contradicted by a sizable number of people of all ages engaging in an astonishing variety of sanctioned and unsanctioned sexual behaviors. The work of Masters and Johnson discredited many earlier hypotheses by objectively illuminating the basic anatomical and physiological facts of orgasm.

Although many people would argue that the sexual revolution affected primarily attitudes rather than behavior, it seems safe to say that expressions of sexuality today are more differentiated, sophisticated, and open. Formerly furtive or carefully hidden activities such as oral-genital sex or homosexuality are practiced by a number of people in our society.

The continuing sexual revolution raises some important questions. Do the observed patterns of contemporary sexual behavior represent genuine changes, or are they merely reflections of "coming out in the open?" There is no consensus about the extent of changes. Has the sexual revolution cut through all ages and classes, embracing all levels of education and income, or is sexual liberation confined to or the prerogative of the young, unmarried, and college-educated? We have too little information at present to decide whether being sexually liberated strengthens interpersonal or love relationships or weakens them. We also do not know whether further revolutionary changes, whatever they may be, will help to create a healthy, sexually sophisticated society or a generation of men and women frantically chasing after novel sensations and kicks.

We do know, however, that it is presently too early to evaluate the impact of the sexual revolution. In order to accomplish this task, we need extensive data on people who grew up during the latter part of the 1960s and 1970s, in an atmosphere presumably free of the sexual taboos and inhibitions of the past. Given the wide range of present manifestations of human sexuality, the spectrum of future possibilities beyond a relatively short span of five to ten years is rather difficult to predict.

References

Bergler, E. *Selected papers by Edmund Bergler.* New York: Grune & Stratton, 1969.

Bernard, J. "The fourth revolution." *Journal of Social Issues,* 1966, 22, 2, 76-87.

Brecher, E. "The sex researchers." Boston: Little, Brown, 1969.

Broverman, I., Vogel, S., Broverman, D., Clarkson, F., and Rosenkrantz, P. "Sex-role stereotypes: A current appraisal." *Journal of Social Issues,* 1972, 28, 2, 59-78.

Coyner, S. "Women's liberation and sexual liberation." In S. Gordon and R. Libby (eds.). *Sexuality today and tomorrow.* North Scituate, Mass.: Duxbury Press, 1976.

Croake, J. and James, B. "A four-year comparison of premarital sexual attitudes." *Journal of Sex Research*, 1973, 9, 91-96.

Frankl, G. *The failure of the sexual revolution*. London: Kahn and Averill, 1974.

Greer, G. *The female eunuch*. New York: McGraw-Hill, 1971.

Heiman, J. "The Hite Report." *Archives of Sexual Behavior*, 1978, 7, 1, 69-71.

Hite, S. *The Hite Report*. New York: Dell Books, 1976.

Hunt, M. *Sexual behavior in the 1970's*. Chicago: Playboy Press, 1974.

Hyman, H. and Barmack, J. "Special review: Sexual behavior in the human female." *Psychological Bulletin*, 1954, 418-427.

Kinsey, A., Pomeroy, W., and Martin, C. *Sexual behavior in the human male*. Philadelphia: W. B. Saunders, 1948.

Kinsey, A., Pomeroy, W., Martin, C., and Gebhard, P. *Sexual behavior in the human female*. Philadelphia: W. B. Saunders, 1953.

Levin, R. and Levin, A. "The Redbook Report on premarital and extramarital sex." *Redbook Magazine*, October, 1975.

Lipton, L. *The erotic revolution*. Los Angeles: Sherbourne Press, 1965.

Lunneborg, P. "Stereotypic aspects in masculinity-femininity measurement." *Journal of Consulting and Clinical Psychology*, 1970, 34, 113-118.

Macklin, E. "Cohabitation in college: Going very steady." *Psychology Today*, November, 1974.

Masters, W. and Johnson, V. *Human sexual response*. Boston: Little, Brown, 1966.

Masters, W. and Johnson, V. *Human sexual inadequacy*. Boston: Little, Brown, 1970.

Millett, K. *Sexual politics*. New York: Avon, 1969.

O'Neill, W. *The American sexual dilemma*. New York: Holt, Rinehart & Winston, 1972.

Packard, V. *The hidden persuaders*. New York: David McKay, 1957.

Pietropinto, A. and Simenauer, J. *Beyond the male myth*. New York: Times Books, 1977.

Pomeroy, W. "Alfred C. Kinsey: Man and method." *Psychology Today*, March, 1972.

Reich, W. *The sexual revolution*. New York: Simon & Schuster, 1974.

Reiss, I. "The sexual renaissance in America." *Journal of Social Issues*, 1966, 22, 2, 1-140.

Reiss, I. *The social context of premarital sexual permissiveness*. New York: Holt, Rinehart & Winston, 1967.

Rinzema, J. *The sexual revolution*. Grand Rapids, Mich.: W. Eerdmans, 1976.

Robinson, P. *The modernization of sex*. New York: Harper & Row, 1976.

Slater, P. "Sexual adequacy in America." *Intellectual Digest,* December 1973.

Steinman, A. and Fox, D. *The male dilemma.* New York: Jason Aronson, 1974.

Travis, C. and Jayaratne, T. "How women really feel about the 'New Feminism.'" *Redbook,* January 1973.

Chapter 4
Theories of Human Sexuality

Psychology is an extremely broad discipline that includes subareas such as physiological psychology, clinical psychology, social psychology, and several other specialties. What links these specialty areas together is a focus on human behavior. A second characteristic of psychology is that it tends to concentrate on the individual as opposed to groups of people. Psychologists recognize that certain principles from a variety of disciplines apply to people in general, but the psychologist is primarily interested in understanding how these factors act, and interact, in determining the behavior of the individual. In the endeavor to understand these factors, most psychologists believe that it is helpful to work within the framework of a theory. This chapter will discuss the influential and widely accepted theories: psychoanalysis and social learning theory.

The role of a theory is twofold. First, a theory must organize and condense existing facts and information. After this stage is completed, the theory should allow for the prediction of future events. Thus a theory is a conceptual system that increases understanding of a phenomenon so that we may extend our knowledge and application of that phenomenon. As an example, atomic theory has been extremely productive in generating technological developments and has altered our conceptualization of the universe.

A good theory suggests to researchers where to look for additional information. Consider, for example, the issue of gender identity. Many theorists are interested in learning how people come to think of themselves as men or women. This interest will lead researchers into various areas of research. For example, the researcher interested in psychological theories will focus on such factors as the relationship between the parents and the child. The biological theorist may be interested primarily in hormone levels or genetics. Through the process of generating hypotheses and gathering evidence,

researchers endeavor to support and extend their theories.

Theories can be a hindrance at times as well as a help. In the above example, psychological theorists may overlook biological factors because of their commitment to their own theory. There is always the danger that theory will turn into dogma and prevent researchers from being open to new knowledge. The true scientist, however, is willing to discard a theory if it fails to receive support from empirical research.

Theories are of immense importance to behavioral scientists interested in human sexuality. The range of observable sexual behaviors is so diverse as to be incomprehensible without the aid of a theory. Theories of sexuality make it possible to discover the sexual nature of some forms of behavior that appear, on the surface, to have little relation to sex. For example, Freud suggested that certain neurotic disorders could be traced to sexuality. And, finally, theories allow us to devise methods for alleviating problems that are associated with sexuality.

Psychoanalytic Theory

It is probably not possible for current researchers to appreciate the contributions of Sigmund Freud. The bulk of his writing and research was done in Europe in the late 1800s and early 1900s. The prevailing view of sexuality at that time was conservative, to say the least. In fact, when Freud presented his ideas regarding infant sexuality, he was condemned by his colleagues as a moral degenerate. The magnitude of his breakthroughs can be evaluated only in the context of the society in which he worked. Freud displayed great courage in continuing his work in the face of such intense hostility. Let us now examine the major components of Freud's theory of personality.

Psychoanalysis as Libido Theory

All comprehensive theories of human behavior offer explanations of the forces that motivate human beings' conduct. Freud's answer to this question was the concept of drives. He thought of drives as genetically determined behavioral predispositions. These drives may be influenced by the environment, but they exist regardless of the conditions in which one lives.

Early in his career, Freud hypothesized that two drives were primarily responsible for motivating human behavior. These were the life instincts, called the libido, and the drive for self-preservation. Shortly after this original formulation, he decided that self-preservation was not so important after all. For a period of some twenty-five years, then, the development of his theory was based on the notion that the primary source of human behavior was the libido. The sexual drive, which was broadly defined by Freud, was the most important component of the libido. The destructiveness and savagery of World War I prompted Freud to add the concept of death instincts to the theory. Nonetheless, psychoanalytic theory is in many respects a theory of human sexuality. In fact, in 1920, Freud pointed to ". . . the importance of sexuality in all human achievements" (Freud, 1953).

The Mental Apparatus

In order to explain how the libido influenced behavior, Freud postulated several psychological mechanisms. The first of these is called the mental apparatus. It consists of the id, ego, and superego. The id was thought to consist of the innate drives (the libido and the death instincts) and was present at birth. As the child develops and begins to become socialized, some of the energy originally supplied by the id is transferred to the ego and

Figure 4.1
Sigmund Freud (Bettman Archive Inc.)

the superego. The extent and nature of this redistribution of energy plays an important role in personality development.

The id is best observed in the infant's demands for instant gratification. When the infant is hungry, thirsty, or wet, he or she wants immediate attention. Of course, instant gratification is rarely possible, so the infant must develop other types of functioning in order to survive psychologically.

As infants begin to learn of the realities of the objective world, they begin to develop the ego. The child begins to learn that certain desires must wait for gratification. The development of the ego allows the child to achieve a balance between the demands of the id and the constraints of the objective world. It is the ego that allows the individual to plan ahead and to satisfy drives in a socially appropriate fashion.

The third part of the personality is called the superego, which develops during the socialization process. Most parents attempt to teach their children the traditional standards of the society they live in. If children internalize these standards and come to believe and feel the rightness of these values, the superego is said to have developed. Thus the superego is sometimes referred to as the internalized parents or the conscience. It is concerned with doing "what is right" and not with the gratification of instincts.

Freud believed that the healthy and mature personality is dominated by the ego. Such a person is able to satisfy the sexual needs but in a socially appropriate fashion. Problems could exist if either the id or the superego were dominant. The person with a dominant id is likely to be impulsive. Such a person seeks immediate sexual gratification with little thought about the consequences of such behavior. Indiscriminate promiscuity or rape are examples of such impulsive behavior.

A dominant superego can be equally destructive. This person may have such restrictive standards of right and wrong that it is virtually impossible to realize his or her sexual potential. A dominant superego results in sexual guilt and anxiety that can hinder the establishing of relationships and can interfere with sexual responses in a sexual relationship (see Chapter 18).

The Discovery of Infantile Sexuality

Around the turn of the century virtually all theorists maintained that one's sexuality lay dormant until the time of puberty. Freud shocked both the public and his scientific colleagues by asserting that sexuality is active from the moment of birth. The way in which the sexuality of the child is expressed is influenced by what Freud called the psychosexual stages of development. The first three stages, and the most crucial, are the oral stage, the anal stage, and the phallic stage. During each of these stages, Freud believed, different erotogenic or erogenous zones of the body are the site of sexual gratification. During the oral stage, stimulation of the mouth, lips, and gums provides the child with sexual pleasure. In the anal stage, the child receives pleasure by learning to control and expel the feces. In the phallic stage, the genitals become the most important erotogenic zone. Freud believed that these three parts of the body— the mouth, the anus, and the genitals—are predestined to be erotogenic zones. Under certain conditions, however, any part of the skin or the mucous membrane can acquire the functions of an erotogenic zone.

An important aspect of the theory of infantile sexuality was the notion that a person's behavior as an adult would be influenced by the failure to undergo a transference of the erotogenic zones. For example, Freud (1953) suggested that adults with intensified oral desires would ". . . become epicures in kissing, (or) will be inclined to perverse kissing." The anus as a primary erotogenic zone was thought to be related to some forms of sexual deviation. The psychologically mature individual, according to Freud, considers the genitals the most important erotogenic zone. It is ironic that today many sex therapists believe that many problems can stem from an overemphasis of the genitals (see Chapter 14).

The Oepidal Conflict

The phallic stage of psychosexual development is probably the most influential in shaping sexual behavior. It is during this stage (between the ages of three and five) that the all-important Oedipal conflict occurs. Freud believed that the way in which individuals resolved this conflict would influence their sexual interests and behavior. The precise nature of this conflict is somewhat different for boys and girls, so each sex will be considered separately.

As boys enter into this period of their lives, they typically have warm, affectionate feelings toward their mothers. However, as they become aware of their sexuality, their warm, affectionate feelings for their mothers become sexualized, that is, boys develop a desire to possess their mothers. These feelings place the boys in the position of competitors with their fathers for the mothers' affections. This perceived competition is frightening because of the fathers' strength and power. The boys fear that sexual longing for their mothers will bring retaliation from their fathers, which would take the form of damage to the genitals. Freud suggested that the boys' fear of retaliation would result in castration anxiety.

This conflict is resolved through the process of repression and identification. Fears of castration cause boys to repress their sexual feelings for the mother and their hostility for the father into the unconscious. This process initiates the process of identification with the father. The sexual feelings toward the mother are converted to feelings of tender affection, and feelings of hostility

---

Does Your Unconscious Choose Your Spouse?

As we have indicated in the text, psychoanalysts believe that unconscious processes influence much of our behavior—sexual and otherwise. As an illustration of this process, psychiatrist Lilly Ottenheimer (1971) has discussed the role of unconscious factors in the choice of a mate. She contends, that for some individuals, marriage is doomed from the start because unconscious motives have replaced the person's capacity to love.

In one example, she discusses the case of men who, as children, became aware of the sexual activity of their parents. This knowledge could lead to the following beliefs: (a) the mother is engaging in immoral activity against her will; (b) the mother needs to be saved from this immoral activity; (c) the child should be the one to save the mother.

According to Ottenheimer, this rescue fantasy leads to feelings of inferiority because the child has selected a task that cannot be carried out. To repair his self-respect in adulthood the man will be attracted to women of "easy virtue." Marriage to a prostitute or a sexually active woman may be based on the repressed rescue fantasy. By saving a woman from immoral behavior, the man can compensate for his failure to rescue his mother.

Women are not immune from the effects of the unconscious, either, according to psychoanalytic theory. As an example, Ottenheimer describes the case of a little girl whose seductive overtures to her father during the Oedipal conflict were met with ridicule. This results in the creation of hostility, which the girl cannot express toward her father for fear of repercussion. The outcome could be a hostile, vengeful attitude toward men in general. As an adult, such a woman may select a mate whom she considers to be clumsy, ineffectual, or in some other way, nonmasculine. She cannot respond sexually to such a man, because of her unconscious motives, but she is responsive to other men whom she considers masculine. These liaisons can be used to humiliate her husband and thus express the woman's repressed hostility toward her father.

Needless to say, other theorists, such as the social learning theorist, would disagree with such interpretations. There is little doubt that childhood experiences can influence the sexual and interpersonal behaviors of the adult, but there is disagreement concerning the underlying mechanisms of such influences.

---

and fear toward the father turn to affection and a desire to be like the father.

If the boy is able to resolve the Oedipal conflict satisfactorily, he is able to progress to more mature psychosexual levels. However, some men are thought to be fixated at this level, which can have profound effects on their behavior as adults. Such men, having failed to deal effectively with their castration anxiety, are said to overvalue their penis (Blum, 1953). This may result in excessive variety in selecting sexual partners and exhibitionism. They seem to have a need to prove that they are "real men." One example is the Don Juan type who feels he must demonstrate his virility continuously by conquering every woman he meets. (See Chapter 18 for a more detailed description of this phenomenon.) Even men who pass through the Oedipal complex satisfactorily are influenced by it. The nature of their friendships, attitudes to authority figures, and romantic and sexual relationships are all affected by the way in which it is resolved. Freudian theorists believe that the popularity of songs such as "I want a girl just like the girl that married dear old Dad" is no accident.

According to Freud, the process of this conflict is quite different for girls. Their Oedipal conflict (sometimes referred to as the Electra complex) is initiated when they become aware that boys have something they lack—a penis. Freud believed that this led to feelings of resentment toward the mother, who was blamed for bringing them into the world with a "deficiency." Girls then shift their affections from the mother to the father because he has the prized organ. Initially, girls desire to share the father's penis, but this is later transformed into fantasies of having a baby by the father. In fact, the theory suggests that women prefer male babies because to some extent this would satisfy the desire for a penis.

As is the case with men, the Oedipal conflict sets the stage for the adult behavior of women. A crucial issue concerns penis envy. The relationships that women have with men are thought to have elements of envy because they, men, possess a penis. Chapter 18 provides an illustration of the potential pathological consequences of this conflict.

The way in which girls are thought to resolve this conflict is not entirely clear. Unlike boys, whose castration anxiety causes enormous repression, the Oedipal complex tends to persist for girls. Realistic barriers that prevent girls from gratifying their sexual desires for their fathers modifies it somewhat, however. Freud believed that this contrast between boys and girls was the basis for many psychological differences between the sexes.

One example of such a difference concerns the development of the superego, which is thought to have its origins in the phallic stage. Freud suggested that for boys the mechanism underlying the Oedipal conflict made the development of a healthy superego possible, but that girls were destined to have weak superegos. Consequently, Freud believed that women were incapable of having a strong sense of objectivity and justice. Needless to say, this notion has not been received uncritically. It has been pointed out that Freud lived in a highly patriarchal society in which women were viewed as second-class citizens. Well-known neo-Freudian Karen Horney (1937) criticized Freud's ideas regarding women on many points. She believed that women did not envy the man's penis, but his status and power. It is not the biological differences that produce psychological differences, she said, but the cultural traditions of Western society. (The issue of sex differences will be discussed in Chapter 17.)

Psychic Determinism and the Unconscious

Perhaps Freud's most important contribution was the notion that much of human behavior is influenced by factors of which people are unaware. He suggested the analogy of an iceberg as an aid in conceptualizing the human mind. The tip of the iceberg, which is above the water line, represents the region of consciousness. The much larger mass below the surface can be thought of as the unconscious. This level of the mind is the depository of repressed ideas, feelings, urges, desires, and fantasies. Freud believed that although human beings are completely unaware of these influences, they nonetheless exercise control over conscious thoughts and behavior.

It was through the principle of psychic determinism and the unconscious, Freud believed, that much of human behavior that seemed self-defeating or incomprehensible could be understood. Events that occurred during childhood, although long forgotten, continued to exert an influence. For example, Freud had as patients many young women with physical complaints. These women's problems, such as paralysis of the limbs, had no apparent medical basis. This condition, called hysteria, Freud believed to be caused by unconscious sexual conflicts. That is, these women had experienced as children some traumatic event related to sexuality, and the memories of these events were repressed. When the women were faced with a situation that involved sex, such as an impending wedding, unconscious feelings were expressed in the form of a physical symptom, and the medical problem delayed the marriage. Freud therefore came to believe that it was the unconscious that protected individuals from anxiety.

Because the prevailing view of sex was quite conservative at the time Freud began formulating his theories, Freud became convinced that a substantial portion of the unconscious was concerned with sexuality. This led to his theory that much of human behavior, either directly or indirectly, is motivated by sexuality.

Social Learning Theory

While there are a number of variants of social learning theory, all theorists working within this framework contend that virtually all human behavior is strongly influenced by learning. These theorists do not deny the importance of genetics, physiology, biological drives, or the like, but they do believe that the way in which one's biological heritage is expressed will be determined by learning. With regard to sexuality, most social learning theorists agree that human beings are born with sexual drive, but the manner in which this drive is expressed depends largely on the environment they are exposed to. Thus, for the most part, people learn to be homosexual, heterosexual, or bisexual. They learn to be celibate, to restrict themselves to one partner, or to have a variety of sexual partners. And they learn to become sexually aroused at the sight of their naked partner, at the smell of a particular cologne, or at the sight of certain articles of clothing. The social learning theorist believes that the same laws of learning that apply to subjects in experimental laboratories apply to all behavior. That is, sexual behavior, both typical and variant, can be understood by principles of learning.

Social learning theory is essentially an extension of traditional learning theories. Early theorists, largely in reaction to the "mentalism" that was popular in the early twentieth century argued that a science of behavior should concern itself only with observable events. They believed that personality concepts, such as Freud's id, ego, and superego, added nothing to our understanding of human behavior. This tradition yielded two important concepts: classical conditioning and operant conditioning. After several years of research with these two types of learning, many psychologists began to realize that many behaviors were difficult to understand if theories were to be limited to observable events. Thus they began to include what are called organismic variables to their hypotheses and theories. They believed that concepts such as expectancy, values, memory, and numerous other unobservables allow us to deal more effectively with the complexities of human behavior. Learning theories that incorporate these organismic variables into their framework have come to be known as social learning

theories. Let us examine some of the highlights of this framework.

Classical Conditioning

Every student of introductory psychology knows of the Russian physiologist Ivan Pavlov's experiments, which elucidated the process of classical conditioning. Pavlov presented dogs with meat powder, which caused them to salivate. He found that if he sounded a tone at the same time the dog was given the meat powder, the dog would eventually salivate in response to the tone alone. In this experiment the meat powder is called an unconditioned stimulus because it brings about an innate, unlearned reflex response—the salivation. The tone is called a conditioned stimulus because it acquired the ability to elicit salivation from the dog only after it had been paired with the meat powder a number of times.

The concept of classical conditioning has been used to explain how people come to be sexually aroused by a variety of stimuli. For example, psychologists have suggested that masturbatory conditioning can result in unusual sexual preferences (McGuire, Carlisle, and Young, 1965). Psychologist Jack S. Annon described a case history of pedophilia that illustrates the mechanism involved. The case involved a man who was compulsively attracted to girls between the ages of six and twelve. The man reported having had his first sexual experiences at the age of eleven when he played "striptease" with boys and girls of his own age. The game generally ended with the children engaging in mutual manipulation of the genitals.

These activities ceased abruptly when the man's family moved to a distant city. After puberty, when he learned to masturbate, his fantasies centered on a nine-year-old girl who had played "striptease." When he was nineteen, he attempted to have sex with an aging prostitute. The circumstances and the woman were so unappealing that from then on he was repelled by the idea of having sex with mature women. In the following years he became increasingly obsessed with the idea of having sex with young girls.

In this case several learning factors were involved, but a key element was the young man's fantasies during masturbation. By associating images of young girls with orgasm, the man became increasingly aroused by the sight of prepubescent girls. It is likely that had his parents not moved and had he been able to continue his sex play with his peers, his problem would not have developed. When he began to masturbate, his fantasies probably would have centered on girls his own age (Staats, 1975).

Operant Conditioning

The term operant conditioning is most likely to bring to mind the name of psychologist B. F. Skinner. In 1938 Skinner published *The Behavior of Organisms*, which described the basic principles of operant conditioning. He believed that this form of learning could explain those behaviors not explained by classical conditioning. Simply stated, operant conditioning suggests that behavior is influenced by its consequences. Behavior followed by a reward or pleasurable consequences is likely to reoccur. Behavior followed by punishment is likely to diminish in frequency.

The principles of operant conditioning can be useful in understanding a variety of forms of sexual behavior—both typical and variant. For example, it has been found that mothers of transvestites reward their sons for dressing in girls' clothing (Stoller, 1967). Also, typical adolescent sexual behavior is reinforced not only by physical pleasure, but also by the interest, attention, and admiration of one's same-sexed peers.

The most important point about operant conditioning is that its principles suggest that

Figure 4.2
B. F. Skinner (Photo by Joel Stern courtesy of B. F. Skinner)

it is not necessary to understand what is going on inside the individual—that is, one's thoughts, feelings, or fantasies. While there is little doubt that the principles of operant conditioning do make many forms of sexual behavior understandable, few theorists would argue that it alone is sufficient as a theoretical framework. As we shall see below, what goes on inside the person, that is the cognitive variables, can have an important influence on sexual behavior.

Observational Learning

People have known for generations that a good way to learn certain skills is to observe others perform them. However, it has been only in the past two decades that psychologists have focused their attention on observational learning. The work of Albert Bandura (1962, 1969), which demonstrates that obser-

Figure 4.3
Albert Bandura (Photo courtesy of Albert Bandura)

vational learning can be useful in the acquisition of behaviors as well as the treatment of problem behaviors, has been largely responsible for the current interest in this form of learning.

Many behaviors related to sex are undoubtedly acquired via observational learning. Watching actors and actresses on television or in the movies provides ideas about how to modify behavior in order to be more successful in sexual relationships. Observational learning can also be important in influencing attitudes and values regarding sex. Many sex educators have pointed to the importance of the parents' behavior in transmitting attitudes to their children. Parents who feel free to show affection for one another in front of the children are likely to communicate attitudes different from parents who avoid any type of public physical contact. Some degree of sex education inevitably occurs in the home. Parents who refuse to discuss sex with their children are, in fact, serving as models for their children.

The children are likely to learn, through observation, that sex is something not to be talked about.

Cognitive Events

The early learning theorists insisted that a science of human behavior should focus only on observable events. This viewpoint implied that it is possible to understand human behavior without taking into consideration one's thoughts, attitudes, or values. With the advent of social learning theory, these variables, called cognitive events, have gained respectability. Social learning theorists such as Julian Rotter (1954) and Walter Mischel (1973) have suggested that inclusion of these "unobservables" enables us to have a greater understanding of the complexities of human behavior. One such cognitive event is that of expectancy. Social learning theorists suggest that behavior is influenced not only by actual reinforcements or punishments but also by one's expectations of obtaining rewards or receiving punishment. For example, we might approach a person to whom we are attracted because we expect that we will be favorably received. Or, on a first date, we might refrain from making a sexual advance if we expect to be rebuffed.

One's expectancies can also have an effect on sexual arousal. In a recent study, psychologist Dan Briddell and his colleagues asked college men to listen to tape recordings of couples engaged in various kinds of sexual activities. Half the men were given an alcoholic beverage before listening to the tapes. The other group of men was given a nonalcoholic beverage that they thought was alcoholic. The men who believed they were given alcohol were significantly more aroused sexually (measured by penile tumescence and subjective reports) regardless of the actual contents of the beverage. Thus it was not the alcohol *per se* that increased sexual arousal but the belief that one was drinking alcohol (Briddell, *et al.*, 1978). Findings such as this have suggested why the belief in aphrodisiacs and anaphrodisiacs (e.g., the legendary saltpeter) have persisted for too long. They seem to work because people expect them to work. (See Chapter 10 for further discussion of sexual arousal.)

Psychoanalysis and Social Learning Theory Compared

Psychoanalysis and social learning theory tend to have opposite strengths and weaknesses. Psychoanalysis' greatest strength lies in its comprehensiveness. Freud was primarily interested in psychopathology, but he also applied his theory to a variety of "everyday" phenomena such as dreams, humor, slips of the tongue, war, and death—to name just a few. In fact, there is probably no aspect of human behavior that has escaped the attention of psychoanalytic theorists.

Social learning theory is not nearly so comprehensive. Much social learning theory research has involved relatively simple behaviors that are studied in laboratory settings. While there are notable exceptions (Rotter, 1954; Staats, 1974), social learning theorists have not attempted to develop comprehensive theories of human behavior in general, or of sexual behavior in particular. For the most part, theorists such as Rotter and Mischel (1973) attempt to use the social learning framework to increase understanding of relatively circumscribed aspects of behavior.

The strength of social learning theory (and the weakness of psychoanalysis) lies in its sensitivity to the importance of empirical validation through scientific research. Its concepts and hypotheses are defined precisely and in ways that make it possible to subject them to empirical test. Many concepts of psychoanalysis, on the other hand, are much too ambiguous even to attempt to submit them to empirical test. For example, the concept of castration anxiety has been invoked to ex-

plain behaviors as diverse as homosexuality, Don Juanism, and erectile failure. Such ambiguity eliminates any scientific value the concept may have.

Psychoanalysis and social learning theory were selected for discussion because they are the two most influential conceptual systems in use today. A substantial number of behavioral scientists, although perhaps not identifying themselves completely with social learning theory, are sympathetic to this approach. Psychoanalysis, although declining in prestige in academic circles, remains a major force in clinical settings. Also, the public, although probably unaware of it, is influenced by psychoanalytic theory. This can readily be seen in such lovelorn columns as that of Ann Landers. When a reader writes that her husband cannot have intercourse unless he wears women's underclothing or that there is a "funny" uncle in the family, Ann invariably suggests that such behavior is indicative of "deep" personality problems. This view originated with Freud who, as we saw earlier, believed that childhood trauma was repressed and later expressed in the deviant behavior of the adult without his or her awareness.

This example represents what is perhaps the most crucial difference between psychoanalysis and social learning theory. The psychoanalyst would suggest that many forms of sexual behavior are determined by unconscious processes that have their origins in the early childhood years. People are thus unaware to a large extent of why they behave the way they do—sexually and otherwise. Social learning theorists tend to believe that patterns of sexual behaviors are relatively straightforward and are governed by the same principles that influence the development of normal behaviors. Through the processes of classical and operant conditioning and imitation learning people learn to behave in certain ways. This means that a pattern of sexual behavior is not indicative of underlying personality processes, but results from specifiable learning histories that include, but are not limited to, the early childhood years.

Research Methods in the Study of Human Sexuality

The essence of science is that its theories and hypotheses be subjected to empirical test. The behavioral scientist has an obligation to conduct research that tests the validity of his or her ideas about human sexuality. Conducting research on many aspects of human behavior is difficult, but human sexuality is certainly one of the most difficult of all. The value-laden nature of human sexuality creates a set of problems that make it nearly impossible to arrive at any conclusive facts. The best that we can hope for is to accumulate evidence, however limited it may be, that will increase our confidence in the validity of our theories and hypotheses. Rarely, however, can we be certain of any assertions regarding this topic. Let us now examine the major research strategies that have been used in the study of human sexuality and consider the problems and limitations associated with each.

Case Study Method

Case studies involve intensive investigations of a single person, a group of persons, or a society. Freud relied upon this method to generate data for his theory of psychoanalysis. He based his theory on discussions with his patients, whom he saw several times a week for periods of up to two or more years.

Another example of this type of research is a project conducted by sociologist Laud Humphreys (1975) in which he conducted an intensive study of a small group of homosexual men. In the first phase of the project, he made detailed observations of homosexual behavior in public restrooms. During the second phase, wearing a disguise, he conducted in-depth interviews with several of these men. The subjects were under the impression that it was a routine survey unrelated to sexuality. Although Humphreys' observations are of interest, several researchers have questioned the appropriateness of such methods.

A last example, a variant of the case study method, concerns detailed observations of societies such as those made by cultural anthropologist Margaret Mead. This type of research has proved to be extremely valuable because it often discounts theories of sexuality popular in our society. For example, the common belief that a homosexual orientation is resistant to modification is seriously questioned by anthropological findings. It has been found that in some societies adolescent boys engage in exclusive homosexual behavior for a period of time. Once they become adults they are expected to marry and are subsequently exclusively heterosexual.

There are several problems associated with the case study method. First of all, in many cases the experimenter must rely on what the subjects say about their behavior, and their accounts may not necessarily correspond to what they actually do. Most people are reluctant to discuss certain aspects of their personal lives, and sex is one of the most personal areas of human experience. In addition, failure to remember and psychological defenses such as repression are bound to occur. Thus people may have a sincere desire to report past experiences accurately but may simply be unable to do so. This point has been the basis of severe criticism of Freud's theory. He developed his theory of psychosexual development by talking to adults about their childhood experiences. It is likely that what they recalled was distorted by the passage of time and psychological defenses.

A second problem is that the observations made by experimenters are likely to be influenced by their own values and interests. Thus, while a Freudian is likely to find evidence of an Oedipal conflict, a social learning theorist would probably have little difficulty in identifying pertinent reinforcement histories in the same client. Expectancies operate for the layperson and the scientist alike. We tend to observe what we expect to observe.

It has also been pointed out that a therapist subtly influences the kind of experience the client discusses (Marmor, 1962). For example, Freud reported that his clients often began their recollections of their childhood years by discussing sexual traumas. It is quite possible that Freud encouraged his clients to do this without awareness on Freud's part or on the part of the client. Nonverbal language, such as a nod of the head or leaning forward in a chair, can influence the client's conversation. Therapists using the case study method should recognize the possibility that their behavior can influence the subject in ways that insure that their hypotheses will be confirmed. For these reasons, most scientists believe that the case study method should be thought of as a starting point in research. It is useful in generating hypotheses, but these hypotheses should be tested with more sophisticated methods.

Survey Methods

Surveys are generally concerned with obtaining a relatively limited amount of information from a large number of people. The purpose of such research is to provide generalizations about sexuality to the general population or to some specific population. The best-known example of survey research is that of Alfred Kinsey and his associates. His research was invaluable not only because it was the first reliable information about how people behaved sexually, but because it had a decided influence on psychological theories.

For example, Kinsey's finding that 62 percent of women eventually masturbated and that 85 percent of them relied primarily on labial and clitoral stimulation cast serious doubt on Freud's notion that women who had clitoral orgasms were immature. The theory of mature vaginal orgasm entered its terminal stage with Kinsey's surveys. This myth received its death blow with the publication of Masters and Johnson's *Human Sexual Response* (1966).

Survey research deals with many of the same problems associated with the case history method. The researcher must rely on the subjects' desire to answer honestly and the accuracy of the subjects' memory. The former issue can be circumvented to some extent. Kinsey, for example, constructed his interviews to include several cross-checks to determine if subjects were intentionally distorting their experiences. It is possible to determine the effects of memory by interviewing the same person twice and comparing his or her responses. Kinsey did this with 319 subjects, allowing a time interval of eighteen months between interviews. It was found that information regarding incidence (e.g., have you had oral sex?) was highly consistent, but that information regarding frequency (e.g., how often do you have intercourse?) was much less consistent.

Two major issues associated with survey research are the representativeness of the sample and nonresponse. Representativeness concerns the composition of the sample; it should approximate the composition of the population to which the researcher wishes to generalize. For example, if a researcher wishes to generalize to the entire United States population, his or her sample must include the same representation of people from various social classes that occurs in the general population. The same is true for such variables as age, religion, ethnic group membership, and a host of others, since these variables have been found to be related to sexual behavior. For example, younger people are more likely to have had premarital intercourse than older people. If young people are overrepresented in the sample, inaccurate conclusions regarding the general population could be made.

Another characteristic of a good sample is that everyone in the population, or some subgroup of the population, should have an equal probability of being included. The survey researcher often uses techniques, such as a flip of a coin, a toss of a die, or a table of random numbers, to generate what is known as a probability sample. This requirement is one that Kinsey chose to ignore, and he has been criticized for it. Kinsey's samples were selected in a haphazard, but not random, manner.

For any number of reasons many people selected for inclusion in a random sample decline to participate. This creates problems, because it is likely that participants differ from nonparticipants in important ways. For example, those who agree to participate in surveys of sexual behavior may have more liberal attitudes than those who do not. Thus we can never really be sure if survey results accurately reflect the values, attitudes, and behavior of the entire population.

This problem of nonresponse is particularly evident in a major survey commissioned by the Playboy Foundation and reported by Morton Hunt (1974). The researchers selected names at random from telephone books and asked these people to participate in the project. Only 20 percent agreed to do so. It is likely that this group differed in important ways from the 80 percent who declined to participate.

Laboratory Research

A wide variety of behaviors related to sex have been investigated in laboratories. Perhaps the most dramatic of these projects, and probably the most valuable, was directed by Masters and Johnson. They observed the sexual behavior of several hundred women and men in a laboratory setting and measured a variety of physiological variables during acts of masturbation and intercourse. To some people the most shocking aspect of their research was an artificial coition machine. It included a clear plastic phallus that contained photographic equipment. This device made it possible to detect changes in the vagina that occurred during sexual response. Although their research was greeted with controversy and outright hostility, it is credited with laying to rest many myths, particularly those about female sexuality (LoPiccolo and Heiman, 1977).

Although the work of Masters and Johnson is invaluable, it is not possible to generalize from their results to the general population. Most of their subjects were recruited from the academic community affiliated with a St. Louis university hospital. These people were well above the national average in terms of intelligence and socioeconomic status.

More typical laboratory research involves studies of psychological processes that are related to sex but do not involve explicit sexual behavior. For example, some researchers have attempted to test psychoanalytic theories by examining the relationship between personality characteristics of men and their preferred feminine body types. The researchers first administer psychological tests to the men to identify relevant personality characteristics. They then show the men silhouettes of women who vary in terms of size of breasts, buttocks, thighs, and so on. Using Freud's notion of oral personalities, it might be hypothesized, for example, that personality differences exist between men who prefer large-breasted women and those who prefer small-breasted women. In fact, such personality differences have been found (Wiggins, Wiggins, and Conger, 1968). Men in the study who preferred large breasts tended to date frequently and were active in sports. Men with a preference for small breasts were submissive, mildly depressed, and had fundamentalist religious beliefs.

One difficulty associated with laboratory research concerns the representativeness of the sample. This issue was mentioned earlier in the discussion of Masters and Johnson's research, but it applies to virtually all laboratory research. Much of the research in this country occurs on the campuses of universities and colleges, and a majority of the subjects are recruited from introductory survey courses. Needless to say, college students taking introductory psychology or sociology are not representative of the general population. In fact, it has been pointed out by many critics that our science of human behavior might be referred to more accurately as the science of the college sophomore.

A major advantage of laboratory research is that it allows for precise control of relevant variables. In the example of body preferences cited above it is possible to construct silhouettes of women in such a way that the researcher can be certain about precisely what characteristics are important. For example, one silhouette may have large breasts, large buttocks, and small thighs. A second may have large breasts, small buttocks, and small thighs. In other words, it is possible to have all possible combinations of these body parts. Needless to say, it would be quite difficult to do the same sort of research with women in naturalistic settings. It would be nearly impossible to find women with all these combinations of body parts who would be willing to pose before college men.

Laboratory techniques that lend themselves to precise control often have the disadvantage of sacrificing realism. To use the example of the silhouettes, we cannot be certain that a man who indicates a preference for a large-breasted silhouettes will, in fact, prefer large-breasted women in everyday life. He may prefer large-breasted women in the abstract, but breast size may be irrelevant when it comes to making choices in dating and marriage. In other words, there is always the question of whether one can generalize from laboratory findings to real-life situations.

Correlational versus Experimental Research

The goal of science is to formulate cause-and-effect statements. That is, scientists want to be able to make statements such as "testosterone is responsible for sexual drive." Unfortunately, it is virtually impossible to make such statements about human sexual behavior. In order to do so, one would have to conduct what is called experimental research. Basically, this involves working with a group of subjects that are as nearly identical as possible. These subjects are then randomly assigned to a control group and an experimental group. The experimental group receives some special treatment but in all other respects is treated identically to the control group. If there are subsequent differences between the two groups, one can conclude that the special treatment caused the difference.

In the example of testosterone (a male sex hormone) and sex drive, it would be possible to conduct such research with animals. A group of rats could be selected and raised under identical conditions in order to control the effect of experiences. At maturity, the rats' gonads could be removed and the experimental group could receive controlled dosages of the testosterone. If differences in copulatory behavior between the two groups were observed, the researcher could be confident that testosterone is responsible for sex drive.

Obviously, the above research would never be performed on humans. Consequently, researchers must rely heavily upon the correlational method. This method involves identifying the relevant variables and determining if they are related to sexual behavior. In the case of sex hormones, this has been done by examining the sexual behavior of men who are castrated through accident or who for medical reasons are chemically castrated. If, in fact, these men show a decrease in sexual activity, it can be concluded that there is a relationship between hormones and sexual behavior. However, it is not possible to arrive at a cause-and-effect relationship.

To further illustrate the nature of correlational research, consider one of the findings of Kinsey's surveys: social class and sexual attitudes are related. All we can say is that a relationship between these variables exists. We cannot conclude that social class causes certain sexual attitudes. It would be equally illogical to assert that sexual attitudes determine one's social class. It is probably true that some third variable causes both sexual attitudes and social class.

Conclusions

The foregoing was intended to illustrate the constraints within which the sex researcher must work. All research strategies have their limitations, and these make it nearly impossible to arrive at any conclusive statements about human sexuality. The researcher is obliged to use a variety of methods and continually repeat those findings. If the results of case histories, surveys, and laboratory studies of the same phenomenon are consistent, then the researcher can begin to have confidence in the findings. If these results are arrived at by other independent researchers, then confidence increases even more. This state of affairs is certainly not the most desirable, but it is the best that the researcher can hope for.

One word of caution should be noted. In many research studies the authors point out the limitations of their work but then go on to report the results as if they had completely

forgotten their own caveats. The reader should not forget them. It is important to read any work on sexuality with a critical eye. Much of our knowledge has come from people who have refused to accept the assertions of "experts."

Summary

This chapter has discussed two psychological theories of sexual behavior and research methods used to test theories. The psychoanalytic theory originated with the work of Sigmund Freud, who believed that sex is a primary motive for many forms of human behavior. Before Freud it was thought that memories associated with sex could be repressed into the unconscious, but Freud asserted that these memories continued to exert an influence on behavior. The most controversial aspect of psychoanalysis concerns infantile sexuality. Freud believed that children possess sexual feelings at birth and the way in which these feelings are expressed is shaped by psychosexual stages of development. These stages are oral, anal, phallic, latency, and genital. Adult behavior is strongly influenced by trauma experienced during the first three stages.

The social learning theorists argue that the principles of learning derived from experimental laboratories can be used to understand sexual behavior. Three important types of learning are classical conditioning, operant conditioning, and observational learning. Recently, social learning theorists have begun to emphasize the role of cognitive events in influencing sexual behavior. For example, the effect of alcohol on sexual responsiveness depends largely on what one anticipates.

All theories of human behavior must be subjected to empirical testing. Three research methods for collecting data have been discussed: the case study method, the survey method, and the laboratory method. Each method has its advantages and disadvantages. One problem associated with all research methods in sexuality is the difficulty of carrying out experimental research. This type of research is valuable because it allows for the formation of statements of causation. Unfortunately, sex researchers must usually rely on correlational methods, which allow only statements of relationships to be made. To obtain reliable results, researchers in sexual behavior must rely on a variety of research methods to provide support for their theories.

References

Bandura, A. "Social learning through imitation." In M. R. Jones (ed.), *Nebraska symposium on motivation: 1962.* Lincoln: University of Nebraska Press, 1962.

Bandura, A. *Principles of behavior modification.* New York: Holt, Rinehart & Winston, 1969.

Bieber, I., *et al. Homosexuality—a psychoanalytic study.* New York: Basic Books, 1962.

Blum, G. S. *Psychoanalytic theories of personality.* New York: McGraw-Hill, 1953.

Briddell, D. W., Rimm, D. C., Caddy, G. R., Krawitz, G., Sholis, D., and Wunderlin, R. J. "Effects of alcohol and cognitive set on sexual arousal to deviant stimuli." *Journal of Abnormal Psychology,* 1978, 87, 418-430.

Freud, S. "Three essays on sexuality." In *The standard edition of the complete psychological works.* Vol. VII. London: Hogarth Press, 1953 (first German edition, 1905).

Horney, K. *The neurotic personality of our time.* New York: W. W. Norton, 1937.

Humphreys, L. *Tearoom trade: Impersonal sex in public places,* 2nd ed. Chicago: Aldine, 1975.

Hunt, M. *Sexual behavior in the 1970's.* New York: Dell Books, 1974.

LoPiccolo, J., and Heiman, J. F. "Cultural values and the therapeutic definition of sexual function and dysfunction." *Journal of Social Issues,* 1977, 33, 166-183.

McGuire, R. J., Carlisle, J. M., and Young, B. G. "Sexual deviations as conditioned behaviour: A hypothesis." *Behaviour Research and Therapy,* 1965, 2, 185-190.

Marmor, J. "Psychoanalytic therapy as an educational process: Common denominators in the therapeutic approaches of different psychoanalytic schools." In J. H. Masserman (ed.), *Science and psychoanalysis, Vol. 5. Psychoanalytic education.* New York: Grune & Stratton, 1962.

Mischel, W. "Towards a cognitive social learning reconceptualization of personality." *Psychological Review,* 1973, 80, 252-283.

Ottenheimer, L. "Unconscious factors in choice of a mate." *Medical Aspects of Human Sexuality,* March 1971, pp. 130-143.

Rotter, J. B. *Social learning and clinical psychology.* Englewood Cliffs, N. J.: Prentice-Hall, 1954.

Skinner, B. F. *The behavior of organisms.* New York: Appleton, 1938.

Staats, A. W. *Social behaviorism.* Homewood, Ill.: Dorsey, 1975.

Stoller, R. J. "Transvestites' women." *American Journal of Psychiatry,* 1967, *124,* 333-339.

Wiggins, J. S., Wiggins, N., and Conger, J. C. "Correlates of heterosexual somatic preferences." *Journal of Personality and Social Psychology,* 1968, 10, 82-90.

Chapter 5

The Biology of Human Sexuality

From a biological point of view, human sexual behavior is far better understood than the psychosocial forces that act upon and interact with the biological foundations of sexuality. Genetics, hormones, anatomy, and physiology have been extensively studied as biological determinants for the psychological and social development of male and female sexuality.

Although the human species shares a number of biosexual functions with other mammals, sexual behavior in animals differs from that of humans in that it is characterized by highly instinctive and stereotypical patterns, evoked directly by hormonal and cyclic changes. Typically, in infrahuman species, the estrus ("heat") cycle, which is under the control of neuroendocrine mechanisms, regulates female sexual behavior; ovulation, as well as copulation, occurs only during estrus, which marks the peak period of sexual activity in many mammals. However, in phylogenetically more evolved species, such as primates or humans, the role of hormonal control over sexual arousal and motivation diminishes. Sexual behavior among men and women can occur at any time through mutual interest and stimulation, independent of the cyclic fluctuations in sex-hormone balance. The important difference between the effects of hormones on the sexual behavior of animals and people is not so much that hormonal influences are inconsequential for human sexuality but, rather, that nonhormonal determinants play a much greater role. The sexual identity of men and women is by and large shaped by psychosocial forces that determine the overt expression of sexuality.

In order to gain an understanding of the complex and multifaceted interaction of biological and psychosocial forces, a basic knowledge of the biological foundations of sexual behavior is paramount. The relevant biophysical aspects of sexuality may be conveniently grouped into the following five categories (Money, Hampson, and Hampson, 1955): (1) chromosomal sex indicated by the presence or absence of *sex chromatin*; (2) hormonal sex associated with the differentiation and development of internal and external sex characteristics; (3) gonadal sex as indicated by morphology; (4) internal genital morphology; and (5) external genital morphology. In accord with these biological factors, this chapter is intended to provide basic information concerning genetic, hormonal, anatomic and physiological differences between the sexes. Genetic and hormonal or endocrine factors exert their primary influence on the differentiation and development of internal and external sex characteristics. Internal and external morphology, in turn, influence psychosexual aspects of sex, such as sex rearing, sexual identity, and gender roles.

Chromosomal Sex

Sex Chromosomes and Sex Determination

Sex determination in higher animals, as well as in humans, occurs at the moment of conception and is the result of chromosomal mechanisms. The nucleus of every human cell contains twenty-two pairs of autosomal chromosomes and one pair of sex chromosomes. One member of each pair of these twenty-three sets of chromosomes is inherited from each parent. At fertilization, the complement of twenty-three chromosomes found in the father's sperm cell is paired with a second set of twenty-three chromosomes borne by the mother's egg, resulting in the fertilized egg or *zygote*, which, under circumstances of normal development, contains the full chromosomal complement of twenty-three pairs or forty-six single chromosomes.

The sex chromosomes are of particular importance for the genesis of sexuality. In contrast to the autosomes, which contain twenty-three pairs, the sex chromosomes carry twenty-three single chromosomes, including an X in the ovum in the case of a female and either an X or a Y in the male sperm. In normal females the complement consists of two X chromosomes, designated XX, with one X chromosome contributed by each parent. Normal males, designated XY, on the other hand, have but one X chromosome inherited from the mother and one Y chromosome contributed by the father. Figure 5.1 represents the process of sex determination, showing that the sex of the child depends on whether the sperm cell carries an X or Y chromosome. It is important to note that the genes on the Y chromosomes confer the qualities of maleness. In other words, it is the father who determines the genetic sex of the offspring, because it is the Y-bearing sperm that carries the genetic material for the differentiation of the embryonic sex organ or *gonad* into *testes* rather than *ovaries*. In the absence of the Y, sex differentiation will proceed along female lines of development. Male sex differentiation has been said to follow the additive principle (Money, 1977). That is, in order to be born male, something must be added. At the genetic level, this extra is the Y chromosome, representing the first manifestation of the additive principle, which will be encountered again in hormonal and neural sex differentiation.

While the role of the X chromosome in sex determination has been known since the early part of this century, the male determin-

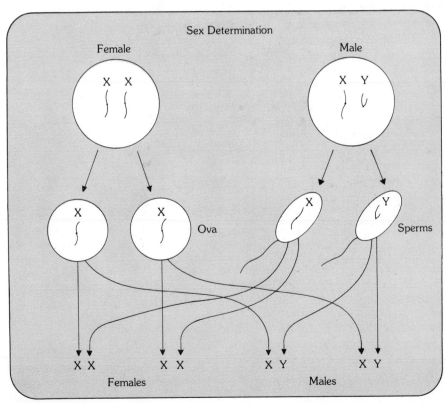

Figure 5.1
Sex determination.

ing effect of the Y chromosome was not recognized until 1959. Only since then has it been certain that the Y chromosome causes the development of the fertilized ovum into a male and that its absence leads to female differentiation (Stern, 1960).

For the most part, it appears to be a matter of chance whether an X- or Y-bearing sperm will fertilize the ovum. There are, however, some differences between the two types of sperms. In general, X-bearing sperms appear to have greater viability and tend to reach the ovum faster. Y-carrying sperms, on the other hand, occur in greater preponderance, as indicated by the ratio of male to female conceptions. According to miscarriage estimates, as many as 140 XY fetuses are conceived for every 100 XX. These differential miscarriage rates leave a birth ratio of about 105 boys to 100 girls. Even at the genetic level the principle of masculine vulnerability is a well-established clinical phenomenon that continues throughout the life span. National averages indicate that within the first twenty-eight days after birth, about 25 percent more male than female infants die. Similarly, while the forty-year-old population in the United States is almost equally balanced in terms of men and women, women clearly outnumber men during the latter part of the life span. Among people sixty-five years of age and older, for instance, the ratio is about seventy men for every one hundred women. Thus the idea of women as the "weaker" sex is certainly not substantiated from a biological point of view.

Sex Differentiation

Once a male or female program has been laid down genetically, the internal and external sex characteristics differentiate and develop, according to the genetic plan, from a common embryonic beginning—the neutral, undifferentiated gonad. The primordial gonad consists of a genital tubercle, a

urogenital opening, and a pair of genital folds. In addition to the pair of generalized sex glands, the primitive gonad is also equipped with a double, that is, male and female, set of sex ducts. These internal structures are, respectively, the *Wolffian* and *Müllerian* ducts. Figure 5.2 shows the undifferentiated genitalia with the Wolffian and Müllerian ducts that give rise to the male and female sex organs respectively.

At this early stage of development, which encompasses the first seven weeks of intra-

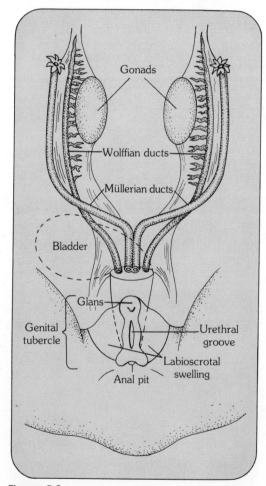

Figure 5.2
Undifferentiated sex organs showing the male (Wolffian) and female (Müllerian) ducts.

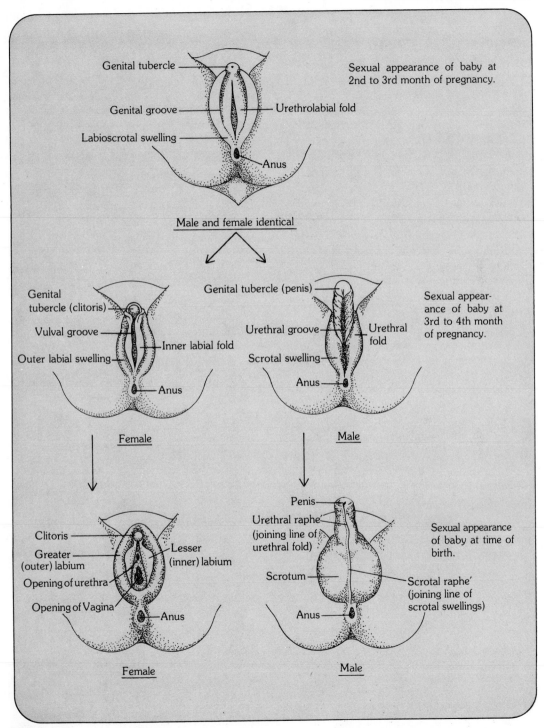

Figure 5.3
Differentiation of the external sex organs.

uterine life, the fetus is essentially bisexual in nature; the undifferentiated gonad is neither a testis nor an ovary. The bipotentiality of the undifferentiated gonad, however, refers only to the potential phenotypic expression of developing along male or female lines because the tissues are already programmed genetically toward maleness or femaleness.

Jost (1973) advanced the idea that maleness is imposed on basically female structures and that male development is a deviation from a basic female pattern. According to this notion, the embryonic gonad initially develops as an ovary. After the intrusion of the Y chromosome, however, the growth of male testes is initiated. Jost's theorizing is certainly contrary to prior hypotheses; it implies that sex differentiation results from two genetically different developmental systems, the Wolffian and Müllerian ducts. According to the more conservative view, both sets of differential sex ducts are held in readiness for the time when sexuality is externally declared as a function of the release of sex hormones. If the embryo is to develop into a male, hormones are necessary to inhibit the development of the Muellerian duct and prevent the regression of the Wolffian structure. The idea of a basic female growth pattern is, however, supported by several workers in the field (Money, 1972; Sherfey, 1972), who also suggest a transformation of female structures into male sex organs by the action of fetal androgens.

Morphologically, the genital tubercle has to enlarge and enclose the urogenital opening if the embryo is to develop along male lines. The genital folds then form the *scrotum*, which will contain the testes after birth. On the other hand, if the embryo is programmed to become a female, the genital tubercle remains small to form the clitoris.

In the normal course of development, one of the ducts undergoes progressive development, whereas the other one is suppressed and becomes vestigial. At the end of the undifferentiated phase, rudimentary male or female genitalia can be clearly distinguished as the opposite potential degenerates in the process of differentiation. If sex differentiation proceeds along the male line, the major portion of the Wolffian ducts are transformed into the vas deferens and the ejaculatory duct. In the case of female differentiation, the Müllerian ducts develop into the uterus, oviducts, and part of the vagina. It is usually clear by the tenth to twelfth week of embryonic development whether the undifferentiated gonad has been programmed to become a testis or an ovary.

In an orderly course of events, birth takes place some 270 days after conception, resulting in an infant whose genetic sex is phenotypically expressed according to the genetic plan. In the absence of male sex hormones, development will proceed innately in the female direction. The remainder of sexual development is collectively controlled by sex hormones, or *gonadotropins*, which determine the final growth and functioning of male and female sex organs.

Hormonal Sex

Male and Female Sex Hormones

The involvement of the X and Y chromosome in the genetic determination of sex is restricted to the differentiation of the embryonic sex organs. Whereas sex chromosomes trigger the developmental direction of the originally neutral gonad, the remaining differentiation is under the control of sex hormones. All sex hormones are released by the anterior pituitary gland located at the base of the brain. Hormone production, once genetically programmed, is controlled and activated by the brain.

Sex hormones play two major roles in determining behavioral outcomes: (1) before and just after birth, hormones serve an organizational function in shaping the development of male and female sex organs. Because of their organizational functions, hormones act directly upon the genetic determinants of sex and complete sex differentiation according to the genetic blueprint. (2) During puberty and adulthood the sex hormones are instrumental in activating the development of secondary characteristics. Therefore, they are said to perform an activational function.

As in the case of the sex chromosomes, the additive principle also applies in the hormonal differentiation of sex. Once again, something must be added for maleness to occur. At the hormonal level the additional requirement involves the presence of the male sex hormone *androgen*. If androgen production fails, the embryonic gonad will differentiate externally as a female, regardless of chromosomal sex. Whereas female sex differentiation is independent of the release of hormonal substances, maleness is determined by the secretion of androgen. In the absence of the androgenic hormone, a male infant may be born with a fully differentiated uterus and fallopian tubes. If, on the other hand, androgen is present in excessive quantity even an XX fetus will be destined to develop into a male regardless of genetic sex. Faulty hormone production, then, leads to the development of morphological characteristics of opposite sex characteristics in both males and females.

Contrary to popular belief, men and women secrete some of all sex-relevant hormonal substances: *androgen, estrogen,* and *progesterone.* The difference in hormone secretion between the sexes is not of an absolute or all-or-none type, but rather a matter of relativity or degree. It has not only been demonstrated that androgenic and estrogenic hormones are produced by both sexes but, more important, that it is androgen

rather than the female sex hormones estrogen or progesterone that provides the active component for sexual desire and erotic feeling in women (Sopchak and Sutherland, 1960; Waxenberg, 1963). Similarly, Foss (1951) reported that androgen administration heightened the sex drive in women who were previously characterized as lacking or possessing a minimal degree of sexual desire. Taken together, these data support the now widely held view that androgen is "the" hormone involved in the activation of sexual behavior in both men and women (Money, 1961).

The following gonadotropins play the major organizational role in completing the process of differentiation of the internal sex organs: the *follicle-stimulating hormone* (FSH), which initiates the normal growth of the testes and ovaries. In its activational capacity, the FSH hormone later acts as the basic factor in ovulation. It causes the *follicles,* each of which contains a developing ovum, to secrete estrogen. In addition, the same hormone also plays a role in *spermatogenesis,* or the process of sperm production in the male.

The second pituitary product is the *luteinizing hormone* (LH), which works in conjunction with FSH in the final stage of follicular growth. The corresponding male hormone is the *interstitial cell-stimulating hormone* (ICSH). LH and ICSH refer to the same hormone that has different functions in the two sexes. LH is the luteal cell stimulator in females and is thus primarily associated with progesterone production. In males, the same hormone stimulates the interstitial (outside of the seminiferous tubules) cells to produce androgen, which in turn induces the development of secondary sex characteristics in pubescent boys.

Finally, the third major gonadotropic hormone is the *lactogenic hormone* (LTH), or luteotrophic hormone, which contains

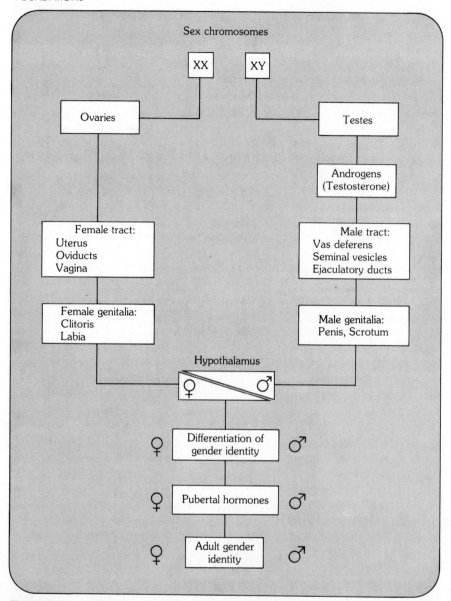

Figure 5.4
Summary of genetic and hormonal sex differentiation.

prolactin and stimulates the secretion of milk by the mammary glands at the end of pregnancy. In concert, the gonadotropins exert primary control over the internal organization of male and female reproductive systems, as well as being responsible for the basic physiological differences between the sexes. Since the hormonal regulation of the male and female sex cycle is different, the influence of the activating functions of gonadotropins will be considered separately for both sexes in the following two sections.

Hormonal Regulation of the Male Sexual Cycle

In men, FSH stimulates spermatogenesis in the seminiferous tubules of the testes at puberty. Sperm production is influenced directly and indirectly by two gonadotropins: FSH and ICSH. After a number of cell divisions, which are under the control of FSH, the mature sperm, or *spermatozoon*, is formed; it consists of a tail, or *flagellum*, and a head, with the neck and body between them.

Although sperm production is initiated in the testes under the influence of FSH, ICSH also operates to stimulate the production of *testosterone*, the second major hormone in males. Virtually all aspects of male reproductive function are either directly controlled or indirectly influenced by testosterone or the anterior pituitary gonadotropins FSH and LH. In addition to stimulating spermatogenesis in the testes, testosterone is also involved in the development of accessory sex organs, the secondary sexual characteristics, sexual behavior, and organic metabolism in general.

The male hormonal cycle and the release

Men Have Their Cycles, Too

Since Freud made his famous statement that "anatomy is destiny," women's behavior and emotions have been correlated with the ebb and flow of hormonal rhythms. It has been suggested, for example, that women lack the calm and consistent behavior of men because they suffer from "periodic lunacy" imposed by their monthly cycles. Because of this biological instability, certain personality characteristics, such as unpredictability or lack of leadership ability, have been ascribed to women. Given the notion of the male as the biologically superior sex, male cycles have been virtually ignored.

Although male cyclicity appears to be less dramatic, there is sufficient evidence for the existence of men's monthly cycles. Among several other investigators, Reinberg and Lagoguey (1978) detected daily or "circadian" cycles in men with testosterone levels being the highest early in the morning and the lowest after midnight.

Ramey (1972) reported a sixteen-year, carefully conducted Danish study in which male urine was tested for the fluctuating amounts of male sex hormones. The results revealed a pronounced thirty-day rhythm, with subtle changes in mood and behavior of which the men were not aware. Other studies that have investigated mood changes as a function of fluctuating hormones in men have revealed startling cycles. During periods when testosterone was low, male behavior was characterized by apathy, indifference, and a tendency to magnify minor problems out of proportion. Conversely, high periods were marked by feelings of well-being, energy, and a decreased need for sleep. Although the men studied tended to deny that they were more or less irritable, more or less amiable, standardized psychological tests at different points of their cycle clearly established that the men responded differently to the same life stresses at different times of their cycles. Men are seldom aware of the subtle changes in mood and behavior induced by fluctuating sex hormones.

As might be expected, men respond to their cycles differently than women do. Because of their culturally conditioned self-image, men are likely to deny or play down their monthly cycles, while many women have a tendency to accentuate the effects of their "periods." At the present time, our knowledge of the relationship of testosterone concentration in men and their sexual activities at peaks or low ebbs of sex hormones is largely unknown. However, it seems safe to assume that biological rhythms in men have important implications in the treatment of various diseases or sexual dysfunctions. So far, we have paid relatively little attention to the significance of cyclic hormonal changes in men.

of FSH and LH, spermatogenesis and testosterone secretion proceed normally at a rather fixed, continuous rate during adult life. This is unusual for hormonal systems and differs in an important way from the large cyclical swing of endocrine activity that characterizes the female hormonal cycle.

Hormonal Regulation of the Female Sexual Cycle

Menstruation, ovulation, and associated monthly body changes constitute the female sexual cycle, which is controlled by hormonal changes initiating in the anterior pituitary gland. In women, the follicle-stimulating hormone (FSH) acts on the ovarian follicular cells, stimulating the enlargement of follicles and the growth of the egg contained within the follicle. As the ovum matures, the surrounding cells of the follicle secrete estrogen, the ovarian hormone that triggers the first menstrual flow (*menarche*) and accounts for most of the characteristic features of the sexual cycle; estrogen also controls the development of secondary sex characteristics in pubescent girls. In addition, differential skeletal growth, particularly the wide pelvis, the development of the breasts and the general "rounding" of female body contours are functions of estrogen release.

Menstrual Cycle

Hormonal control of the menstrual cycle involves a complex interplay between pituitary and ovarian hormones. The increase in concentration of estrogen inhibits the secre-

tion of FSH from the pituitary while it simultaneously stimulates an increased production of the luteinizing hormone (LH) from the anterior pituitary lobe. LH, on the other hand, acts in concert with FSH to precipitate ovulation, which generally occurs in only one follicle at a time.

During menstruation periodic discharges of bloody fluid take place when the superficial layer of the *endometrium* or uterine lining is shed. Under the influence of FSH, one of the ova-containing ovarian follicles matures, and estrogen production by the ovary increases. The menstrual phase is followed by a period of increased estrogen production. At the same time, LH stimulates the development of the *corpus luteum* ("yellow body") and the secretion of progesterone. Figures 5.5a and 5.5b describe the menstrual cycle and the effects of female sex hormones on the ovarian and uterine cycles.

Ovulation, or the release of the ovum, occurs when the secretion of FSH reaches its peak and the production of LH decreases to a minimal level, typically about fourteen days after the onset of menstruation. As a consequence of the release of FSH, the pressure of the fluid inside the follicle housing the ovum rises, causing the follicle to burst and ejecting the egg into the funnel of the uterine tube. Following ovulation, the emptied follicle is transformed into a knot of yellow tissue known as the corpus luteum, which becomes a new endocrine organ responsible for the secretion of the second female hormone, progesterone.

Through the release of progesterone the final preparation of the endometrium, or

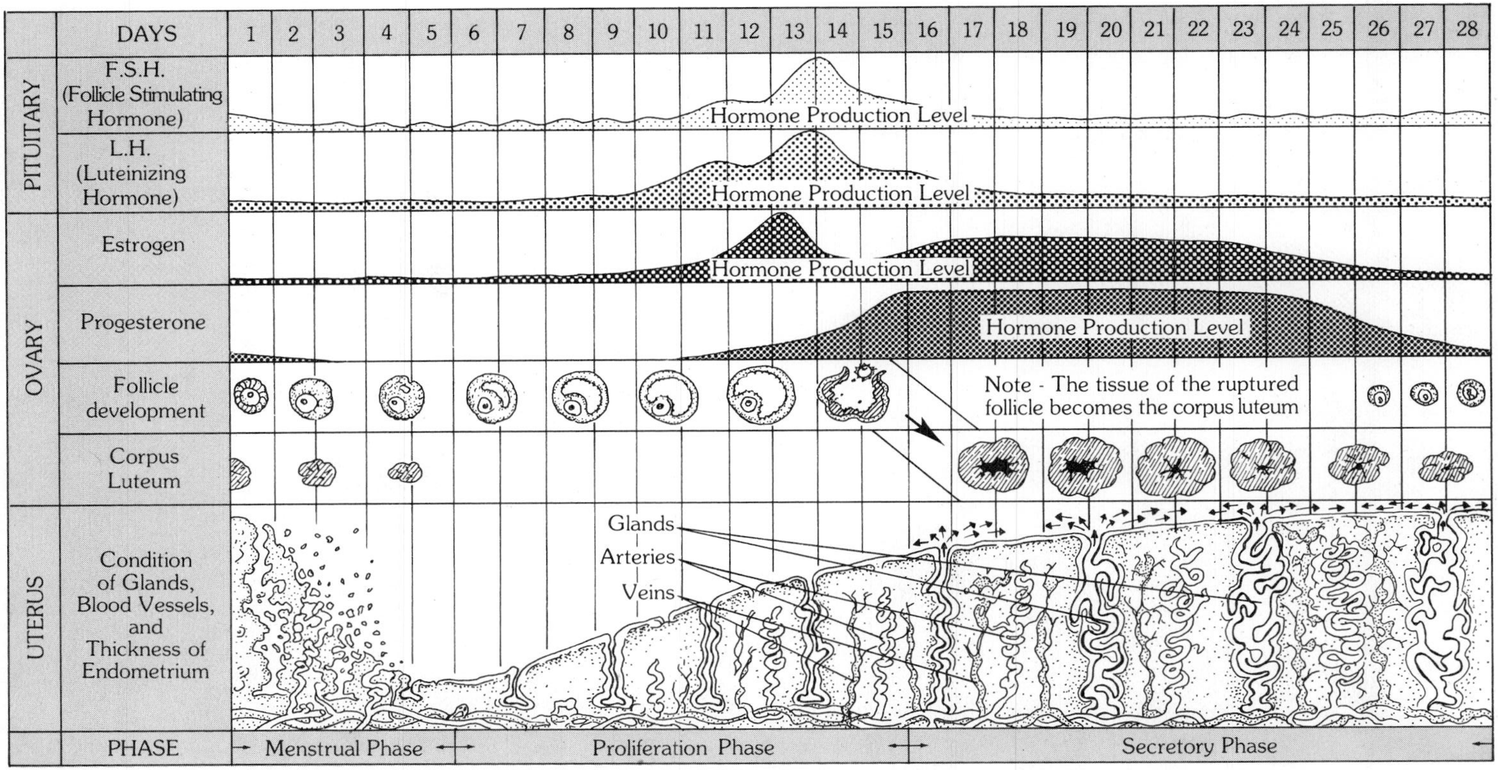

Figure showing the interrelationship of female sex hormones and the ovarian and uterine cycles, with columns for Days 1–28.

		DAYS: 1 2 3 4 5 6 7 8 9 10 11 12 13 14 15 16 17 18 19 20 21 22 23 24 25 26 27 28
PITUITARY	F.S.H. (Follicle Stimulating Hormone)	Hormone Production Level
	L.H. (Luteinizing Hormone)	Hormone Production Level
OVARY	Estrogen	Hormone Production Level
	Progesterone	Hormone Production Level
	Follicle development	
	Corpus Luteum	
UTERUS	Condition of Glands, Blood Vessels, and Thickness of Endometrium	Glands / Arteries / Veins
	PHASE	Menstrual Phase — Proliferation Phase — Secretory Phase

Note – The tissue of the ruptured follicle becomes the corpus luteum

Figure 5.5a
Interrelationship of female sex hormones and the ovarian and uterine cycles.

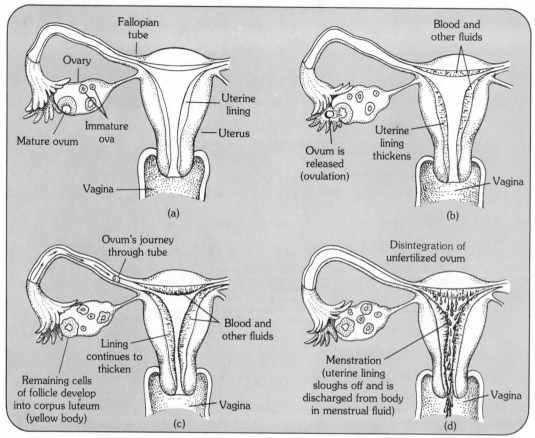

Figure 5.5b
The menstrual cycle.

uterine lining, to receive the fertilized egg is accomplished. As the level of progesterone falls, the uterine lining deteriorates and menstruation ensues. If, on the other hand, fertilization occurs and the ovum is implanted, the corpus luteum continues to be active for several months in the production of progesterone. Ovulation normally occurs as a result of the combined actions of FSH and LH, secreted at critical times during the cycle. If no ovum is available during the ovulatory phase when intercourse occurs, there will be no conception. Table 5.1 summarizes the hormonal effects on sexual maturation.

Anatomical Sex

Sexual development in men and women subsequent to the period of genetic and hormonal differentiation passes through a period of growth that culminates in fully mature and functioning sex organs in late adolescent boys and girls. Although the male and female reproductive systems develop from identical anatomical beginnings and according to the same plan, the mature sex organs are structurally and morphologically different enough in men and women to be considered separately.

Table 5.1

Summary of the Hormonal Effects on Sexual Maturation

Hormone	Principle Site of Action	Sexual Processes Affected
Follicle-stimulating hormone (FSH)	ovaries	development of follicles, secretion of estrogen
	testes	spermatogenesis
Luteinizing (LH) or interstitial cell-stimulating hormone	ovaries	ovulation, formation of the corpus luteum, secretion of progesterone
(ICSH)	testes	secretion of testosterone
Lactogenic or luteotrophin (LTH)	mammary glands and ovaries	secretion of milk, maintenance of the corpus luteum, secretion of progesterone

The Male Reproductive System

The male reproductive system (Fig. 5.7) consists of two testes producing sperm and androgens and the following bilateral structures: the *epididymis, vas or ductus deferens, seminal vesicles, ejaculatory ducts,* as well as the single organs of penis and *prostate gland.*

The testes are suspended outside the abdominal cavity in a pouch of loose skin, the *scrotum.* Each testis is an oval white body, about the size of a small egg, and is attached to an overlying structure, the epididymis, which in turn is continuous with the vas deferens or duct of the testis. A cross-section of the testis reveals a subdivision of several hundred lobules containing the tiny, coiled *seminiferous tubules.* The walls of these tubules are lined with germinal tissue and are the site of sperm production. Once spermatogenesis is completed and the fully mature sperm are formed, spermatozoa are moved out of the testes into the duct system of the epididymis.

In the normal healthy male the process of sperm formation takes about 72 days and is an ongoing process. In addition to the influence exerted by the two pituitary gonadotropins FSH and ICSH, spermatogenesis is also dependent on body temperature. Normally, the testes descend from an abdominal position into the scrotum a few weeks prior to birth. They must remain in this site thereafter if normal sperm formation is to be initiated at puberty and maintained in adulthood. Artificial elevation of body temperature in men for short periods of time, which also raise the thermal level in the testes, markedly reduces the sperm count in the ejaculate. Similarly, states of high fever may temporarily render a man sterile. All the available evidence suggests that normal spermatogenesis can proceed only at a temperature below that of the body and that the scrotum plays a crucial role in the thermoregulation of the testes.

Surgical removal of the testes or *castration* destroys the male's ability to produce sperm as well as the secretion of testosterone. If castration occurs prior to puberty, secondary sex characteristics fail to develop. Castration after puberty, however, has a less predictable effect on sexual behavior, since androgens are also produced by the adrenal gland in addition to the testicular hormone production. In the case of sufficient hormone production from the adrenals, the effect of castration on sexual behavior may be negated.

The *epididymis* starts in the testes as a series of small ducts that become convoluted after they leave the testis and subsequently unite to form a single tube, the ductus epididymis. The epididymis extends into the *vas* or *ductus deferens,* which forms the bilateral continuation of the canal of the epididymis. The upper end of the vas deferens joins the *seminal vesicles* and broadens to form the ampulla, which serves as a

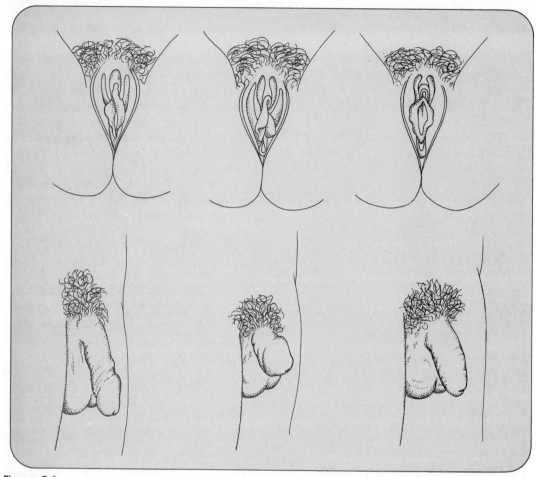

Figure 5.6
Normal genitals of men and women can take on a variety of forms.

storage reservoir for the completely matured sperm.

The *ejaculatory duct* is formed by the union of the vas deferens and a duct of the seminal vesicle at the same side. The two ejaculatory ducts then descend between the lobe of the prostate gland to the urethra into which they open and discharge their content. Thus the male urethra has both reproductive and excretory functions.

The *prostate* gland is a firm body approximately the size of a chestnut. Its main function is to secrete a thin, milky alkaline fluid

that enhances the motility of the sperm. The prostate is a common site of infection among younger men. In older men, cancer of the prostate occurs fairly frequently, accounting for 2 to 3 percent of all male deaths. Malignant tumors of the prostate may be treated surgically by castration; the growth of tumor cells may also be inhibited by the administration of estrogen.

The last male sex organ we consider is the penis, also referred to as the executive organ of male sexuality. The human penis, contrary to that of many other species, has no bone or intrinsic muscles. When sexually aroused, the penis becomes firm and erect (tumescent). If the erection is lost, the blood which had temporarily filled the spongy tissues slowly leaves the penis, returning it to the flaccid or detumescent, that is, nonerect state.

At the end of the penis there is a slight enlargement known as the *glans penis* containing the most sensitive part of the male sex organ. At birth the glans is covered with a fold of skin, the *prepuce* or foreskin. The foreskin is attached to the glans on the lower surface by a thin midline tissue known anatomically as the *frenum*. Occasionally, the prepuce may fit so tightly that it cannot be drawn back over the glans. This condition is referred to as *phimosis* or constriction of the foreskin. It

may be prevented or treated by the surgical removal of the foreskin, or *circumcision*, which leaves the glans permanently exposed. Figure 5.9 illustrates the anatomical structure of the penis.

Circumcision rites are common in many primitive as well as culturally advanced societies. In some cultures circumcision serves as a puberty rite, marking the adolescent's passage into adulthood (*see* Chapter 9). In others, such as among the Jews, circumcision is practiced as a religious ritual, passed down from generation to generation. Today, except for religious reasons, the main justification for the operation is its presumed effectiveness as a prophylactic measure. For example, the uncircumcised penis has been associated with both cancer of the penis and

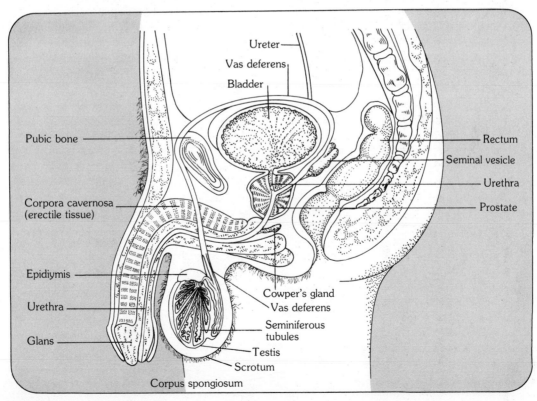

Figure 5.7
The male reproductive system.

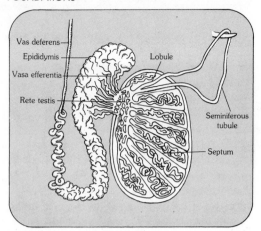

Figure 5.8
The internal structure of the penis.

the prostate gland. Similarly, wives of uncircumcised men have been found to be more susceptible to cancer of the cervix. However, a recent study of Lebanese Christians and Moslems failed to support the contention that wives of uncircumcised men develop cervical cancer.

The long-standing phallic myth, according to which the circumcised male is more rapidly aroused and maintains superior ejaculatory control compared with the noncircumcised male, fails to be substantiated by current evidence. In spite of the controversy over routine operations, advocates of neonatal circumcision seem to be in the majority and the preponderance of medical opinion supports the removal of the foreskin immediately after birth as an important aspect of preventive medicine.

Concern about the dimensions of their penises is almost universal among men. Typically, the larger penis is associated with a

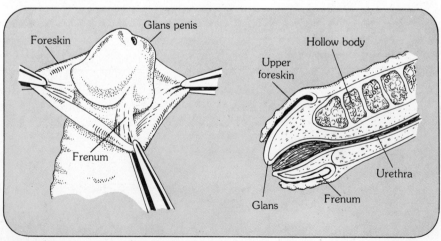

Figure 5.9
The foreskin and glans penis.

higher degree of masculinity and vitality. Adolescents in particular are conditioned by peer-conducted sex education and exposure to supersized genitals in pornography to equate sexual prowess with inordinately large penises. Actually, there is no relationship between penis size and sexual adequacy, since the vagina can, except for rare cases of dysfunction, accommodate penises of various sizes. Furthermore, the comparative differences between penises in their flaccid state tend to be compensated for during erection. That is, a small flaccid penis usually becomes more distended and increases proportionately more during sexual stimulation than a larger penis in its flaccid state. Thus there is little relationship between a nonerect and an erect penis.

The size and the dimension of the penis are shaped by genetic factors, and nothing can be done medically to enlarge it. According to recent data contributed by Masters and Johnson (1966), the length of the average penis ranges from three to four inches (seven to eleven centimeters) in the flaccid state to five to six and a half inches (fourteen to eighteen centimeters) in the erect state. In spite of the considerable variations in penis size from man to man, these differences are independent of overall body size, sex drive, or skin color.

Erection and Ejaculation

The primary components of the male sexual act are *erection* of the penis, which permits entry into the vagina, and *ejaculation* through which the semen (the ejaculatory fluid) is deposited into the vagina. Erection is accounted for by the dilation of the erectile tissue during sexual excitement. As the vascular spaces of the erectile tissue become engorged with blood, the penis becomes rigid. Thus erection of the penis is primarily a vascular phenomenon.

Ejaculation, on the other hand, is basically a spinal reflex. When the level of sexual stimulation reaches a critical peak, the genital ducts contract, emptying their contents into the urethra (emission). Rapid rhythmical muscle contractions then expel the semen from the penis, resulting in the orgasmic experience. The average volume of fluid ejaculated is three milliliters containing approximately 300 million sperms. However, the range of normal values is extremely large among men. The entire sequence of sexual excitement, erection, penetration, emission, and, finally, ejaculation is a product of complex sequential and coordinated actions of the muscular and nervous systems.

The Female Reproductive System

Anatomically speaking, the female reproductive system is built on the same basic plan as the corresponding male sex organs, consisting of an internal and external group of structures. Figure 5.10 shows the major parts of the female reproductive system. The internal sex organs are located within the pelvis and consist of two ovaries, bilateral uterine tubes, and the single structures of the uterus and the vagina. The external genitalia, sometimes collectively referred to as vulva, include the *mons pubis* or *veneris*, the *labia* (both major and minor), the *clitoris*, the vestibule of the *vagina*, and the *mammary glands* as accessories to the reproductive system.

The *ovaries* are two almond-shaped bodies located on either side of the uterus and are homologous to the testes. The human ovary, like the testis, serves a dual purpose: (1) production of ova, (2) secretion of the female sex hormones, estrogen and progesterone. As endocrine glands, the ovaries are regulated by the anterior pituitary.

At birth as many as 400,000 primary follicles may be contained in each ovary. However, this number decreases steadily during childhood and early adolescence. During the reproductive span of approximately thirty-

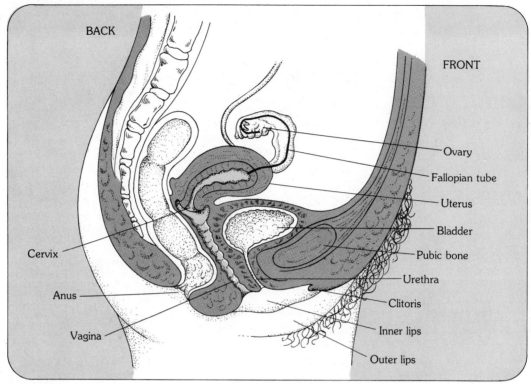

BACK

FRONT

Ovary

Fallopian tube

Uterus

Bladder

Pubic bone

Urethra

Clitoris

Inner lips

Outer lips

Cervix

Anus

Vagina

Figure 5.10
The female reproductive system.

five years, only 300 to 400 follicles reach maturity in the average woman.

The development of the mature ovum follows a path paralleling spermatogenesis. Under the influence of FSH several cell divisions take place, giving rise to a mature ovum with twenty-three single chromosomes. However, the final division is not completed until fertilization takes place.

The *uterine tubes*, also known as *Fallopian tubes* or *oviducts*, convey the ova from the ovaries to the uterus. After ovulation, the released ovum enters the uterine tube. Fertilization of the ovum normally occurs in the outer third of the oviduct, nearest to the ovaries. Occasionally, a fertilized ovum may adhere to the uterine tube, a condition known as *ectopic pregnancy*.

The *uterus* is a thick-walled, hollow, mus-

cular organ whose cavities communicate with those of the uterine tube above and with that of the vagina below. Structurally, the pear-shaped uterus is divided into two parts: the body, which constitutes the upper portion, and a lower constricted section, the *cervix*. Functionally, the uterus is the organ of the female reproductive system in which the embryo develops and grows until the time of delivery.

Attached to the cervix of the uterus is a muscular tube, the *vagina*. Its walls are made up of smooth connective tissue that is highly distensible to accommodate the penis during intercourse. The major sexual functions of the vagina are related to the reception of the penis and holding the semen. As an erotic center, the vagina is of minor importance because of its insensitivity. Kinsey (1953), for

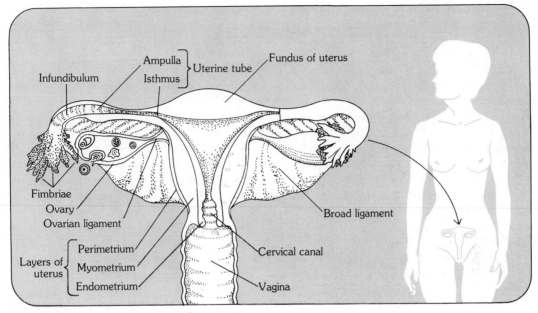

Figure 5.11
The internal structure of the female sex organs.

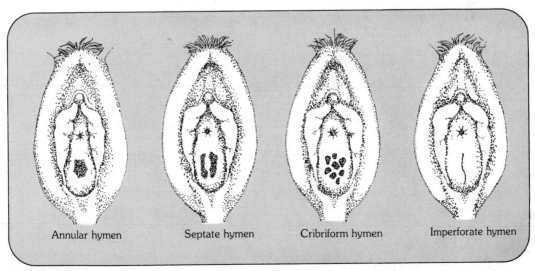

Annular hymen   Septate hymen   Cribriform hymen   Imperforate hymen

Figure 5.12
Several types of hymen.

instance, reported that less than 14 percent of women were conscious of tactile stimulation of their vagina.

At the lower end of the vagina there is a thin fold of tissue, the hymen, which partially closes off the vaginal opening. The intact hymen is often, although erroneously, regarded as a sign of virginity. Although the hymen can be ruptured during first intercourse, many other factors—such as repeated insertion of tampons, strenuous exercise, or sexual experimentation—can also tear the hymen. Consequently, the existence of an intact hymen does not necessarily serve as a reliable criterion of virginity.

The *mons pubis* or *veneris* is part of the external female genitalia, consisting of a rounded pad of fat under dense skin, which, at puberty, becomes covered with hair. It partially surrounds the *labia majora* (outer lips), arising as two prominent folds of skin from the mound of fatty tissue that forms the mons pubis. The labia majora are the homologues of the scrotum and, like it, contain large sweat glands that become pigmented after puberty. Between the outer

lips are the *labia minora* (inner lips). Anteriorly, they are united to form the prepuce, a small hood of skin that partially covers the clitoris.

The *clitoris* is an erectile structure homologous to the penis. As in the case of the penis, there are great variations in the dimensions of the clitoris, which again bear no relationship to sexual responsiveness. Since the clitoris is highly sensitive, it may retract to an inaccessible position under the hood with direct and intense sexual stimulation. In Figure 5.14 the external portions of the female reproductive system are represented.

It has been suggested that a woman achieves two types of orgasms, vaginal and clitoral, experiencing them as separate anatomic entities. At one time psychoanalytic theory proposed that in the course of normal psychosexual development the adolescent girl initially experiences immature clitoral orgasms as a result of masturbation. With the practice of heterosexual intercourse, the orgasmic center is transferred from the clitoris to the vagina, which in turn produces a more mature orgasm. The work of Masters

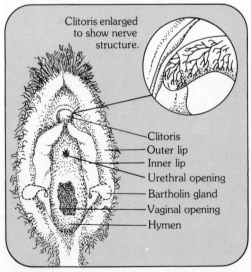

Figure 5.13
The structure of the clitoris.

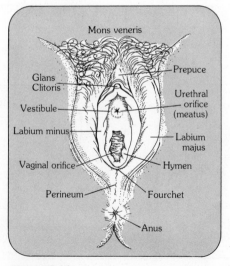

Figure 5.14
The external sex organs of the female.

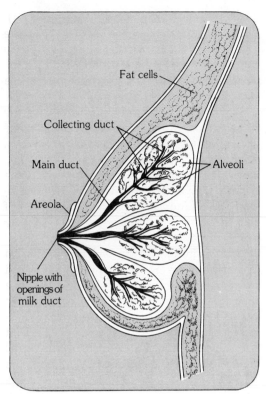

Figure 5.15
Internal structure of the breast.

Fat cells

Collecting duct

Main duct

Areola

Alveoli

Nipple with openings of milk duct

amount of glandular tissue in the breast varies; this causes its size and shape to vary as well. Most women have approximately the same amount of glandular tissue when compared at the same points of their reproductive cycle. Differences in breast size are determined by the amount of fat collected over and between the sections of the gland.

Physiology of the Male and Female Sexual Response

The preceding section focused on the anatomical structure of the internal and external sex organs of men and women. Our next concern is with the functional aspects of the anatomical structures or the physiology of sex.

The Sexual-Response Cycle

Biological changes resulting from sexual stimulation are reflected in a series of physiological alterations summarized as the *sexual-response cycle,* which culminates in *orgasm.* The sexual-response cycles for men and women have been conveniently divided into four phases (Masters and Johnson, 1966) to provide a framework for the description of bodily changes in response to sexual stimulation.

The sexual-response cycle is usually independent of the type of sexual stimulation or sexual activity that produces it. Physiologically, sexual arousal and orgasm follow the same pattern whether brought about by direct stimulation such as masturbation or intercourse, or indirect sexual activities such as exposure to erotic literature or pornographic literature. Many of the physiological reactions occurring during the sexual-response cycle are of such short duration that they may be confined to a specific phase of the cycle. Other physiological consequences of sexual arousal develop to such a

and Johnson (1966) seriously questioned the distinction between these two types of orgasm. Anatomically and physiologically, the orgasmic response is identical, regardless of the source of sexual stimulation. The "mature" vaginal orgasm has been relegated to the status of a myth.

Finally, the *mammary glands* or breasts are functionally related to the reproductive system since they secrete milk after parturition. The gland is made up of milk-producing areas and ducts leading to the nipple. With the great increase of sex hormones during adolescence, the glandular tissues in the breast begin to increase in size. Because sex hormone levels change during the menstrual cycle, with the starting and stopping of birth control pills, and during pregnancy, the magnitude that they can be observed throughout the entire cycle. Differences resulting from various types of stimulation typically do not affect the fundamental physiological changes of the body but do manifest themselves in the intensity of these responses.

The basic sexual-response pattern that unfolds in men and women leads to two major changes early during sexual stimulation: *vasocongestion* and *myotonia*. Vasocongestion refers to the engorgement of the penis, pelvis, and vulva, which dilate and become filled with blood. Myotonia is the tightening of the muscles. Both reactions are physiological components of sexual arousal in both sexes.

According to Masters and Johnson, the sexual-response cycle may be separated into four consecutive phases: excitement, plateau, orgasm, and resolution.

Excitement Phase. Sexual stimulation usually starts the excitement phase of the response cycle. Typical male reactions include penile erection and partial elevation of the testes. In women, one of the earliest signs of sexual arousal becomes evident when the fibers of the breast nipples contract. Many men also experience nipple erection, although not as frequently. In addition, vasocongestion increases and the uterus becomes elevated. Both men and women may show a flushing of the skin, which takes on a rosy color. If the sex flush occurs, it starts late in the excitement phase and then spreads rapidly during the later phases until it reaches maximum distribution just prior to orgasm.

Plateau Phase. If sexual stimulation is effectively maintained, the plateau phase develops as the advanced stage of sexual arousal in which high tension is maintained for a while prior to orgasmic release. The male responds to increasing sexual arousal with an increase in penile circumference and

further elevation of the testes. In women, the orgasmic platform begins to form as the outer third of the vagina becomes engorged. The clitoris retracts under the hood. During the plateau phase the full subjective feeling of sexual arousal reaches its peak.

Orgasmic Phase. Following the plateau phase of the sexual response, there are involuntary spasms of a number of skeletal muscles supplying the pelvic area. In males, orgasm is initiated by the phasic contractions of the accessory sex organs of vas deferens, seminal vesicles, and prostate, which contract regularly to provide the seminal fluid necessary for ejaculation. For men, ejaculation and orgasm are separate processes. The sensations of orgasm are associated with the feeling that ejaculation is coming and that it is no longer under voluntary control. In women contractions of the vaginal platform and the uterus progress toward the lower uterine segment and are associated with a 50 percent increase in uterine size because of vasocongestion.

Resolution Phase. After orgasm there is a rapid disappearance of the sex flush, the orgasmic platform, and the erection. The resolution phase marks the return to the nonaroused state. Swelling of the internal and external genitals decreases, and the muscles of the pelvic floor relax. When the physiological residuals of sexual arousal dissipate, male and female sex organs assume their unstimulated position. The resolution phase may last thirty minutes or more.

Although the fundamental events of the response are identical for both sexes, there are a number of differences in the physiological responses of men and women. In the male cycle orgasm is followed by a *refractory* period that extends into the resolution phase. The refractory period is characterized by a lack of sexual responsiveness. Even though in principle a man is capable of multiple or at least repeated orgasms at the end of the

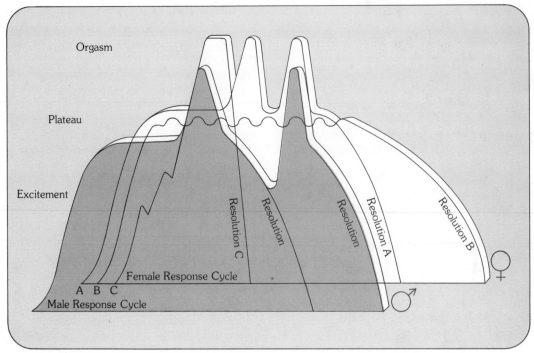

Figure 5.16
The male and female sexual response cycle.

refractory period, his capacity to experience more than one orgasm is limited in practice. Women, on the other hand, do not experience a distinct refractory response but can easily experience repetitive orgasms. This multiorgasmic capacity of women represents a major difference between the male and female response cycle.

A second major sex difference concerns the range of variability of sexual responses in men and women. Figure 5.16 shows a single sequence characterizing the male pattern but much more variability in women. Pattern A in Fig. 5.16 is essentially the female response associated with the basic male pattern. In addition, at least two alternatives exist. In Pattern B the plateau and orgasmic phases fuse, resulting in a series of sustained orgasms. Pattern C reflects an orgasmic experience without a plateau moving directly from excitement to climax. Figure 5.16

summarizes the male and female sexual-response cycle. The corresponding Table 5.2 lists the physiological reactions during the four phases of the sexual response cycle for men and women.

In spite of these physiological differences, men and women experience orgasm as highly pleasurable. It is generally assumed, however, that the psychological concomitants of orgasm also differ among the sexes. The male orgasm is more sudden and explosive in nature, whereas the female counterpart is sustained longer and is less violent. Robertiello (1970) argues in favor of two distinct and easily distinguishable kinds of orgasms experienced subjectively by men and women. However, little attention has been paid to an examination of male and female orgasms within the total life experiences of men and women living in a particular society. Differences in expectations, as well as in the

Table 5.2

Summary of the Physiological Reactions During the Female and Male Sexual Response Cycle

Excitement Phase	Plateau Phase	Orgasmic Phase	Resolution Phase
Vaginal lubrication	Continued vaginal expansion	Contractions of uterus	Loss of vaginal vasocongestion
Thickening of vaginal walls and labia	Uterine and cervical elevation	Contractions of orgasmic platform	Loss of orgasmic platform
Elevation of cervix	Secretion from Bartholin's gland	External rectal sphincter contractions	Loss of clitoral tumescence and return to position
Swelling of clitoris	Withdrawal of clitoris	Hyperventilation	Loss of sex flush
Nipple erection	Generalized muscle tension	Rapid heartbeat	
Sex-tension flush	Hyperventilation		
	Rapid heartbeat		
Penile erection	Increase in penile circumference	Contraction of accessory organs of reproduction: vas deferens, seminal vesicles, prostate	Loss of penile erection
Elevation of scrotal sac	Full testicular elevation	Ejaculation	Loss of sex flush
Partial elevation of testes	Secretions from Cowper's glands	Loss of voluntary muscle control	Loss of vasocongestion
Nipple erection	Myotonia		
	Sex flush	Contractions of penile urethra and anal sphincter	
	Generalized muscle tension	Hyperventilation	
	Hyperventilation		
	Rapid heartbeat	Rapid heartbeat	

degree to which attainment of orgasm and pleasure and satisfaction in sex are equated, are at least in part culturally determined.

Neural Mechanisms of Sexual Behavior

A biological perspective of human sexuality would be incomplete without a considera-tion of the neural mechanisms controlling sexual behavior. The last section of this chapter will therefore examine the role of the brain and the central nervous system in mediating sexual and sex-related responses.

Neural mechanisms have been imple-mented in the regulation of sexual behavior in two important ways. First, some parts of the central nervous system, notably specific

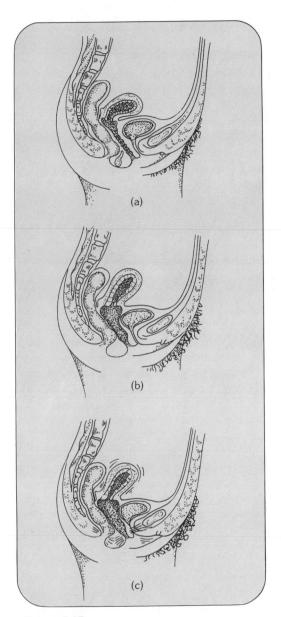

Figure 5.17
The sexual response of the female genitals; (a) the female genitals in the unaroused state; (b) the female genitals in a highly aroused state (plateau); (c) the female genitals during orgasm.

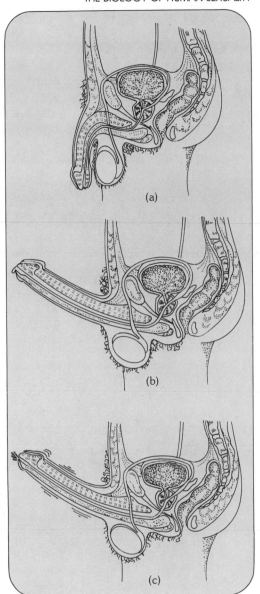

Figure 5.18
The sexual response of the male genitals: (a) the male genitals in the unaroused state; (b) the male genitals in a highly aroused state; (c) the male genitals during orgasm.

hypothalamic regions, control the functional activity of the sex organs by acting through the anterior pituitary gland and mediating the release of sex hormones. Since hypothalamic neurons are in direct contact with the posterior portion of the pituitary, the gland is under direct control of the brain. It has been suggested that special types of neurons in the hypothalamus secrete "releasing factors" or "releasing hormones", which in turn stimulate or inhibit the pituitary gland to release its gonadotropic hormones into systemic circulation.

The central nervous system exerts an additional influence on sexual behavior through discrete structures in the brain that are involved in the sensory and perceptual reception and integration of sexually relevant stimuli, as well as in the organization and motivation of sexual responses. These areas of the brain control sexual arousal and the corresponding motor responses.

Until recently, little was known about the specific structures of the brain responsible for genital reflexes such as penile erection and vaginal lubrication. Presently, clinical evidence is accumulating from animal research and from observations of individuals who have been accidentally deprived of certain areas of the brain to provide a link between certain areas of the central nervous system and sexual behavior.

Most of the available evidence suggests that many aspects of sexual behavior are integrated at the hypothalamic level. Of vital importance in maintaining and regulating the secretion of gonadotropins from the anterior pituitary, the hypothalamus ultimately controls the functional state of the ovaries and testes. However, there is a major functional difference in the male and female hormonal secretion patterns. Men secrete sex hormones at a tonic, more or less constant level, whereas in the female pattern the release of estrogen occurs in a cyclic fashion resulting in the rhythm of ovulation, formation of the corpus luteum, or menstruation.

A review of the relevant animal research of the past two decades suggests that the difference in the tonic male hormone secretion and the cyclic release of female hormones reflects a differentiation in the brain (Whalen, 1977). Evidence to support the notion of a "male" vs. "female" brain comes from ovarian transplants into male animals. The resultant production of the ovarian hormone estrogen, however, proceeds at the steady, tonic rate typical of the male secretion pattern. Similarly, a female pituitary transplanted into a male animal will activate hormonal secretions at a more or less constant level. In the reverse case, transplanting a male pituitary into a female organism causes the characteristic cyclic release of gonadotropins. These data clearly suggest that the secretion of male and female sex hormones is not a function of pituitary control. Instead, the findings from hormonal implants indicate that organized systems in the brain respond to hormones and that males and females differ with regard to these systems.

Recent sex research (Money, 1972) investigating the influence of fetal hormones on hypothalamic centers implies that neural mechanisms of sexual behavior follow the same additive principle that determines chromosomal and hormonal differentiation. Money suggests that at the neural level once again nature's basic premise is programmed for female development. And once again the element being added is a male sex hormone. The notion of a "male" vs. "female" brain had been postulated earlier when Harris (1964) found that the presence of a male hormone led in both genetic males and females not only to the emergence of a male genital tract but also stimulated the development of a central nervous system different from the brain of an organism lacking the male hormone.

Supportive evidence comes from a series of animal studies (Gorski, 1971) in which the path of a radioactive male hormone was followed through the central nervous system, including cells in the hypothalamus. When the hormone was administered to female animals during the critical period of differentiation, the hypothalamic cells became masculinized. Consequently, they never released the neurohormonal messages to the pituitary to activate the typical female cycle. Behavioral effects of masculinization also included disoriented sexual responses often repulsed by the male animal. The findings have been repeated with male animals that were castrated during the critical period before androgen leaves its imprint on the hypothalamus. The sexual behavior of these animals in adulthood is distinctively feminine.

Another major area of research relating sexual behavior to neural mechanisms concerns the search for localized areas of the brain that control specific sexual functions. Most of the early work focused on the identification of neural "sex" or "pleasure" centers as suggested by studies employing electrical stimulation of the brain. Subjective reports of patients whose brains were electrically stimulated in the region of the temporal lobe indicate that electrical stimulation has sexual overtones; the experience was described as an erotic pleasure and orgasm-like event.

Recent evidence from brain lesion techniques, however, refutes the notion of one or more centers controlling sexual responsiveness and sexual performance. Instead, a complex set of neural subsystems exists at all levels of the central nervous system, ranging from the spinal cord to the cerebral cortex. Brain-lesion studies revealed that hormone-insensitive systems exist in addition to those areas of the brain responding to sex hormones.

Both animal research and observations of patients who have sustained spinal cord injury have shown that the spinal cord mediates genital reflexes. For example, genital stimulation has elicited sexual movements and posture in female cats even after the transection of the spinal cord below the brain (Beach, 1967; Hart, 1969). At least some elements of sexual behavior are apparently arranged at the level of the spinal cord.

In addition, the reflex mechanism responsible for the control of penile erection and the emission of semen is apparently located in the spinal cord. Human males with spinal cord damage may retain their genital reflexes and can produce an erection and ejaculate (Money, 1960). For instance, Comarr's

---

Sexual Behavior of Spinal Cord-injured Women

Spinal cord injuries may result from a number of different sources including automobile accidents or degenerative diseases directly affecting the spinal cord. The effects of spinal cord injury are not only neurological but also involve psychological and social consequences. Until fairly recently, persons with spinal cord injury have been viewed as asexual, having lost all ability and interest in sexual function (Cole, 1975).

Recent research has shown, however, that women with spinal cord injuries have the same sexual capacities as prior to injury. For example, Bregman (1973) reported that spinal cord-injured women were able to engage in satisfying sexual relationships and to experience orgasm. Their sexual interests seemed to be similar to what they had been prior to injury. Moreover, spinal cord-injured women have been found to have normal menstrual cycles and deliveries.

In a recent investigation (Fitting, Salisbury, Davis and Mayclin, 1978) the authors examined the differences in the sexual response in women before and after spinal cord injury. The majority of the women interviewed reported that sex was enjoyable before as well as after injury, and most of them had been involved in sexual relationships since their injury. This is not to say, however, that the self-image of these women had not changed. Interestingly enough, the majority of the women perceived themselves as being more assertive, more independent, more active as a sexual partner, and honest with themselves after the injury. One woman commented:

> "It has been a growth maturing type process. I am happy in my marriage and children and truly enjoy my work. I feel like a very effective human being and injury has little to do with it, except, pehaps, it made me mature faster and gave me an outlook which doesn't get hung up on little things." (Fitting *et al.,* p. 153)

In contrast to men whose reproductive capacities may be impaired after spinal cord injury, such injury is not as devastating to women. The major complaint of women was the lack of genital sensations. Nevertheless, many spinal cord-injured women "report orgasms in spite of complete denervation of all pelvic structures" (Cole, 1975).

(1970) examination of hundreds of patients with spinal cord injury revealed that more than 90 percent of men with upper motor neuron lesions still had erections, whereas only 25 percent of the patients with lower motor lesions retained erections. Interestingly, however, the reverse was true for ejaculation. Orgasm, that is, the psychological experience accompanying ejaculation is typically lost after spinal cord injury although some men reported orgasmic experiences in the absence of erection.

The hypothalamus is not only important in controlling the secretion of releasing factors but has also been implemented in the regulation of sexual drive. Hypothalamic lesions of the ventromedial area have been applied to men in order to decrease the activity of sex offenders (Roeder and Mueller, 1969). Similarly, Whalen (1977) quoted cases of men with long histories of pedophilic homosexuality who were subjected to unilateral lesions of the hypothalamus, which successfully reduced their intense sex drive.

The operation in both cases apparently suppressed many forms of sexual behavior.

Some of the most interesting data suggesting neural control of sexual behavior come from observations of the effects of temporal lobe lesions. In the classical study conducted by Kluever and Bucy (1939), male rhesus monkeys displayed a variety of dramatic symptoms including hypersexuality as reflected in autoerotic behaviors, the mounting of unusual objects, such as members of other species, or even a boy after temporal damage. Since then a variety of males of other species have been found to exhibit hypersexual behavior after temporal damage. In all instances, the males mated at inappropriate times, in inappropriate places, or with inappropriate objects. Temporal lobe lesions affect perceptual rather than motivational systems since none of the afflicted animals engaged in sexual activities with greater frequency or intensity. Instead, their perceptions of appropriate location for mating and appropriate sex object choices were altered as a result of the temporal lobe lesion.

In addition to hypersexuality, bizarre fetishes have also been associated with temporal lobe dysfunction. A particularly striking case was reported by Mitchell, Falconer, and Hill (1954). A young man with epilepsy suffered from a safety pin fetish. His compulsion to gaze at safety pins, in turn, would trigger his seizures, at the end of which he would dress in his wife's clothing. Surgical removal of the man's temporal lobe corrected his epilepsy, and the transvestism disappeared simultaneously. A number of similar cases may be found in the literature (for example, Hunter, Logue and McMenemy, 1963; Epstein, 1960; and Walinder, 1965). Furthermore temporal lesions have been employed in the treatment of epilepsy where seizures originated from localized irritative lesions in the temporal lobes. Here again, removal of the affected tissues sometimes resulted in hypersexuality (Blumer, 1970). Finally, a relationship between sexual disorders such as voyeurism, sadomasochism, and impotence and temporal damage has been found, especially if the tissue destruction occurred early in life (Kolarsky, Freund, Machek, and Polak, 1967).

At the highest level of neural integration, the cerebral cortex exerts some influence over sexual functions. Cortical lesions disrupt copulatory behavior in the male of the species, while the sexual activities of females remain by and large uninhibited (Larsson, 1964). The disparity in the role of the cortex can be accounted for by the fact that the physical role of male animals is more complicated in mating behavior; his sexual arousal depends on a higher degree of analysis of sensory (such as sight and smell) information. Male arousal principally depends on the sight and smell of a receptive female, whereas female responsiveness is determined by hormonal conditions. Consequently, cortical damage exerts a greater influence on the sexual behavior of male animals. In humans, one would expect cortical damage to disrupt the sexual behavior of both men and women. At present it is difficult to provide clear and concise summary of the brain functioning in the control of sexual behavior. Nevertheless, it seems safe to say that the spinal cord contains the neural circuits for some basic sexual reflexes such as erection, ejaculation, and pelvic thrusting. The hypothalamus regulates these reflexes and removes them from inhibitory control under the appropriate circumstances. The temporal lobe appears to be particularly important in the analysis of what circumstances are appropriate for sexual activities. Finally, the cortex plays an important role in the perceptual organization of sex-relevant sensory and motor functions.

Summary

This chapter has examined the major biological factors involved in the expression and manifestation of human sexuality. Biological forces may be said to operate at the genetic, hormonal, and neural level to organize male and female sex organs anatomically and to determine the physiological concomitants of the sexual response cycle.

At conception the genetic choice is determined by whether the ovum will be fertilized by a sperm carrying an X or Y chromosome. In the former case the resulting fetus will have the XX chromosomal complement characteristic of females, whereas in the latter case a male with the XY genetic constellation will begin embryonic life. After the chromosomal sex has been established, gonadal differentiation begins at the critical period of approximately six weeks after fertilization. In the XX embryo the undifferentiated gonad proliferates to form an ovary, whereas in the XY conception the undifferentiated core develops into the testes. In both cases the opposing ducts regress and become vestigial. Genetic sex differentiation is paralleled by the action of sex hormones that have a dual influence on the remainder of sexual differentiation. Before birth, hormones act in an inductive way to organize the primitive gonad along male or female sexual morphology, internal as well as external. During puberty and adulthood, the gonadal hormones—activated by the central nervous system—are responsible for the final maturation of sex organs and secondary sex characteristics for both sexes. Ultimately, the male and female reproductive systems are the result of the complex interaction of genetic and endocrine factors. Each stage of chromosomal and hormonal differentiation represents a choice point, and errors may occur leading to atypical conditions. Some of the genetic and hormonal aberrations are described in Chapter 6.

The neural mechanisms involved in sexual behavior are complex, incorporating subsystems at all levels of the central nervous system, ranging from the spinal cord to the cerebral cortex. Both hormone-sensitive and nonhormonal elements control one or more stages of the sexual act. There appears to be no single sex center in the brain, contrary to suggestions based on early research employing electrical stimulation of the brain. Instead, interacting neural subsystems mediate different facets of sexual activities. Biological control of sex differentiation, then, not only forms the basis of sexual organization in men and women. It also influences the final determination of psychosexual differences, which ultimately are the results of interacting biological, psychological, and social forces.

References

Beach, F. "Cerebral and hormonal control of reflexive mechanisms involved in copulatory behavior." *Physiological Review*. 1967, 47, 289-316.

Blumer, D. "Hypersexual episodes in temporal lobe epilepsy." *American Journal of Psychiatry*, 1970, 126, 1099-1106.

Bregman, S. "Behaviors relating to feminine attractiveness and sexual adjustment among women with spinal cord injuries." Unpublished Master's thesis. Los Angeles: California State University, 1973.

Cole, T. "Sexuality and physical disabilities." *Archives of Sexual Behavior*, 1975, 4, 389-403.

Comarr, A. "Sexual function among patients with spinal cord injury." *Urologia Internationalis*, 1970, 25, 134-168.

Diamond, M. "Biological foundations for social development." In F. Beach (ed.), *Human sexuality in four perspectives*. Baltimore: Johns Hopkins University Press, 1977.

Epstein, A. "Fetishism: A study of its pathology with particular reference to a proposed disorder in brain mechanism as an etiological factor." *Journal of Nervous and Mental Diseases*, 1960, 130, 107-110.

Fitting, M., Salisbury, S., Davis, N., and Mayclin, D. "Self-concept and sexuality of spinal cord injured women." *Archives of Sexual Behavior*, 1978, 7, 2, 143-156.

Foss, G. "The influence of androgens on sexuality in women." *Lancet*, 1951, 260, 667-669.

Gorski, R. "Gonadal hormones and the perinatal development of neuroendocrine functions." In L. Martin, and V. Ganong (eds.), *Frontiers of neuroendocrinology*. New York: Oxford University Press, 1971.

Harris, G. "Sex hormones, brain development and brain function." *Endocrinology*, 1964, 75, 627-648.

Hart, B. "Gonadal hormones and sexual reflexes in the female rat." *Hormones and Behavior*, 1969, 1, 65-71.

Hunter, R., Logue, V., and McMenemy, W. "Temporal lobe epilepsy supervening transvestism and fetishism." *Epilepsia*, 1963, 4, 60-65.

Jost, A. "'Maleness' is imposed upon a basically female fetus." *Science Digest*, 1973, 73, 4.

Kinsey, A., Pomeroy, W., Martin, C., and Gebhard, P. *Sexual behavior in the human female*. Philadelphia: W.B. Saunders, 1953.

Kluever, H. and Bucy, P. "Preliminary analysis of functions of the temporal lobe in rhesus monkeys." *Archives of Neurology and Psychiatry*, 1939, 42, 979-1000.

Kolarsky, A., Freund, K., Macheck, J., and Polak, O. "Male sexual deviation: Association with early temporal damage." *Archives of General Psychiatry*, 1967, 17, 735-743.

Larsson, K. "Mating behavior in male rats after cerebral cortex ablation." *Journal of Experimental Zoology*, 1964, 155, 203-214.

Masters, W. and Johnson, V. *Human sexual response*. Boston: Little, Brown, 1966.

Mitchell, W., Falconer, M., and Hill, D. "Epilepsy with fetishism relieved by temporal lobectomy." *Lancet*, 1954, 2, 626-630.

Money, J. "Phantom orgasm in the dreams of paraplegic men and women." *Archives of General Psychiatry*, 1960, 3, 373-382.

Money, J. "Components of eroticism in man: The hormones in relation to sexual morphology and sexual drive." *Journal of Nervous and Mental Diseases*, 1961, 132, 239-248.

Money, J. "Determinants of human sexual identity and behavior." In C. Sager and H. Singer Kaplan (eds.), *Progress in group and family therapy*. New York: Bruner/Mazel, 1972.

Money, J. "Sexual dimorphism and homosexual gender identity." In N. Wagner (ed.), *Perspectives on human sexuality*. New York: Behavioral Publications, 1977.

Money, J., Hampson, J., and Hampson, J. "Examination of some basic sexual concepts: Evidence of human hermaphroditism." *Bulletin of Johns Hopkins Hospital*, 1955, 99, 301-319.

Ramey, E. "Men's cycles (They have them too, you know)." *Ms. Magazine*. Spring 1972, 8-14.

Reinberg, A. and Lagoguey, M. "Circadian and circannual rhythms in sexual activity and plasma hormones of five human males." *Archives of Sexual Behavior*, 1978, 7, 1, 13-27.

Robertiello, R. "The clitoral versus vaginal orgasm controversy and some of its implications." *Journal of Sex Research*, 1970, 6, 307-311.

Roeder, F. and Mueller, D. "The stereotaxic treatment of pedophilic homosexuality." *German Medical Monthly* (English Language Monthly), 1969, 14, 265-271.

Sherfey, J. *The nature and evolution of female sexuality*. New York: Random House, 1972.

Sopchak, A. and Sutherland, A. "Psychological impact of cancer and its treatment." *Cancer*, 1960, 13, 528-531.

Stern, C. *Principles of human genetics*. San Francisco: W. H. Freeman, 1960.

Walinder, J. "Transvestism: Definition and evidence in favor of occasional derivation from cerebral function." *International Journal of Neuropsychiatry*, 1965, 1, 567–573.

Waxenberg, S. "Some biological correlates of sexual behavior." In G. Winokur (ed.), *Determinants of human sexual behavior*. Springfield, Ill.: Charles Thomas, 1963.

Whalen, R. "Brain mechanisms controlling sexual behavior." In F. Beach (ed.), *Human sexuality in four perspectives*. Baltimore: Johns Hopkins University Press, 1977.

Chapter 6

Biological Disorders of Sex

In the preceding chapter we discussed the fundamental genetic and hormonal determinants of sex, tracing them from the undifferentiated embryonic structure to the fully developed male and female sex organs. Although in most individuals sexual development unfolds normally according to the genetic blueprint reinforced by the appropriate hormone secretions, there are a number of sex chromosome abnormalities and hormonal aberrations that lead to atypical expressions of sexual behavior. Many abnormalities of sexual anatomy or physiology are rooted in genetic mistakes. However, as we shall see later in this chapter, sex hormones administered for medical reasons have inadvertently resulted in abnormal sexual morphologies.

In addition to the genetic and hormonal disorders of sex, there is a second major category of sexual diseases that is usually classified as venereal infection. Unfortunately, the term venereal disease still carries loaded moral connotations, and the stigma attached to it often prevents people from seeking medical treatment.

In this chapter, we shall examine the major biological disorders of sex—genetic, hormonal, and infectious—and their behavioral consequences.

Chromosomal Sex Aberrations

Chromosomal sex has been defined by the characteristics of the twenty-third pair of chromosomes. According to this definition, the presence of two X chromosomes characterizes genetic females, whereas one X and one Y chromosome identify the genetic male. The common test of genetic sex is based on the presence of *sex chromatin* or Barr body, a darkly staining spot found in the cells of females of many species (Barr and Bertram, 1949). Because of the presence of the Barr body, females are said to be sex chromatin

positive. Males, on the other hand, are sex chromatin negative since their cells do not contain a Barr body. Identification of genetic sex is easily determined by a smear of the oral mucosa, which is examined under the microscope.

Under normal circumstances, genetic sex is in agreement with other sexual criteria such as internal sex organs or secondary sex characteristics. However, there are several clinically recognized conditions in which nuclear or genetic sex is not congruent with internal or external sex. Aberrations of sex chromosomes may involve the loss or addition of sex chromosomes, resulting in women who are sex chromatin negative and men who are sex chromatin positive. Consequently, sex characteristics of the opposite sex may develop, or male and female components of sex may fail to emerge.

There are four major clinical syndromes in which the number of sex chromosomes deviates from the normal XX or XY pattern: Klinefelter's syndrome, Turner's syndrome, the XYY syndrome, and the triple X syndrome. Let us examine these conditions in more detail.

Klinefelter's Syndrome

Klinefelter's syndrome is an example of a chromosomal deviation in which 47 chromosomes instead of the normal 46 are found. The condition was first described in 1959 (Jacobs and Strong, 1959; Ford, Jones, Miller, et al., 1959a) and designated cytogenetically as 47,XXY. Because of the presence of the Y chromosome, the individual tends to be phenotypically male but, with two X chromosomes, which are typically characteristic of females, he is also sex chromatin positive. Because internal and external genital differentiation is male, the condition is usually not recognized until puberty when female secondary sex characteristics begin to develop.

Physical characteristics of males with

Klinefelter's syndrome include small testes and prostate gland, and underdevelopment of pubic, facial, and body hair. Many afflicted males also have enlarged breasts. Typically, their sexual drive is reduced. Moreover, mental retardation is present in approximately 25 percent of affected men (Mertens, 1975), and various forms of psychopathology tend to be more common with them than among the general population. Prominent among psychological disorders are the psychosexual pathologies such as gender identity confusion and various manifestations of homosexuality or bisexuality (Money and Pollitt, 1964). Men with Klinefelter's syndrome have also been found to dress in the clothes of women (*transvestism*) or to live in the role of the opposite sex after attaining hormonal, surgical, and legal sex reassignment (*transsexualism*). Money and Ehrhardt (1972) conjectured that the extra X chromosome introduces an element of instability into brain functioning that may manifest itself as a vulnerability to psychological impairment. Although some men with Klinefelter's syndrome may appear normal physically and mentally, all are usually sterile because they are unable to produce sperm. Figure 6.1 shows a young man with Klinefelter's syndrome.

The 47,XXY chromosome constitution is the most frequent sex chromosome aberration with an incidence* rate of two cases per 1,000 male births (Hamerton, 1971). Variations of Klinefelter's syndrome occur in essentially the same clinical condition and can include a second (48,XXXY) or even third (49,XXXXY) additional X chromosome. Males with the 48 or 49 chromosome

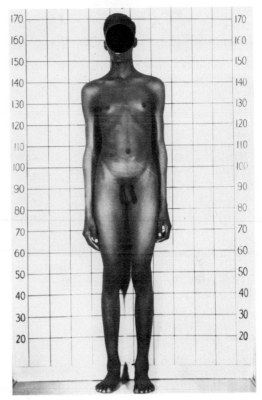

Figure 6.1
Man with Klinefelter's syndrome. (J. Money and A. Ehrhardt. *Man and woman, boy and girl.* Johns Hopkins University Press, 1972)

constitutions do not differ markedly from 47,XXY men, although they tend to be more severely affected. Many of them have additional abnormalities including skeletal malformations and severe mental deficiency.

Turner's Syndrome

Whereas Klinefelter's syndrome in males is typically characterized by one or more additional X chromosomes, Turner's syndrome is caused by the loss of a sex chromosome and occurs only in females. In Turner's syndrome only a single X chromosome is present. Consequently, the condition is designated as 45,XO. This chromosome constitution, also

*The terms incidence and prevalence are two related but independent concepts. Incidence refers to the number of people who *become* ill in a particular time period. Prevalence describes the number of people who *are* ill at the same time. Prevalence is measured by the number of people in mental hospitals. The difference between the two rates is determined by the duration of the disorder. If the disorder is one from which people recover quickly, then incidence and prevalence are very close.

known as *ovarian dysgenesis*, was first described by Ford and his co-workers (1959b). Apart from Klinefelter's syndrome, Turner's syndrome is the best known sex chromosome abnormality.

Phenotypically, people with Turner's syndrome look like girls and have external female genitals (see Figure 6.2). However, they are without ovaries, which are represented by narrow streaks of nonfunctional tissue. The absence of ovaries has pronounced effects on later sexual development since ovarian deficiency is responsible for the lack of body changes at puberty. Turner's girls do not experience the normal pubertal development. Without hormonal replacement therapy secondary sex characteristics

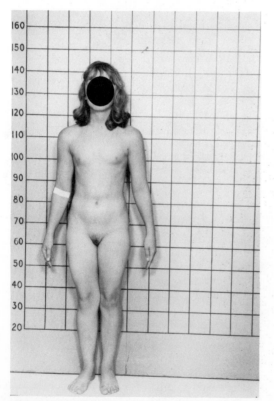

Figure 6.2
Girl with Turner's syndrome. (J. Money and A. Ehrhardt. *Man and woman, boy and girl.* Johns Hopkins University Press, 1972)

such as breast development, pubic hair, and female body contours fail to emerge. Since the ovaries produce ova as well as female sex hormones, their presence is necessary for the beginning and regulation of the menstrual cycle.

The genetic abnormality of not maturing sexually also has psychological consequences. Being flat-chested and unable to menstruate deprives the Turner's girl of the feeling of being "normal," especially at a period of her life when peers exert strong pressure and demand conformity to peer standards of sexual behavior. Budding breasts and the experience of the first mysterious menstruation are part of peer definitions of sexuality. Like the Klinefelter's males, girls with Turner's syndrome are sterile, although they may have a normal uterus and can menstruate if provided with estrogen substitution therapy to induce puberty.

Turner's girls not only fail to mature sexually but also rarely attain an adult height of more than five feet. Because the administration of estrogen tends to inhibit the growth of the long bones of the body, hormone therapy is often delayed until age sixteen or seventeen to permit the girl to grow as tall as possible. Judicious timing of the onset of a hormonally induced puberty can offset the failure of sexual maturation, as well as assure maximal growth.

In addition to the shortness of stature, the cosmetically most conspicuous disfigurement involves flabby folds of extra skin at the neck. Typically, breasts are underdeveloped with widely spaced nipples. Sexual hair is scanty and the external genitalia are infantile. As in the case of Klinefelter's syndrome, Turner's girls may or may not show intellectual deficit.

In spite of their sterility, women with Turner's syndrome are unequivocally female and conform to the style of femininity idealized by traditional cultural definitions of womanhood. Turner's girls not only differentiate a clearly female psychosexual identity but also develop strong feminine interest patterns and behaviors (Ehrhardt, Greenberg, and Money, 1970). For example, Ehrhardt (1969) showed that Turner's girls either equaled or slightly surpassed normal girls in maternal play and interest ratings. Similarly, they did not differ in romantic interests: most Turner's girls studied described daydreams and fantasies of romantic courtship, marriage, and sometimes of heterosexual acts. In contrast to males with Klinefelter's syndrome, who frequently experience confusion over gender identity, the genetic abnormalities associated with Turner's syndrome apparently do not interfere with the differentiation of feminine psychosexual identity. As Beach (1965) has noted, Turner's condition indicates that an important component of feminine psychosexual orientation may be operating despite the total absence of any estrogenic hormone. Feminine identity is therefore not entirely dependent on the presence of the second X chromosome (Money and Mittenthal, 1970).

Clinical studies of girls with Turner's syndrome have repeatedly demonstrated that our concepts of gender role and sexual orientation arise from the kinds of learning experiences we are exposed to. We may conclude from these cases that sexual identity and responsiveness are governed by psychological and social experiences. Because sexual identity involves deep, intense, and personal feelings, it has often been assumed that it must be innately or biologically determined. However, the study of girls with Turner's syndrome indicates that this assumption is erroneous because it underestimates the impact and importance of learning experiences on gender identity.

The XYY Syndrome

The 47,XYY chromosome constitution became well known following its discovery by Jacobs and his colleagues (1965). They examined the genetic make-up of inmates of a maximum-security state hospital in Scotland and found a prevalence rate of nearly 3 percent of XYY men. This was an extraordinarily high percentage for a rare chromosomal disorder. Many surveys have since been reported on inmates of prisons, mental institutions, and detention homes, where hundreds of XYY men have been identified (Price and Whatmore, 1967; Welch, Borgaonkar, and Herr, 1967).

Whereas Klinefelter's syndrome is characterized by two female and one male chromosome typically producing a somewhat demasculinized man, researchers in the past expected the double Y condition, in turn, to lead to supermasculinity. This premature conclusion was partially supported by the fact that XYY males tend to have tall stature (six feet and over), as shown in Figure 6.3.

The clinical picture of men with the XYY syndrome, however, does not indicate increased masculinity. On the contrary, XYY men tend to have unusual sexual preferences, often including homosexuality (Money, Gaskin, and Hull, 1970). Sperm production is often reduced, sometimes to the point of actual sterility. Interestingly enough, the extra Y chromosome in XYY men appears to be a genetic accident in males with normal chromosome counts, since the condition is not transmitted genetically from father to son (Mertens, 1975).

In addition, XYY males are frequently below average in intelligence and display personality disorders that prevent them from functioning adequately in society. XYY males often have a history of antisocial behavior, violence, and conflict with the police and educational authorities (Telfer, Baker, Clark, and Richardson, 1968). Behaviorally, the most important consequence of the double Y syndrome is found in its linkage to criminal and aggressive acts. Since the mid-1960s, the XYY male has become notable for his attempts to avoid the legal consequences of his actions because of bad heredity (the extra Y chromosome exerts a potentially antisocial

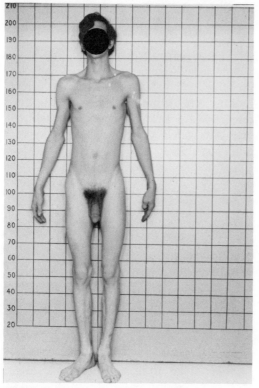

Figure 6.3
The XYY syndrome. (J. Money and A.
Ehrhardt. *Man and woman, boy and girl.* Johns
Hopkins University Press, 1972)

effect). Although not born as criminals, males with the XYY error have considerably higher chances of becoming involved in aggressive acts (Casey et al., 1966; Conan, 1968). Although there is no doubt that genes do influence to some extent the development of behavior, the behavioral manifestation of the XYY syndrome cannot be accounted for solely in biological terms. Several cases of XYY males who had no apparent behavioral disturbances and were of bright average intelligence have been reported (Leff and Scott, 1968; Weiner and Sutherland, 1968). These cases support the idea that the XYY male can lead a normal life. In general, XYY men demonstrate wide variations in abilities and behavior covering the entire spectrum from normal to severely disorganized per-

sonalities, from men with superior intelligence to those with mental retardation. Research conducted during the 1970s generally revealed lower incidence rates of XYY patterns among criminals than did earlier investigations.

The XYY syndrome has been extensively studied in population surveys. The incidence rate is estimated as 1.8 in 1,000 unselected infants. Among inmates of the various penal and mental institutions, however, the prevalence of XYY males is 10 percent in 1,000 (NIMH, 1970). Obviously, XYY men run a higher risk of being institutionalized—mentlly or criminally—than do XY males. Unfortunately, there is a considerable sampling bias in studies on the XYY syndrome; the reported cases have come primarily from prisons and mental hospitals where chromosomal surveys have been conducted.

The Triple X Syndrome

In some women, one or two additional X chromosomes have been observed (47,XXX or 48,XXXX). Although there is nothing exceptionally feminine in these women, they are sometimes referred to as superfemales. In most cases, there are no sexual abnormalities, and many XXX women have children. However, in most instances affected individuals are mentally retarded, and the degree of retardation seems to be related to the number of extra chromosomes. The more additional chromosomes, the greater the tendency toward more pronounced intellectual deficits.

The four major sexual aberrations that are genetically determined are summarized in Table 6.1.

Sex Errors

Hermaphroditism

Sex errors typically involve chromosomal and hormonal factors that interact to pro-

Table 6.1

Chromosomal Abnormalities of Sex

Clinical Syndrome	Sex Chromosome Constitution	Phenotypic Sex Characteristics	Estimated Incidence
Turner's syndrome	45,XO	sterile female	1 in 500
Klinefelter's syndrome	47,XXY	sterile male	1 in 400
Double Y syndrome	47,XYY	fertile male	1 in 500
Triple X syndrome	47,XXX	fertile female	1 in 800

duce a biological disorder. One clinical condition that has been known since antiquity and which is found among humans as well as animals is *hermaphroditism*. The word comes from the Greek name Hermaphroditus, the legendary son of the gods Hermes and Aphrodite, who produced a child with both male and female sex characteristics. The hermaphrodite is a person in whom external sex characteristics and internal reproductive structures and/or sex-chromatin patterns are contradictory. In this relatively rare clinical condition, the embryonic gonad fails to differentiate. As a result, ovaries and testes develop independently within the same individual.

The first systematic classification of hermaphroditism was made by Klebs in 1873 (Money, 1961). It included the classical true hermaphrodite, who possesses elements of the sexual anatomy of both sexes, and *pseudohermaphrodites*, people who have both male and female sex organs but who have the sex glands (ovary or testicle) of only one sex and are thus fundamentally male or female.

The hermaphrodite is characterized by ambiguous external genitalia and confused gender identity. Usually, infants who are diagnosed as true hermaphrodites at birth are assigned the sex that correlates with their external genital appearance. Corrective surgery can easily be performed under the age of eighteen months before the child develops a sense of gender identity. Medical management of hermaphroditism involves surgical and hormonal restructuring to remove am-

biguous sex organs and tissues so that the child can be assigned to one sex or the other. Sex reassignment after eighteen months of age presents a greater psychological risk, since most children have established some degree of gender identity by the age of two.

Not all hermaphrodites are recognized at

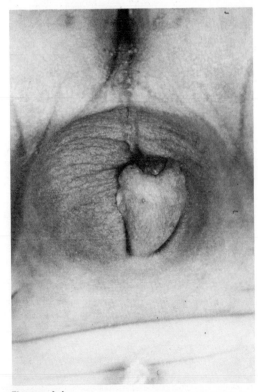

Figure 6.4
Ambiguity of sexual organs in a genetic male. (J. Money and A. Ehrhardt. *Man and woman, boy and girl.* Johns Hopkins University Press, 1972)

birth or shortly thereafter, however. Hampson (1965) reported the case of a seventeen-year-old girl who was sent for surgical consultation by the school physician because of mildly troublesome hernias. During surgery it was discovered that the vagina of the girl was a blind pouch. Chromosomal analysis revealed a male sex-chromatin pattern.

Sex reassignment is not only complicated by the fact that older children may retain sexual interests and identity regardless of the surgical reconstruction of their genitals. Often, they are also afraid of aversive social consequences. Many people express negative reactions or even horror when they learn that a person possesses sexual structures of both sexes. In the mind of many, hermaphroditism is at best equated with perversity. More often, however, the hermaphrodite is seen as some kind of a sexual monster, being both man and woman.

As in the case of the chromosomally determined disorders of sex, evidence from the study of hermaphrodites indicates that psychological masculinity or femininity is not attributable to any single variable of sex such as internal or external sex organs. By and large, postnatal experiences override biological factors and are the chief determinants of sexual identity.

Hormonal Sex Aberrations

The Female Androgenital Syndrome

The female androgenital syndrome is a variety of female hermaphroditism representing a hormonal disorder of sex. Women with this condition have female internal sex organs but mature with the secondary sex

---

Norman: Trapped Between Two Sexes

As long as Norman could remember, he had thought of himself as a boy. At age three and a half his gender identity was questioned.

When Norman was born, his mother was told that the sex of her baby was uncertain. However, by the third day she was unequivocally assured that she had a boy. The child was subsequently reared as a boy, and the family never questioned his identity although the mother had longed for a girl instead of a fourth son.

The ambiguity of Norman's sex came up again when he was referred to the hospital for corrective surgery. Since age one, he had undergone several operations to provide him with an adequately functioning penis. At this time, it was discovered that he had female internal sex organs.

By the time he was three and a half, he had become rather penis-conscious. At the hospital he told the staff that he had been there before because "the nurse cut on my wee-wee." Once, during a long-distance telephone conversation with his older brother, Norman asked him to bring back a new wee-wee for him.

Behaviorally, Norman was quite unlike little girls of his age and very much like little boys. At the hospital the children accepted him as a boy. Norman was alarmed by the prospect of a surgical altering of his genitals and was greatly relieved when it was explained to him that when he got bigger his penis would not be taken away, but finished so that he could stand up to urinate (adapted from Money, Hampson, and Hampson, 1955).

This case illustrates the conflict between biological and psychological sex. In Norman's case, social and cultural factors had already strongly affirmed the boy's gender identity. He had come to see himself as male in spite of his contradictory internal and external sex organs.

---

characteristics of a male. The condition is the result of excessive androgen production, usually stemming from a malfunction of the adrenal gland. As a result, the person has, along with ovaries and uterus, external genitalia that are masculine in appearance. This masculinization can range from an enlarged clitoris to a normal appearing penis with an empty scrotum in extreme cases (Ehrhardt, 1973). Figure 6.5 depicts a typical case of a

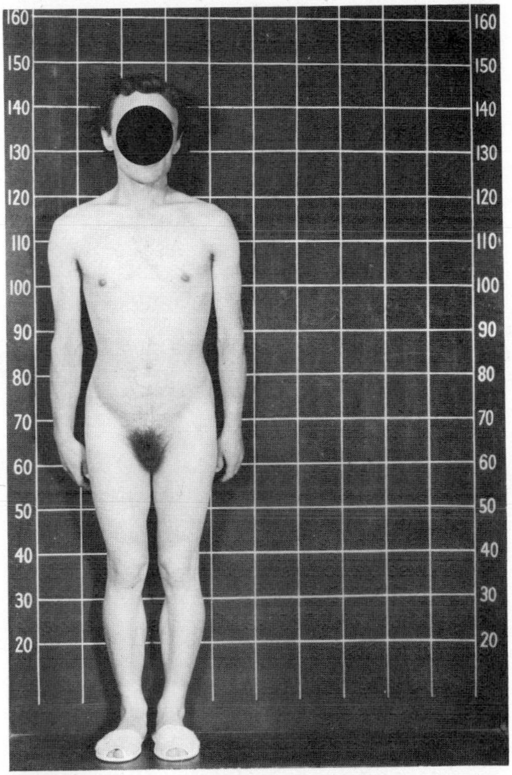

Figure 6.5
Woman with the androgenital syndrome. (J. Zubin and J. Money. *Contemporary sexual behavior: Critical issues in the 1970's.* Johns Hopkins University Press, 1974)

woman with the androgenital syndrome. If the condition is recognized at birth and treated with the hormone cortisone, the masculinizing effects of androgen can be reversed. If detected later, the androgenital syndrome requires surgical reconstruction of external genitals.

The Male Androgen-Insensitivity Syndrome

The androgen-insensitivity syndrome or *testicular feminization* is a well-defined clinical entity that approximates the female androgenital syndrome. The condition is the result of a lack of sensitivity to androgen in genetic males. Although the fetal testes produce normal amounts of both androgen and estrogen, the body responds only to estrogen. As a result, the person with the androgen-insensitivity syndrome has a typically female appearance with well-developed breasts (Figure 6.6). The condition tends to occur in members of the same family. There are indications from animal research that the gene for testicular feminization is located on the X chromosome (Lyon and Hawkes, 1970).

In spite of a feminine appearance, the person has testes that are usually located in the abdomen. If the condition is recognized at birth, there is no indecision about the sex of the infant. The baby is definitely female. Consequently, it is reared as a girl in spite of the genetic maleness. However, individuals with androgen insensitivity do not menstruate and are sterile. Nevertheless, they stand out as strongly feminine on a number of criteria of sex such as eroticism and marriage (Masica, Money, and Ehrhardt, 1971). Although the

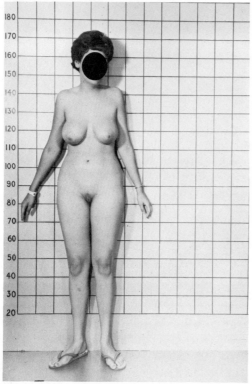

Figure 6.6
The androgen insensitivity syndrome in a genetic
male. (J. Money and A. Ehrhardt. *Man and
woman, boy and girl.* Johns Hopkins University
Press, 1972)

women studied were resigned to their permanent incapacity for pregnancy, several had
adopted children and displayed a good sense
of motherhood. Again, as in the case of the
hermaphrodite, androgen insensitivity leads
to psychosexual identity contrary to genetic
sex.

The clinical syndromes reviewed in this
section suggest that gender differentiation is,
for the most part, accomplished through interaction with the social environment. Because of the discrepancy of genetic sex and
sex of rearing, these conditions are of particular interest.

Venereal Disease

In addition to the chromosomal and hormonal sexual abnormalities, there is a second group of sexual disorders that is not
genetically determined. Rather, these disorders are transmitted from person to person. Collectively they are referred to as
venereal diseases (VD). "Venereal" is derived from the Latin word *venus,* referring to
love or lust and indicating that the biological
disorders in this category can be contracted
through sexual contact.

Venereal diseases are communicable infections, many of which are sexually transmitted. VD may be caused by a variety of
bacteria, viruses, and other organisms, most
of which thrive in warm, moist environments
such as the vagina, penis, mouth, or rectum.
Transmission can occur through any type of
sexual activity—vaginal, anal, or oral. Homosexuals as well as heterosexuals can spread
VD. For example, a study by the American
Health Association in 1971 showed that 23.3
percent of sexual contacts named by syphilis
patients were of the same sex as the patients.
The high risk of venereal infection among
males engaging in homosexual acts has been
illustrated by a study of 291 prisoners, of
which 28 percent were infected with syphilis
at the time of examination (Smith, 1965).
Contrary to popular notion, the possibility of
catching VD from toilet seats, drinking cups,
or doorknobs is quite remote.

As shown in Figure 6.7, the cycle of catching and treating VD occurs in five stages
(Darrow, 1976). First, it is necessary to have
sexual contact with an infected person. Second, in order to become infected by a person
who already has the disease, intercourse has
to take place. (Regardless of how many different sexual experiences a person has with a
number of different sexual partners, he or she
will not acquire VD unless the other person
is infected at the time of contact.) The third

Common Myths About VD

1. You can go to jail for VD.

   No. It is a disease, not a crime.

2. You can treat yourself safely for VD.

   No. Most VDs, with the exception of scabies, require prescription drugs.

3. Masturbation causes VD.

   No, unless a second person is involved.

4. You cannot get syphilis and gonorrhea at the same time.

   Yes, you can.

5. You cannot catch VD more than one time.

   No. You can be reinfected a number of times.

6. VD is incurable.

   No. With the possible exception of Herpes, most common forms of VD can be treated with antibiotics.

7. You can get VD from toilet seats, drinking cups, or door knobs.

   No. The transmission of VD requires physical contact.

8. You cannot get syphilis by kissing someone who already has it.

   Yes, you can. VDs can be transmitted through any kind of physical contact, vaginal, oral, or anal.

9. You can get VD only from someone of the opposite sex.

   No. VD is transmitted heterosexually or homosexually.

10. You can tell when a person has VD.

    No. Even physicians have to use tests to find out.

Adapted from Gordon, 1974

phase, following sexual contact, involves the actual transmission of the disease. Exposure to another person with VD does not ensure infection because sufficient pathogens must be transmitted for infection to occur. During the fourth stage, the infected person develops the symptoms of venereal disease. Finally, the treatment phase completes the cycle. If left untreated, the symptoms may go away. However, that does not mean that the person is cured.

Although venereal diseases have plagued many countries for centuries, public health officials are concerned because the incidence of VD increases each year despite the fact that effective antibiotic treatment is readily available. Today sexually transmitted diseases have reached their highest levels in American history. *Syphilis*, for instance, increased about 8 percent in 1970, while *gonorrhea* showed a growth rate of 16 percent. The highest rates of syphilis and gonorrhea are found in the seventeen-to-twenty-four-year-old age group of both men and women (DHEW, 1974). However, on the average, patients with gonorrhea tend to be several years younger than people with syphilis. Homosexually transmitted VDs are more frequently associated with syphilis infections than with gonorrhea.

Kinsey and his colleagues (1948) were the first investigators to examine the relationship

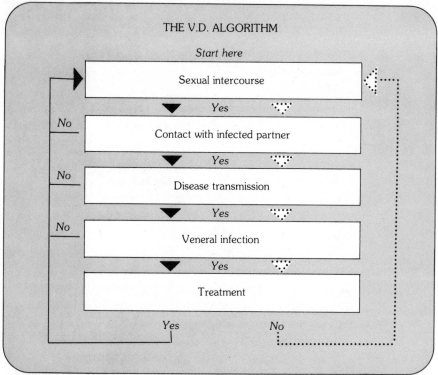

Figure 6.7
Becoming a VD patient. (W. Darrow. "Social and behavioral aspects of the sexually transmitted diseases." In S. Gordon and R. Libby, Eds. *Sexuality today and tomorrow.* Duxbury Press, 1976)

between VD and social status. They found that Americans with low levels of educational achievement and low occupational prestige carried a disproportionate share of VD. This finding has been consistently repeated (Darrow, 1971). However, most of the studies examining the relationship between the incidence of VD and social class are biased because the data typically are collected in hospitals and public clinics. Middle and upper class people with VD usually seek private medical treatment, whereas people from lower socioeconomic strata are more likely to turn to public facilities for help.

In addition to the social-class differences in VD rates, there also seem to be ethnic differences. Young blacks, for instance, who initiate sexual intercourse earlier than whites (DHEW, 1972) also tend to have disproportionately higher rates of infectious syphilis.

At one time, many professionals working on VD control anticipated a relationship between VD and prostitution, especially in view of the fact that most men have had sexual experiences with prostitutes (Kinsey et al., 1948). In addition, it has been estimated that as many as 90 percent of all prostitutes can be expected to catch VD during their careers (Winick and Kinsie, 1971). Unpublished data collected in 1973, however, indicated that only 1 percent of all people with infectious syphilis were prostitutes. Apparently prostitution has contributed little to the present VD epidemic.

Syphilis

Syphilis is a sexually contagious disease that is rarely acquired by any other means than intercourse. It is caused by a cork-screw shaped (spirochete) bacterium called *Treponema pallidum* shown in Figure 6.8. Usually, the syphilis germs enter the body through the soft lining of body openings involved in sexual intercourse. After a person has become infected, syphilis may go through a number of separate disease stages.

Symptoms. During the first stage of syphilis, also referred to as primary syphilis, an open sore called *chancre* develops on the skin where the germs invaded the body. The chancre usually appears ten to ninety days after sexual contact. In 90 percent of the cases the chancre develops on the genitals. In females the sores may develop inside the vagina. Many times the infected person is not aware of the sores and transmits the disease to others without knowing it.

During the primary stage, the germs spread all through the body but especially through the skin. After a few weeks to a month, a widespread rash may occur, which usually does not itch. In addition to the skin disorder, the lymph nodes in the groin are frequently enlarged. The symptoms last for about two weeks and then disappear. Although the person is symptom-free during this latent stage, he or she still has the disease.

In the second phase, or secondary syphilis, moist and highly infectious flat warts may appear around the genitals. Low fever, headaches, and a sore throat may accompany the rash. Very often these signs are mistaken for the symptoms of a common cold.

During the second stage, the body produces a number of protective antibodies. As a result of these natural defenses, some people show a spontaneous cure. In most infected people, however, tertiary syphilis develops after many symptom-free years.

During the third stage, or tertiary syphilis, the germs become quite dangerous because they may affect the brain and/or spinal cord. Over the next five to twenty years, the disease may spread to the heart and other organs, inducing large ulcerlike sores. Brain damage and heart trouble may accompany syphilis that has progressed to the tertiary stage.

Syphilis is not only transmitted sexually but can also be passed via the blood of a pregnant woman to the fetus. This condition is known as congenital syphilis. It has been almost eliminated in the United States because all pregnant women are given a routine blood test for syphilis. Infected individuals are treated before the child is born. Untreated women with syphilis may give birth to infants who are severely affected at birth or appear well but later show severe illness.

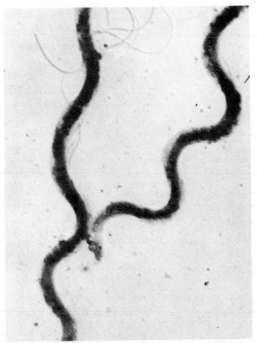

Figure 6.8
Treponema pallidum, the spirochete that causes syphilis. (Atlanta Disease Control Center)

Diagnosis and Treatment. Different blood tests are available for the identification of syphilis. In most of these serological tests the doctor will search for spirochetes in the blood. Very early syphilis can be treated easily with penicillin. However, once the germs have left their marks, the damage cannot be repaired. Syphilis can be caught more than one time.

Gonorrhea

The second best-known and most-feared VD is gonorrhea (from the Greek word meaning flow of seed). It is an extremely contagious, sexually transmitted disease that is caused by a coffee-bean shaped bacterium called *Neisseria gonorrhea*. The bacteria mainly attack the tissues in the genital and urinary passages. The throat, but not the mouth, may also be affected.

According to health statistics, gonorrhea affects mostly people in the sixteen-to-forty-year-old age group. The World Health Organization has ranked gonorrhea as the most prevalent communicable disease, second only to the common cold. Statistically, males

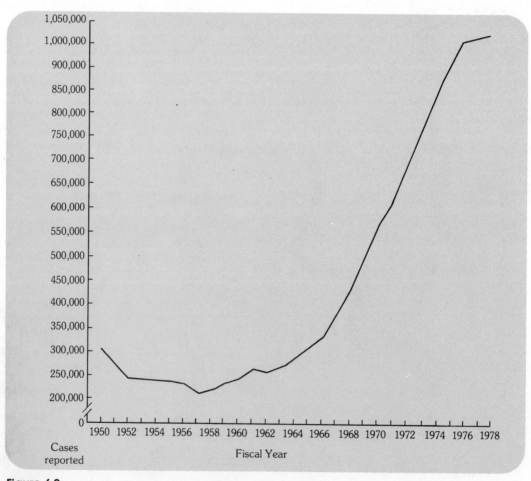

Figure 6.9
Increase in reported cases of gonorrhea (W. Darrow. "Social and behavioral aspects of the sexually transmitted diseases." In S. Gordon and R. Libby, Eds. *Sexuality today and tomorrow*. Duxbury Press, 1976)

who contract gonorrhea outnumber females by three to two, but only 20 percent of infected females show the symptoms. Figure 6.9 shows the steady increase in reported cases of gonorrhea over the last two decades.

Symptoms. Males notice a yellowish-white pus discharge from the penis, which causes discomfort when urinating. Females with gonorrhea essentially complain about the same symptom. However, most women who have contracted the disease (60 to 80 percent) are symptom-free. Even if there are signs of the disease, they are not readily detectable.

The symptoms usually develop within five to eight days after exposure to an infected person. However, the incubation period, that is, the time from the initial exposure to the appearance of the first symptoms, may extend to three weeks.

Asymptomatic females can unwillingly transmit gonorrhea. If left untreated, the disease may spread to the cervix, uterus, and Fallopian tubes. Untreated gonorrhea is also one of the most common causes of sterility in women.

Diagnosis and Treatment. The diagnosis of gonorrhea is made by finding the responsible bacterium in a smear taken from the male or female urethra, rectum, or throat. Penicillin remains the treatment of choice for gonorrhea. However, as in the case of syphilis, there is no immunity against further infection, and many people suffer repeated attacks of the disease.

Herpes

Herpes is caused by a virus that occurs in two different types. *Herpes simplex virus* (HSV) Type I causes infections above the waist, whereas Herpes simplex Type II occurs below the waist. However, each type of the virus can occur outside its territory.

Betty and Brian: "From Siff to Clap"

Betty, a college freshman, felt more than the usual discomfort in her abnormal psychology class discussions. She wondered if she could have appendicitis or just a cold. Between classes, she suddenly collapsed and blacked out. Betty was taken to the hospital; the physician on call was unable to contact her mother who was working some forty miles away from the college.

Upon further examination, blood tests at the hospital revealed that Betty had an advanced case of gonorrhea. However, there was more to Betty's story. A rash she had worried about earlier proved to be even more dangerous than her present gonorrhea, since it was diagnosed as a latent sign of syphilis. Blood tests confirmed the syphilis infection.

Asked about her sexual relationships, Betty revealed the following story. She had been dating a fellow student, Brian, who unknowingly caught syphilis from another girl. Since he was afraid to discuss his symptoms—stinging, burning sensations, drips in his underwear—with his parents, Brian bought some pills from a friend who had experienced the same "problem." Even though Brian's drips and stings were cured, his syphilis was not cured.

Betty and Brain had sexual intercourse on their second date, exchanging VDs. Betty traded Brian's "siff" (syphilis) for her "clap" (slang word for gonorrhea).

Adapted from Chiappa and Forish, 1976.

**Jennifer: A Baby
Dies from Herpes**

Jennifer, aged eight weeks, died on May 9. Although she appeared normal and healthy at birth, she was infected by Herpes simplex virus (HSV).

Jennifer was born on March 13 and brought home after a five-day stay at the hospital. Within the first two weeks she displayed symptoms unusual for a new-born. She was listless; her eyes were red. She slept for long periods of time and was hard to wake up. Jennifer's parents were concerned because she did not take her milk very well. They also noticed jerking motions in her arms and legs, which were identified as seizures when her parents took her to the hospital. There, all sorts of tests were done, and it was found that she had herpes. With this diagnosis, her parents were told that she would die in a matter of days.

However, Jennifer did not die that week. The doctors could do little for her except to see that she was tube-fed. When she died after eight weeks, an autopsy was performed; it revealed that Jennifer had Type 1 herpes. The cause of death was herpes encephalitis, a viral infection of the brain. Active herpes were not only found in the brain but had also spread to the liver and spleen.

Jennifer's mother did not know that she had herpes. A culture done three weeks after delivery showed no trace.

Herpes has become much more common than many types of sexually transmitted diseases, including syphilis. It is currently exploding through the population and causing genuine alarm among mental health experts. It is the venereal disease of the new morality, said one investigator (Subak-Sharpe, 1977).

Symptoms. The symptoms of genital herpes usually appear about six days after sexual contact with an infected person. Irritating spots and blisters develop into painful ulcers of varying sizes. Fatigue, swelling in the legs, and difficult urination may also occur. In women the blisters form inside the vagina or on the cervix. The blisterlike lesions frequently open, ulcerate, and are extremely painful.

Herpes can also be transmitted during childbirth. Infected women have a miscarriage rate more than three times that of the general population. Even when the pregnancy is extended to full term, delivery through an infected birth canal may expose the infant to the virus, causing death or irreversible brain damage. The disease is fatal in 70 to 90 percent of these cases. Many survivors include children who are blind or mentally retarded.

The danger in herpes infections is further increased by the possible link between herpes and cancer. There is a strong, although not proven, suspicion that the infection may lead to cancer of the prostate and cervix.

Diagnosis and Treatment. Herpes can be detected by microscopic examination of material from a pap smear, or the virus can be cultured in a special medium. Many physicians can simply diagnose the infection by direct examination of the blisters. There is, however, no totally effective way of testing for herpes through blood tests, since the virus presumably buries itself in nerve endings between outbreaks and cannot be detected in the bloodstream.

Numerous treatments have been tried with herpes, but none of them is 100 percent effective. One of the more common but controversial treatments entails painting the infected area with a red dye and subsequently exposing the area to light. Although this method seems to inactivate the virus and shorten the duration of the outbreak, it has been criticized as a potential danger. Experiments with hamsters have shown that the red-dye treatment can cause cancer. In the meantime, an intensive search is under way for a vaccine to forestall recurrent herpes attacks, much like smallpox or TB vaccinations.

Chancroid

Chancroid is a less common VD in the United States. It is a tropical and subtropical disease caused by a virus. Males are more often affected than females and frequently catch chancroid from European prostitutes who may have no symptoms.

The first sign of chancroid is a group of sores that resemble the symptoms of syphilis. Typically, the sores appear on the genitals and bleed very easily. Although chancroid may cause painful local damage, it seldom leads to complications as severe as in syphilis or gonorrhea. As in the case of most venereal infections, chancroid can be treated easily with antibiotics.

Genital Warts

Warts on the genitals are painless growths caused by a virus. They vary in size from a pinhead to a walnut. The wart virus can be passed from one person to another sexually, or it may be spread locally by the fingers. Warts usually take several weeks to grow. Medically, they present no problem since they can be easily treated with a chemical wart paint or by cauterization.

Scabies

Scabies, or the "itch," is a common skin disease found mainly among poor, overcrowded families whose personal hygiene is inadequate. The disease is contagious and may be sexually transmitted, as well as being spread by dirty clothing, towels, and bed linens.

Nonspecific Urethritis

Nonspecific urethritis (NSU) is a form of venereal infection entirely confined to males. It is sexually transmitted, with the symptoms appearing from three to six weeks after sexual contact.

The infection resembles gonorrhea in many respects. In addition, there is a mild irritation in the urethra, and chronic inflammation of the prostate may follow NSU. Like many other VDs, NSU is treated with antibiotics.

Prevention of Venereal Diseases

Technological advances in birth control have accelerated the incidence of venereal infections. Although the pill and other birth control methods afford protection against unwanted pregnancy, they do not protect against VD. One way of curbing the rate of sexually transmitted diseases is through VD prophylaxis. Brecher (1975) reviewed a number of methods of prevention, all of which reduce the likelihood that the infection will be passed on when a man has sexual relations with an infected woman or when a woman has sexual relations with an infected man.

One way of reducing the risk of infection is for male sexual partners to wear a *condom*. The effectiveness of the condom in preventing VD transmissions is well established (Medical Letter, 1971). New condoms, made of plastic with good heat transmission, do not interfere as much with male and female sensory pleasure as did traditional condoms.

Studies in the 1970s have also shown that contraceptive foams and jellies can also be a deterrent to venereal infections (Singh, Cutler and Utidijian, 1972). One of these researchers hopes to popularize contraceptive foams and jellies as "pro-cons," that is, serving the dual purpose of VD prophylaxis and contraception.

Hygiene also helps in the prevention of VD. Thorough washing of the penis with soap and water as soon as possible after sexual contact has been recommended by public health authorities as a prophylactic measure (Buchan, 1973). Washing does little to help women in the prevention of venereal infections but a douche of a tablespoon of vinegar in a quart of warm water may help. In some European countries, the bidet, a low basinlike bath for cleansing genitals, takes the place of the douche. In France, the low rate of gonorrhea has been attributed, at least in part, to the prompt use of the bidet after sexual contact.

Medical researchers are currently working to perfect a vaccine or pill to prevent VD. For instance, the Japanese have developed a tablet composed of antibiotics which may be inserted into the vagina before intercourse (Ohno, Kato, et al., 1958).

Presently, the rate of fresh gonorrhea cases is estimated at 2.5 million per year. If VD prophylaxes can be popularized over the next few years, venereal infections can be reduced considerably. Lee and associates (1972) discuss a method of gonorrhea prevention that is only 50 percent effective. But if it is used by even only 20 percent of the population at risk, it will reduce the incidence of gonorrhea in that population by 90 percent in less than two years.

Summary

Two major categories of biologically determined sexual disorders have been discussed in this chapter. The first group dealt with genetically determined aberrations of sex. Included in the discussion were descriptions and psychological consequences of Klinefelter's and Turner's syndromes as well as the double Y and triple X conditions. In these four clinically recognized disorders, the chromosomal abnormality may lead to profound alterations in sexual behavior and personality functioning. Confused gender identity and intellectual deficits frequently accompany these conditions.

The study of individuals with hermaphroditism, the androgenital syndrome or testicular feminization, reveals that psychosexual identity is a psychosocial phenomenon rather than the result of biological factors.

The second section of the chapter examined the major forms of sexually transmitted diseases. In addition to the description of the symptoms of the common venereal diseases, methods of identification and treatment were discussed. With the availability of effective treatment with antibiotics, prevention of venereal infection has become a major concern of mental health professionals.

References

Barr, M. L. and Bertram, E. G. "A morphological distinction between neurons of the male and female, and the behavior of the nucleolar satellite during accelerated nucleoprotein synthesis." *Nature,* 1949, 163, 676-677.

Beach, F. A. *Sex and Behavior.* New York: John Wiley & Sons, 1965.

Brecher, E. M. "Prevention of the sexually transmitted diseases." *Journal of Sex Research,* 1975, 11, 318-328.

Buchan, W. *Domestic medicine: a treatise on the prevention and cure of diseases.* Boston: printed by Joseph Bumstead for James White and Ebenezer Larkin, 1973.

Casey, M., Blank, D., Street, L., Segall, L., McDougall, H., McGrawth, R., and Skinner, J. "XYY chromosomes and antisocial behavior." *Cancer,* 1966, 2, 859-860.

Chiappa, J. and Forish, J. *The VD book.* New York: Holt, Rinehart & Winston, 1976.

Conan, P. "Males with an XYY chromosome complement." *Journal of Medical Genetics,* 1968, 5, 341-359.

Darrow, W. *Social class, infectious syphilis, and patient behavior.* Atlanta: Center for Disease Control, Venereal Disease Branch, 1971.

Darrow, W. "Social and behavioral aspects of the sexually transmitted diseases." In S. Gordon and R. Libby, (eds.). *Sexuality today and tomorrow,* North Scituate, Mass.: Duxbury Press, 1976.

Department of Health, Education, and Welfare, Public Health Service, Health Services and Mental Health Administration, Center for Disease Control, State and Community Services Division, Venereal Disease Branch, *VD Fact Sheet.* DHEW Publication No. 72-8085, Washington: U.S. Government Printing Office, 1972.

Department of Health, Education, and Welfare, Public Health Service Center for Disease Control, Bureau of State Services, Venereal Disease Control Division. *VD Statistical Letter,* 120, 1974 (August), 15-16.

Ehrhardt, A. A. "Die Wirkung foetaler hormone auf intelligent und geschlechts-spezifisches verhalten" (The effect of fetal hormones on intelligence and gender indentity). Inaugural dissertation, Düesseldorf, 1969.

Ehrhardt, A. A. "Maternalism and fetal hormonal and related syndromes." In J. Fubin and J. Money, *Contemporary sexual behavior: critical issues in the 1970's.* Baltimore: Johns Hopkins University Press, 1973.

Ehrhardt, A., Evers, K., and Money, J. "Influence of androgen and some aspects of sexually dimorphic behavior in women with the late treated androgenital syndrome." *Johns Hopkins Medical Journal,* 1968, 123, 115-122.

Ehrhardt, A., Greenberg, N., and Money, J. "Female gender identity and absence of fetal hormones: Turner's syndrome." *Johns Hopkins Medical Journal,* 1970, 125, 237-248.

Ford, C. E., Jones, K. W., Miller, O. J., Mittwoch, U. L., Penrose, L. S., Ridler, M., and Shapiro, A. "The chromosomes in a patient showing both mongolism and Klinefelter syndrome," *Lancet,* 1959a, 1, 709-710.

Ford, C., Jones, K., Polani, P., Almeida, J., and Briggs, J. "A sex-chromosome anomaly in the case of gonadal dysgenesis." *Lancet,* 1959b, 711-713.

Goldstein, B. *Introduction to human sexuality.* New York: McGraw-Hill, 1976.

Gordon, S. "VD: If you are old enough to get it, you are old enough to read about it." *Ms. Magazine*, June 1974.

Hamerton, J. L. *Human cytogenetics*, vol. 2, *Clinical cytogenetics*. New York: Academic Press, 1977.

Hampson, J. L. "Determinants of psychosexual orientation." In F. A. Beach, *Sex and behavior*. New York: John Wiley & Sons, 1965.

Jacobs, P., Brenton, M., Melville, M., Brittain, R., and McClemont, W. "Aggressive behavior, mental subnormality and the XYY male." *Nature* (London), 1965, 208, 1351-1353.

Jacobs, P. and Strong, J. "A case of human intersexuality having a possible XXY sex-determining mechanism." *Nature*, 1959, 182, 302-303.

Kallman, F. J. "Genetic apsects of sex determination and sexual maturation potentials in man." In G. .Winkur (ed). *Determinants of human sexual behavior*. Springfield, Ill.: Charles C. Thomas, 1963.

Kinsey, A., Pomeroy, W., and Martin, C. *Sexual behavior in the human male*. Philadelphia: W. B. Saunders, 1948.

Lee, T., Utidijian, H., Singh, B., and Cutler, J. "Potential impact of chemical prophylaxis on the incidence of gonorrhea." *British Journal of Venereal Diseases*, 1972, 48, 57-64.

Leff, J. and Scott, P. "XYY and intelligence." *Lancet*, 1968, 1, 645.

Lyon, M. F. and Hawkes, S. C. "X-linked gene for testicular feminization in the mouse." *Nature* (London), 1970, 227, 1217-1219.

Masica, D., Money, J., and Ehrhardt, A. "Fetal feminization and gender identity in the testicular feminizing syndrome of androgen insensitivity." *Archives of Sexual Behavior*, 1971, 1, 131-142.

Medical Letter. "Treatment and prevention of syphilis and gonorrhea." *Medical Letter on Drugs and Therapeutics*, 1971, 13, 87.

Mertens, T. R. *Human genetics*. New York: John Wiley & Sons, 1975.

Mittwoch, U. *Genetics of sex differentiation*. New York: Academic Press, 1973.

Money, J. "Hermaphroditism." In A. Ellis and A. Abarbanel (eds.). *The encyclopedia of sexual behavior*, Vol. 1. New York: Hawthorn, 1961.

Money, J., Ehrhardt, A., and Marica, D. "Female feminization induced by androgen insensitivity in the testicular feminizing syndrome: effect on marriage and maternalism." *Johns Hopkins Medical Journal*, 1968, 123, 105-114.

Money, J., and Ehrhardt, A. *Man and woman, boy and girl*. Baltimore: Johns Hopkins University Press, 1972.

Money, J., Gaskin, R. J., and Hull, H. "Impulse, aggressive and sexuality in the XYY syndrome." *St. John's Law Review*, 1970, 44, 220-1235.

Money, J., Hampson, J. G., and Hampson, J. L. "Hermaphroditism: recommendations concerning assignment of sex, change of sex, and physiologic management." *Bulletin of the Johns Hopkins Hospital*, 1955, 97, 285-300.

Money, J. and Mittenthal, S. "Lack of personality pathology in Turner's syndrome: relation to cytogenetics, hormones and physique," *Behavior Genetics*, 1970, 1, 43-56.

Money, J. and Pollitt, E. "Cytogenetic and psychosexual ambiguity: Klinefelter's syndrome and transvestism compared." *Archives of General Psychiatry*, 1964, 11, 589-595.

National Institute of Mental Health Center for Crime and Delinquency. *Report on the XYY chromosomal abnormality* (U.S. Public Health Service Publication No. 2103). Chevy Chase, Md.: National Institute of Mental Health, 1970.

Ohno, T., Kato, K., Nagala, M., Hattori, N., and Kanakawa, H. "Prophylactic control of the spread of venereal disease through prostitutes in Japan." *Bulletin of the World Health Organization*, 1958, 19, 575-579.

Price, W. and Whatmore, G. "Behavior disorder and the pattern of crime among XYY males identified at a maximum security hospital." *British Medical Journal*, 1967, 1, 533.

Singh, B., Cutler, J., Utidijian, H. "In vitro effect of vaginal contraceptive and selected vaginal preparations in candida albicans and trichomonas vaginalis." *Contraception*, 1972, 5, 401-411.

Smith, W. H. "Syphilis epidemic in a southern prison." *Journal Medical Association of Alabama*, 1965, 35, 392-394.

Subak-Sharpe, G. "The venereal disease of the new morality." In *Focus: Human Sexuality 77/78*. Guilford, Conn.: Dushkin Publishing Group, 1977.

Telfer, M., Baker, D., Clark, G., and Richardson, C. "Incidence of gross chromosomal errors among tall criminal American males." *Science*, 1968, 159, 1249-1250.

Weiner, S. and Sutherland, G. "A normal XYY man." *Lancet*, 1968, 2, 1352.

Welch, J., Borgaonkar, D., and Herr, H. "Psychopathy, mental deficiency, aggressiveness and the XYY syndrome." *Nature* 1967, 214, 500-501.

Winick, C. and Kinsie, P. *The lively commerce*. Chicago: Quadrangle, 1971.

Chapter 7
Conception, Childbirth, and Contraception

Childbirth is a profoundly significant and creative experience in the lives of many women. Women react to the discovery of pregnancy with a variety of feelings, ranging from ecstatic joy to deep depression. Positive feelings are often associated with increased sensuality, a deepened sense of being in love, or strong feelings of being special, creative, and feminine. Women who never felt particularly sexually desirable before perceive themselves as sexually attractive and voluptuous. Negative feelings are equally relevant. Women sometimes experience shock when they realize that pregnancy and having children entail sacrifices—giving up some of their individuality, leisure time, independence, or career for a period of time. Negative emotions naturally revolve around inadequate preparedness for motherhood or a lack of understanding of the physiological processes of childbirth.

In many women, positive and negative feelings about childbirth are combined, resulting in an ambivalent attitude toward pregnancy. Simone de Beauvoir (1953) described some of the conflicting feelings regarding childbirth. Although proud of the new life that is going to manifest itself, a woman begins to realize that she is no longer herself alone, but herself plus another person. For nine months the developing child is part of her, and this gives the woman a unique relationship with it—different from her relationships with her lover, husband, or friends. At birth the child is separated from her, and her task then is to support the child's development as an independent individual.

Ambivalence may also be created by the medical establishment. Childbirth is a highly personal, compassionate, and emotional experience. Yet many hospital settings create sterile, impersonal environments that may be disillusioning for a couple wanting to share the experience of birth. In many hospitals the pregnant woman is still treated as though she were ill. For instance, she is usually taken to the maternity ward in a wheelchair. Delivery rooms with their bright lights, medical odors, and surgical equipment further depersonalize the atmosphere. In sharp contrast to the traditional management of pregnancy are innovative alternatives that permit or encourage natural or family-centered childbirth.

Childbearing is a period of growth, change, the giving up of independence, and the acceptance of new responsibilities. It represents the future and the couple's willingness to extend themselves into the next generation. Some psychologists (Erikson, 1963) suggest that our ability to care for the next generation is an important milestone in adult personality development.

Pregnancy not only has a profound influence on the woman who is carrying the child but affects her relationship with her partner, as well as with her mother. Psychologist Grete Bibring (1975) has discussed the changes that may occur in the interpersonal relations between a couple as a result of pregnancy. Many couples find their relationship enhanced or deepened, especially if pregnancy is planned and wanted. Many parents have reported feelings of accomplishment from the experience of having children. On the other hand, there are couples who experience pregnancy as an intrusion or a stress factor that may hamper their adjustment. This is especially true for recently married couples, couples living together prior to marriage, or couples living in disharmonious marriages. The hope that problems in disturbed partnerships may be resolved by the addition of a third person usually fails to materialize. On the contrary, the advent of a child may disrupt a former relationship of marginal adequacy.

A couple's relationship will be redefined during pregnancy, depending on the point of view that both partners take regarding some important issues. Many questions will arise during this time, and their answers will inevitably bring about changes in the couple's relationship. Many a woman asks herself whether she or her partner will be able to cope with parenthood or how strong the emotional ties of both parents will be to the child. Is the man willing to share responsibilities as a father? For some couples the question of single parenthood will arise as a viable option. These and many other unique issues may call for adjustments during pregnancy reflecting the psychosocial aspects of childbearing.

Some women find that their relationships with their own mothers change during pregnancy. For instance, the Bibring study showed that women who were somewhat dependent upon their mothers (reflected in their seeking advice regarding the management of their households) became more independent during pregnancy. Statements such as "Now I know what my mother was going through" or "I really can understand my mother now" indicate that the pregnant woman, maybe for the first time, identified with the problems her mother had been faced with.

Regardless of the extent or intensity of the physical changes that accompany pregnancy, we can say that childbearing and childbirth by far transcend the biological and physiological factors involved, leaving a profound mark on the interpersonal relationships of the couple. In the following sections we shall review the sequence of biological events leading to childbirth. More important, however, are the psychological ramifications of this experience, which need to be considered by a couple with aspirations for parenthood.

Fertilization

From Conception to Implantation

Fertilization takes place when a sperm (Fig. 7.1) and a mature egg meet and fuse. During ejaculation millions of sperm (an estimated 100 million per milliliter of seminal fluid) are deposited into the vagina and move up the uterine tube. They are transported

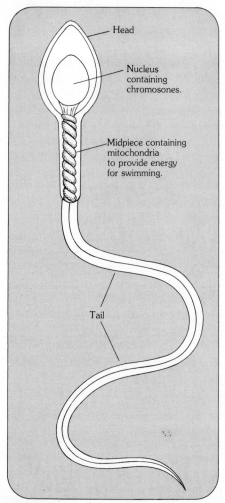

Figure 7.1
The structure of a mature human sperm.

either by the sperms' whiplike movements called *flagellation* or as a result of uterine or tubal contractions. The sperm can, under ideal circumstances, reach the distance from the opening of the vagina to the Fallopian tubes, which amounts to approximately six inches, within forty-five minutes. Of the millions of sperm that are deposited in a single ejaculate, a few hundred may reach the egg but only one is necessary for fertilization.

Successful conception requires a mature

ovum, usually released from the ovaries about fourteen days preceding the onset of menstruation. Figure 7.2 illustrates the sequence of events from ovulation to pregnancy. If conception is to take place, the egg must be fertilized relatively soon after ovulation; the projected life expectancy of the ovum is thought to be about 24 hours. A second prerequisite for successful impregnation is a sufficiently high sperm count. It has been estimated that males with fewer than 100 million active sperm per milliliter often have difficulty impregnating a woman, probably because low-sperm density reduces the chances of a sperm encountering an egg. Thus male potency is often directly related to the number of active, motile sperm released during ejaculation.

Fertilization usually takes place in the middle section of the Fallopian tube. After the fusion of the sperm and the egg, the fertilized ovum, now called the zygote, begins to move down the Fallopian tube toward the uterus. By the time the egg reaches the uterine cavity it has become a hollow ball of cells, which is now referred to as the *blastocyst*. The blastocyst will bury itself in the lining of the uterus, which has been hormonally prepared to receive the growing organism. This is the process of *implantation*; it occurs on about the twentieth day of the cycle. The developing tissues, once attached to the endometrium, together with the maternal tissue, will form the *placenta*. The placenta is the structure that transports nourishment from the mother to the developing embryo and

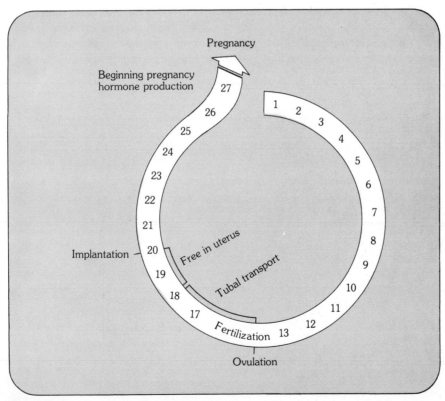

Figure 7.2
Time sequence from ovulation to implantation.

carries waste products from the embryo into the maternal bloodstream.

Immediately after implantation, hormonal secretions are released. They help to maintain the corpus luteum and its hormonal products, estrogen and progesterone. These hormonal secretions are known as *chorionic gonadotrophins* and are released by the placenta. As a result of this new hormone output, ovulation and menstruation are prevented. Figure 7.3 diagrammatically presents the time sequence from ovulation through fertilization, transport through the Fallopian tube into the uterus, and implantation.

Controlling the Baby's Sex

Many couples wish that they could influence the sex of their child. Old wives' tales and superstitious beliefs offer suggestions for couples desiring a child of a given sex. For example, in many societies intercourse during a full moon has been associated with the conception of a male. Notions like this are based on wishful thinking or superstitions, rather than on biological realities, but at least one geneticist, Dr. Landrum Shettles, claimed in the early 1960s to be able to help couples to control the sex of their offspring. Shettles' theory is based on a chromosomal study of sperm. In his quest to help people have babies of the sex they prefer, Dr. Shettles examined the sexual identities of sperm and came to the conclusion that two different types of sperm are found in a man's semen. One type is a relatively small, round-headed sperm that carries a Y chromosome and therefore is the male-producing sperm. Dr. Shettles labeled this sperm *androsperm*. Since the larger, oval-shaped sperm supposedly carries the female-producing X chromosome, it was called *gynosperm*. Both types of sperm have distinct advantages. For example, because of their smaller size, androsperms are more mobile and can move with greater speed than the gynosperm. Their big-

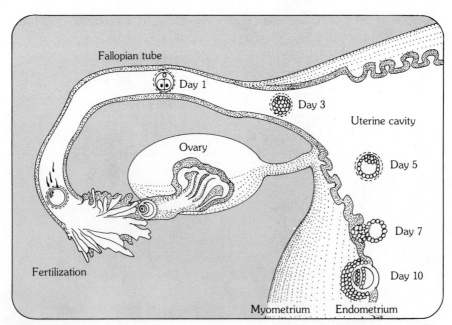

Figure 7.3
From conception to implantation.

gest asset is that they will probably win the race to the egg. Gynosperms, on the other hand, seem to have greater durability and are better able to survive in vaginal environments of less than optimal conditions.

After the discovery of the sexual identity of the sperm, Dr. Shettles and his co-worker (Rorvik and Shettles, 1970) have the following recommendations for couples interested in conceiving a child of the preferred sex.

In order to have a male child, a couple should remember the following points. First, since Y-bearing sperm are less viable than X-bearing sperm, the woman must be able to identify her exact time of ovulation, and intercourse should be timed as closely as possible to the moment of ovulation. This is because the androsperm, once ejaculated into the vagina, usually dies within twenty-four hours. Perfect timing of ovulation and intercourse are therefore crucial if a male conception is desired.

A second known factor, namely that androsperms are sensitive to the natural, acid secretions of the vagina, may also be used to increase the likelihood of conceiving a male. To counteract the normal acidity of the vagina, Rorvik and Shettles recommend that the vaginal area be neutralized to reduce its acidity. This neutralization can be very easily accomplished by douching with a solution consisting of two tablespoons of baking soda in a quart of water prior to intercourse.

Another suggestion for increasing the chances of conceiving a male is for the woman to reach orgasm before her partner ejaculates. Orgasm tends to increase the alkaline secretions of the vagina, thereby favoring the androsperms. Furthermore, certain intercourse positions seem to permit androsperms to reach the ovum faster than others. For example, penetration from the rear is recommended to promote the deposition of sperm at the mouth of the cervix. This position, and especially deep penetration from the rear, shortens the sperm's trip to the ovum and decreases the amount of time spent in the vagina.

Finally, a last hint for conceiving baby boys: a couple should refrain from intercourse a few days prior to the woman's calculated time of ovulation. Abstinence tends to increase the sperm count, thereby ensuring a maximum number of androsperms in the semen.

For a couple desiring the conception of a female, the following procedures may be helpful. Since the gynosperms, because of their greater life expectancy, may live for a couple of days, the last intercourse should occur two or three days prior to ovulation. This will guarantee that by the time the ovum is released, only the longer-living gynosperms will be available for fertilization. Another way of reducing the number of androsperms is to take an acid douche consisting of two tablespoons of vinegar in a quart of water. Because of the greater sensitivity of the androsperms, many of them will not survive, leaving the gynosperms to head for the egg.

Just as certain intercourse positions favor male conception, other positions enhance the chances of female conception. The face-to-face male superior position seems to be the best because of its relatively shallow penetration. Also, sperm deposited this way are required to swim through most of the vagina, a trip that will take its greatest toll on the androsperm. The missionary position will be even more effective if the woman avoids having orgasm, leaving the vagina in its natural acid environment. And, finally, a man who frequently ejaculates will have a low sperm count that favors the survival of gynosperms and, as a result, female conception.

Although Rorvik and Shettles' procedures for choosing the sex of a baby have been exposed to scientific criticism, there is some anecdotal evidence supporting the recommended prescriptions. For centuries, Orthodox Jews have been required to practice abstinence from intercourse prior to one week following the woman's menstrual cycle.

And for centuries, Orthodox Jews have been proud of the unusually high proportion of male births, because it was believed that abstinence during certain periods of the menstrual cycle increases the likelihood of male offspring.

Prenatal Development

Signs of Pregnancy

The symptoms of pregnancy may be divided into three different categories, grouped according to increasing reliability. Usually, the first sign of pregnancy is the lack of menstrual flow—one of the earliest *presumptive signs*. However, having missed one period is by no means a reliable indication of pregnancy. Other presumptive signs may include nausea and vomiting ("morning sickness"), tender and unusually full breasts, and an increased frequency of urination. Some women complain about unusual fatigue.

Missing a second menstrual period is frequently considered a *probable sign* of impregnation. Among other probable symptoms are an enlargement of the abdomen and changes in the uterus. Finally, there is the category of *positive signs*, which, however, are only detectable after the fourth month of pregnancy. Positive signs include the detection of fetal heartbeat and the perception of fetal movements.

Many women, anxious to learn whether or not they are pregnant, request a pregnancy test after the first missed period. Most common pregnancy tests are based on the presence of a specific hormone called the human chorionic gonadotrophin (HCG), which can be detected in the urine of a pregnant woman as early as fourteen days after fertilization. Injecting urine containing HCG into laboratory animals such as rabbits or mice will cause them to ovulate. Pregnancy may also be established by combining a drop of urine with an antiserum. If the HCG hormone from the placenta is present, the mixture will not coagulate. This failure to clot is considered a positive result indicative of pregnancy. And, finally, a doctor can identify a pregnancy through pelvic examination. Even in the early stages, the uterus of a pregnant woman is very soft and makes a bulge over the site of implantation. Once the pregnancy has been confirmed, the date of delivery can be estimated.

Prenatal Periods

Prenatal development falls roughly into three stages: the period of the ovum, the period of the embryo, and the period of the fetus. During the first two weeks after conception, the *period of the ovum*, the fertilized egg is primarily engaged in cell division. It has been estimated that the zygote takes about three days to progress through the Fallopian tube, where it floats freely for another three or four days. During this time the cluster of cells continues to differentiate until it reaches the stage of the blastocyst. The blastocyst, in turn, undergoes further cell divisions, giving rise to the *amnion* and *chorion*, the inner and outer sacs that surround and protect the developing organism. Another structure that results from cell differentiation during this stage is the placenta, the organ through which the developing organism receives nourishment and discharges wastes.

By the end of the period of the ovum, the organism is ready to anchor itself to the lining of the uterine wall, which has been prepared for that event beforehand by the secretion of maternal hormones. Implantation terminates the period of the ovum.

In the six weeks following the period of the ovum, the organism begins to take shape, and its various organ systems are formed. This stage, the *period of the embryo*, witnesses the emergence of the heart, which is

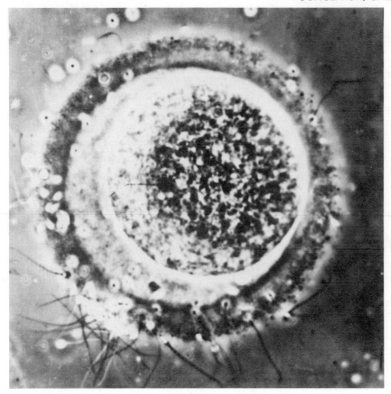

Figure 7.4
Living human ovum at the moment of fertilization. (Dr. Landrum B. Shettles)

usually beating by early in the fourth week. There is a simple brain, rudimentary kidneys, a liver, a digestive tract, and a primitive umbilical cord. The one-month-old embryo is only about one-fifth of an inch long and looks very much like that of other animals. For instance what looks like gill slits of a fish are actually the rudimentary structures in the neck. And what seems to be a primitive tail eventually becomes the tip of the adult spine. The tail reaches its maximum length at about six weeks and thereafter recedes.

The rudimentary forms of the amnion and the placenta continue to develop. The amnion becomes filled with fluid, which transports nutritional material, keeps the temperature even, and serves as a buffer to absorb physical shock experienced by the mother. The placenta develops fully into the organ of exchange between the embryo and the mother, since both embryonic and maternal bloodstreams open into the placenta. However, the two systems are always separated by cell walls within the placenta. Various nutritional substances from the mother's blood—sugars, fats, and certain protein elements—pass through the placental barrier. At the same time, waste products from the embryonic system are carried into the maternal bloodstream through the placenta. In addition to nutrients and waste products, many other substances can cross the placental barrier. Since the rudimentary organ systems are formed during the period

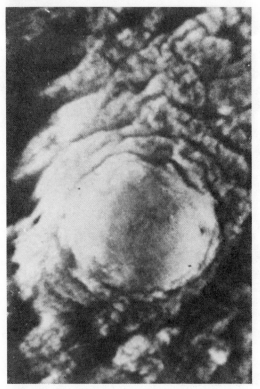

Figure 7.5
Implantation of a human embryo at 12 days after fertilization (Dr. Landrum B. Shettles)

are just beginning to form during this phase, it is difficult to distinguish male from female embryos by inspection. Overall, the embryo is still a very primitive organism that must develop for several months before it can be considered fully functional.

From approximately twelve weeks after conception until birth, the embryo is called a *fetus*. During this phase many body systems that have existed in rudimentary form in the embryonic stage become functional. By the end of the third month, the fetus is about three inches long and weighs about an ounce. During this month, nails begin to appear on already well-developed fingers and toes. The external sex organs have undergone marked changes that make it possible to determine the sex of the fetus by inspection. Some fetuses are quite active. They can kick their legs, turn their feet, and close their fingers; some squint and frown.

The head, which has been disproportionately large, takes on a different appearance when the growth of the lower part of the body

of the embryo, any chemicals with adverse effects—narcotics, tranquilizers, alcohol, nicotine, to name a few—may interfere with the normal growth of the embryo and lead to physical and/or mental abnormalities.

Toward the end of the embryonic period the developing organism has a definite human appearance, with an unmistakably human face, arms and legs, stubby fingers and toes. The head is still disproportionately large compared with the rest of the body. At this point, the embryo measures about one inch in length and weighs approximately one-thirteenth of an ounce. The brain already coordinates the functioning of the other organ systems, and the endocrine system is functioning. However, since the sex organs

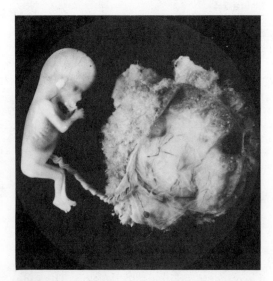

Figure 7.6
Human fetus at 12 weeks showing the umbilical cord and the developing placenta. (Dr. Landrum B. Shettles)

accelerates during the fourth month. At this time, fetal movements can be readily felt by the mother. The first fetal movements are known as *quickening*. The fetus now weighs about four ounces and is seven inches long. During the rest of the gestation period, the process of perfecting the form and functioning of internal and external organs takes place, along with increasing size and weight. By the fifth month, for example, the fetus has developed a sleeping and waking pattern that closely resembles that of a newborn. Although a five-month-old fetus may survive briefly outside the mother's body, it usually dies because of its inability to maintain the necessary breathing movements. In the sixth month, on the other hand, the fetus is able to make slight, irregular breathing movements.

The seventh month is important because, if born at this time, the fetus has a chance of

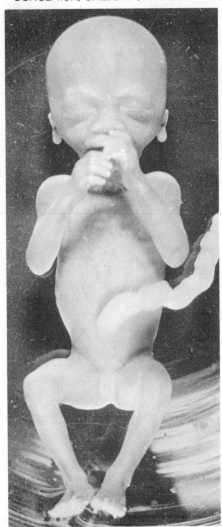

Figure 7.8
Human fetus at 30 weeks. (Dr. Landrum B. Shettles)

surviving in a highly sheltered environment such as an incubator. The fetus now measures about fifteen inches in length and weighs approximately two-and-a-half pounds. The nervous, circulatory, and other bodily systems are sufficiently developed for survival. Nevertheless, the fetus is highly sensitive to infections.

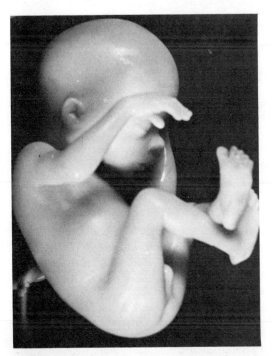

Figure 7.7
Human fetus at 20 weeks. (Dr. Landrum B. Shettles)

Amniocentesis
Amniocentesis is a relatively new and simple procedure used to detect genetic abnormalities in the developing fetus during the first three months of prenatal life. In amniocentesis a needle is inserted into the uterus of the pregnant woman

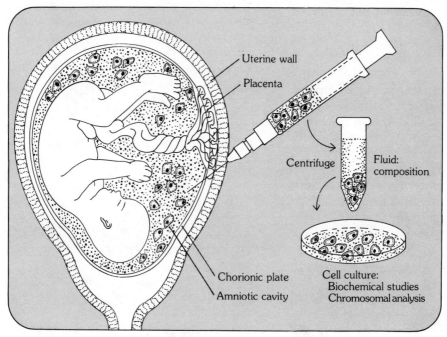

Figure 7.9
Amniocentesis.

to withdraw a sample of the amniotic fluid that bathes the fetus. Cells from the fluid are then grown in a tissue culture and can be analyzed for chromosomal aberrations.

The remainder of the prenatal phase, from twenty-eight weeks to birth at full term (forty weeks) is marked by rapid weight gains. About 50 percent of fetal weight is added during the last two-and-a-half months in the uterus. By the thirty-eighth week the fetus is called a term fetus, and all the finishing touches have been put on the organs. At this time, the fetus has definite periods of alertness and cries when hungry or disturbed.

At birth, when the filling-out process is completed, a normal-sized baby may be expected to weigh approximately seven pounds (though the weight may vary from seven to twelve pounds) and be about twenty inches long.

Environmental Influences on Prenatal Development

The developing organism, which is under genetic control, is also influenced by the external environment. In contrast to the relatively stable and constant intrauterine environment, a multitude of external factors, including the physical and emotional state of the mother, determine the quality of the prenatal environment. Although it is difficult to state exactly what constitutes an optimal prenatal environment, a good prenatal environment is certainly affected by the following factors.

Diet and Maternal Health. The developing fetus must, in the course of nine months, grow from a single cell to a highly complex organism. The ability to develop normally depends, at least in part, on the nourishment supplied by the mother. Poor nutrition may either directly affect the fetus by not meeting its nutritional needs or indirectly affect the fetus by increasing the mother's susceptibility to disease. Malnutrition not only can cause physical weakness, miscarriage, or stillbirth, but can also produce mental deficiency. Malnourished mothers typically come from an environment of poverty, inadequate medical care, and inferior sanitary conditions.

The old saying that a pregnant woman must eat for two is one of those half-truths that probably has done more harm than good. In spite of the considerable variations in nutritional needs among pregnant women, some generalizations can be made about dietary requirements. A good maternal diet must include a variety of food elements, particularly proteins, minerals, and vitamins. A varied diet rich in natural foods such as milk, eggs, fruits, and green vegetables is recommended. Most physicians advocate a substantial increase in protein in the diet. Protein can come from a variety of sources: animal sources include eggs, fish, milk, milk by-products, and meats; plant sources include beans and nuts. Fresh fruits and vegetables provide an important source of minerals and vitamins. Because of the difficulty of

meeting all nutritional needs by natural foods, most obstetricians prescribe iron and vitamin supplements.

Increases in weight may vary from fifteen to more than forty pounds. Most obstetricians set the upper limit at twenty-five pounds; some limit their patients to fewer than fifteen. A minimal weight gain in a normal pregnancy can be broken down as in Table 7.1.

Increases in weight of thirty pounds or more are undesirable for a number of reasons. In the first place, they represent unnecessary poundage, which may cause complications during labor and delivery. One such complication, *toxemia*, or the retention of toxic body wastes, is associated with excessive increments in weight. Large weight gains are also a common cause of backaches and pains. And, finally, large gains in weight require rigorous dieting after delivery if they are not to become a permanent acquisition. Ideally, a pregnant woman should restrict her weight gain while carefully watching the quality of her diet.

A number of studies have shown that women who maintained good diets were not only in better health during pregnancy but also gave birth to infants who had a better health record during the first few weeks of postnatal life. These infants also had a lesser incidence of minor diseases (colds, bronchitis) during the first six months.

Table 7.1

Distribution of Weight Gain During Pregnancy	
baby	7 pounds
afterbirth	1 pound
amniotic fluid	1 1/2 pounds
increase in weight of uterus	2 pounds
increase in blood	3 pounds
increase in weight of breasts	1 1/2 pounds
	16 pounds

Drugs. Because of the transport of chemicals between the mother's and the fetus's bloodstream, the infant receives some proportion of whatever a pregnant woman consumes. It is important to understand that any substance—food, medication, and drugs— passes through the placental barrier. There have been many dramatic cases of damage to the child as a result of drugs taken by the mother. For example, mothers who regularly used opiate drugs (heroin, morphine) during pregnancy have given birth to addicted infants. As a result, the addicted newborn had to pass through all the withdrawal symptoms (tremors, fever, convulsion, and breathing difficulties) that adults experience when they "dry out" (Brazelton, 1970). Similarly, babies born to alcoholic mothers can also suffer from withdrawal symptoms after birth. In addition, there is some evidence linking chronic drinking with congenital heart defects.

The specific effects of a drug will vary, depending not only on which drug is involved but also on the quantity used and the stage of pregnancy at which it is taken. This was clearly demonstrated several years ago when pregnant mothers took thalidomide to relieve minor discomforts. Thalidomide affects genes that control the development of the appendages. When taken twenty-one to twenty-two days after conception, thalidomide may prevent the external part of the ears from developing. When ingested twenty-four to twenty-nine days following conception, arms and legs fail to develop. From a developmental point of view, the most dangerous time for the new organism is two or three months after conception. This does not mean, however, that deformities or abnormalities cannot occur at any time during development.

Current interest in the harmful effects of smoking, quite apart from pregnancy, have resulted in concern over the possible harmful effects of nicotine on the fetus. Smoking by the mother has been shown to lower the birth weight of the baby, with infants born to women who smoke weighing about one-half pound less than babies of nonsmoking women. Low-birth-weight babies have, of course, more survival difficulties.

Irradiation. Irradiation can be harmful to the fetus, even if administered therapeutically to pregnant women. Several studies of women subjected to therapeutic X rays found infants with physical or mental abnormalities that could not be attributed to any source other than the treatment. Perhaps the most dramatic illustration of the effect of radiation on the fetus was seen after the dropping of the atomic bomb on Hiroshima in Japan. If a woman pregnant less than twenty weeks lived within a half-mile of the center of the explosion, she was likely to give birth to a physically or mentally abnormal child (Plummer, 1952).

Maternal Emotional States and Attitudes. Maternal diet and the consumption of potentially dangerous agents are not the only factors that may influence the mother's overall health and thereby the quality of the prenatal environment. Equally important are the mother's attitudes toward the baby and her emotional well-being. Old wives' tales would have us believe that happy mothers give birth to happy children and that a fearful mother may have a child with a birthmark in the shape of the object or animal that frightened her during pregnancy. Several researchers have shown that there may be some truth to these superstitions. A mother's emotional state can bring about changes in her body chemistry. Emotions such as anger or anxiety, for example, may liberate into the bloodstream certain hormones that can be irritating to the fetus. It is not the emotions that influence the baby but the physiological changes associated with emotions. Prolonged emotional stress during pregnancy may have enduring effects on the child.

The expectant mother's attitude toward her pregnancy and motherhood are also related to the health of the infant and may set the stage for later behavior patterns. A woman who resents being pregnant is likely to be emotionally upset during pregnancy and often hostile toward the baby after birth. Women with positive attitudes have been found to have beneficial effects on the development of the infant after birth. The emotional state of the pregnant woman, then, seems to be an important predictor of her behavior as a mother.

Pregnancy

The average duration of human pregnancy is about nine calendar months, or 280 days, when calculated from the first day of the last menstrual period. However, variations of a couple of weeks either way are not uncommon. In view of the wide variations in the length of pregnancy, it is often impossible to predict the expected delivery date with any precision.

The Three Trimesters of Pregnancy

Just as the prenatal period consists of three different stages, the nine months of pregnancy can be divided into periods of three months or *trimesters*. During that time, many changes occur in the woman's body, primarily because of increased hormonal activities.

During the first trimester (the first twelve weeks after conception), there are relatively few body changes except the usual signs of early pregnancy. Some women feel nauseated; others experience irregular bowel movements or have to urinate more often because of the increased pressure of the growing uterus. Usually, a woman does not

feel the changes occurring in her body during the first trimester.

In addition to physical changes, a woman's feelings may fluctuate considerably during the early months of pregnancy. Sometimes she feels positive toward her pregnancy, at other times, negative. Feelings of joy and excitement may give way to doubts and fear. It is important to know that these mood changes are common and not indicative of negative attitudes toward childbearing.

By the beginning of the second trimester, which extends from the thirteenth to the twenty-sixth week, the annoying aspects of early pregnancy are over. Nausea and fatigue usually subside. Since the second trimester is a period of rapid fetal growth, pregnancy becomes increasingly obvious at this time, with abundant evidence of dramatic body changes. As the abdomen expands and grows larger, the skin may stretch, leaving reddish or pink streaks ("stretch marks"). These striations can be minimized by applying generous amounts of baby oil or cocoa butter. Breasts, stimulated by sex hormones, enlarge and are functionally ready for nursing. They begin to produce a sticky, yellowish substance called *colostrum*, a watery precursor of milk.

Fetal movements can usually be felt from the sixteenth week on. At first, they are only felt by the mother, but later they can be felt by others if they place a hand on the woman's abdomen. Some infants are extremely active and may become so rambunctious that they keep their mothers awake at night. For many women the second trimester is a period of psychological well-being marked by joyous anticipation and emotional exhilaration and excitement.

The third trimester (the twenty-seventh through the thirty-eighth week) often means return of physical discomforts. Many women complain about insomnia and indigestion. Water retention (*edema*) is another common problem of late pregnancy, causing swollen hands and feet. Exercise and the elimination of salt and carbohydrates from the diet help to reduce water retention.

In the last few weeks before birth the baby settles into the birth position. This event is called *lightening*, since it takes considerable pressure off the stomach.

Sex During Pregnancy

Sexual activities and interests are closely related to the physical and emotional changes during pregnancy. During the early stages of pregnancy some women report a decreased interest in sexual intercourse. Morning sickness, fatigue, and some minor and annoying symptoms can make sex less enjoyable. Masters and Johnson (1966) have described the first trimester as a time of decreased sexual activity in women. Sometimes, the woman's partner does not understand the physi-

cal and emotional changes accompanying pregnancy and may appear uninvolved in the new circumstances of their relationship. Until fetal movements become perceptible, a woman's partner usually does not experience pregnancy as a reality. Lack of communication and misconceptions or ignorance may force a couple into unnecessary abstinence. For example, a man may be afraid of hurting or causing damage to the unborn child and refrain from intercourse. For the vast majority of women, there is no physical danger in having sex during pregnancy. Nevertheless, some obstetricians impose unrealistic restrictions on sex, which tend to immobilize the couple's relationship.

In contrast to the first trimester, the second is usually associated with heightened sexual desires. Many women who by that time have developed habits of eating well and caring for themselves experience high levels

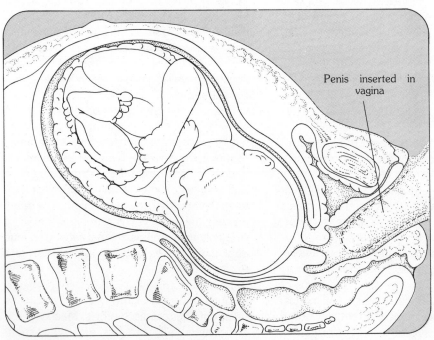

Penis inserted in vagina

Figure 7.10
Intercourse during the advanced stages of pregnancy.

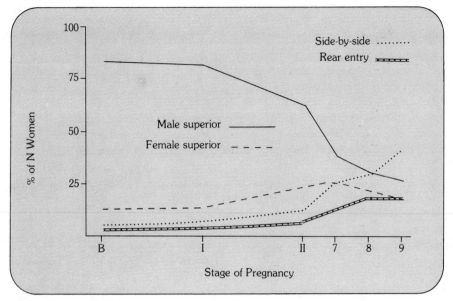

Figure 7.11
Graph of most frequently used positions of intercourse during pregnancy.

of sensual arousal, often exceeding prepregnancy excitement. Even the later stages of pregnancy are by no means a time of sexual incapacitation. Couples who modify their sexual activities continue to derive enjoyment from intercourse even in the last weeks before delivery. Obviously, certain positions are no longer safe or possible. Typically, the missionary position has to be abandoned. Also, deep penile penetration may be painful for some women during the last trimester. Some physicians recommend sexual abstinence after lightening has occurred and the baby has assumed the birth position.

Solberg, Butler, and Wagner (1974) studied female sexuality during pregnancy to provide some information about specific sexual behaviors. In their study they interviewed 260 women immediately after they had had their babies. For the purpose of their investigation, sexual activities were studied in terms of the following stages: (1) B, or baseline, sexual behavior during the year of becoming pregnant; (2) sexual activities during the first

trimester (I); (3) sexual behavior during the second trimester (II); and (4) the pregnant women's sexual interests during each of the three months of the last trimester (labeled 7, 8, and 9). Table 7.2 shows the distribution of sexual activities over the entire period of pregnancy. Overall, Solberg and his co-workers found a general decrease in the strength or intensity of orgasm compared with the orgasmic level before pregnancy. However, in spite of the general decline of sexual interest, a consistent percentage of the women reported an increase in the intensity of intercourse at all stages of pregnancy.

Women who reported reduced sexual activities gave a number of reasons for the decrease, including physical discomfort, fear of injury to the baby, awkwardness because of unfamiliar positions during intercourse, and a feeling of unattractiveness. Many women feel less appealing, especially in the latter stages of pregnancy. When the woman's abdomen becomes large, familiar positions, such as face-to-face intercourse, may have to be modified. Rear entry, with the man approaching from behind while both partners lie on their sides, is one of the preferred positions in the advanced stages of pregnancy. As the Solberg study indicates, there is a general decrease in the use of the male superior position and an increase in other positions, particularly the side-by-side position, as pregnancy progresses. Emotionally and physiologically, the last months of pregnancy provide some unique opportunities for more gentle erotic pleasures.

The Birth Experience

Stages of Labor

There are probably as many ways of experiencing childbirth as there are women having babies. The entire process of childbirth or

Table 7.2

Distribution of Sexual Activities over the Entire Period of Pregnancy

Frequency of Coitus at Different Stages of Pregnancy.

Stage of Pregnancy*	No. of Women	Frequency of Coitus (%)			
		None	< wk	1-5/wk	>5/wk
B	255	1	7	81	12
I	259	2	11	78	9
II	259	2	16	77	5
7	259	11	23	63	2
8	257	23	29	46	2
9	247	59	19	23	1

Rating of Sexual-Interest Level in Each Stage of Pregnancy as Compared to B.

Stage of Pregnancy*	No. of Women	Sexual-Interest Level (%)		
		Increased	Unchanged	Decreased
I	226	23	48	28
II	226	24	32	44
7	226	16	19	65
8	224	14	14	71
9	215	13	11	75

Various Rates of Orgasm with Coitus at Each Stage of Pregnancy.†

Stage of Pregnancy*	No. of Women	Rate of Orgasm (% of Women)		
		<25%	25-75%	>75%
B	233	13	36	51
I	235	20	36	45
II	237	23	41	36
7	218	40	30	30
8	186	51	25	24
9	98	57	19	23

*I and II refer to the first and second trimesters of pregnancy.
†Excludes women not orgastic or abstaining from coitus.

Table 7.2 (cont.)

Rating of the Strength or Intensity of Orgasm as Compared to Intensity in Stage B for Each Stage of Pregnancy.*

Stage of Pregnancy	No. of Women	Ratings of Orgasm (% of Women)		
		Intensity Increased	Intensity Unchanged	Intensity Decreased
I	223	17	66	17
II	211	10	62	28
7	179	12	46	41
8	151	11	37	52
9	91	11	41	48

*Excludes women not orgastic or abstaining from coitus.
Source: Solberg, D., Butler, J., and Wagner, N. "Sexual Behavior in Pregnancy." In Wagner, N., *Perspectives on Human Sexuality*. Behavioral Publications, Inc., 1974, p. 402. Reprinted by permission of Human Sciences Press.

parturition occurs in three stages. When it is time for delivery, the mother begins to experience interim contractions marking the onset of labor. At first, the contractions are at infrequent intervals and not very intense. Later they become more intense and more frequent, eventually setting a rhythmic pattern. As labor progresses, the cervix stretches and becomes dilated and the fetus descends through the birth canal into the vagina.

The first phase of the birth process is referred to as the *first stage of labor*. It begins with the first contractions leading to the dilation of the cervix and lasts until the cervix is sufficiently dilated to allow the head of the fetus to pass through the vaginal canal. During this phase, the cervix is thinned or stretched so that the opening enlarges much like the diaphragm of a camera being opened. Figure 7.12 shows the actual dilation of the cervix from the beginning of labor to full dilation. The pregnant woman may hear the doctor using the medical term, "She is dilating nicely."

Figure 7.13 shows the movements of the fetus during labor and delivery. The first stage is the longest period of labor; for

women having their first child it may last as long as twelve hours. For women who have had children, the first stage seldom lasts longer than eight hours. Several typical signs suggest that labor is progressing. Uterine contractions begin to occur at regular intervals of fifteen or twenty minutes. The cervical plug, a seal of mucus protecting the uterus from infection, comes away as a slightly blood-stained discharge. This is sometimes referred to as the "show." Next, the amniotic membrane, or "bag of waters," may rupture. Many women feel as if they are suddenly losing control of their bladders when the amniotic membrane breaks and releases its clear fluid.

The *second stage of labor* begins with the full dilation of the cervix and terminates with the expulsion of the baby from the woman's body. During this phase, the baby's head (or presenting part) moves through the birth canal. In order to accommodate the passage of the infant's head and shoulders, which are the largest parts of its body, the opening of the vagina must stretch tremendously. During this stage, many women experience the compelling urge to push the infant

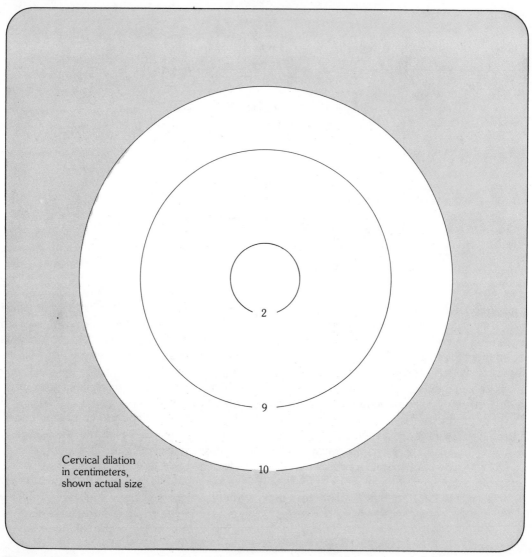

Cervical dilation
in centimeters,
shown actual size

2

9

10

Figure 7.12
Dilation of the cervix shown in actual size.

down into the birth canal. It must be remembered that the delivery of an infant is by and large brought about by the action of abdominal and respiratory muscles. Accordingly, at this stage of labor, a woman may be asked to exert these muscular forces and "bear down" with each contraction.

In the past, many doctors anesthetized women for the second stage of labor. Although the value of anesthetics in complicated deliveries is indisputable, blanket administrations of drugs to eliminate the sensations of labor and delivery are no longer desirable. Many women have described the

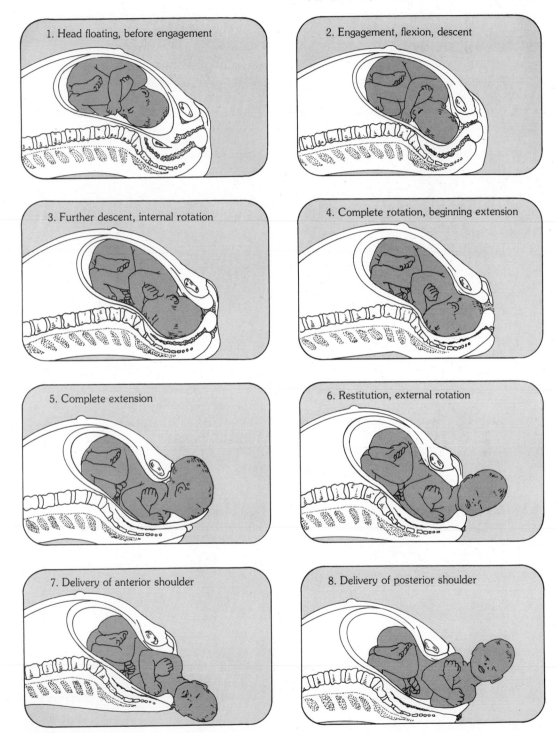

Figure 7.13
Movements of the fetus during labor and delivery.

second stage of labor as hard work but also as a worthwhile effort, since with each contraction the baby descends a little farther.

A common intervention during the second stage of labor is a surgical incision called *episiotomy* (Figure 7.14), performed to en- large the birth canal and forestall the possible tearing of the vaginal area. The episiotomy, usually performed between contractions under local anesthesia, involves a small cut in the pelvic floor. Most women do not feel the cut, which is immediately stitched up after

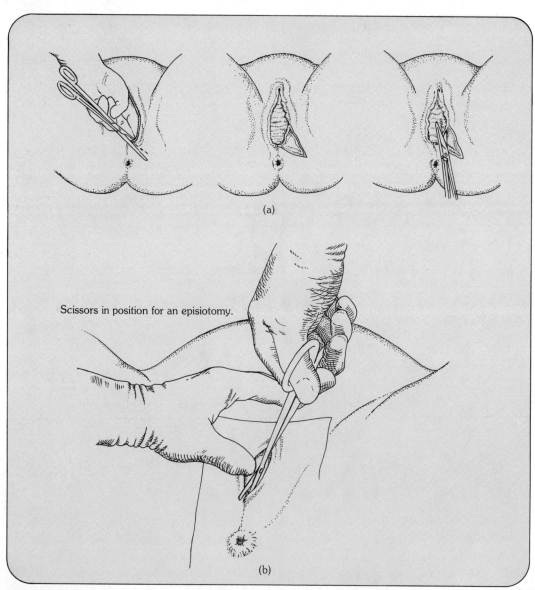

(a)

Scissors in position for an episiotomy.

(b)

Figure 7.14
The episiotomy.

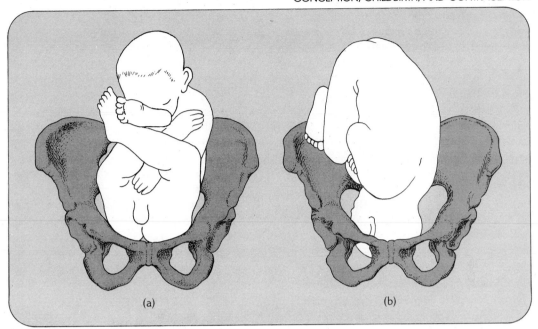

(a)   (b)

Figure 7.15
Possible position of the fetus during birth: (a) a breech presentation; (b) a normal, head-first presentation.

the baby's passage. An increasing number of obstetricians believe that the advantages of episiotomies are not sufficient to warrant their routine use. Healing of the incision may be painful and intercourse may be difficult when a couple resumes sexual activities after childbirth.

Following the delivery of the head, the shoulders, arms, trunk, and legs will pass quite easily through the birth canal. Since these parts of the infant are soft and pliable, delivery of the rest of the body is usually accomplished in a minute or two.

The *third and final stage of labor* is sometimes referred to as the placental stage; it involves the delivery of the *afterbirth*, which consists of the placenta, the amniotic membrane, and part of the umbilical cord. This part of the birth process usually occurs within ten minutes after the birth of the infant.

Today there are a number of options for the conduct of labor. The most commonly used method for enhancing maternal comfort is the administration of analgesics to relieve pain and anesthetics, which deaden all sensations. There seems to be a general trend away from general anesthetics that create a temporary but complete loss of consciousness toward a greater use of local anesthesia when necessary. Local anesthetics work by temporarily interrupting the pathways that carry pain and other sensations to the brain. There are a number of methods of producing local anesthesia, each with different action sites. All anesthetic techniques for delivery, however, tend to impair a woman's ability to work with her contractions and limit maternal participation in the childbirth process.

The New Methods of Childbirth

Many couples view childbirth as a highly personal experience and look for ways to overcome the impersonality of the hospital with its atmosphere of illness. Two new childbirth methods have recently gained popularity. One is the Read method developed by the British physician Grantly Dick-Read (1953), who argued that the pain of childbirth could be minimized by overcoming the fear of it. Dick-Read was firmly convinced that childbirth without medication and with minimal medical interference is desirable for the infant under normal circumstances. He also thought that a woman's awareness and participation during labor and delivery are a crucial component of the childbirth experience.

Dick-Read devised a series of exercises to help women cope with their labor and to deliver while fully conscious. With the publication of Dick-Read's book, *Natural Childbirth*, the term caught on and came to mean preparation for childbirth through understanding the physiological and psychological processes involved in giving birth.

In the 1950s, a French doctor, Fernhand Lamaze, introduced the *psychoprophylactic method of childbirth* first developed in Russia. This method is one of pain relief through conditioned *reflex* and is based on the work of the Russian physiologist Pavlov. As with the Dick-Read approach, the Lamaze method educates the woman to dissociate pain sensations from childbirth. At the same time, she is required to learn a series of exercises and breathing techniques to help her uterine contractions and to participate actively and effectively in the actual delivery. Rather than viewing childbirth as unbearable, a woman comes to appreciate that nature has ingeniously prepared her for the event.

The most recent childbirth method was proposed by Frederick Leboyer (1975), an outspoken critic of traditional delivery techniques. Glaring lights in delivery rooms, loud noises, and strange odors, says Leboyer, are a traumatic reception for the infant making the transition from the warmth of the mother's body to the outside world. Leboyer's delivery techniques include soft, dimmed lights and voices that whisper. After birth, the infant is placed on his mother's body and gently massaged. When the umbilical cord is cut, the baby is put in a lukewarm bath to simulate the intrauterine environment as closely as possible.

Women who choose natural methods of childbirth consider the presence of the father indispensable. The natural childbirth partner is an informed and competent man who wants to become part of an experience once considered strictly female business. In preparatory classes he has acted as a coach while the woman learns breathing and exercise techniques. Because he has learned what to expect, he is permitted to remain with the woman throughout the birth process. The new childbirth methods make the birth experience a family affair.

Some Western European countries are practicing a family-centered approach to childbirth by moving the hospital to the house of the pregnant woman and supporting the birth process with obstetrical "flying squads." These mobile medical units carry all the necessary surgical equipment in case of complications.

With the growing popularity of natural childbirth methods, the first studies comparing the psychoprophylactic method with traditional, medicated childbirth have become available. Tanzer (1977) demonstrated that natural-childbirth women reported mostly positive feelings of happiness, excitement, and joy. Couples who have shared the birth experience have called it a "peak experience," a rapturous gratification of sharing and togetherness. They experience birth as a unit and embark on parenthood as a dual involvement and responsibility. The statements of women in Tanzer's control group, most of whom received some type of medication to control their labor, did not describe birth as a happy experience. Their descriptions were characterized by sensations of fear and hostility. Uninvolved fathers who did not participate in the birth process often described themselves as feeling "left out" and not ready for parenthood.

The Postpartum Period

The postpartum period encompasses the time immediately following birth until the woman's reproductive organs have returned approximately to their nonpregnant state. This is a period—about six weeks—of physical as well as emotional adjustment. Especially with the first child, drastic changes are necessary to accommodate the totally dependent infant. These new demands are so anxiety-provoking for some women that they may experience the *"postpartum blues,"* characterized by irritability, crying spells, constant fatigue, or fear of failure as a mother. Other women complain about inability to concentrate, spells of physical or emotional letdown, or failure to understand why they cannot maintain the emotional high experienced at birth. In most cases the postpartum blues are temporary and give way to less emotional upset and better coping with new situations.

Breast-Feeding

One important determinant of the mother's physical and psychological state during this period is the ease or difficulty with which a feeding schedule is established. *Lactation* is the production of milk, usually beginning within three days after childbirth. Milk production is triggered by two hormones, prolactin and oxytocin. *Prolactin* stimulates milk production, while *oxytocin*, the same hormone involved in uterine contractions, forces the milk into the ducts of the breasts and acts as the milk-releasing hormone. The sucking action of the infant at the breast stimulates lactation, and frequent nursing increases the milk supply. If a woman continues to breast-feed beyond the postpartum pe-

riod, menstruation and ovulation may be delayed. However, the absence of menses provides no guarantee that conception cannot take place. Although the lactating woman is less likely to become pregnant, breast-feeding cannot be depended upon as a reliable contraceptive method.

Breast-feeding was very popular at the beginning of the century, when 90 percent of infants were nursed for at least a few months. Since then, its popularity has declined, and by 1966 only 20 percent of mothers were breast-feeding (Mayer, 1972). Although there has been an increase in breast-feeding in the last decade, especially because of the growing popularity of natural-childbirth methods, probably less than 50 percent of American women choose to breast-feed today. Those who do find nursing physically and emotionally gratifying. Masters and Johnson found that sexual stimulation induced by the nursing infant frequently reaches plateau levels of sexual excitement. In a few instances some women experienced orgasm while breast-feeding.

Successful breast-feeding has been closely related to the mother's attitude toward the child, as well as her attitude toward sexuality. Newton's (1968) findings indicated that mothers who were successfully breast-feeding by the time they left the hospital showed stronger interest in and more positive feelings toward their babies than nonnursing women. The nursing mother was also more accepting in her attitude toward sexuality. For instance, Sears, Maccoby, and Levin (1957) reported that nursing mothers were more tolerant of sex play and masturbation in their children. Similarly, Masters and Johnson (1966) noted that the highest level of sexual arousal in their laboratory was experienced by nursing mothers during the first three months after delivery. As a group, these women reported a strong interest in as rapid a return as possible to active intercourse with their husbands.

If a mother decides not to nurse, milk production will cease and the breasts will return to the prepregnant state. Among the reasons given by contemporary American women who choose not to breast-feed are inconvenience, greater physical freedom, modesty, and a fear of spoiling the shape of the breasts.

Contraception

Contraceptive practices and devices come in many different forms, some of which are as old as history. In ancient Egypt, for example, camel-dung pebbles were placed in the woman's uterus to prevent fertilization. The condom has been known at least since the eighteenth century.

Choosing a method of contraception is a very personal matter. Some people find the insertion of a diaphragm annoying, while others consider the condom unattractive. Still others feel that withdrawal spoils their sexual fun or find that abstinence during certain days of the menstrual cycle is an irritating imposition. The choice of birth control is further complicated because any method inevitably involves the needs of two individuals, both of whom have rights and responsibilities with regard to birth control.

Contraception involves emotional and social factors, including the type of relationship between two people, the frequency of intercourse, and religious attitudes. In recent years social pressures have increasingly supported birth control with the recognition that children extract a high price in effort, time, and money. And the changing role of women in contemporary society has demonstrated that female identity is no longer exclusively determined by motherhood. Although most women want to experience childbirth and the role of mother, a lifelong dedication to the family and home are no longer realistic expectations for many women. Career interests and the economic needs of the family have

begun to take precedence over lifelong caring for children. And, finally, the emergence of more egalitarian male-female relationships and the worldwide population crisis seem to justify birth control more than ever before.

Technically, anything that interferes with the fertilization of the egg by the sperm can be termed contraception. Generally, conception can be avoided by blocking the sperm from entering the vagina (condom, diaphragm), killing the sperm (contraceptive foams, jellies), preventing ovulation (oral contraceptives), or limiting intercourse to a period in the female reproductive cycle when no mature egg is available for fertilization.

In our discussion of contraceptive methods and devices we shall divide contraceptive techniques into the following classes: natural methods of birth control, mechanical methods, chemical methods, oral contraceptives, surgical methods, and experimental approaches to birth control. Abortion, although not a contraceptive technique, will also be discussed.

Natural Methods of Contraception

Both *withdrawal* by the male during intercourse and *rhythm control* by the female are two of the simplest and oldest means of preventing pregnancy. With the withdrawal method (*coitus interruptus*), the male withdraws his penis from the vagina just prior to ejaculation, thus preventing semen from being deposited within the vaginal canal. *Coitus interruptus* is a rather unreliable method of birth control, depending on considerable self-control on the part of the male. If even the smallest amount of semen finds its way into the vagina, fertilization can occur. The withdrawal method may be characterized by faith in luck. If withdrawal fails and pregnancy occurs, a woman is likely to blame her partner for the "accident." If withdrawal is practiced as a regular contraceptive method, a couple may find their sexual relationship

Table 7.3

Choosing Contraceptives

Method	Type	Available from	Theoretical Effectiveness
Oral contraceptive Pill (combination)	Medical	Family planning clinic/GP	Virtually 100%
Oral Progestogen (Progestin)	Medical	Family planning clinic/GP	98%
IUD	Medical	Family planning clinic/GP	98%
Diaphragm & Spermicide (barrier)	Medical	Family planning clinic/GP	96%
Condom & Spermicide (barrier)	Non-medical	Family planning clinic across the counter	96%
Spermicide (foams, gels)	Non-medical	Family planning clinic across the counter	60-90% (not recommended for use on their own)
Rhythm Method (calendar)	Non-medical		75%
Coitus Interruptus	Non-medical		
Sterilization			
female	Medical	Hospital	Virtually 100%
male	Medical	Family planning clinic/ GP/Hospital	Virtually 100%

Source: The visual dictionary of sex. New York: A Jc W Publishers, Inc., 1977.

unsatisfactory because of the lack of sexual pleasure and fulfillment.

The *rhythm method* is used by a substantial number of women who are limited by their religious beliefs to "natural methods of birth control," methods that do not interfere artificially with the natural course of procreation. The rhythm method is the only form of contraception approved by the Roman Catholic Church.

In the calendar rhythm method the woman determines the time of ovulation in her menstrual cycle and then abstains from intercourse during her fertile period. Since a mature egg is available for fertilization only for a relatively short period of time, the minimum period of abstinence may be as short as two-and-a-half days before ovulation and one-and-a-half days afterward in women with perfectly regular cycles of twenty-eight days (Figure 7.16). However, because of the variations in the length of menstrual cycles, more

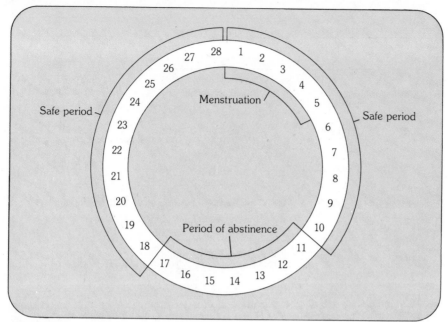

Figure 7.16
Rhythm system for a 28-day menstrual cycle.

days in the middle of the cycle must be re-garded as unsafe. Most women who practice birth control with the rhythm method prefer not to engage in intercourse between the tenth and eighteenth days of their cycle, when conception is most likely to occur.

Although the rhythm method appears quite simple in theory, its application is complicated by two factors. First, many women not only have difficulty in determining their exact date of ovulation but also have menstrual cycles that fluctuate from month to month. The second uncomfortable factor in the rhythm method is its unreliability. Sperm can survive in the oviducts for as long as forty-eight hours. Thus, if intercourse takes place two days prior to ovulation, it might possibly result in fertilization. Similarly, the egg is available for twelve to fourteen hours after ovulation and can be fertilized during this extended period.

A second method of predicting ovulation

is with the *temperature rhythm method.* This approach is based on the fact that a woman's temperature drops slightly at the time of ovulation and then rises to a high level immediately afterward. Women using this birth control method take their temperature daily and record it on a special chart. The major drawback of the temperature rhythm method is that it cannot be used to indicate the safe period before ovulation. Combining the calendar and temperature rhythm methods increases the effectiveness of these two birth control procedures.

At least one researcher (House, 1973) has suggested that a woman's personality may dictate her choice of contraceptive methods. Women using the rhythm method were char-acterized as rigid in their religious and social attitudes. They also suffered from low self-esteem and a pervasive sense of guilt. In addi-tion, many of them had negative attitudes to-ward sexuality or considered sex a duty.

They had chosen the rhythm method, at least in part, to escape intercourse or to punish their partner for arousing them sexually. In spite of the numerous limitations of the rhythm methods, women who cannot use other means of contraception continue to use them as a birth control method.

Mechanical Devices of Contraception

The most widely used male contraceptive device is the *condom*, a sheath of rubber that is placed over the penis before sexual contact. The condom holds the sperm after ejaculation, preventing it from being deposited in the vagina.

One of the main advantages of the condom is its easy availability. Condoms do not require medical supervision and can be bought over the counter from druggists, barbers, and are often available from coin-operated machines. The condom is a highly reliable contraceptive if used properly. Condoms are now manufactured in many colors and shapes; several gimmicky brands promising "extra sensitivity" are on the market. Because the condom serves as a thin mechanical barrier between the penis and the vagina, it also provides protection against sexually transmitted diseases.

The *diaphragm* is a contraceptive device used by women to prevent the sperm from entering the reproductive tract. Diaphragms look like caps that are placed over the cervix. All diaphragms must be initially fitted by a physician to determine the right size of the cap. Before insertion a woman must put contraceptive cream or jelly inside and along the rim of the diaphragm. The diaphragm is put into place several hours before intercourse and should not be removed for at least six hours afterward. It is inserted with a finger by pushing it to the top of the vagina and put across the cervix. Once in place, the diaphragm is held there by the tension of a metal

ring. After proper insertion, a woman should not be able to feel the diaphragm. With the removal of the cap, it should be washed and checked for cracks or holes. The diaphragm can be used for several months.

Some people do not like to use a diaphragm because, as in the case of the condom, it may interfere with the spontaneity of sexual intercourse. The major advantages of the diaphragm are that it is relatively inexpensive and virtually free of side effects or long-term health hazards. Used together with foams or jellies, the diaphragm is a very reliable form of birth control, second only to the pill.

The *intrauterine device* (IUD) is a contraceptive method whose mode of action is not fully understood. It has been suggested that IUDs either cause the egg to pass down the Fallopian tube too rapidly to be fertilized, or that they lead to a chronic, low-grade inflammation of the endometrium, thereby interfering with implantation. Figure 7.17 shows some of the common shapes of IUDs.

The IUD must be inserted by a physician during an office visit. It is made of soft plastic or a combination of plastic and copper. When the IUD is free in the uterine cavity it assumes its original loop, ring, spiral- or bow-shaped form. As long as the IUD is in place, it is about 98 percent effective in preventing pregnancy. However, only about 80 percent of the women using IUDs are able to practice this method of birth control on a long-term basis. The rest have to choose alternative means because the IUD can be expelled without the woman's knowledge. It has been estimated that one-third of the pregnancies with IUDs are due to the expulsion of the device.

The major advantage of the IUD is that it frees the woman from having to remember to take special precautions prior to intercourse. Once inserted, the IUD can be more or less forgotten. A second advantage stems from the fact that the IUD leaves the female hormone cycle unchanged and avoids some of

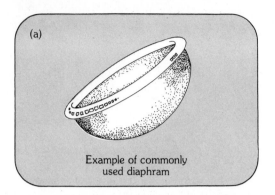

(a)

Example of commonly
used diaphram

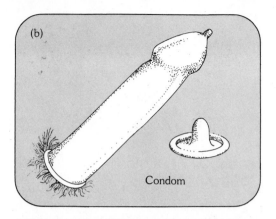

(b)

Condom

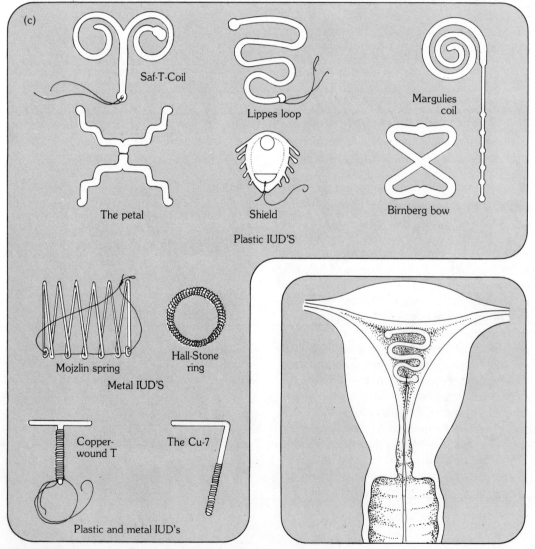

(c)

Saf-T-Coil

Lippes loop

Margulies
coil

The petal

Shield

Birnberg bow

Plastic IUD'S

Mojzlin spring

Hall-Stone
ring

Metal IUD'S

Copper-
wound T

The Cu-7

Plastic and metal IUD's

Figure 7.17
Examples of commonly used contraceptive devices.

the side effects associated with the pill. Major complaints about IUDs are increased or irregular menstrual flow, cramping, and perforation.

Chemical Methods of Contraception

Perhaps one of the oldest and least effective methods of birth control is the *vaginal douche*. With this method a relatively large amount of water (one to two quarts) is sprayed into the vagina immediately after intercourse. As a birth control technique, the douche is ineffective because active sperm can travel so fast that even the most agile woman cannot "wash them out" with a douche.

Spermicides are contraceptive foams, creams, or jellies containing chemicals that will kill the sperm. Most of these preparations are available in tubes or aerosol dispensers with a special applicator to be deposited into the vagina just prior to intercourse. Some spermicides are inserted into the vagina in tablet form, where they dissolve in the vaginal secretion producing a foam barrier.

Spermicides have a failure rate of 20 percent mainly because they can be washed away during prolonged foreplay. Since the vagina is secreting when a woman is sexually aroused, the spermicide may be rendered ineffective at the time of orgasm. Although the lack of major side effects appeals to some people, others are reluctant to use spermicides because of their messiness and annoyance prior to intercourse.

Oral Contraceptives

Oral contraceptives or "the pill" are the only reversible method of birth control that virtually always prevent pregnancy (if taken as directed). The pill has had an enormous influence on contemporary sexual behavior, liberating many women from the fear of unwanted pregnancy. In less than two decades the pill has become the most widely used method of birth control (Garcia, 1970).

The most commonly used oral contraceptive is the *combination pill* containing synthetic forms of the female hormones estrogen and progesterone. The combination pill is taken in twenty-eight cycles, twenty-one or twenty-two pills followed by seven or six pill-free days. The synthetic hormones mimic the natural female reproductive cycle and produce a physical state similar to pregnancy. Ovulation is inhibited so that the implantation of the egg is prevented. In addition, progesterone makes the lining of the uterus unreceptive to a fertilized egg so that even by some mistake (such as one forgotten pill) it is unlikely that pregnancy will result.

Reactions to the pill vary considerably from woman to woman. For many women the pill alleviates menstrual problems such as heavy periods or skin complaints. Many women also experience an increase in sexual interest once the fear of pregnancy has been removed.

However, there are some women who cannot use oral contraceptives for medical reasons, such as diabetes or high blood pressure. Also, oral contraceptives are not the preferred birth control method for women over forty years of age. Some younger women choose not to take the pill because of some potential side effects. Over the past few years there have been some alarming findings concerning the side effects of oral contraceptives. A relatively well-documented risk involves an increased risk of blood clotting. Some less harmful, nonhazardous side effects include nausea, weight gain, and fluid retention.

Additional evidence indicates that the pill may influence emotional states in women. Grant and Pryse-Davies (1968) found that high estrogen compounds affect mood states in a positive way, while high progesterone compounds are more likely to produce depressive mood states. The majority of studies

Table 7.4

Adverse Side Effects of the Pill—Most Commonly Reported

Side Effect	Confirmed	Suggested
Weight ↑		×
*Fluid retention		×
Engorgement and fullness of breasts		×
Breast tenderness and soreness		×
Headache	×	
Libido ↓		×
*Depression ↑		×
*Vitamin B₆ ↓	×	
Vitamin C ↓		×
*Nausea and vomiting	×	
*Discoloration of skin (chloasma)	×	
†Breakthrough bleeding	×	
Infertility after going off pill		×
Thrombophlebitis (inflammation of a vein causing obstruction of blood flow)	×	
Pulmonary embolism (obstruction of blood vessel in lungs with blood clot, air bubble, bit of sloughed off tissue from another vessel, etc. Obstructing material originates in another region of body. Obstructing blood clot or dead tissue may come from an inflamed vein.)	×	
Cerebral thrombosis (blood clot originating within a vessel supplying the brain and causing obstruction of blood flow to brain)	×	
*Blood pressure ↑	×	
Change in populations of vaginal microorganisms (bacteria, yeast, etc.)	×	

*Estrogen may need to be decreased.
†Progestogen activity or dose may need to be increased.
Key: ↓ = Decrease
      ↑ = Increase
Source: B. Goldstein. Introduction to human sexuality. New York: McGraw-Hill Book Co., 1976.

examining the possible side effects of oral contraceptives, however, are inconclusive, and we do not know how the present findings will be altered once longitudinal studies of the pill become available.

In spite of the attention directed at the possible undesirable side effects associated with the pill, the fact remains that oral contra-ceptives provide almost 100 percent protection against pregnancy.

Surgical Methods of Contraception

The methods included in this category of contraceptive techniques represent permanent means of birth control through sterilization. They are usually requested only when the desired family size has been attained. Many doctors will not perform the operation on young people because, for the most part, sterilization is difficult to reverse.

Male sterilization is achieved by *vasectomy* (Figure 7.18), a minor procedure performed in the physician's office. Vasectomies can be performed relatively quickly (in ten to fifteen minutes) under local anesthesia and are fairly inexpensive compared with female sterilization. The operation consists of cutting or tying a small section of the vas deferens. Ejaculation occurs exactly as it did before the vasectomy, and sexual activities remain unaltered; the man has no difficulty in achieving an erection or ejaculation. However, since sperm are no longer transported by the vas deferens, the ejaculate contains no sperm.

Attempts are presently being made to improve vasectomy techniques by making them reversible. Research with animals has

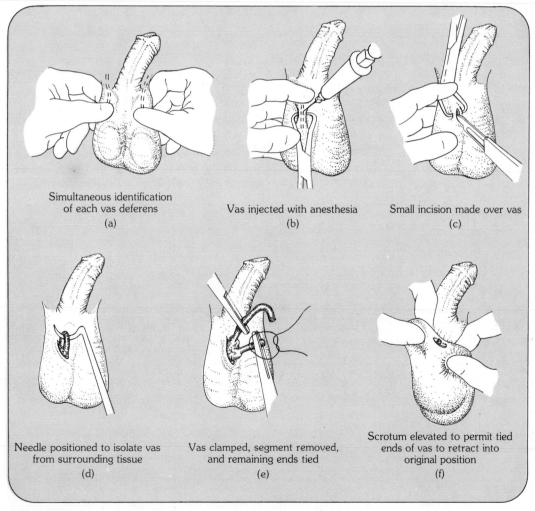

Simultaneous identification of each vas deferens
(a)

Vas injected with anesthesia
(b)

Small incision made over vas
(c)

Needle positioned to isolate vas from surrounding tissue
(d)

Vas clamped, segment removed, and remaining ends tied
(e)

Scrotum elevated to permit tied ends of vas to retract into original position
(f)

Figure 7.18
The procedure for doing a vasectomy.

shown that "on-off" valves have successfully worked on guinea pigs, and it may only be a question of time until reversible vasectomies are available for men.

Female sterilizations are more complicated operations because a woman's reproductive organs are located inside her body. The operation, called *tubal ligation* (Figure 7.19), involves tying off the uterine tubes, thereby preventing the egg from traveling to the uterus or the sperm from reaching the egg. Tubal ligations require a small incision in the abdomen. A short hospital stay, up to ten days, is usually necessary.

A relatively new procedure, *laparoscopy*, is being performed by an increasing number of obstetricians. In this procedure the physician views the Fallopian tube through a telescopic instrument, the laparoscope, which enables him to cut and cauterize the Fallopian tube. Laparoscopy is performed in clinics on an out-patient basis or requires an overnight stay if performed in a hospital.

All current sterilizations have to be considered as irreversible. Johnson (1972) suggested that the need for reversible sterilizations may be exaggerated, since it has been estimated that only one in 1,000 cases of female sterilization and one case in 400 vasectomies requested a reversal of the operation. A review of the literature regarding the psychological effects of sterilization indicates that most couples are satisfied with the results of their surgery and do not experience negative emotional consequences (Rodgers and Ziegler, 1973). Successful adjustment to sterilization is influenced by family size, an understanding of the operation and its implications, the attitude of the partner toward sterilization, and whether or not the operation is voluntary.

Experimental Methods of Contraception

A number of approaches to birth control are currently under investigation. For example, now available, on a limited basis, are injectable hormones that can be administered once every month or once every three

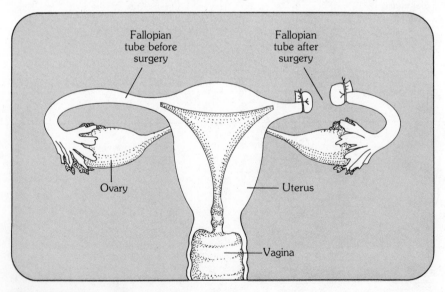

Fallopian tube before surgery

Fallopian tube after surgery

Ovary

Uterus

Vagina

Figure 7.19
Schematic representation of a tubal ligation. In actual sterilization the surgery is performed on both Fallopian tubes.

months. These preparations slowly release their hormones to block ovulation. In their present form these long-lasting preparations have several side effects, including headaches, nausea, and depressive moods.

The *"morning-after pill"* is prescribed in emergency situations, for example, for rape or contraceptive failure. The drug diethylstilbestrol (DES) is a massive dose of estrogen that presumably prevents the implantation of the fertilized egg (Morris and Van Wagenen, 1973). The "morning-after pill," containing approximately the equivalent amount of hormones found in a thirty-five-to-forty-year supply of the pill, must be taken within seventy-two hours following intercourse. The drug is given over a period of five days and is almost 100 percent effective if taken within the prescribed time period. The use of DES, however, has been approved by the Food and Drug Administration only in emergency situations. An alternative to the "morning-after pill" is the experimental *"morning-after coil."* Insertion of this type of IUD after unprotected intercourse has been found to bring on a menstrual period without unpleasant side effects.

There has been much speculation about the possibility of a male contraceptive pill. At this time, a male pill is not commercially available, although quite a few research efforts have been directed to the development of such a preparation (Jackson, 1973). Particularly promising as a contraceptive is testosterone, the male hormone. Researchers are hoping that testosterone will block fertility in men in a manner similar to the way the pill works in women. At present the work with testosterone is controversial because there is the potential danger that it may cause cancer of the prostate. Since it seems inevitable that a male contraceptive pill will be available during the next decade, it will be interesting to see whether males will accept responsibility for birth control as readily as women have.

Another approach to contraception that is very much in the experimental stages is the immunological method. With this type of contraception a woman would be vaccinated against sperm or a man against sperm production in much the same way as a smallpox vaccination. Or antibodies may be given to immobilize sperm. From this experimental research it appears that future methods of contraception will be different from existing techniques.

Abortion

Although abortion is not a method of birth control in the sense of preventing conception, it may be viewed as a fertility control for women who have "accidentally" become pregnant. Abortion has been legal throughout the United States since the Supreme Court ruled in 1973 that neither federal, state, or local governments may interfere with a woman's decision to interrupt a pregnancy. Although abortions during the first three months of pregnancy are considered a personal and private matter, the Court maintained that states may prohibit abortions during the last trimester unless the physical or mental health of the mother is at stake. In this chapter we are concerned only with various abortion techniques. The psychological and moral issues surrounding the abortion controversy are discussed in Chapter 19.

Abortions are now a relatively safe procedure. At the present time, most abortions can be performed without complications until the twelfth week of pregnancy. One of the most commonly used procedures is *vacuum extraction* or *aspiration* (Figure 7.20). It involves the introduction of a cannula, a small tube connected to a source that literally sucks out the content of the uterus. The actual abortion takes an average of five to ten minutes with recovery time between one and three hours. Uterine extractions can be safely performed up to the eleventh week

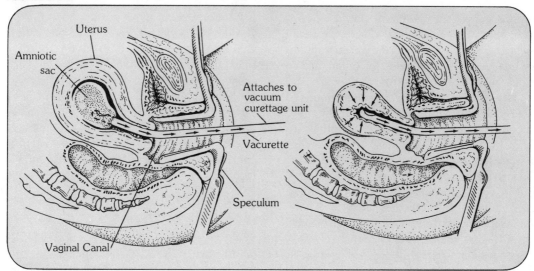

Figure 7.20
A vacuum suction abortion.

of pregnancy. Afterward, the size of the embryo is generally too large for the suction apparatus.

The vacuum aspiration technique has more or less replaced the D & C technique, the abbreviation for *dilation and curettage*, also known as the "scrape method." In D & C terminations of pregnancy the content and lining of the uterus are removed after dilation of the cervix.

When pregnancy has advanced to the second trimester, the uterus is so enlarged that techniques like vacuum aspiration or D & C can no longer be safely used. The usual method of inducing abortion during the second trimester is by *saline injection*. In this procedure the woman receives a local anesthetic, and a small needle is inserted into the amniotic cavity. A small quantity of amniotic fluid is withdrawn and replaced by a similar quantity of a saline solution. As a result of this injection, labor is induced within twenty-four hours and the fetus is expelled. With pregnancies terminated during the second trimester, most fetuses are stillborn. Clearly,

when termination of pregnancy is considered, the procedures that can be performed during the first trimester are preferable and less traumatic than saline injection.

The increasing acceptance of abortion, particularly after its legalization, has resulted in fervent arguments presented by opponents and proponents of abortion. The "prolife partisans" and "right-to-life" advocates have organized antiabortion groups to seek prosecution of abortionists. These groups are devoted to the preservation of human life, born or unborn. They claim that any society spending millions of dollars on atomic bombs and space exploration should be able to care for unwanted children. Proponents, on the other hand, defend the necessity of abortions, especially in view of the psychological stress and socioeconomic problems involved with unwanted children. From a moral/ethical viewpoint, the Commission on Population Growth (1972) concluded that legal restriction against abortions are an obstacle to the exercise of individual freedom. The Commission argued that women should be allowed control over their fertility and be able to make moral choices based on personal values.

Apart from the legal and ethical issues involved in abortions, the psychological effects of terminating a pregnancy have also received attention. Smith (1973) concluded that the majority of his sample (90 percent) did not report negative emotional consequences of a degree that might require psychological help. Although some women expressed feelings of guilt and depression, the majority expressed relief from the emotional stress often accompanying unwanted pregnancies.

Summary

In this chapter we have examined the impact of conception, childbirth, and contraception on male and female sexuality and found that pregnancy and childbirth can have a profound effect on a couple's interpersonal relationship. We have traced the sequence of the biological events beginning with fertilization through the three stages of prenatal development. Each of these stages, the period of the ovum, the embryo, and the fetus, is characterized by distinctive developmental events. The period of the ovum encompasses the trip of the fertilized egg down the Fallopian tube into the uterus and is completed at the moment of implantation. The following period of the embryo is of crucial importance because it represents the time of organ formation when the developing organism is particularly susceptible to environmental influences. Among the important factors affecting the quality of the prenatal environment are maternal diet and health, drugs, irradiation, and the woman's emotional state and her attitudes toward pregnancy and motherhood.

Most women modify their sexual behavior during pregnancy in accordance with the physical and emotional changes marking the various stages of pregnancy. Honest communication, freedom of misconceptions, and change of positions during intercourse can enhance sexual pleasures even during the later stages of pregnancy.

All birth experiences, whether traditional medicated childbirth or the recent methods of natural childbirth, have in common a number of features, for example, the different stages of labor and the postpartum period with its unique problems and adjustments.

Closely related to conception and childbirth is the control of fertility. The discussion of the commonly used contraceptive methods revealed that all the approaches to birth control have advantages and disadvantages. Although research data suggest that oral contraception and the intrauterine device are the most effective methods of preventing pregnancy at present, some people practice less effective methods of birth control. Disadvantages common to the less effective techniques—the diaphragm, condom, foams and jellies—are that the person must be highly motivated to use these methods and must use them consistently before engaging intercourse. However, after reading in the lay press some of the more sensational articles about the complications caused by the pill or the IUD, some women will consider barrier methods or periodic abstinence as their method of birth control. Sterilization in the form of vasectomy for males or tubal ligation and laparoscopy for females provide alternatives to birth control, especially for couples who consider their families complete. Safe and legal abortions are available to women who select the less effective but safer methods of contraception that might result in contraceptive failures or accidental pregnancies. The birth control revolution, which began with the advent of the pill, is now exploring new frontiers in the form of once-a-month pills or injections, capsules and implants, antipregnancy vaccines and antisperm drugs, the male pill, and reversible sterilization. Most of these methods, now in the testing stage, are expected to be available in the 1980s.

References

Bibring, G. "Some specific psychological tasks in pregnancy and motherhood." In S. Hammer (ed.). *Women: Body and culture.* New York: Penguin Books, 1975.

Brazelton, T. "Effects of prenatal drugs on the behavior of the neonate." *American Journal of Psychiatry,* 1970, 126, 1261-1266.

Commission on Population Growth and the American Future. *Population and the American Future.* Superintendent of Documents. Washington: Government Printing Office, 1972.

De Beauvoir, S. *The second sex.* New York: Alfred A. Knopf, 1953.

Dick-Read, G. *Childbirth without fear.* New York: Harper & Row, 1953.

Erikson, E. *Childhood and society.* New York: W. W. Norton, 1963.

Garcia, C. "Clinical aspects of oral hormone contraception." In M. Calderone (ed.). *Manual of family planning and contraceptive practice.* Baltimore: Williams and Wilkins, 1970.

Grant, E. and Pryse-Davies, J. "Effect of oral contraceptives on depressive mood changes and on endometrial monoamine oxidase and phosphates." *British Medical Journal.* 1968, 777-780.

House, A. "What contraceptive type are you?" *Ms. Magazine,* March 1973.

Jackson, H. "Chemical methods of contraception." *American Scientist,* 1973, 61, 188-193.

Johnson, D. "Female sterilization: Prognosis for simplified outpatient procedures." *Contraception,* 1972, 5, 155-163.

Leboyer, F. *Birth without violence.* New York: Alfred A. Knopf, 1975.

Masters, W. and Johnson, V. *Human sexual response.* Boston: Little, Brown, 1966.

Mayer, J. "Better educated mothers lead trend toward breastfeeding." *Houston Post,* August 20, 1972.

Morris, M. and Van Wagenen, G. "Interception: The use of postovulatory estrogens to prevent implantation." *American Journal of Obstetrics and Gynecology,* 1973, 115, 101-106.

Newton, M. "Breastfeeding." *Psychology Today,* 1968, 34, 68-70.

Plummer, G. "Anomalies occurring in children exposed in utero to the atomic bomb in Hiroshima." *Pediatrics,* 1952, 10, 687.

Rodgers, D. and Ziegler, F. "Psychological reactions to surgical contraception." In J. Fawcett, (ed.). *Psychological perspectives on population.* New York: Basic Books, 1973.

Rorvik, D. and Shettles, L. *Your baby's sex: Now you can choose.* New York: Dodd, Mead, 1970.

Sears, R., Maccoby, E., and Levin, H. *Patterns of childbearing.* Evanston: Row, Peterson, 1957.

Smith, E. "A follow-up study of women who request abortion." *American Journal of Orthopsychiatry,* 1973, 43, 575–585.

Solberg, D., Butler, J., and Wagner, N. "Sexual behavior in pregnancy." In N. Wagner (ed.). *Perspectives on human sexuality.* New York: Behavioral Publications, 1974.

Tanzer, D. "The psychology of natural childbirth." In H. Chiang and A. Maslow (eds.). *The healthy personality.* New York: D. Van Nostrand, 1977.

Chapter 8
Human Sexuality from an Intracultural Perspective

Although human sexual behavior is determined in part by genetic, biological, and constitutional factors, the most apparent variations in sexual styles and standards are influenced by psychological and sociocultural factors. Manifestations of sexuality, modes of sexual expressions, and the symbols and imagery associated with sex are particularly subject to cultural conditioning, embedded in the social matrix of a given culture. Davenport (1977) has argued that in every society sex is anchored in two directions.

> . . . in one direction it is moored to the potentialities and limitations of biological inheritance. In the other direction, it is tied to the internal logic and consistency of the total culture. . . .

In other words, although biological determinants define the potentialities of sexual behavior, it is through socialization and exposure to culturally specific norms that biological potentialities are shaped into distinctive expressions of sexuality.

In all cultures—primitive, illiterate, or postindustrial—society defines the boundaries between behaviors regarded as sexual and those considered nonsexual. Each culture dictates what is appropriate and inappropriate, normal and abnormal sexual behavior and prescribes who interacts with whom sexually. Society also determines how social norms and sexual behaviors are related to each other and to what degree the norms governing sexual practices change over time. For example, in Chapter 3 we noted that social norms regulating premarital intercourse have changed over the last two decades, resulting in a liberalization of sexual attitudes, particularly for females. Finally, in each society children are indoctrinated into the sexual ideology of their particular culture. Although societies differ substantially in what is prescribed, permitted, and proscribed sexually, most forms of sexual behavior are normatively regulated in all societies.

Sex and Society

If we are interested in why people in one particular culture or subculture think and behave differently sexually from people in another society or subgroup, we are entering the domains of sociology and anthropology. The sociologist departs from the assumption that society and its subunits, that is, families, communities, and subcultures, depend upon procreation and sexual relationships. Without sexual relationships no society could survive beyond one generation. One of the fundamental axioms of the sociological perspective is that we are social animals. Consequently, the social aspects of our sexual interactions account for the distinctiveness of human sexuality.

In addition to research comparing the sexual behavior of different cultures, studies of the sexual behavior and practices of different social groups have been made. These groups were classified according to certain social indices such as education, occupation, or religious affiliation. Both the studies and research have shown that absolute standards of sexual conduct do not exist. Instead, all forms of sexual behavior are culturally relative. Sexual practices permitted or encouraged among one segment of the population may be prohibited in another group.

Looking at sexual behaviors and values from a sociocultural perspective—intracultural as well as cross-cultural—can be helpful in surmounting the limitations imposed by our own individual standards as well as those prescribed by our culture. We have previously traced the historical, theoretical, and biological foundations of human sexuality. In this chapter, we shall focus our attention on sociocultural expressions and meanings of sexuality. We are concerned here with comparisons of different patterns of sexual behavior among people who are socially stratified according to class, religious conviction, urban or rural residence, and ethnic group membership. Our survey of intracultural differences in this chapter and our sampling of the sexual customs of different societies in the next chapter will illuminate certain universal aspects of sexuality that exist despite a multitude of idiosyncratic sexual habits. Both the intracultural and the cross-cultural view will help us to understand that members of a given society or subgroup do not select their sexual practices arbitrarily. Rather, in each culture or subculture, patterns of sexual behavior develop in relation to the customs, traditions, and beliefs of that culture.

The idea of intracultural differences in sexual attitudes and behaviors is based on the assumption that certain subgroups within our society display unique aspects of sexual behaviors. In addition, it is also assumed that members of different subcultures respond to cultural norms and expectations differently. If we categorize men and women according to certain social dimensions such as social class, religious affiliation, or ethnic background, we find that a single pattern of American sexual behavior does not exist. Sexual standards are defined according to the norms prevailing among a particular segment of the population. Within each group, whether middle class, Protestant, or black, specific sexual attitudes and practices are sanctioned, and members of the group are expected to conform to these standards. Behavioral discrepancies do exist, however; the Catholic Church's laws regarding contraception and Catholics' observance of these laws are not synonomous.

Indices of Social Class

By far the most commonly used social index is a person's class status. The concept of social class presumes that people can be ranked in hierarchal order according to one or more social indices such as income, occupation, or education. Of these three indices, income is usually regarded as a poor index of social class, since a person's social status is not necessarily determined by economic power. Many people among the working classes, for instance, have considerably higher incomes than, let us say, high school teachers, who belong to the middle class. In spite of their greater economic power, most men and women in the working classes usually do not enjoy or share the social status of a teacher.

Social class is a broad concept, and any definition necessarily encompasses a considerable number of people within one category. Frequently, the differences observed indicate tendencies toward different behavior rather than sharp distinctions. It is also important to remember that even though a person's behavior may be atypical for his or her class, it is nonetheless significantly influenced by the behavioral norms typical for the class.

For our discussion of the effects of social class on sexual behavior, we are assuming a multidimensional index of class commonly employed by social scientists. This index is based upon two dimensions of classification that appear to be most important in contemporary American society, namely, the level of education and occupational class. Both factors are, of course, related, since educational achievement determines to some degree the range of occupations a person can choose. In addition, educational and occupational levels are also associated with a variety of other factors, ranging from income to conceptualizations of masculinity and femininity.

For convenience, we have adopted a social class model according to which society is subdivided into four relatively discrete social classes. The first two are a "lower class," comprised largely of unskilled manual workers, and a "working class" of manual workers in semiskilled and skilled occupations. (At times, when clear-cut definitions of the laborer or semiskilled categories are difficult to make, these two classes will be referred to collectively as "the lower classes.") The third social group is made up of white collar workers and professionals who are categorized as "middle class." Socially, the middle class represents a rather heterogeneous category, ranging from a lower middle class of small shopkeepers, sales persons, and clerks to the upper middle class of professionals, managers, and proprietors, most of whom have at least some college training. Finally, there is a social elite or "upper class," differentiated from the middle class not so much in terms of occupational status as by wealth and lineage.

People in each of these social classes have a corresponding proportion of financial resources, prestige, and education—factors that are used to justify the class stratification. However, in spite of the class distinctions, there is considerable blurring and overlapping in our present class structure. In the case of sexual behavior, especially, it is often impossible to draw a rigid line between the sexual standards of the lower and the middle/upper classes; basic sexual attitudes do not alter as rapidly as place of work or income.

Comparison of Sexual Behavior in Lower and Upper Classes

Sociocultural studies investigating the relationship between social class and sexual behavior have concentrated on only a few areas, among them, marital and premarital intercourse, certain sexual practices, and specific sexual variations. Although these concerns are legitimate aspects of sexuality, having considerable social consequence, we must bear in mind that they reflect only a small proportion of the total scope of sexual expressions and styles.

The most comprehensive comparison of sexual activities and attitudes of men and women of different social classes was conducted by Kinsey and his associates (Kinsey et al., 1948; Kinsey et al., 1953). At the time he wrote the volume on male sexual behavior,

Kinsey was convinced that social class was more significant than any other factor affecting a person's sex life. As a matter of fact, Kinsey contended that differences in sexual practices and morals between lower and upper classes were as great as those existing between different cultures.

Using the combined education/occupation index of social class, Kinsey classified his respondents as follows (educational level was broken down into three categories):

1. 0-8 years of schooling
2. 9-12 years of schooling
3. 13+ years of schooling

In addition, the following occupational classes were recognized:

1. Underworld
2. Day labor
3. Semiskilled labor
4. Skilled labor
5. Lower white collar group
6. Upper white collar group
7. Professional group
8. Business executive group
9. Extremely wealthy group

According to the Kinsey reports, the sexually most active group consisted of males who had attended high school but did not go beyond the tenth grade and had no further education. On the other hand, college males emerged as the least active portion of the male population. The same distribution occurred among married men, with high school-educated males more sexually active than their college-educated counterparts. Overall sexual activity was measured by totaling various sexual behaviors, such as pre- and marital intercourse, masturbation, petting or homosexual contacts, into what Kinsey termed "total sexual outlets."

When the data were analyzed on the basis of occupation as the social class index, a similar differentiation was observed among the different occupational levels. Men who were categorized as semiskilled workers (occupational class 3) reported the greatest amount of sexual activity, whereas the skilled workers showed the lowest rates. Among the female sample the level of overall sexual activity was less strikingly affected by educational background or social class. As a matter of fact, not even premarital sex, which, as we will see, was most significantly influenced by social class among men, showed significant variations among women of different social backgrounds. The same was true for other sexual behaviors, for example, masturbation, petting, and intercourse. Kinsey hypothesized that females are less pressured to conform to the norms of a social group than males are. The failure to detect any marked social class differences among women, however, may have been obscured by the biases in Kinsey's male and female samples; they were proportionately unequal with respect to social class.

Masturbation and Social Class Differences

In addition to comparing men and women from different social classes in terms of their overall involvement in sexual activities, Kinsey and his colleagues also analyzed differences in specific sexual practices. It was found, for instance, that the highest frequencies of masturbation occurred among single males of college level and in the professional group. More specifically, during the late adolescence and early twenties, college-educated males masturbated nearly twice as often as did men of comparable age who never went beyond grade school. During these years masturbation accounted for 80 percent of the orgasms of the college group, compared with 52 percent of orgasms for males of lower edu-

cational and occupational levels. Among married men the differences in masturbation between lower and middle/upper class males were equally significant. More recently, Reiche (1971) has demonstrated that masturbation is still more frequently associated with a middle class background and less common among lower classes, who tend to view autoeroticism as a poor or "unnatural" substitute for heterosexual intercourse.

The frequency of masturbation is greater among higher socioeconomic groups for several reasons: (1) men and women from the higher social classes tend to have their first intercourse at a later date and therefore may practice masturbation longer; (2) masturbation requires imagination, a characteristic that tends to be associated with educational status; (3) cultural taboos against masturbation have less effect among the well educated than the poorly educated.

In spite of the considerable social class differences, masturbation emerged at Kinsey's time as the second most important source of sexual gratification in the life of the average American male in all social classes, second only to heterosexual intercourse. As might be expected, several other factors also influenced the frequency of masturbation. Among the more important ones were marital status, religious conviction, and family background.

A second sexual activity characteristic primarily of high school- and college-level men was heterosexual petting, which also occurred less frequently among males of lower and working classes. A generation after Kinsey, however, the social class differences in relation to masturbation and petting to climax are no longer quite as apparent. As a matter of fact, Hunt (1974) failed to find inhibitory effects of lower education on masturbation or petting.

Similar social class differences are documented in the Kinsey reports when attitudes toward oral sex and nudity are considered. Whereas many members of the upper social strata consider a certain amount of oral eroticism as a fundamental part of lovemaking, lower class people engage in oral sex less frequently. Although there has been a dramatic increase in oral-genital stimulation since Kinsey's generation (Hunt, 1974), social class differences still exist. For example, in the 1970s oral sex had become part of the sexual repertory of approximately 55 percent of males at the high school level compared with 63 percent for college-educated males. Although comparative data from the lowest classes are missing, we may assume that oral-genital sex is even less popular at the lower- and working-class level.

Nudity and Social Class Differences

With regard to nudity, Kinsey found that there is a greater acceptance of nudity among the middle and upper social levels than among the lower classes. At least a generation ago nudity was an essential erotic component of intercourse for higher status people (90 percent in Kinsey's sample reportedly made love in the nude regularly), whereas only 43 percent of the men and women who never went beyond grade school regularly experienced intercourse without clothing. Twenty to twenty-five years ago, attitudes toward nudity were more closely tied in with social class than they are today. Typically, many more upper class people had the opportunity to visit other countries such as France with its burlesque shows or the nudist colonies along the North Atlantic beaches, where mores regarding the nude body were more relaxed. In addition, more men and women at higher levels of education have developed an appreciation for artistic representations of the nude male or female body. Among the lower classes nudity was always closer to perversion and rarely appreciated as a source of sensual stimulation.

Many sociologists have argued that the in-

sistence on intercourse with some clothes on is not so much a result of the lack of privacy that often exists in the small, restricted quarters of lower-class people but a reflection of a different underlying attitude, namely, that nudity is obscene. In the absence of recent data assessing lower-class attitudes toward nudity, we can only assume that traditions against nude intercourse have probably relaxed among the younger generation as a result of more liberal sexual attitudes in all social classes.

Premarital Sex and Social Class Differences

Of all sexual activities, social class differences in premarital intercourse have attracted most of the research attention (Figure 8.1). The first Kinsey report provided a wealth of data supporting the notion that persons of higher socioeconomic classes were more conservative in their premarital sexual relations, while persons of lower social status were more liberal. Only about two-thirds of Kinsey's college males, for instance, had experienced sex before marriage compared with nearly all the males who never went beyond high school. Similarly, Kinsey found that by the age of twenty-five only 10 percent of the unmarried males with eighth-grade educations were virgins compared with 16 percent of men with high school educations and 36 percent of college males who reportedly never had premarital intercourse. Furthermore, the college educated males who had had premarital sex engaged in intercourse with the girl they intended to marry, while lower class males were much more indiscriminate in their premarital relations. For example, at all ages, men with grade school educations engaged more frequently in premarital sex with prostitutes than did men at the high school or college level.

A second major social class difference in premarital sex concerned the age when inter-

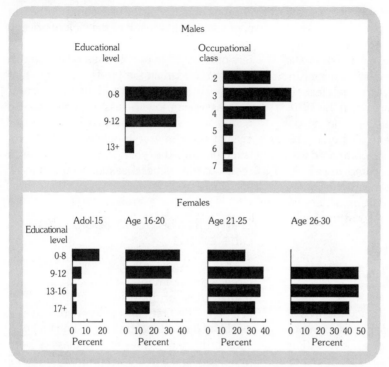

Figure 8.1
Social class differences in premarital intercourse: (a) males; (b) females.

course was first engaged in before marriage. Characteristically, men with little education started having premarital intercourse five to six years earlier—in many cases in preadolescence—than those with more education.

Although the social class differences among women were far less striking, they followed a similar pattern. The less-educated women had experienced intercourse earlier than those with high school or college educations. For example, between the ages of sixteen and twenty, 82 percent of the girls who were entering colleges had not had intercourse compared with 62 percent who did not go to college. However, at the time of marriage the relationship reversed itself, and a greater proportion of college girls had experienced premarital sex compared with the less-educated women. The reason for this reversal stems from the fact that women from

lower social strata marry at an earlier age, whereas girls from higher social classes encounter their first sexual relationship later.

Given the smaller social class differences for girls, a number of observations are noteworthy. First, lower-class girls experienced more frequent premarital intercourse than upper middle class boys. Second, although lower-class boys have much of their sexual experience with a limited number of girls (prostitutes or promiscuous girls), lower-class girls still had more premarital sexual encounters than girls from higher classes.

Reiss (1963) contributed additional data regarding premarital permissiveness of women from lower-class backgrounds. He found that upward mobility, that is, aspiring to move toward a higher social class, is an important factor in influencing the premarital behavior of lower-class women. In Reiss's study, upwardly mobile women were more restrictive in their premarital sexual activities than the women in the class they were moving toward. Apparently, these women are reluctant to engage in sexual behaviors that might interfere with their mobility. This finding provides an interesting contrast to an earlier study (Kanin and Howard, 1958), which reported that the incidence of premarital sex was highest for couples in which the husband was of higher social class than his wife, intermediate for couples in which both spouses came from the same class, and lowest for couples in which the wife was from a higher social class than the husband.

A possible explanation for these seemingly contradictory results may be found in the different sociocultural climates of the 1950s and the 1960s. During the 1950s it was possible for a woman from a lower socioeconomic background to marry into a higher social class, thereby elevating her social status, by granting her partner sexual favors that would have been denied by women of his own class. In other words, premarital permissiveness in the 1950s served as a means to achieve upward mobility. In the 1960s, however, many voices, particularly those of the feminist movement, vehemently rejected the treatment of women as sex objects. Women moved up the social ladder for different reasons: personal competence or professional achievement.

When reexamining the relationship between social class and premarital sexual behavior based on a national adult sample and a two-state student sample (New York and Virginia) in the 1960s, Reiss (1965) failed to observe the negative correlation between premarital permissiveness and social class. Neither sample, adult and college, demonstrated the expected relationship. This suggested that the differences found by Kinsey may have been obscured by other sociocultural factors. Reiss commented that a person's general attitudes toward premarital sex

may vary along a conservative to liberal continuum for the different social classes. This general attitudinal outlook may have at least as much influence on sexual beliefs as a person's socioeconomic position. In other words, a person with liberal sexual attitudes is more likely to condone or engage in premarital intercourse than a person with conservative attitudes, regardless of social class membership. Viewed this way, the differences between Kinsey's and Reiss's results are at least in part a function of differences in the two samples. Kinsey's sample, for instance, especially in the upper class, was disproportionately involved in conservative settings, including fraternities, social clubs, and religious groups that maintained a strong censorship over premarital sex.

A second difference in the two studies revolves around attitudes toward premarital intercourse and premarital sexual behavior. In the Reiss study attitudes were measured, whereas Kinsey's inquiry was measured by the frequency of intercourse before marriage. It is conceivable that the frequency of premarital sex is negatively related to social class while attitudes toward sex before marriage are not. According to this idea, middle- and upper-class people may behave less permissively than they feel is proper, whereas lower-class people behave more permissively than they believe is proper.

Although Reiss failed to elucidate similar class differences, as Kinsey did, his study did reveal one important difference between upper and lower classes. Higher-status people stressed affection as a prerequisite in premarital relationships, while men and women from the lower classes were much less concerned with the emotional component of the relationship.

Use of Contraceptives in Different Social Classes

Social class differences in premarital sex are also reflected in the use of contraceptives.

Kanter and Zelnik (1974), for example, found that greater and more consistent use of contraceptives is typically associated with higher socioeconomic status. In their investigation of the contraceptive behavior of a national sample of never-married women between the ages of fifteen and nineteen, they reported that two-thirds of the women whose parents were college educated had used contraception at last intercourse compared with less than one-third of the girls of parents with elementary school educations. Furthermore, the girls from the lower social strata were more likely not to use any method of contraception at all. Increase in social status generally meant more reliance on the pill as the preferred means of contraception. Middle- and upper-class girls not only tended to use contraceptive methods more often, but also selected the more effective technique in comparison with lower-status girls.

Since the use of contraceptives is less consistent and effective among lower-class girls, the probability of premarital pregnancy is relatively high. Premarital pregnancy is inversely related to social class (Lowrie, 1965). It has been estimated that as many as one-half of lower-class girls are pregnant at some time before marriage.

Marital Satisfaction and Social Class Differences

For all social classes in the Kinsey reports marital intercourse represented the major type of sexual activity for most men and women. Furthermore, at all social levels the belief prevails that the missionary position is most appropriate for marital intercourse. In the Kinsey studies few differences were found attesting to significant variations in marital intercourse at different social levels. However, even though the frequency of marital sex does not differ significantly, there are some interesting qualitative variations among lower- and middle- and upper-class couples. Men and women in the lower classes usually make love in the missionary position and show little versatility in positional variations. According to the Kinsey data, 35 percent of college-educated women used the female superior position, while only 17 percent of the couples with grade school education indicated that they had used this position. Lower-class males especially consider the female-above position a perversion. They also rationalize that the female superior position is degrading because the male loses his powers of control and authority under such circumstances.

Rainwater (1966) noted that couples from lower, working, and middle classes also evaluated marital sex differently, expressing dissimilar views about the gratification and dissatisfactions experienced in marital intercourse. In the range from higher to lower social class, it was shown that the proportion of men and women who show strong interest and enjoyment of sex declines. Among men the proportion expressing only mild interest in marital relations increased from middle to lower class, while the proportion of women who were not affirmative in their sexual attitudes increased systematically from the middle to the lower-lower class. According to these findings, social class affects the way in which couples regard marital sex as a meaningful activity.

A major factor relevant to these class differences concerns the quality of the role relationships among husbands and wives in different classes. Middle-class couples have been found to emphasize joint activities in and around the home, while the role relationships of lower-class couples stress the separate responsibilities and interests of husbands and wives. Lower-class males, for instance, have been found to show more reluctance about sharing household tasks—considered the exclusive domain of women. In addition, they have a greater need to

Table 8.1

Social Class Differences in Attitudes Toward Marital Sexuality (in percentages)

Attitude	Social Class		
	Middle	Upper-Lower	Lower-Lower
Husbands			
Highly positive	78	75	44
Mildly positive	22	25	56
No. of cases	56	56	59
Wives			
Highly positive	50	53	20
Mildly positive	36	16	26
Slightly negative	11	27	34
Totally negative	3	4	20
No. of cases	58	68	69

Adapted from Rainwater, L. "Some aspects of lower class sexuality." *Journal of Social Issues,* 1966, 2, 96-107.

adhere to the masculine stereotype of toughness and dominance, and their women tend to be more passive than their middle-class counterparts. The traditional belief in the inequality of the sexes is still firmly entrenched in the lower and working classes.

To explain these qualitative differences in marital relationships, Rainwater introduced the concept of "conjugal role relationships" to account for social class differences in marital sex. Couples who showed a high degree of separateness in their roles as husband and wife were classified as "highly segregated," whereas couples whose relationship was characterized by joint participation and involvement were labeled "jointly organized." Between these extremes were those marriages in which some degree of separateness (intermediate) determined the role relationship of husband and wife. Lack of interest in marital sex and rejecting attitudes toward marital relations occurred mostly among couples who assigned highly segregated and specific tasks to each spouse. Couples who emphasize individual activities and responsibilities in their daily interactions also seem to carry this segregation into their sexual relationships.

Highly segregated couples were mostly found among the lower classes, where hardly any joint-participation patterns were observed. Since lower-class husbands place little emphasis on mutual gratification during intercourse and make few efforts to assist their wives in achieving sexual gratification, it is not surprising that lower-class wives are more likely to complain about their husbands' lack of consideration during intercourse. Forty percent of the lower-class wives in the highly segregated marital relationships indicated that their husbands were inconsiderate of them during lovemaking, compared with only seven percent of the wives whose marriages were based on sharing, cooperative relationships. In addition, women in segregated marriages were more likely to look upon sex as a duty or a means of physiological relief rather than emphasizing the emotional component of marital sex stemming from closeness and love.

In the area of marital sex, then, we find considerable qualitative differences among lower- and upper-class couples, in spite of the fact that the frequency of marital intercourse shows few variations among men and women from different social backgrounds. Among middle- and upper-class couples, joint involvement in each other's activities seems to facilitate a marital relationship in which both partners express more interest in sexual relations than lower-class couples do. Since the overall marital relationship is built on togetherness, sharing, and mutual involvement, these qualities also extend into the sexual relationship, encouraging husband and wife to pursue mutual gratification in the sexual sphere as well.

The picture that emerges from the research relating sexual behavior to social class reflects a lower-class sexual style that differs qualitatively from that of the middle and upper class. The sexual behavior of lower-class men and women may be characterized by an emphasis on genital performance, compared with the more varied and diverse sex life of individuals of higher social status. In addition, in the lower classes, intercourse is viewed primarily as a male activity, something many women feel they must "put up with." Whereas many people in the lower class prefer simplicity, directness, and a relatively straightforward approach to sex, men and women in the higher social strata are sexually more elaborate and versatile. They engage in a wider range of sexual activities, are aroused by a greater variety of sexual as well as nonsexual stimulation, and are more devoted to the art of love. Sex among the lower classes, by contrast, is focused primarily on ejaculation, with little interest in foreplay or afterplay. Members of the middle and upper classes are more likely to look upon sex as a positive, fulfilling force in life, whereas sex for the lower-class person is often an isolated activity, divorced from the total context of living. Greater freedom from

economic concerns gives upper-class people more time and opportunity to participate in sexual activities for the sake of pleasure. For the lower-class person, sex is not so much engaged in for its own sake but for such functional purposes as relief from tension.

Although the origins of diverse sexual philosophies in the lower and middle/upper classes are not completely understood, they probably can be ascribed, at least in part, to the intellectual advantages of men and women in higher social strata. With more education, men and women often develop a finer sense of imagination, which makes them more receptive to genital as well as nongenital stimuli. In addition, the educated person is more open to less traditional interpretations of the male and female role in sexual relationships. For example, it has been shown that lower-class people still place a great deal more emphasis on "the double standard" than people from higher social classes. The double standard condones certain sexual activities for males but discourages them for women. According to working-class philosophy, boys are expected to engage in sexual relations whenever the opportunity arises and pride themselves on their sexual conquests. There is a lot of bragging, quite often exaggerated, among slum adolescents about their sexual prowess. Such prowess represents a valuable currency within the peer group.

Lower-class women, however, are often evaluated rather rigidly according to the extent of their promiscuity. The "one man's woman" is respected to some extent by her peers, especially when she ultimately marries the man with whom she has had premarital sex. Women who have premarital intercourse with several men are often labeled "promiscuous" or an "easy lay." The continued adherence to the double standard tends to ridicule or penalize lower-class women when they deviate from the prescribed pattern. Thus the lower-class woman finds herself in the difficult position of having to use sex in order to maintain her relationship with her man, but does so at the risk of losing both the man and her reputation. Consequently, lower-class sex norms tend to be much more rigid and less open to individual interpretation than those of men and women further up the social scale. Since people in the upper classes have greater freedom to make more effective choices in professional as well as recreational activities, they are less rigidly restricted by traditional stereotypic conceptions of masculinity and femininity.

Finally, each social class seems to rationalize its sexual behavior differently. Upper and middle class sexual morality is usually based on what is right and wrong, and many sexual practices are evaluated as moral issues. At the lower social levels sexual behavior is most often rationalized on the basis of what is "natural or unnatural" (Kohn, 1969). Masturbation and oral sex, for instance, are unnatural substitutes for heterosexual intercourse, where premarital sex is considered natural and hence accepted.

Since the publication of the Kinsey reports, several authors (Reiss, 1963; Sears, Maccoby, and Levin, 1957) have argued that social class is no longer as important a factor in sexual behavior and attitudes as once thought, partially because social class distinctions are no longer as rigidly adhered to as in the past. Although many people still marry within their social class, crossing class lines is no longer uncommon. More men than women, however, have selected a spouse from a lower social class. Conversely, more women than men have raised their social status by marriage since it is usually the husband who establishes the social position of a couple. Finally, over the last decade men, and to a somewhat lesser extent women, have also been able to elevate their social status by economic or professional excellence.

The subtle shifts in social structure, changing conceptualizations of masculine and feminine roles in all areas of life, and the increasing commitment of women to careers rather than homemaking have created a need to redefine our approach to the study of the relationship between social class and sexual behavior. More specifically, we have to produce social groups that actually share a common style of life. Men and women who generally agree on a conservative or liberal approach to sexuality are probably more likely to engage in similar sexual behaviors than people who earn a comparable salary or have gone to school the same number of years. This is not to say that a person's life and sexual style are not in part a consequence of income and education. However, at different socioeconomic levels sexual mores and practices may reflect a set of attitudes and values that varies independently of conventional indices of social status. In other words, it seems reasonable to assume that our social and moral values have at least as much influence on our sexual beliefs and standards as does our socioeconomic position.

Sex and Religion

Religious background is another criterion for distinguishing relatively discrete social groups. For many people religious dogma offers a major source of official sexual values. Most religious teachings impose restrictions on the sexual behavior of their followers, claiming that the church's official sexual code will not only protect the sanctity of the home but also guarantee a high level of sexual gratification over a long period of time. Recognizing a couple's twenty-fifth or fiftieth wedding anniversary exemplifies the church's sanction of marital sex.

Christian and Jewish Doctrines of Procreational Sex

Both Christian and Jewish doctrines interpret sex in the context of procreation. Al-

Figure 8.2
Religious doctrines may exert a restraining
influence on sexual behavior. (Metropolitan
Museum of Art, Cloisters Collection, Purchase.)

quently, masturbation, premarital sex, extramarital sex, and homosexuality are considered sinful and hence condemned by many
Western religions. In recent years, however,
many churches have relaxed some of their
restrictions. Some religious communities (at
least in their official publications) are expressing the view that masturbation for both men
and women may be considered as a complementary sexual experience at appropriate
times in their lives. Only 29 percent of priests,
for instance, are willing to say that adolescent
masturbation is a serious sin (Greeley, 1972).
Today, the main difference among religious
groups is not so much in the lack of tolerance
expressed toward masturbation but in how
much guilt it arouses in the religious person.

In spite of some fundamental similarities in
sexual morality among various religions, different churches express divergent opinions
about specific issues related to sexuality. On
the issue of divorce, for instance, the differences range from rigid prohibition to some
acceptance. Catholicism regards the preservation of the family and home as paramount
and rejects the dissolution of a marriage.
Among Protestants and Jews, on the other
hand, there is a greater leniency.

Religious Views of Contraception and Abortion

The Catholic church is equally conservative in regard to contraceptives and abortion.
In the past, the use of all contraceptive procedures except abstinence and the rhythm
method was regarded as sinful. Recently,
however, Catholicism and the Jewish religion
have become more tolerant of birth control.
Protestant denominations generally allow the
use of contraceptives for family planning.
Both the Catholic as well as the Jewish religion strongly opposes abortion. Since the
Catholic church holds the view that human
life begins at the moment of conception, a
human being is "murdered" in the process of
abortion. Therefore, even therapeutic abor-

though the orthodox Jewish code and the
traditional Catholic interpretation of sexual
morality are quite dissimilar, they share the
view that sexual activities that do not offer the
possibility of procreation within the context
of marriage are morally wrong. Conse-

tions performed to save the life of the mother have usually been discouraged. Among Jews, abortions were forbidden as a means of limiting family size, but were acceptable when the life of the mother was endangered or when the fetus was deformed or defective. In spite of the different viewpoints espoused by the various churches in relation to contraception and abortion, statistics from birth control and abortion clinics show that there are no differences in the number of Protestant, Catholic, or Jewish women who come for assistance.

Effects of Religious Devoutness on Sexual Behavior

The restraining influence of religious devoutness is reflected in a number of empirical studies. Kinsey et al. (1948) reported that the sexually least active individuals in any age and educational group were orthodox Jews, devout Catholics, and churchgoing Protestants (in that order). Conversely, the most active were nonchurchgoing Catholics, noninvolved Protestants, and nonreligious Jews (in that order). Religiously active men and women engage in intercourse less frequently and adhere to more conservative sex norms. The negative relationship between religious conviction and sexual morality is much stronger for women than for men. As a matter of fact, among Kinsey's female sample religion emerged as the only social factor of unquestionable importance. At all age levels religious devoutness had a powerful and inhibitive influence on the sexual behavior of women. Religious women had significantly lower rates of masturbation, petting, and intercourse and achieved orgasm less often than nonreligious women. Kinsey intuitively blamed "frigidity" on the moral restraints imposed by religion. Masters and Johnson (1966) later substantiated Kinsey's hypothesis when they found that religious orthodoxy was a major factor in a number of sexual dysfunctions (see Chapter 14).

Among the married women of the Kinsey study there was little relationship between sexual behavior and religious devotion. This is not surprising, since intercourse between husband and wife is the one form of sexual activity that many churches not only condone but also impose as a duty. Reiss (1965) basically confirmed Kinsey's findings. Religious devotion was measured by church attendance, and frequent attendance was defined as attending religious services more than once a month. Frequent attendance, according to this definition, was associated with conservative sexual standards. For example, only one-third of regular churchgoers accepted premarital intercourse, compared with the two-thirds who attended church less often.

One of the most outspoken critics of the restrictive sexual code advocated by many Christian denominations and Judaism was Freud (1961). He was firmly convinced that religions are responsible for neurotic rather than mature solutions of conflicts involved in sexual adjustment and the attainment of sexual maturity.

Recently, there has been a considerable effort on the part of many religious denominations to formulate a basis for ethical judgment of sexual behavior that would accommodate changes in our thinking about sexuality. Many church leaders are reexamining religious teachings and official positions in matters of sex. A number of churches are beginning to abolish their restrictions on private sexual acts and are becoming more accepting of different sexual life-styles. Similarly, only 40 percent of the priests in this country still support official church teachings on birth control. Today many churches provide their members with factual information on human sexuality and an equal number support sex-education programs in public schools. In a recent position statement, Smith (1974), speaking primarily for the Protestant church, emphasized the need to provide guidelines for sexual decisions in specific situations, rather than prescribing universal rules for sexual conduct.

Sex and Place of Residence

The social index of residence raises the question of whether men and women living in cosmopolitan areas differ in their pattern of sexual behavior from people who reside in less populated rural areas. Unfortunately, there is little systematic research comparing the sexual activities of people living in large urban areas with those of nonurban populations. The Kinsey reports showed that people in rural populations had fewer sexual contacts, such as petting or premarital intercourse, primarily because of the lack of opportunity. Kinsey also reported that about 17 percent of farm boys, mainly adolescents, had sexual relations with animals for either intercourse or masturbation. Erotic excitement was also experienced from fondling and stroking animals. Rural boys have also been found to act in a sexually aggressive way toward farm animals, prodding them both rectally and vaginally with long sticks to such a degree that the animals needed medical attention. In most cases, however, sexual activities involving farm animals represent isolated events during adolescence and usually do not preclude heterosexual satisfactions later (see Chapter 15). Among urban adolescents, house pets are rarely used as sexual objects.

A generation after Kinsey, Harrison, Bennett, Globetti, and Alsikafi (1974) found in their study of a rural Mississippi community that differences in sexual behavior between rural and urban populations are largely a matter of attitudes and values. Youth, particularly those living in isolated rural areas, tend to adhere to more conservative sexual standards and are more likely to support the double standard of male dominance than young people raised in cities.

Sex and Ethnic Background

On the basis of the foregoing discussion we have examined different sexual styles and forms of sexual morality among various social groups. These groups differed in terms of level of education, occupational class, religious affiliation, and place of residence. A final intracultural dimension is ethnic background. Many ethnic groups, first-generation Americans and originally immigrants, are usually conservative in their attitudes toward sexuality. There are, however, considerable differences among subcultures of different cultural heritages. These differences are a result not only of historical experience but also of the educational and economic opportunities afforded them after integration into American society.

Stereotypes of Black Sexuality

Black Americans represent a large ethnic group in contemporary society. Over the past few years a popular myth of "black sexuality" has developed. The black male especially is often portrayed as a supermale whose virility and sexual drive far exceeds the abilities of white males. In popular music, folklore, and the media the black male is depicted as a "stud" with huge genitals and insatiable sexual cravings.

The literature on black sexuality has long stressed the greater degree of permissiveness among blacks. Kinsey (Kinsey et al., 1953), for instance, reported that black girls in their teens had had premarital intercourse three to four more times than white girls from the same social class. In black ghetto communities, for instance, more than 60 percent of grammar school-educated girls had had intercourse by the age of fifteen (Rainwater, 1966). Similarly, Broderick (1965) found that black boys between twelve and thirteen years showed a high incidence of heterosexual involvement; white boys of the same ages, on the other hand, displayed a greater degree of sexual reserve. Black men and women generally experience intercourse earlier, a greater number of illegitimate and extramarital pregnancies, higher divorce, separation, and desertion rates than do whites of comparable socioeconomic classes.

The greater degree of permissiveness among blacks has been viewed as a consequence of a long-standing tradition. Black men and women, it has been suggested (Reiss, 1965), have been always more permissive since they have less social standing to lose. According to this view, the differences between the races reflect a general difference between more or less permissive ethnic subgroups in our society. The interpretation of more or less permissive subcultures is further supported by differences between two extreme groups—black men as the most permissive and white women as the least permissive. White women's permissiveness is affected by church attendance and romantic love, whereas the behavior of black men is not influenced by these variables.

Interracial Sexual Relationships

Sexual relationships between white and black people usually evoke strong societal reactions from both races. These may range from stares and expressions of curiosity to overt acts of hostility or violence. Mixed couples reportedly have been attacked by strangers in the streets. All studies of racial attitudes emphasize the continuing resistance to interracial sexual relations. Despite the threats and barriers, however, interracial sex occurs even in parts of the country where legislation prohibits black-white relations.

In view of such resistance, it is interesting to examine the motives of men and women who form interracial sexual relations. Masters (1962) cited the lure of the forbidden, the naturalness and primitive sensuality of black people as important elements in the attrac-

Figure 8.3
Interracial couple. (United Press International, Inc.)

tion of mixed couples. In some cases, black men of higher occupational positions enter into sexual relationships with lower-class white women for whom the union obviously means an otherwise unattainable upward move. According to the exchange theory of interpersonal attraction, the social status of the black men is exchanged for the women's white skin, much in the same way as relevant commodities are traded in the economic marketplace.

The literature on interpersonal adjustment of mixed couples is very sparse. In one study of black-white couples residing in New York City (Smith, 1966), none of the participants revealed any sexual experiences that would substantiate popular beliefs about the existence of unusual sexual attraction between the two races. All the couples agreed that there is little basis in fact to support the notion of the allegedly greater virility of the black male. Reportedly, individual personality characteristics outweighed the importance of sexual attraction. Most of the participants described their relationship in terms of high levels of communication and intimacy rather than its sexual aspects.

Black sexuality is varied in nature and does not subscribe to a uniform code of sexual behavior. From the limited data available it seems that black men and women feel less pressure to conform to traditional conceptualizations of masculinity and femininity. Black working-class males, for instance, have been found to be more expressive in their relationships with women than white lower-class men. Similarly, among educated blacks who have attained economic or educational success, women seem to experience less conflict over achievement and career aspirations than white women do.

Sexual Ideology of Mexican Americans

Mexican Americans represent an ethnic group whose sexual values are determined by a male superior-female inferior ideology. The sexual ideal of this ethnic group is epitomized in the concept of machismo, an exaggerated concept of masculinity. The term reflects the overbearing attitude of Latin-American men toward women, which demands menial services and subservience. The machismo concept not only imposes a rigid role structure upon males but forces women into equally inflexible roles. The female must accept the high value placed on fertility and childbearing, tolerate male opposition to birth control and the extramarital affairs of Mexican American men. Because many women of this culture feel inferior to men, they tend to perpetuate the myth of the hypermasculine male. A comparison of the stereotype of the black supermale and the Mexican American who is *muy macho* provides an interesting example of how two different subcultures can subscribe to an almost identical male image. In both cultures, however, the male-female relationship is governed by altogether different sociosexual norms: black women have con-

siderably more sexual freedom than Mexican American women. Although these two groups—black, and Mexican Americans—represent only a limited sample of ethnic variations in our society, they demonstrate that social, political, and cultural forces influence sexuality in intricate and important ways.

Summary

In this chapter we have seen that expressions of sexuality are subject to constant modification as a result of social and cultural experiences. Social factors combine and interact with biological determinants of sexual behavior to produce divergent sexual styles.

A complex society like ours includes not a single culture of sex but many different subcultures that influence segments of the population. The Kinsey studies investigated the sexual behavior of men and women who were classified in discrete social groups according to education, occupational class, or religious affiliation. In Kinsey's day, social class emerged as the single most important factor, influencing sexual activities such as petting, masturbation, premarital intercourse, or homosexual contacts. Differences in sexual behavior, according to Kinsey, were a result of varying socioeconomic strata, ranging from the lower working class to the elite upper class. This was true regardless of whether social class was categorized on the basis of educational level or occupational class. By contrast, religious affiliation had a marked effect on the sexual behavior of women in the female sample. Religiously devout women were considerably more sexually inhibited than nonreligious women.

Since Kinsey's work, other less extensive studies have revealed sexual codes endemic to urban or rural populations, racial or ethnic minorities. Various broad differences among different social groupings, first pointed out by

Kinsey, have remained relatively constant. These include the positive correlation between frequency of masturbation or length of foreplay and the upper class, early sexual experience and the lower class, and homosexuality and the middle class. However, the majority of variations in sexual patterns among the different segments of our population occur in the area of sexual attitudes and values rather than in actual differences in frequency of types of sexual expression. Many popularly perceived differences in sexual behavior, such as the supervirility of the black male, are based on misconceptions or prejudices.

Research that focuses on sociocultural aspects of human sexuality, particularly from the intracultural perspective, needs to be redirected to more meaningful social factors. Level of education and occupational class, long considered the most relevant social factors, are not the most significant indices to contemporary society. Recent shifts in social structures, the increased opportunities for members of all social strata to move up and down the social ladder, and the effects of the women's liberation movement on the sociosexual attitudes of men and women seem to suggest that social classification is becoming more and more complex.

References

Broderick, C. "Social heterosexual development among Negroes and whites." *Journal of Marriage and Family.* 1965, 27, 2, 200-203.

Davenport, W. "Sex in cross-cultural perspective." In F. Beach (ed.), *Human sexuality in four perspectives.* Baltimore: Johns Hopkins University Press, 1977.

Freud, S. *The future of an illusion.* In *The complete psychological works Sigmund Freud,* Vol. 21, pp. 5-56. London: Hogarth Press, 1961.

Greeley, A. *Priests in the United States.* Garden City, N.Y.: Doubleday, 1972.

Harrison, D., Bennett, W., and Alsikafi, M. "Premarital sexual standards of rural youth." *Journal of Sex Research,* 1974, 10, 4, 266-277.

Hunt, M. *Sexual behavior in the 1970's.* New York: Dell Books, 1974.

Kanin, E. and Howard, J. "Postmarital consequences of premarital sex adjustments." *American Sociological Review,* 1958, 23, 556-562.

Kanter, J. and Zelnik, M. "Contraception and pregnancy: Experience of young unmarried women in the United States." In N. Wagner (ed.), *Perspectives on human sexuality.* New York: Behavioral Publications, 1974.

Kinsey, A., Pomeroy, W., and Martin, C. *Sexual behavior in the human male.* Philadelphia: W. B. Saunders, 1948.

Kinsey, A., Pomeroy, W., Martin, C. and Gebhard, P. *Sexual behavior in the human female.* Philadelphia: W. B. Saunders, 1953.

Kohn, M. *Class and conformity.* Homewood, Ill.: Dorsey, 1969.

Lowrie, S. "Early marriage: premarital pregnancy and associated factors." *Journal of Marriage and Family,* 1965, 27, 48.

Masters, R. *Forbidden sexual behavior and morality.* New York: Julian Press, 1962.

Masters, W. and Johnson, V. *Human sexual response.* Boston: Little, Brown, 1966.

Nicassio, P. "Social class and family size as determinants of attributed machismo, femininity, and family planning: A field study in two South American communities." *Sex Roles*, 1977, 3, 6, 577-598.

Rainwater, L. "Some aspects of lower class sexuality." *Journal of Social Issues*, 1966, 2, 96-107.

Reiche, R. *Sexuality and class struggle*. New York: Praeger, 1971.

Reiss, I. "Sociological studies of sexual behavior. In G. Winokur (ed.). *Determinants*. Springfield, Ill.: Charles C. Thomas, 1963.

Reiss, I. "Social class and premarital permissiveness: A re-examination." *American Sociological Review*, 1965, 30, 747-756.

Sears, R., Maccoby, E., and Levin, H. *Patterns of childrearing*. New York: Harper and Row, 1957.

Smith, C. "Negro-white intermarriage: Forbidden sexual union." *Journal of Sex Research*, 1966, 2, 3, 169-177.

Smith, L. *Religion's response to the new sexuality*. SIECUS Report, 1974, 4, 2. New York: Sex Information and Education Council of the U.S., Inc., 1974.

Chapter 9
Human Sexuality from an Intercultural Perspective

A book on human sexuality would not be complete without some consideration of the sexual behavior of people in other cultures. Although there are distinctive variations among the different subcultures in our own society, the differences between American sexual ideology and the sexual practices and mores of other Western and non-Western societies are even more striking.

Anthropological research testifies that great variations in sexual-behavior patterns exist among people of different cultures. One of the earliest important descriptions of the sexual practices of a foreign culture was presented by anthropologist Bronislaw Malinowski (1884-1942), who lived for several years during World War I on the island of Boyawa, the largest of the Trobriand Islands, northwest of Guinea. Malinowski was particularly interested in comparing two South Pacific societies located in close proximity to each other, the Trobriand and the Amphett islanders. The inhabitants of these two islands are very similar in race and language. Yet the Trobrianders had considerably more sexual freedom than the Amphett group which lived under strict prohibitions. Malinowski found neurotic behavior to be low among the Trobrianders but high among the Amphett islanders. He viewed his findings as evidence in support of Freud's hypothesis that sexual repression is a critical factor in neuroses (Malinowski, 1929).

Collaborating on a study of sexual behavior in 191 different societies, Ford and Beach (1951) have provided us with a broad perspective of many divergent and culturally unique aspects of sexuality. Their survey particularly emphasized the importance of cross-cultural studies of sexuality as an unparalleled means of enlarging our understanding of sexual behavior. The authors pointed out that the intercultural perspective affords us a much broader and more diversified view of sexuality than the perspective offered by our own culture.

Sexual behavior means many different things among the peoples of various cultures. Even the meaning of the word sexual and the behaviors summarized under this appellation are highly cultural. Erotic behaviors in one culture may be entirely unrelated to sex in another society. For example, among the French, a kiss and an embrace among members of the opposite sex are considered a simple act of greeting, whereas in our own society the kiss is part of our sexual-behavior repertory. By the same token, there are cultures, past and present, in which most aspects of sexuality are considered sinful and ugly, while other societies regard the same behaviors as beautiful. Patterns of human sexual behavior viewed from a cross-cultural perspective cover a vast spectrum of sexual expressions, ranging from the "puritanical" Irish of Inis Beag (the pseudonym for a small community on an island off the coast of Ireland) at one extreme to the Polynesians of the South Pacific, who are renowned for sexual freedom.

Universally, most cultures are concerned in some ways with social control over the sexual behavior of its members. Again, different societies display tremendous variations in the extent to which they tolerate or prohibit various sexual activities. In some cultures premarital intercourse is virtually enforced, whereas it may be severely penalized in others. However, such premarital relations cannot be equated with promiscuity since they are subject to some control within the culture. In most societies that condone or encourage premarital intercourse, gaining sexual experience before marriage is viewed as a necessary part of maturational learning.

Similarly, homosexuality may be entirely absent in some societies, for example, among the Mangaians of the South Seas (Marshall, 1971); yet homosexual acts may occur extensively in other societies, for example, among the Melanesians of East Bay, where nearly every male is predominantly homo-

Figure 9.1
The traditional Polynesian "Fia-Fia" dance on the island of Niue in the South Pacific. (United Nations)

sexual at some time in his life. Ford and Beach (1951) were able to gather information about the incidence or lack of homosexuality in seventy-six societies of their total sample of 191. They reported that in 64 percent of these cultures at least some form of homosexual behavior was socially condoned or encouraged. In the other societies, social reactions following the discovery of homosexual acts ranged from ridicule to the death penalty. Among many societies, such as the Trobrianders, homosexuality is not so much a societal taboo as a subject for jokes and social ostracism.

In other societies the man who assumes the feminine role in homosexual relationships is regarded as a powerful shaman. Among the Siberian Chukchee, such a person puts on female clothing, mimics feminine mannerisms, and may assume the role of the "wife" of another man. In still other societies, such as the Koniag, a powerful tribe on the Alaskan coast, some male children are reared from infancy to occupy the female role. They are trained in feminine duties and crafts and wear women's clothes and ornaments. When such a male reaches maturity he becomes the "wife" of an important member of the community. Because he is credited with magical powers, he is usually accorded a great deal of respect.

Male homosexuality in most societies usually involves anal intercourse; mutual masturbation and oral-genital contacts are relatively rare. Furthermore, exclusive or nearly exclusive homosexuality appears to be rarer in preliterate societies than among more civilized cultures.

Marital intercourse also reflects cultural and situational conditioning. Positions of intercourse and attitudes toward experimentation with novel positions vary from one culture to another and are controlled to some extent by the prevailing customs. In most societies a desire for privacy during intercourse is prevalent, although it may be difficult to achieve in many tribal or primitive cultures. Fortunately, privacy is culturally defined and can be achieved for intercourse as well as for other intimate behaviors without the couple actually being alone.

Except for the first weeks of marriage, the frequency of marital intercourse for most people around the world seems to range from two to five times per week during sexually active years. However, there are great cultural variations. The frequency of marital intercourse seems to decline almost universally with age. A notable exception are the Bala people of the Congo, who are reported to have marital coitus more than seven times per week in their fifties and sixties (Merriam, 1971).

Deviations from the sexual norms of a given society are also treated very differently by those societies. In contrast to our contemporary society, which demands relatively strict adherence to the prevailing sexual ideology, many cultures have a much higher tolerance for different and even deviant sexual styles; they permit people to continue functioning as accepted members of society. Among the numerous small societies populating the many islands of the South Pacific or the Bala of the republic of Congo in Africa, driving out a sexual deviant would deprive the tribe of an otherwise useful and perhaps even gifted individual. Rather than

punishing or persecuting sexual behavior that is incongruent with the social norms of the culture, these people have adopted a relatively high degree of tolerance of unusual sexual behavior as defined by concepts of sexual normality and deviance prevailing in the particular culture. In still other societies socially undesirable or deviant sexual behavior is minimized by a rigid separation of the sexes, allocating separate quarters for men and women.

Regardless of the degree to which different cultures condemn, condone, punish, or encourage various sexual practices, virtually all societies have implicitly or explicitly developed certain rules and regulations to govern the sexual activities of their members. For example, there is probably no society that does not attempt to affect the outcome of pregnancy or interfere with reproductive processes under certain conditions. In almost all cultures part of the jural system is concerned with the reproductive consequences of sexual behavior (Davenport, 1977). Through their jural systems societies define sexual rights and obligations, delineate the kinds of permissible sexual unions and the conditions under which they may be established, and determine which authorities should be allowed to allocate sexual rights. However, in most cultures sexual regulations are not exclusively confined to sexual acts or aspects of human reproduction. Instead, sexual norms are intimately linked with other aspects of social life, among them, courtship, marriage, family, and the sociosexual training of children.

In every culture there is a well-defined erotic code, consisting of sexual language and symbolism that conveys erotic messages or arouses expressions of sexuality. For instance, physical beauty is an important component of erotic symbolism in primitive as well as technological societies. However, physical features considered sexually attractive vary markedly from one culture to another. In most cultures the use of decorative adornments is a widely practiced means of enhancing sexual attraction. In some societies these bodily decorations may even take on the form of cosmetic deformities. One well-known technique is tattooing. Sometimes male symbols, such as anchors, snakes, or daggers are tattooed on the arm muscles; at other times, the tattoo may be flagrantly sexual. Many men of primitive African tribes color their penises in unusual patterns or designs. Women of the East Bay society in the South Pacific consider the inside of the thigh a highly erotic area and increase the attractiveness of this part of the body by wearing a tattoo there. For the male an occasional glimpse of the tattoo is highly arousing. East Bay women, aware of the stimulating properties of their thighs, wear long skirts to cover them, allowing men only a rare glimpse. The custom of tattooing is also found among Western women, particularly among wives and girl friends of sailors who wear a tattoo with the man's name, often in intimate places; this symbolizes a sense of domination as well as of protection.

In all cultures the sight or display of sexual organs is associated with sexual arousal. In only a few societies, however, do men and women go entirely naked throughout their lives. The Aborigines of Australia are an example; nudity is favored. Nevertheless, there are strict rules forbidding both men and women to stare at the genitals of the opposite sex. Women are expected to sit cross-legged to hide the vaginal opening.

Other primitive societies are so modest that they come close to prudishness. The people of East Bay, for instance, hardly ever remove their clothes during the daily bath in the sea except under the water. By the same token, garments are washed and put on again under water and replaced with dry ones only upon returning to the village. Even among their own sex, men and women never expose themselves to each other. Among primitive tribes that generally disdain clothing, there often exists a high degree of modesty.

People of most cultures are required to cover their sex organs fully or partially. However, the degree to which coverings are socially necessary varies greatly. In Africa and Asia males of some tribes wear a penis sheath of wood or leather to conform to social norms but also to attract female eyes to the decorated organ. By contrast, women in many Arabic societies cover their bodies completely, leaving only an opening for the eyes and part of the face.

In many societies the main purpose of wearing clothes has always been to protect the human body from the discomforts of the environment. If modesty had been born only out of the necessity to cover the genitals, however, males should be more modest than women, since female sex organs are already protected by nature. Nevertheless, it seems to be a universal law that women are more concerned to cover their genitals than men. Although rules of sexual modesty are observed universally, they are not only highly variable but also relatively inconsistent between the sexes.

Also widespread is the observation that societal regulations of sexual behavior are different for men and women. In most cultures rules about sexual conduct are usually specific for women. Cross-cultural research, as well as the intracultural data presented in the previous chapter, indicate that the double standard is nearly universal. With relatively few exceptions, males are viewed as sexual aggressors and initiators of sexual activities. One of the few notable exceptions is the Trobriand women who go on ceremonial escapades into other villages to seek out males. They also form groups in order to make orgiastic assaults on men who are fair game for their sexual violence and obscene cruelty (Malinowski, 1929). Almost universally, however, women's interest in sex and their sexual acitvities are more closely regulated than men's by what is culturally appropriate.

The few examples cited reveal that sexual behavior often becomes loaded with special cultural meanings completely divorced from the satisfaction of sexual desire or the role of sex in the reproductive cycle. In this chapter we shall present some examples of cultural diversity in sexual practices and beliefs. In addition, we shall be looking for certain universal aspects of human sexuality. Davenport (1977) has called our attention to two different types of similarities that he encountered when studying the sexual behavior of many diverse cultures. First, we can expect some cross-cultural similarities in certain sexual activities such as intercourse position or masturbation techniques. Beyond these, however, we can also assume that cultures share similarities in the relationship of sexuality to the structure and function of society as a whole. This second type of similarity reflects the view that the sexual behavior of individuals can be thoroughly understood only when it is viewed in relation to the general social framework in which it occurs.

Three Sexual Cultures

In order to gain a glimpse of the vast diversity of cultural expressions and manifestations of sexuality, we shall focus on three particular societies whose sexual-behavior patterns provide a sharp contrast to our own view of sexuality. The first, the Mangaians of the South Seas, reflect the prototype of a highly permissive, sensual approach to sexuality characteristic of many Polynesian societies. The second example, a small Irish subculture, represents probably the most repressive sexual style of our times. Finally, we have included a brief summary of the traditional Chinese Taoist sexology that has been part of Oriental heritage for thousands of years.

Mangaia: A Prototype of Sexual Freedom

> Listen to the great calm nature here, to the eternal and monotone sound of the waves breaking over coral reefs; look at the grandiose scenery, the basalt hillocks, the forest amid the sombre hills, all lost in the boundless and majestic solitude of the Pacific.
> Pierre Loti

The islands of the South Pacific have often been called the Garden of Eden. Travelers, artists, and explorers often described their exposure to the South Seas as a voyage through paradise. The islands of the South Pacific have been praised as a perfect illustra-

Figure 9.2
Portrait of a young Polynesian woman adorned with hibiscus blossoms. (United Nations)

tion of tropical magnificence and the home of bewitchingly beautiful women.

The Polynesian cultures of the central Pacific have long been famous for their open, liberated approach to sexuality. A free, happy love life is very important for Polynesians and particularly the Mangaians who live on the tiny island of Mangaia located at the southernmost part of the Cook Islands in the South Pacific. Sex is not only an integral part of interpersonal interactions but is a major theme in folklore, religion, and social life. Concern with sexuality is reflected in the language; it contains numerous words for intercourse, sexual activities, and the sex organs of men and women.

Masculine and feminine beauty are worshipped, very much as in ancient Greece. Perfumes and heavily scented flowers are used in abundance. Erotic symbolism is lav-

ishly expressed in artistic forms in song and dance. The Polynesian dancers are sexual acrobats. Explorer James Cook observed a love dance in Tahiti that actually consisted of sexual intercourse set to music.

Boys as well as girls are indoctrinated early into the sexual ethos of the Mangaians. Infantile and juvenile expressions of sexuality are viewed as manifestations of curiosity. Exploratory sex play is encouraged in children of both sexes. Similarly, masturbation is advocated and premarital sex is accepted and widely practiced. As a matter of fact, Mangaian parents encourage their daughters to interact sexually with a number of men. In his extensive study of the Mangaian people, Marshall (1971) reported that the average "nice girl" had three to four successive boyfriends between her thirteenth and fourteenth year. Most boys in this age bracket

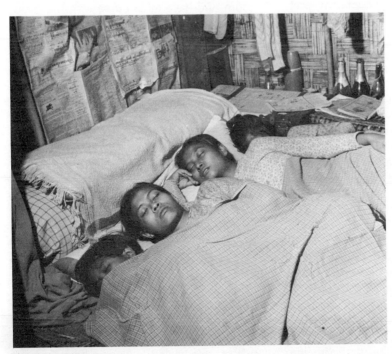

Figure 9.3
In many South Pacific societies the entire family shares the bedroom.
(United Nations)

typically have had ten girl friends; the most active ones are said to have been intimate with sixty to seventy girls. Part of the sexual prowess of Mangaian boys is reflected in tattoos; the highly promiscuous boy will have a penis tattooed on his thigh or a vagina on his penis.

Typically, the young Mangaian boy is initiated into the pleasures of love after the rites of passage to manhood, which are represented in the *superincision*, an extreme form of circumcision. In the superincision ceremony a cut is made along the length of the penis, and the skin is folded back and covered with a herbal powder. Although no skin is removed during the operation, the skin is rearranged in such a fashion that the scar tissue will leave the glans of the penis permanently exposed. Performed with a razor, the procedure is reportedly extremely painful. Often, a group of boys is assembled for the superincision ritual in a secluded spot, preferably near the shore. When the procedure is finished, the boys like to run into the ocean to obtain relief from the pain. Proclamations of "Now I am really a man" often accompany the dip into the water.

After the superincision the boy is given some formal training in the art of loving. Sex instructions include explanations of what to do with women and how to do it as well as practical demonstrations and exercises. The boy is taught how to avoid ejaculation before the woman has climaxed several times, as well as various techniques of coitus. The expert also helps the boy to find an experienced partner who will have sex with him during the finale of the superincision rite, the goal of which is to remove the superincision scab by actual intercourse.

Girls also receive oral instructions from older women. Afterward, they have intercourse with an older male relative. So important is this preparation that a young woman who is a virgin is despised by men and society in general.

Among the young Mangaians sexual inti-

macy is initiated with few preliminaries. A flick of an eye, a raised eyebrow in a crowd are invitations for heterosexual intercourse, which can take place without social contacts or dating. Typically among Mangaians, sexual intercourse precedes interpersonal intimacy. The reverse is common in our culture. Affection is often regarded as a necessary prerequisite for sexual intimacy and is used to justify premarital sex (Reiss, 1967).

Intercourse occurs nightly among young men and women in their twenties. Many times it takes place in the single room of the hut where five to fifteen family members of all ages may be sleeping. The young women may receive a succession of nightly visitors with whom they make love. This custom is known as *motoro*, the sleep-crawling tradition common in several Polynesian societies. It is part of a larger courtship custom that challenges young men to slip into the family sleeping room and have intercourse with the young woman in the midst of her family. Although the parents pretend to be asleep, they actually are anxiously listening for the "wet" sounds of orgasm and for their daughter to laugh, a sign that her partner had satisfied her. Overly vigilant behavior on the part of the parents is met with little tolerance. As a matter of fact, parents are warned that their intrusiveness may cost their daughter a husband.

Another typical Mangaian notion is the belief that sexual encounters are designed to lead to heterosexual contact. Both men and women believe that intercourse is the main reason for coming together. The sexual activities of the Mangaians are dominated by the idea that men and women must have a variety of regular sexual experiences, including premarital, marital, and extramarital encounters. For the male it is essential to be able to continue his sexual activities over long periods of time while the woman keeps moving her hips like "a washing machine." Both men and women place high value on sexual pleasure, and nothing is more despised than a passive partner. A woman who does not actively participate in the sexual act is considered deviant; she is behaving in a way contradictory to female training. Many times the sexual act is accompanied by expressions of passion and intense involvement. Biting of the partner's body is used by both sexes, as is oral-genital intercourse. For the Mangaian male the most important aspect of making love is to give pleasure to his girl. The more often the girl experiences the heights of orgasm, the more likely she will pass on his "good name."

Anthropologist Donald Marshall, who studied the people of Mangaia from 1951 to 1958, described the ease with which young couples reach climax, usually three to four times in the course of a lovemaking session (Marshall, 1971). He also reported that the Mangaians expressed great concern when they learned that some women in Western cultures do not achieve orgasm regularly. For the Mangaians this is not only a strange state of affairs but can be attributed only to some malfunctioning of a woman's sex organs. Frequent orgasm is a natural and universally achieved event among the Mangaians, who have not built up the elaborate concern with climax that characterizes some Western sexual partnerships. Although the Mangaian language has a wide repertory of words depicting various aspects of sexual anatomy and different sexual activities, words for multiple or simultaneous orgasm are unknown.

Extramarital relationships are widely acknowledged and openly practiced. Two forms of extramarital sex are particularly common. One involves the Mangaian young woman's inclination after her marriage to return to the man with whom she first had intercourse. Extramarital activities for traveling men are also socially sanctioned, based on the belief that regular heterosexual intercourse is essential for normal human functioning.

How alien the Christian view of sex life is to Polynesian ideas is illustrated by an anecdote about one of the first bishops in New Zealand. On a journey through a new diocese the bishop came late one evening to a remote Maori village where he was naturally received as a guest of honor with endless speeches and a huge banquet. When the bishop and a young clergyman who was his sole companion had endured the entire ceremony and were at last ready to retire for the night, the chief, according to good Polynesian custom, sent for a woman for the bishop. The young cleric, who happened to overhear the chief's order, stopped him and said indignantly, "What do you mean? A bedfellow for the bishop?" The chief could not imagine more than one explanation for this outburst of anger and hastened to repair his error by shouting loudly to his servants, "Give the bishop two women!"

In spite of the uninhibited sexual freedom enjoyed by men and women on Mangaia, the culture is characterized by a unique modesty about exposure of adult sex organs. For example, Mangaians were horrified when they heard about the casualness with which some men in Western societies expose their penises when urinating.

Inis Beag: A Prototype of Sexual Repression

Women pray and men masturbate.
(Title of a painting by Paddy Graham exhibited at a Dublin gallery in 1974)

At the opposite end of our cross-cultural spectrum we find the people of Inis Beag, a pseudonym (chosen to protect the inhabitants) of a rural community of approximately 350 people living on a small island off the western shore of Ireland. The population lives in seventy-two cottages in four villages. The people of Inis Beag were studied by anthropologist John Messenger (1971), who visited the island between 1958 and 1966. The

What Can We Learn from the Polynesian View of Sex?

We probably have something to learn from the Polynesians in the following respects.

1. Positive Attitude Toward Sexuality

The most conspicuous difference between life in Polynesia and some of our Western societies is the appreciative attitude toward sexuality prevailing among most islanders in the South Seas. While in Polynesia religion and sexuality go hand in hand, Christian and Jewish teachings have often declared sexual impulses to be base and sinful.

2. Sexual Instruction

Many times the failures of both unmarried young men and women and married people to achieve happiness in sexual relationships are due to ignorance or incompetence in sexual matters. Without advocating practical instructions, it is certainly possible to effect improvement by means of open discussion and first-class textbooks on sexual techniques; these methods of instruction can show that sexual skill is not an innate gift but an art that, like many others, can be learned. This discovery is not unique among Polynesian societies but was also recognized by such ancient civilizations as the Hindus and Chinese.

3. Realistic Conception of Love

Whereas sexual relationships in our own and many other Western societies are often based on the concept of romantic love, the Polynesians attach great importance to such definite qualities as sexual skills, physical beauty, and even temperament.

majority of the people are described as poor, living off meager agricultural products procured from the soil.

The people on Inis Beag represent a society that severely represses and frustrates basic sexual needs. Men and women practice an ethos of sexuality that negates the existence of any sexual urges. Consequently, all forms of sexual behavior are relatively rare. Sex is never discussed in the home when children are around. Sexual repression is evident in parent-child relationships, where the seeds for sexual denial are planted early. Although mothers are affectionate with their children, they do not express their feelings through physical contact such as kissing or hugging. Emotions are expressed only verbally. Equally rare among the women of Inis Beag is breast-feeding, not only because of its

sexual implications but also because it involves "indecent" exposure.

Sex education takes place through the peer group and by observing animals copulate. It is commonly assumed that after marriage nature will take its course indoctrinating the young into the "facts of life."

Even among adults, sexual matters are rarely discussed. By contrast, members of both sexes are in constant surveillance of each other to discourage gossiping about sex. Even the slightest sexual overtones in conversation are objected to. All behaviors suggestive of sex, such as dancing or nudity, are restricted. Recreation never involves both sexes. Instead, there is a sharp separation of the sexes, men interacting mostly with men and women with women, before as well as after marriage.

Body modesty is equally extreme. The islanders on Inis Beag abhor nudity. Both men and women leave their underclothes on when they do have intercourse. Personal hygiene is poor because children and adults avoid revealing parts of their bodies other than faces, lower arms and hands, and lower legs and feet. Many men and women do not learn to swim because it would mean dressing scantily. The pathological fear of physical exposure has cost a number of lives in drownings. Equally puritanical is the attitude of sick men who refuse to see a female nurse because it might require exposing part of their bodies to a woman.

Another manifestation of ultimate sexual repression is the absence of sexual humor. The tradition of dirty jokes—an integral part of the sexual folklore of most societies, past and present—is completely lacking on Inis Beag. Instead, people have a myriad of misconceptions about sex, including the belief that sexual intercourse is debilitating. The lack of sexual knowledge among adults makes the people of Inis Beag one of the most sexually naive and inhibited in the world.

As a result of the denial and repression of sexuality, there is no courtship or dating pattern on Inis Beag. Marriage comes relatively late, with a mean age of thirty-six for men and twenty-five for women. Typically, marriages are contracted by elders with little or no concern for the preferences of the groom or bride. Women are taught that marital sex is a duty that must be "endured." The teachings of the Catholic Church perpetuate the notion that refusal of marital sex is a mortal sin. As elsewhere in Ireland, bachelorhood and spinsterhood are prevalent on Inis Beag.

The only purpose of marital sex is reproduction. Foreplay is brief and limited to kissing and rough fondling of the lower body, especially the buttocks. Women never initiate sexual activities. With the exception of the male superior position, all other forms of sexual expression are considered deviant. The male achieves orgasm almost immediately and reportedly falls asleep instantaneously. In contrast to the women on Mangaia, who reach climax frequently, female orgasm is unknown on Inis Beag—or at least considered an abnormal response. Any attempt to experiment with marital sex or introduce more liberated sexual behaviors would bring about strong social reactions. Men on Inis Beag will not have intercourse with their wives the night before they have to do a strenuous job. There are also strong taboos against marital sex during menstruation and for months before and after childbirth.

The people of Inis Beag share with many primitive and Western societies the belief that men by their nature have stronger sexual desires than women. The Irish version of the double standard is probably best summarized by the stock phrase, "The lads are in the pub, the women in the kitchen." The extreme separation of the sexes leads to many manifestations of the double standard. For example, male masturbation is a major escape from the frustrations generated by the repression of sex. The only escape for women is the occasional consummation of marriage. In addition, the high incidence of drinking among Irish men in general is another escape valve. One in thirteen persons is an alcoholic. Men are said to drink so they can face their girl friends or acquire the courage to ask a girl for a dance.

Messenger (1971) suggested that the denial of sex on Inis Beag is at least in part the result of an indoctrination with a particularly rigid and ascetic version of Catholicism. It is an ethos of sexuality that comes close to blotting out all the cultural ramifications of sexuality (Davenport, 1977).

The Art of Oriental Love

The male belongs to Yang
Yang's peculiarity is that he is easily aroused

But also he easily retreats
The female belongs to Yin
Yin's peculiarity is that she is slow to be
aroused
But also slow to be satiated

Wu Hsien

Ever since ancient times people in Eastern cultures have recorded instructions in the art of love. The most famous and earliest classified description of intercourse variations is contained in the Sanskrit classic, the *Kama Sutra* ("Love Doctrine"), dating from some time in the first five centuries A.D. and based on still older writings. Much of the text deals with advice on general social conduct and marriage, but its title has become synonymous with "positions." The part that deals with sexual practices discusses the size of genitals, touching, kissing, and how to vary positions.

The Hindu, Chinese, and Japanese have a rich treasure of classical works on erotology that gives detailed advice on how to rise to the heights of sexual pleasure. Bedside books also tell of an infinite variety of physical love, how to increase pleasure and virility. In Japan, the Bridal Rule pasted on the walls of the bedroom was intended to instruct the bashful newlywed. Oriental erotic prints and paintings are extremely explicit and can be studied by Westerners who are interested in improving their sexual techniques.

More so than in Western civilizations, Oriental sexuality is linked to the overall psychological well-being of a person. *Taoism* in China supports the belief that sexual activity is the secret to longevity and to health itself (Chang, 1977). Hindu philosophy fuses sexuality and religion. The necessity of sexual activity is stressed in the attainment of nirvana or ultimate peace. Similarly, Hindu religious culture is filled with erotic elements that serve to enhance and embellish unrelated theological concepts (Davenport, 1977).

Taoism is a sexual culture of particularly longstanding tradition concerned with Chinese sexology, ancient and contemporary. For the ancient Chinese, man was a Yang force, while woman was a Yin force. Although

---

Passages from the Kama Sutra

Man is divided into three classes, the hare man, the bull man, and the horse man, according to the size of his lingam. Woman also, according to the depth of her yoni, is either a female deer, a mare or an elephant.

The deer-woman has the following three ways of lying down:

> The widely opened position
> The yawning position
> The position of the wife of Indra (Indrani).

When she lowers her head and raises her middle part, it is called the "widely opened position." When she raises her thighs and keeps them wide apart and engages in congress, it is called the yawning position. When she places her thighs with her legs doubled on them upon her sides, and thus engages in congress, it is called the position of Indrani and this is learnt only by practice.

When a man enjoys many women altogether, it is called the "congress of a herd of cows."

(Translated by Sir Richard Burton
1821-1890)

Yang and Yin are separate forces, they are essentially components of the same ultimate unity. A common analogy mentioned frequently in Chinese texts likens Yang and Yin to fire and water. Fire belongs to Yang and, though quick to ignite, is typically overwhelmed and extinguished by water, a Yin force.

The Swiss psychologist Carl Jung (1953) adapted the Chinese principle of Yang and Yin to his own thought and translated them into *animus* and *anima*. In Jung's theory a woman's animus (Yang) accounts for the masculine side of her personality and is responsible for qualities such as rational judgment, discipline, and aggressiveness. Similarly, a man's anima embodies the Yin aspect. It is the side of a man's personality that is responsible for his capacity for relatedness, his emotionality and spontaneity. The Yin and Yang, or anima and animus, motivate each sex to respond to and understand members of the opposite sex.

Both the Tao masters and Jung agreed that some characteristics of the opposite sex may be found in men and women. This idea has recently found support in a number of areas of research. For instance, John Money at Johns Hopkins University demonstrated that both men and women secrete male and female sex hormones (see Chapter 5 for the biological dimorphism of sexuality). On a psychological level we also find masculine and feminine characteristics in both sexes. The work of Sandra Bern (1974) showed that many individuals are *androgynous*, that is, they possess both masculine and feminine traits. In addition, Bem, Martyna, and Watson (1976) found that men and women markedly androgynous are characterized by better psychological adjustment and mental health than those who exhibit predominantly male or female behaviors (see Chapter 17).

Returning to Chinese Taoism, we now examine some of the principle tenets of Chinese sexology. The basic principles of the Tao of Loving include control over ejaculation, the importance of female satisfaction, and the understanding that male orgasm and ejaculation are not the same thing (Chang, 1977). These three basic themes are aspects of sexuality that have been addressed by the scientific studies of Kinsey, Masters and Johnson, and other sex researchers.

The most important part of the Tao of Loving is the control and regulation of ejaculation. In order to attain ultimate peace of mind and superb tranquility, harmony of the Yang and Yin must be reached. This is possible only through frequent sexual intercourse because it allows a man to profit from a woman's Yin essence and the woman from the man's Yang essence. The man is advised, however, to withhold his semen and to ejaculate infrequently. The Tao prescribes a locking method for the control of ejaculation, according to which a man simply withdraws his penis when he is at the verge of ejaculating. In this way, the Tao masters point out, he not only wards off ejaculation but also loses a good percentage of his erection. According to the Tao, the more a man makes love, the more he benefits from the harmony of Yin and Yang, and the less he ejaculates, the less he loses the advantages of this harmony. This pattern of lovemaking is said to provide the path for longevity. For the Taoist sex is not only to be enjoyed and savored but is also considered wholesome and life-preserving.

The Tao of Loving describes twenty-six positions of intercourse, all variations of four basic positions:

1. close union (male superior)
2. unicorn horn (female superior)
3. intimate attachment (male-female face to face but side by side)
4. sunning fish (male entry from the rear)

For the Taoist, uninhibited experimentation with the various coital positions is the spice of loving. Successful lovemaking entails not only sampling endless variations of intercourse positions but also making sure that the woman is completely satisfied. Taoism stresses female gratification as one of its cardinal principles because it brings about the harmony of Yin and Yang.

Tao masters also emphasize that love and sex should not be separated. Love without sex is said to be unhealthy and frustrating, while sex without love is simply a biological function which does not bring two people closer to serenity.

The Tao of Loving also includes a sensitive description of sexual relationships between younger women and older men, referred to as May-September partnerships. Such relationships are mutually gratifying because the young woman produces ample lubrication and has a tight vagina, which the older, experienced lover finds exciting. The older man, on the other hand, achieves an erection slowly and is slow to finish, thereby contributing an atmosphere of confidence that very few unexperienced lovers could command.

Although most of the instructions contained in the Tao of Loving are directed at men to improve their sensitivity and lovemaking skills, women can also learn much from the Tao masters. For example, it is important that a woman understand the Tao or she might misunderstand the man who retains his semen. She may think that she has failed to satisfy him or does not please him.

The Oriental art of loving combines frankness and explicitness with sensitivity and detailed instructions. It allows men and women to make the most of their lovemaking and also to gain great personal enrichment.

Culturally Specific Sex Practices

Our brief survey of three divergent sexual cultures has provided us with an overall idea of the manifold possibilities of cultural expressions of sexuality. We shall now turn our attention to some highly specific sexual customs and practices. Some of these sexual customs are shared by several civilizations, while others represent idiosyncratic or unique manifestations of sexuality found only in one particular society.

Sexual Taboos

Many societies curtail sexual activities during menstruation, lactation, and pregnancy in spite of the fact that there are relatively few biological reasons to eliminate intercourse during these times. Mohammedan laws, for instance, forbid the embrace during menstruation. Similarly, the men in many African tribes avoid women if they become pregnant, when they are weaning children, and during menstruation. During these times women often have to live in separate quarters.

Among many Australian tribes severe restrictions are placed on menstruating or pregnant women. If a woman is married during her menses she is forced to sleep alone and cannot share food and drink with anyone else. No one will consume food or drink touched by her because it is believed that it would cause violent gastric disturbances.

In some cultures males are also prohibited from engaging in heterosexual intercourse at certain times. These include before and after hunting, before going to war, and before or after harvesting crops.

An almost universal taboo prohibits sexual relations among immediate members of a family. Such relations are considered to be incest, which includes sexual contact between brothers and sisters or parent and child. As far as kinship relations are concerned, however, incest taboos vary considerably from culture to culture.

There is probably no other country with as strict incest prohibitions as Australia. Among certain tribes a man is not permitted to marry within the tribe of his mother, grandmother, or one who speaks his dialect. If a love affair between two people of the same family is discovered, the relatives or brothers of the young woman beat her unmercifully. The young man is dragged to the chief of the tribe and punished severely.

On the other hand, some societies allow sexual union between family members that would be considered incestuous, or at least improper, in our own culture. Among the Polynesians and some African tribes, a man can marry the widow of his brother or the sister of his dead wife. If the husband dies, an unmarried brother is expected to marry the woman. Sexual relations among closer kin in these societies are viewed not so much as sexual deviations but as an indication of moral incapacity closely related to insanity (Davenport, 1977).

Puberty Rites

Many societies celebrate maturational transitions with ceremonies that contain sexual overtones. Elaborate ceremonies mark the rites of passage, boys entering manhood and girls becoming women. Practically all Australian tribes permit men to marry only after they have been initiated. The reaching of manhood is celebrated by carrying a young man to a place far away from his home. During the night the priests and medicine man, who are painted in glowing colors and decorated with feathers, begin the rites, which include the painful extraction of the two upper front teeth. After this torture the boy is hidden in a hut of tightly compressed branches through which no light can enter. Outside the hut the women dance, carrying flaming torches. For a whole month the young man is permitted to see only the priests and medicine man; should a woman see him during this period it is considered a certain sign that the adolescent will die shortly thereafter.

The Polynesian people of the Eastern Solomon Islands also recognize the transition from adolescence to adulthood by separating boys from girls. Boys between the ages of ten and twelve must undergo a lengthy ritual of separation, sometimes lasting a year, during which they are indoctrinated into the sacred activities that only men are allowed to perform in this culture. Thereafter, a gala reintroduction into the social life of the community is staged in the form of a wedding for each initiate with a girl of his age. However, in most cases the boys and girls are too young to understand the sexual meaning of what they are told to do.

Defloration Ceremonies

Girls are also subjected to mandatory rituals during transition ceremonies. In Hawaii, when a girl became of marriageable age and was spoken for as a wife, she used to be taken to the chief who would end her virginity.

In Samoa in the South Pacific, deflorations were carried out in public with members of the community invited to view the event. As soon as the guests had assembled at the site where the ceremony was to take place, the bride was led in. Some of the elderly women assisted her in taking off her clothes. Then, she was seated with her legs crossed on a snow-white mat spread on the ground. The chief approached the girl and silently seated himself directly in front of her. Then came the critical moment. Placing his left hand on the girl's right shoulder the chief inserted two fingers into the vagina while two women held the girl around the waist. The spectators eagerly watched for the drops of blood; at the sight of them the crowd proclaimed the virtue of the bride. To the cheers of the visitors, the girl, still naked, was paraded around to exhibit the blood that trickled down her thighs.

In Cambodia a priest usually performed the defloration ceremony with his fingers dipped in wine. Some say that the relatives and parents of the husband drank of the wine. Among some Australian tribes a girl's virginity was taken in rather brutal ways, performed by several older men who ruptured the hymen with a stone or stick.

In societies where the bride must be a virgin at the time of marriage, girls have invented means to restore their virginity with a few stitches through the labia majora. In other cultures a young woman may inject some drops of blood from doves as part of the preparation for the wedding night. In still other cultures, girls who are no longer virgins deliberately chose for their marriage night the last day of their menstruation to mimic the breakage of the hymen.

Body Piercings and Mutilation of the Sex Organs

Body piercing is a form of physical adornment practiced in several cultures to enhance the sex appeal of men and women. Pierced ears for pendants, for instance, are a popular personal decoration among women in our own society. Among tribal and primitive societies body piercings often involve the sex organs and are more sexually explicit than in Western societies. Apparently the practice is as old as mankind. Among the "penis-enhancers" described in the *Kama Sutra*, for instance, perforating the penis to insert various hard objects is specifically mentioned. It is claimed that this increases sensitivity during intercourse.

Rings and studs may be inserted through many parts of the skin, including the nipples of both sexes, the labia, the male foreskin, and even the head of the penis itself. These adornments are considered erotically exciting in several Asian, African, South American, and Oceanic cultures. In addition, many Hindu men wear nose rings of precious metals or gemstones.

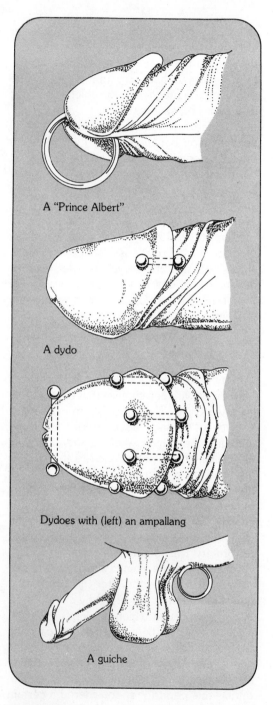

A "Prince Albert"

A dydo

Dydoes with (left) an ampallang

A guiche

Figure 9.4
Body piercings are thought to be sexually appealing in some primitive societies.

An elaborate pattern of body decoration is found among the Bala women of the Congo: they are covered with geometrically patterned *keloid* or scar tissue markings (Marshall and Suggs, 1972). Like most other body decorations, beautification, increasing attractiveness, and sex appeal are the major purposes of the procedure. These markings cover the body from above the breasts, down between them, and across the stomach just below the navel. In most cases the markings are made by the mother or an older sister when the girl is still quite young, usually before the age of eight. First, the design is traced on the body with charcoal if the girl has a light skin tone or with a white liquid in the case of a dark-skinned girl. Then the girl's skin is pinched between thumb and forefinger and cut with a razor blade following the tracings. Thereafter black charcoal is rubbed into the cuts, which not only irritates the wound but also causes swelling. The operation is an ordeal, especially since it is performed in a single session. Although the little girl is allowed to cry, crying is considered shameful.

After the cuts have healed, the design appears as a pattern of skin elevations. The most important criteria by which keloid markings are evaluated are the aesthetic quality of the design and a moderate degree of swelling. If the design does not show properly after the wounds have healed, they may be recut later.

The keloid markings of Bala women do not carry any social implications such as rank or status. They are always covered by clothing and not shown to anybody other than the husband or other Bala women. However, females without keloid markings are considered to be sexually less attractive, since Bala men like to touch and run their hands over the pattern as part of foreplay. Although the custom was recorded as early as 1897, there is some indication that today this tradition is going out of fashion among younger girls.

While most forms of body piercing are not meant to restrain sexual intercourse, *infibulation* is a specific technique for restricting sexual intercourse. The procedure is used for both males and females and involves the piercing of the foreskin or the labia, which is then permanently kept together by a seam. In Nubia and the Sudan, infibulation assures the chastity of women and results from the idea of a wife as property. Although little research has been done in this area, it seems that sadomasochistic motivation (see Chapter 15) lies behind some of the body-piercing practices, especially those that result in cosmetic deformities.

Polygamy and Polyandry

While contemporary American society formally recognizes only one form of sexual partnership, namely, *monogamy* or the legal marriage of one man to one woman, from a cross-cultural perspective this custom is relatively rare. As a matter of fact, the studies by Ford and Beach (1951) disclosed that only twenty-nine societies (or less than 16 percent) out of 185 groups about whom information could be obtained were designated as monogamous.

In 84 percent of the 185 cultures, men were permitted to have more than one wife at a time. These relationships are known as *polygamy* or polygamous marriages. The word polygamy is certain to conjure up visions of Arabic or Eastern harems with innumerable veiled wives or bring back recollections of a newsreel showing the dethroned Sultan of Morocco about to board an airplane with his twenty-three favorite wives. Polygamy on such a grandiose scale is actually rare. Polygamy on a smaller scale is common in a number of societies. Among African tribes, for instance, the first wife has authority over all the others. In most cases, she asks the husband to take as many wives as he can so that the work may be divided among the women of the household.

Most of the time the husband must be able to afford to support the women he brings into the household and must pay equal attention to all of them. Recognizing this particular obligation, the husband usually spends his nights in some kind of rotational order that guarantees each wife equal opportunities for sexual relations.

In Polynesia polygamy occurs, with few exceptions, only among the nobility (Danielsson, 1956). About 20 percent of the marriages are polygamous with the number of wives being relatively modest—2.1 wives per chief on the average. In addition, many societies that sanction multiple wives for a man recognize only the sisters of the first wife as permissible mates.

There are probably few customs that have been so fundamentally misunderstood and misjudged in Western societies as polygamy. Three particular misconceptions seem to be prevalent in the minds of many people. One deals with the notion that a man who keeps several wives needs them in order to satisfy his sex drive. If this were true, it would more likely lead to a frequent change of wives rather than the relatively permanent assembly of several wives that is characteristic of polygamous marriages.

In many societies another major reason for polygamy is family consideration. All men in primitive societies, but particularly the chiefs, desire male heirs to continue the family line. Furthermore, many chiefs want as many male children as possible to maintain economic or political advantages.

Another misconception is that in polygamous marriages women are treated as slaves by their husbands. Rather than diminishing the freedom of each wife, polygamy divides the burden of work among the women. In addition, among illiterate societies, many wives are glad to have a substitute within the family during pregnancy or menstruation when sexual intercourse is avoided.

In many cultures women see nothing humiliating or irrational in living in polygamy. Handy (1952) has described a situation in Hawaii where a wife might say to her husband, "I love my cousin so much that I do not want her to go away; so you take her for your wife." At the same time, she might say to her cousin, "Let him be our husband."

A third misconception is the assumption that jealousy and quarrels are common in polygamous marriages. With few exceptions, jealousy is rather rare among wives. As a matter of fact, it has been suggested that jealousy is a function of the exclusive sexual monopoly that men and women impose upon each other in traditional Western marriages.

In many polygamous marriages the possibility of friction and controversy is reduced by a number of simple family arrangements that typically include:

1. placing the wives in order of rank (usually the first wife has authority over the others)
2. dividing the work evenly between them
3. giving the different wives separate houses or sleeping quarters
4. the husband visiting his wives in turn

Polyandry, a marital arrangement in which a woman has sexual relations with a number of different men who are members of the same household, is not nearly as frequent as polygamy or monogamy. Polyandrous unions occurred among the Tibetans and the Marquesas islanders of Polynesia and are still considered an anthropological curiosity. Since in primitive as well as literate societies the belief prevails that males are polygamous "by nature" and women are genetically predisposed to be more monogamous, polyandry represents a cultural phenomenon. At times polyandry has been linked to a surplus of males or the superior social status of a woman who had the liberty of taking as many husbands as she pleased. In a ruling class of Hawaii, according to Malo (1951), polyandry was practiced at the request of the priest with regard to high-class women.

Like polygamous marriages, polyandrous unions subordinate second and third husbands to the first or chief husband. Usually, the chief husband divides the work among the remaining males. Additional husbands are typically allocated sleeping quarters away from the main house and are allowed to spend the night with their wife only at the consent of the first husband. Furthermore, the chief husband is always regarded as the father of all the children of the wife. Danielsson (1956) has suggested that it would be more accurate to say that a polyandrous marriage consists not so much of a woman who is married to several men but a man who is married to a woman and several other men.

Many other examples of culturally idiosyncratic sexual behaviors could be cited. For instance, most preliterate societies allow some forms of extramarital relations, with many of them clearly delineating the type of permissible liaisons. The Chukchee of Siberia furnish an interesting example: traveling Chukchee men are usually granted sexual access to the wives of their hosts. Similarly, among the Eskimos, extramarital rights are legitimized in the custom of offering a male visitor the host's wife as part of hospitality. Contrary to the current fad of spouse swapping in the United States, the Eskimo custom of "wife lending" is socially approved and legally sanctioned.

Universal Aspects of Human Sexuality

Despite a diversity of sexual practices and mores, all cultures share a number of similarities. Virtually all men and women believe that sexual activities are necessary, although the motivation for sexual behaviors varies.

It is also widely believed that after a childhood and early-adolescent phase of masturbation and sociosexual experimentation the majority of men and women make heterosexual intercourse their chief sexual activity. Equally common is the assumption that male sexual needs exceed those of females, a belief that prevails even in cultures granting equal sexual privileges to both sexes.

Marriage in all societies in one form or another, usually is an institution with particular privileges and obligations. Again, the reasons for entering into marital unions vary from culture to culture, ranging from economic considerations to emotional and/or sexual gratification.

The cross-cultural view of human sexuality shows that, without exception, societies shape, structure, and constrain the expression of sexual desires. Seldom, if ever, are all forms of sexual behavior in a given culture regarded only on the basis of their biological or psychological dimensions. Within the general context of a given culture most people share similar interests, desires, frustrations, loves, sorrows, and joys that are part of sexual behavior.

Summary

In this chapter we have broadened our perspective of human sexuality by looking at the sexual practices of various cultures. Although there are many cross-cultural similarities, there are as many if not more intercultural differences. At the beginning of the chapter, we discussed several cultural views of homosexuality, and this allowed us to make several generalizations concerning sexual-behavior patterns. First, there is a wide divergence of social attitudes toward many kinds of sexual activities. Second, no matter how a particular society treats certain sexual taboos or prohibitions, some people still engage in these behaviors. And, finally, it seems that most human expressions of sexuality are the product of the learning experiences of men and women raised and living in different societies. As Ford and Beach point out, socially controlled learning is not only responsible for cross-cultural similarities but also for many of the differences between societies.

Our survey of three culturally distinct societies, the island populations of Mangaia in the South Pacific, the Inis Beag in Ireland, and the Oriental approach to sexuality demonstrated that social learning is an important source of cultural variations of sexuality.

In the last part of the chapter we contrasted some culturally specific expressions of sexuality with universal aspects. While some societies practice unique sexual habits, such as puberty rites or infibulation, most of them have a system of rules, values, and regulations that govern sexual behavior. In most societies the biological aspects of sex are overruled by social sanctions that determine to a large degree a person's sexual behavior.

To avoid the pitfalls of universalities we come to the conclusion that no two societies think or behave alike sexually. Every society has its culture of sex. Large societies vary from one subgroup to the next, and there are variations from one generation to another. At the same time, the study of the sexual behavior and standards of other cultures seems to reinforce the view that our own interpretation of sexuality is culturally conditioned. No other society can actually provide a model for us; we cannot extract the most appealing sexual customs from another societal context and implant them into our own social framework, just as we cannot transplant an exotic flower into Nordic soil. But we can integrate aspects of other cultures into our own when we recognize the limitations of our culture.

References

Bem, S. "The measurement of psychological androgyny." *Journal of Consulting and Clinical Psychology*, 1974, Vol. 42, 2, 155-162.

Bem, S., Martyna, W., and Watson, C. "Sex typing and androgyny: Further explorations of the expressive domain." *Journal of Personality and Social Psychology*, 1976, 34, 1016-1023.

Chang, J. *The Tao of love and sex.* New York: E. P. Dutton, 1977.

Danielsson, B. *Love in the south seas.* New York: Reynal, 1956.

Davenport, W. "Sex in cross-cultural perspective." In F. Beach (ed.). *Human sexuality in four perspectives.* Baltimore: Johns Hopkins University Press, 1977.

Ford, C. and Beach, F. *Patterns of sexual behavior.* New York: Harper & Row, 1951.

Handy, C. "The Polynesian family system in Kau, Hawaii." *Journal of the Polynesian Society*, 1952, 3 and 4.

Jung, C. "Anima and animus." In *Two essays on analytic psychology*, collected works (Vol. 7, pp. 188-211). Princeton: Princeton University Press, 1953 (originally published 1928).

Malinowski, B. *The sexual life of savages in North-Western Melanesia.* New York: Halcyon House, 1929.

Malo, David. *Hawaiian antiquities.* Honolulu: Mau Publishers Inc., 1951.

Marshall, D. "Too much in Mangaia." *Psychology Today*, 1971, Vol. 4, 9, 43-47.

Marshall, D. and Suggs, R. *Human sexual behavior, variations in the ethnographic spectrum.* Englewood Cliffs, N.J.: Prentice-Hall, 1972.

Merriam, A. "Aspects of sexual behavior among the Bala (Basongye)." In D. Marshall and R. Suggs (eds.), *Human sexual behavior*. Englewood Cliffs, N.J.: Prentice-Hall, 1971.

Messenger, J. "Sex and repression in an Irish folk community." *Psychology Today*, 1971, Vol. 9, 4, 41-49.

Reiss, I. *The social context of premarital sexual permissiveness.* New York: Holt, Reinhart & Winston, 1967.

Part Two

Sexual Behavior and Relationships

Chapter 10

Sexual Arousal and Intercourse

For most people sexual intercourse is what comes to mind when the topic of human sexuality is mentioned. Sexual intercourse is just one aspect of human sexuality, of course, but none can deny that it is a very important aspect. Probably no other kind of human behavior has as much potential for affording pleasure—both physical and psychological. In fact, the physical pleasure associated with orgasm is enhanced by the psychological satisfaction derived from feelings of closeness, tenderness, and intimacy with one's partner.

Sexual intercourse is similar to other human behaviors in that its techniques are learned. While the drive to express sexuality is influenced by biological factors, the manner in which the drive is expressed is strongly influenced by social and psychological factors. Thus, if one is to derive maximum pleasure from sexual intercourse and wishes to give one's partner maximum pleasure, a knowledge of human sexual arousal and sexual techniques is necessary. This knowledge, in combination with sensitivity to the feelings and wishes of one's partner, provides the basis for a satisfying sexual relationship. These factors have more to do with making one a "good" lover than does physical appeal or prowess.

Motives for Sexual Intercourse

That there are many motives for having sexual intercourse can be seen readily in the terms we use to describe the act: coitus, fornication, screwing, fucking, scoring, getting laid, banging, copulation, and making love. All these terms refer to the same behavior, but they suggest that people have sex for different reasons. And any one person is likely to have different motives for different acts of sexual intercourse. Gerhard Neubeck, a specialist in family studies, has discussed the myriad motives for sex (1974). Let us review his list of possible reasons for having sex.

Affection. Sex can be connected with a cluster of feelings such as love, intimacy, affinity, and romance. It may be symbolic of the desire to bridge the gap between oneself and one's partner, that is, to achieve unity with another human being. Affection tends to be viewed as the most noble of motives for having sex in our society.

Animosity. Some people regard sex as a means of inflicting pain or degradation upon their partner. People who are indoctrinated with the view that sex is dirty or disgusting may wish to have intercourse to express their hostilities toward their partner.

Anxieties. The desire to have sex can arise from nonsexual frustrations and fears. A sexual partner may be providing a vehicle for the displacement of such feelings. Intercourse may provide a momentary relief from anxieties. In Chapter 8 we saw that this was an important motivation for people in lower socioeconomic groups.

Boredom. The desire to have sex may arise simply from being bored. The pleasure and excitement associated with sex may provide temporary escape from an uninteresting and dull environment.

Duty. Many people have sex out of a sense of obligation. The man or woman who no longer finds the spouse interesting but wants to maintain the marriage, or the person whose date has spent a great deal of money may feel a responsibility to have sexual relations. Any pleasure derived from the encounter is likely to occur as a result of having "gotten it over with." This sense of duty can arise from feelings of sexual guilt (see Chapter 18) or from a loss of interest in the relationship.

Mending Wounds. Many couples find sex to be an effective way of making up after an argument.

Adventure. Sex can be creative. The desire to know another person better or the wish to learn more about oneself can provide the impetus for sex. Neubeck suggests that an adventurous approach to sex can provide a genuine growth experience. The desire for sexual adventure can be seen in the increasing popularity of encounter groups that emphasize sexual development.

Recreation. Sex is fun. One can have sex with the sole aim of experiencing and producing pleasant sensations.

Lust. Sexual hunger or passion can be a motive for sex. Imagery, fantasy, and expectations are focused on the body, and there is an urgent need to consummate the desire.

Self-affirmation. Sex can be a means of confirming one's ideas about one's sexual role. The man who views himself as a great lover may be motivated to seduce every woman he meets. The woman who views herself as a temptress may need to have a string of sexual conquests.

Altruism. In many cases sex is not a fifty-fifty proposition. One partner may engage in sex with the desire to provide the partner with pleasure and not out of a concern for his or her own satisfaction.

Power and Acceptance. There are two important motives for sex that Neubeck neglected to discuss. First, sex can be motivated by the need for power. It has been suggested, for example, that the "strutting masculinity" of many poor young males is an expression of power. The flaunting of sexual prowess is a substitute for their lack of economic and political power (Fullerton, 1974). For some women, sex may be the only available expression of power. The withholding and judicious giving of sex can be a vehicle for satisfying other needs and desires. Sex can

be used to gain some measure of control over others.

Second, sex can be a vehicle for gaining acceptance by peers of the same sex. Family specialist Lester Kirkendall's investigation of high school and college men who visited prostitutes illustrates this phenomenon (1974). He noticed that boys never visited prostitutes alone. They went in pairs or groups after there had been much kidding about who would be too "chicken" to do it. Visiting the prostitute was essentially a male group experience designed to test masculinity; the prostitute and the sexual act were of less significance. Similarly, some young women may have a sexual encounter in response to the taunts of their friends about being the only virgin in the school.

Sex is more than hormones and genitals; it is a vital aspect of our whole being. Motives as diverse as passion and boredom, affection and animosity not only provide the impetus for sex but emphasize the need to approach the topic of human sexuality in the context of the total person.

The Science of Sexual Arousal

A popular saying suggests that sexual arousal is a combination of fantasy and friction. While there may be much truth to this adage, behavioral scientists are just beginning to acquire factual information about the factors that influence sexual arousal. Until recently, the moral climate of our society prevented laboratory research in this area. And it will probably be some time before researchers can conduct the type of research that will provide conclusive answers. Masters and Johnson have provided basic information about the physiology of the sexual response cycle (see Chapter 5), and psychologists are conducting exploratory studies to identify circumstances that lead to sexual arousal in men and women. But because sexual behavior in general, and sexual arousal specifically, is such a complex phenomenon, it probably will be quite some time before we have all the answers.

Problems of Measurement

One problem in conducting research in this area is that sexual arousal is difficult to measure. Research conducted in the 1960s and early 1970s relied on the personal reports of subjects who were asked by researchers to describe how aroused they were. Since then, technological advances have made possible the physiological assessment of sexual arousal. In men, the *penile plethysmograph* can be fitted around the penis to detect changes in penile volume. A similar device, called a *penile strain gauge*, is placed around the penis to detect changes in circumference. For women, a device called a photopletysmograph can be inserted into the vagina to detect physiological changes, (for example, blood volume and pressure pulse) that accompany sexual arousal (Sintchak and Geer, 1975).

A typical experiment might involve the exposure of men or women to sexual stimulus materials and then measuring their arousal level physiologically and by personal report. The problem with this method is that the various indices do not always agree with one another (O'Grady and Janda, 1980). For example, in a recent study of the effects of alcohol on sexual arousal in women, it was found that alcohol reduced physiological arousal but increased women's feelings of arousal (Wilson and Lawson, 1978). The question, therefore, becomes: which is the more relevant psychologically—measured physiological arousal or personal reports of arousal? Ethics permitting, we could perhaps answer this question by introducing a sexual partner into the situation. But that might raise even more questions. For instance, does the nature of the relationship influence the type

of sexual arousal? Could it be that physiological or genital arousal is crucial to satisfaction in casual sexual relationships? In more intimate relationships, the perception of arousal may be the more important factor. There is some evidence that women who have difficulty in reaching orgasms have lower levels of physiological arousal in laboratory settings than orgasmic women (Wincze, Hoon, and Hoon, 1976). As of yet, however, the implications of inconsistencies between personal reports of and measured physiological arousal in orgasmic women are not known.

Research is still sparse in this area. Although it has been crucial in debunking many myths (for example, vaginal orgasms), this research has raised more questions than it has answered. Thus we must still rely to a large extent on the opinions and reports of men and women about the factors that lead to sexual arousal. Scientific knowledge of sexual arousal is growing, but much remains to be learned.

A Cognitive Perspective of Sexual Arousal

One question confronting behavioral scientists is how people learn to become aroused by such a wide variety of stimuli. Some men find tall, willowy women sexually appealing, while others find more well-endowed women desirable. Many women are attracted to scholarly, intellectual men; others find athletic men more attractive. There are other denominators in sexual arousal. Many people become stimulated by inanimate objects, such as shoes, rubber raincoats, or underwear. Others cannot become aroused unless sex is associated with an emotion or activity, for instance, violence or aggression.

The almost infinite variety of stimuli that elicit sexual arousal suggests that response to certain stimuli is a learned behavior. This was noted some three decades ago by sex researchers Ford and Beach (1951) and Kinsey and his colleagues (Kinsey, et al., 1953). Both groups of researchers argued that humans are born only with the anatomy and physiology necessary to respond sexually. The kinds of stimulations and the types of situations that elicit sexual arousal are largely determined by learning.

A recent article by psychologists Karen Rook and Constance Hammen (1977) attempts to explain how this learning occurs. They begin by pointing out that sexual arousal is an emotion and may be acquired in much the same way that other emotions are. One theory regarding the experience of emotion was proposed by social psychologist Stanley Schachter (1964). He suggested that the experience of emotion depends on two factors: (1) perceptible autonomic arousal and (2) situational cues that suggest a label or name for an emotional state. That is, once individuals experience physiological arousal, they will look at their environment for cues that suggest what emotion they are experiencing. (See Chapter 11 for a detailed description of Schachter's theory.) Rook and Hammen argue that the Schachter theory of emotion can be applied to the experience of sexual arousal.

Research in this area is still in the preliminary stages, but one experiment does offer support for a cognitive theory of sexual arousal (Dutton and Aron, 1974). In this experiment, college males were asked to meet an attractive female experimenter. To do so, they had to cross a wobbly wooden bridge that was 230 feet above jagged-looking rocks. In line with a cognitive theory of sexual arousal, the authors hypothesized that these men would be more sexually aroused and attracted to the experimenter than control subjects who either crossed a safe-looking bridge ten feet above a stream or were going to meet a male experimenter. It was thought

that the first bridge would induce physiological arousal, that is, fear, and that once the subject was in the presence of an attractive woman, he would label his arousal as sexual. The results supported the hypothesis. The experimental subjects did tell more sexually oriented stories about a TAT picture (a psychological test intended to measure one's needs) and made more attempts than those in the control group to contact the experimenter after the experiment was completed.

This process of linking physiological arousal to subjective labels probably occurs in children and adolescents. Early sexual experiences are likely to occur in relatively ambiguous circumstances, so that there can be a great deal of variability in the kinds of cues that elicit sexual arousal. For example, many men could recall experiences of attempting to sneak looks at "girlie" magazines on newsstands when they were eleven or twelve years of age. Because of the risk of being discovered, they were likely to be somewhat aroused physiologically. While looking at the pictures, they identified their arousal as sexual. These early experiences probably had an influence on the types of stimuli that elicited feelings of sexual arousal in later life. In fact, psychologist Arthur Staats (1975) has suggested that a case can be made for "normal" pornography. If adolescents have their initial experiences with pictures depicting deviant sexual activities, they may later find these activities the most arousing.

This cognitive or labeling theory of sexual arousal, while potentially useful, does not explain all cases of sexual arousal. It can be applied only in those situations in which it is unclear to the individual what emotion is associated with the physiological arousal. In many cases, people will anticipate or seek arousal in explicit ways; in these cases any subtleties in situational cues will be irrelevant.

Many theorists have speculated about other mechanisms of sexual arousal. The psychoanalytic notion of the Oedipal stage in

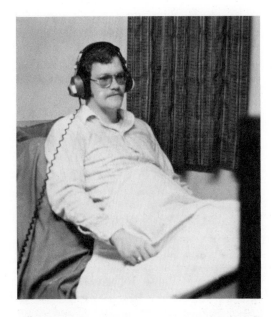

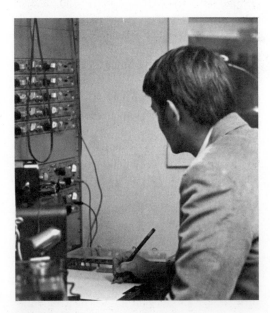

Figure 10.1
Recent laboratory research has provided much information about sexual arousal. (Dwyer and Zinkl)

children and the idea of masturbatory conditioning (see Chapter 4) may offer clues. Also, the influence of peers undoubtedly plays a major role in sexual response. The adolescent girl who hears her friends talk about how sexy a movie star or singer is, is likely to have her patterns of sexual arousal shaped. However, we are still in the speculative stage. Behavioral scientists will be occupied for years to come attempting to understand fully patterns of sexual arousal.

Aphrodisiacs

The search for substances to increase sexual appetite is a centuries-old preoccupation. And the list of substances that purportedly are effective as *aphrodisiacs* is almost endless. Pine nuts, powdered rhinoceros horn, a mixture of bat's blood and donkey's milk, the fat from a camel's hump, and the blood of executed criminals are just a few of the substances once thought to augment sexual arousal. More mundane foods, such as tomatoes, oysters, and potatoes, have also been thought to be aphrodisiacs.

To the dismay of many people, no true aphrodisiacs have been discovered. Nonetheless, each substance mentioned above, and many others, are thought to be effective by at least some people. The cognitive perspective of sexual arousal allows us to understand how such substances may increase the sexual appetites of some individuals. Let us review some substances that currently are thought to have aphrodisiac properties and consider how these substances seem to work.

The search for substances to increase or intensify sexual arousal continues in our own time. Marijuana and cocaine are reported to enhance sexual pleasure, but any effects these drugs may have are likely to be indirect. They may alter perceptions of reality and hence produce idiosyncratic changes in the perception of sexual experiences. That is, these drugs' effects depend to a large extent upon a person's expectations or cognitions. Long-term and heavy use of these drugs may actually detract from the sexual experience. It has been found recently that men who smoked four to five marijuana cigarettes a week had significantly lower testosterone levels (Kolodny, et al., 1974). The side effects of cocaine, such as dryness and inflammation of the vagina and feelings of nervousness and exhaustion, are incompatible with sexual gratification.

Amyl nitrite ("poppers") is a substance that seems to be growing in popularity. This drug produces a drop in blood pressure and a feeling of giddiness. Taken just before orgasm, amyl nitrite supposedly intensifies and prolongs the pleasurable sensations. It is not without side effects, however, and should be used only under medical supervision.

The substance cantharides (Spanish fly) is widely reported to have aphrodisiac properties. Made from a beetle from southern Europe, cantharides irritates the urinary tract and dilates the associated blood vessels. In males it can produce an erection, although it may not be accompanied by sexual desire. This substance, however, is a dangerous drug that can result in death if taken in excessive doses.

The drug most widely thought to have aphrodisiac properties is alcohol. Until recently, scientists and laymen alike believed that there is a link between alcohol and sexual arousal and behavior. It was thought that alcohol influenced sexual arousal and behavior by reducing sexual inhibitions. Many "experts" have commented on this phenomenon. In the scientific literature one can find assertions that alcohol is related to illegitimate pregnancies (Beigel, 1967), child molestation (Gebhard, et al., 1965), rape (Rada, 1975), and numerous other socially undesirable sexual behaviors. Surveys also point to the belief that alcohol can increase sexual

desire. A survey of 20,000 men and women found that some 60 per cent of the respondents enjoyed sex more after drinking (Athanasiou, et al., 1970). So, until recently, the link between alcohol, taken in moderate doses, and sexual activity seemed firmly established.

The problem with most of the evidence suggesting a relationship between alcohol ingestion and sexual behavior is that it is correlational in nature. As shown in Chapter 4, correlational research can demonstrate that a relationship between two variables exists, but it says nothing about causation. Thus, while there was much evidence that suggested a relation between alcohol and various forms of sexual behavior, there was no evidence that alcohol actually *caused* these activities. It was assumed by the scientist and layperson alike that alcohol did in fact cause these behaviors.

Only in the past few years have scientists begun to conduct the type of experiments that allow us to determine if alcohol is directly responsible for changes in sexual arousal. A typical experiment of this type usually involves four conditions or situations. The first includes a group of people who are given alcohol and accurately informed about the contents of the drink. A second situation consists of people who are given alcohol but are led to believe that the beverage is nonalcoholic. The last two groups are not given alcohol: one group is accurately informed about the contents of their beverage, but the other group is led to believe that they are drinking alcohol. After drinking the beverage, all subjects are exposed to sexual stimuli and physiological measures and personal reports of their level of sexual arousal are taken. This type of experiment allows the researcher to assess the independent and interactive effects of alcohol and the subjects' beliefs or expectancies regarding the effects of alcohol.

Recently, clinical psychologist G. Terrence Wilson and his colleagues have been using this type of experiment to examine the effects of alcohol on sexual arousal in both men and women. The results for men are relatively straightforward. Men who *believed* they had consumed an alcoholic beverage had stronger erections and reported more sexual arousal than men who believed they had consumed a nonalcoholic beverage (Briddell, et al., 1978, Wilson and Lawson, 1976). The alcohol itself had no effect. Thus it seems that, for men, beliefs about the effect of alcohol are the crucial factor. In line with this finding, it has been suggested that alcohol provides a convenient excuse for socially unacceptable behaviors. The man who makes a pass at his secretary (or the woman who succumbs) at the office Christmas party can blame it on the drinks.

The effects of alcohol on sexual arousal in women appear to be more complex. In a recent experiment it was found that women who consumed alcohol, regardless of what they thought they drank, showed decreases in sexual arousal as measured physiologically. Interestingly, personal reports of sexual arousal were highest for those subjects who believed they had consumed alcohol, regardless of what they had actually drunk (Wilson and Lawson, 1978). Thus it would seem that although alcohol actually inhibits sexual arousal in women, they believe that it increases it.

The research with men hints at why many substances are thought to be effective aphrodisiacs. If men believe or expect a substance to increase their arousal or potency, then it may very well do so. Many substances may be effective aphrodisiacs because of their psychological properties rather than their physiological properties. This hypothesis is consistent with a cognitive view of sexual arousal.

This is not to say that a physiologically effective and safe aphrodisiac will not be discovered eventually. It is conceivable that drugs could be found that affect the same brain centers that influence sexual arousal.

And, in fact, every now and then, the medical community believes it has found one. A recent example was a drug named L-dopa that is used in treating Parkinson's disease, a neurological disorder. A number of reports appeared, claiming the drug sexually rejuvenated men in their sixties and seventies. Unfortunately, scientific evidence confirming the anecdotal evidence of the effectiveness of L-dopa has not been forthcoming. The search for an effective aphrodisiac will undoubtedly continue.

Techniques of Sexual Arousal

Making love is a cooperative enterprise. While this statement may seem blatantly obvious, many people seem to be unaware of the truth it expresses. With the introduction of numerous "how-to" books in the past decade, many men and women have become overly concerned with technique and whether or not they are "good" lovers. The fact of the matter is that it is impossible to have good technique or be a good lover by oneself. One can be "good" only in relation to another person. It is true that a basic knowledge of bodily responses and functions is helpful, if not essential; the most important sexual "technique," however, is communication between the partners.

One of the ironies associated with human sexuality is that people are reluctant to tell others what makes them feel good. Any mental health professional who has counseled couples on their sex lives can attest to this. Many wives complain that some of their husbands' techniques irritate them, but they wouldn't dream of telling them. Husbands may want their wives to stimulate them in certain ways, but cannot bring themselves to mention it. As every introductory-psychology student knows, feedback is essential if learning is to take place. If couples wish to increase their sexual satisfaction, the most important thing they can do is provide each other with such feedback. By telling each other what they like and what they don't like, what feels good and what doesn't, they are well along the road to having a gratifying and rewarding sex life.

Reluctance to discuss sexual preferences with one's partner is, at times, understandable. Because feelings of self-worth and skill at lovemaking are intertwined for many people (particularly for men), suggestions for changing one's approach may be taken as a personal attack. This reaction can be minimized if the suggestions are made tactfully. The woman who says, "I really like it when we take longer for foreplay" is not as likely to hurt her partner's feelings and more likely to get rewarding results than the woman who says, "You're a lousy lover." Nonetheless, there are some people who cannot tolerate any hint that they are not completely proficient lovers. No matter how tactfully suggestions are made, they perceive them as criticisms. In such cases, the couple should have a frank and open discussion about their feelings and attitudes toward their sexual relationship. Professional counseling can be helpful in resolving such issues.

Foreplay

As we have indicated before, sexual relations do not occur in a vacuum. They are inextricably intertwined with our total being. Thus, our cultural standards, sense of morality, and personalities influence the way in which we go about having sexual relations. In the past (see Chapters 2 and 3) these factors have led individuals to believe that certain types of sexual activity were immoral, perverted, or sinful. These attitudes were reflected in laws that prohibited many forms of sexual behavior, even for married couples (see Chapter 19). While most of these laws have been repealed or remain unenforced,

attitudes associated with them have not completely changed. Even today, many couples restrict their range of sexual techniques because they feel that some may be improper.

Most modern experts in the field of human sexuality argue that there is nothing that adults should not feel free to do together in private, as long as both parties agree. That is, no sexual act or technique is inherently good, bad, moral, or immoral. If the couple enjoys a specific practice, they should feel free to engage in it as long as they are not impinging upon the rights of others. In fact, the ability to experiment and try new techniques is characteristic of the psychologically mature individual.

In the next two sections we shall provide a brief overview of techniques of foreplay and positions for sexual intercourse. The interested reader should view the material presented here as a starting point and consult one of the many popular "how-to" books for more detailed information. However, since many of these books are inaccurate in one way or another, the reader should view such material critically. One manual with a high level of sophistication is Alex Comfort's *The Joy of Sex* (1972).

The term "foreplay" suggests that it is only a means to an end. That is, it implies that people engage in some preliminary activities prior to getting down to the business of having intercourse. This is unfortunate because such a view is incompatible with the greatest pleasure. Masters and Johnson (1970) have reported that many individuals with a sexual dysfunction tend to look ahead to intercourse during foreplay (see Chapter 14). This inhibits the pleasure they could derive from such activities. Foreplay should be viewed as an enjoyable activity in itself rather than as merely preparatory to the "real thing."

Men, much more so than women, are likely to be guilty of paying insufficient attention to foreplay or "pleasuring" their partners. The Hite Report (Hite, 1976), while of dubious scientific value, did illustrate that large numbers of women are dissatisfied with the degree of foreplay they have with their partners. Men would be well advised to attend to this common complaint if they are truly interested in helping their partners achieve satisfaction.

There is some evidence that people are becoming more aware of, and taking more delight in, foreplay. Kinsey reported that college-educated men spent an average of from five to fifteen minutes in foreplay, while less-educated men engaged in only the briefest bodily contact before intromission. Twenty-five years later, Hunt (1974) reported that the duration of foreplay had increased considerably, particularly for less-educated men. This development has undoubtedly been a factor in the increase in the incidence of female orgasms.

If there is one common complaint that men have always had about their partners, it is that they are too passive. This disposition has changed considerably during the past decade, however, with the advent of women's liberation and the demand for sexual equality. Women have begun to realize that they can feel free to pleasure their partners and initiate sexual relations. Most men prefer active and enthusiastic partners.

The number of ways in which foreplay can be initiated is almost limitless. A couple may build up to it slowly, beginning with a romantic evening out. Or they may begin on the spur of the moment, with one of them making a rather explicit suggestion. Couples who know each other well may initiate foreplay with a "knowing" glance or when one of them wears a particular article of clothing, such as

Figure 10.2
A romantic dinner can be an effective form of foreplay. (Dwyer and Zink l)

a nightgown. Part of the fun of sex comes from employing a variety of approaches to communicate one's desire to make love.

Actual physical contact often begins with kissing. The couple may start with a light, delicate touch and proceed to more vigorous and passionate kissing. The tongue and mouth play an important role. One may stroke the partner's lips with the tongue and eventually explore the partner's mouth with it. (The use of the tongue during kissing is often called "French kissing," but it is unlikely that it originated in any single culture.)

Kissing, of course, is not restricted to the mouth. Some parts of the body are especially susceptible, and erotic response can be stimulated with kisses. These erogenous zones, as they are called, include the neck, earlobes, fingertips, breasts, abdomen, and the inside of the thighs. As always, communication between the partners is essential in order to ensure that the most sensitive areas of the body are properly caressed. It should be remembered that while there are similarities among people, erotic response is an individualistic matter. What one person finds stimulating may leave another cold.

Tactile stimulation is an important part of foreplay. Sexual partners enjoy using hands to explore all parts of the body. In fact, more than one "expert" has declared the hands to be the most important sexual "tools."

Two important erogenous zones are the breasts and the genitals. Most women enjoy having their breasts, particularly the nipple, stimulated—both with the hand and the mouth. Size of the breasts bears no relation to erotic response, so it should not be assumed that women with small breasts do not enjoy this activity. Although not as well known, men's nipples also are a sensitive area; some men enjoy having their nipples caressed or kissed.

Stimulation of the genitals is probably the most exciting form of foreplay for most people. For women, the clitoris and the labia

minora are the most sensitive areas. Stimulation is likely to be most effective if it is gentle and rhythmic. Masters and Johnson (1966) found that many women find direct stimulation of the clitoral glans to be painful. It may be more effective, therefore, to stroke the clitoral shaft or provide indirect stimulation by manipulating the mons area as a whole. A vibrator may be used in clitoral stimulation as in Fig. 10.3. Communication between partners is essential to discover the method that affords the most pleasure.

Manipulation of the penis can be initiated by gently stroking the glans and frenulum. As arousal becomes more intense, the woman may grip the shaft and move her hand over it in a "milking" manner. Some men report that the extreme sensitivity of the glans makes vigorous stimulation of this area unpleasant. It is up to the man to give his partner feedback about what is enjoyable.

In general, tactile stimulation is likely to be most effective if it begins gently, and gradually becomes more vigorous. As always, there is a wide range of individual variability. Some people want rough handling, while others may prefer to maintain a slow gentle pace throughout foreplay. Communication between sexual partners is essential. The person who has preconceived ideas about how to please a sexual partner is likely to be wrong as often as he or she is right. In addition, any one person may crave a variety of approaches to foreplay. For instance, a woman may have a preference for a slow, gentle, "teasing" style of foreplay, but there may be times when she wants her partner to be more vigorous and forceful in his approach. The man who typically wants only minimal foreplay is likely to want his partner to spend more time in stimulating him on other occasions. The ability to communicate with and be sensitive to the needs of one's partner is more important to sexual compatability than specific techniques.

Oral-genital stimulation can be a highly

effective form of stimulation. In the past, a substantial proportion of the population found this type of foreplay unacceptable, but it is becoming increasingly common (see Chapter 3).

Oral stimulation of the woman's genitals, called cunnilingus, involves gentle stimulation of the clitoris and labia minora. Fellatio, or oral stimulation of the penis, involves stroking the glans and frenulum with the tongue and lips. As arousal becomes more intense, the woman may suck the penis while the man engages in coital movements. Couples may engage in mutual oral-genital stimulation ("sixty-nine") as a form of foreplay or for its own sake (Fig. 10.4).

The anus also has the potential for erotic response. Both men and women may find manual or oral stimulation of the anus pleasurable. The growing acceptance of anal foreplay represents a major shift in attitudes. A generation ago such practices were viewed with general disgust and suspicion. Kinsey, for example, failed to collect any publishable data regarding anal sex. In the 1970s, anal techniques are openly discussed in a number

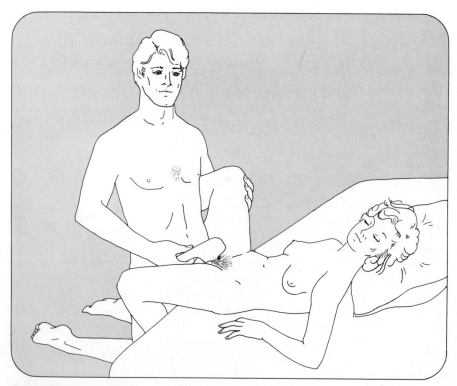

Figure 10.3
Use of a vibrator in clitoral stimulation.

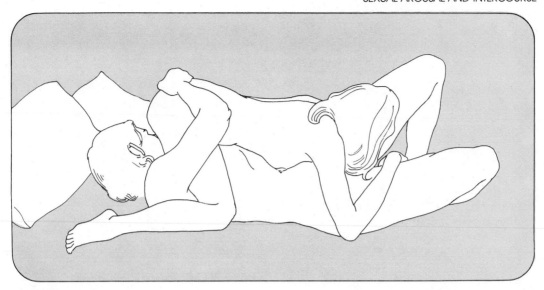

Figure 10.4
Mutual oral-genital stimulation.

of sex manuals. Hunt (1974) reported that half of young married couples surveyed indicated that they would find manual anal foreplay acceptable with someone they loved. Over one-third indicated their acceptance of oral-anal practices.*

The duration of foreplay varies from couple to couple and from occasion to occasion for a given couple. Generally, it is desirable to prolong foreplay until both partners are ready for intercourse. Unfortunately, it is often the case that one person requires or desires much more foreplay than the other. The couple with mutual respect and affection will be able to discuss such issues and arrive at a resolution satisfactory to both.

Sexual Intercourse

The number of coital positions is limited only by the imagination. The position se-

*Hygiene becomes an important consideration when anal techniques are used. The penis or hand should be thoroughly washed before moving from the anus to the vagina.

lected for any occasion will depend on a number of factors. The setting, degree of privacy, psychological needs, and physical limitations of the couple will all play a role. In this section four basic positions will be presented, and the advantages and disadvantages of each will be discussed. One should keep in mind that there are numerous variations of each of these basic positions.

Face-to-Face, Man-Above Position. This position, illustrated in Figure 10.5, is referred to as the *missionary position*. It is by far the most common one in European and American cultures. In fact, a generation ago, about 70 percent of Americans had never had intercourse in any other manner (Kinsey, et al., 1948). Currently, less than one-fourth of the population restrict themselves to this position (Hunt, 1974).

This position usually makes intromission quite easy when the woman has her legs apart and knees bent. Some couples like to place a pillow under the woman's buttocks. This helps to adjust the slant of her vagina for

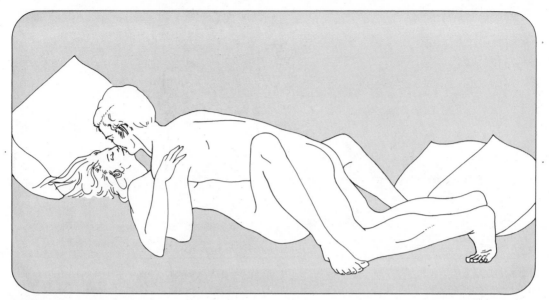

Figure 10.5
Man above coital position.

easy and deep penetration.* As always, the woman should guide the penis into the vagina with her hand since she knows exactly where the penis goes. This has the dual advantage of communicating her interest and enthusiasm and reducing any anxiety her partner may experience during a difficult intromission.

After intromission the woman can change the position of her legs to vary the sensations she and her partner experience. By pulling her knees to her shoulders, or placing her legs on her partner's shoulders, deeper penetration can be achieved. She may extend her legs or close them between her partner's. This constricts the vaginal opening and walls, which in turn provides more friction to her partner's penis. This technique is useful when the man has less than a full erection.

*The vagina must be thoroughly lubricated if intromission is to be easy and painless. If natural lubricants are insufficient, a number of commercial products are available. Many people enjoy using these products, even when there are sufficient natural lubricants, because of the sensations that can result from their use.

The man may avoid putting his full weight on his partner by partially supporting himself on his elbows and knees. Because he is largely in control of bodily movements in this position, he must be sensitive to his partner's desires and responsiveness. It is generally helpful to maintain pressure on the woman's pubic bone; this provides stimulation for the clitoris.

The advantages of this position are largely psychological. Many people feel that this position is the most "natural," and therefore are likely to be less inhibited and derive more pleasure. The missionary position does allow for the couple to kiss, caress, and observe each other's facial expressions. Also, for couples who want a child, this position increases the likelihood of conception, particularly if the woman's knees are drawn forward (see Chapter 6). An important advantage concerns the ease of intromission in this position. In fact many couples achieve intromission in this position before shifting to another.

The disadvantages of this position lie

chiefly in the woman's restricted range of movements: it is difficult for her to be an active participant, and she has little control over the depth of penetration. The man-above position is difficult when the partners are obese and may be unadvisable for women in late pregnancy. While this position is highly stimulating for most men, it makes it difficult for him to control ejaculation. Sex therapists often recommend other positions when the couple wishes to prolong the duration of intercourse (Masters and Johnson, 1970).

Woman-Above Position. This position, illustrated in Fig. 10.6, is probably second in popularity. Hunt (1974) reported that nearly three-fourths of all married couples used this position at least occasionally. Intromission can be achieved by having the woman lower her body over her partner and guiding his penis into her vagina. Many couples, however, find it easier to achieve intromission in the man-above position; they then roll over into this position.

The advantages of the woman-on-top position are many. It allows the woman to an active participant. Because she can control the tempo, movements, and depth of penetration, many women find this position to be the most stimulating. Men may like this position because it requires little exertion or strain on their part. This may allow a man to delay his orgasm. An important advantage is that the man's hands are free to caress his partner's body. As in the man-above position, partners are able to observe each other's reactions (see Fig. 10.7).

The disadvantages of the woman-above position are mainly psychological. Some men may feel that their passive role in this position is feminine. And some women may be too inhibited to take the active role in intercourse. However, as can be seen in Hunt's data, younger people are much less likely to be bound by traditional notions of sex roles. This position does have the disadvantage of restricting the man's movements. Because he is not in control of the coital movements, it is not uncommon for the penis to slip out of the vagina on occasion. With practice, the couple is usually able to overcome this problem.

Face-to-Face, Side Position. Many couples use this position, illustrated in Figure

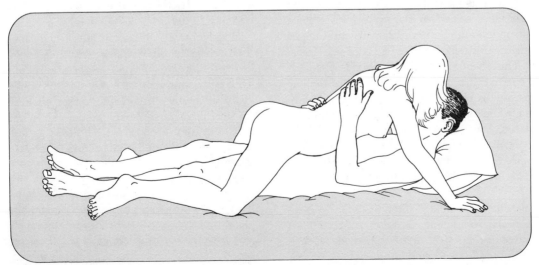

Figure 10.6
Woman above coital position.

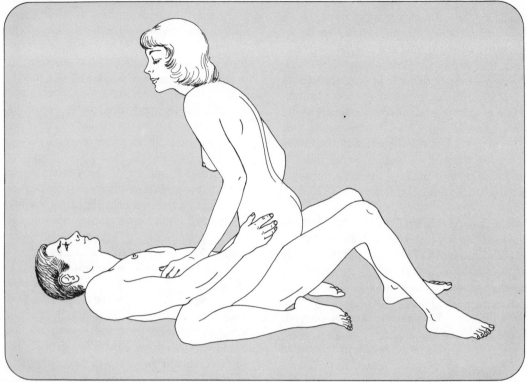

Figure 10.7
Woman on top coital position.

10.8, when they wish to have slow, relaxed, and leisurely intercourse. Generally, however, it is easier for the couple to achieve intromission in another position and then to roll on their sides.

The advantages of this position lie chiefly in its relaxed approach to intercourse. Neither partner is pinned down, so problems of fatigue and muscle cramping are virtually eliminated. Both partners have the freedom to control pelvic thrusting. This position is especially desirable when one or both of the partners are fatigued, in poor health, or obese. When one partner is considerably taller than the other, the couple often prefers this position. These advantages, taken together with the close body contact it provides, have prompted Masters and Johnson to refer to it as "the most effective coital position available

to man and woman." They believe that once a couple has tried this position, they will utilize it about 75 percent of the time.

Disadvantages of this position lie in the fact that it is difficult to have vigorous pelvic thrusting or to achieve deep penetration. Thus some couples may find it uncomfortable or insufficiently stimulating.

Rear-Entry Position. There is a variety of ways in which the man can effect intromission from behind the female (see Figure 10.9). Both partners can lie on their sides with the woman's back against the man's chest. Also, the woman can lie on her stomach, or kneel with her weight resting on her knees and elbows. Or the woman can sit in her partner's lap with her back to him.

This position can be highly exciting be-

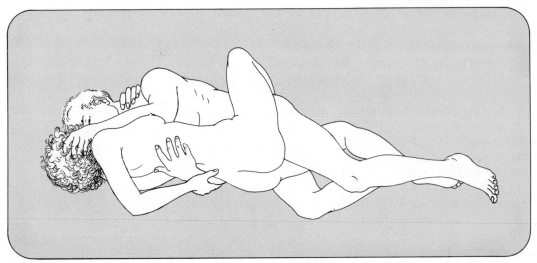

Figure 10.8
Side-by-side coital position.

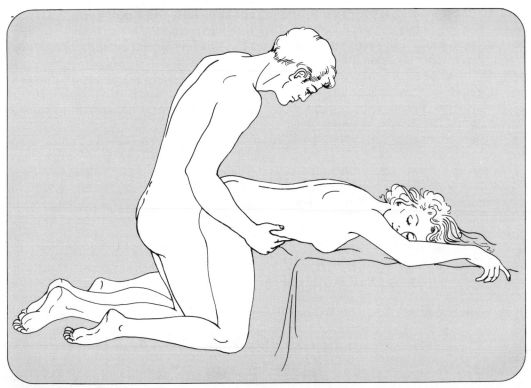

Figure 10.9
Rear-entry coital position.

cause it shortens the woman's vagina, making deep penetration possible. Many men like this position because they find the pressure of their partner's buttocks against their body stimulating. The man also has the freedom to use his hands to further stimulate his partner.

One important disadvantage, particularly with the sitting positions, is that the deep penetration it allows may be uncomfortable or even painful to the woman. Some couples object to this position because its lack of face-to-face intimacy makes sex seem impersonal. There may be psychological barriers that prevent others from using this position. Because it is the typical position used by animals, some may feel that it is degrading or perverted. Needless to say, such objections have no basis in reality.

Coital Movements. The manner in which sexual partners move once intromission has been effected is every bit as important, if not more so, than the position selected. The general pattern of movement involves thrusting (in and out), which gradually increases in tempo until orgasm is reached. While this may be the most "natural" pattern, it certainly can be improved upon.

The most skillful lovers are those who are willing to take advantage of the infinite degree of variety possible during coitus. Shallow thrusting can be alternated with deeper thrusts. A period of rapid thrusting can be followed by several minutes of slow, teasing thrusting. After a period of deep thrusting, many couples find it highly stimulating if just the glans of the penis moves across the introitus. Another variation is to place the penis deep inside the vagina and then to rotate the pelvis. Both the man and the woman should attempt to provide their partners with variety of movements. Couples who are sensitive to each other can discover ways of moving that

provide novel sensations even after years of marriage.

Orgasm

One goal, although certainly not the only one, that most people have in mind when they engage in sexual activity is to reach orgasm. As you recall from Chapter 5, the physiology of orgasm is relatively straightforward. The psychology of orgasm, however, is much more complex, and a plethora of popular books published in recent years have offered advice on how men and women can increase the intensity and frequency of their orgasms.

Several experts, such as Masters and Johnson, have suggested that many people place too much emphasis on orgasm. In their attempt to have orgasm or bring their partner to orgasm, some people may have been rendered sexually dysfunctional (see Chapter 14). Masters and Johnson believe that people should view sexual activity as a process to be enjoyed rather than as a means to an end—namely orgasm. If people focus on the process, then the orgasms will follow with little difficulty.

An important point is that all orgasms are not the same. Different positions produce different sensations, and different types of orgasms will inevitably result. Also, the variety of motives for having intercourse discussed at the beginning of this chapter are likely to result in different types of orgasms. The person who has intercourse for reassurance and emotional closeness is likely to experience orgasm quite differently from the one who is motivated by lust. And, importantly, a subdued orgasm that helps one feel closer to his or her partner can be as satisfying emotionally as more intense orgasms that are associated with lust. Perhaps the most adaptive approach is to value the psychological differences that can exist between orgasms rather than striving for ever better orgasmic experiences.

The Problem of Sexual Monotony

Sexual monotony is an issue that most couples with long-term relationships must face at one time or another. This fact has not been lost on popular writers who have published hundreds of books containing thousands of ways to enrich one's sexual life. While many of these manuals are of dubious scientific value, the general principles suggested by them are often similar to those involved in the treatment of sexual dysfunction. Three of these principles are communication between partners, a greater emphasis on foreplay, and an openness to new experiences.

As we have indicated earlier, the first principle, open communication between sexual partners, may be the most crucial. Openness is just as important in an established relationship, as in a newly developed relationship. Couples who communicated openly in the early stages of their relationship may have grown reluctant to suggest changes or to express concerns several years later. Sexual monotony will probably not be overcome if a couple is not able to discuss the subject with each other.

The second general principle concerns foreplay. Often, couples in the early stage of a relationship delight in spending extended periods of time in foreplay. As the relationship progresses, however, they may have a tendency to view foreplay as merely a preparation for intercourse. This approach tends to turn sex into little more than an exercise in tension reduction. Needless to say, such an approach is bound to contribute to sexual monotony. Couples would be well advised to view foreplay as a pleasurable activity in its own right rather than as a means to an end.

The third principle, openness to new experiences, is given the most attention by many current sex manuals. They often suggest an endless number of activities to be engaged in with oneself, with a partner, with multiple partners, with mechanical devices, and so on. While many of these recommendations are unacceptable to the average couple, many other suggestions do have merit. Variety in coital positions, for example, has much to recommend it. Many couples experiment with a variety of positions early in their relationship, but then fall into the habit of relying on a limited number. It is possible for a couple to use a different position every time they have intercourse. Of course, such acrobatic extremes are not necessary, but experimentation with new techniques can bring novelty to even the longest-lasting relationships.

Variety can also be introduced by changing the setting for intercourse. Many married couples virtually never have intercourse except after the late news and before going to sleep. Initiating or having sex in the kitchen, in front of a fireplace, or even the back seat of a car can introduce novelty into the relationship. Many married couples find that a weekend away from the children can do wonders for their sex life.

There are numerous other ways in which a couple can reduce monotony. For example, many couples find that sharing their sexual fantasies can be highly stimulating. Psychologists are well aware of the important role that fantasy plays in sexual arousal. It has been found that men and women become more aroused when asked to fantasize than when they view erotic pictures (Byrne and Lamberth, 1971). Sharing fantasies, however, must be done with tact and sensitivity. Not everyone is secure enough to accept a partner's fantasies with equanimity. The couple that enjoys this activity, however, may like to share each other's fantasies.

Those concerned with the issue of sex-

Fantasy and Sexual Arousal

"Sue considers herself happily married. She enjoys sexual intercourse with her husband and usually reaches orgasm. However, just as she approaches the peak she imagines that she is tied to a table while several men caress her, touch her genitals, and have intercourse with her. It is a fleeting image; as she passes into orgasm it disappears" (Hariton, 1973).

Had Sue related her fantasy to a psychiatrist a decade or two ago, she probably would have been told that she was in dire need of therapy. Freud believed that fantasies were symptoms of neuroses and sexual maladjustment, and this view persists even today. Currently, however, most therapists recognize that sexual fantasies need not be a sign of pathology, but may represent a heightened sense of sexuality. Men and women who enjoy sex are likely to have a rich sexual fantasy life. In fact, many therapists will encourage dysfunctional individuals to develop and use sexual fantasies while making love.

Kinsey reported that half of all women and nearly three-fourths of men fantasized most of the time during masturbation. Men and women are likely to share many fantasies, but there are some differences in themes (Hunt, 1974). The most common male fantasy was to have intercourse with a stranger (47 percent), while women were most likely to fantasize about sexual activities that they would never engage in, in reality (28 percent). Men were more likely to have fantasies about forcing someone to have sex (13 percent), while women were more likely to fantasize about being forced to have sex (19 percent). An analysis of the differences between men's and women's fantasies has suggested that both sexes use fantasies to express their sexual desire and appeal. Men fantasize about situations in which they are powerful and aggressive and entice women to have impersonal sex with them. Women are likely to imagine that their sexual desirability incites strange men to force them to have sex, while at the same time making efforts to excite and satisfy her.

In a study of women's fantasies during intercourse it was found that 65 percent of the women had fantasies while having intercourse with their husbands (Hariton and Singer, 1974). The two most common themes were having sex with an imaginary lover and being overpowered or forced to have sex. Contrary to psychoanalytic theory, women who fantasized were well adjusted and satisfied with their sexual relationship with their husbands. There have been no comparable studies of men's fantasies during intercourse, but, based on information about their fantasies during masturbation, they are more likely to fantasize during intercourse than women.

ual monotony may wish to consult other sources, such as *The Joy of Sex* and *More Joy*, for additional ideas. While it is possible to increase the novelty of most on-going sexual relationships, it is probably unrealistic for a couple to expect to maintain the high level of excitement experienced in the early stages of their lovemaking. Most people feel, however, that there are more than sufficient compensations in having a long-term, stable relationship. Feelings of closeness, intimacy, and emotional interdependency develop fully in such a relationship.

Masturbation

Most everyone, given their choice, would prefer to have sex with another person. But virtually everyone has periods in which no sexual partner is available. During these times, a substantial number of people use self-stimulation, or masturbation, as a means of achieving orgasm. Hunt's data indicated that 94 percent of males and 63 percent of females had had experience with masturbation (1974). These figures clearly indicate that masturbation is an important form of sexual activity.

As we indicated above, the most important reason for masturbating is probably the unavailability of a sexual partner. Adolescents who have yet to have their first sexual relationship, adults who are between relationships, and adults whose regular partner is unavailable for such reasons as illness or travel, can be expected to desire gratification of their sexual drive. In fact, Hunt reported that the most commonly cited reason for masturbation in his sample was release from sexual tensions. Thus, it would seem that masturbation is a relatively simple and straightforward matter.

The topic of masturbation has received considerable attention from physicians and psychiatrists, and, until recently, very little good was said about it. Around the turn of the century, masturbation was thought to cause almost every imaginable physical and psychological ailment. As recently as the 1960s, substantial numbers of medical students believed that masturbation caused insanity. Freud and his followers added a new dimension. They suggested that masturbation was evidence of arrested psychological development (see

Chapter 4 for further discussion of this topic). With this history, it is not surprising that Hunt reported that even among educated people a great deal of ambivalence exists regarding masturbation. People who are aware that there is nothing physically or psychologically dangerous about masturbation, and that the person who has never masturbated is more unusual than those who have, still feel embarrassed about the practice. It is difficult for many people to feel comfortable with the role self-stimulation plays in their sexuality.

The fact that more than half of married people masturbate (Hunt, 1974) indicates that sexual deprivation is not the only reason for doing so. An examination of the fantasies that people have while masturbating suggests an additional motive: it may provide a safe means of expressing sexual interests that a person is unwilling or unable to experience in real life. The most common fantasy involves sexual encounters with a loved person, but substantial numbers of both men and women engage in more daring fantasies. Having sex with acquaintances and strangers in a variety of settings, having sex with several partners, being forced to have sex, forcing someone to have sex, and homosexual experiences are all relatively common fantasies (Hunt, 1974).

While people can become intensely aroused while fantasizing unusual sex practices, it does not necessarily follow that they would like to have the actual experience. For example, many women masturbate to fantasies of rape, but they do not want to have to undergo such an experience. In fantasies one can control the appearance of the partner, the setting, the approach, and all the other relevant details. The violence and degradation of a real-life rape is quite another matter.

Some mental health professionals, particularly those with a psychoanalytic orientation, suggest that fantasies during masturbation represent unconscious conflicts. However, this is a difficult proposition to prove. Most experts argue that indulgence in unusual fantasies is not harmful as long as a person clearly distinguishes fantasies from reality.

Changes in attitudes toward masturbation have been an important part of the sexual revolution. "Experts" who warn of the dangers of masturbation are increasingly rare. Most mental health experts agree that learning to masturbate is a normal part of growing up. In his book *Boys and Sex*, Dr. Wardell Pomeroy (1968) advised boys to masturbate as much as they want to. He also suggested that rather than doing it as fast as they could, they should try to do it slowly, since this would be good practice for when they became lovers. In a similar book for girls, he gave essentially the same advice, but suggested that girls not delay orgasm if they wished to have successful intercourse in the future (Pomeroy, 1969).

Summary

This chapter has discussed motives for sex, scientific knowledge of sexual arousal, techniques of foreplay and intercourse, the problem of sexual monotony, and masturbation. Sexual acts can be motivated by a number of factors. Affection, animosity, anxiety, boredom, and a sense of duty are just a few of the reasons people have sex. It is likely that the motives of any particular person will vary from occasion to occasion.

Behavioral scientists are just beginning to acquire accurate information about sexual arousal. Research has been hampered by prevailing moral and social standards and by the fact that, until recently, there was no objective way to measure sexual arousal. The development of the penile plethysmograph and strain gauge and the photoplethysmograph now makes it possible to detect physio-logical sexual arousal in both men and women. These devices should stimulate more research in this area.

One theory of sexual arousal emphasizes cognitive factors. This theory suggests that people learn to become aroused in response to certain stimuli by looking at their environment. There, they find cues that allow them to label their state of physiological arousal. Other factors, such as social learning and peer influence, also play a role. A cognitive theory of sexual arousal helps to explain the phenomenon of aphrodisiacs. If people believe a particular substance increases sexual arousal, whether it is powdered rhinoceros horn or alcohol, it will probably do so.

We have also described sexual techniques of foreplay and intercourse. The most important "technique" is communication between sexual partners. Foreplay generally begins with kissing and proceeds to tactile stimulation of the erogenous zones. Foreplay should continue until both partners are ready for, and desire, intercourse. There are numerous positions for intercourse, but most of them are variations of four basic positions: (1) man above; (2) woman above; (3) side by side; (4) rear entry. Each position has its advantages and disadvantages.

It is probably impossible for a long-term sexual relationship to remain as exciting as it was in its early stages, but couples can do a number of things to minimize problems of sexual boredom. Variety, increased emphasis on foreplay, and the sharing of fantasies are effective for many people.

Masturbation is generally viewed as a substitute for having sex with another person. While many people use it in this way, it can nonetheless be an important source of gratification. The use of fantasy during masturbation can make it a vehicle for the expression of sexual interests that many people are unable or unwilling to express in real life.

References

Athanasiou, R., Shaver, P., and Tavris, C. "Sex." *Psychology Today*, January, 1970, pp. 37-52.

Beigel, H. "Illegitimacy." In A. Ellis and A. Abarbanel (eds.). *Encyclopaedia of Sexual Behavior*. New York: Hawthorn Books, 1967.

Briddell, D. W., Rimm, D. C., Caddy, G. R., Krawitz, G., Sholis, D., and Wunderlin, R. J. "Effects of alcohol and cognitive set on sexual arousal to deviant stimuli." *Journal of Abnormal Psychology*, 1978, 87, 418-430.

Byrne, D. and Lamberth, J. "The effects of erotic stimuli on sex arousal, evaluative responses, and subsequent behavior." In technical report of the *Commission on Obscenity and Pornography* (Vol. 8). Washington, D. C.: U.S. Government Printing Office, 1971.

Comfort, A. (ed.). *The joy of sex*. New York: Crown, 1972.

Dutton, D. and Aron, A. "Some evidence for heightened sexual attraction under conditions of high anxiety." *Journal of Personality and Social Psychology*, 1974, 30, 510-517.

Ford, C. S. and Beach, F. A. *Patterns of sexual behavior*. New York: Harper & Row, 1951.

Fullerton, C. P. "Commentary: The myriad motives for sex." In L. Gross (ed.), *Sexual Behavior: Current Issues*. Flushing, N.Y.: Spectrum Publications, 1974.

Gebhard, P. H., Gagnon, J. H., Pomeroy, W. B., and Christenson, C. V. *Sex offenders*. New York: Harper & Row, 1965.

Hariton, B. E. "The sexual fantasies of women." *Psychology Today*, 1973, 6 (10), 39-44.

Hariton, B. E. and Singer, J. L. "Women's fantasies during sexual intercourse: Normative and theoretical implications." *Journal of Consulting and Clinical Psychology*, 1974, 42, 313-322.

Hite, S. *The Hite report*. New York: Macmillan, 1976.

Hunt, M. *Sexual behavior in the 1970s*. New York: Dell Books, 1974.

Kinsey, A. C., Pomeroy, W. B., and Martin, C. E. *Sexual behavior in the human male*. Philadelphia: W. B. Saunders, 1948.

Kinsey, A. C., Pomeroy, W. B., Martin, C. E., and Gebhard, P. H. *Sexual behavior in the human female*. Philadelphia: W. B. Saunders, 1953.

Kirkendall, L. A. "Commentary: The myriad motives for sex." In L. Gross (ed.), *Sexual behavior: Current issues*. Flushing, N.Y.: Spectrum Publications, 1974.

Kolodny, R. C., Masters, W. H., Kolodner, R. M., and Toro, G. "Depression of plasma testosterone levels after chronic intensive marihuana use." *New England Journal of Medicine*, 1974, 290, 872-874.

Layman, W. A. "The 'saint or sinner' syndrome: Separation of love and sex by women." *Medical Aspects of Human Sexuality*, August, 1976, pp. 46-53.

Masters, W. and Johnson, V. *Human sexual response.* Boston: Little, Brown, 1966.

Masters, W. and Johnson, V. *Human sexual inadequacy.* Boston: Little, Brown, 1970.

Mathis, J. "The madonna-prostitute syndrome." *Medical Aspects of Human Sexuality,* January, 1971, p. 202.

Neubeck, G. "The myriad motives for sex." In L. Gross (ed.), *Sexual behavior: Current issues.* Flushing, N.Y.: Spectrum Publications, 1974.

O'Grady, K. E. and Janda, L. H. "Sex guilt: A review of the literature." Unpublished Manuscript, Old Dominion University.

Pomeroy, W. B. *Boys and sex.* New York: Delacorte Press, 1968.

Pomeroy, W. B. *Girls and sex.* New York: Delacorte Press, 1969.

Rada, R. T. "Alcohol and rape." *Medical Aspects of Human Sexuality,* 1975, 9, 48-65.

Rook, K. S. and Hammen, C. L. "A cognitive perspective on sexual arousal." *Journal of Social Issues,* 1977, 33, 7-29.

Schachter, S. "The interaction of cognitive and physiological determinants of emotional state." In L. Berkowitz (ed.), *Advances in experimental social psychology.* New York: Academic Press, 1964.

Sintchak, G. and Geer, J. "A vaginal photoplethysmograph system." *Psychophysiology,* 1975, 1, 113-115.

Staats, A. W. *Social behaviorism.* Homewood, Ill.: Dorsey, 1975.

Wilson, G. T. and Lawson, D. M. "Expectancies, alcohol, and sexual arousal in male social drinkers." *Journal of Abnormal Psychology,* 1976, 85, 587-594.

Wilson, G. T. and Lawson, D. M. "Expectancies, alcohol, and sexual arousal in women." *Journal of Abnormal Psychology,* 1978, 87, 358-367.

Wincze, V., Hoon, E., and Hoon, P. "A comparison of the physiological responsivity of normal and sexually dysfunctional women during exposure to erotic stimulus." *Journal of Psychosomatic Research,* 1976, 20, 44-50.

Chapter 11

Interpersonal Attraction and Romantic Love

In the middle 1970s a well-known Senator from the Midwest criticized the National Science Foundation for funding research to study romantic attraction. His objections to such a scientific pursuit rested on the assumptions that scientists could never unravel the "mystery" of love and, even if they could, people wouldn't want to know the answers. The Senator went so far as to assert that as far as romantic attraction is concerned "ignorance is bliss."

It is difficult to understand how anyone could actually believe that people are not interested in knowing answers to questions about relationships between men and women. Love is big business in our society. People spend millions of dollars every year on books, magazines, fortune tellers, astrologers, and even professional counsellors in an attempt to find answers. It seems safe to assume that questions about romantic relationships are near the top of the list of questions that people want to have answered.

Only in recent years have behavioral scientists begun to collect the kind of information that provides definitive answers to these questions. Social psychologists—those who have done most of the research in this area—began to study interpersonal attraction some twenty years ago. The study of romantic love is barely a decade old. While much remains to be learned, we are beginning to understand the factors that can lead to mutual attraction and romantic love. Let us review the current state of knowledge.

Interpersonal Attraction

Much of the research conducted by social psychologists has involved situations in which two strangers meet for the first time. By varying the setting and the type of information available to those involved, much has been learned about the factors that lead to initial attraction. Let us explore these findings.

Familiarity

Familiarity may breed contempt on some occasions, but in general it appears to lead to attraction. We have a tendency to like and develop relationships with those with whom we have contact. This principle is illustrated in a now classic study by Leon Festinger and his colleagues (Festinger, 1951). They investigated the formation of friendships in a new housing project for married students. The project consisted of small houses arranged in U-shaped courts. All of the houses faced onto a grassy area except the end houses, which faced the street.

The investigators concluded that the major factors influencing friendship formation were the distance between houses and the direction in which the houses faced. Friendships were most common between next-door neighbors, somewhat less common between people whose houses were separated by another house, and so on. In addition, the people who lived in the end houses had fewer than half as many friends as those whose houses faced the court area. (It is somewhat disconcerting to know that one's social life depends so heavily upon the location of one's house.)

This *proximity factor*, as it is called, also has an effect upon mate selection. A number of studies have demonstrated that the closer single men and women live to one another, the more likely they are to meet and marry. In summarizing this line of research Kephart (1961) has concluded that notions of romantic love and the "one and only" notwithstanding, the chances are better than fifty-fifty that a person will marry someone within walking distance.

Because proximity can lead to hostility as well as attraction, it might be speculated that proximity simply provides an opportunity to acquire information about those who live nearby. Depending on the type of information acquired, either strong positive or strong

Figure 11.1
The proximity factor suggests that men and women living in the same building are likely to form relationships. (Dwyer and Zinkl)

negative feelings can develop. Researchers have considered this possibility and conducted experiments to test it. The answer seems to be that proximity is more likely to lead to attraction than hostility.

To illustrate this theory, Ellen Berscheid and her colleagues (Berscheid, et al., 1976) demonstrated that even the anticipation of proximity or familiarity can lead to attraction. They told college men and women that they wanted to study romantic relationships. To this end, the students were asked to agree to date exclusively the person who was selected for them for either one week or six weeks. After making the commitment, the students were allowed to view a videotape of their prospective date participating in a group discussion. Ratings of the group members indicated that the longer the student expected to

date the other person, the more positively that person was rated. The researchers concluded that mere anticipation of interaction with another person can lead to a desire to find positive qualities in him or her.

Reciprocity of Liking

A second basic principle of interpersonal attraction is that we like those who like us. A number of experiments have shown that we tend to like those who do favors for us (Jennings, 1959), make flattering comments about us, and indicate that they like us (Jones, 1964). The power of the reciprocity-of-liking effect is evident by the fact that philosophers and interpersonal-relations "experts" have been aware of it for some time. In the second century B.C. the philosopher

Hecato wrote that those who wish to be loved should love others. In more recent times, Dale Carnegie has advised those who wish to win friends and influence people to greet others enthusiastically and to use generous amounts of praise (1937).

As is usually the case with human behavior, things are not quite so simple. A number of additional factors can mediate the reciprocity-of-liking effect. One such factor is one's own self-esteem. The fact that many people do seem to get married on the rebound suggests that when our self-evaluation is particularly low, we are especially susceptible to the attention of others. This idea is supported by several experiments.

In one example, Walster (1965) asked a number of women to participate in an experiment. On the way to the experimental session, each woman "accidentally" bumped into a man who was really a confederate of the experimenter. During the conversation that ensued, the man made it clear that he was romantically interested in her and asked her for a date for the following week. Following this, each woman was asked to take several psychological tests. In order to manipulate the self-esteem of the women, half the subjects were told that the tests indicated that they were immature and lacked capacity for successful leadership. The remaining women were given extremely positive feedback. Each was told that she possessed "one of the most favorable personality structures analyzed by the staff."

The results were as predicted. Women with lowered self-esteem (those who received the negative feedback) indicated that they liked the man they had met earlier "extremely much" or "fairly much." Women with raised self-esteem were relatively neutral about their prospective date.

A second factor that mediates the reciprocity-of-liking rule is the constancy of favorable feedback. Social psychologist Elliot Aronson (1969) has argued that increasing re-

wards for behavior has more impact than constant rewards. For example, suppose you overheard two strangers talking about you at a party. One said positive things about you, while the second person said rather negative things. Imagine that the following week you again encountered the two strangers and again you overheard the first one saying positive things about you, but this time the second stranger was saying somewhat less negative things. At several subsequent parties, the first stranger continued to make positive remarks, and the second stranger's remarks became increasingly positive. Which person would you be most attracted to? In a study using a very similar paradigm, it was found that people liked a person whose comments moved from negative to positive more than a person whose comments were always positive (Aronson and Linder, 1965). Conversely, a person whose remarks shifted from positive to negative was disliked more than one whose comments were consistently negative.

This *gain-loss theory*, as it is called, can also be applied to situations in which friends and strangers make either positive or negative remarks. For example, a husband's remark to his wife that she looks attractive may have little impact because she is accustomed to having him say nice things about her. The same woman, however, may feel extremely flattered if a stranger or acquaintance pays her the same compliment; coming from him, it represents a "gain." Conversely, an unkind remark from a husband should have more impact than the same remark from an acquaintance; it represents a "loss." This phenomenon has been found in laboratory settings (Harvey, 1962).

Those who take Dale Carnegie seriously and wish to use the reciprocity-of-liking rule to their own benefit should be warned that it may not always work. Although it is generally true that we like others who flatter us and like us, we do not like those who do so with an ulterior motive. For instance, most people would be suspicious of the salesperson who is overly friendly or complimentary. They would suspect (with some justification) that such behavior was merely a prelude to the hard sell. Thus, when friendliness and flattery are viewed as ingratiating, they are not likely to be successful in eliciting liking or attraction (Jones, 1964).

Attitude Similarity

Perhaps the most firmly established rule of interpersonal attraction is that we tend to like those who we perceive as being similar to ourselves. Put more simply, "birds of a feather flock together." Psychologist Donn Byrne and his colleagues have conducted much of the research that establishes this principle. The typical experiment involves having subjects complete an attitude questionnaire that taps opinions about religion, politics, and so on. Later, subjects are given information about the attitudes of another person and are then asked to indicate their liking for and attraction to that person. By varying the proportion and number of similar and dissimilar attitudes, the researcher can

Figure 11.2
A sharing of interests is a basis on which men and women may form relationships. (Dwyer and Zinkl)

specify the nature of the relationship between attitude similarity and interpersonal attraction. A substantial body of research has shown that attraction is linearly related to the proportion (rather than number) of similar attitudes. That is, the more similar another person's attitudes are to our own, the more we will like him or her (cf. Byrne, 1974).

A corollary to this "law of attraction" is that people tend to assume similarity of attitudes exist when they are attracted to a person on some other basis (Byrne and Wong, 1962). For example, it has been found that husbands and wives assume that they are more similar than they actually are (Byrne and Blaylock, 1963). Many a man, attracted to a woman on the basis of her appearance, assumes that she is perfect for him, only to discover later that they cannot agree on anything.

There are several explanations for why attitude similarity leads to attraction. Byrne (1974) has argued that we need to validate the "correctness" of our attitude. Since everyone likes to be right, any source that validates attitudes will be rewarding. One source of validation is the opinions and attitudes of others. Thus we may choose to associate with others having similar attitudes because they provide "evidence" that our own are correct. As Byrne says, we avoid those with dissimilar attitudes because disagreement raises the possibility that we are "stupid, uninformed, immoral or insane."

An alternative explanation for liking those with similar attitudes is that we anticipate sharing mutually rewarding activities (Berscheid and Walster, 1978). If we learn that another person shares our love of sports, theater, and so on, we are attracted to that person because we expect to enjoy those activities with him or her.

A third explanation is our assumption that people with similar attitudes will like us; following the reciprocity-of-liking rule, we like them in return. Walster and Walster (1963) found that students who were told to select a group in which others would probably like them, chose to participate in a group discussion with other college students rather than groups consisting of factory workers or psychologists. Available evidence suggests that all three factors play a role in the "similarity leads-to-attraction phenomenon."

The effects of similarity are not limited to attitudes. Similarity also seems to be important when it comes to a number of physical and psychological characteristics. It has been found that husbands and wives tend to be similar in physical attractiveness (Berscheid and Walster, 1974), stature (Pearson and Lee, 1903), and physical disabilities, such as deafness (Harris, 1912). Husbands and wives are also similar in terms of intelligence (Reed and Reed, 1965), education (Garrison, Anderson, and Reed, 1968), and a variety of social characteristics (Burgess and Wallin, 1943).

There is one important exception to the similarity effect. As an illustration of this exception, Byrne (1974) posed the question: How would you feel if someone just like yourself was more successful than you? Or conversely, how would a person feel if someone similar was insane or a failure? In these cases, the evidence shows that we prefer dissimilar individuals (Novak and Lerner, 1968). It is easier to rationalize if our "true love" rejects us for someone completely different from ourselves than for one who is nearly identical. We might also feel threatened if we learned that someone quite similar to ourselves had a history of emotional disturbance.

Physical Attractiveness

Although we may be reluctant to admit it, physical attractiveness is an important factor in interpersonal attraction. Folk sayings such as "You can't judge a book by its cover" and "Beauty is only skin deep" imply that it is somehow unfair that attractive people should have an advantage, but the fact is they do.

One of the earliest and most ambitious experiments illustrating the importance of physical appeal involved 750 college freshmen and a computer dance (Walster, et al., 1966). The students completed questionnaires with the belief that a computer would select their date for the dance. Prior to the dance, the students responded to a variety of questionnaires and psychological tests. When they purchased their tickets to the dance, ratings of their physical attractiveness were taken. In order to examine the effects of a number of variables, researchers assigned dates in a random manner.

The researchers were testing a matching or similarity hypothesis. They predicted that students would be most attracted to dates who were similar in social desirability: high, medium, or low. Contrary to what was expected, all students, regardless of their own attractiveness, preferred the most attractive dates.

Although many studies show that people, given an ideal world, prefer physically attractive partners (Janda, O'Grady, and Barnhart, in press; Walster, 1970), things seem to work somewhat differently in the real world. In a typical dating situation, students are concerned with the possibility of rejection. And rejection is a real possibility if one approaches a too-desirable partner. This suggests that when one is required to choose a partner, in contrast to having a partner assigned—as in the computer dance—matching is likely to occur. This has been found to be true (Berscheid, et al., 1971). Dating couples are likely to be quite similar in physical attractiveness (Murstein, 1972).

The pervasiveness of the physical-attractiveness effect has led to the postulation of a "what-is-beautiful-is-good" stereotype that operates to influence our first impressions (Dion, Berscheid and Walster, 1972). Physically attractive people are believed to have more favorable personality characteristics, to lead happier, more suc-

Figure 11.3
Physical attractiveness plays an important role in interpersonal attraction. (Dwyer and Zinkl)

cessful lives, to be more emotionally stable, and on and on. This applies to both men and women, as perceived by both men and women. This stereotype begins in early childhood and continues through adulthood (cf. Berscheid and Walster, 1974).

Although some studies have found that the attractiveness of one's partner is just as important to women as to men (Walster, et al., 1966), it does seem to be the case that men tend to be somewhat more guilty of believing the "what-is-beautiful-is-good" stereotype than women (Janda et al., in press). Schwartz (1975) has argued that our society places more emphasis on women's attractiveness than on men's. The media may be guilty of transmitting the subtle message that men are judged on a number of characteristics—

intelligence, occupation, and so on—while women have little to offer but their appearance. Interestingly, a man who is seen with an attractive woman is evaluated more favorably than when he is seen with an unattractive woman (Bar-Tal and Saxe, 1976). The appearance of a woman's partner has little effect on the evaluations made of her.

The *equity theory* provides a framework for understanding the differential importance of appearance. This theory suggests that two people enter into a relationship when it is profitable for both of them. Thus the more desirable a person is, the more desirable a partner he or she can attract. This notion has been stated bluntly by Goffman (1952):

> A proposal of marriage in our society tends to be a way in which a man sums up his social attributes and suggests to a woman that hers are not so much better as to preclude a merger or partnership in these matters.

Traditionally, since the man has played the role of provider in our society, his range of social attributes may be somewhat broader than those of the woman. In the past, women may have had little to exchange but their attractiveness in return for financial security. Although this basis for exchange may still operate in many circumstances today, the blurring of sex roles will probably give women greater bargaining power in the future (see Chapter 17).

Establishing Contact

Social psychologists have learned a great deal about the factors that influence interpersonal attraction, but there is very little information about how a particular man and a particular woman get together. We really do not know much about the process of how people meet and come to the mutual decision to have some type of relationship.

In the past, and, to a large extent, today, men had the responsibility of taking the first step. The high school boy was expected to phone the girl for a date. At nightclubs or dances it was up to the man to ask the woman to dance. In other words, it was the man's prerogative to indicate initially that he was interested in making contact.

Although men may have believed it was up to them to take the first step, women have probably always known that they had a fair amount of control over whether or not that first step was taken. A study by psychologist Mark Cary (1974) documents this. He was interested in how conversations began when one person was sitting in a room and another person entered. The results were clearest when a man entered a room in which a woman was seated. Typically, the two people would look at each other. Then, if the woman looked at the man a second time the man would initiate a conversation. This prompted Cary to suggest that women serve as the "gatekeeper" in initial contacts with men.

Other research suggests that women have other ways of indirectly communicating their feelings of attraction for men in initial conversations. It has been found, for example, that men are more likely to like women who call them by their first name frequently and have high levels of eye contact. Interestingly, women do not care for men who behave in similar ways (Kleinke *et al.*, 1972; 1973). Even though women have been encouraged to initiate relationships in recent years, it may well be the case that they have always had a great deal of control in such matters.

Romantic Love

Although *romantic love* has been a focus of speculation for countless centuries, there is virtually no agreement about how it should be defined or how it can be recognized. In fact, there is so much disagreement that one observer remarked, "Love is such a tissue of paradoxes, and exists in such an endless variety of forms and shades that you may say anything about it that you please, and it is likely to be correct" (Finck, 1902).

Only in the past ten years or so have psychologists entered the fray in an attempt to untangle the web of inconsistent and often contradictory notions of love. A working definition of romantic love has been offered by Walster and Walster (1978):

> A state of intense absorption in another. Sometimes "lovers" are those who long for their partners and for complete fulfillment. Sometimes "lovers" are those who are ecstatic at finally having attained their partner's love, and momentarily, complete fulfillment. A state of intense physiological arousal.

Let us review what has been learned about this mysterious state.

Liking versus Loving

One issue that behavioral scientists have confronted (and have not yet conclusively answered) is whether liking and loving fall on the same continuum or whether they are qualitatively different. In other words, if we begin to like someone more and more, will we ever love that person? Are liking and loving different, meaning that despite how much we like a person, we may never love him or her? Although many theories of interpersonal attraction imply that loving is merely a case of extreme liking, there appear to be compelling arguments to the contrary.

Berscheid and Walster (1978) are among those who argue that liking and loving are distinct phenomena. They point out that there are at least three differences between them. First, fantasy seems to play a much more important role in love than it does in liking. Most people may enjoy fantasizing about an ideal lover, but few spend much time having fantasies about an ideal friend. Also, as Berscheid and Walster point out, passions aroused by partners who are barely known or who are not known at all are often more intense than reactions to real-life love objects.

A second difference is that love is much more likely to be associated with conflicting emotions. To illustrate this point, Berscheid and Walster reported that when college students were allowed to ask psychologists one question about love, the inquiry "Can you love and hate someone at the same time?" was near the top of the list. Novels, songs, and movies have suggested that loving and liking are independent. How many heroes and heroines have fallen in love with someone guaranteed to bring them unhappiness. And how many fictional (and real) characters have uttered the phrase "I love you but I don't like you." Love seems to be a much more turbulent emotion than liking.

Third, the effects of time upon liking and loving appear to differ. Whereas liking usually increases as we spend more time interacting with another person (Homans, 1961), romantic love appears to be a rather short-lived

---

When Love and Sex Are Separated

For most people love and sex belong together. Most of us believe that sex is much more meaningful and gratifying if it is with someone we love. There are, however, some people who separate the two. They cannot respond sexually to those whom they love.

Psychiatrists have coined a term for people who separate love and sex. In men, this phenomenon is referred to as the Madonna-Prostitute syndrome (Mathis, 1971). In women, it is called the Saint-or-Sinner syndrome (Layman, 1976).

These men and women have usually grown up in families that thought sex was dirty or vulgar. They develop conflicts about their sexuality and resolve these conflicts by dividing people into two categories: "nice" people, who are not thought of as sexual objects, and the not-so-nice people, who can be viewed as sexual objects.

These syndromes can range from mild to severe. A man with a mild Madonna-Prostitute syndrome may become sexually excited by his wife only when she wears black fishnet stockings or exotic underwear. This may be enough for him to transform, psychologically, the "pure, mother-type" woman into the promiscuous, prostitute-type female. Men with more severe problems may be impotent with their wives but highly aroused by prostitutes. In one of the most dramatic reported cases, a young man made no sexual advances toward his wife for several months after their marriage. Then, while on a picnic in a secluded spot, the man virtually raped her. The setting and the nature of the sexual act was such that his image of his wife as a "pure" woman was untarnished. The wife was disconcerted by the experience but hopeful that it marked the beginning of a sex life. The man, however, refused to talk about what happened and made no further sexual advances. The wife sought psychiatric help when the picnic scene was repeated a few months later.

The Saint-or-Sinner syndrome can take a variety of forms in women. In milder cases, women prefer to have sex with their husband when he is unshaven and dirty or may encourage him to use "dirty" words during foreplay and intercourse. Many single women report that they react quite differently to the eligible men they meet, depending on how they perceive them. If the man seems to be unsuitable as a prospective husband, they may be willing to have a casual sexual relationship with him. If, however, the man seems "nice," they will proceed slowly with the thought of withholding sex until marriage. Often, these women find themselves unable to respond sexually once they do marry.

One hopeful note is that these syndromes are more common in older people. The increasing acceptance of human sexuality as a normal and valued aspect of our lives may be making it unnecessary for people to separate love and sex.

---

emotion. An impressive number of experts argue that couples who base their relationship or marriage on romantic love will inevitably be disappointed (McCary, 1978; Reik, 1944; Van Den Haag, 1973). Many family and marriage specialists have suggested that liking is a better basis for marriage because it lasts, while romantic love fades with time.

Social psychologist Zick Rubin (1974) has provided empirical support for the idea that love and liking are distinct emotions. He constructed separate personality scales to measure liking and loving and administered them to 182 dating couples. The results suggested that for men, liking and loving their partners was only moderately related ($r = .56$), while for women the relationship was even smaller ($r = .36$). Thus, while there was a tendency for liking and loving to go together, it was clear that loving one's partner did not ensure a liking for that person.

On the basis of the above ideas, the conclusion arrived at by most behavioral scientists is that love qualitatively differs from liking. This may not seem to be a very profound thought, but it is an important beginning. It suggests that the factors discussed earlier with regard to interpersonal attraction cannot be applied directly to the concept of love. These factors, such as proximity, reciprocity, and similarity, are undoubtedly important, but they probably interact with other variables to influence the course that love may take. As is always the case in the behavioral sciences, a good theory helps to increase understanding of complex processes. Let us examine one theory of love that currently has much credibility.

The Two-Component Theory of Love

Psychologist Stanley Schachter (1964) has proposed a two-component theory of emotion. He has argued that before an emotion can be experienced two conditions must be met. First, a state of bodily arousal must exist, and, second, the individual must apply a label or name to the state of arousal. Because bodily arousal is often ambiguous, the specific situation a person is in will influence the label applied to the arousal. To illustrate, suppose a man notices that he has a rapid heart beat and sweaty palms. If he is at a football game in which the home team is driving for the game-winning touchdown, the arousal will probably be labeled excitement. The same bodily response experienced before making a class presentation may be given the label of anxiety.

To test this hypothesis, Schachter conducted an ingenious experiment in which both the setting and physiological arousal were manipulated. First the subjects were given an injection that contained either epinephrine, which produces palpitations, tremor, flushes, and rapid breathing, or a placebo. Then the students were asked to

take a seat in a waiting room where another "subject" was seated. The second subject, actually a confederate of the experimenter's behaved in either an angry or euphoric fashion. Schachter found that only those subjects who received the epinephrine and who were not told what to expect, mimicked the behavior of the confederate. That is, the subjects who experienced bodily arousal and believed that it was appropriate to experience anger or euphoria in this particular situation were the ones who felt the most intense emotions (Schachter and Singer, 1962).

Walster and Walster (1978) have suggested that Schachter's two-component theory of emotion may be useful in understanding the emotion of love. Using Schachter's model, they reasoned that people should be especially susceptible to love when they experience a state of physiological arousal and find themselves in a situation that suggests the word love is an appropriate label for what they are feeling. This hypothesis is appealing because bodily arousal can be caused by either positive or negative experiences. Thus frustration, fear, and rejection, as well as more positive experiences such as sexual arousal, excitement, and joy may influence the intensity of love. This theory would explain the apparent paradox of love—that it can lead to agony as well as ecstasy. Let us examine how various experiences can create feelings of romantic love.

Fear. To test the hypothesis that fear can lead to feelings of romantic attraction, psychologists Donald Dutton and Arthur Aron (1974) invited college men to participate in a learning experiment. Upon arriving at the laboratory, the men were pleasantly surprised to find that their "partner" for the experiment was a beautiful woman. Their joy, however, quickly turned to fear when they were told that the experiment would require them to receive a series of electric shocks. Half the men were told that the shocks would

Figure 11.4
Feelings of excitement may be interpreted as feelings of love. (Mimi Forsyth,
Monkmeyer Press Photo Service)

be quite intense and painful (fear condition), while a control was told that the shocks would be a barely perceptible tingle. As expected, the men who became fearful were more romantically attracted to the woman than men in the no-fear condition. It seems that the men believed that their bodily responses were caused by the sexiness of the woman.

Frustration. The idea that frustration increases love is of long standing. Women have always been advised to play "hard to get." The assumption is that men will appreciate a woman more if she provides a challenge or, to some extent, frustrates her suitors. Freud (1925) essentially agreed. He believed that obstacles are necessary to swell the tide of libido. He argued that if love is to be enjoyed, barriers must be overcome to obtain it.

Scientific research has only partially confirmed this observation. Elaine Walster and her colleagues (Walster, et al., 1973) conducted a series of experiments to test the hypothesis that men would be more attracted to a "hard-to-get" woman than a woman who was enthusiastically receptive. Several of their initial experiments failed to support the hypothesis. In one rather dramatic example, the role of experimenter was taken by a prostitute. In one situation she played "hard to get," explaining to her client that she could see only a limited number of men and had to be selective in choosing her customers. In the "easy-go-get" role she let the customer assume she would accept any and all clients. The woman's estimate of how much her client liked her, the fee paid by the client, and the length of time before he called for a second appointment made up the measure of attraction. It was found that the prostitute was liked equally well, regardless of which role she played.

In a final experiment it was concluded that the selectively hard-to-get woman was the one men liked the most. That is, men like a woman who is hard for all other men to get, but easy for them to get, more than the consistently hard-to-get or easy-to-get woman.

Perhaps Ann Landers needs to revise her advice.

A second common source of frustration is parental interference. To their dismay, many parents have found that when they attempt to point out the unsuitability of their son's or daughter's partner, the relationship only intensifies. Like Romeo and Juliet, many couples become even closer when faced with opposition from their families. Science has now provided parents with empirical evidence that they should keep their opinions to themselves lest they inadvertently strengthen a relationship they would like to see dissolved.

Driscoll, Davis, and Lipitz (1972) interviewed ninety-one married and forty-two dating couples on two occasions six to ten months apart. They found that if parents increased their interference during that time, the couple's love intensified. When parents became more accepting of the relationship, the couple began to feel less intense about each other. Ann Landers was right this time.

Because these data are correlational and not experimental, it is not possible to state that parental interference *causes* intensification of love. That such a correlation was found, however, certainly suggests that parents can influence the course of their children's courtship.

Learning to Recognize Love

Numerous scientific studies support the idea that a variety of experiences can intensify love. One puzzling question is why we should have so much difficulty in distinguishing between love and other emotions. Why do men mistake fear for feelings of romantic attraction? Why do women have difficulty in distinguishing sexual arousal from romantic love?

Berscheid and Walster (1978) suggest that the answer to this puzzle is that we receive little training from our parents in learning to recognize feelings of love. Parents teach their children emotions by observing their behavior and then suggesting a label to explain what the child is feeling. If a child sees a large growling dog, begins to sob, and clings to the parent's legs, the mother or father is likely to say, "Don't be afraid." Consequently, the child learns that fear is an appropriate label for that feeling.

Parents are less likely to provide feedback about feelings of love. The small boy who comes home talking about nothing except the virtues of his pretty new teacher is not likely to be told, "I think you're in love with Miss Jones." If such feelings are acknowledged by the parents, they may do it in a lighthearted or teasing manner. The boy may be told that he has a case of puppy love or infatuation, or that he has a "crush" on his teacher. But it is a rare parent who teaches the child that he may be experiencing feelings of romantic love.

This confusion is reflected in the difficulty many adults have in distinguishing among emotions such as romantic love, infatuation, affection, sexual attraction, and so on. A common query received by Ann Landers is "How do I know when I am really in love?" The usual answer—that a person just knows when it's the real thing—is not really accurate. Romantic love is intertwined with a variety of emotions, and most people receive poor training in recognizing feelings of love. Therefore, it may be impossible to know precisely what one is experiencing while involved in a relationship. It has been suggested that such judgments are related to the state of the relationship. People use the term romantic love to describe relationships that are in progress and terms such as infatuation or sexual attraction to describe relationships that have ended (Ellis and Harper, 1971).

Men, Women, and Romance

Many people in our society subscribe to the stereotype that women are more romantic than men. Casual observation, in fact, would seem to offer more than ample support for such a hypothesis. Romance magazines such as *True Confessions*, and television soap operas are aimed at women, while men seem to prefer explicit sex magazines and televised sports events. Surprisingly, however, empirical evidence suggests just the opposite: men are more romantic than women.

The differences are readily apparent in attitudes toward marriage. In one study, 1,000 college students were asked: "If a man (woman) had all the other qualities you desired, would you marry this person if you were not in love with him (her)?" Not very many men or women said they would (11 percent and 4 percent); yet, while 65 percent of the men answered no, only 24 percent of the women ruled out this possibility. The remaining men and women were undecided (Kephart, 1967). Men also show greater adherence to what has been called the romantic ideal (Rubin, 1973). Men are more likely to agree with such statements as "A person should marry whomever he loves regardless of social position" and less likely to agree with such statements as "Economic security should be carefully considered before selecting a marriage partner."

The above findings suggest that men more than women, are likely to believe that love is a necessary and sufficient condition for marriage. There may be, however, good reasons for such a difference in attitudes. As Waller (1938) suggested a number of years ago:

> There is a difference between the man and the woman in the pattern of bourgeois family life: a man, when he marries, chooses a companion and perhaps a helpmate, but a woman chooses a companion and at the same time a standard of living. It is necessary for a woman to be mercenary.

Perhaps women suppress their romantic natures because marriage has a greater impact on their standard of living than it does on men. It will be interesting to see if women become less practical as they achieve greater economic independence.

There is, however, additional evidence to suggest that men are more romantic than women. In his studies of dating couples, Zick Rubin (Hill, Rubin, and Peplau, 1976; Rubin, 1973, 1974) has found that men tend to fall in love more readily than women and women tend to fall out of love more readily than men. Interestingly, men are more likely to enter a relationship based on the "desire to fall in love" than women are.

Rubin has also investigated the nature of breakups before marriage. Again, his results were consistent with the hypothesis that men are the more romantic sex. Women are more likely to initiate the breakup, and men tend to take the breakup harder. They are more likely than women to report feelings of depression, loneliness, unhappiness, and guilt after the relationship has ended. Rubin found that fairly common reaction among men was the failure to accept the fact that the relationship was over. They often harbored the hope that the woman would realize she really loved him after all.

Romantic Love and Marriage

In our society most people assume that they will fall in love and get married, that is, they subscribe to what has been called the romantic ideal. They believe that romantic love is both a necessary and sufficient basis for marriage.

Societies with this view of marriage, however, are in the minority. Throughout history the prevailing practice has been to arrange marriages on an economic and social basis. Sociologist John Finley Scott (1966) has commented that the nuclear family prevails because it is socially useful, not because it satisfies individual needs. It carries out the functions of reproduction, child care, and economic cooperation with great efficiency.

Because of the importance of these functions, marriages in most parts of the world have been arranged by matchmakers and parents instead of being left to romantic choice.

Many critics have been harsh in their treatment of the ideal of romantic love. European social critic Denis de Rougemont (1949) has commented that it is "one of the most pathological experiments that a civilized society has ever imagined, namely, the basing of marriage, which is lasting, upon romance, which is a passing fancy." de Rougemont and many others believe that the romantic ideal is at least in part responsible for spiraling divorce rates. The intense passion a man and woman feel for each other when they are first married will be of little use when decisions must be made about how to discipline their child, whether to buy a new house or save for the future, and countless other practical considerations. It has been suggested by many writers that a couple should base their decision to marry on practical matters rather than on the ephemeral emotion of romantic love.

As we have seen in Chapter 2, many societies in the past have provided rituals for enjoying the experience of romance and passion outside of marriage. The view that romance should be independent of marriage received official sanction in twelfth-century Europe when Marie, Countess of Champagne decreed: "We declare and hold as firmly established that love cannot exert its powers between two people who are married to each other. For lovers give each other everything freely, under no compulsion of necessity, but married people are duty bound to give in to each other's desires and deny themselves each other nothing." Although this view of romance and marriage may seem cynical and even immoral to many people in our society, it should be remembered that the practice of basing marriage on romantic love is relatively unusual and of recent origin.

Companionate Love

What binds couples together for a lifetime if romantic love is doomed to fade and slowly disappear? This is a question that is probably best left to philosophers, but psychologists Ellen Berscheid and Elaine Walster (1978) have coined the term companionate love to describe the affection that couples in long-lasting unions feel for one another. They define companionate love as "the affection we feel for those with whom our lives are deeply intertwined." In contrast to romantic love, Berscheid and Walster believe that companionate love is on the same continuum as liking. It differs from liking only in intensity of feelings and the extent to which lives are intertwined.

As we mentioned earlier, research in the area of romantic love has only just begun. Research in the area of companionate love, with a limited number of exceptions, has yet to begin. We have little scientific evidence that allows us to state what factors are involved in a satisfactory long-term relationship. There is an abundance of speculation, based largely on clinical observations, but these speculations have yet to be confirmed, or disconfirmed, by more systematic observations. Let us review briefly some current speculations about marital satisfaction and the available empirical evidence.

A Filtering Model

Many theorists have expressed reservations about the type of research on interpersonal attraction described in the first part of this chapter. It has been argued that such factors as attitude similarity and physical attractiveness may be crucial in determining initial attraction, but other factors gain importance as the relationship develops. This view has been referred to as a "filtering model" (Kerckhoff and Davis, 1962). It suggests that when two people meet, they evaluate each other according to broad categories, for example, similarity of background and appearance. If they pursue the relationship, more specific characteristics become important. These may include similarity of attitudes and values. Still later in the development of the relationship, other factors, such as emotional needs, achieve paramount importance.

Kerckhoff and Davis offer one variation of a filtering model. They hypothesize that early in a relationship the couple's *value consensus* is of critical importance: later in the relationship, however, the extent to which they share complementary needs is responsible for the stability (or lack of it) of the relationship. For example, in the early stages of a relationship, agreement on issues such as religion, child-rearing practices, sex roles, and so on, would have to exist if the relationship were to progress. In the next stage, the relationship of couples who have complementary needs would flourish, that is, the dominant person would pursue a relationship with a submissive mate. The dependent person finds a relationship with a paternal or maternal spouse rewarding.

The theory of complementary needs has received some support (Kerckhoff and Davis, 1962; Winch, 1958). However, numerous studies, carefully designed to test the complementary-need hypothesis, have failed to support it (cf. Berscheid and Walster, 1978). In fact, the bulk of the research seems to indicate just the opposite: need similarity is the important factor.

Nonetheless, many theorists are reluctant to abandon the complementary-need hypothesis. It does have a great deal of intuitive appeal. It seems reasonable to expect that couples with highly similar needs might have difficulties in getting along with one another. If both the man and woman were highly competitive or extremely dominant, it is possible that neither would have their needs satisfied.

On the other hand, similarity may be more rewarding for some needs, while complementary needs may produce the most gratifying results in other cases. For example, it seems unlikely that a generous person would be happy with a stingy, tightfisted spouse. And it seems logical that a person who requires a great deal of love and reassurance would be most satisfied with a spouse who is nurturing. Perhaps it is possible to confirm empirically a more complex complementary-need hypothesis, but at present the weight of the evidence points to the importance of similarity in stable relationships.

Selecting a Mate

When reviewing the literature dealing with interpersonal attraction, romantic love, and mate selection, one cannot help being struck by an apparent inconsistency. On the one hand, our society seems to subscribe to the romantic ideal—that one day we will fall passionately in love, get married, and live happily ever after. On the other hand, scientific evidence seems to suggest that people's attractions and mate selections are not completely emotional, but rational. We do, in fact, seem to follow de Rougemont's advice to base marriage on factors such as suitability of temperament and background.

Occasionally, one does read reports of a couple who meet, fall madly in love, and marry all within a day or two, but such cases are rare. Surveys indicate that less than 10 percent of men or women recall feeling a strong physical attraction for their partner within one or two days of their meeting. It is much more common for a couple to decide that they are in love after knowing each other for many months (Burgess and Wallin, 1953). Morton Hunt (1959) summarized this paradox when he wrote:

> Americans are firmly of two minds about it all, simultaneously hardhearted and idealistic, uncouth and tender, libidinous and puritanical. They believe implicitly in every

tenet of romantic love and yet they know perfectly well that things don't really work that way.

Perhaps de Rougemont and other critics of the American romantic ideal may have set up a strawman. Even though most people in our society profess faith in the value of romantic love, their selection of a mate is usually made with eyes open.

A variation of a filtering model proposed by Murstein (1976) seems to allow for both romance and the more practical considerations that provide the basis for the development of companionate love. His hypothesis, called the *Stimulus-Value-Role theory* of marital choice proposes three distinct phases. The first, the "Stimulus" stage, occurs when we first meet another individual. In this stage, appearance is crucial. If the person is attractive and creates a good impression, we are interested in developing a relationship. Our feelings in this phase may be characterized as romantic love. A physical attraction may exist, but we do not yet know much about the person.

The second and third stages involve more practical considerations. In the "Value" stage the couple beings to learn whether they share similar values and attitudes. In the "Role" stage, the two people discover if they are compatible in the various roles they will be required to fulfill. Murstein's point is that a couple will never progress to the second or third stages if the initial attraction does not occur. Perhaps people do not marry on the basis of romantic love, but, rather, romantic love serves as an impetus to explore a relationship further to determine if marriage is a realistic alternative.

Summary

Social psychologists have contributed a great deal to our understanding of the factors that contribute to interpersonal attraction.

We are most likely to develop relationships with those who are in close proximity to us. We generally like those who like us. We are attracted to those with whom we share similar attitudes, personality traits, and physical characteristics. We also place great value on physical attractiveness. Although we know that these factors lead to interpersonal attraction, little is known about how a particular man and a particular woman make contact. It is generally assumed that men have the responsibility of taking the first step, but it may be that women serve as "gate-keepers" in these matters.

Behavioral scientists are just beginning to investigate romantic love. Most theorists agree that romantic love differs qualitatively from liking. There are at least three major differences: fantasy is much more important to romantic love than liking; love is a more turbulent emotion than liking; although liking tends to increase with time, love tends to fade.

A current theory of love involves two components. First, a person experiences a state of physiological arousal; second, environmental cues suggest the label of "love" for the arousal. This theory explains how unpleasant experiences, such as fear or frustration, can serve to intensify feelings of love.

Both men and women in our society tend to believe that marriage should be based on romantic love (although it has been found that men are somewhat more romantic than women). Many critics have suggested that, because romantic love does not last, marriage should be based on more practical considerations, such as background and similarity of attitudes. Societies that adhere to the romantic ideal are in the minority; in most societies marriages are still arranged.

The term companionate love describes the bond that exists between two people in a long-lasting union. Although very little is known about the development of companionate love, a "filtering model" is useful in understanding it. One such model suggests that men and women are initially attracted to one another because of similarity of values. A couple that has complementary needs is likely to have a more enduring relationship. While such a model has much appeal, it lacks empirical support.

Although Americans may profess a belief in the romantic ideal, they do attend to practical considerations when selecting a mate. Perhaps romantic love serves as a motivation to explore a relationship further to determine if marriage is a realistic alternative.

References

Aronson, E. "Some antecedents of interpersonal attraction." In W. Arnold and D. Levine (eds.), *Nebraska symposium on motivation* (Vol. 17). Lincoln: University of Nebraska Press, 1969.

Aronson, E. and Linder, D. "Gain and loss of esteem as determinants of interpersonal attractiveness." *Journal of Experimental Social Psychology*, 1965, 1, 156-171.

Bar-Tal, D. and Saxe, L. "Physical attractiveness and its relationship to sex-role stereotyping." *Sex Roles*, 1976, 2, 123-133.

Berscheid, E., Brothen, T., and Graziano, W. "Gain/loss theory and the 'law of infidelity': Mr. Doting vs. the admiring stranger." *Journal of Personality and Social Psychology*, 1976, 33, 709-718.

Berscheid, E., Dion, K., Walster, E. and Walster, G. W. "Physical attractiveness and dating choice: A test of the matching hypothesis." *Journal of Experimental Social Psychology*, 1971, 7, 173-189.

Berscheid, E. and Walster, E. "Physical attractiveness." In L. Berkowitz (ed.), *Advances in experimental social psychology*. New York: Academic Press, 1974, 7, 158-216.

Berscheid, E. and Walster, E. *Interpersonal attraction*, 2nd ed. Reading, Mass.: Addison-Wesley, 1978.

Burgess, E. W. and Wallin, P. "Homogamy in social characteristics." *American Journal of Sociology*, 1943, 49, 109-124.

Burgess, E. W. and Wallin, P. *Engagement and marriage*. Philadelphia: Lippincott, 1953.

Byrne, D. "Interpersonal attraction and attitude similarity." *Journal of Abnormal and Social Psychology*, 1961, 62, 713-715.

Byrne, D. *An introduction to personality*, 2nd ed. Englewood Cliffs, N.J.: Prentice-Hall, 1974.

Byrne, D. and Blaylock, B. "Similarity and assumed similarity of attitudes between husbands and wives." *Journal of Abnormal and Social Psychology*, 1963, 67, 636-640.

Byrne, D. and Wong, T. J. "Racial prejudice, interpersonal attraction, and assumed dissimilarity of attitudes." *Journal of Abnormal and Social Psychology*, 1962, 65, 246-252.

Carnegie, D. *How to win friends and influence people.* New York: Simon & Schuster, 1937.

Cary, M. S. "Nonverbal openings to conversations." Paper presented at meeting of Eastern Psychological Association, Philadelphia, 1974.

de Rougemont, D. "The crisis of the modern couple." In R. N. Anshen (ed.), *The family: Its function and destiny.* New York: Dryden, 1938.

Dion, K. L., Berscheid, E., and Walster, E. "What is beautiful is good." *Journal of Personality and Social Psychology,* 1972, 24, 285-290.

Driscoll, R., Davis, K. E., and Lipitz, M. E. "Parental interference and romantic love. The Romeo and Juliet effect." *Journal of Personality and Social Psychology,* 1972, 24, 1-10.

Dutton, D. and Aron, A. "Some evidence of heightened sexual attraction under conditions of high anxiety." *Journal of Personality and Social Psychology,* 1974, 30, 510-517.

Ellis, A. and Harper, R. A. *A guide to rational living.* Englewood Cliffs, N. J.: Prentice-Hall, 1971.

Festinger, L. "Architecture and group membership." *Journal of Social Issues,* 1951, 1, 152-163.

Finck, H. T. *Romantic love and personal beauty: Their development, causal relations, historic and national peculiarities.* London: Macmillan, 1902.

Freud, S. "The most prevalent form of degradation in erotic life." In E. Jones (ed.), *Collected Papers,* 4. London: Hogarth Press, 1925.

Garrison, R. J., Anderson, V. E., and Reed, S. C. "Assortative marriage." *Eugenics Quarterly,* 1968, 15, 113-127.

Goffman, E. "On cooling the mark out: Some aspects of adaptation to failure." *Psychiatry,* 1952, 15, 451-463.

Harris, J. A. "Assortive mating in man." *Popular Science Monthly,* 1912, 80, 476-492.

Harvey, O. "Personality factors in resolution of conceptual incongruities." *Sociometry,* 1962, 25, 336-352.

Hill, C. T., Rubin, Z., and Peplau, L. A. "Breakups before marriage: The end of 103 affairs." *Journal of Social Issues,* 1976, 32, 147-168.

Homans, G. C. *Social behavior: Its elementary forms.* New York: Harcourt, Brace and World, 1961.

Hunt, M. M. *The natural history of love.* New York: Alfred A. Knopf, 1959.

Janda, L. H., O'Grady, K. E., and Barnhart, S. A. "Effects of sexual attitudes and physical attractiveness on person perception of men and women." *Sex Roles,* in press.

Jennings, H. *Leadership and isolation,* 2nd ed. New York: Longmans, Green, 1959.

Jones, E. *Ingratiation: A social psychological analysis.* New York: Appleton-Century-Crofts, 1964.

Kephart, W. M. *The family, society, and the individual.* Boston: Houghton Mifflin, 1961.

Kephart, W. M. "Some correlates of romantic love." *Journal of Marriage and the Family,* 1967, 29, 470-474.

Kerckhoff, A. C. and Davis, K. E. "Value consensus and need complementarity in mate selection." *American Sociological Review,* 1962, 27, 295-303.

Kleinke, C. L., Staneski, R. A., and Weaver, P. "Evaluation of a person who uses another's name in ingratiating and noningratiating situations." *Journal of Experimental Social Psychology,* 1972, 8, 457-466.

Kleinke, C. L., Bustos, A. A., Meeker, F. B., and Staneski, R. A. "Effects of self-attributed and other attributed gaze on interpersonal evaluations between males and females." *Journal of Experimental Social Psychology,* 1973, 9, 154-163.

Layman, W. A. "The 'saint or sinner' syndrome: Separation of love and sex by women." *Medical Aspects of Human Sexuality,* August, 1976, 46-53.

McCary, J. L. *McCary's human sexuality.* 3rd ed. New York: D. Van Nostrand, 1978.

Mathis, J. "The madonna-prostitute syndrome." *Medicine Aspects of Human Sexuality,* January, 1971, 202.

Murstein, B. "Physical attractiveness and marital choice." *Journal of Personality and Social Psychology,* 1972, 22, 8-12.

Murstein, B. *Who will marry whom? Theories and research in marital choice.* New York: Springer, 1976.

Novak, D. W. and Lerner, M. J. "Rejection as a function of perceived similarity." *Journal of Personality and Social Psychology,* 1968, 9, 147-152.

Pearson, K. and Lee, A. "On the laws of inheritance in man. I. Inheritance of physical characteristics." *Biometrika,* 1903, 2, 372-377.

Reed, E. W. and Reed, S. C. *Mental retardation: A family study.* Philadelphia: W. B. Saunders, 1965.

Reik, T. *A psychologist looks at love.* New York: Farrar and Rinehart, 1944.

Rubin, Z. *Liking and loving: An invitation to social psychology.* New York: Holt, Rinehart & Winston, 1973.

Rubin, Z. "From liking to loving: Patterns of attraction in dating relationships." In T. L. Huston (ed.), *Foundations of interpersonal attraction.* New York: Academic Press, 1974.

Schachter, S. "The interaction of cognitive and physiological determinants of emotional state." In L. Berkowitz (ed.), *Advances in experimental social psychology,* I. New York: Academic Press, 1964.

Schachter, S. and Singer, J. "Cognitive, social and physiological determinants of emotional state." *Psychological Review,* 1962, 69, 379-399.

Schwartz, P. "The social psychology of female sexuality." Paper presented at the Conference for New Directions for Research on the Psychology of Women. Madison, Wis., 1975.

Scott, J. F. "Marriage is not a personal matter." *New York Times Magazine*, October 30, 1966.

Van Den Haag, E. "Love or marriage?" In M. E. Lasswell and T. E. Lasswell (eds.), *Love, marriage, family: A developmental approach*. Glenview, Ill.: Scott, Foresman, 1973.

Waller, W. *The family: A dynamic interpretation*. New York: Dryden, 1938.

Walster, E. "The effect of self-esteem on romantic liking." *Journal of Experimental Social Psychology*, 1965, 1, 184-197.

Walster, E. "Effects of self-esteem on liking for dates of various social desirabilities." *Journal of Experimental Social Psychology*, 1970, 6, 248-253.

Walster, E., Aronson, V., Abrahams, D., and Rottman, L. "The importance of physical attractiveness in dating behavior." *Journal of Personality and Social Psychology*, 1966, 4, 508-516.

Walster, E., Berscheid, E., and Walster, G. W. "New directions in equity research." *Journal of Personality and Social Psychology*, 1973, 25, 151-176.

Walster, E. and Walster, G. W. "Effect of expecting to be liked on choice of associates." *Journal of Abnormal and Social Psychology*, 1963, 67, 402-404.

Walster, E. and Walster, G. W. *Love*. Reading, Mass.: Addison-Wesley, 1978.

Winch, R. F. *Mate selection: A study of complementary needs*. New York: Harper & Row, 1958.

Chapter 12

Intimate Relationships

In the past, the most accepted sexual intimacy was that which took place between married couples. The model of the conventional marriage is based on the idealized notion that one man and one woman should marry to satisfy all of each other's physical, sexual, and emotional needs. Recently, a wide range of variations of traditional marriage and alternate life styles has emerged which challenges the assumptions underlying our traditional model of marriage. Changing male and female role relationships suggest that we need to examine how the new role conceptualizations influence intimate relationships between men and women.

In the last chapter we discussed some of the salient factors such as proximity, perceived similarity of attitudes and values, complementary needs, and chance as being important in attracting two people to one another. We have also seen that many of these factors also operate in mate selection. Although, theoretically, people have an almost unlimited choice in the selection of marriage partners, the field of eligibles is in reality considerably reduced by social selection in terms of similarity and propinquity.

Sociologists refer to the concept *homogamy,* which means, literally, marrying alike. Very often people select more or less permanent partners who resemble themselves in certain ways. Again, we are looking at the "birds of a feather flock together" principle discussed in the last chapter. In the selection of a marriage partner, *age homogamy* operates most effectively among young couples considering their first marriage. In other words, young people generally tend to marry someone roughly their own age. Among older persons marrying for the first time and men and women who remarry, however, the age differences tend to be larger (Leslie and Leslie, 1977).

Traditionally, racial, religious, and social class homogamy have been equally powerful factors in mate selection when strong social pressures forced many men and women to marry someone of similar background. Not only were couples expected to select their partner from their own social circles, but they were also supposed to marry according to the *mating gradient.* The mating gradient is a concept which proposes that men tend to marry downward in age, education, and social class, whereas women are more likely to marry upward. As we have seen in Chapter 8, crossing social class barriers into higher status groups has been typically more common and less difficult for women than for men.

Today society is undergoing rapid change in this area because young people are increasingly challenging the traditional homogamous views. In fact, a recent national survey showed that the mating gradient is largely a function of the prevailing upward social mobility of our entire population. Rather than utilizing the mating gradient as an explanatory process operating in mate selection, the survey pointed out, most people marry while their social class membership is still indefinite. That is, most men and women marry before their final social class destination is clear and, as they grow older and consolidate their occupational or professional status, their social position also tends to rise (Glenn, Ross, and Tully, 1974).

Although partner selection between persons of widely disparate status such as interfaith or interracial marriages has become more acceptable in recent years, young people contemplating such partnerships often face conflicting parental and social pressures.

Next to homogamy, residential proximity acts as the second important factor in social selection, further reducing the field of theoretically available partners to a relatively small group of potential mates. With the exception of factors such as living in similar neighborhoods, living on the same campus, and participating in the same activity group, partner selection thereafter proceeds on the basis of personality characteristics.

As we saw in Chapter 11, people are initially attracted to each other on the basis of external stimulus characteristics such as physical attractiveness. Verbal interactions exploring each other's attitudes and values are then instrumental in establishing the degree of compatibility. After the mutual assessment of the degree of value similarity, couples compare and share their perceptions and expectations of a future spouse, forecasting their possible roles as marital partners ("role" phase of Murstein's stimulus-value-role, SVR, theory; see Chapter 11). Mutual role fit should be rewarding and result in the desire to ensure continuity of the relationship by putting it on a more permanent basis.

Combining the concepts of interpersonal attraction (proximity, compatibility, value similarity), filter, and SVR theory with the homogamy assumption, we arrive at the model of partner selection presented in Figure 12.1.

Marriage

Assumptions Underlying Monogamous Marriage

Marriage holds many different meanings for different people. Monogamous marriage is traditionally viewed as representing the optimal environment for intimate relationships. Both sexual exclusivity and permanence are required in marriage as institutionalized in our society (Libby and Whitehurst, 1977). All interpersonal attachments must occur within the marriage. Monogamy, like many other conventions, is held together by external controls and internal restraints.

Traditionally, marriage had four major functions: (1) economic provisions for its members; (2) reproduction; (3) psychological and emotional security; and (4) socialization of children. Historically there has been an important shift from emphasis on economic

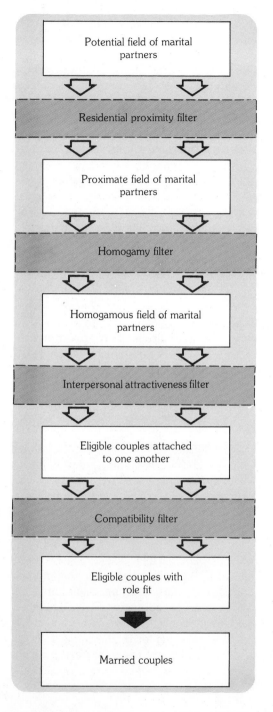

Figure 12.1
Selection of marriage partners.

survival and procreative goals in marriage to interpersonal aspects of the relationship involving intimacy and a high degree of companionship. Erikson (1963) defined the ideal of adult sexuality and love as "mutuality of orgasm with a love partner of the opposite sex with whom one is willing to share mutual trust and with whom one is willing to regulate the cycles of work, procreation and recreation" (p. 26). A tall order indeed!

Traditional marriages were usually founded upon complementarity rather than similarity. The more recent companionate forms of marital relationships, on the other hand, are based on ideals of sharing and intimacy. The traditional marriage has been associated with a working-class background while companionate marriages have been found among couples with a college background (Long Laws and Schwartz, 1977). One of the most difficult problems for young people approaching marriage is to develop a life pattern in which both husband and wife recognize and meet their marital responsibilities and, at the same time, have equal freedom and opportunity to enhance their individual personality development.

As marriage has currently evolved, its implicit assumptions are increasingly difficult to accept for young couples, especially when they enter marriage with the expectation that each person must be able to fulfill every need, sexual or otherwise, of the other. Despite the increased availability of sexual partners outside marriage and the rising number of unmarried couples living together, the majority of young men and women are overwhelmingly in favor of marriage. And although many of the old reasons for marriage, as religious or sexual pressures, conventionality or romantic notions have lost importance, the percentage of men and women marrying has not dropped off. A recent survey (Pietropinto and Simenauer, 1977) found that the majority of young men and women consider monogamous marriage as the ideal condition.

Early Marital Adjustments

As sociologist Jessie Bernard (1972) indicated, "dwindling" into a wife takes time. It involves a redefinition of one's self and a reshaping of one's personality to conform to the needs, wishes, and demands of the husband. The central developmental problem for many couples during the initial phase of marriage is how to preserve and enhance one's sense of individuality and self-esteem while at the same time making the compromises necessary for building an enduring intimate relationship. No matter how rationally and maturely a couple may have managed their courtship, marital adjustment inevitably involves a period of settling down.

Adjustments of many different kinds—personal, sexual, and social—have to be worked out during the initial phase of marriage. Developing a harmonious relationship between young married couples and their parents takes time and some quarreling for the young couple to find ways of treating both sets of parents equally. Financial values are closely linked to other personal values and differences in financial values may also cause problems at the personal level. One spouse may view saving and systematic investment as means of guaranteeing security, while the other's philosophy is to enjoy the present as fully as possible. Differences in basic attitudes toward money management must be worked out. All new marriages face a period of adjustment during which such conflicts need to be resolved.

In many cases, each spouse comes to recognize the fact that the partner cannot meet the needs of the other person at all times. One spouse, for instance, may have to study for an exam while the other wants to go out, or one person may want to go to sleep after a tiresome day while the other wants to make love.

During the early phases of marriage the process of mutual adjustment must take place for the marital relationship to "jell." Idiosyncrasies not discovered during dating and courtship, such as not wiping the sink after cutting hair or drying hose over the shower rod, may turn into major issues. Rights and responsibilities—who carves the roast at family gatherings, who manages the budget, who is responsible for household repairs—need to be clarified. Although some of these issues seem to be trivial, they tend to be invested with expectations and traditions and may be unexpectedly difficult to compromise.

Other disappointments may involve more subtle assumptions about the marital relationship which a dating couple may not have discussed during courtship. A young woman or man, for instance, who for the past twenty years has observed her or his parents' marriage, may compare the spouse to the mother or father. Or, as suggested by the complementary needs theory (Kerckhoff and Davis, 1962), a woman who has a domineering father may choose a gentle, somewhat passive husband. Similarly, the husband may

perceive his wife like his mother. Even if the relationship is based on value consensus and need similarity, potentialities for escalating frustrations and resentment are obvious. Often it becomes apparent only in retrospect that a marriage has been built on mutual misperception.

Another source of disappointment stems from our culturally prescribed courtship pattern. Traditionally it was assumed that the man takes the initiative, both in dating and arriving at the decision to marry, whereas the woman only had the power to assent or refuse. Not only do our socially prescribed roles involve a lot of role playing but they are also often deceitful. A husband may find himself wishing that he did not always have to be the initiator of sexual relations while nevertheless conforming to stereotypic male behavior. Or the wife may find the passive role obsolete but will not discuss this matter with her husband for fear he might find her "unfeminine." While many young wives come to the marriage bed with greater experience and

Figure 12.2
Newly wed couple seeking advice from a marriage counselor. (Dwyer and Zinkl)

with greater expectations than in times past, it does not seem that the movement toward equality of the sexes has gone far enough for men to appreciate wives who will teach them about sex (Peterson, 1975).

Negotiating roles and role expectations to allow for more flexible assumptions of responsibilities, initiative, and assertiveness provides an important basis for mutual understanding—especially early in marriage. Among college youth there is a noticeable change toward less stereotypic behavior. Young women today feel freer to initiate social and sexual contacts while young men are less reluctant to accept "unmasculine" tasks such as washing dishes or doing laundry. The traditional notion that a woman acquires status and a sense of personal worth vicariously through her husband is increasingly being rejected by college girls. Although a more egalitarian approach in a marital partnership may necessitate more complicated decisions, harder work, and less immediate gratifications for both partners early in marriage, it seems to be worthwhile if it leads to a sense of greater mutuality.

Regardless of how well two people have known each other—including having lived together—some disillusionment will be encountered in marriage. The degree of disappointment is directly proportionate to the unreality that went into marriage. Young men and women who marry in the full throes of romantic love may find the initial marital phase totally disappointing, whereas couples who really came to know each other before marriage may experience little or no disillusionment.

Marital Sex

Since marriage in our society is the context in which sexual behavior has the most legitimacy, we can expect that marital sex is one of the most common forms of sexual expression. There are, however, no sexual "norms" in marriage regarding the frequency of marital sex. Whatever is satisfying and comfortable for both partners—based on clear communication and fair negotiations—establishes the pattern of sexual interaction within a marriage. Nevertheless, the question of how frequently a couple should have sexual intercourse often arises. Kinsey and his co-workers (1948, 1953) found that at each point of the life cycle married men and women had more sexual intercourse than unmarried men and women. Younger married couples reported having intercourse two to three times per week on the average. Among women, the Kinsey statistics indicated that the duration of orgasmic regularity increased with the duration of marriage, continuing up to about twenty years of marriage. Finally, the Kinsey surveys reported that for both married men and women the frequency of intercourse gradually declined over the years.

Recent studies (Bell and Bell, 1972; Hunt, 1974; Westhoff, 1974) indicated that married couples today have intercourse more often than couples used to. The increase in marital intercourse can be seen in Figure 12.3, which compares the data collected by Kinsey (1948, 1953) and Hunt (1974). Westhoff (1974) compared two samples of over 5,000 married women, once in 1965 and again in 1970, questioning them on how often they had had intercourse during the preceding four weeks. The women questioned in 1970 reported a 14 percent higher frequency of intercourse than those questioned in the 1965 survey.

Several factors may account for the increases in marital sex over the past two decades. Greater sexual awareness and accessibility to sexual information allow partners to bring in freer attitudes. Increases in the frequency of marital intercourse are also related to educational levels and the use of contraception. Women with at least some college in Westhoff's (1974) study reported having intercourse an average 8.7 times in

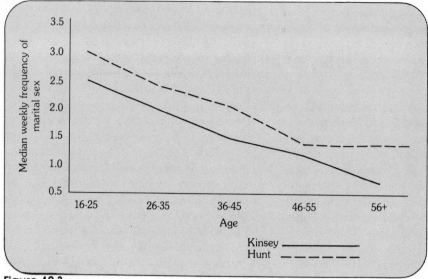

Figure 12.3

Frequency of marital sex: A comparison of the Hunt and Kinsey surveys.

four weeks, compared to only 7.4 times for married women who had not completed high school. With more favorable social attitudes toward premarital sex, partners bring in broader premarital experience and more reliable means of contraception, factors which have contributed to more frequent marital intercourse.

As in the Kinsey studies, all recent surveys showed a gradual decline in lovemaking with increasing duration of the marriage. In the absence of definitive research we can only speculate about the reasons for this decline. Perhaps continued access to a sexual partner reduces sexual excitement. Since there is little evidence that the majority of couples are very innovative in their sexual techniques, marital intercourse may become routine. Married couples in long-term relationships seem to become accustomed to each other and may cease to be satisfying lovers.

More important than average frequencies of sexual intercourse is the wide variability that exists. Some young couples have intercourse daily, some more frequently, others

once a week or less. There is no magic standard. Each couple needs to establish a pattern that is most satisfactory to both partners. One writer suggested that the most fortunate women are those who desire intercourse as often as their husbands and exercise their right of refusal rarely and only when lovemaking would turn out so poorly that both partners would be disappointed (Hunt, 1962).

Most couples negotiate their sexual interactions. A husband's casual "Honey, how about it?" may set the stage for an evening of leisurely lovemaking. A wife's statement, "I have a splitting headache," may clearly rule out sex for that day. Vincent (1971) studied husbands' communications reflecting requests for making love. A sample of the findings:

1. "It's about time! . . ."
2. "I'll see you upstairs . . ."
3. "I think I'll go and take a shower . . ."
4. "It's Thursday night . . ."
5. "Let's go out to dinner . . ."

In addition to sexual intercourse, masturbation has become an acceptable variation within marriage. The survey conducted by Hunt (1974) indicated that about 72 percent of young husbands and about 68 percent of young wives masturbated. For some couples, learning how the other partner masturbates can be exciting as well as enhance their knowledge of each other's sexuality.

One common reason for sexual problems in marriage stems from the inability of one or the other partner, or both, to communicate sexual needs and likes. Many times, husbands and wives fail to tell each other how they would like to experience the sex act and what gives them sexual satisfaction. If a wife asks a husband to scratch her back and he complies, she does not hesitate to give him instructions: "Not so hard, now over to the left, slow down, easier." Sexual communications are rarely as explicit or directive. Frequently, each partner may have to know the sexual desires of the other intuitively. Failure to communicate sexual likes and dislikes openly may lead a person to believe that the techniques of the partner are satisfactory when they are not.

Sexual Satisfaction in Marriage

It is difficult to measure the quality of marital sex and individual fulfillment or dissatisfaction. Nevertheless, we do know that one apparent consequence of the liberalization of sexual attitudes in recent years has been an increase in sexual satisfaction in marriage. Apparently, married couples not only have intercourse more often but they also seem to enjoy it more. Concern about the quality of marital sex, however, is more common among higher educated couples. There are a number of studies indicating that for a large number of less educated women marital sexuality is still seen as positively related to the husband and negatively to the wife (Bell, 1970).

The overall emotional and psychological climate of a marriage is inevitably reflected in the degree of sexual satisfaction. Gebhard (1966) found wives who reached orgasm in 90 to 100 percent of their marital intercourse were found more commonly in happy marriages than in other marriages. Similarly, Clark and Wallin (1965) found that women whose marriages were happy were increasingly likely to be sexually responsive with the passage of time. Women who were sexually responsive initially but whose psychological relationships with their husbands changed from positive to negative were less likely to maintain their sexual responsiveness.

In addition to the psychological quality of the marital relationship, age also appears to be a factor. Generally, younger couples are more satisfied with their sexual relationships than older couples. In the Hunt (1974) survey, 60 percent of the women under forty-five stated that intercourse during the preceding year had been "very pleasurable," whereas fewer than 38 percent of the women over fifty-four answered affirmatively.

Research on marital satisfaction indicates that couples are satisfied with their marriages as long as their expectations are met (Laws, 1971). Recently, emphasis on sexual performance, leading to higher expectations, has been found to be anxiety provoking. The working-class women in Rubin's (1976) study, for example, indicated they felt inadequate because they were not as orgasmic as they thought they were supposed to be. Sexual demands of "liberated" women have also been found to cause anxiety in men, leading to dysfunctional marriages (Moulton, 1977).

The relaxation of sex role stereotypes and the greater freedom of choice for women in terms of career and life styles have not only brought expanded opportunities but may also place increased demands on marital satisfaction. Many couples today, and women in particular, are asking whether it is not possible for both partners to share with friends those personal interests that cannot be shared with the spouse (Saline, 1975). The problem is, of course, how to manage such relationships. As one marriage counselor put it, "The time to cool any relationship is when you start having bedroom fantasies with your friend in the starring role. That's a sign that you are drifting away from your spouse." In order for cross-sexed relationships to enhance the marriage, the nature and boundaries of these relationships must be clear. Despite the intention of friends, however, male-female relationships outside marriage are difficult to handle because sexual interests may surface once empathy has been established.

Good sexual adjustment in marriage implies that both partners are satisfied with what they give and receive sexually. Since it is probably rare to find a married couple where the sexual needs of each partner are exactly the same, sexual adjustment rests upon compromise, at least on some occasions. Given the vast variations in sexual interests and abilities in each sex, the assumption that each partner can reach an optimal level of satisfaction is often unrealistic.

Sexual relations are an important source not only of sexual satisfaction but also of marital conflict. DeBurger (1975) found that more husbands (42.1 percent) than wives (20.6 percent) cited sexual relations problems as the major cause of their marital difficulties. The pattern was reversed in the closely related area of affectionate relations with wives complaining more (31 percent) about emotional problems than the husbands (11.5 percent). These data seem to indicate that women are more concerned with the romantic and men more with the erotic aspects of the marital relationship.

In the majority of marriages, sexual satisfaction is a growth process requiring compromise, open communication, and honesty. In order to be successful, each person has to rework his or her sense of sexuality to accommodate the needs and desires of the partner.

Open Marriage

Open marriage, a term coined by Nena and George O'Neill in their best-selling book, *Open Marriage* (1972), refers to a marital pattern which emphasizes role equality and flexibility, allowing husbands and wives the need for stimulation, variety, and novelty in interpersonal relations. Since neither partner is locked into a stereotypic role, marital obligations are shared according to real convenience and talent rather than according to some predetermined role or 50-50 arrangement. In open marriage the focus is on equality and the partners' increased freedom to define themsevles and their interests individually.

In their concept of open marriage, the O'Neills accept cross-sexed friendships and recognize that each partner may have friends and interests which the other may or may not share. The role of sex in such relationships is deemphasized, however. It is suggested that the cross-sexed friendships of a husband or wife be of a variety that can be comfortably related to one's spouse. In this way outside dating can be used to enhance and enrich the marital relationship without the complications of romance or intercourse.

The work of the O'Neills is aimed at producing openness, honesty, and trust while simultaneously developing more autonomy and personal expression within the marriage. Although the O'Neills do not promote sexual openness, they do not advise people to avoid sexual relations. Open marriages can be sexually open if a couple has the necessary trust, identity, and open communication. Whitehurst (1974) investigated sexually open marriages which were based on the mutual agreement not to be sexually exclusive. The couples involved in sexually open marriages found that the better fulfillment of personal needs, the excitement of new experiences, both social and sexual, and the security of being together enhanced their self-esteem as well as their marital closeness. Among the major problems mentioned by husbands and wives in sexually open marriages were jealousy, time-sharing problems, occasional resentment over the importance of the outside partner, and difficulty in finding private meeting places. Both Whitehurst (1974) and Knapp (1976) agreed that sexually open marriages are not advisable for people who are not emotionally equipped to handle freedom, time alone, complex interrelationships, and the inevitable struggle of possessiveness versus autonomy.

Serial Monogamy

Serial monogamy involves the familiar pattern of marriage and divorce, remarriage and subsequent divorce (Delora and Delora, 1972). While nobody wants a divorce, divorce has become so common that most couples realize that it might happen to them. The number of divorces in the United States has been rising steadily for the past decade. On the average, one marriage out of every three will end in divorce (England and Kunz, 1975; Glick, 1975).

Infidelity is no longer cited as frequently as a reason for dissolving a marriage. A study of six hundred couples applying for divorce in Cleveland, Ohio, reported the various complaints that brought couples to the divorce court (Levinger, 1966). As can be seen from Figure 12.4, mental cruelty, neglect of home and children, financial problems, and drinking were reported more frequently than infidelity. Generally, wives' complaints outnumbered those of husbands by a wide margin. Marriage counselors are in strong agreement that other qualities and benefits of the marriage are of greater importance and that often husband or wife will go to great lengths to pretend ignorance or ignore evidence of extramarital affairs.

Delora and Delora (1972) suggested that serial monogamy can be advantageous to the individual provided that the divorce involves no pain or guilt and the new marriage is a rewarding one. From a societal perspective,

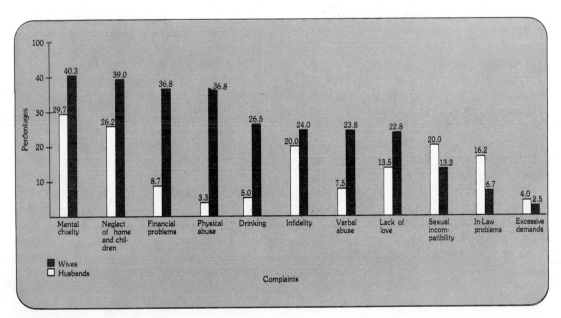

Figure 12.4
Complaints of divorcing couples about their marriage.

however, such a marital pattern is dysfunctional because it interferes with the adequate socialization of the children of such unions.

The Future of Marriage

In view of the steadily rising divorce rate, there are many people today who are questioning the value of preserving marriage as an institution. While the traditional, monogamous marriage may no longer be the only acceptable environment for intimate relationships, it is still a status-giving, socially prized institution. Recognizing that the divorce rate is high, we must also note, however, that the remarriage rate is high. Thus the idea of marriage is still powerful and appealing since it represents emotional commitment, security, trust, and convenience.

One of the greatest changes in American marriages has been the result of women achieving greater and greater equality. One area of this increased equality has been in the sexual realm. Today young women enter marriage with the assumption that they have the right to sexual fulfillment and they take responsibility to secure sexual satisfaction. With the general reduction in sex role differences, the sexual needs and desires of men and women will become more and more alike. In the future we can anticipate that both partners will have a similar vested interest in giving and receiving sexual satisfaction.

Extramarital Relationships

Clinical experience as well as reflections of literature and popular wisdom indicate that

Figure 12.5
Young couple balancing out their budget. (Dwyer and Zinkl)

there are a number of men and women who harbor desires for sexual contact with someone other than their spouse. In our society the extramarital relationship is thought of as cheating and dishonesty, as a transgression of the marriage contract. It is viewed as a sure sign that one really does not love his or her spouse or as a clear indication that something serious is wrong with the marriage. The less frequently used term adultery summarizes many of the negative connotations surrounding extramarital sex.

Types of Extramarital Experiences

Clanton (1973) proposed a threefold typology of extramarital relationships which are arranged according to the extent to which the spouse knows and approves of the relationship. In *clandestine* extramarital affairs the spouse is unaware of extramarital involvement. This is the type of relationship that the word adultery frequently connotes. *Consensual* extramarital sex is based on the knowledge and approval of the spouse. Extramarital affairs are accepted by both husband and wife as part of their life style. Several different types of consensual affairs exist. We have already discussed one form of consensual extramarital sex—namely, the sexually open marriage. Swinging and group marriages are also forms of consensual extramarital sex. The third category includes *ambiguous* extramarital relationships, in which the spouse knows about the affair but may not be able to approve of it. The extramarital involvement is tolerated as preferable to divorce.

Frequency of Extramarital Sex

As with other forms of sexual behavior, figures are essentially meaningless except to confirm the obvious—extramarital sex is a very common phenomenon. Kinsey and his coworkers (1948, 1953) found that by the age of forty, one-half of the married men and one-fourth of the married women had at least one experience with extramarital intercourse. Among the various subgroups of the Kinsey samples many variations existed. Husbands, for instance, engaged about twice as often in extramarital relations as wives. Extramarital intercourse was found to be lowest among the most highly educated men, but highest among the most educated women.

The *Playboy* survey (Hunt, 1974) concluded that the sexual liberation had little effect on extramarital sex because extramarital affairs apparently are no more common today than they were during Kinsey's time. The results of the *Redbook* survey (Levin, 1976) reported that college-educated wives were less likely to have extramarital relations until age forty, after which they were more likely to become involved in extramarital affairs. Wives who stayed at home were less likely to have extramarital experiences than working wives. Currently it is estimated that by age forty about one-third of all married women and about 60 percent of all married men have had an extramarital sexual experience.

There are basically two categories of extramarital relationships. According to Sprey (1975), one of them is symptomatic of disorganized, deteriorating marriages. Here we find husbands and wives with personality traits that tend to make them poor risks in close interpersonal relationships. Goldberg (1978) discussed three personality patterns that may foster extramarital desires. The first is described as a *narcissistic personality*, referring to the type of person who has a great need for attention although he or she is generally unable to give much in return. Such a person is apt to have intense desires for extramarital involvement because the spouse's attention is never enough. A second personality pattern reflects *compulsiveness as a dominant personality trait*. Typically such a person conforms to the social standards of proper sexual behavior most of the time. Every so often, however, he or she feels a great need to break out of the conformity and engage in some very nonconforming behaviors such as extramarital affairs. This category of extramarital behavior is associated with relatively stable marriages where extramarital affairs are experienced as actually being supportive of the marriage. A third person who may be prone to an extramarital relationship is the *sexually dissatisfied husband or wife.*

Reasons for Extramarital Involvement

One of the major reasons for becoming involved in an extramarital relationship is the desire for variety of sexual experiences. The traditional, sexually monogamous, permanent marriage places a heavy restriction upon our capacity for sexual variety. The desire for variety in all kinds of interactions, not only sexual, exists even in relatively compatible marriages. One general effect of an extramarital relationship is that it provides variety, which tends to make love more exciting. Regardless of whether it satisfies, produces conflict, or destroys or uncovers new dimensions, it certainly produces variety. For some people, an affair may provide temporary respite from problems at home; for others it may help to expand their sexual and emotional repertory. For still other men and women, extramarital relationships may help overcome marital boredom or stagnation.

Although most people think that the major reason for extramarital sexuality is a poor sexual relationship in the marriage, several studies have shown that emotional needs may be more important than sexual ones. Whatever the reason for the extramarital affair, the person involved in such a relationship is seeking fulfillment of certain emotional, social, or sexual needs that are not being met in the marriage.

Effects of Extramarital Relationships

According to the popular view, extramarital sex is always destructive. In recent decades different interpretations of extramarital relationships have surfaced. Kinsey's classic studies gave the first concrete evidence that extramarital relations may be viewed as a positive experience. Similarly, in *The Significant Americans*, Cuber and Harroff (1966) came to pointed conclusions about the positive character of some extramarital relations among upper-middle-class couples. More recently, Myers and Leggitt (1975) also called attention to the potentially positive aspects of extramarital relations. "Constructive adultery," as these authors label positive extramarital affairs, is related to maturity, personal growth, and, consequently, better marriages. The authors point out that there are as many kinds of extramarital relationships as there are marital relationships and that not all marriages are blissful nor are all affairs sick and painful. Ziskin and Ziskin (1973) argued that the practice of extramarital sex does not necessarily deny the importance of marriage but merely redefines the marital ground rules.

The ultimate effect of an extramarital affair depends on how the spouse interprets the behavior. On the negative side, affairs may create communication barriers, destroy trust, and lead to feelings of insecurity and inadequacy. In the case of a positive experience, an extramarital relationship may renew the marital dialogue. Obviously, a husband or wife who believes that extramarital involvement means that the spouse no longer loves him or her will feel and react differently from the husband or wife who believes that it is just a sexual attraction which will most likely burn itself out in due course (Sprey, 1975).

At present there is no scientific evidence that sexually monogamous couples are psychologically healthier or happier than couples who have explored extramarital relationships, nor is there any scientific proof for the common assumption that extramarital involvements are always destructive to marriage (Libby and Whitehurst, 1977). As long as the benefits and rewards of a sexually committed marriage are not available within the marriage, some husbands and wives will seek them in extramarital relations. For husbands and wives who are psychologically "ripe" for an extramarital affair, factors of chance and opportunity will play an important role in establishing an intimate relationship outside of their marriage.

Alternate Forms of Intimate Relationships

While traditional marriage expects a single bonding relationship for life, most alternatives to traditional marriage go beyond sexual exclusivity and require less permanence. Each of these alternate styles of intimate relationships reflects a relaxation of the strictures of the traditional marriage while retaining part of the conventional framework. A wide variety of male-female relationships has emerged, some of which have gained acceptance while others represent controversial forms of living. Today's alternatives to marriage encompass a broad range of sexual styles, including swinging, group marriage, and communal arrangements which we will examine in this section. Most alternatives to traditional marriage rest on the assumption that monogamous marriages may be incompatible with the personal needs of marital partners because monogamy cannot always satisfy the desire for variety, challenge, and romance.

Swinging

Swinging was one of the earliest departures from the conventional monogamous marriage. Also referred to as mate-swapping,

swinging as an alternate sexual style can give spouses both security and sexual variety. In this context, swinging refers to a couple having sexual relations with at least one other person. By definition, swinging is consensual extramarital sex. Although swingers may or may not be married, they usually swing in couples. Smith and Smith (1970) have coined the term *co-marital sex* to refer to a sexual relationship which violates the monogamous contract but which takes place in a highly structured way and is guided by specific rules and expectations. Although swinging violates deeply entrenched ideas of sex and marriage, it has been estimated that several million people populate the swinging scene.

Two anthropologists, Charles and Rebecca Palson (1972), have formulated a typology of swinging couples based on their observations of swingers.

1. The Eversearcher. Couples falling into this category typically married young and neither husband nor wife has had much sexual experience. Both partners seek sexual activities outside marriage because marital sex is seen as too routine. They find swinging rewarding and keep it a secret activity which none of their friends are aware of.

2. The Close Friends. This couple becomes involved in swinging as an extension of close emotional relationships with other couples. Usually they swing with people they have known for quite some time. The swinging relationship resembles a second marriage in conjunction with the primary marriage.

3. The Sharers. In most cases the husband or wife has been involved in a clandestine extramarital affair before they decide to swing. Typically, this type of couple prefers to introduce their friends to swinging by "courting" other couples. They often swing with one couple exclusively over an extended period of time.

4. The Racers. Couples in this category are highly successful and competitive and tend to retain their competitiveness in swinging. Frequently they are jealous of each other's sexual activities and may have to break off the outside liaison in order to protect the marriage.

5. The Successes. Husbands and wives in this category are usually older and have comfortable homes and secure jobs. Although they have accomplished much, they are looking for more stimulating experiences. For them, swinging represents a life style.

Symonds (1967) divided swingers into two types: "recreational" and "utopian." The recreational swinger is someone who uses swinging as some sort of play or diversion, much like playing cards. This person does not want to change the social order. The second type, the utopian swinger, views swinging as a means to build a new social order.

Getting Together. Members of the swinging scene meet in key clubs or form private groups which meet in the home of different members at regular intervals. In addition, swinging bars provide a convenient meeting place. The swinging bar serves essentially a function similar to the gay bar, providing a place of social support and an environment in which swingers can be relatively open and free.

Several underground newspapers advertise for sexual partners. *SELECT*, one of the largest swingers' publications, had 3,500 advertisements in a recent issue, over 40 percent of which were placed by married couples looking for swinging partners. A typical ad might read:

> B-056-CA/C attractive wife, 27, 36C-24-36, and goodlooking husband seek contact with attractive, broadminded couples. Will entertain at home or meet at beach cottage. Phone and photo please.

Most swinging publications use a code system to ensure secrecy and to set restrictions on who should apply. Frequently used codes are: French culture (cunnilingus and fellatio), Roman culture (orgies), Greek (anal intercourse), AC-DC (bisexual). Disappointments are common among respondents since advertising couples often shave off a few years of their age, a few pounds of their weight, and add a few inches to the bust of women (Denfeld, 1974).

Usually, men initiate the sexual exchange. Through advertisement in swinging magazines they learn about the availability of other couples and may begin correspondence with them before telling their wives. Many times the real selling point is to send a photograph of the wife in a sexy outfit. Farrell (1974) noted that in responding to swinging ads with photographs, the men are usually shown in business suits while women are seen in negligees or scanty underwear. In other words, men present themselves as success objects and women as sex objects in such pictures. Selectivity in swingers is mainly based on the wife's physical attractiveness and immediately obvious aspects of personality rather than of shared attitudes or values.

In addition to swinging bars, clubs, and publications, some couples meet compatible swingers through reference from another couple. Of the various ways of meeting other swingers, Bartell (1970) feels that couple-to-couple seduction is the least popular method.

Usually, the first meeting of swinging couples does not involve sexual contact. If it is decided at that point that they want to get together, the arrangements are made and the participants meet later either at a motel or the home of one of the couples. The premises of getting together are simple, since sexual investment is all that is expected from participants.

Rules of the Swinging Game. Although no swinging group has yet become organized enough to draw up a set of by-laws, informal rules governing what is and what is not acceptable in swinging regulate the behavior of swinging couples. One of the most important implicit rules prohibits emotional involvement and outside dating among swinging partners. The basic philosophy of swingers is that love and sex can be separated and that sex without the emotional component is enjoyable as recreation. In order to guarantee a minimum of involvement, the repeated choice of one partner is frowned upon, as is romantic conversation without sexual activity. Those who adhere to the dictum of swinging only once with another person end up collecting sexual experiences like trophies in an endless search of new, beautiful partners.

For most swingers, exchanging spouses is not considered as a substitute for the marital relationship. It is "in addition to" and frequently viewed as a different kind of sexual experience with significantly different physical and emotional dimensions (O'Neill and O'Neill, 1970). Despite the basic ground rule that sex must be impersonal and physical, many swingers seem to be searching for intimacy with others besides their spouses.

Wives usually go along with the arrangements set up by the husband. Women do not initiate sexual contacts at swinging parties. In many cases, wives express initial reluctance to join the swinging scene but, once the practice is initiated, they tend to enjoy swinging more than their husbands do. This is particularly true if they believe that swinging will not endanger their marriage (Gilmartin and Kusisto, 1973). After various ice-breaking processes partners pair off in twos, threes, or more and have sex in the same (open swinging) or separate (closed swinging) rooms.

Often, men set up a homosexual contact between the women. It has been estimated that almost 100 percent of female swingers engage in some kind of homosexual behavior in the course of their swinging activities (Palson and Palson, 1972; Bartell, 1971). In one study (Bartell, 1970) 65 percent of the women said that they enjoyed their sexual relations with other women to the point where they preferred them to heterosexual relations. Most men avoid sexual contact with each other in swinging and tend to see female sexual involvement as a performance for their own pleasure.

When it comes to sexual equality, swingers frequently disavow the double standard. What is permissible for one spouse is also acceptable for the other. Each person is free to engage in any and all kinds of sexual acts without disapproval. If the wife cannot participate in a "social" because she is menstruating, the husband is also expected to forego the event.

All swinging activities are usually kept secret and this discretion ensures the couple's respectability in the community. Couples with children are particularly careful in hiding swinging literature and photographs and plan their get togethers either in motels or at home on weekends when children can stay with relatives or friends.

Personality Characteristics of Swingers. All the studies, whether conducted by psychologists, sociologists, or anthropologists, agree that swinging couples differ not only from traditional couples but also from traditional adulterers. Most participants of the swinging scene are middle-class suburban couples who, with the exception of their sexual activities, lead relatively conventional lives. They tend to be well educated and the majority of them are white and under forty. Swinging—rather than being practiced by deviant or far-out men and women—reflects white middle-class attitudes and values with most participants being married and socially conventional with the exception of their sex lives.

Given the apparently greater sexual interests of swingers, Bartell's (1971) finding that 90 percent of the swinging males read *Play-*

Table 12.1

Problems Reported by Ex-swingers

Problem	Number of Couples
Jealousy	109
Guilt	68
Threat to the marriage	68
Outside emotional attachments	53
Boredom and loss of interest	49
Disappointment	32
Divorce or separation	29
Wife's inability to accept swinging	29
Fear of discovery	15

Source: Denfeld, D., "Dropouts from swinging." *The Family Coordinator*, 1974, 23, 46-47.

boy and 10 percent were confirmed nudists seems to support the notion that swingers are more preoccupied with sex than other women and men. The swingers in this study also became romantically interested and involved with the opposite sex significantly earlier in life than nonswingers. They passed through stages of increasingly intense dating and sexual involvement earlier in life and faster than nonswingers. In general, the swingers developed a stronger and earlier need for social heterosexual interactions than did the control couples. Despite their extramarital relationships, swingers engage in sex with their spouses quite frequently and enjoy better than average sexual relations.

Bartell (1970) also reported that the swinging men and women in his study had few or no interests other than sexual. Their reading was restricted to newspapers and magazines. This is in striking contrast to the swinging ads and correspondence which list a variety of hobbies and recreational activities such as dancing, theater, sports, and travel. Of the women, 90 percent of the sample remained housewives.

Investigating early family relationships of swingers, Gilmartin (1974) found that relations with parents during the formative years

were significantly less happy for the swingers. As adults, their ties with relatives (other than spouse and children) were less close and consequently swingers viewed their relatives as being significantly less important in their lives than a comparable group of nonswinging couples. The author hypothesized that swingers may engage in and enjoy deviant behavior because their parents failed to inspire the internalization of traditional values and norms which usually occurs in families. In addition to being alienated from relatives, the swingers also had little contact with other social institutions such as the church.

Swinging Failures. There are several studies in the literature which examine the problems experienced by swingers. Denfeld (1974), for instance, sent a questionnaire to marriage counselors who assisted couples with their marital relationships after they gave up swinging. The problems reported by the clients shed interesting light on the less often talked about dynamics of swinging. Table 12.1 indicates that jealousy was the most frequently encountered problem. Feelings of jealousy are, of course, contradictory to the basic philosophy of swingers. Somewhat surprising guilt feelings were the next common difficulty experienced. Apparently, some swingers are not as liberated and unconventional in their sexual morality as the literature on swinging suggests. The third common complaint, "threat to marriage," may stem from feelings of jealousy and guilt which can augment marital problems. Sixty-eight percent of the couples indicated that they fought and quarreled more frequently since they joined the swinging scene than before. Finally, the data show that one of the fundamental rules of swinging—namely, avoidance of emotional involvement and outside dating—was violated in fifty-three cases. Couples who experienced this as a problem expressed their concern over the lack of emotional closeness between sexual partners which interfered with their sexual enjoyment and/or their ability to perform adequately. As can be seen from the remaining problem categories, swinging emerged as a source of additional marital difficulties leading to disappointment and separation and divorce in some cases.

Swinging and Marital Adjustment. Several attempts have been made to evaluate the impact of swinging upon the marriage. Sympathetic accounts that view swinging as a valid challenge of the normative order of sexual relationships have been published. Potentially positive contributions may include the following.

1. Escape from boredom. Swinging provides an outlet for the need of a variety of sexual encounters to overcome marital monotony and to satisfy sexual curiosity. It is presumed that additional stimulation from others will enhance the sexual relationship within the marriage. Since swinging involves common planning and preparation and provides a subject matter for conversation before and after, it could potentially consolidate the marriage.

2. Sexual honesty. Some couples recognize that, because extramarital affairs may be inevitable, they may as well be incorporated into the marital relationship to control the circumstances under which they can take place (O'Neill and O'Neill, 1972). In traditional affairs, the disruptive forces of extramarital sex are believed to be the betrayal of the partner, the emotional involvement of the participants, and the jealousy of the spouse (Cole and Spanier, 1974). Advocates of swinging assume that sexual honesty will circumvent these complications. Swingers believe that if cheating and lying—the most damaging aspects of extramarital affairs—are removed, comarital sex can be beneficial to the marital bond. In other words, "those who

swing together stay together" (Brecher, 1969).

3. Sexual fun. Some swingers believe that married couples take sex too seriously and that monogamous marriage takes most of the fun out of sexual activities. In marriage, sex may become routine. Swinging, on the other hand, is seen as exciting, exotic, and sexually educative.

4. Personal growth. Finally, it has been suggested that the sexual exclusivity of traditional marriages fosters petty emotions such as possessiveness which curbs personal growth. Additional sexual experiences are seen as a means to greater self-fulfillment that can actually increase the commitment of husbands and wives to one another (Denfeld and Gordon, 1970).

In swinging, then, intimacy, not sex, is the threat to the stability or permanence of the marriage. People who enjoy swinging must be willing to share their partner without feelings of jealousy and possessiveness. Despite the presumed sexual emancipation among swinging couples, these requirements are still cumbersome for some swingers to accommodate. Since most swingers are committed to an otherwise conventional life style, they keep their sexual activities secret. Given this secrecy, it is difficult, if not impossible, to gather representative samples of swingers. Presently the results regarding the effects of swinging are ambivalent. Proponents of swinging consider comarital sex as a valid alternative to the traditional monogamous marriage, while opponents view it as a deviant behavior reflective of a decaying society. We can only conclude at this time that sexual mate-sharing itself cannot harm or help a marital relationship. What is of vital importance again is how the husband and wife view their extramarital sexual activities. If both partners see sexual variety as an important part of their relationship and are emotionally satisfied in a swinging situation, then this type of sexual expression is unlikely to have negative effects on the marital relationship.

Group Marriage

Group marriages may be defined as intimate relationships involving three or more people, each of whom is regarded as married or strongly committed to at least two other members of the group. Larry and Joan Constantine (1971), a computer scientist and his wife who conducted the most extensive research on group marriage, proposed the term multilateral marriage to refer to the complexities of relationships in such arrangements.

It appears that most group marriages originate with couples who have an established friendship. Unlike swinging, in which the husband is usually the instigator, both members of a couple seem to be equally motivated to enter into a multilateral marriage. Presumably the bonds between the group members are genuinely intimate and the hope is that the commitment will be permanent. However, permanence is not prescribed and provisions are made for opting out. Although research on group marriage is still in its infancy, participants seem to be committed to openness in personal as well as in sexual relationships.

Formation of the Group. One of the first problems is finding compatible people who share the belief that the group marriage represents an improvement over traditional marriages because they offer greater security—both material and psychological—wider sexual variety, and greater potential for personal growth. In establishing and maintaining multilateral relationships, a high degree of openness and honest expression of feelings is necessary.

Some group marriages evolved out of a good experience with swinging, whereas others jelled on the basis of mutual friend-

ships. The Constantines (1973) described the case of two couples whose friendship eventually led to a multilateral marriage. Joe and Mark had gone to the same high school and had become good friends through work. Both had been married for a couple of years. Joe and Jessica had dated a few times but Jessica ended up marrying Mark and Joe married Bev. Since the two men shared many interests, all four became good friends, enjoying different activities together. When Mark and Jessica moved into a new apartment, Bev and Joe helped with the moving. Because it got very late that night, all four climbed into the only bed to get some sleep. The following day Mark asked his wife Jessica what she would do if Joe ever asked her to go to bed with him and he (Mark) would not mind. Jessica's immediate answer was negative, but she eventually decided that it was not such a bad idea.

Both couples started discussing the idea of living together. All four read Rimmer's (1966, 1969) utopian novels *The Harrad Experiment* and *Proposition 31* and after months of discussions and phone calls, the two couples decided to try group marriage.

Sexual Aspects of Group Marriages. Sexual variety is one of the major reasons for people entering group marriages. Eighty-eight percent of the participants studied by the Constantines indicated that variety of sexual partners was among their main reasons for living together. However, sex was not the most important determinant. Personal fulfillment and opportunity for personal growth were quoted as most noteworthy.

Most sexual contacts in multilateral marriages occur in heterosexual pairings. Homosexual activities are relatively rare and group sex takes place only occasionally.

Sexual relations are dealt with in a variety of ways. Early in the history of many groups the exchange of partners is determined by a rotating schedule typically allotting three to four days with each partner. At least theoretically, rotation equalizes sexual opportunity and forestalls jealousy and possible rejection. Having assigned partners may, however, cost spontaneity. Another way of allocating partners is by free choice, which allows spontaneity but increases the likelihood of rejection.

Advantages and Problems in Multilateral Marriages. Theoretically, the group marriage answers many of the difficulties encountered in traditional marriages. A wide variety of sexual needs can, at least in theory, be satisfied within the context of multilateral relationships. The group provides not only sexual variety but also security. It relieves the men from the sole responsibility of the provider role and women are not expected to solely take care of child rearing and housekeeping tasks. Presumably, both sexes share equal responsibilities. The children are supposedly the major benefactors, thriving on the multiplicity of adult models (Constantine and Constantine, 1973). Because of shared responsibilities, parents themselves are more relaxed and less harried.

The group may also offer economic and emotional security. It is less expensive to live as a group than as a couple. A quarrel with a partner is not as devastating and less likely to lead to emotional isolation in a group. Shared feedback in conflict resolution and consensual decision making can be important sources for interpersonal learning.

In spite of the egalitarian philosophy, participants in most group marriages pay lip service to emancipation. In the ten multilateral marriages studied by the Constantines, it was always the male who functioned as the leader. Similarly, in the group marriages analyzed by Clanton and Downing (1975), not only was it the male who initiated the arrangement but it was the male who subsequently retained direction over virtually all aspects of the relationship until the group dissolved.

A major source of stress is generated by the delegation of responsibilities. In spite of the best intentions, there is often little concensus when it comes to the distribution of labor. Many group marriages are also beset by financial problems, with budgets involving a multitude of items and priorities. Finally, the precarious legal status—group marriages are illegal in most states—is a source of social harassment and ostracism.

Sexual variety does not always come easy and personal jealousies are a strain in many multilateral relationships. In addition, the intensity of feelings generated by multiple emotional involvements may turn into a "sensory overload" that may be difficult to process. Sexual jealousy is not, as the Constantines seem to think, drastically reduced in group experiences.

Since it is rare that two people are matched perfectly in terms of intellectual compatibility, sexual interests and values, and psychological and social status, differences among four to six individuals living together probably require more effort to be worked out. Thus multilateral marriages may accentuate problems of a two-person marriage. Instead of having to adjust to the idiosyncracies of one person, several people have to be taken into consideration.

Although group marriage appeals to the need for novelty, intimacy, and security, the majority of these relationships did not survive longer than a few weeks or months and most of them eventually dissolved. Presently, it is unlikely that multilateral relationships will turn into a mass form of marriage in the near future.

Communes

Communes initially coalesced around the hippie scene during the late 1960s. The term commune applies to a life style, not to a form of marriage. While in multilateral marriages the emotional relationship is the basis for living together, in communes the basis is economic and ideological. Many women and men who choose the communal life style are people who find our technological society intolerable. Often they are people who find it impossible to enter into permanent relationships. In the commune they set themselves the goal of creating a social structure that overcomes alienation and promotes sexuality as the primary focus of life.

Given the diversity in ideology and structure within communes, it is not surprising that there is as much variety with regard to sexual relations. Some communes include married couples who retain their conventional monogamous relationship. Others include one or both sexes among whom liaisons form and dissolve but they are not committed to one another.

Twin Oaks, a commune of fifty members set on two hundred acres of rolling farmland in central Virginia, may serve as an example. The ideology is formally based on B. F. Skinner's novel *Walden Two*. Twin Oaks is a highly structured commune in which the labor for all work is shared on the basis of a complex labor credit system that assigns credit for labor on the basis of psychological desirability (Conover, 1975). Women and men have equal access to all work: women did 31 percent of the "masculine" work and men performed 34 percent of "feminine" activities.

As in most communes, sexual practices in Twin Oaks varied widely. Several couples were sexually monogamous; others were committed to threesomes. There were celibate and quasi-celibate members, and the rest practiced free love. An occasional mating game was sometimes set up to stimulate

Figure 12.6
The communal life style has become an alternative to traditional marriage for some men and women. (Sam Falk, Monkmeyer Press Photo Service)

more variety of sexual relations. It was also reported that jealousy or the inability to establish sexual relationships was an important cause of some of the membership turnover.

As in most variant forms of intimate relationships, proponents of communes advocate gender equality. Nevertheless, women have a hard time in many communes because they are likely to find themselves as saddled with stereotypic chores as in conventional households. Estallachild, V. (1972), who lived in several communes, described the state of affairs on Crow Farm, a commune of between thirty and fifty people in Oregon. The commune spread over 310 acres financed by loans and parents. All members deposited their welfare check in the communal bank to cover the $2,500 monthly expenses. Egalitarianism of the sexes was still only an ideal. Most of the men were engaged in pruning trees and servicing cars and the women took care of babies and washed the dishes.

Among the factors that play a role in the failure of communes are the lack of an overriding constructive goal, male chauvinism, and the rapid turnover of people. During the summer, especially, transients go to communes and often break down the stability that might have existed. Many times communes are too fluid to create any sense of security or continuity. It is interesting to note that two of the major goals espoused by a large number of people who are considering alternate life styles—namely, independence of women and gender role equality—often fail to be achieved in alternate intimate styles.

The Single Life

Traditionally, singlehood was just a way-station to couplehood. Since adulthood has been synonymous with marriage and parenthood, the prevailing attitude was that those who remain single must be inadequate in some way. In other words, single people were usually defined in terms of their relationship to marriage. Although the single status is still occupied by a relatively small proportion of the adult population it is becoming increasingly acceptable both to society and individuals. The adult single population which jumped by 2 million a year during the 1960s approached 49 million in 1974 (Jacoby, 1974). It is probably too early to tell whether the sharp rise in the single population reflects a new life style or simply a shift in the timing of marriage. There has been a marked trend over the last few years to delay marriage until some degree of occupational or professional stability has been attained.

Many men and women who prefer to remain single today oppose the generally held view that single people are not single by right or by choice. They also object to the two common stereotypes of singles. According to one, singles are viewed in the old-fashioned image of unmarried people as lonely losers. The current media, on the other hand, depict a picture of "swingles" who cavort through an endless round of bars, parties, and no-strings-attached sexual relationships (Jacoby, 1974).

Like most men and women involved in intimate relationships, singles are searching for human interactions that provide the basic satisfactions of intimacy, sharing, and continuity. Although many singles emphasize the importance of variety and change, they also believe in the value of close, caring friendships that last over a period of time. Many single men and women, including the divorced, oppose early or hasty marriage rather than marriage itself.

Men and women who choose to be single offer several reasons for doing so—including more and better sexual experience, economic independence and personal freedom, continued opportunities to meet other people, or the desire to experiment with alternatives to monogamous marriage. Both men and women consider sexual availability an important motivation for remaining single. They enjoy the stimulation and variation of an open dating pattern and tend to see their cross-sexed relationships in terms of friendships rather than romance (Stein, 1975).

Singlehood is not, however, conflict-free. Many single persons experience contradictions which stem from the clash between traditional values stressing marriage and parenthood and alternate life styles which emphasize the need to renegotiate sexual partnerships when they are no longer mutually satisfying. A young woman referred to this type of conflict when she remarked that she grew up with the attitude "don't sleep with a man unless you know he is going to marry you." Yet the reality of her present life in a large suburban single complex was that she would not have an opportunity for marriage unless she did sleep with men.

In addition to being exposed to contradictory values, the social identity of singles is often uncertain. Overt forms of social pressure are ilustrated by Linda, who at age twenty-eight has never been married and does not plan to marry in the near future. However, she feels that her parents and some of her married friends are pressuring her and she is concerned about what others think about her: "When I tell people that I am 28 and not married they think there's something wrong with me. Some feel sorry for me, others think I am a lesbian."

Depending on how powerful a person's own definition of marriage is, he or she may consider singlehood or alternate options for intimate relationships as viable alternatives. Although the majority of people will continue to choose monogamous marriage as the preferred sexual style, we can expect that the alternatives to marriage will become more visible in the future.

The Future of Intimate Relationships

The plurality of life styles available today offers men and women the potential for satis-fying not only needs of intimacy and security but needs for sexual variety. Perhaps the central meaning of the sexual revolution is found in the changing norms of sexuality rather than in the total liberation of everyone. People have become much more accepting of a broader range of sexual expressions and styles in others, if not in themselves.

We are living in an era now where we can be at least informed about the options that are open to the person who chooses to deviate from the predominant sexual norms —i.e., the sexually monogamous, permanent marriage. Instead of one dominant style of living we can expect an increasing number of more diffuse sexual styles to emerge. In the future, men and women who find one of the variant forms of intimacy appropriate for them will find more support in subcultures and in the literature to help them make their choices. Sociocultural changes—including the gradual relaxation of the double standard, changing concepts of sex roles and female sexuality, and greater tolerance for alternate life styles—will continue to mold intimate relationships into new patterns. However, even when alternate forms of sexual relationships are no longer seen from the viewpoint of deviance but are instead considered within the perspective of cultural and social change, many people will continue to have deep fears about deviating from the traditional pattern.

Considering the network of intimate relationships, including open marriage, multilateral marriage, communal arrangements, cohabitating couples, swinging, and other experimental alternatives, it seems clear that increasing numbers of people are questioning the validity of an exclusive sexual relationship with one other person throughout the life span. Couples who continue to prefer monogamy can expect a greater variety of marital styles existing concomitantly. Many monogamous couples will opt for more egalitarian and open marriages. Although the growth of egalitarianism and flexibility will not solve all the problems encountered in traditional marriages, they may help to reduce the complaints of sexual monotony. While monogamy will remain the most popular choice in the near future, we can anticipate a redefinition of our traditional model to include intimacy, even if this does not necessarily include sexual intimacy. Libby and Whitehurst (1977) see tomorrow's marriage as "emotional caring, companionship with the other sex and flexibility for both spouses in the work and leisure worlds which will provide a basis for expanding one's patchwork of intimates and for some, the sexual expression of these feelings" (p. 369).

Divorce rates in the future will continue to rise, despite the offsetting effect of extramarital liaisons. Swinging apparently seems to be on the decline since the mid-1970s, along with the multilateral and communal arrangements. Open marriage, singlehood, and cohabitation seem to be increasing in popularity. Many of the unconventional alternatives will probably become more visible over the next generation. Exactly how strong a support in the larger culture these emerging sexual styles will gain is difficult to predict.

Summary

In this chapter we examined the nature and implications of intimate relationships across a variety of life styles. Until recently the monogamous marriage has been the only environment where sexual intimacy has been socially and legally approved. The model of the traditional marriage calls for a lifelong one-to-one union in which husband and wife are sexually faithful and emotionally committed to each other. It has been conceded that our traditional marriage imposes considerable limits on the individual freedom and growth needs of each marital partner. As a result, some couples find themselves caught between the desire for a multitude of sexual experiences and the obligation to adhere to the restrictions imposed by the traditional marriage.

Many of the alternate forms of intimacy which we discussed in the second part of this chapter can be viewed as an attempt to resolve this conflict. Most of them presume that sexual exclusivity and permanence in intimate relationships are obsolete prerequisites of the past. The sexually open marriage, extramarital relationships and swinging represent non-monogamous intimate styles which do not necessarily negate the commitment to marriage. An even more radical attack on our marriage system is seen in the multilateral marriages and communal arrangements which are experimental forms of living that combine the search for sexual freedom and novelty with the search for a new social ideology. The ideal in many of the variant forms of intimacy is complete sexual freedom, genuine commitment to another person, freedom from jealousy, and gender role equality.

In spite of the many signs of contemporary revolt against marriage, as a social institution marriage is very plastic. Most of the contemporary assaults upon marriage as the only legitimate form of intimacy are not so much efforts to destroy it, but attempts to modify and remold it.

Hot and Cool Sex: Fidelity in Marriage Robert and Anna Francoeur (1974, 1976) suggest that many married couples in this country live the tension between the traditional and new sexual images and relations. Inspired by the initial conceptualizations of hot and cool sex described by McLuhan and Leonard (1967), the Francoeurs expand the concepts into a model of sexual relations that compares to the closed and open marriages analyzed by Nena and George O'Neill (1972).

Hot sex is associated with the belief that sex is nothing but a penis and a vagina. Hot sex mentality is exemplified in the blown-up picture of the Playmate of the Month or the preoccupation with "perfect" sexual techniques. It lives by possessing and conquering sex objects and pressuring females to satisfy the male ego with mutual, or better, mutual and multiple orgasms. Hot sex, as it soon becomes evident, is part and parcel of the traditional pattern of thought which views men and women in terms of unchanging, sexist stereotypes. Hot sex, in a few words, is male-oriented, double standard, property oriented, and obsessed with genital sex.

Cool sex is a term used to describe an emerging pattern of sexual values and attitudes in which men and women become conscious of themselves as individuals with a real existence outside their socially stereotyped roles. Cool sex means considering and accepting for oneself and others the possibility of real alternatives to the traditional hot sex stereotypes of breadwinner, housewife, married couple. Since men and women in cool sex relationships do not define themselves in terms of their gender or roles, they are free to express their personalities in nonstereotypic ways. Sexuality is not restricted to genital sex but integrates a wide range of intimacies and sensuality along with genital intercourse into a holistic framework of daily living. Cool sex, in short, is egalitarian, single standard, and oriented toward intimacy and open relations with others.

Applying these two concepts to marital relationships, we find that in a hot sex marriage it is the husband who controls the relationship. Marital fidelity is synonymous with genital exclusivity. Monogamy, life-long and sexually exclusive, is the way of adult life. The emphasis is on husband and wife as a couple, not a man and a woman who happen to be married.

In the hot sex and traditional marriage it is assumed that two individuals will continue to grow on parallel tracks in this exclusive relationship for thirty, forty, or more years.

Marital relationships in a cool sex partnership are based on the premise that given the complexities of today's life, the varieties of personal backgrounds and expectations, it may be difficult for a spouse to satisfy all the partner's needs completely and totally. Cool sex partnerships accept a variety of intimate relationships on all levels, for both husband and wife. It is an open, flexible marriage which recognizes the need for "satellite" relationships to compliment primary relations.

The parallels between options of hot versus cool sex and closed versus open marriages are striking. Based on the combined writings of the Francoeurs (1974, 1976) and the O'Neills, Table 12.2 presents some of the salient comparisons between the two models.

As can be seen from Table 12.2, both the Francoeurs and O'Neills are convinced that two different patterns of marital relationships exist and that we will be increasingly confronted with making choices between the two patterns. Both open marriages and cool sex relationships are viewed as growth-promoting trends leading to new values of fidelity and commitment, new risks and new challenges.

Table 12.2

Parallels between models of hot and cool sex, closed and open marriage

Comparative Feature	Model			
	Hot Sex	Closed Marriage	Cool Sex	Open Marriage
Definitions	clear sex-role stereotyping; highly structured; sex equated with genital intercourse; male-female relationships governed by male dominance	static framework; rigid role perceptions	little, if any stereotyping, flexible structure; diffuse sexuality; male female relationships governed by egalitarianism	dynamic framework; flexible roles; spontaneity
Values	patriarchal; double standard morality	unequal status of husband and wife; personhood subjugated to couplehood	egalitarian; single standard morality	equality of status, personal identity
Concerns	orgasm obsessed; fidelity means sexual exclusiveness; extramarital relations are an escape	limited love; deception and game playing; conditioned static trust; exclusion of others	wide range of sexual communications; fidelity means commitment; satellite relationships with or without sexual involvement	open love; honesty; open trust; additive relations with others in an expanding system

References

Bartell, G. "Group sex among mid-Americans." *Journal of Sex Research*, 1970, 6, 2, 113-131.

Bartell, G. *Group sex: A scientist's eyewitness report on the American way of swinging.* New York: Peter H. Wyden, 1971.

Bell, R. R. "Sex as a weapon and changing social roles." *Medical Aspects of Human Sexuality*, 1970, 6, 6, 99-106.

Bell, R. and Bell, P. "Sexual satisfaction among married women." *Medical Aspects of Human Sexuality*, 1972, 6, 12, 136-144.

Bernard, J. *The future of marriage.* New York: World Publishing, 1972.

Brecher, E. *The sex researchers.* Boston: Little, Brown, 1969.

Clanton, G. "The contemporary experience of adultery: Bob and Carol and Updike and Rimmer." In R. Libby and R. Whitehurst (eds.), *Renovating marriage.* Danville, Calif.: Consensus Publishers, 1973.

Clanton, G. and Downing, C. *Face to face: An experience in intimacy.* New York: Dutton, 1975.

Clark, A. and Wallin, P. "Women's sexual responsiveness and the duration and quality of their marriage." *American Journal of Sociology*, 1965, 71, 187-196.

Cole, C. and Spanier, G. "Comarital mate sharing and family stability." *Journal of Sex Research*, 1974, 10, 21-31.

Conover, P. "An analysis of communes with particular attention to sexual and genderal relations." *Family Coordinator*, 1975, 24, 4, 453-464.

Constantine, L. and Constantine, J. "Sexual aspects of multilateral relations." *Journal of Sex Research*, 1971, 7, 204-225.

Constantine, L. and Constantine, J. *Group marriage.* New York: Macmillan, 1973.

Cuber, J. and Harroff, P. *The significant Americans.* Baltimore: Penguin, 1966.

DeBurger, J. "Sex in troubled marriages." In L. Gross (ed.), *Sexual issues in marriage.* New York: Spectrum Publications, 1975.

Delora, J. and Delora, J. (eds.). *Intimate life styles.* Pacific Palisades, Calif.: Goodyear, 1972.

Denfeld, D. "Dropouts from swinging." *The Family Coordinator*, 1974, 23, 45-49.

Denfeld, D. and Gordon, M. "The sociology of mate swapping." *Journal of Sex Research*, 1970, 6, 85-100.

England, L. and Kunz, P. "The application of age specific rates to divorce." *Journal of Marriage and the Family.* 1975, 37, 40-46.

Erikson, E. *Childhood and society.* New York: W. W. Norton, 1963.

Estellachild, V. "Hippie communes." In J. Delora and J. Delora (eds.), *Intimate life styles.* Pacific Palisades, Calif.: Goodyear, 1972.

Farrell, W. *The liberated man.* New York: Random House, 1974.

Francoeur, R. and Francoeur, A. *The future of sexual relations.* Englewood Cliffs, N.J.: Prentice-Hall, 1974.

Francoeur, R. and Francoeur, A. *Hot and cool sex: Cultures in conflict.* Canbury, N.J.: A. S. Barnes, 1976.

Gebhard, P. "Factors in marital orgasm." *Journal of Social Issues*, 1966, 2, 88-95.

Gilmartin, B. "Sexual deviance and social networks: A study of social family and marital interaction patterns among co-marital sex participants." In J. Smith and L. Smith (eds.), *Beyond monogamy.* Baltimore: Johns Hopkins University Press, 1974.

Gilmartin, B. and Kusisto, D. "Personal and social characteristics of mate-sharing swingers." In R. Libby and R. Whitehurst (eds.), *Renovating marriage.* San Ramon, Calif.: Consensus, 1973.

Glenn, N., Ross, A., and Tully, J. "Patterns of intergenerational mobility of females through marriage." *American Sociological Review*, 1974, 39, 683-699.

Glick, P. "A demographer looks at American families." *Journal of Marriage and the Family*, 1975, 37, 15-26.

Goldberg, M. "Extramarital desires." *Medical Aspects of Human Sexuality*, 1978, 12, 11, 32-47.

Hunt, M. *Her infinite variety*. New York: Harper & Row, 1962.

Hunt, M. *Sexual behavior in the 1970's*. New York: Dell, 1974.

Jacoby, S. "49 million singles can't all be right: The truth lies between lechery and loneliness." *New York Times Magazine*, February 17, 1974.

Kerckhoff, A. and Davis, K. "Value consensus and need complementarity in mate selection." *American Sociological Review*, 1962, 27, 295-303.

Kinsey, A., Pomeroy, W., and Martin, C. *The sexual behavior of the human male*. Philadelphia: W. B. Saunders, 1948.

Kinsey, A., Pomeroy, W., Martin, C., and Gebhard, P. *Sexual behavior in the human female*. Philadelphia: W. B. Saunders, 1953.

Knapp, J. "An exploratory study of seventeen sexually open marriages." *Journal of Sex Research*, 1976, 12, 3, 206-219.

Laws, J. "A feminist review of the marital adjustment literature: The rape of Locke." *Journal of Marriage and the Family*, 1971, 33, 3, 483-516.

Leslie, G. and Leslie, E. *Marriage in a changing world*. New York: John Wiley & Sons, 1977.

Levin, R. "The Redbook report on premarital and extramarital sex: The end of the double standard." *Redbook Magazine*, 1976, 145, 6, 38.

Levinger, G. "Sources of marital dissatisfaction among applicants for divorce." *American Journal of Orthopsychiatry*, 1966, 36, 803-807.

Libby, R. and Whitehurst, R. *Marriage and alternatives*. Glenview, Ill.: Scott, Foresman, 1977.

Long Laws, J. and Schwartz, P. *Sexual scripts*. Hinsdale, Ill.: Dryden Press, 1977.

McLuhan, M. and Leonard, G. "The future of sex." *Look Magazine*, July 25, 1967.

Moulton, R. "Some effects of the new feminism." *American Journal of Psychiatry*, 1977, 134, 1, 1-6.

Myers, L. and Leggitt, H. "A positive view of adultery." In L. Gross (ed.), *Sexual issues in marriage*. New York: Spectrum Publications, 1975.

O'Neill, G. and O'Neill, N. "Patterns in group sexual activity." *Journal of Sex Research*, 1970, 6, 101-112.

O'Neill, N. and O'Neill, G. *Open marriage*. New York: Evans, 1972.

Palson, C. and Palson, R. "Swinging in wedlock." *Society*, 1972, 9, 4, 28-37.

Peterson, J. "Nagging and sex." In L. Gross (ed.), *Sexual issues in marriage*. New York: Spectrum Publications, 1975.

Pietropinto, A. and Simenauer, J. *Beyond the male myth.* New York: New York Times Book Co., 1977.

Rimmer, R. *The Harrad experiment.* New York: Bantam, 1966.

Rimmer, R. *Proposition 31.* New York: New American Library, 1969.

Rubin, L. *Worlds of pain.* New York: Basic Books, 1976.

Saline, C. "Why can't married women have men as friends." *McCalls,* January 1975, 67, 132-133.

Skinner, B. *Walden two.* New York: Macmillan, 1969.

Smith, J. and Smith, L. "Co-marital sex and the sexual freedom movement." *Journal of Sex Research,* 1970, 62, 131-142.

Sprey, J. "Extramarital relationships." In L. Gross (ed.), *Sexual issues in marriage.* New York: Spectrum Publications, 1975.

Stein, P. "Singlehood: An alternative to marriage." In M. Sussman (ed.), *Variant family forms. The Family Coordinator,* 1975, 24, 4, 489-507.

Symonds, C. Pilot study of the peripheral behavior of mate swappers. Masters thesis. Riverdale: University of California, 1967.

Vincent, C. "Prerequisites for marital and sexual communication." In D. Grummon and A. Barclay (eds.), *Sexuality: A search for perspective.* New York: Van Nostrand Reinhold Co., 1971.

Westhoff, C. "Coital frequency and contraception." *Family Planning Perspectives,* 1974, 136-141.

Whitehurst, R. "Swinging into the future: Some problems and prospects for marriage." In R. Caven (ed.), *Marriage and family in the modern world.* New York: Thomas Crowell, 1974.

Ziskin, J. and Ziskin, M. *The extramarital sex contract.* Los Angeles: Nash, 1973.

Chapter 13
Sexuality in Later Life

Sexuality is a concern of people of all ages including middle-aged and older people. Childhood is a period of sexual experimentation, sex role learning, and the establishment of gender identity. The physical changes of puberty reinforce gender identity and prepare the adolescent for adult sexuality. Late adolescence and early adulthood are the beginnings of sexual initiation and active genital sexuality. It is during that period that sexual experiences are integrated into a person's sexual identity and the image of his or her sexual self is shaped. The script of psychosexual development does not end with adulthood but goes further into the later years. Psychosexual development is an ongoing process in which people, including the elderly, rework their sense of sexual identity as part of their psychological development throughout life.

As a developmental period, the later years involve learning to cope with being replaced, with not being needed. It is a period when some or all of the children have left home and parents are becoming grandparents. That their children have sexually come of age places parents in the "older generation." Although there is no question that older parents are often deeply needed, a reversal of roles often takes place eventually. Consequently, it is not unusual for older people to feel depressed because of the realization that their children have become sexual adults at a time when they are feeling less sexual than they did when they were younger (Berman, 1978).

Older men and women have to confront many problems. Some of them are physiological, others economic; some are real, others are myths. Because of physical or financial limitations, many older people are forced to adjust to a different life style, one which offers not only less responsibility and structure but also fewer challenges and rewards. With the exception of some of the natural changes inherent in the aging process, many of the burdens of old age are

unnecessary. However, as long as they are misunderstood, they will complicate the adjustment to old age.

One of the most significant developments in the area of aging is the steady growth of our older population. Whereas at the beginning of this century only 40 percent of the population reached or lived beyond the age of sixty, during the decade of the 1970s the corresponding figure is estimated at 75 percent. There are now more than 25 million people in the United States past the age of sixty, and the number is growing rapidly. A large population over sixty is an important social phenomenon of our times. It is the result of advances in medical and health care, improved nutrition, and a generally higher stan-

Figure 13.1
Many people believe that sex and intimacy have no place in the life of elderly men and women. (Mimi Forsyth, Monkmeyer Press Photo Service)

dard of living among many segments of our society. Not only are people living longer, but they do so with good health and vitality.

As survival into old age becomes increasingly more commonplace, mental health professionals are becoming deeply concerned with the quality of life during the later years. One aspect of life that has received insufficient consideration by researchers and clinicians until recently is the sexual behavior of older people. Even today, relatively little scientific information is available with regard to the range and scope of sexuality in old age.

Traditionally, old age and sex have been considered mutually exclusive. Whereas in the past the failure of society to recognize the sexual needs of older people may have been serious but not crucial, today, with the growing older population, we can no longer afford to ignore or misconstrue the sexual lives of the elderly.

In this chapter we will turn our attention to the major physiological and psychosocial factors which shape the expression of sexuality in men and women during the advanced years. Let us begin with a discussion of the physiological changes underlying the aging process.

Physiological Changes of Aging

It is virtually impossible to specify an age when a person begins to become old. Some people are sexually old before they reach middle age, whereas others—for example, the highly creative and productive people of our times such as Picasso and Casals—are still "young" beyond the age of eighty.

Generally people do not change much; they just grow older. As with most of our physical abilities, erotic capacities and desires also change with time. However, in most older people, assuming the absence of physically disabling conditions or chronic diseases, these changes are consistent with a person's

earlier sex life. Several studies have suggested a correlation between early sexual activity and a continued active sex life in later life (Kinsey, Pomeroy, and Martin, 1948; Freeman, 1961). Men and women who were sexually active during their younger years will continue these pursuits later in life. By the same token, individuals with little interest in sex early in life usually abandon sexual activity in old age regardless of physical capacities. A wife, for example, who was raised in an era when sex was only for making babies and who never enjoyed the "duty of sex" is likely to use aging, ushered in by menopause, as an excuse to give up sex completely. If satisfactory sexual adjustment is to be achieved in old age, it must be initiated before middle age. Couples who have looked upon a good sexual relationship as an important aspect of their total relationship do not expect it to change because the body undergoes changes.

As the body ages most physiological processes become progressively slower and weaker. The physiological functions involved in the sexual response prove no exception. Both men and women undergo distinctive changes as they grow older, but the physiological changes associated with aging take a different course and have different importance for men and women.

Menopausal and Postmenopausal Years

In a society which traditionally equated sexuality in women with the ability to have children, menopause was thought to mean the end of sexual pleasures or even the total end of a woman's sex life. As a distinctively demarcated physiological event, menopause or the so-called change of life signalled a woman's advance into middle and old age.

Many myths have surrounded menopause in the past as well as in the present. Fear of insanity and depression have been associated with the event. For women who are not emotionally prepared for it, the end of menstruation may be a traumatic experience if menstruation has been the badge of femininity and the symbol of youth (Rubin, 1963). As we will see, the idea that a woman loses sexual interests or is less capable of sexual functioning after menopause is a myth that has no anatomical or physiological basis.

Physiologically, *menopause* refers to the cessation of the menstrual cycle. A distinction is necessary here between two terms that are often used interchangeably: menopause and *climacterium*. Whereas menopause refers to the cessation of the menses, the term climacterium in women applies to the gradual involution of the ovaries and the psychosocial processes accompanying this process.

Basically, menopause involves the gradual decrease in the cyclic release of estrogen which usually begins several years before the end of menstruation. As women approach their fifties, the blood supply to the ovaries decreases and as a result the glands begin to wither. Most women are aware that menopause is coming closer because their menstrual periods become shorter and farther apart with scantier flow. Sometimes whole months are skipped.

It is not possible to predict the exact age at which a woman will begin menopause, although it usually happens between forty-eight and fifty-two years, but with a wide normal range spanning the two decades from thirty-five and fifty-five. Women of today typically experience menopause nearly ten years later than women at the beginning of the century (Committee on Human Sexuality of the American Medical Association, 1972). Apparently there is no correlation between the onset of menarche and menopause, that is, girls who begin menstruating earlier than average do not necessarily go through menopause earlier than average.

Menopause itself is manifested by menstrual periods of highly unpredictable se-

quences. In the absence of the cyclic hormonal stimulation, the endometrium begins to atrophy so that menstruation finally ceases. One of the most common symptoms of the menopausal period are "hot flashes," which are sudden sensations of heat, particularly in the upper part of the body. Some women have described hot flashes as "being hot all over" or being "flooded by heat and sweat." Other women have described them as being similar to looking into a hot oven or staying in a sauna for too long. Sometimes these heat sensations are accompanied by patches of redness of the skin that look like a rash. Usually hot flashes last from several seconds to a minute, often involving profuse perspiration. Many women feel chilly when they are over.

The physiological processes responsible for the appearance of hot flashes are not fully understood. One factor quoted by medical authorities is that the pituitary increases its production of the ovary-stimulating hormone FSH (see Chapter 5) in response to the decreased production of estrogen. Consequently, the unusually large amount of FSH in the blood may cause an imbalance and hot flashes may occur as the body's attempt to adjust to the new hormonal level. Another explanation suggests that hot flashes result directly from estrogen deprivation in the vascular system (blood vessels). The observation that hot flashes typically diminish once a woman's body has adjusted to the lower estrogen levels seems to be consistent with the second explanation.

A second menopausal symptom which is a direct consequence of the withdrawal of estrogen is the increased dryness and decreased elasticity of the vaginal walls. Since in some older women the vagina produces less lubrication and its tissues lose subtleness, intercourse can be painful. However, in most instances, vaginal dryness does not set in until the latter part of menopause and can easily be counteracted by applying substitute lubrication such as the water soluble lubricant K-Y jelly to prevent uncomfortable friction.

Other symptoms of menopause may include weight gain, particularly a shift of fat deposits to the lower regions of the body, headaches, fatigue, and sleeplessness. In addition, palpitations and dizziness may be related in some yet undefined way to the body's adjustment to a different level of estrogen. So far, medical research has not proven that any of the symptoms, with the exception of vaginal dryness and hot flashes which are a direct response to the decrease in estrogen, are clearly linked with menopause.

Although this catalog of symptoms may justify the notion that menopause should be a genuinely dreaded process, it leaves out one important consideration: of every five women, one will have only minor or no menopausal symptoms, and only 15 percent of all women suffer severe menopausal symptoms (Gadpaille, 1975). Although many women experience some bothersome symptoms, most of them will require no treatment. For those who do, physicians treat menopausal symptoms in a variety of ways.

Sleeping pills or tranquilizers may be prescribed for symptoms such as sleeplessness or anxiety, if warranted. A more controversial treatment involves the prescription of *estrogen replacement therapy* (ERT), which is administered in the form of injections or pills containing estrogen, sometimes along with progesterone. Medical authorities differ sharply over whether ERT should be given routinely after menopause or whether it should be reserved for those symptoms clearly linked with estrogen deficiency. Many physicians warn against the indiscriminate use of ERT because it does involve a risk. Of particular concern has been the speculative role of estrogen in increasing the likelihood of certain forms of cancer. Although valid clinical evidence connecting ERT and cancer is missing, ERT is not given to women who have

a history of cancer, recurrent cysts, or blood clots. As in the case of oral contraceptives (see Chapter 7), ERT increases the risk of blood clots which, in turn, increase with age. A second group of women for whom ERT is not recommended are women with kidney and liver disturbances because estrogen has a tendency to cause salt and water retention in the body.

It is worth repeating that many women pass through menopause with little or no feelings of physical or emotional upset. Most of the time postmenopausal production of estrogen is sufficient, and no ERT is indicated. In many cases, vaginal dryness can be alleviated by artificial lubricants or estrogen creams applied to the vagina, thereby avoiding the possible dangers of oral ingestion which may affect the entire body. For women with severe menopausal symptoms the goal of ERT is to prescribe as small an amount of estrogen as possible, sufficient to relieve the symptoms and bring about a sense of well-being but without precipitating any side effects.

Although most research evidence regarding the etiology and dynamics of menopausal symptoms has been guided by an endocrine factor theory which attributes the physiological changes to a disturbance in hormonal balance, emotional factors are equally important. Women who have maintained an active and fulfilling sex life before menopause are likely to accept the physiological changes without denying themselves sexual enjoyment. In fact, most women maintain that menopause has no effect on their sexual activities. This was convincingly demonstrated by sociologist Neugarten (1963) who interviewed one hundred premenopausal, menopausal, and postmenopausal women between the ages of forty-three and fifty-three about their menopausal expectations and experiences. The women came from working- and middle-class backgrounds. All of them were married, lived with their husbands, and had at least one child. When asked how menopause affected their sexual lives, 65 percent of the women replied that there was no effect. Interestingly enough, women with more severe menopausal symptoms did not view menopause any more negatively than those with less severe symptoms. On the other hand, women who described earlier sexual experiences such as masturbation or first sexual intercourse as well as pregnancy and childbirth in negative terms were also those who reported more severe menopausal symptoms. Thus, Neugarten's findings clearly demonstrated the importance of a woman's premenopausal sex life in accounting for the nature and severity of menopausal symptoms.

Since a woman's reproductive system is governed by the cyclic ebb and flow of estrogen, the loss of this hormone manifests itself in further changes during the postmenopausal years. Masters and Johnson (1966) noted that the lining of the vagina becomes thin and atrophic. There is also a shrinking of the labia majora leading to a constriction of the opening of the vagina. The uterus and breasts begin to shrink. In women past the age of sixty these physiological changes are quite evident. The effects of hormonal adjustment are not, however, the crucial factors in the sexual adjustment of older women. Sexual capacity and performance depend far more on the regularity of intercourse than on hormonal balance. It is, according to Masters and Johnson, the key to sexual responsiveness for aging women and men.

Once the drastic changes of menopause have passed and adjustment to postmenopausal levels of estrogen has taken place, many women experience a renewed interest in erotic activities. Most of the problems connected with raising a family have been resolved so that women can devote more time to their sexual partners. As a result, some older couples actually go through a "second honeymoon" during their late fifties.

In general, we can conclude that a particular woman's menopausal experience is less determined by biological changes than shaped and colored by her prior sexual attitudes and cultural expectations. Most adverse psychological reactions of menopause result from poor premenopausal sexual adjustment and societal misconceptions. Sexually fulfilled and secure women who are able to maintain a compatible and satisfying relationship with their partner are usually able to pass through menopause with minimal distress. For women whose major role in life has been motherhood, a close relationship with their children is also important during these years. After the menopausal period has been successfully negotiated, many women experience increased sexual and marital satisfaction.

Male Climacterium

While men do not go through a definite or pronounced "change of life" as women do, they do experience, but at different ages, a gradually diminishing virility and slackening of their sexual capacity. However, in men there is no absolute end to fertility. Consequently, the male climacterium appears to be less traumatic and is more representative of a generalized fear of aging. Nevertheless, there are a few men who actually develop menopausal symptoms—hot flashes and the like—in the same way as some men develop pregnancy symptoms when their wives are pregnant.

In contrast to the hormonal changes in women, the male climacterium has a questionable hormonal basis. There is, for instance, no sudden decline in testosterone production at any age. The output of androgen and testosterone diminishes very gradually. Secretions of androgen, for instance, dwindle insidiously over a period of thirty years from about 55 units per 24 hours in a man of thirty, to about 8 units in a man of sixty

(McCary, 1973). Thus, for men there is no automatic cut-off point at which fertility suddenly ceases and which would allow us to assume that old age is entering the picture. This does not mean, however, that men do not age sexually. They do, but much more slowly than usually thought, with aging being linked more to general physical and social factors rather than specific hormonal changes.

The changes taking place in the sexual response pattern of older men are well documented. Usually the first symptom of the male menopause has to do with having an erection. Elevation of the penis takes a longer time and more physical stimulation is required to produce an erection. Once he has achieved an erection, the older man can maintain it. As a matter of fact, the plateau phase can be prolonged voluntarily for a considerable time providing that ejaculation does not occur. Hence, men who were premature ejaculators in their younger years may not be troubled with the problem as they grow older.

A man does not lose his facility for erection as he ages unless physical illness or emotional illness interferes with his sexual functioning. Many men over sixty are usually satisfied with one or two ejaculations per week, but can enjoy and satisfy a partner more frequently because erections are possible given adequate sexual stimulation. Older men who lose interest in sex or become impotent do so for a variety of factors other than the ability to achieve an erection.

Even with longer arousal periods before orgasm, many older men often do not ejaculate during intercourse. Usually the expulsion of semen is less powerful than in younger years and the volume of the semen decreases. After orgasm there is a rapid loss of erection; in fact, in old men the penis often collapses immediately after climaxing. Finally, the refractory period in men (see Chapter 5) is extended—that is, a longer interval is required between erections. This is probably the greatest change in the sexual response cycle of men because the refractory period is altered from minutes to hours, lasting between eight and twenty-four hours in men over sixty.

With the gradual drop in the level of testosterone, male reproductive organs also undergo physical changes over the years. The testicles become smaller and the semen becomes thinner and less plentiful. Testosterone replacement therapy is available and has been successfully employed to revive the sex drive and erectile potency in older men. However, it is not as widely used as ERT with women. For men, the power of suggestion seems to be more important than the hormone itself. Men who have been given placebos and were convinced they took testosterone have reported elevated sexual interests.

Canadian and American researchers (de Martino, 1969; McCary, 1973) have called our attention to some of the potential sexual advantages the older man can have over his younger counterpart. Since sexual arousal occurs more slowly, the older man is likely to approach orgasm with less urgency than a younger man. He can be less hurried during foreplay and more concerned to provide his partner with ample stimulation after intromission. Equipped with accurate information about his sexual potential, the older man can delay ejaculation, allowing a woman to reach complete orgasmic fulfillment before pursuing his own. Older men who experience their sex drive as less urgent often feel that good sex is more a part of a total relationship than the strictly genital demand it was when they were younger.

The older man is not only less consumed by the need to ejaculate but also has gained sexual finesse and sophistication over the years, which can make him an imaginative, considerate lover who is willing to subordinate his own sexual satisfaction to that of his partner. Finally, many older men, at the height of their professional or business career, can afford the means and time to "go places" or "do things" with their sexual partners, thereby adding new dimensions of romance and variety to the relationship (McCary, 1973).

The sexual advantages of older men elucidated by contemporary researchers echo the descriptions and are reminiscent of "September love" found in the writings of the ancient Chinese *Tao of Love* (see Chapter 9). In view of these potential advantages, it is unfortunate that many sexual relationships between older couples are described as dull, monotonous, and mechanical.

Physiological changes related to aging in men develop not only more slowly and gradually than in women, but also take place about ten years after the female menopause. As with women, it is difficult to separate the relative impact of physiological changes involved in the climacterium from psychosocial influences. A productive man, for instance, who is forced into mandatory retirement may show changes in sexual functions unrelated to physiological changes.

An active enjoyable sex life for men and women depends upon having established such a pattern earlier. A lack of a satisfying sex life in the formative and adult years does not lend itself to reversal later in life. Successful adjustment to the physiological changes of aging requires an understanding and sexually interested partner and a willingness to accept the "givens" of nature without conforming to the myth of a "sexless old age."

Social Attitudes and Stereotypes

More important than our understanding of the physiological changes of aging is a careful evaluation of the psychosocial factors shaping and coloring the aging experience of any given person. Many people experience anxiety about getting older in our society, which confers high prestige upon youth. In adoles-

cence, age thirty seems to be the end of life. After thirty-five any mention of age is a reminder for many that life is closer to the end than to the beginning. The thirty-ninth birthday can be particularly traumatic since society lets us presume that the person is then standing at the threshold of middle age. After the fourth decade has been ushered in, many men and women give themselves another ten years before succumbing to "old age." Our youth-oriented society is not an easy culture to grow old in. Despite the many improvements in health care and life style, aging remains a crisis for many people, a long crisis indeed.

Stereotypes of Middle and Old Age

Aging, as difficult and stressful a process as it is, is further complicated by the many confusing and stereotypic attitudes concerning the sexual lives of older people. On one hand, society perpetuates the myth of a sexless old age. At the same time, given our present preoccupation with sex, old people are inundated with the notion of sex being the ultimate experience. However, old people presumably cannot share this ultimate experience. Because their sex drive is presumably gone, they are expected to relinquish all sexual pleasures.

Many old people grew up in a Puritan era but ultimately discovered for themselves that sex is pleasurable. Now they are led to believe that sex "at their age" is perverse, dirty, or indecent at best. The older person who protests becomes the butt of jokes. Old men are often ridiculed as impotent, lechers, or dirty old goats when they talk about sex. A California bumper sticker, protesting such notions, reads: "I am not a dirty old man, I am a sexy senior citizen."

Another common stereotype reveals the tendency of many people to exaggerate unusual types of sexual behavior among older people, especially in men. Many older men, for instance, are seen as potential molesters of young children. This is paradoxical because sexual offenses of older men tend to be relatively harmless and not seriously damaging. Abrahamsen (1960) noted how aggressive assaults such as rape and rape-murder are almost strictly the province of younger sex offenders. Older men are more liable to be involved in exhibition or pedophilic activities (see Chapter 15), fondling, and caressing young children without causing physical injury. Many of the unusual sexual practices of older men are related, in part, to their struggle to maintain something that had been a valued part of their self-image for a good part of their lives—namely, their sexual capacities (Whiskin, 1970).

Many people, young and old alike, are astonished at the idea of men and women making love in their seventies or eighties. Our culture has perpetuated the notion that sex is for young people only and consequently has little tolerance for sexual expressions of older people. Several surveys have shown younger people to believe that the elderly do not have a sex life. Golde and Kogan (1959) asked students at Brandeis University, ranging in age from seventeen to twenty-three, to complete the sentence: "Sex for most old people is . . . ." Almost all replied "negligible," "unimportant," or "past." It has been suggested that with the creation of the stereotype of a sexless old age, younger people perhaps seek to eliminate older persons as sexual competitors (Butler and Lewis, 1973).

The notion of older people as an asexual group exists not only in the minds of the young. Many older people give up intercourse even when it is mutually enjoyable because they feel it is "indecent" at their age. Often the elderly are victims of cultural values they helped devise and their own earlier beliefs that sex has no place in later life. Bowman (1963) noted:

Men and women often refrain from continuing their sexual relations or from seeking remarriage after the loss of a spouse because they themselves have come to regard sex as a little ridiculous, so much have our social attitudes equated sex with youth. They feel uncertain about their capacities and very self-conscious about their power to please. They shrink from having their pride hurt (p. 372).

Often the older person conforms to the stereotypic notion of an asexual old age because he or she is afraid that having sex will lead to scandal or ridicule. Many times old men and women are ashamed of their sexual desires and consequently deny them. They refuse to be a lecherous man or a shameless old woman (de Beauvoir, 1972). Many elderly people, unsure about their role in a period of life for which they have been poorly prepared, are ignorant of their sexual capacities and consequently give up sex.

Too often older people find themselves in a setting that provides little or no opportunity for sexual expression. Clinical experience in hospitals and institutions has shown that people working with and caring for the aged too have a tendency to accept taboos against sexuality in old age, thereby underlining the powerful effects of negative cultural expectations. For example, the staff in many nursing homes or other residential facilities for the elderly typically assures that men and women (even if they are married to each other) are rigidly separated by assigning them to different wings. There are no provisions for privacy. Sexual expression, regardless of age, however, requires privacy. In many of the facilities for the elderly there seems to be an agreement that old people must be prevented from having sexual contacts. When they resort to masturbation the nursing staff responds with indignation.

The problem is no less difficult for older persons living with their children or in the homes of friends. Often the elderly are embarrassed to admit to their children or friends that they have sexual feelings. Many adults have a tendency to overprotect their elderly parents as they do pre-school age children. Consider the following case:

Case 13.1
The Case of Joe and Laura

An elderly couple consulted their physician for advice. The husband, seventy-two years old, had a heart infarct four years ago but had made satisfactory recovery. His seventy-year-old wife had a mild case of diabetes which was controlled by small amounts of insulin and a dietary regimen. The couple reported enjoying intercourse about three or four times a month. It was not their sex life, however, that troubled them, but her daughter's reaction to it. They lived with a married daughter in her forties who overheard them making love one night. The daughter apparently was embarrassed at the thought of her parents having intercourse. She expressed her embarrassment as concern over the parents' state of health and suggested the old couple stop "the foolishness."

Not only do young people, elderly peers, and children of older people reinforce the asexuality of old age, but sometimes the old person encounters the same reaction from physicians when seeking help for diminishing sexual responsiveness. The next case will illustrate this situation:

Case 13.2
Sexual Complaints in Old Age

An eighty-five-year-old man sought the advice of his doctor because of impotence. He complained that he had not been able to perform sexually although he had weekly morning erections and masturbated occasionally. His eighty-year-old wife still wanted to have intercourse but found his inability to maintain an erection frustrating. The doctor, trying to

put the old man at ease, wrote off the man's problem with the statement: "That's only natural at your age."

The taboos and stereotypes surrounding sexual behavior in old age affect not only the older population or the helping professions, but are also reflected in research endeavors. Gathering data about the sexual interests and activities of the aging has not been an easy task. Several investigators (Kinsey, Pomeroy, and Martin, 1948; Kinsey et al., 1953; Masters and Johnson, 1966; Newman and Nichols, 1960) have commented on the difficulty of recruiting aged people for studies that are clearly sexual in nature. At times when the elderly were glad to participate in such research, relatives became upset and insisted on withdrawal. Or, when cooperation was finally gained, the data collected were of a limited variety because the investigators were hamstrung by their own and society's attitudes toward sexuality in old age.

As we have seen, various segments of our population, including the elderly themselves, assume that old persons have no sexual desires. It is often believed that the older person could not make love, even if he or she wanted to, because of physical disabilities, frailty, or the possibility of hurting themselves during intercourse. Older men in particular are warned that they are jeopardizing their life span by having sex because the loss of semen presumably drains a man's vitality and thereby shortens his life. Since old people are often afraid of losing their sexual capacities and becoming sexually undesirable, they often uncritically accept social prescription of an asexual old age.

Rubin (1973) has been a particularly outspoken critic of the "sexless older years" which he views as a socially harmful stereotype. The notion of a sexless old age coupled with the notion that aging is a disease rather than a normal process makes the social stereotype of aging especially powerful, causing many old men and women to curtail their sexual activities.

The Double Standard of Aging

One of the functions of later life is stock-taking, deciding where one has been and where one wants to go. Frequently, taking stock is more painful for women than for men. For women, taking stock can be a poignant reminder of the inevitability of aging, the loss of physical attractiveness, and undeniable disappointments. Although men may experience similar emotions, aging often operates in their favor. Many men have reached the plateau of their professional or business career, in great contrast to most women. Achievement, recognition, money, and power are sexually enhancing for men, whereas women with similar accomplishments may intimidate men or turn them off sexually.

In many ways women in our culture are more severely penalized for aging. Loss of physical attractiveness in women is much more traumatic because being physically attractive accounts for much more in a woman's life than in a man's. Gray hairs and wrinkles in a woman's face are pitied blemishes of aging, whereas in a man's face the same features are taken for "character," indicative of emotional strength and maturity.

Most of the physical characteristics regarded as attractive in women, the smooth, slim physique of the late teens and early twenties, wane much earlier than the physical qualities making for good looks in men. Butler and Lewis (1973), in discussing the stereotype of the older woman as seen in the public eye, describe her as a person who has mysteriously metamorphosized from a desirable young sexy "thing" to a mature, sexually interesting woman; finally, somewhere around the age of fifty, she declines into sexual oblivion. The recognition of this image of old women is movingly represented in a statue by the French sculptor Rodin called "Old Age" which opens this chapter: a naked old woman, seated, pathetically contemplating her flat, sagging body.

The notion that physical aging affects women more painfully than men is reinforced by the fact that women lie more about their age than men do. More women also try to combat the aging process; after all, the majority of clients for plastic surgery are women. Once past youth, women who can afford to fight cosmetic battles enlist in elaborate efforts, trying to close the gap between the image of female attractiveness put forth by society and the evolving facts of nature (Sontag, 1976). Since a woman's appearance, far more than a man's, for whom good looks may be a bonus, is dependent on being at least "acceptable" looking, a greater part of her self-esteem is threatened by the experience of getting old. Social standards of male attractiveness are less intimately linked with youthful appearance, allowing a man to look older with less penalty. Consequently, men rarely panic about aging in the way women do.

The sexual behavior of older men and women also mirrors the double standard. Elderly women become sexually ineligible at a much earlier age because their sexuality is more related to reproductive ability and looks than actual performance. Old women are often considered sexually repulsive. A man, even an ugly man, however, can remain sexually eligible well into old age as long as he can make love. As a matter of fact, many men have more success romantically in their fifties and sixties than they did in their twenties. Although the sexual attractiveness of the older man may not be dazzling, it is understood that other attributes—power, money, experience—can make him a viable trader in the sexual marketplace (Long Laws, and Schwartz, 1977). Since a man's sexual value is more determined by what he does than how he looks, the older, successful man is still

Figure 13.2
Some young women find older men particularly attractive, especially if they have attained prestige.
(United Press International, Inc.)

a desirable partner for a young attractive woman. The woman past age forty, on the other hand, regardless of how radiant, lively, healthy, and sexy she may be, is a "has-been" by social definition. Female sexuality in later years is socially evaluated in terms of a woman's attractiveness to men and her fertility rather than in terms of a woman's own sexual identity or the sexual gains she has made over the years.

The terms our language uses to describe the status of elderly women and men who choose not to marry tell the same story. The older woman who remains single is pitied because of her presumed lack of sexual activity and labeled an old maid or spinster. The older man who never married is allocated the status of a bachelor. As a matter of fact, our langauge does not have an equivalent term for single old males that would carry the same emotional loading as spinster or old maid.

Although aging is less of a developmental crisis for men than for women, this is not to say that men do not experience anxiety when growing older. They too are concerned about their physical attractiveness and sexual performance, worry about the loss of sexual vigor or becoming impotent. Men too are prone to periodic bouts of depression about aging. However, the social role of the older man is much more clearly defined than that of a woman of the same age.

Our contemporary culture maintains a set of ambiguous and conflicting attitudes toward older women who were told to devote their lives almost totally to children as long as they were at home, but leave them almost totally alone once they are grown. A woman's main role as a mother is likely to run out at a time when women feel themselves in a race against the calendar, a time when customary rewards are being withdrawn. In short,

Figure 13.3
Becoming a grandparent is one of the many challenging tasks in later
life. (Dwyer and Zinkl)

whereas a woman's sexual value drops steadily in the public eye as soon as she is no longer young, physically attractive and fertile, the older man may actually benefit from the aging process.

Since sexual behavior is largely a reflection of individual expectations shaped by cultural norms, the widespread acceptance of taboos against sex in old age becomes a self-fulfilling prophecy for many older people of both sexes. As a result, many aging men and women undergo an identity crisis when thinking of themselves as aging and sexless. Ausubel (1954) noted that the transition into old age resembles in many respects the period of adolescence. During both periods of the life span a person is in the marginal transition of having lost an established, rec-

ognized status without having acquired a new, consolidated position. Like the adolescent, the older person undergoes role confusion during which he tends to behave in accordance with social stereotypes in sexual as well as in other areas of behavior (Berlin, 1976).

As we have seen, aging is much more a social judgment than a biological reality. More defeating than the loss of youth and attractiveness or even the waning of sexual interests are social attitudes which make getting older a long tragedy. Psychologist Erikson (1963), in his optimistic and creative view of personality, presented us with the concept of the emerging person challenged by various crises of the life span, each of which may bring success or failure. Erikson suggested that we are programmed to go through various developmental stages from birth to death. To move from one stage to another means struggle because there is always some sort of conflict in the transition from stage to stage. One of the major conflicts in later life arises from the necessity of having to accept the narrowing scope of personal activities and functions. Successful adjustment to this period requires the ability to accept the progressive simplification that usually accompanies aging.

Erikson labeled the developmental period of later life "generativity" (meaning successful adjustment to aging) vs. "stagnation" (failure to cope with the developmental tasks of the period), and viewed this stage as a period of great potential, productivity, maturity, and enrichment.

By and large, sexuality aside for a moment, the later years can provide many opportunities for productive endeavors for the person who has successfully resolved the role crisis of this particular period. The older person who is free from parenting responsibilities, illness, or other disabling condition can devote his or her energies and the knowledge and wisdom gathered over the years to aid the next generation, thereby transcending immediate, self-related interests. For the well-adjusted older person, Erikson's criteria of generativity—productivity, maturity, parental pride—add a new rewarding dimension in the series of adult responsibilities—namely, concern for the next generation. Aging parents and grandparents are surrounded by an ever-expanding number of persons with whom they can identify. Children, grandchildren, and great-grandchildren offer opportunities for vicarious fulfillment and a sense of meaningful extension into the future. Elderly individuals who either outlived their children or never had any can also experience generativity by finding meaning and satisfaction in the memory of their contributions.

Sex in the Life of Older Men and Women

Physiological changes and cultural expectations and stereotypes combine in many different ways to determine the specific effects of aging on sexual behavior. Some older people in whom physical aging takes its normal course without leading to disabling conditions cannot find sexual happiness in old age because they feel pressured to conform to social expectations. Others who had several heart attacks, vascular breakdowns, or underwent disfiguring surgery, such as removal of the breasts because of cancer, are able to resume their sexual activities even though their sex life might require some modifications.

When Freud first presented his findings about infantile and childhood sexuality the public was shocked and responded with incredulity and resistance. The findings of later life sexuality have and are still stirring up similar reactions in many people. The old person, just as the innocent infant, is simply not expected to have sexual feelings. In the case of the elderly, the general prejudice of aging in a youth-oriented culture combines with the belief that sex is the exclusive province of the young, thereby creating attitudes of rejection when it comes to the sex life of old people.

A good part of our knowledge regarding sexual activities of elderly and aged men and women rests on three major investigations: the Kinsey findings, the research of Masters and Johnson, and the Duke University longitudinal studies. Let us review the highlights of this research along with some additional evidence.

Sexual Activities in Old Age

The Kinsey data of twenty-five years ago provided the first empirical evidence debunking the myth of sexless later years. Kinsey and his colleagues (1948, 1953) reported to the skeptic public that 75 percent of their males beyond the age of sixty-five were sexually potent and that couples in their sixties and beyond were engaging in weekly intercourse. The Kinsey data for males documented a continuous weakening of sexual responses with increasing age. Morning erections, for instance, which averaged 4.9 per week in the early years, dropped to an average of 1.8 at sixty-five, and to 0.9 at the age of seventy-five. Despite the general decline of sexual responsiveness, it was emphasized that providing regularity of sexual activities in a stimulating climate with an interested partner, a healthy man can express his sexual potential in his seventies and eighties. It should be noted, however, that Kinsey's elderly male sample was relatively small. Although over 10,000 sexual histories of men were collected during the Kinsey investiga-

tions, only 106 males over sixty and 18 over seventy were included in the interviews.

With regard to older women, Kinsey and his coworkers found little evidence indicating any pronounced effect of aging on women's sexual capacities. Although the strength and intensity of the sexual response diminishes with age, women can still reach orgasm in old age when properly stimulated. As mentioned before, many women freed from the burden of child-rearing and obligatory parenting find themselves interested again in sex later in life. In fact, some women first discover orgasm after menopause, when fears of pregnancy are gone (Pfeiffer, Verwoerdt, and Wang, 1969).

The Kinsey findings that men and women remain sexually active well into the advanced years were further substantiated by the physiological studies of the sexual response cycle by Masters and Johnson (1966). In their

Figure 13.4
Sexual interests and desires are not the privilege of the young. This man enjoys his daily girl watching. (United Press International, Inc.)

clinical work with older men, Masters and Johnson found six general categories of factors which tend to reduce sexual responsiveness. Although these factors were originally only applied to men, we have expanded them so that many of them are relevant for women also.

1. *Monotony* or *"psychologic fatigue."* This factor essentially translates into being bored with one's sexual partner after a repetitious sex life without much novelty or variation over a long period of time. Sex is bound to get dull for a couple after thirty or forty years of marriage if one or the other partner is unwilling to experiment sexually. Older people (see Chapter 11), like younger couples, simply become bored by sexual routine.

2. *Preoccupation with career or economic success,* a factor more likely to apply to older men who may be more involved in professional than sexual relationships. Men who have attained the peak of their career are faced with the necessity of giving up the reins of power shortly. Retirement may make a major change not only in daily activities but also in the self-esteem of older men. Many men experience a sense of generalized restlessness, dissatisfaction, or searching around the time of retirement. Being forced by social conventions to curtail regular activities often affects the sex life of an older man too.

3. *Mental or physical fatigue.* This factor applies to both older men and women and usually results from stressful personal, family, financial, or occupational commitments. People in their fifties and sixties usually have to face many changes in work and family life—getting along on less than one was used to, finding a different living arrangement, becoming dependent upon children. Many of these demands often go beyond a person's physical and mental resources. Confronted with all these changes the older person often feels unable to control the situation and falls into helplessness and depression. This mental and physical fatigue tends to dampen sexual interests.

4. *Overindulgence of food and drink.* Many elderly people become increasingly preoccupied with food or drink. Particularly, the heightened enjoyment of food is a continuing temptation the elderly have to strongly resist in order to avoid obesity which is quite common among old people. Being overweight reduces both sexual attractiveness and activity.

5. *Physical or mental disability.* We cannot overlook the reality factor that older age brings an increasing incidence of minor infirmities as well as chronic illnesses. For example, diabetes mellitus is common in old age and may cause impotence in men or render women nonorgasmic. Cardiac and circulatory diseases are another category of physical condition that affect a large number of middle aged and elderly women. Both men and women have their share of sexual problems during later life. By far the most common sexual problem of aging men is trouble with the prostate gland which becomes infected or tumorous. In women, removal of the uterus or ovaries is often necessary. Most of these physical conditions have sexual side effects, many of which are imagined or emotional. Inappropriate fear of sexual dysfunction is often more damaging than the illness itself. Nevertheless, as in the case of mental strain, physical fatigue or health problems make it difficult for many older people to sustain sexual responsiveness.

6. *Fear of failure.* The lack of knowledge of normal age changes in sexual functioning often leads older people to give up sex long before it is necessary. This factor is often based on misconceptions about

what is normal in old age. After an occasional failure during intercourse an older person may not attempt coitus again because he or she found the failure humiliating.

In many older people, several of these factors probably combine to make them sexually less active.

At the Duke University Center for the Study of Aging and Human Development, a longitudinal, interdisciplinary study of older persons has been carried out since 1954 and is still in progress (Newman and Nichols, 1960; Pfeiffer, Verwoerdt, and Davis, 1972). From the data gathered, two major conclusions were drawn. First, consistent with Kinsey's and Masters and Johnson's findings, the Duke studies showed that sexual interest and intercourse are by no means rare in people beyond sixty. More than half of the older sample (54 percent), ranging in age from sixty to ninety-three, said they were

sexually active with a frequency of one to three times a week. The Duke findings were replicated by one of the largest surveys of the sexual behavior of old men conducted by *Sexology Magazine* (Rubin, 1966). Questionnaires were mailed to highly successful and distinguished men over sixty-five who had attained enough eminence to be listed in *Who's Who in America*. Of the more than 800 men who answered, 70 percent were married and indicated that they engaged in intercourse with some regularity and found it generally satisfying. The remaining 30 percent were impotent. Even in the group of 104 men between the ages of seventy-five and ninety-two, almost one-half reported satisfaction with their sex life and 6 had intercourse more than eight times a month.

The second major finding of the Duke studies concerned the marked differences in patterns of sexual interests and activities for men and women. As can be seen from Table 13.1, only 6 percent of the men said that they

Table 13.1

Frequency of sexual intercourse (in percentages) among middle-aged and elderly men and women

Group	Number	None	Once a month	Once a week	2-3 times a week	More than 3 times a week
Men						
46-50	43	0	5	62	26	7
51-55	41	5	29	49	17	0
56-60	61	7	38	44	11	0
61-65	54	20	43	30	7	0
66-71	62	24	48	26	2	0
Total	261	12	34	41	12	1
Women						
46-50	43	14	26	39	21	0
51-55	41	20	41	32	5	2
56-60	48	42	27	25	4	2
61-65	44	61	29	5	5	0
66-71	55	73	16	11	0	0
Total	231	44	27	22	6	1

From Pfeiffer, E., Verwoerdt, A., and Davis, G. "Sexual behavior in middle life." *American Journal of Psychiatry*, 1972, 128, 10, 1262-67.

no longer had any sexual feelings compared to 33 percent of the women. Similarly, whereas 12 percent of the men indicated strong current interest, only 3 percent of the women responded positively to this question (Pfeiffer, Verwoerdt, and Davis, 1972).

The investigators also inquired about the reason why the elderly couples stopped having sexual relations. Women overwhelmingly attributed the reason to their husbands—his death, illness, his inability to perform sexually. Men, on the other hand, generally held themselves responsible for the cessation of intercourse with loss of interest in sex and diminished sexual capacity as the major reasons given.

The greater sexual decline in women is, as we shall see in the next section, by and large one of circumstance—namely, the shortage of sexual partners.

Widows and Widowers

Most of the research discussed so far has been based on the study of married older couples. Marital status has emerged as one of the most important factors determining the level of sexual activity of older men and women. Obviously, sexual intercourse is much more frequent among married elderly couples because married life provides continued opportunity for sexual stimulation. Widows and widowers, on the other hand, faced with the need to find an available sexual partner, have much more difficulty in satisfying their sexual needs.

Aging widows, widowers, and single elderly people make up an increasingly large segment of our population. They are particularly prone to isolation and depression. Their sexual contacts are very limited. In the survey reported by Newman and Nichols (1960), only 7 of 101 single, divorced, or widowed men over sixty reported any sexual activity. Let us take a closer look at the problems elderly unmarried people are facing.

Eventually one partner in every surviving marriage is confronted with widowhood. Of the more than 22 million people in the United States who are sixty-five years and older, almost one-half of the women and one-fifth of the men have lost their marital partners (Leslie and Leslie, 1977). Proportionately, there are four times as many widows as widowers. In 1970 there were 11.7 million widows and widowers; 9.6 million were women and 2.1 million were men. Because of the differential longevity of men and women, we can expect an increasing preponderance of widows in the aged population over the years to come.

The loss of a spouse by death invariably produces trauma or conflicting emotions. Questions about the meaning of life and the significance of the passage of time can lead the surviving spouse to shut off from sexual activities, sometimes temporarily, sometimes forever. During widowhood many elderly men and women are inclined to adhere to the strict sexual customs of their youth—no sex outside of marriage—and are therefore forced into celibacy regardless of personal inclination.

Many authors who write about widowhood must assume that most widows and widowers have relinquished all sexual interests because there are many books on the subject without a word concerning sex. A notable exception are Kreis and Pattie (1969), two widows who worked as a team collecting data on sexual problems during widowhood. They noted once the initial shock, grief, and suffering are over, the sexual appetite of healthy men and women is rekindled. The authors give many examples showing how widows and widowers handle their feelings about sex during and after bereavement. Some are plagued with feelings of guilt when attempting to separate sex from marriage, whereas others, particularly widowers, can work out this problem without entering into another permanent relationship. Women who establish a new sexual relationship after a period of

Figure 13.5
Many widows experience isolation and loneliness in later life. (Irene Bayer, Monkmeyer Press Photo Service)

mourning are likely to either remarry or form a new stable partnership with a man they considered a boyfriend (Clayton and Bornstein, 1976).

The double standard of aging is also apparent in the differential options available for widowed men and women. Society at large clearly views remarriage or a continued sex life in some other type of arrangement more favorably for widowers than widows. The widowed man, although not without problems, still has distinct advantages. Because widows outnumber widowers considerably, the widower is, in effect, in a buyer's market. The chances of remarriage for older widows are slim, whereas the widower has a choice of possible partners. Socially, the widower is an asset; the widowed woman is a liability. As widows become older, the pool of available men to marry shrinks continuously. The sex differential in mortality rates may create a real shortage of partners for women in their sixties and older. Someone has seriously suggested legalizing polygamy in old age as a way of resolving the dilemma.

Even the Social Security system favored widowers over widows because it was the widow who was forced to give up her husband's benefits when she remarried. Economically, there was a greater incentive for the widow to live with her partner rather than marry him. The practice of elderly widowed people living together has been described as the "Social Security Sin," in which widows and widowers live together to preserve their pension. Recently, the problem was recognized by Congress and legislation was passed allowing a widow to retain her previous pension or choose her new husband's benefits, whichever sum is greater.

In addition to the greater opportunities to remarry, the widower can choose nonmarital affairs, sexual fantasies, or masturbation. Most of these expressions of sexual interests are disapproved of socially for widows, who are expected to devote themselves to their children or grandchildren, volunteer services in the community, and the memories of their husbands. While many assume that the elderly widowed man needs a woman to look after him, this assumption is no longer valid in the case of the elderly widow.

Both widowers and widows complain that society does not provide suitable outlets for them to express sexual needs relevant to old age and widowhood. For senior citizens without available partners, masturbation has become a major alternative to gain release from sexual tension. Still, many men and women feel that there is something wrong for people of their age to engage in this practice.

Although widows and widowers are faced with many problems in their attempt to find sexual happiness in their later years, many of them remain vigorous people who are not willing to surrender a meaningful relationship with someone of the opposite sex.

Summary

In this chapter we emphasized that successful, mutually satisfying sexual activity can and should continue from adolescence to old age. Sexual enjoyment is available throughout life. In the absence of age-dependent problems that do interfere with sexual functioning, old age does not need to take away the joys of sex. In the later years as during any other period of the life span, sexual adjustment can evolve in many directions based on individual attitudes, appetites, and opportunities. As we have seen, the best prescription for a rewarding sex life in later years is the establishment of satisfying sexual partnerships earlier in life. Just as the truly healthy old person requires a sound diet, adequate exercise, and continued intellectual stimulation, so he or she requires continued sexual activity.

Age can and does reduce the sexual capacities of men and women. As a matter of fact, physical aging seems to narrow the differences between the sexes. In men and women the sexual response becomes less intense and intercourse is less frequent as physical and sexual powers decline. Physiological age changes cause distinct changes in the male and female sexual anatomy. None of the physical changes accompanying aging, however, justify the social stereotype of a sexless old person. Although the capacity for sexual response does slow down gradually along with other physical abilities, it is usually not until actual senility that there is a marked loss of sexual function.

A full and rewarding sex life throughout the life span is an important ingredient of the quality of late life that Erikson called final integrity. However, it should be clear from our discussion that unless society recognizes the need and importance of continued sexual expressions during the later years, it will be difficult for older people to express themselves without feeling guilty or immoral.

Ideally sexual expression would be considered in the overall context of successful aging. The fragmentary research indicates not only that men and women continue to be sexually active into old age, but there is also strong reason to believe that staying in training sexually will also help to improve the quality of life in the advanced years. Staying in training can take many forms other than intercourse: caressing, touching, physical closeness, or emotional bonding. Free of worry blocks and social stereotypes, older men and women can continue to enjoy a full sexual life until the end of their lives.

References

Abrahamsen, D. *The psychology of crime.* New York: Columbia University Press, 1960.

Ausubel, D. *Theory and problems of adolescent development.* New York: Grune & Stratton, 1954.

Berlin, H. "Effects of human sexuality on well-being from birth to aging." *Medical Aspects of Human Sexuality,* 1976, 10, 7, 10-27.

Berman, E. "Transition periods in sexual-marital life: An adult developmental perspective." *Medical Aspects of Human Sexuality,* 1978, 12, 11, 125-136.

Bowman, K. "The sex life of the aging individual." In M. DeMartino (ed.), *Sexual behavior and personality characteristics.* New York: Citadel, 1963.

Butler, R. and Lewis, M. *Aging and mental health.* St. Louis: C. V. Mosby, 1973.

Clayton, P. and Bornstein, B. "Widows and widowers." *Medical Aspects of Human Sexuality,* 1976, 10, 9, 27-48.

Committee on Human Sexuality of the American Medical Association. *Human sexuality.* Chicago: American Medical Association, 1972.

de Beauvoir, S. "Joie de vivre." *Harper's Magazine,* January 1972, 33-40.

De Martino, M. *The new female sexuality.* New York: Julian Press, 1969.

Erikson, E. *Childhood and society.* New York: W. W. Norton, 1963.

Freeman, J. "Sexual capacities in the aging male." *Geriatrics,* 1961, 16, 37-43.

Gadpaille, W. *The cycles of sex.* New York: Charles Scribner's Sons, 1975.

Golde, P. and Kogan, N. "A sentence completion procedure for assessing attitudes toward sex." *Journal of Gerontology,* 1959, 14, 355.

Kinsey, A., Pomeroy, W., and Martin, C. *Sexual behavior in the human male.* Philadelphia: W. B. Saunders Co., 1948.

Kinsey, A., Pomeroy, W., Martin, C., and Gebhard, P. *Sexual behavior in the human female.* Philadelphia: W. B. Saunders Co., 1953.

Kreis, B. and Pattie, A. *Up from grief.* New York: Seabury Press, 1969.

Leslie, G. and Leslie, E. *Marriage in a changing world.* New York: John Wiley & Sons, 1977.

Lewis, M. and Butler, R. "Why is the women's lib ignoring old women?" *Aging and Human Development,* 1972, 3, 223-231.

Long Laws, J. and Schwartz, P. *Sexual scripts.* Hinsdale, Ill.: Dryden Press, 1977.

McCary, L. "Sexual advantages of middle aged men." *Medical Aspects of Human Sexuality,* 1973, 7, 12, 139-146.

Masters, W. and Johnson, V. *Human sexual response.* Boston: Little, Brown, 1966.

Neugarten, B. L. "Women's attitudes toward menopause." *Vita Humana,* 1963, 6, 140.

Newman, G. and Nichols, C. "Sexual activities and attitudes in older persons." *Journal of the American Medical Association.*

Pfeiffer, E., Verwoerdt, A. and Davis, G. "Sexual behavior in middle life." *American Journal of Psychiatry,* 1972, 128, 10, 1262-1267.

Pfeiffer, E., Verwoerdt, A., and Wang, H. "The Natural History of Sexual Behavior in a Biologically Advantaged Group of Aged Individuals." *Journal of Gerontology;* 1969, 24, 193–198.

Rubin, I. "Sex over 65." In H. Beigel (ed.), *Advances in sex research.* New York: Harper & Row, 1963.

Rubin, I. "Sex after forty and after seventy-five." In R. Brecher and E. Brecher, *An analysis of the human sexual response.* New York: Signet Books, 1966.

Rubin, I. "The 'sexless old years': A socially harmful stereotype." In McCreary Juhasz (ed.), *Sexual development and behavior.* Homewood, Ill.: Dorsey Press, 1973.

Sontag, S. "The double standard of aging." In S. Gordon and W. Libby (eds.), *Sexuality today and tomorrow.* North Scituate, Mass.: Duxbury Press, 1976.

Whiskin, F. "The geriatric sex offender." *Medical Aspects of Human Sexuality,* 1970, 4, 4, 125-130.

Chapter 14

Sexual Dysfunction

The term sexual dysfunction refers to an impairment in the ability to obtain gratification from sexual intercourse. These disorders probably produce as much anguish and sorrow in those who suffer from them as any psychological disorder. Many people cannot help but feel that their masculinity or femininity or even their worth depends on their sexual prowess and responsivity. Because of this prevailing attitude, those who suffer from some form of sexual dysfunction not only fail to obtain sexual gratification but are likely to suffer psychological side effects as well. Thus, a thorough understanding of sexual dysfunction is important for a person's general psychological well-being as well as for his or her sex life.

Forms of Sexual Dysfunction

Three major forms of dysfunction in men are erectile failure, premature ejaculation, and ejaculatory incompetence, and two major dysfunctions in women are orgasmic dysfunction and vaginismus. Let us examine the nature of these problems.

Erectile Failure

Erectile failure, commonly called impotence, is the inability on the part of a male to achieve or maintain an erection for a period of time long enough to complete sexual intercourse. The term erectile failure will be used here instead of impotence because the latter has acquired much excess meaning over the years. It tends to have pejorative connotations, whereas the term erectile failure is more precise and free from surplus meaning.

The specific form that this disorder takes can vary greatly from man to man. The man loses his erection when he becomes anxious. The precise aspect of sexual activities that produces the anxiety varies among men.

Some men are never able to have an erection when in the presence of a willing sexual partner. Others will have an erection when engaged in light petting, but will lose it when they take their clothes off. Some may be able to have an erection during some sexual activities, such as oral sex, but are not able to have one when attempting intercourse. Still others will be able to initiate intercourse, but will become flaccid (nonerect) shortly after beginning. Erectile failure may be specific to one's partner as well. Thus, some men are potent with their wives but unable to have intercourse with other women. On the other hand, some men are able to have extramarital sex, but are unable to have intercourse with their wives.

Masters and Johnson (1970), who have conducted extensive research in the area of sexual dysfunction, distinguished between two forms of erectile dysfunction. The first is called primary impotence. This term refers to men who have never successfully completed sexual intercourse. They may, however, achieve erections in other ways, such as masturbating. The second form is called secondary impotence. Impotence is secondary in men who have had one or more successful experiences with sexual intercourse. It is often the case that such men have a history of many years of successful functioning before developing potency problems.

It is important to keep in mind that sexual functioning is not an "all or none" phenomenon. Many people will have some occasions when they are not able to respond sexually. Fatigue, worry over business or money, or any number of situational factors can result in failure experiences. Thus, the man who is only occasionally dysfunctional is not necessarily experiencing a sexual dysfunction. Masters and Johnson recognize this and defined secondary impotence as dysfunction in 25 percent of attempts at intercourse. Although this figure is arbitrary, it does acknowledge that occasional incidents of erectile dysfunction are within the range of normal sexual functioning.

Premature Ejaculation

It is difficult to arrive at a satisfactory definition of premature ejaculation. In general, it refers to the man who ejaculates before he would like to. Experts, however, do not agree as to how long the period of time between beginning intercourse and having an orgasm should be when defining premature ejaculation. Common definitions suggest that men who cannot last from thirty to sixty seconds after intromission are suffering from premature ejaculation. One self-proclaimed expert, psychiatrist David Reuben (1969), has stated that the man who cannot last for five to ten minutes is sexually inadequate. Reuben's definition is interesting because Kinsey reported that three out of four men reach orgasm within two minutes after intromission. Thus, Reuben seems to be suggesting that at least 75 percent of all men are sexually inadequate.

Actually, any attempt to define premature ejaculation in terms of time is likely to be misleading. Many couples find brief intercourse to be highly gratifying. For these people, thirty seconds may be sufficient to produce mutual gratification. It would seem unreasonable to label a man as suffering from premature ejaculation because he does not last for more than thirty seconds when both he and his partner are satisfied with their sexual pattern.

Psychiatrist Helen Singer Kaplan (1974) has suggested that time is not really the crucial issue. She suggests that this dysfunction involves an absence of voluntary control over the ejaculatory reflex. While other theorists seriously question whether any man can exercise voluntary control of ejaculation, Kaplan argues that what separates premature ejaculators from others is the inability to tolerate high levels of sexual excitement. The premature ejaculator has his orgasm almost immediately after reaching the plateau stage in the sexual response cycle. Thus, such men not only have their orgasm sooner than they would like, but they have a reduction in the pleasant sensations that accompany intercourse. Kaplan reports that men who have been successfully treated for this dysfunction report a considerable increase in pleasure during intercourse.

Although it is probably impossible to define premature ejaculation in such a way to satisfy all experts, many men clearly suffer from this problem. Some may ejaculate at the sight of an unclothed body of a desirable partner. Others may have an orgasm while their partner fondles their genitals. Still others may ejaculate during intromission or seconds later. Regardless of the definition used, these men would be suffering from premature ejaculation. Such a pattern of sexual response greatly diminishes their potential pleasure and virtually insures that their partner will not reach orgasm through coitus.

Ejaculatory Incompetence

Ejaculatory incompetence, also called retarded ejaculation, refers to an inability on the part of the male to have an orgasm during intercourse. Masters and Johnson (1970) have reported that this is a relatively rare disorder, but other sex therapists believe that it is becoming increasingly prevalent (Kaplan, 1974).

The severity of this disorder can vary considerably. Some men have only occasional experiences during which they find it difficult to have an orgasm. These experiences may be related to anxiety-provoking situations. For example, some men may have difficulty with one particular woman but have no problems with others. Other men may not be able to have an orgasm with their wives when they are staying at their parents home. At the other extreme, there are some men that have never been able to have an orgasm—either via intercourse, masturbation, or other forms of stimulation. Somewhere between these extremes are cases in which men are unable to have an orgasm during intercourse, but are able to have one via manual stimulation or oral sex. Some of these men may have intercourse until their partner is satisfied and then the woman will manually stimulate the man to orgasm. For other men, the mere sight of their partner is enough to inhibit ejaculation. They may wait until they are alone and obtain gratification via masturbation.

Orgasmic Dysfunction

Orgasmic dysfunction is an inability on the part of a woman to have an orgasm during sexual intercourse. Masters and Johnson offered this term as a substitute for the older, commonly used term frigidity. They believe, with some justification, that the term frigidity has come to be pejorative. That is, calling a woman frigid is often more a nasty remark than a clinical diagnosis. Many men have the unfortunate tendency of labeling a woman as frigid if she does not respond in the manner they feel she should. It is not unusual for a man to think of a woman as being frigid if she does not respond breathlessly to his advances although she may respond this way to other men. At any rate, the term orgasmic dysfunction does not have the excess meaning that the term frigidity has acquired over the years.

As is the case with all sexual dysfunctions, the severity of orgasmic dysfunction can vary widely. Some women never feel erotic sensations and may view sexual intercourse as their rather unpleasant duty to their husbands. To them, sex may be so distasteful that they continually search for excuses to avoid such encounters. Other women, who have no erotic feelings, may enjoy intercourse because of the feelings of closeness to their partner and the emotional satisfaction it affords.

At the other end of the continuum, some women will become highly aroused during foreplay and intercourse. For some reason, however, they get to the plateau phase of the sexual response cycle but are often unable to reach orgasm. According to Masters and Johnson, a diagnosis of orgasmic dysfunction is appropriate when a woman fails to have an orgasm during 50 percent of her sexual encounters. This, of course, assumes that she has an adequately functioning partner.

A distinction can be made between primary and secondary orgasmic dysfunction. The condition is diagnosed as primary when the woman has never had an orgasm. The woman who has had some history of successful functioning would be said to be secondarily dysfunctional. She may have had orgasms with her husband early in her marriage but after several years was no longer able to. Or, the dysfunction may be specific to a particular partner. Some women have orgasms readily in extramarital relationships but are unable to do so with their husbands.

Earlier we suggested that the woman who has no erotic sensations whatsoever and the woman who can have orgasms via manual stimulation but not during intercourse are two extremes on the same continuum. That is, they have the same basic problem, and they differ only in terms of the severity of the problem. Kaplan, on the basis of her clinical observations, has suggested that they are in fact discrete conditions. She believes that the woman who has no erotic feelings is truly suffering from a sexual dysfunction. Kaplan uses the term frigid to describe this woman. On the other hand, the woman who becomes aroused but fails to reach orgasm may be within the normal range of female sexuality. This woman is said to be suffering from an orgasmic dysfunction. According to Kaplan, such women should not necessarily be thought of as having a problem. They are simply exhibiting a pattern that is normal for them.

Although there may be some merit to Kaplan's hypothesis, it is always extremely difficult to distinguish between what is normal and what is abnormal. Such judgments, particularly with regard to human behavior, tend to be philosophical rather than scientific. There are some people in our society who might claim that the woman who experiences no erotic feelings is normal whereas the woman who becomes highly aroused is abnormal. It was not too many years ago that some wives tried to conceal any pleasure they derived from intercourse so that their husbands did not think they were "that kind of woman." In short, it is legitimate and appropriate for scientists to search for techniques to allow both "frigid" and orgasmically dysfunctional women to change their response pattern if they so desire. It is questionable whether scientists should label anyone as normal or abnormal.

Vaginismus

Vaginismus is a disorder that involves an involuntary contraction of the muscles surrounding the vaginal entrance. The contraction of the muscles can be so severe as to make sexual intercourse impossible. Many women who seek treatment for this disorder have not consummated their marriages—some after several years of marriage. The contraction can occur in response to imagined, anticipated, or attempted sexual intercourse.

Women who seek treatment for this disorder can vary greatly in terms of their general level of sexual responsiveness. Some may find any form of sexual contact unpleasant and experience no erotic sensations whatsoever. Others, may be highly responsive except in sexual intercourse. They may want sexual contact, and may even have orgasms in response to clitoral stimulation.

Their involuntary muscle contractions, however, make it extremely difficult, if not impossible, for them to complete coitus.

According to Masters and Johnson, a diagnosis of vaginismus can be made only on the basis of a pelvic examination. However, other therapists have noted that the contractions can be specific to certain situations. That is, some women may experience the problem only when attempting intercourse; others may experience the contractions only during a pelvic examination. The *exam* can be useful, though, since some women may have a phobia regarding sexual intercourse, and a therapist may mistakenly conclude that she has vaginismus based on her verbal description of her reaction. If she does in fact have vaginismus, it may be readily observed during a pelvic exam. A local anesthetic may be required to complete such an examination.

Causes of Sexual Dysfunction

The most complete information available about the causes of sexual dysfunction is provided by Masters and Johnson in *Human Sexual Inadequacy* (1970). In this book they summarize the cases of 733 individuals with some form of sexual dysfunction. Thorough histories were taken for all clients which provide information about the factors that can operate to cause a sexual dysfunction. In this section the factors that these researchers identified will be summarized.*

While each case of sexual dysfunction may be associated with specific factors, most, if not all, of those with such a problem have fears of performance. These fears, also called performance anxiety, cause a person to approach a sexual encounter with a concern of how he or she will perform. Men might worry

*Although most cases of sexual dysfunction result from psychological factors, about 5 percent of cases can be traced to physical or medical origins. These factors are discussed in Chapter 6.

about whether they will have an erection. If they have, they may worry if it is hard enough —or will it last long enough. Women worry about whether they will have an orgasm. If they do not have one, they fear that something is wrong with them or that their partner will think of them as unresponsive.

Performance anxiety is extremely destructive because it turns one's attention away from enjoying potential pleasant sensations. If individuals are worried about performing it is not likely that they will become aroused to the point that they will be able to perform. Performance anxiety can rapidly develop into a vicious cycle. If a man worries about his sexual performance, he is likely to fail. This failure serves to increase his fears which means that he will approach his next sexual encounter with an even higher level of anxiety. This, of course, results in another failure experience. In a short period of time, the sexual dysfunction will be firmly established. It is ironic that while sexual drive is so strong, sexual response is so fragile. Masters and Johnson suggest that the specific factors that can be found in the backgrounds of dysfunctional individuals generally operate by generating fears of performance.

Before the research of Masters and Johnson is discussed further, a word of caution should be given. Their work is based on the case-history method, and this approach has serious limitations. The most serious problem is that we cannot feel confident about the relationships that are identified by this method. For example, Masters and Johnson conclude on the basis of their research that religious orthodoxy is a major factor associated with sexual dysfunction. They arrive at this conclusion because a large percentage of the clients they saw were from such backgrounds. However, their research does not answer several crucial questions: How many people in the general population have religious orthodox backgrounds? How many individuals with no sexual problems have

such a background? It is possible that a large majority of those from religious orthodox backgrounds never experience any sexual difficulties. If this were found to be the case, then Masters and Johnson's conclusion would be highly questionable.

Masters and Johnson have made a contribution whose importance almost defies description. However, their findings should not be accepted uncritically. We hope their efforts will serve as a starting point for further research which will undoubtedly confirm many of their hypotheses.

In their earlier research on human sexual response, Masters and Johnson (1966) found that the similarities between male and female sexuality were more striking than the differences. In light of this, it is not surprising that many of the factors that are found in the backgrounds of women with sexual dysfunction are quite similar to the factors found in the backgrounds of sexually dysfunctional men. Let us review some of Masters and Johnson's findings.

Religious Orthodoxy

Extreme religious orthodoxy was a common element in the backgrounds of both men with primary and secondary impotence and ejaculatory incompetence and women with orgasmic dysfunction and vaginismus. These individuals typically grew up in homes where any form of sexual expression was severely condemned. They were taught that the only legitimate justification for sex was to have children. Along with their feelings of sexual anxiety and guilt, the clients had virtually no knowledge of sexual functioning. The problem was confounded by the fact that they typically married individuals from similar backgrounds. Their untutored attempts to have intercourse were often unsuccessful, and in other cases were only marginally successful. In the former case, the result was several years of unconsummated marriage.

In the latter instance, there was a period of several months to several years of alternating successes with failures. Finally, the dysfunction of the husband or wife or both would dominate the sexual relationship and they would discontinue their attempts at intercourse. Case 14.1 provides an example of the effects of extreme religious orthodoxy.

Case 14.1
The Case of Mr. and Mrs. A

Mr. and Mrs. A. were referred to Masters and Johnson for treatment after their marriage of nine years had not been consummated. Mrs. A. came from a family in which the father was seen as a godlike figure whose opinion was absolute law. The father assumed the responsibility of enforcing standards of moral behavior which were drawn from a fundamentalist Protestant religious orientation. A part of this orientation was dedicated to the concept that sex and sin were one and the same.

The family environment was described as cold, formal, and controlled. Much importance was placed on privacy and Mrs. A. could not recall ever seeing her brother, sister, mother, or father undressed. The subject of sex was never discussed, and all newspapers were evaluated by the father to ensure that other family members were not exposed to suggestive material.

Mrs. A. described her mother as a very rigid, unemotional woman who never seemed to find pleasure in her family or life in general. The mother was of no help to Mrs. A. when she experienced her first menstrual period. Her mother, who was embarrassed by the incident, told Mrs. A. that this was a "curse" to be suffered every month. It was also explained that this curse would be accompanied by severe illness and pains in the stomach which Mrs. A. experienced beginning with her second menstrual period. The only time the mother discussed sex with Mrs. A. was on her wedding day. Mrs. A. was instructed to remember that she was now committed to serve her husband and that it would be her duty to allow her husband privileges. These privileges would cause Mrs. A. a great deal of pain but her reward would be having children.

The wedding night was described as a struggle devoted to divergent purposes. The husband frantically searched for the proper place to insert his penis while Mrs. A. was determined to maintain her modesty with her nightclothes. It never occurred to Mrs. A. that she might cooperate in the effort. Initially, there were nightly attempts to consummate the marriage. During the last three years prior to treatment such attempts occurred once every three to four months (adapted from Masters and Johnson, 1970).

Homosexual Orientation

A second factor found in the backgrounds of both men and women experiencing sexual dysfunction was homosexual orientation. Often these individuals had had some homosexual experience during their teens. They subsequently married, either in an attempt to reverse their homosexual orientation or for economic and social reasons. Some men had a period of successful functioning but became impotent because they had little interest in such relationships. Women were typically dysfunctional throughout the marriage. A serious problem in such cases was that frequently the dysfunctional partner had little interest in reestablishing a physical relationship. They were motivated to maintain their marital relationship for economic and social protection.

Early Experience with Prostitutes

Several cases of erectile failure and premature ejaculation were traced to early experiences with prostitutes. Four men treated for primary impotence had their initial sexual encounter with prostitutes from the most debilitated sections of the cities in which they were living. They were so repulsed by the surroundings, the lack of appeal, and the matter-of-fact approach of the women, that they were unable to achieve an erection. They interpreted their failures as indicating their own inadequacies rather than as reflecting the unappetizing nature of the situation. Case 14.2 provides an additional example of primary impotence.

Case 14.2

The Case of Jim R.

Jim R. was a twenty-eight-year-old office manager when he sought treatment for his sexual problem of impotence. He was reared by his mother and father in a small community. His parents were not unusual except for the importance they placed on school and religion. Mr. R. was taught that it was important to study hard if he was to get anywhere in life, and it was equally important to remain

faithful to the teachings of his church. During adolescence, Mr. R. was allowed to date only girls that belonged to the local church. His parents told him that any other girls were likely to be wild and would be a bad influence. The only sex education received by Mr. R. consisted of warnings to stay away from loose girls.

At the age of seventeen Mr. R. left home to attend the state university. He joined a fraternity and took a great deal of kidding from his older brothers about his sexual inexperience. During his second year, his fraternity brothers, determined that he lose his virginity, arranged a date with a local girl who was willing to have sex with most anyone. That night at the party, Mr. R. had several drinks in an attempt to calm his nerves. Finally, he was told that his time had come and he and his date were ushered into the bedroom. With his fraternity brothers shouting encouragement from the next room, and the girl teasing him about his inexperienced,

Figure 14.1
Masters and Johnson found that sexual problems of older men could often be traced to early experience with prostitutes. (Bettman Archive Inc.)

fumbling approaches, Mr. R. was not able to have an erection. The final humiliation occurred when his date informed everyone at the party of Mr. R.'s failure.

Mr. R. did not attempt to have intercourse again until after he graduated from college and fell in love. The woman had some prior sexual experience and was understanding about Mr. R.'s problem. However, after three attempts and three failures at intercourse, he became quite upset and depressed and broke off the relationship. For the next three years he did not date at all and became increasingly withdrawn and despondent. He finally decided to seek treatment after reading a magazine article about successful treatment for problems such as his.

Men with premature ejaculation who visited prostitutes for their early experiences developed this pattern at the woman's urging. Because her income was dependent on rapid turnover, the prostitute discouraged these men from showing any interest in her reactions. A similar pattern occurred with men who had their initial experiences with women in their peer group. They were likely to have intercourse in situations in which there was a possibility of being discovered—such as the back seat of a car at the drive-in movie or in the parents' home. In these situations there would be a premium on quickness with little concern with the satisfaction of the woman. Masters and Johnson argue that early attempts at intercourse that are characterized by the man's concern to have his orgasm as quickly as possible are sufficient to establish an enduring pattern.

One important concern with premature ejaculation is that it can lead to secondary impotence. More than one-fourth of men treated by Masters and Johnson for secondary impotence had a history of premature ejaculation. The typical pattern of these men was that they were married to women who were initially understanding and supportive.

In the early stages of the marraige they were convinced that with time and experience, the problem would be solved. However, after months, or years, went by with little improvement, the wife became increasingly frustrated. She felt used, and was convinced that her husband had no concern about her feelings. She began to verbalize her anger and frustration, her husband began to question his adequacy. If he became preoccupied with these thoughts during a sexual encounter, he was likely to lose his erection. This might have moved him into the vicious cycle that ended in erectile failure.

Alcohol-Induced Failure

Perhaps the most common factor in the backgrounds of men with secondary impotence is a failure experience associated with an excessive intake of alcohol. Masters and Johnson present a composite case history of

Figure 14.2
Excessive intake of alcohol is the most common factor associated with secondary impotence. (Jean Shapiro)

a man between the ages of thirty-five and fifty-five. He is typically a college graduate whose occupation demands high levels of psychosocial performance. His rate of alcohol consumption has steadily increased over the years to the point where the two-drink business lunch and the evening cocktail hour are considered essential. After this pattern has been established for several years, he attends a party at which he has too much to drink. That night he attempts to have intercourse with his wife, but his high blood-alcohol level results in inevitable failure.

The next day he begins to wonder if he might be developing a problem. He ponders this for a few days and then decides to test everything out one night. Since the sexual encounter is viewed as a test, it will probably have unfortunate results. And so he is likely to be frightened and to avoid sexual encounters. His avoidance of his wife causes her to be concerned about her desirability. She may begin to make more sexual demands, thereby increasing the pressure on the husband. Finally sexual encounters are avoided altogether, and the husband's and wife's inability to communicate their fears about their sexuality generalizes to all aspects of the relationship.

Parental Dominance

Maternal or paternal dominance was identified in the backgrounds of several men with either primary or secondary impotence. Some mothers were overtly seductive with their sons; others completely dominated the household. As adults, these men were likely to be intimidated by women and their feelings of insecurity would carry over into their sexual functioning until they finally developed erectile problems. Men with domineering fathers had developed the feeling that they could never be as successful as their fathers. They were particularly sensitive to any perceived failure. They would have a history of

successful sexual functioning; however, at some point an attempt at intercourse would end in failure. This failure would convince them that sexual inadequacy was just another one of their many shortcomings and this belief was enough to establish a pattern of erectile failure in a short period of time.

Special Problems of Women

Along with many of the above factors women face two additional handicaps. First, in our society, for the most part, female sexuality carries an implication of shame. It is generally recognized, even among the most puritanical, that young men experience sexual feelings. Young women, on the other hand, are thought to be relatively free from such feelings by a large segment of our population. It may be acceptable for a young woman to have romantic feelings and fantasies, but for the most part "nice girls" are not taught to value their sexuality in anticipation of opportunities for expression in the same way that boys are.

Thus many women begin their sexual lives with a definite handicap. They have spent their formative years trying to live up to the "good girl" facade imposed by our society. This has caused them to try to repress or remove their sexual feelings because they are thought to be bad, dirty, sinful, and the like. After several years of functioning within such a value system, it is extremely difficult to make a sudden transition. A marriage ceremony cannot instantly reverse a woman's attitudes toward sex. Society may now condone the sexual needs and feelings of the woman, but is likely to take her some time to assimilate these values.

Masters and Johnson imply that the generally negative view society holds toward female sexuality may actually serve a purpose. They point out that women have a physiological capacity for sexual response that infinitely surpasses that of men. Perhaps society's negative view of female sexuality serves to create a balance between the sexes. Someone once suggested that while many men have the fantasy of being alone on a deserted island with a nymphomaniac, the reality of the situation would be a nightmare. If women behaved sexually in accord with their physiological capacities, there would be few men who would not feel threatened.

A second factor that women must contend with concerns the adequacy of their partner. Men only require a partner that is physically available in order to achieve sexual release. The woman may have no sexual feelings whatsoever, but as long as she is there, the man will be able to have an orgasm. A woman, on the other hand, requires a partner that functions sexually at an adequate level if she is to have any chance for sexual fulfillment. If the woman's partner suffers from premature ejaculation or impotence, then her chances of consistently reaching orgasm are greatly impaired. This is highlighted by the fact that in nearly half of the cases treated by Masters and Johnson, both the husband and wife suffered from some form of sexual dysfunction.

The problems of the woman who is married to a man who suffers from either premature ejaculation or impotence are obvious. The man who ejaculates upon intromission or after a few thrusts is not likely to bring his partner to orgasm. The man with erectile problems, of course, has no chance whatsoever of eliciting orgasm via sexual intercourse. The woman who brings a history of orgasmic response via masturbation into this type of relationship, does have the choice of returning to this mode of release. Many women, however, with no history of orgasm, cannot accept the idea of either masturbation, manual, or oral stimulation by their partner as a means of tension reduction. In this situation, both the man and the woman would require treatment.

Multiple Factors

In many cases of sexual dysfunction, more than one of the factors discussed above can be identified. In fact, it is probably rare that any case of sexual dysfunction can be traced back to a single cause. For example, a man with the problem of secondary impotence may have a religious orthodox background. He may have functioned normally until his erectile problem was triggered by a failure experience associated with alcohol. A combination of factors is often responsible for sexual dysfunction in women. A woman whose parents conveyed the attitude that sex was sinful may develop a high level of responsivity if her partner is sexually knowledgeable and adequate. However, if she marries a man with premature ejaculation, her potential for orgasm might rapidly diminish.

Along with stressing the fact that many disorders have multiple causes, Masters and Johnson emphasize the importance of the relationship between the sexual partners. You may recall that of 510 couples accepted for treatment, 223 cases involved both the husband and wife suffering a problem. Also, in many of the cases in which only one person had a specific dysfunction, the problem may have been prevented if the partner had been more knowledgeable or understanding. Sex is a social enterprise and the interpersonal aspects must be considered.

Theories of Sexual Dysfunction

Masters and Johnson do not identify with any particular theoretical approach. However, other experts in the field are committed to a certain theoretical framework and their commitment generally influences the type of factors they believe to be important, and the meaning they attribute to sexual dysfunctions. Let us briefly review two major theories—the psychoanalytic and the social-learning approaches. (See Chapter 4 for a more detailed discussion of theories of sexual behavior.)

Psychoanalytic Theory

There are two very important implications of the psychoanalytic view of sexual dysfunction. The first is that the dysfunction itself is not the problem. It is only a symptom of a deeper, underlying pathology. The second implication is that since the dysfunction is a symptom, it is symbolic of the type of underlying conflict or pathology. Thus, the form of dysfunction that a client exhibits is thought to be a clue to the nature of the conflict that produced the symptom. For example, a psychoanalytic interpretation of premature ejaculation suggests that the man with this problem has intense, but unconscious, feelings of hatred toward women. Such a man supposedly has his orgasms so rapidly because it satisfies his sadistic impulses. It allows him to "defile and soil" the woman while at the same time ensuring that she will receive no pleasure from the sexual act.

There are similar psychoanalytic interpretations of sexual dysfunction in women. As one example, vaginismus is viewed as one way a woman may deal with her penis envy—which is thought to be a phenomenon that occurs in all girls during the phallic stage. Women with vaginismus supposedly harbor a hatred toward all men. Their problem is an expression of their unconscious desire to castrate their partner.

We discussed the limitations of psychoanalytic theory earlier. Often it can be a source of rich insight, but many of its hypotheses are not and are unable to be substantiated by empirical evidence. It may be true that a few men with the problem of premature ejaculation have unconscious sadistic feelings toward women. However, only the strictest followers of psychoanalysis would

insist that this is generally the case. Most men who have this problem and most women with vaginismus are extremely upset by it. They would welcome any form of treatment that would help them get over it.

One strong point of psychoanalysis is that it attempts to deal with the question of why some individuals who are exposed to an unfortunate sexual experience develop a problem whereas others who are exposed to the same situation do not. For example, one young man whose first sexual partner makes a disparaging comment about the size of his penis may be rendered impotent. A second man may simply laugh at such a comment and be completely unaffected by it.

The psychoanalyst would explain this apparent inconsistency by suggesting that the comment elicited repressed conflicts in the first young man. His partner's comment may have reminded him, at an unconscious level, of his childhood sexual feelings toward his mother. This in turn could bring back fears of punishment, that is fear of castration, from the father. It was this fear then, that resulted in impotence. The merits of such an interpretation are debatable, but it does at least recognize the issue.

Social Learning Theory

Perhaps the most important implication of this approach is that sexual dysfunctions are viewed as learned disorders rather than as symptoms of an underlying personality disturbance. The dysfunctional man or the orgasmically dysfunctional woman would be viewed in pretty much the same way as, say, the person with public-speaking anxieties. They were all exposed to environments that taught them to be anxious in a particular situation.

Another difference between the psychoanalytic and social learning approaches is that the latter theory does not include the belief that all aspects of an individual's behavior can be understood in terms of a single, coherent pattern. For example, the psychoanalyst would suggest that a man's sexual problem, his interpersonal relations with women, and his attitudes toward his parents are all understandable in relation to a single underlying conflict. The social learning theorist would suggest that each aspect of the man's functioning might be caused by separate factors. The man's feelings toward women in general and his sexual problem may be unrelated. Perhaps his interpersonal style was firmly established during his adolescent years, whereas his sexual dysfunction developed in response to a traumatic experience that occurred later in life. Such an approach would seem to fit in better with the diversity of backgrounds found in those with a sexual dysfunction.

Although Masters and Johnson do not identify themselves as such, their approach fits in nicely with social learning theory. They are interested in identifying the environmental determinants of specific forms of sexual dysfunction. They recognize that many factors can operate together to produce a sexual dysfunction. And they reject the notion that it is necessary to invoke the concept of psychosexual developmental stages to understand sexual dysfunction.

Psychosocial Effects of Sexual Dysfunction

Sexual dysfunctions can be particularly destructive disorders because they not only impair or eliminate sexual pleasure, but they can also have psychological side effects. Both men and women who suffer from some form of sexual dysfunction are likely to be generally more anxious, more depressed, and to have lowered self-esteem. The psychological effects can be profound for those who have not established a stable relationship. As was illustrated in Case History 14.2, a dysfunctional man may avoid forming relationships with women because eventually he will have to face additional evidence of his "inadequacy." Similarly, the woman with a fear of sex may choose to delay or avoid marriage so that she will not have to deal with this issue. Such self-imposed isolation will understandably add to one's feelings of misery.

For those whose problem occurs in the context of a stable relationship, the partner and the relationship itself are likely to be affected as well. The man who is married to the orgasmically dysfunctional woman will wonder if he is inadequate in some way. Perhaps his technique is poor, or perhaps his penis is not large enough. The woman married to the dysfunctional man is likely to wonder if he finds her unattractive. Or she may view his problem as a sign that he does not love her.

Because it is so difficult for many people to discuss their sexual concerns with their partner, the quality of the relationship may be eventually undermined. The man with the problem of premature ejaculation may begin to avoid sexual encounters because they serve to reinforce his feelings of inadequacy. His wife, who already is feeling insecure about her sexuality, tacitly agrees to avoid sex because it has proved to be a frustrating experience for her. Their inability to communicate about this one issue may generalize to other issues. Their avoidance of sexual contact may generalize to avoidance of all physical contact until their relationship becomes devoid of any signs of affection. Before long, they may find their relationship totally empty and without meaning. Masters and Johnson described several cases in which the foundations of marriages of ten to thirty years' duration were destroyed by the occurrence of a sexual dysfunction. That many of these effects are largely preventable make the situation particularly unfortunate.

Treatment of Sexual Dysfunction

At the present time, the scientific literature suggests that sexual dysfunctions are highly amenable to treatment. Such has not always been the case. As recently as the middle 1960s widely respected psychologists such as Coleman (1964) and Hastings (1967) expressed the view that sexual dysfunctions were extremely difficult to treat. Once again Masters and Johnson are largely responsible for this about-face in attitude. Let us begin this section by examining their approach.

The Masters and Johnson Approach

Masters and Johnson consider the relationship between the sexual partners as the "patient" even though one member may be clearly dysfunctional and the other is not. Consequently, both the husband and wife are required to participate in the treatment program. The couple is required to move near the Reproductive Research Biology Foundation in St. Louis for the two-week treatment program conducted by a male-female therapist team.

The treatment procedure consists of three phases. The first phase, which lasts three days, involves history taking—both medical and psychological. The goal is to learn as much as possible about the clients' lives and personalities. The second phase consists of a roundtable discussion among the husband and wife and the co-therapists. The therapists offer their hypotheses about possible causes of the sexual dysfunction and correct any misconceptions the couple may have. Another purpose of the discussion is to promote communication between the husband and wife. Often a sharing of vulnerabilities will elicit the partners' support and understanding which has therapeutic value of its own.

The third phase consists of training in sensate-focus exercises and supplemental techniques designed for the particular disorder. Sensate-focus involves having the clients provide each other with sensual pleasure that is not explicitly sexual. The couple is instructed to simply explore each other's body with their hands. These exercises allow many clients to feel sexually aroused for the first time in years. Because they have become preoccupied with the act of intercourse and potential failure, they are likely to feel anxious the moment their partner touches them. With the pressure of intercourse removed, they can relax and enjoy their partner's caresses. The supplemental techniques for each disorder are described below.

Erectile Failure.   The first step involves engaging in the sensate-focus exercises with instructions not to attempt intercourse immediately. This reduces the man's fears of performance and allows him to feel sexually stimulated by his partner. Typically, the erective response returns after about a week. LoPiccolo (1978) finds that it is helpful to instruct the man to attempt to *not* have an erection. This advice often has the paradoxical effect of making it easier for him to become erect since it decreases performance anxiety. At this point, the couple is asked to engage in the exercises until the husband has an erection. They are instructed then to rest for a short period of time until the husband becomes flaccid. They are to then once again engage in the exercises so that the man regains an erection. This procedure helps the man to overcome the common fear that if he loses his erection, it is gone for the night. He learns that as long as he relaxes and doesn't try to "will" an erection, it is likely to reoccur.

Additional instruction is given regarding sexual positions. At first the couple is asked to use the female superior position. The woman is given responsibility for inserting the penis and is instructed to engage in nondemanding movements. Many men lose their erection when they have difficulty at intromission. Because the woman knows exactly where the penis goes and the man often is not sure of the exact location, the woman's acceptance of this responsibility further reduces the pressure felt by her partner. Masters and Johnson successfully reversed 59.4 percent of cases of primary impotence and 69.1 percent of cases of secondary impotence.

Premature Ejaculation. The basis of treatment for premature ejaculation is the squeeze technique. The wife is instructed to stimulate her husband until he has a full erection. At this time, the wife squeezes the penis (see Figure 14.3) for three to four seconds. This causes the man to immediately lose his urge to ejaculate. After a period of fifteen to thirty seconds the procedure is repeated. After the first day's session the couple may

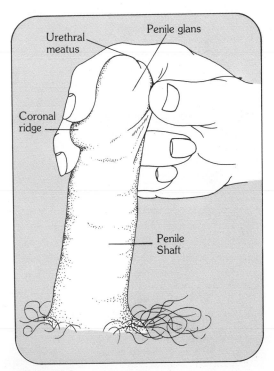

Figure 14.3
The squeeze technique.

have engaged in fifteen to twenty minutes of sex play without the man ejaculating—something that may be a first for them.

Additional instruction in non-demanding sexual positions is offered. The female-superior position is used and the wife is discouraged from initially making any vigorous movements. This allows the man to become accustomed to the sensations associated with intra-vaginal containment. If the husband develops the urge to ejaculate he communicates this urge to his wife. She then elevates herself and utilizes the squeeze technique before proceeding with intercourse. These techniques were successful in 97.3 percent of the cases. LoPiccolo has found that a "pause" technique may be equally effective. With this technique the man is instructed to pause or cease coital movements as soon as he becomes aware of the urge to ejaculate. By beginning with slow movements, with intermittent pauses, and gradually progressing to full thrusting, many men can learn to delay ejaculation relatively rapidly. The woman must be supportive of the process since the stop-and-go nature of the technique could prove frustrating for her.

Ejaculatory Incompetence. The wife of the man with this problem is instructed to manually manipulate his penis to the point of ejaculation. Once this response has been established, she manipulates the penis just short of ejaculation and then inserts it into her vagina. Typically, a few vigorous thrusts bring the man to orgasm. Once the man's mental block against ejaculating into the vagina has been cracked, he will require decreasing amounts of manual stimulation before initiating intercourse. Eighty-two percent of these cases were successfully treated.

Orgasmic Dysfunction. The early stage of treatment for orgasmic dysfunction involves non-demanding sexual play. The man is given detailed information about the basics of effective genital play. For example, many men stimulate the clitoris directly even though women often respond with feelings of irritation or pain to this tactic. Figure 14.4 illustrates a recommended position for the early stages of treatment. This position provides the man access to his wife's entire body and also seems to provide women with feelings of warm security. After the couple experiences success with manual stimulation, they are given instruction in coital positions that allow the woman freedom of movement so that she can respond in accord with her level of sexual tension. Two of these positions are female-superior (Figure 14.5) and the lateral coital position (Figure 14.6). Surprisingly, the success rate was higher for primary orgasmic dysfunction than it was for situational orgasmic dysfunction. The percentages were 82.4 and 75.2, respectively.

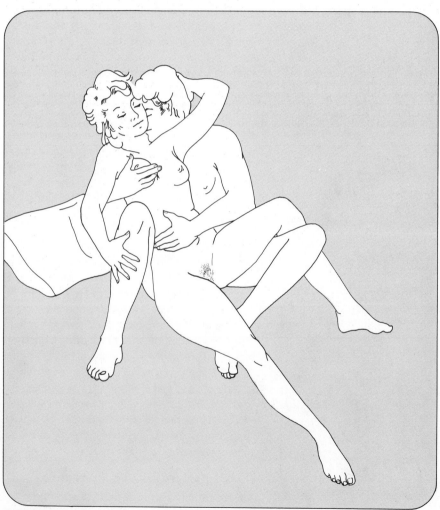

Figure 14.4
Pleasuring position.

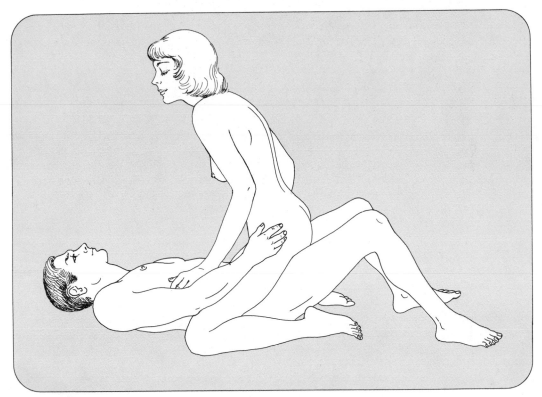

Figure 14.5
Woman above coital position.

Vaginismus. The most important aspect of treatment for vaginismus is demonstrating the involuntary vaginal spasm to both the husband and wife. To do this, the wife is placed in the standard gynecological examining position and the physician makes an attempt to insert a finger. The resulting spasm is often more of a surprise to the wife than to her husband. The husband is also gloved and encouraged to demonstrate to his own satisfaction the severity of the spasm.

After the nature of the disorder is convincingly demonstrated to both the husband and wife, they are provided with a set of graduated dilators. In the privacy of their bedroom, the husband successively inserts larger and larger dilators. The larger-size ones are left in the wife's vagina for several hours each night. The involuntary spasms are typically eliminated within three to five days. Use of the dilators may be required prior the the first few attempts at intercourse. The success rate

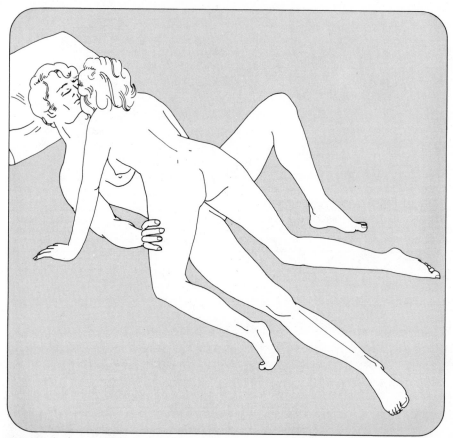

Figure 14.6
Side-by-side coital position.

was 100 percent in overcoming the vaginismus. Of the twenty-nine women treated for this disorder, twenty-six were orgasmic within six months after treatment.

The overall success rate for the 790 cases treated was 80 percent. This figure is particularly impressive because it represents a very conservative estimate. The results should not be accepted uncritically, however. The limitations of the case study approach were discussed earlier and these same considerations apply regarding of treatment outcome. In any therapy situation, expectancy and placebo effects can play a role in the outcome. If clients believe they are receiving meaningful treatment and expect that treatment to be effective, it is possible that they will show some improvement on that basis alone. Without appropriate control groups, it is impossible to unequivocally conclude that it was the treatment per se that was responsible for the success. Such an interpretation of Masters and Johnson's results is made unlikely by the fact that over 50 percent of their cases had previous psychotherapy which proved to be unsuccessful. Furthermore, other researchers have achieved the same results in several hundred cases with a similar treatment program (Hartman and Fithian, 1972). It seems highly likely that future, well-controlled research, will confirm the efficacy of Masters and Johnson's treatment approach.

Psychotherapy

Psychotherapy is a broad term that can include any number of specific approaches, but we shall concern ourselves only with dynamically oriented psychotherapy. This approach, based on psychoanalytic theory, assumes that sexual dysfunctions are symptoms of underlying personality conflicts. Thus, the focus of therapy is not on the sexual dysfunction itself, but on the structure of the client's total personality.

It is impossible to briefly summarize the process and techniques of dynamic psychotherapy,* but perhaps the most important element is that of transference (Meyer, 1976). Transference occurs when the clients' feelings and reactions toward the therapist replicate their feelings and reactions toward other important people in their lives. If a person's dysfunction has its roots in the client's childhood relationship with the father, it is assumed that the client will relive this relationship with the therapist. This provides the therapist with the opportunity to help the client understand the unconscious motives that are influencing his or her behavior. For example, a dysfunctional man in therapy may begin to show concern that the therapist dis-

*Irving B. Winer has provided a highly readable description of dynamic psychotherapy in *Principles of Intensive Psychotherapy.*

approves of him. The therapist would make interpretations that illustrated to the client that such feelings had their origin in painful interactions with the father. If such memories were repressed, however, they may have continued to influence the client's behavior. It is believed that once the client understands the source of his or her conflict, he or she will no longer have the "unconscious need" to be dysfunctional.

Interestingly, the goal of dynamic psychotherapy is not necessarily the cure of dysfunctional behavior patterns. Respected psychoanalytic theorist Freida Fromm-Reichman (1950) has stated that the therapist should make no promises of cure. The goal is to increase self-understanding and to bring to consciousness the origins of intra-psychic conflict. If these goals are being met, it is thought that improvement in the client's problems will occur almost as an aside.

It is difficult to establish the effectiveness of dynamic psychotherapy in the treatment of sexual dysfunction. Although there are reports of success in isolated cases, there is very little information regarding the treatment of large numbers of cases. One study, however, suggests that the results are not encouraging. O'Connor and Stern (1972) examined the cases of sixty-one women and thirty-five men treated at the psychoanalytic clinic of Columbia University. Without specifying the form of sexual dysfunction, they reported that 25 percent of the women and 57 percent of the men were cured.

The relative ineffectiveness of this approach is evidenced by the fact that there seems to be a growing acceptance among dynamic theorists that not all sexual dysfunctions result from intrapsychic conflict. As an example, psychiatrist Helen Singer Kaplan has published a book entitled *The New Sex Therapy.* Although some of her "new" techniques have appeared in the literature twenty years ago (see Ascher and Phillips, 1975), she does recognize that it is not always necessary to treat intrapsychic conflict that underlies the sexual dysfunction. Any psychoanalyst who made such a statement ten years ago would probably have been considered a heretic by his or her colleagues.

Behavior Therapy

Although Masters and Johnson do not label themselves as behavior therapists, their program incorporates many fundamental behavioral principles. Providing factual information, dispelling misconceptions, improving communication skills, and gradually extinguishing performance anxiety are techniques that behavior therapists have used for years. In fact the concept of sensate-focus as a means of reducing anxiety is highly similar to the behavior technique of *in vivo* desensitization which was introduced more than twenty-five years ago (Wolpe, 1954). In addition to these techniques, several other procedures have been devised.

One behavioral technique that is widely used is systematic desensitization. This requires the client to imagine a series of graduated scenes of the specific fear or anxiety (see Chapter 18 for a complete description of this technique). Once the clients are able to imagine sexually related activities without experiencing anxiety, they feel more comfortable in the actual situation. This procedure has been demonstrated to be effective on several occasions (Lazarus, 1963; Wolpe, 1969).

There have been several modifications of the desensitization procedure that have led to treatment success. Brady (1971) used Brevital, a fast-acting barbituate, in conjunction with desensitization to increase the clients' level of relaxation during the treatment procedure. This procedure, with a success rate of about 67 percent, proved superior to traditional psychotherapy.

A second modification was suggested in a case study by Caird and Wincze (1974). They successfully treated a twenty-four-year-old woman who had experienced feelings of discomfort and disgust during sexual intercourse. The woman was asked, while in a state of deep relaxation, to view a series of videotapes that varied in degree of sexual explicitness—from a man and woman conversing to their having sexual intercourse. After seven treatment sessions, the woman was free of unpleasant emotions during intercourse and was orgasmic on several occasions.

Behavior therapists Charles Lobitz and Joseph LoPiccolo (1972) have put together a treatment package that has been highly effective in preliminary findings. The first step involves having the clients keep detailed records of their sexual behavior. This is

---

Group Treatment of Sexual Dysfunction

In the last few years we have come to realize that a variety of factors can lead to sexual dysfunctions. These factors can vary greatly in terms of the degree to which they are incorporated into an individual's personality or behavior. At one extreme a case of sexual dysfunction may be traced back to a childhood in which the parents created doubts in their child about his or her adequacy. At the other extreme, a couple may experience sexual dissatisfaction because they are concerned that certain sexual practices that they would like to engage in are not proper or may be immoral.

In recognition of the various levels at which sexual problems can operate, psychologist Jack Annon (1974) has developed what he calls a PLISSIT model that can be useful in approaching treatment. This model provides four levels with each successive level requiring increasing professional experience and competence. The levels are as follows:

1. Permission. Some individuals need assurance from an authoritative source that it is permissible to think, read, talk, and fantasize about sex. They need to be told that it is okay to masturbate, to experiment and to express likes and dislikes.

2. Limited Information. At this level, clients will have their myths dispelled and will be given accurate information about sexual functioning.

3. Specific Suggestion. Methods such as the squeeze technique for premature ejaculation, will be explained to clients at this level.

4. Intensive Therapy. This level is necessary for those individuals for whom the first three levels are ineffective or who have pervasive psychological or relationship problems.

One advantage of this model is that it suggests that not all dysfunctional individuals require intensive (and thus, expensive) therapy such as that provided by Masters and Johnson. As an illustration, sex therapists Lawrence Baker and Frances Nagata (1978) have successfully utilized the first three levels of the PLISSIT model to treat couples with a sexual problem in a group therapy setting. Through the use of audio-visual aids, group discussion of common sexual concerns, and discussion of specific techniques, they were able to effect improvement in about 75 percent of the couples treated. With innovations in treatment techniques such as this, it is possible to reach large numbers of people and to provide services at reasonable cost.

---

essential so that the therapist can know precisely what behaviors need to be changed, the degree to which the clients are following the therapeutic program, and what, if any, progress is being made. Many clients find such detailed record keeping tedious so to increase their motivation to do so, a substantial refundable deposit is required. Violations of the agreement made between the therapist and the client result in forfeiture of a portion of the deposit.

To enhance the level of sexual arousal, the client is instructed to masturbate while fantasizing and/or reading erotic literature and looking at erotic photographs, then, just prior to orgasm, switch to fantasies of the usual partner. For women who have never experienced orgasm, a nine-point masturbation program has been developed.

Lobitz and LoPiccolo confirm Masters and Johnson's observation that many dysfunctional couples suffer from communication deficits. To deal with this, the behavioral techniques of modeling and role playing are used. The therapist may model or demonstrate an appropriate way of expressing a feeling or desire. The client is asked to practice with the therapist before trying it with the partner.

A final technique is aimed at the disinhibition of sexuality. This technique is based upon a report of a female physician who advised her patients to feign orgasm in order to satisfy their husbands (Hillard, 1960). For many of these women, what began as a pretense, turned out to be a reality. Lobitz and LoPiccolo advise women to feign orgasm, not to deceive their partners but to overcome their fears about losing control and showing intense sexual arousal. The results of the treatment program were very encouraging. Of a total of thirty-four cases there were only eight failures.

Behavior therapists recognize that oftentimes the entire individual requires treatment rather than just his or her sexual behavior. Perhaps the best example of this broad spectrum approach is in the work of Arnold Lazarus and what he calls multi-modal behavior therapy (Lazarus, 1976). Lazarus argues that in any clinical case, the therapist should assess a variety of aspects of the individual. These include behavior, affect, sensations, imagery, cognitions, interpersonal relations, and the need for medication. In line with this conceptualization Lazarus believes that it is crucial to use a variety of techniques to treat all aspects of the individual. To illustrate, he successfully reversed a case of primary impotence using desensitization and sensate-focus (Lazarus, 1976a). However, he also noted that the couple had a number of other trouble spots that might eventually lead to a relapse of their sexual functioning. To alleviate these difficulties, Lazarus used imagery and role playing techniques to help the man become more assertive and self-confident and the woman to become more independent and overcome a variety of anxieties.

The cautionary note that was sounded about Masters and Johnson's results apply to other behavioral techniques as well. For the most part, the research is of the case study variety which does not control for nonspecific effects such as expectancy and placebo. Nonetheless, the work of Masters and Johnson and the other behavior therapists is responsible for the prevailing attitude among professionals that sexual dysfunctions respond well to treatment. Twenty years ago, the individual with a sexual problem was virtually doomed to a life of deprivation and misery. Today, such a person has an excellent chance of establishing a pattern of effective sexual functioning, which invariably leads to an enriched life and increased feelings of dignity and self-worth.

Summary

In this chapter, five forms of sexual dysfunction were discussed. Impotence, premature ejaculation, and ejaculatory incompetence are disorders found in men. Orgasmic dysfunction and vaginismus are disorders found in women. All of these disorders impair or eliminate the satisfaction one can attain from sexual intercourse.

Masters and Johnson have identified a number of factors that are commonly found in the backgrounds of those with a sexual dysfunction. These include religious orthodoxy, parental dominance, failure experiences associated with alcohol, and homosexual involvement. It is believed that these factors operate by increasing one's performance anxiety. When individuals become concerned about the adequacy of their performance, their sexual responsivity is likely to be impaired.

The question of whether sexual dysfunctions are indicative of a more general personality disturbance was raised. Psychoanalytic theorists typically view sexual dysfunctions as symptoms of underlying intrapersonal conflict that has its origins in early psychosexual developmental stages. Social learning theorists believe that sexual dysfunctions are acquired on the basis of unfortunate learning experiences and are learned in much the same way that "normal" sexual behaviors are.

Behavior therapy and the treatment approach developed by Masters and Johnson appear to be highly effective in reversing sexual dysfunction. These approaches provide factual information and they correct misconceptions about sexual behavior. They strive to increase the degree and quality of communication between sexual partners. They promote a view of sex as a process to be enjoyed, reduce performance anxiety, and recommend techniques to maximize potential pleasure. Dynamic psychotherapy, which focuses on hypothesized underlying conflicts, has not been demonstrated to be as effective.

References

Annon, J. *The behavioral treatment of sexual problems*, Vol. 1. Hawaii: Enabling Systems, 1974.

Ascher, L. M. and Phillips, D. Review of Kaplan, H. S., The new sex therapy. *Journal of Behavioral Therapy and Experimental Psychiatry, 1975, 6, 1975.*

Journal of Behavior Therapy and Experimental Psychiatry, 1975, 6, 175.

Baker, L. D. and Nagata, F. S. "A group apporach to the treatment of heterosexual couples with sexual dissatisfactions." *Journal of Sex Education and Therapy,* 1978, 4, 15-18.

Brady, J. P. "Brevital-aided systematic desensitization." In R. D. Rubin, H. Fensterheim, A. A. Lazarus, and C. M. Franks (eds.), *Advances in behavior therapy.* New York: Academic Press, 1971.

Caird, W. K. and Wincze, J. P. "Videotaped desensitization of frigidity." *Journal of Behavior Therapy and Experimental Psychiatry,* 1974, 5, 175-178.

Coleman, J. C. *Abnormal psychology and modern life.* Chicago: Scott, Foresman, 1964.

Fromm-Reichman, F. *Principles of intensive psychotherapy.* Chicago: University of Chicago Press, 1950.

Hartman, W. E. and Fithian, M. A. *Treatment of sexual dysfunction.* Long Beach, Calif.: Center for Marital and Sexual Studies, 1972.

Hastings, D. W. "Sexual potency disorders of the male." In A. M. Freedman and H. I. Kaplan (eds.), *Comprehensive textbook of psychiatry.* Baltimore: Williams and Wilkins, 1967.

Hillard, M. *A woman doctor looks at love and life.* New York: Permabook, 1960.

Kaplan, H. S. *The new sex therapy.* New York: Brunner/Mazel, 1974.

Lazarus, A. A. "The treatment of chronic frigidity by systematic desensitization." *Journal of Nervous and Mental Diseases,* 1963, 136, 51-53.

Lazarus, A. A. *Multi-modal behavior therapy.* New York: Springer, 1976.

Lazarus, A. A. "Sex therapy and the basic id." In A. A. Lazarus (ed.), *Multimodal behavior therapy.* New York: Springer, 1976a.

Lobitz, W. C. and LoPiccolo, J. "New methods in the behavioral treatment of sexual dysfunction." *Journal of Behavior Therapy and Experimental Psychiatry,* 1972, 3, 265-272.

LoPiccolo, J. "Direct treatment of sexual dysfunction." In J. LoPiccolo and L. LoPiccolo (eds.), *Handbook of sex therapy.* New York: Plenum Press, 1978.

Masters, W. and Johnson, V. *Human sexual inadequacy.* Boston: Little, Brown, 1970.

Meyer, J. K. "Individual psychotherapy of sexual disorders." In B. J. Sadock, H. I. Kaplan, and A. M. Freedman (eds.), *The sexual experience.* Baltimore: Williams & Wilkins, 1976.

O'Conner, J. and Stern, L. "Results of treatment in functional sexual disorders." *New York State Journal of Medicine,* 1972, 72, 1927.

Reuben, D. *Everything you always wanted to know about sex but were afraid to ask. New York: Bantam, 1969.*

Wolpe, J. "Reciprocal inhibition as the main basis of psychotherapeutic effects." *Archives of Neurology and Psychiatry,* 1954, 72, 205-226.

Wolpe, J. The practice of behavior therapy. New York: Pergamon, 1969.

Chapter 15

Variations in Sexual Behavior and Relationships

What is Sexually Normal?
The Statistical View of Sexual Normality
The Clinical View of Sexual Normality
The Moral/Legal View of Sexual Normality
The Personal View of Sexual Normality
The Sociocultural View of Sexual
Normality

Classifications of Unconventional Sexual Behavior

Variations in Sex Object Choices
Pedophilia
Zoophilia
Incest
Fetishism
Necrophilia

Variations in Sexual Activities
Voyeurism
Exhibitionism

Sadomasochism
Rape

Gender Identity Disturbances
Transvestism
Transsexualism

Modification of Unconventional Sexual Behavior
Psychodynamic Approaches
Behavioral Approaches
Aversive Conditioning in a Case of
Fetishism
Elimination of Sadistic Fantasies by
Counterconditioning
Modification of Gender Identity in a
Transsexual

Summary

References

Many different terms have been used over the years to describe the sexual behavior of people who engage in strange or unusual sexual activities. Labels such as "perversion," "deviance," or "abnormality" have been employed. When we are dealing with sexual behaviors it soon becomes evident that many of these labels have little utility. Normality, for instance, is not a very useful concept because there is simply no norm for human sexuality. Moreover, the word normal has not one, but several meanings. It may mean prevalent in the sense that it is normal for women to menstruate. Or it may refer to behaviors that occur with a certain degree of frequency in the general population. By this definition, frequently occurring conditions, such as nail biting or drug abuse, would be considered normal. Being normal sexually is a crucial concern for many people who scrutinize themselves and their friends in the hope of making sure that their sexual activities are normal.

What Is Sexually Normal?

In order to understand some of the factors involved in discussions of sexual normality we have selected five different models that emphasize different aspects of normality.

The Statistical View of Sexual Normality

This approach to normality views normal sexual behavior from a statistical perspective. Normal is what most people do. Abnormality, on the other hand, is defined in terms of the deviation from the average. Perhaps the largest amount of statistical data regarding sexual behavior is found in the Kinsey surveys. If we would interpret some of the Kinsey findings in accordance with the statistical criterion of normal sexuality, we would label the homosexual and the eighty-five-

year-old woman who enjoys an active sex life abnormal because only a small percentage of the total population displays these behaviors.

Being labeled sexually normal is comforting and reassuring for many men and women. A young woman who masturbates, for instance, may be relieved to learn that at least 68 percent of other women do so. Or a man who had a single homosexual experience during adolescence may be less alarmed when he finds out that almost 50 percent of American males have had similar encounters. While the knowledge of falling within the normal range may be encouraging, deviations from the average can cause concern in a person. A young girl who reads that 60 percent of her peers have had premarital intercourse may begin to wonder about her virginity. The problem with the statistical model is that frequent occurrence of a given type of behavior may not necessarily be healthy, desirable, or normal. And similarly infrequent behaviors may not always be abnormal or deviant.

The Clinical View of Sexual Normality

According to this model, normality is equated with mental or emotional health. Sexually normal behavior, according to the clinical view, means freedom of disabling conditions and efficient adaptation to various sexual experiences. By this definition, then, people who are sexually deprived, unsatisfied, or inefficient must be considered abnormal.

The Moral/Legal View of Sexual Normality

Both moral as well as legal definitions of normal sexual behavior seem to be relatively clear-cut. The moral model proposes that abnormal sexual behavior equals sin. If the moral definition serves as the exclusive criterion for judging normal sexual behavior, many people would be abnormal. By the traditional standards of most religious doctrines, sexual activities such as pre- or extramarital sex, are immoral.

From a legal standpoint, a sexual deviate is any person who breaks a law and is apprehended by law enforcement officers. Although this seems to be a clear-cut definition, legal criteria of sexual normality are actually inconsistent and confusing. Sexual acts that are considered misdemeanors in one state might lead to a prison sentence in another; sexual practices considered normal under some circumstances may be unlawful under others. Thus, having sexual intercourse with one's spouse is not illegal but having sex with one's mate in full view of onlookers is a legal offense.

The Personal View of Sexual Normality

The fourth model of normal sexual behavior defines sexuality in highly subjective terms. The subjective approach is illustrated by the Quaker saying, "Sometimes I think everyone is queer save thee and me and sometimes I wonder about thee!" This philosophy acknowledges the fact that each of us can make independent judgments of normality without regard for statistical, legal, or moral criteria. People such as exhibitionists or peeping Toms are often convinced that their sexual activities are indeed normal. Similarly, Kinsey and Masters and Johnson reported that their male study subjects generally considered their frequency of masturbation—whether it was once a day or once a month—normal. Greater or lesser frequencies, however, were believed to have ill effects. The subjective model thus defines sexual normality on a highly personal and idiosyncratic basis.

The Sociocultural View of Sexual Normality

Many people would agree with Marmor (1971) that concepts of normal and deviant sexual behavior cannot be divorced from the value system of our society. Each culture in turn evolves its own sexual mores and customs. Many behaviors that have been condemned as an offense by one group or another or at one time or another have been accepted by other cultures during different eras. Homosexuality, for example, was an acceptable and fashionable expression of sexuality in ancient Greece, where it served a distinctive pedagogic purpose. In our own society, on the other hand, the same behavior was labeled a disease as recently as 1974, when the American Psychiatric Association ceased to classify homosexuality as a mental disorder.

In many forms of sexual variations the interaction between the individual and his or her particular culture or subculture determines the evaluation of the atypical behavior. Sexuality is, after all, a social construction that is learned in interactions with others. Chapters 8 and 9 highlighted this notion by showing that within our own culture we disagree sharply in regard to socially acceptable or unacceptable sexual behavior. Moreover, different societies show an almost incredible range of differences in what is considered normal sexually. Since social value systems are always fluctuating and changing, we must face the possibility that some sexual activities currently labeled deviant or abnormal may not always be regarded so. Consequently anthropologists, psychologists, and sociologists, keenly aware of the culture relativity of sexual norms, insist that we must define sexual variations within the confines of a given society.

Normality in sexual behavior, then, becomes a testing ground where subjective, legal, moral, clinical, statistical, and cultural views of sexuality are explored in the hope that we can assess and gain an understanding of the functions of unusual forms of sexual expression. Of the five models described, none in itself is able to accommodate the complex and diverse nature of human sexuality. Each model, while making specific and significant contributions to our understanding of normal or deviant sexual behavior, has problems of its own.

Gagnon and Simon (1968) call our attention to the many problems that confront us when we try to apply models of normality and abnormality to sexual behavior. They state:

> There is no form of sexual activity that is not deviant at some time, in some location, in some specified relationship, or with some partner. Truly one can say that sexual deviance covers a multitude of sins. As a consequence of this variety, sexual deviance as a category includes behaviors that call forth societal responses that range from tacit encouragement to almost incalculable ferocity. It is important that the term "sexual deviation" should be approached somewhat less globally (p. 107).

Sexual behavior can be normal or abnormal depending on (1) the context in which it occurs and (2) the viewpoint from which the judgment is made (Johnson and Fretz, 1974). The question of what is sexually normal thus proves to be meaningless. The answer typically is: "Well, it all depends."

Classifications of Unconventional Sexual Behavior

According to the Diagnostic and Statistical Manual of the American Psychiatric Association (DSM-II, 1968) the term "sexual deviation" applies to

individuals whose sexual interests are directed primarily toward objects other than people of the opposite sex, toward sexual acts not usually associated with coitus, or toward coitus performed under bizarre circumstances as in necrophilia (sexual contacts with corpses), sexual sadism and fetishism. Even though many find their practices distasteful, they remain unable to substitute normal sexual behavior for them. This diagnosis is not appropriate for individuals who perform deviant sexual acts because normal sexual objects are not available to them (p. 44).

This definition recognizes Freud's (1905) scheme of sexual variations. In Freud's system, unusual sexual behaviors were examined in terms of the sex object chosen and the sexual activity engaged in. For example, if a person has sexual relations with a close relative, we call the behavior *incest.* Or if someone chooses an inanimate object, such as a woman's black lace stocking, for sexual arousal, we are dealing with *fetishism.* Instead of engaging in heterosexual intercourse, a person may also prefer to observe others undress, which is *voyeurism;* expose his or her genitals to an audience, which is *exhibitionism;* obtain sexual gratification forcibly, which is *rape;* inflict pain, which is *sadism;* or endure pain, which is *masochism.*

Two other forms of unconventional behavior which do not fit into these two major categories are *transvestism,* or dressing in the clothing of the opposite sex, and *transsexualism,* which refers to the belief that one is actually a member of the opposite sex trapped in the wrong body.

We have chosen to refer to atypical sexual expressions as sexual variations or unconventional sexual behavior rather than sexual deviations. For us, the former terms reflect some of the changes we have evidenced in our society that allow or encourage us to approach unusual or strange forms of sexu-

PSYCHOSEXUAL DISORDERS
Gender Identity Disorders

Indicate sexual history in the fifth digit of
Transsexualism code as 1 = asexual,
2 = homosexual, 3 = heterosexual,
4 = mixed, 0 = unspecified.
302.5x Transsexualism
302.60 Gender identity disorder of
childhood
302.85 Other gender identity disorder of
adolescence or adult life

Paraphilias
302.81 Fetishism
302.30 Transvestism
302.10 Zoophilia
302.20 Pedophilia
302.40 Exhibitionism
302.82 Voyeurism
302.83 Sexual masochism
302.84 Sexual sadism
302.89 Other

Psychosexual Dysfunctions
302.71 with inhibited sexual desire
302.72 with inhibited sexual excitement
(frigidity, impotence)
302.73 with inhibited female orgasm
302.74 with inhibited male orgasm
302.75 with premature ejaculation
302.76 with functional dyspareunia
306.51 with functional vaginismus
302.79 other

Other Psychosexual Disorders
302.01 Ego-dystonic homosexuality
302.90 Psychosexual disorder not elsewhere classified

Figure 15.1
Classification of the sexual variations accord-
ing to the latest version of Diagnostic and
Statistical Manual of Mental Disorders (DSM III).

ality in a more objective and scientific manner
as compared with the highly moralistic and
pejorative approach of previous generations.

Sexual variations are often described as
clearly distinct clinical phenomena. In actu-
ality, however, there is a frequent overlap
among the various forms. A fetishist, for instance, may also display exhibitionistic tendencies or a transvestite may also be engaging
in sadomasochistic practices. Although people who prefer unconventional sexual behaviors show many different personality characteristics, many of them have difficulties in
establishing or maintaining satisfactory relations with a mature partner of the opposite
sex. Most of the people, the majority of whom
are males, engage in unconventional sex practices in an attempt to achieve sexual gratification which cannot be attained in a more
conventional way.

Variations in Sex Object Choices

For most men and women, a compatible
person of the opposite sex is the most frequent
choice for a sex partner. However, in addition,
a person may also decide to have a sexual relationship with himself or herself (masturbation). Or a person may decide to enter into a
sexual relationship with someone of the same
sex (homosexuality), or choose a sex partner
as a business arrangement (prostitution). In
our culture, masturbation, homosexuality,
and prostitution are no longer considered to
be socially harmful forms of sexuality.

In this section we will focus on unusual
choices of sex objects, a category of unconventional sexual behavior which can be broken down further to differentiate between
persons who prefer either animate or inanimate sex objects. The choice between these
two categories results in a number of sexual
variations that are listed in Table 15.1.

Let us take a closer look at these sexual
object choices.

Table 15.1

Unconventional Sex Object Choices

Animate	Inanimate
Pedophilia (child) Zoophilia (animal) Incest (relative)	Fetishism (object) Necrophilia (corpse)

Pedophilia

In pedophilia, the preferred sex object is a child. Most pedophiles are men who seek sexual contact with and/or gratification from children. The pedophilic act itself may involve sexual contact, penetration of the child, or sex games. Many older pedophiles do not attempt intromission but encourage the child to fondle or to manipulate their genitalia.

Legally, pedophilia is a deviant act which is referred to as child molestation. It is viewed by society as one of the lowest forms of criminal behavior. As a matter of fact, many people react much more strongly to men who have sexual relations with children than to rapists. As a legal offense pedophilia can result in severe penalties.

In a study of fifty-eight young adult males who had committed sexually deviant acts against children, three different patterns of pedophilia were suggested (Cohen, Seghorn, and Calmas, 1969). The *fixated pedophile* had never been able to develop or maintain mature interpersonal relationships with either male or female peers. He is socially comfortable only with children and seeks them out as companions. In most instances the child victim is known to the offender and the sexual play occurs only after a period of developing friendship. In their classic study of sex offenders, Gebhard and his colleagues (1965) also noted that many pedophiles know the children they molest, often being a friend of the family, a next door neighbor, or relative.

For the *regressed pedophile*, a history of apparently normal adolescence with good peer relationships and some appropriate dating and heterosexual behavior (including marriage, in some cases) preceded the pedophilic act. Presumably, however, feelings of masculine inadequacy existed under the surface appearance. When social, occupational, or marital stress occurred, the person fell back on more immature expressions of sexuality. A common precipitating event in this form of pedophilia was the man's discovery that his wife or girlfriend was having an affair with another man. The victim for the regressed pedophile is ordinarily not a familiar neighborhood child and the sexual act is typically impulsive. Many pedophiles in this category were in their mid-thirties and had developed serious mental and social maladjustments—including alcoholism, which was frequently associated with the act (Mohr, Turner, and Jerry, 1964).

For the *aggressive pedophile*, young boys are often the target of aggression, which may be expressed in cruel and vicious assaults on the genitals and anal areas of the child.

These different behavioral patterns provide a sense of the existing variations in pedophilia. In spite of these differences some similarities exist among pedophiles. It has been suggested that the pedophile is a sexually anxious person who has deep doubts about his sexual performance. Often he is a weak, inadequate individual unable to succeed in the adult world, socially and sexually. Many pedophiles also tend to be rigidly religious and highly moralistic. Afraid of being rejected because of his personal and sexual inadequacies, the pedophile avoids sexual contacts with adult females and concentrates on children instead because they are more trustworthy. The child is not only sexually inexperienced but also gives the pedophile a sense of power and domination. Because many children do not have the same concept of right and wrong as adults, they often comply with the will of the pedophile, who in turn enjoys the unspoiled quality of the child.

It should be pointed out that not all pedophilic acts result from initiation by an adult. Occasionally, precocious children display a large measure of sexual curiosity which may tempt an older person. At other times a child's innocent, uninhibited show of affection may arouse an older, sexually deprived person.

Zoophilia

Zoophilia, or bestiality, is the technical term for sexual contacts between humans and animals. It is a form of sexual behavior that has been known throughout history. Although zoophilia is not very common in our society, it is not highly unusual either, particularly in rural areas. Kinsey et al. (1948) reported that 15 percent of boys had sexual contacts with farm animals. Farm workers for whom few or no women were available as sexual partners experienced sexual excitement from fondling, striking, or actual intromission with the animal. Most commonly used for sexual gratification were farm animals such as cows, goats, and dogs. In most cases reported by Kinsey and his coworkers sexual contacts with animals were restricted to adolescence and the person turned to more appropriate sex objects later. In some cases, however, zoophilia became an end in itself. Heterosexual satisfaction was excluded.

The practice of zoophilia is not restricted to unskilled farm laborers but also occurs among upper- and middle-class couples who are part of the swinging scene (see Chapter 12). At this level, there are couples who identify themselves as "animal lovers" in swinging maga-

Figure 15.2
The ghostly lover. (Institute for Sex Research, Bloomington)

zines who use small dogs trained to have oral sex with their mistresses. In one such case, an "animal loving couple" traveled several hundred miles to spend the weekend with another couple with "similar interests"; their Alsatian dog, John, performed oral sex on the two wives while the husbands looked on.

Incest

Incest, or sexual relations among family members, is a pervasive theme in the literature, mythology, and folklore of many civilizations. Some forms of incest have been condoned among the royal families of ancient Egypt, Peru, and Hawaii. Cleopatra, Queen of the Nile in ancient Egypt, for instance, was a direct descendent of six generations of brother-sister marriages. In spite of her stormy love affair with Caesar, she continued the tradition by taking her brother as a husband. Incest historically occurred in rich and powerful families whose dynastic interests required the conservation of power and wealth as a monopoly of the royal family. Many times the royal families considered themselves as the descendents of the gods who gave them special power that needed to be preserved and perpetuated. Although incest is almost universally prohibited today, there are a few primitive cultures that still allow and regulate incest.

Incest taboos vary from culture to culture, but in all cultures there seems to be a hierarchy in incest prohibitions. The most unacceptable and abhorred incestuous relationship is between mother and son, then father-daughter, then brother-sister, followed by relations among the various second-order relatives such as cousins and uncles.

Incidence. The occurrence of incest has been notoriously difficult to establish because incest takes place within a close family circle under conditions of secrecy. According to Forward and Buck (1978) somewhere between 10 and 20 million people—victims and aggressors—participate in the "family crime nobody talks about." Whatever the final figures, it seems safe to assume that the frequency of incest is much greater than any statistics can reveal. Because in many cases the incest victim is a young girl who does not have the strength of will or initiative to shake off the father's domination, incestuous family relationships often do not come to the attention of the authorities (Hughes, 1964). The shame and guilt experienced by the family may be sufficient to keep the incestuous relationship hidden.

The Victims of Incest. Sexual relationships between father and daughter have received the most attention. Weinberg (1955) studied 203 Illinois cases and reported 159 (78 percent) incidents of father-daughter incest, 37 (18 percent) cases of brother-sister incest, two (1 percent) of mother-son incest, and five (3 percent) cases of multiple incestuous relationships.

Several descriptions of incestuous relationships between fathers and their daughters lend support to the idea that fathers involved in incest share certain common tendencies (Forward and Buck, 1978; Poznanski and Blos, 1975; Weinberg, 1955). They are generally weak, ineffective men, both within and outside the family. Within the family, they frequently have poor relationships with their wives and demonstrate little emotional or economic responsibility. Especially when the victim is a young girl, the father rarely has to resort to violence to achieve his incestuous ends because the child thinks: "If daddy says it's all right, then it must be all right."

Some investigators noted that the daughter often does not fit the description of the "innocent" victim. Weinberg (1955) found the girls to be precocious and eager to assume the adult role. Moreover, they were gratified by the parental attention and used the incestuous relationship to express their hostility toward their mother. A pathological relationship between mother and daughter is almost always a sine qua non for the existence of father-daughter incest (Poznanski and Blos, 1975).

Gagnon (1977) speculated that an incestuous relationship between a father and daughter begins when the father is under considerable stress outside the home and yet receives insufficient emotional and sexual support from his wife. Under these circumstances he turns to the available daughter who takes on the role of a substitute wife. In some families, father-daughter incest occurred after prolonged absence of the father from the home who, upon his return, found an estranged aging wife and an attractive, young, and tempting daughter.

The mother also plays a crucial role in father-daughter incest. Many times it is her response that determines whether or not the incestuous relationship continues. In the interest of keeping the family together the mother may choose to ignore what is going on. She may simply not "see" the sexual fondling in the home or she may deliberately go out leaving father and daughter alone. In one instance, a mother set up an incestuous situation when she sent her husband upstairs into the single bedroom of their daughter to paddle her. The paddling led to sexual contact. The mother never questioned the silence which ensued and subsequently closed her eyes denying any responsibility. Thus, while the mother may be a silent partner and technically nonparticipating in the sexual act, her permission is a key factor.

Mother-son incest is probably the least understood and most complex and traumatic of all forms of incest. The mother-son sexual relationship is, of course, the basis of the Oedipal conflict which is at the heart of the Freudian interpretation of sexuality (see Chapter 4). Because these types of relationships are based on a few isolated case reports it is almost impossible to discuss this form of incest with any type of confidence. Presumably the mother is believed to be a highly dependent woman who needs to relive her marital romance by becoming sexually involved with the son. The son is idealized and the mother's youthful fantasy of a romantic lover is invested in the son. Many times the son is nearing puberty and usually unexperienced sexually (Forward and Buck, 1978). Because of his sexual awakening a boy who might otherwise have resisted his mother's possessiveness revels in it. At the same time he feels guilty about the sexual act and becomes insecure and extremely self-conscious. Also relatively rare clinical cases are brother-sister incest. Usually the victim in this type of incest is the younger sister whose older brother takes advantage of her sexual naïveté.

Incest inevitably creates role distortions— the father becomes the "lover," the son the "husband," or the sister the "mistress." Confusion and conflict may occur—for example, when one participant is not aware that it is *not* parental prerogative to have sexual relations with a child. This was the case with a nineteen-year-old girl from Illinois whose mother died when she was twelve (Renshaw and Renshaw, 1977). She became the housekeeper and regular sexual partner of her father and three older brothers. All of the men drank heavily and none of them had gone beyond the sixth grade. The girl completed high school and attended courses at a junior college where she met a young man who was sexually interested in her. It was only then that she discovered that her sexual behavior was incest.

Interpretations of Incestuous Relationships. Freud (1905) regarded the incest drive as part of human physiology. In the form of the Oedipal complex, psychodynamic theory depicts the instinctual urge to possess the parent of the opposite sex coupled with instinctual rivalry with the parent of the same sex.

Other writers minimized the biological aspects of incest taboos and advanced explanations based on cultural, environmental, or sociological factors. It has, for instance, been suggested that incest is harmful because it ties the individual so tightly to the family thereby restricting general social relationships. Weinberg (1955), in a similar vein, noted that incest tends to occur most frequently either in the family which is so ingrown that its members find it impossible to achieve good social relationships outside the family circle or, conversely, in families which are so loosely organized that individual members never absorbed conventional feelings of rejection of sexual relations within the family.

Viewing incest in a transactional framework, Lustig and his coworkers (1966) proposed that incest is a transaction that serves defensively to protect and maintain a dysfunctional family. The authors defined five conditions of the dysfunctional family which foster the breakdown of the incest taboo: (1) the emergence of the daughter as the central female figure of the household in place of the mother; (2) some degree of incompatibility between husband and wife with unrelieved sexual tension in the husband; (3) unwillingness of the husband to seek a sexual partner outside the family; (4) shared fears of family disintegration; and (5) covert sanction of the nonparticipant mother. In many incestuous families the situation derives from a unique combination of these factors given certain necessities and attitudes of family members. In addition, the probability of incest is augmented by certain situational factors and by participants' capacity to rationalize their violation of the incest taboo (Ferracuti, 1974).

Situational factors associated with the breakdown of the incest barrier are overcrowding, alcoholism, and geographic isolation which make social contacts difficult. The majority of persons involved in incestuous relationships are of lower position, borderline economic means, and unstable work records. Weiner (1962) in an attempt to summarize sociological factors linked with incest found that incest can occur at any socioeconomic level and also under normal or near normal living conditions. Thus, we can only conclude from the available literature that poverty, overcrowding, and social isolation are of secondary etiological importance. Central to all incest situations is a previous interruption of the marital relationship.

Fetishism

Like many forms of sexual behavior, conventional or unconventional, fetishism is a sexual expression of a wide range. The fetishist is a person who attaches sexual significance to objects that are not necessarily sexual in nature. At one end there are men who are sexually aroused by the sight of women in black boots, red underwear, and the like, and the arousal derived from these objects enhances their sexual gratification. In this sense, there is a bit of a clothing fetishist in most males which is actively promoted and reinforced by the fashion industry. Thus, fetishism is present to some extent in many males where it serves a normal excitatory function during foreplay. At the opposite end we find the person for whom the inanimate object becomes sufficient for sexual gratification.

Inanimate objects that are common sources of arousal for fetishists are lingerie, shoes, or high-heeled boots. Clothing fetishists often prefer clothing that has been worn by females.

Many fetishists collect the items or objects that arouse them. Often they present an annoying problem to the police because they will steal in order to obtain the sexually arousing object. The kinds of items stolen and the manner in which the theft is committed characterize the particular person involved. Reinhardt (1957) described the case of a milkman who claimed that his wife liked high heeled shoes and he could not resist stealing them. Upon searching his home, the police found seventy-nine pairs of women's shoes, many of which were not his wife's size. Evidently the milkman, a shoe fetishist, had been investigating homes along his milk route in order to add to this collection.

A second type of fetishism pays exaggerated importance to certain parts of the body —breasts, legs, hair color—and is known as *partialism*. As with fetishism, the partial body part becomes the major arousing stimulus for the man who cannot achieve sexual gratification with a woman who does not possess the valued part of the body. The attraction felt by the person toward the fetishist part of the body is presumably involuntary and irresistible. A man, for instance, may be so attracted to women's ankles that he takes a job as a shoe salesman although he qualifies for a better paying position.

An unusual variation of partialism is a deformity fetish. Some women find ugly, deformed men sexually arousing and people with amputated limbs may strongly attract some men and, much less commonly, women.

How do fetishes arise? According to psychoanalytic theory, the fetishist is warding off anxiety about heterosexual contacts. Usually, he is afraid of being rejected by the person to whom he is attracted and consequently fixates on the article of clothing as on a portion of the body because this fixation does not involve the real person and remains under the fetishist's control. Learning theorists evoke some kind of classical conditioning as in the case of one fetishist who, as a young boy, masturbated to pictures of women dressed in black. Eventually, black apparel became sexually arousing in itself.

Necrophilia

Necrophilia refers to sexual interest in having intercourse with corpses. It often comes as a surprise to learn that there are really people who are sexually attracted to corpses. Like incest, necrophilia has been known throughout history. Some ancient societies, for instance, took great pains to preserve bodies intact for a long time after death and there is evidence that suggests that there were sexual rituals with entombed bodies.

Morbid sexual attraction to corpses is rare. From society's standpoint, the most dangerous and disruptive type of necrophila is the one who kills his victim to obtain the body. The majority of necrophiles, however, are not of this sort. DeRiver (1956) reported that some necrophiles become embalmers so that they can gain access to corpses. One young man, a twenty-one-year-old morgue attendant, had fallen in love with a girl at age eighteen with whom he had had sexual intercourse only once because she was in poor

---

Apotemnophilia: A quest for amputation

Little is known about the sexual attractiveness of amputated limbs. Since there is no official label for an erotic obsession or fetishism for amputated legs, Money, Jobaris, and Furth (1977) created the term apotemnophilia to refer to a sexual attraction to amputees. The authors reported a case of self-demand amputation requested by a man who considered himself as a "cryptic transsexual." Instead of having his sex changed, however, he was absorbed by the obsessive wish to be amputated. As a matter of fact, he found the thought of amputation so arousing that he had fantasies of himself as an amputee in all his sexual contacts. He stated:

> since my 13th year, my conscious life has
> been absorbed, with varying intensity, in a
> bizarre and prepotent wish, desire to have
> my leg amputated above the knee; the image
> of myself as an amputee accompanied every
> sexual experience in my life: auto-, homo-,
> and heterosexual, since, and beginning with
> puberty (Money et al., 1977, p. 117).

Reportedly, the man had several sexual encounters with amputees. One involved a homosexual relation with an older amputee; another, a female amputee with whom he was able to achieve orgasm. While masturbating the man would use photographs of seminude or fully dressed amputees as visual aids.

Although he had been married twice, the man perceived himself as an "amputated homosexual" who repeatedly requested the removal of his leg "to make fantasy real." After having received several negative responses from the medical profession for surgical amputation, he began contemplating various accidents which would injure his leg enough to warrant amputation. When this failed, he began to insert a steel stylus into his leg which caused a serious infection. Eventually his attempts to get rid of his leg became so ritualized that his left leg was almost constantly infected.

In addition to apotemnophilia, the man also had a rubber fetish as well as having homosexual interests in adolescent youths. He changed his job as a designer/engineer in a technical institute for a new career—helping amputees—with the ambition of becoming a voluntary amputee himself. At the last follow-up, the man still had his leg and was working. He expressed feelings of depression over his sexual preferences because he could not resolve his apotemnophilia either by self-amputation or by psychotherapy.

---

health. After the girl died from tuberculosis, he was so upset that he felt an urge to jump into the casket with her. Although the young man had originally planned to go to medical school, he decided to enter a school of undertaking and embalming. At the morgue he became intensely interested in female bodies and began to have intercourse with them.

Over the next few years he violated scores of female corpses. On one occasion, he was so impressed with the corpse of a young girl fifteen years old that when he was alone with her the first night after her death, he drank some of her blood and bit into her buttocks. He then crawled on the cadaver and had intercourse with her.

Although the dynamics of necrophilia are largely unknown, we do know that most necrophiles are timid, nonassertive people whose bizarre sexual behavior seems to be a release of anxieties built up over the years.

Variations in Sexual Activities

In this category we find people who, instead of preferring unusual sex objects, obtain sexual gratification from unconventional activities.

Voyeurism

Voyeurism is difficult to assess because, at one extreme, it is a universal activity. The sexual attraction of watching a nude body is obvious. Striptease shows, topless waitresses, and go-go dancers are common examples of normal manifestations of voyeurism. Many couples experience a natural amount of mutual voyeurism in their sexual relationship. However, they usually restrict their voyeurism to displaying themselves in sexy clothing or in the nude as a prelude to and during love making. The difference between the average person and the voyeur is not one of seeking erotic stimulation but of willingness to assume some risks in obtaining arousing stimuli (Gebhard et al., 1965).

The true voyeur (peeping Tom) is a person who experiences sexual excitement when watching others undress or have sexual intercourse. Excessive interest in peeping at the genitalia or others engaged in having sex is called *scoptophilia*.

An important element in voyeurism is the risk of potential discovery. Most voyeurs—who are almost always men—do not find it particularly exciting to watch a woman undress for their particular benefit. The major thrill is derived from the secret watching of unsuspecting women. For this reason,

voyeurs will creep into the gardens of houses in order to peep into windows, or race over fences to maintain their anonymity.

Virtually all voyeurs are looking for adult females with some degree of physical attraction. The ideal is to observe an attractive woman engaged in some sort of sexual activity. By observing without being observed, the voyeur enjoys sexual stimulation without the threat of rejection or demand for sexual performance.

A typical case of voyeurism was presented by Gebhard and his colleagues (1965). A young man in his twenties, had one heterosexual experience when he was seventeen. His overwhelming fear of rejection kept him from seeking more heterosexual activities which he strongly desired. His fear of rejection could be traced back to a rather traumatic event shortly after puberty when circumstances forced the young man to share a bed with his married sister. He became extremely aroused and wanted to have sex with his sister. Unable to express his wish, he simply showed her his penis. His sister rejected him violently and harassed him at length about being vile. After that, the young man felt extremely awkward about approaching females sexually and took every rejection as a personal rebuff. Eventually, he began peeping regularly, first at his sister through a keyhole and later at other women through windows. Usually he masturbated while looking on. The peeping became a compulsion which he was finally unable to resist, despite repeated arrests.

Exhibitionism

Self-display is a normal and important part of the sexual development of men and women. With today's related attitudes toward nudity, varying degrees of body exposure are socially acceptable. As in the case of voyeurism, tendencies of exhibitionism can take many different forms. Expensive automobiles, flamboyant clothing, or even public appearances could be considered forms of socially acceptable exhibitionism.

Exhibitionism is almost invariably a male practice, although women may expose themselves in more subtle ways. String bikinis and see-through blouses are forms of exhibitionism. Prostitutes expose parts of their bodies to attract customers and strippers do the same because it is an occupational requirement. A quip holds that a man who is surreptiously looking at a nude woman is a voyeur, but that a woman looking at a naked man is watching an exhibitionist. Although behaviors may be considered exhibitionistic in a narrowly defined sense, they lack the compulsive element which characterizes the male exhibitionist.

The exhibitionist obtains sexual gratification from exposing his genitals to unsuspecting women and children. The public stereotype of the exhibitionist is well illustrated in *Playboy* cartoons showing a leering old man dressed in sneakers and a raincoat (hiding the fact that he wears no trousers) who flashes his penis at some horrified, dumbstruck female. Typically, the exposure is made when the woman is alone and in circumstances where she can do little to avoid the man. A woman so confronted can, however, deflate the exhibitionist by refusing to be afraid or ignoring him. Ridicule works even better. Statements such as "yuk, what a terrible little thing you've got" or "be careful you don't catch a cold" can be utterly demoralizing and discouraging to the exhibitionist.

Observing the reaction of the woman constitutes half of the thrill the exhibitionist is experiencing. Because most of the victims he exposes himself to are strangers, anticipation of fear, disgust, horror, or surprise responses constitute an important component of the act. Like the voyeur, the exhibitionist rarely exposes himself to his girlfriend or wife but chooses strange women who would be considered suitable sex partners. Voyeurism and exhibitionism together account for almost the majority of all sexual offenses that come to the attention of the police.

Most men who expose themselves are sexually timid. They are shy, withdrawn people who have great difficulties in developing any sort of relationship with others. Typically, they are unsuccessful in attracting sexual partners or, having attracted a woman, they are unable to make love satisfactorily. Moreover, Mathis (1969) found that exhibitionists tend to lack masculine aggressiveness or self-confidence feeling markedly inferior to other men. Since the exhibitionist is typically unable to display even justifiable levels of anger and hostility, exhibiting his penis to a strange female is about as aggressive as he will become. Body contact between the exhibitionist and his victim is extremely rare. Should the woman respond with interest to the exhibitionist's act, the offender is likely to panic and run away.

The picture that emerges from the clinical analysis of exhibitionists is a description of an ordinary person leading a somewhat dull, isolated life. Personality and background factors consistently show insecurity in social relations and low frustration tolerance. When subjected to obvious criteria of sexuality such as frequency of intercourse, number of lovers, age of first intercourse, the exhibitionist falls far below normal sexual adjustment. Nevertheless, many exhibitionists are married and have children. The following case reported by Bond and Hutchinon (1964) presents a typical history:

Case 15.1

Exhibitionism

The man under consideration was a twenty-five-year-old man of average intelligence. His parents were of Anglo-Saxon stock and quite puritanical in outlook. He recalls his mother's early admonition against childish sexual practices which she described as "evil" and "nasty." He was also instructed to conceal his genitals from females. An incident which increased his sexual guilt tremendously involved punishment by his mother for engaging in a contest with another boy to see how high up the side of a wall each could urinate. He recalled, at this time, feeling "hurt" by the observation that his friend's penis was larger.

His first exposure occurred at thirteen following sex play with a ten-year-old neighbor girl. He felt a desire to perform coitus, but the girl appeared indifferent to his suggestion and had refused. Her indifference hurt him; this was followed by rage, then by exposing his erect penis to her. . . .

Throughout adolescence he suffered feelings of inadequacy and inferiority. His exhibitionism continued, and he indulged excessively in sexual daydreams . . . and it was not unusual for him to expose several times during the day . . .

Attacks of exhibitionism were described as being preceded by a feeling of sexual excitement and dread. He would experience "a grim determination to expose, come what might." He would become tense and an erection would occur . . . When the girl registered shock, "the spell would be broken" and he would flee, trembling and remorseful. His wife, often present during such an attack, described his appearance as one of being "paralized, with glazed eyes" (Bond and Hutchinon, 1964, pp. 80-82).

This case shows the compulsive act quite clearly. As a matter of fact, the young man's police record indicated twenty-four charges of indecent exposure and eleven convictions with nine prison sentences.

Psychoanalytic literature states that the urge to exhibit one's genitals to strangers is a defiance of the threat of castration. Typically, the unsuspecting female represents the mother figure whose reaction reinforces the exhibitionist's masculinity. An interesting learning hypothesis of the development of

Figure 15.3
Streaking has become a socially acceptable form of body exposure in many Western countries. (United Press International, Inc.)

exhibitionism offered by McGuire, Carlisle, and Young (1965) emphasized the reinforcing aspects of masturbation. The authors described the cases of two young men. An attractive woman found them urinating. When they recuperated from their embarrassment, the thought of being discovered in "a private act" aroused them and they began masturbating at the fantasy of the earlier experience. After repeated masturbation to the fantasy of the woman, both men began to exhibit. It was suggested that repeated association of sexual arousal with the fantasy of being seen by the woman classically conditioned the men to become aroused through exhibitionism. More experimental evidence is needed, however, to support clearly a learning explanation of exhibitionism.

With the increasing sexual frankness we are currently experiencing, attitudes, and laws toward exhibitionistic behavior will probably change. With the publication of *Playgirl* magazine with the explicit photograph of the Playboy of the Month, we may reasonably expect that women are becoming inured to the sight of the exposed penis.

Sadomasochism

Sadomasochism involves the paradoxical combination of pain and pleasure. The sadist obtains sexual gratification from inflicting pain upon his partner. The punishment and pain inflicted by the sadist may be physical (kicking, biting, whipping, slapping) or verbal (abusive language, teasing, threatening) in nature. The sadist relishes watching or making others suffer.

Masochism, on the other hand, refers to the enjoyment of pain received. The masochist delights in experiencing torture or cruelty which may be self-inflicted or caused by others (Klein, 1972).

Masochism may be viewed as the opposite of sadism. Many times, sexual partners complement each other with sadomasochistic

tendencies. Sadomasochistic behaviors may also be present in the same person. The common denominator in both is pain, either given or received. Sadomasochism becomes an unconventional sexual behavior when inflicting or experiencing pain serves as a substitute for, or the predominant source of, pleasure in the sexual act. In less extreme forms, sadomasochism may serve as a prelude to heterosexual intercourse. A married couple had worked out the following ritual:

> As a prelude to intercourse, the young man would draw blood by cutting a small incision on the palm of his wife's right hand. She would then stimulate his penis using the blood of her right palm as a lubricant. Normal intercourse would then ensue and the moment the wife felt her husband ejaculating, she was required to dig her nails deep into the small of his back or buttocks (Lazarus and Davison, 1971, pp. 201-203).

The complex connections between pain and restraint on one hand and erotic pleasure on the other are also illustrated in the elaborate set games known as erotic *bondage.* Bondage and discipline (B & D in the vernacular) typically refers to various forms of physical restraint and discipline refers to spanking and whipping. Bondage people use belts, lacings, and wrist straps as restraints for the purpose of inducing sexual excitement. Sadomasochism, like voyeurism and exhibitionism, can range from a mild inclination common to many people to extreme forms dominating a person's approach to sexual gratification.

From a psychoanalytic perspective the sadist is performing "symbolic castration" of his sexual partner. He achieves orgasm by venting his rage upon his sexual partner, making him or her suffer pain. Usually, the sadist needs a partner who permits him or herself to be whipped and humiliated. Freud maintained that masochism was a manifestation of the sadistic impulse turned against the self. Psychoanalytic theory also holds that sadomasochism can be traced to a fixation on an early misinterpretation by the child of the male role in intercourse. This view assumes that the child witnessed intercourse between the parents ("the primal scene") and interpreted the father's behavior as an attack on the mother. Learning theorists again point to a classical conditioning model according to which early pairing of sexual arousal with pain is reinforced by subsequent masturbatory fantasies.

Rape

In rape, as in sadomasochism, aggression and sexuality are closely linked. Rape is defined as the forcible infliction of intercourse on another person. From a legal point of view, this may be interpreted as physical force, mental intimidation, or taking advantage of people who are incapable of making a decision with respect to intercourse (for example, a minor or a mentally retarded person). Although the law attempts to make a clear decision between rape and sexual intercourse, the courts find it difficult to distinguish between a case where the decision to have sex is mutual or where a man forced himself on his partner. Consider the following case:

> A judge in Salt Lake City, Utah reversed the verdict of a jury which convicted a man of raping a young college student. After reversing the verdict, the judge expressed his concern over the conduct of the victim. She was a white girl sitting in a bar with a black man, in a "flimsy dress," eating "his" food and drinking "his" beverages. The judge felt that there was a lot to be said about mutual consent in this case. Although he denied to have a racist or sexist point of view, the judge expressed the attitude that by dressing in a certain way or by going certain places, a woman is fair game for rape.

The crime of rape has become a matter of increasing public concern. It is the fastest growing crime in America: an 80 percent national rise of rape cases was reported between 1968 and 1975 (FBI, 1975). Even more disconcerting than the sharp increase in rape is the fact that the actual figures are estimated at five times the number of reported assaults. In a nationwide study on the causes of violence conducted for the National Commission, it was found that 10 percent of the recorded rapes were between members of the same family. In 29 percent of the cases the rapist and his victim were acquainted; in 53 percent of the cases they were strangers. Moreover, it was found that the vast majority of rapes were planned. In other words, it is a myth to say that rape is the spontaneous act of a man who temporarily loses control over his sexual impulses (Harrington and Sutton-Simon, 1977).

The Rapist. An increasing number of professional efforts have attempted to isolate the rapist's basic motivation and personality traits. Because rape is a mixture of both aggression and sex and because in our culture male sexuality and violence are intimately linked, the motivation of the rapist is difficult to determine.

Gebhard and his coworkers (1965), in their classic study of sex offenders, described several distinct types of individuals who commit rape. Some men were classified as *assaultive* because rape was the explosive expression of pent-up sexual desires. It appeared that, for this type of rapist, the sexual activity alone was insufficient but had to be accompanied by physical violence. The majority of rapists in this category carried out the act to express aggression rather than for sexual gratification. Amir (1971), in his landmark study of rape patterns, also proposed that rape is less an act of sexual expression than it is of aggression. The assaultive rapist was also described as a sadist who arouses most of the fear and concern because he bears tremendous hostility and hatred toward women

(Amir, 1974). He is obsessed by the need to prove his mastery and enjoys causing pain to his victim by great violence.

A second type of rapist was labeled the *amoral delinquent* to describe men who play little heed to social controls. In contrast to the assaultive rapist, the amoral delinquent is not sadistic but simply wants to have intercourse. These men treat women as sex objects whose sole role is to provide the male with sexual pleasures regardless of their own wishes. A third pattern of rape was described as the *drinker aggressor* because drinking is often the precipitating factor in the rape. Gebhard et al. also discussed the *double standard aggressor*, a rapist who categorizes women as decent or "bad." Decent women, according to this rapist's philosophy, are treated with respect while "bad" women do not deserve any consideration. Women who can be picked up easily can be forced into intercourse. The double-standard aggressor feels that force or threat is justified if he judges the woman to be sexually promiscuous or provocative. As is true for most typologies, not all rapists will neatly fit into these categories.

Rada (1978) described a broad spectrum of rapists who might be labeled "masculine identity rapists" because they share in common an actual or felt deficiency in their masculine role. Each rapist in this group has developed a particular style for dealing with his role-identity conflicts. Some are quite timid and shy, whereas others are hypermasculine men who constantly attempt to impress others with their physical and social prowess. The following case illustrates the masculine-identity rapist.

Case 15.2

Rape

John was a 22-year-old married male who readily admitted to a charge of rape. His father was a truck driver who was away from home for long periods of time in his early childhood and deserted the family when he was nine years old. John was raised by his grandmother, mother, aunt, and two sisters. His grandfather was the only male figure in the home while he was growing up. When his grandfather died (John was 15 then), he experienced a serious emotional deprivation. Shortly thereafter, he engaged in his first sexual intercourse. He called a woman whose phone number he found written on the wall of a public men's room. She agreed to meet him and he went to her apartment. Before having intercourse she asked to see his penis and told him that it was "not large, but okay." Although he felt humiliated, he engaged in intercourse but was unable to have an orgasm. He did not attempt intercourse again until he was married four years later. . . .

Although he had strong positive feelings toward his wife, he felt sexually inadequate. His wife was apparently satisfied with the sexual relationship and would reassure him that he was a good lover. She became pregnant and during the late second trimester of the pregnancy desired intercourse less often. He took her lack of sexual interest as a personal rejection and began to fantasize about sexual relations with other women. Nevertheless, he felt incapable of establishing a voluntary relationship and started to think about rape.

One night after work, he and a male friend went to a bar and began drinking heavily. After he left the bar he picked up a female hitchhiker. Several weeks earlier he had placed a knife under the front seat of his car in the event that he should ever "build up the courage" to attempt rape. Shortly after the woman got in his car he asked her if she would "screw" and when she refused, he took out the knife, threatened her, and slapped her several times. The rape was performed quickly, and although he achieved orgasm, he was too frightened to enjoy it. He apologized to the victim, freed her, panicked and drove home (Rada, 1978, pp. 126-127).

The Rape Victim. Most women who are raped are between the ages of fifteen and twenty-four although elderly women and young girls are also subject to rape. While definitions of rape vary greatly in different police jurisdictions, most states assume that a woman is a victim of rape when she submits to real or implied threats of force. But she may also be raped in a legal sense when she consents under the influence of alcohol or drugs of if she claims she was unable to give responsible consent. The moral and legal issues involved in forcible rape are complex and often confusing (see Chapter 19).

One of the most crucial problems for the rape victim is the question of consent. If the existence of a prior relationship with the rapist is established by the court, the suspicion of consent may transform the victim into an accomplice. Many women, and particularly feminists, argue that our law enforcement is sexist in the area of rape because it often assumes that women are to blame for the assault. Susan Griffin (1971) called rape a form of mass terrorism in which the victim is chosen indiscriminately. According to Griffin, the law, supported by propagandists for male supremacy, broadcasts the view that women are raped because they are unchaste. The Amir (1971) study also found that the police tended to believe that a woman with a good reputation cannot be raped. Many times the rape victim feels that *she* is on trial because her sexual motives are questioned. Technically, victims often must prove their moral "purity" to husbands, friends, lovers, and the police (Brownmiller, 1975).

Rape victims are often traumatized by the experience, both mentally and physically. Many women commented on the difficulties they had shaking the memory of rape. Others complained about having lost trust in male-female relationships as well as having lost self-esteem. The sexual humiliation inherent in rape is experienced as psychologically more damaging by most women than the involuntary intercourse.

Gender Identity Disturbances

In this final category, we find two manifestations of unconventional sexual behavior which are essentially the result of gender identity confusion.

Transvestism

Transvestism is a term applied to people who crossdress—that is, wear clothing considered appropriate for the opposite sex. Crossdressing constitutes a role activity rather than a sexual activity (Prince and Bentler, 1972). Almost all known transvestites are males who enjoy dressing in female apparel. The transvestite may be a homosexual in masquerade ("drag queen") or a transsexual who lives routinely in the role of the other sex (Benjamin, 1966). The homosexual transvestite dresses in the clothing of the opposite sex to attract persons of the same sex. The clothing has essentially no value to the wearer and is but a means and not an end in itself.

Our focus here will be on the transvestite who is heterosexual in orientation and has no desire to change his sex. The heterosexual transvestite wears the clothing of the opposite sex for emotional and sexual gratification. Crossdressing in this case is an end in itself.

The heterosexual transvestite is quite compulsive in his crossdressing and makes it patently clear that he is not a homosexual. Many of them start crossdressing in childhood and as adults initially wear female cloth-

Figure 15.4
Female impersonator shown in both male and female attire. (United Press International, Inc.)

ing clandestinely. After the initial excitement of solitary crossdressing is past, the transvestite wants to be seen. Once they have taken up crossdressing, transvestites find great pleasure in being able to mix as "women" among other transvestites or real women. To pass as a woman successfully is a thrill.

Many transvestites are easily recognized because their appearance and behavior is often a caricature of the opposite sex. The male transvestite uses more make-up, wears longer false eyelashes, and louder dresses. At other times the clothing is outdated and obviously out of style, more like the clothes "mother" used to wear.

The following case history describes a heterosexual transvestite, a married man with children, who led an otherwise conventional sex life:

Case 15.3

Transvestism

Diane (Steve) is a salesmanager for a large company and father of three children. He is active in the marine reserves and a devoted football fan. His wife is a pretty woman in her thirties who knows of her husband's crossdressing. She speaks of the need of keeping the marriage together arguing that transvestism is better than adultery.

For almost seven years after they were married her husband kept his crossdressing activities secret. He would sneak out of the house to dress, wait until everyone was gone or go to motels. His wife became suspicious when she discovered American Express bills for local motels and cosmetics in his drawers. Suspecting other women, Steve's wife confronted him and the truth came out. For several months the marital adjustment was tentative until Steve's wife decided that she was better off with him than without him. The children never learned about their father's crossdressing activities.

A number of factors, such as broken homes, poor father image, and domineering mother have been implicated in the development of transvestism (Stoller, 1968). Most transvestites had their first experience at crossdressing prior to adolescence. Lambley (1974) reported a typical case which involved a twenty-six-year-old graduate student who had been crossdressing since the age of ten. When he was younger his crossdressing had taken the form of masturbation while wearing his mother's high heeled shoes. Over the years it extended to the stage where he completely dressed as a woman and masturbated in front of a mirror.

Conventional psychotherapeutic treatments of transvestism has been disappointing but behavior therapy and, in particular, aversive shock treatment have shown considerable success.

Transsexualism

The fundamental difference between the transsexual and the transvestite is that the latter, when crossdressed, still knows that he is a man while the transsexual has the distinct feeling of belonging to the opposite sex. Transsexuals are convinced that nature played an unfair trick on them by trapping them in the wrong body. Transsexualism, or gender dysphoria as it is called recently, may be defined as cross gender identification because the person perceives his or her gender identity and anatomy as incongruous. Transsexualism is thus a psychological condition in which a biologically normal person wishes to change his or her sexual identity into a person of the opposite sex. Accord-

ingly, many transsexuals try to obliterate all traces of their given sex. The desire to negate their biological sex and pass into and be accepted into the opposite gender role is so strong and overwhelming that some transsexuals have sex-change operations. Paula, a preoperative twenty-two-year-old male-to-female transsexual described these feelings as follows:

> I feel that with most transsexuals, including myself, there is the crucial experience of living for many years in the assigned and undesired sex. The more I think and feel it, the more I suspect that someone who has lived through this can never be the same as someone who hasn't. In other words, I have very strong feelings of femaleness, so deep that it changes my body images itself. I desire sex reassignment to bring my physical reality in line with the emotional feeling. Yet, without at all denying the validity of this, if I am honest I must at the same time admit that because I lived for 21 years as a male (with whatever reluctance and frustration), because I have considered my female identity as a goal rather than a given, I can never have quite the same sense of femaleness as a "native." I have a memory bank which is filled with relationships with others as a male. If I honestly want to speak about my feelings, I must say I feel myself to be a female so deeply that I wish to live so and be so (Feinbloom, 1976, p. 151).

While the desire to live as a person of the opposite sex is quite old, surgical and hormonal techniques for sex change did not become possible until this century. Only since the 1930s, when plastic surgery and improved hormonal techniques became sophisticated enough, has it been possible to construct an artificial vagina or penis. After the highly publicized case of Christine Jorgenson (originally an exsoldier, George), who underwent sex reassignment in Copenhagen in 1952, the public became acquainted with the "transsexual phenomenon." Since then, more than 3,000 Americans have undergone sex reassignment.

Sex-Transformation Surgery. Probably the most widely known American institutions for sex reassignment are the Gender Identity Clinics at the Johns Hopkins School of Medicine and at Stanford University. Both institutions subject the person who is requesting the sex reassignment operation to a series of tests. First of all, the client has to present a lifelong history of wishing to live in the body of the opposite sex. Typically, this includes a history of crossdressing, a strong aversion to masculine (or feminine) pursuits, and effeminate (or masculine) behaviors. In order to pass this portion of the screening process, some transsexuals who have been so eager to have the operation memorized the classic case histories from Benjamin (1966) resorting to outright subterfuge to achieve their goals.

Most sex reassignment clinics require the transsexual to be free from marital bonds if he or she has been married. Moreover, hormonal treatment is mandatory for one or two years prior to surgical treatment. As they undergo hormonal therapy, transsexuals are encouraged to live and work in their new sex roles as a proof to themselves that they can meet and enjoy successfully, in reality as well as in imagination, all the exigencies of the changed sex role (Money, 1974). This means that candidates for transsexual surgery must demonstrate that they can live and dress in the role to which assignment is desired. This is a very demanding and extremely difficult test since it may require a person to be able to fake even an employer's medical examination.

The Male-to-Female Conversion. The most commonly requested sex change operation involves a man who believes he should be a woman. There is a ratio of approximately three or four males for every female wanting to reverse her anatomy.

In the first phase of the male-to-female sex reassignment, hormone therapy, consisting of estrogen and prosgesterone, changes the male secondary sex characteristics into their feminized counterparts. Hormone therapy results in breast development which may be augmented by silicone implants. The male beard is usually removed by electrolysis. In order to create a feminine shape of the neck, a prominant Adam's apple in men may require surgical modification. With training, the voice can become more feminine.

The second phase of sex conversion entails the surgical transformation of the male genitalia into their female counterparts. For this purpose the erectile tissue of the penis and the testes are removed and the glands and the scrotal skin are preserved. Parts of these tissues are used to construct an artificial vagina. The skin of the amputated penis, for instance, is stripped off and inserted into the artificial vaginal pouch. The tissues from the penis contain sensory nerve cells which may later on help in achieving orgasm.

After surgery there is a follow up period of about six months during which the "new" vagina must be dilated with a prosthetic device to prevent the artificial pouch from sealing itself. After this time, the male-to-female transsexual can function sexually as a female and have normal sexual relations with a man.

One of the problems experienced in male-to-female conversions results from the fact that the new vagina does not lubricate. Obviously, pregnancy, menstruation, and ovulation are impossible because surgical modifications were made on the external genitalia only. Presently, there is no way of artificially creating functional ovaries and Fallopian tubes.

Psychologically, male-to-female transsexuals tend to be more traditionally feminine than many contemporary women. They want to be housewives and mothers. Many male-to-female transsexuals fail to realize that womanhood is a gender phenomenon rather than a sexual one (Prince, 1978). It must be learned by living, whether by a natural-born female or by someone newly assigned to that status. Although sex conversion surgery can provide genital alterations in a man who wants to be a woman, it cannot construct a woman in the gender sense. The only possible route to such attainment is personal experience and social acceptance.

Working with male-to-female transsexual candidates for conversion surgery, Morgan (1978) pointed out that we might be fostering sex role stereotypes in a time when sexual

---

Changing from a man to a woman

Jan (originally James) Morris, a well-known British journalist published *Conundrum*, a highly sensitive and personal account of her life as a man and her subsequent alteration into a woman. She recalls that although her mother wished for a daughter, as a boy she was never treated as a girl. Nevertheless, all through her childhood Jan prayed to God to let him be a girl.

During World War II James (Jan) joined an English regiment and found himself paradoxically attracted to soldiering. He enjoyed this excursion into the male society but he knew that he could not stay. Aware of his irrational conviction of being a female, he was confused. How could he know how a woman felt? And what did he mean when he said he was feminine?

After he left the Army, Morris focused on self-exploration, finding reassurance in the discovery that other people experienced similar feelings. Morris "trod the long, well-beaten, expensive and fruitless path" to psychiatrists and sexologists. Some assured him that he would grow out of his wish to be a woman; others gave him urine or blood tests. He met with Dr. Benjamin, author of the *Transsexual Phenomenon* (1966), in New York. An endocrinologist, Dr. Benjamin believed that true transsexuals cannot be bullied, drugged, analyzed, or electrically shocked into an acceptance of their body. Morris arranged for a meeting with a physician in London but was apparently not ready for the sex reassignment surgery.

Meanwhile, back in England, he married and had five children. He described his marriage as open, since both he and his wife Elizabeth had their separate lives, chose their own friends, but enjoyed a very affectionate relationship with each other. Although he honored the unspoken obligation of his marriage, his longing to live as a woman grew stronger every year. For a period of over fifteen years the marriage looked like the perfect match from the outside. When the oldest children were in their late teens, Morris told some of his closest friends of his desire to have his sex changed. By the time he was in his late thirties, he loathed his maleness and resented any connection with the male sex. Between the years of 1964-1972 he took hormone pills, estimating that he had swallowed at least 12,000 pills over the eight-year period.

Hormone therapy produced gradual changes. Morris felt younger, "enjoying the dream of the ages, a second youth." His body changed with the waist becoming narrower, the hips broadening, and the breasts developing. Stripped of his clothes, he felt like a chimera, half-male and half-famale. For the next few years he pursued a double life, supposedly male in one place and female in another. It was a confusing time for those who knew him, some people only knew him as a male, others only as a female, and a few as both. With the help of his wife Morris was able to widen the range of his confidants.

The next step was to inform the State—Passport office, department of health and social security—and to have his name changed into Jan. Morris was legally divorced from his wife but redefined his relationship with Elizabeth as a sister-in-law. Telling the children was the hardest problem.

There remained the surgery. In 1972 Morris felt ready for the last hurdle and flew to Casablanca for the sex change operation. Upon return to England, Elizabeth welcomed him as though nothing in particular had happened.

After thirty-five years as a male, ten years in between, Jan at age forty-five experienced the fulfillment of a life's desire. She was a woman. Physically she was satisfied. She was treated as a woman and found herself more emotional and was "ludicrously susceptible to flattery." Family and close friends accepted her in her new identity:

> I suspect the only transsexuals who can really achieve happiness are those of the classic kind, the lifelong puzzlers, who offer no rational purpose for their compulsion, even to themselves, but are simply driven, helplessly toward the operating table.
>
> . . . Nothing I discovered has shaken my conviction and if I were trapped in that cage (the male body), nothing would keep me from my goal. I would search the earth for a surgeon, I would bribe barbers and abortionists, I would take a knife and do it myself, without fear, without calms, without second thought (Morris, 1974, p. 169).

stereotyping is not generally applauded. In other words, the stereotypic behavior pattern of the male-to-female transsexual may not be very adaptive at a time when androgyny (see Chapter 17) is promoted in our society.

The Female-to-Male Conversion. Female-to-male transformation surgery is less frequent and more problematic. Conversion of a woman into a man requires a complex surgical procedure and multiple hospital admissions which may literally take years.

The first step is again a hormone therapy program which involves the administration of androgen. Androgen suppresses menstruation, thickens the vocal cords enough for the voice to become masculine and effects a redistribution of body fat so that the woman's shoulders become broader and the hips narrower. The breasts and internal organs are removed and a scrotum is created from the labial tissues and filled with plastic testicles. The artificial penis is constructed in stages so that finally the clitoris becomes embedded in the penile tissue to retain the capacity for orgasm. At best, the penis is not very large or realistic. Although functional for urination, it is too soft for intercourse. Since the artificial penis cannot become erect to penetrate a vagina, it must be given artificial support. In general, the female-to-male sex conversion appears to be less satisfying aesthetically and sexually, as well as functionally.

Even though the transsexual may be able to convince him or herself completely of the efficacy of the transformation, the real test comes in everyday life and social relationships. A major problem faced by male-to-female as well as female-to-male transsexuals is living with a self-concept that is initially not supported by external cues. How very real the question of coherence and connected information becomes for transsexuals is evidenced by the following report:

> Changing my name was a big step. I had always thought of myself as Margie, not Michael. But when the court order was final and my social security card and my drivers license read Margaret instead of Michael, I was pleased. I had to change my last name too since my family had been vehement about the sex reassignment and had disavowed me. So there I was with a new name and a new identification and for a few days I felt on top of things. . . . I almost hoped a police would ask me for identification so I could show it. Then I started to look for a job and the first place I went they gave me a long form to fill out with places for schools, other jobs, medical history, etc. I froze. I just hadn't stopped to realize that I really did have a past and that a name change alone was nothing. My new name had no transcripts, no references, no award, no pension plan, nothing (Feinbloom, 1976, p. 236).

Although hundreds of sex transformations have been performed, little is known about the long-term postoperative adjustment. Female-to-male transsexuals are likely to drop their former social contacts after surgery and blend into conventional marriages, often with women who have been divorced. After sex change, female-to-male transsexuals usually adopt a traditional male middle-class value system: they are punctual, responsible, pay their bills, and hold steady jobs (Person and Ovesey, 1974).

Male-to-female transsexuals may remain publicly identified as transsexuals after the operation by becoming stage professionals or female impersonators. They are less likely to form stable marital relationships. Frequently, they are characterized by financial independability, lack of vocational goal directedness, transitory relationships with others, and frequent moves between rented rooms.

Although most people who undergo sex reassignment surgery report better personal and social adjustment, at least for the first several years after surgery, cases with poor outcome have also been reported. In one instance, a fifty-three-year-old biological male with a life-long history of gender confusion, although subjectively pleased with the surgery, developed a severe paranoid psychosis (Van Putten & Fawzy, 1976). He claimed that he did not regret the conversion but was disturbed because the surgeons did not turn him into "a gorgeous sexpot pursued and ravished by young Marines." Post operatively, he felt strange in women's clothes, was unable to pass convincingly as a woman and could not secure employment. In the streets he was ridiculed as an "old drag queen." He looked grotesque, was unable to carry himself in a feminine manner, and remained preoccupied with a hopeless quest for becoming a woman through further surgery.

Both psychoanalysts and learning theorists seem to agree that transvestism and transsexualism develop under circumstances in which a person is confused about which sex he or she belongs to. Typically, transsexuals claim for many years that they have the core gender identity of the opposite sex. Green

(1974) has been studying childhood recollections of adult transsexuals comparing them with the childhood memories of fifty young boys with normal anatomy who showed an unusually high degree of feminine behavior. In the case histories of the transsexuals, Green reported that the mother found her infant son unusually attractive and cuddly and fostered a mutually close relationship. The sons began to play with their mothers' clothing and jewelry imitating her. This behavior was reinforced because the mother thought it was cute. Later the father began to feel alienated from his son who refused to engage in rough and tumble play. As a result, the boy relied even more on the mother for guidance and intimacy. Girls became his main friends helping him to solidify his female interests and developing identity. It was usually between the ages of seven and nine that some other person, a teacher or neighbor, expressed concern because by that time many of the boys had developed a pattern of "playing at being girls" by crossdressing. Green suggested that the parents, especially the mother, showed an unusual degree of tolerance for the boy's developing sex role problem and, in fact, actively fostered it by allowing the child to dress in the clothing of the opposite sex.

Despite the plethora of explanations from various theoretical perspectives, the etiology of transsexualism remains unknown. Although some sex change candidates are flagrantly psychotic (Finney et al., 1975), in general transsexuals cannot be said to suffer mental disturbances which could account for their unconventional desire to have their sex changed to conform to the strongly held belief that they are of the opposite sex.

Modification of Unconventional Sexual Behavior

In the case of sexual variations the word "treatment" poses a problem because it implies that there is something wrong with the person that needs to be changed. Some individuals with certain forms of unconventional sexual behavior, however, may be quite satisfied with their sexual adjustment and have little or no motivation to be treated for it. Ethically speaking, the term treatment should be reserved for those people who *wish* to make certain changes in their sexual behavior or preferences. For people who engage in more deviant modes of sexual behavior, such as the rapist or the pedophile, the issue of treatment may involve forced participation in rehabilitation programs.

Psychodynamic Approaches

Essentially, psychodynamic approaches follow the classic psychoanalytic method. The theoretical basis for this approach rests on the assumption that people engaging in unconventional sexual expressions harbor repressed conflicts in the unconscious, are fixated at an earlier stage of psychosexual development or have not been successful in resolving the Oedipal conflict. These repressed conflicts, in turn, are sources of anxiety that interfere with sexual enjoyment.

Of particular importance is the essential transference relationship. According to psychoanalytic theory, the client is prone to develop erotic responses to the therapist. The therapist must be constantly on guard for such a possibility and muster his or her own resources to maintain the transference relationship without yielding to the sexual advances of the client (Meyer, 1975). The central task of the therapist is to help the client overcome his or her fears of rejection and disappointment which prevent the person from becoming involved in an intimate relationship. The anxiety evoked in such situations becomes a barrier to effective sexual responses. Traditional psychodynamic therapies have been successful in some cases where clients were strongly motivated to change their sexual behavior. Many of the sexual variations are highly refractory to psychodynamic intervention.

Behavioral Approaches

The methods used by behavior therapists have been found to be particularly adaptable to the modification of unconventional sexual behavior. The behavior therapist assumes that sexual behavior, whether conventional or unconventional, functional or dysfunctional, is learned. Consequently, it must be amenable to change through directed learning experiences which are the core of behavior therapy (Fischer and Gochros, 1977). Behavioral procedures for dealing with sexual variations have been found to be more effective and less time consuming than psychodynamic techniques.

From the wealth of available data demonstrating effective behavioral intervention, we have selected three different procedures to highly successful modification of problems involving unconventional sexual object choice, unconventional sexual activity, and gender disturbance.

Aversive Conditioning in a Case of Fetishism

Aversion therapy can take many forms and many aversive stimuli have been applied ranging from nausea-inducing drugs to unpleasant scenes presented in imagination. The most frequently used aversive stimulus is electric shock which is typically paired with some form of undesirable sexual behavior.

Kushner (1977) reported a case study of a thirty-three-year-old male with a fetish of twenty-one years' duration. The man recalled that his fetishistic behavior started at about age twelve, when he began masturbating while wearing women's panties that he usually took from clothes lines. If these were not available he masturbated while fantasizing about women wearing panties. As he grew

older he felt increasingly inadequate and unmasculine.

In therapy, electric shock was paired with a number of fetishistic stimuli. For example, a picture consisting of a rear view of a woman from the middle of the back to the knees wearing panties was presented; or an actual pair of panties was placed in the client's hands. Other stimuli involved imaginary situations in which the client was asked to picture himself wearing panties, imagining a clothes line with panties on it, and imagining himself standing in front of a lingerie shop.

The different fetishistic stimuli were presented, immediately followed by shock. The client was instructed to tolerate the shock until it became too uncomfortable and then signal for termination. After forty-one shock sessions (fourteen weeks of therapy) the client reported no longer being troubled by the fetish. He also indicated that he had more and more difficulty in eliciting fetishistic fantasies during his masturbation. The termination of aversive conditioning was coupled with reinforcement sessions and desensitization training to reduce the client's heterosexual anxieties. At the last report, the client enjoyed a full and satisfactory heterosexual life. Although he had occasional fleeting thoughts of the fetish or was reminded of it when exposed to advertisements or window displays, he had no difficulty thinking of other things.

The question of ethics is often raised in conjunction with electric shock. It should be noted that ethics in aversion therapy are no different from those in other forms of therapy, provided it is given with discretion and compassion and with the client's overall needs in mind (Marks, 1976).

Elimination of Sadistic Fantasies by Counterconditioning

In addition to overt sadomasochistic behavior in which sexual satisfaction is associated with inflicting pain upon someone else or having pain inflicted upon oneself, sado-masochistic tendencies may also be expressed in fantasies. Davison (1977) reported a case which utilized client-controlled masturbation sessions in which strong sexual feelings were paired with pictures and images of females in nonsadistic contexts.

The client in this case was a twenty-one-year-old unmarried college senior who described himself as a sadist. He masturbated about five times a week while having sadistic fantasies, specifically inflicting tortures on women. The client reported few heterosexual contacts, recalling having kissed only two girls in his life, with no sexual arousal accompanying these episodes.

The client was instructed to obtain an erection in the privacy of his dormitory room by whatever means possible—usually with a sadistic fantasy. He was then told to begin to masturbate while looking at the picture of a sexy nude woman such as the Playgirl of the Month. His sadistic fantasies were used only to gain an erection, after that he was to focus on the *Playboy* picture while masturbating to orgasm. The therapist impressed on him that he would only be able to eliminate his sadistic fantasies by associating sexual arousal with the female picture. The purpose of this procedure was to attach the client's sadistic fantasies and replace them by sexual arousal to heterosexual stimuli. At the end of therapy, the client had given up his sadistic fantasies and made some initial attempts to establish appropriate relationships with women.

Modification of Gender Identity in a Transsexual

Although no forms of psychological intervention have been shown to be consistently effective in transsexualism, behavior therapy seems to fare better than other approaches. Barlow, Reynolds, and Agras (1973) described the successful modification of sexual identity in the case of a transsexual. The client, a seventeen-year-old boy named Roger had thought of himself as a girl as long as he could remember. Willing to change his transsexual orientation, Roger agreed to the behavioral program after he was assured by the therapist that if this failed he could consider a sex-change operation.

Since his effeminate behavior was a source of much social ridicule, he was taught more masculine ways of sitting, standing, and walking by modeling, videotape feedback, and generous social reinforcement. During this phase of therapy, Roger had to role-play male appropriate social behaviors and was trained to speak in a deeper, more relaxed tone of voice. Nevertheless, his sexual urges and fantasies continued to be transsexual.

Modification of these sexual fantasies was the target of the next phase. Roger was shown pictures of nude females and sexual arousal to slides of women was conditioned. At that time, Roger had made progress toward being able to behave more like a male and began to have more heterosexual urges. At a one-year follow-up his sexual identity change had endured and he was going steady with a girlfriend.

While we do not wish to convey the impression that behavioral techniques are the panacea for all sexual problems, they have been found effective not only in increasing desired sexual responses but also in decreasing undesired sexual behaviors by eliminating fetishistic, transvestite, exhibitionistic and other forms of unconventional sexual behavior.

Summary

Unconventional forms of sexual behavior were the focus of this chapter. After considering a number of different views of normal and abnormal sexual behavior, we discussed the major sexual variations in terms of a threefold classification system: unconventional sex object choices, unconventional sexual activities and gender identity disturbances. The first category included pedophilia, zoophilia, incest, fetishism, and necrophilia. Unconventional sexual activities involved voyeurism, exhibitionism, and sadomasochism. We also presented rape as a violent crime in this category in which aggressive and sexual aims are mixed. At present, we cannot identify the rapist by social, motivational, or personality characteristics.

Under the category of gender identity disturbances, we subsumed to focus on unconventional sexual behavior, transvestism, and transsexualism. The transvestite enjoys wearing the apparel and likes to appear socially as a member of the opposite sex. The transsexual is a person who has undergone a sequence of developmental experiences which

result in the conviction that he or she really belongs to the opposite sex and that something must be done to confirm this conviction, namely hormonal and surgical sex change.

According to psychoanalytic theory, most of these unconventional sexual behaviors are interpreted as defenses against anxiety aroused by the idea of engaging in conventional heterosexual intercourse. Learning theorists often rely on a conditioning model. Both psychodynamic and behavioral approaches have been used in the modification of unconventional sexual behavior. Multifaceted behavioral procedures which combine aversive conditions with reconditioning to appropriate sexual objects or activities have been found particularly effective in many cases.

References

American Psychiatric Association. *Diagnostic and statistical manual of mental disorders* (2nd ed.). Washington, D.C.: American Psychiatric Association, 1968.

Amir, M. *Patterns of forcible rape.* Chicago: University of Chicago Press, 1971.

Amir, M. "Socio-cultural factors in forcible rape." In L. Gross (ed.), *Sexual behavior.* Flushing, NY.: Spectrum Publications, 1974.

Barlow, D., Reynolds, J., and Agras, S. "Gender identity change in a transsexual." *Archives of General Psychiatry*, 1973, 28, 569-579.

Benjamin, H. *The transsexual phenomenon.* New York: Julian Press, 1966.

Bond, J. and Hutchinson, H. "Application of reciprocal inhibition therapy to exhibitionism." In H. Eysenck (ed.), *Experiments in behavior therapy.* New York: Pergamon Press, 1964.

Brownmiller, S. *Against our will: Men, women, and rape.* New York: Simon & Schuster, 1975.

Bryant, C. (ed.). *Sexual deviance in social context.* New York: New Viewpoints, 1977.

Cohen, M., Seghorn, T., and Calmas, W. "Sociometric study of the sex offender," *Journal of Abnormal Psychology*, 1969, 74, 249-255.

Davison, G. "Elimination of a sadistic fantasy by a client-controlled counterconditioning technique." In J. Fischer and H. Gochros (eds.), *Handbook of behavior therapy with sexual problems.* New York: Pergamon Press, 1977.

DeRiver, J. *The sexual criminal: A psychoanalytic study.* Springfield, Ill.: C. C. Thomas, 1956.

Federal Bureau of Investigation (FBI). *Uniform crime reports.* Washington, D.C.: U.S. Department of Justice, November 19, 1975.

Feinbloom, D. *Transvestites and transsexuals.* New York: Delacorte Press, 1976.

Ferracuti, F. "Incest between father and daughter." In R. Friedman, R. Richart, and R. van de Wielde. (eds.), *Sex differences in behavior.* New York: John Wiley & Sons, 1974.

Finney, J., Brandsma, J., Tondow, M., and LeMaistre, B. "A study of trans-sexuals seeking gender reassignment." *American Journal of Psychiatry,* 1975, 132, 962-964.

Fischer, J. and Gochros, H. (eds.), *Handbook of behavior therapy with sexual problems.* New York: Pergamon Press, 1977.

Forward, S. and Buck, C. *Betrayal of innocence: Incest and its devastation.* New York: J. P. Tarcher, 1978.

Freud, S. "Three contributions to the theory of sex," 1905. In A. Brill (ed.), *The basic writings of Sigmund Freud.* New York: Modern Library, 1938.

Gagnon, J. *Human sexualities.* Glenview, Ill.: Scott, Foresman, 1977.

Gagnon, J. and Simon, W. "Sexual deviance in contemporary America." *Annals of the American Academy of Political and Social Science,* 1968, 376, 107-122.

Gebhard, P., Gagnon, J., Pomeroy, W., and Christenson, C. *Sex offenders.* New York: Harper & Row, 1965.

Green, R. *Sexual identity conflict in children and adults.* New York: Basic Books, 1974.

Griffin, S. "Rape: The all-American crime." *Ramparts,* 1971, 10, 3, 26-35.

Harrington, A. and Sutton-Simon, K. "Rape." In A. Goldstein, P. Monti, T. Sardino, and D. Green (eds.), *Police crisis intervention.* Kalamazoo, Mich.: Behaviordelia, 1977.

Hughes, G. "The crime of incest." *Journal of Criminal Law,* 1964, 55, 322-331.

Johnson, W. and Fretz, B. "What is sexual normality?" In L. Gross (ed.), *Sexual behavior.* Flushing, N.Y.: Spectrum Publications, 1974.

Kinsey, A., Pomeroy, W., and Martin, C. *Sexual behavior in the human male.* Philadelphia: W. B. Saunders, 1948.

Klein, H. "Masochism." *Medical Aspects of Human Sexuality,* 1972, 6, 11, 33-53.

Kushner, M. "The reduction of a longstanding fetish by means of aversive con-ditioning." In J. Fischer and H. Gochros (eds.), *Handbook of behavior therapy with sexual problems.* New York: Pergamon Press, 1977.

Lambley, P. "Treatment of transvestism and subsequent coital problems." *Behavior Therapy and Experimental Psychiatry,* 1974, 5, 101-102.

Lazarus, A. and Davison, G. "Clinical innovation in research and practice." In A. Bergin and S. Garfield (eds.), *Handbook of psychotherapy and behavior change: An empirical analysis.* New York: John Wiley & Sons, 1971.

Lustig, N., Dressee, L., Spellman, S., and Murray, T. "Incest: A family group survival pattern." *Archives of General Psychiatry*, 1966, 14, 34.

Marks, J. "Management of sexual disorders." In H. Leitenberg (ed.), *Behavior modification and therapy.* Englewood Cliffs, N.J.: Prentice-Hall, 1976.

Marmor, J. "Normal and deviant sexual behavior." *Journal of the American Medical Association*, 1971, 217, 2, 165-170.

Mathis, J. "The exhibitionist." *Medical Aspects of Human Sexuality*, 1969, 3, 6, 89-101.

McGuire, R., Carlisle, J., and Young, B. "Sexual deviations as conditioned behavior." *Behavior Research and Therapy*, 1965, 3, 21-43.

Meyer, J. "Individual psychotherapy of sexual disorders." In A. Freedman, H. Kaplan, and B. Sadock (eds.), *The comprehensive textbook of psychiatry* (Vol. 2). Baltimore: Williams and Wilkins, 1975.

Mohr, J., Turner, R., and Jerry, M. *Pedophilia and exhibitionism.* Toronto: University of Toronto Press, 1964.

Money, J. "Sex reassignment therapy in gender identity disorders." In R. Friedman, R. Richart, and R. van de Wielde (eds.), *Sex differences in behavior.* New York: John Wiley & Sons, 1974.

Money, J., Jobaris, R., and Furth, G. "Apotemnophilia: Two cases of self-demand amputation as a paraphilia." *Journal of Sex Research*, 1977, 13, 2, 115-125.

Morgan, J. "Psychotherapy for transsexual candidates." *Archives of Sexual Behavior*, 1978, 7, 4, 273-283.

Morris, J. *Conundrum.* New York: Harcourt Brace Jovanovich, 1974.

Person, E. and Ovesey, L. "The psychodynamics of male transsexualism." In R. Friedman, R. Richart and R. van de Wielde (eds.), *Sex differences in behavior.* New York: John Wiley & Sons, 1974.

Poznanski E. and Blos, P. "Incest." *Medical Aspects of Human Sexuality*, 1975, 9, 10, 46-76.

Prince, V. "Transsexuals and pseudo-transsexuals." *Archives of Sexual Behavior*, 1978, 7, 4, 263-272.

Prince, V. and Bentler, P. "Survey of 504 cases of transvestism." *Psychological Bulletin*, 1972, 31, 903-917.

Rada, R. *Clinical aspects of the rapist.* New York: Grune & Stratton, 1978.

Reinhardt, J. *Perversions and sex crimes.* Springfield, Ill.: C. C. Thomas, 1957.

Renshaw, D., and Renshaw, R. "Incest." *Journal of Sex Education and Therapy*, 1977, 3, 2, 3-7.

Rhinehart, J. "Genesis of overt incest." *Comprehensive Psychiatry*, 1961, 2, 338.

Socarides, C. *Beyond sexual freedom*. New York: New York Times Book Co., 1975.

Stoller, R. *Sex and gender*. New York: Science House, 1968.

Van Putten, T. and Fawzy, I. "Sex conversion in a man with severe gender dysphoria." *Archives of General Psychiatry*, 1976, 33, 751-753.

Weinberg, S. *Incest behavior*. New York: Citadel Press, 1955.

Weiner, S. "Incest: A survey." *Excerpta Criminologica*, 1962, 4, 607.

Chapter 16

Homosexuality

Perhaps no other aspect of human sexual behavior is as controversial today as homosexuality. For large segments of our society, homosexuality is severely condemned as being sexually abnormal, perverted, or a sign of mental illness (Weinberg and Williams, 1974). On the other hand, there are those who believe people are not truly liberated until they can have homosexual as well as heterosexual relations. For example, in a book written for women, feminist sex counselor Carmen Kerr (1977) discusses the pros and cons of homosexual relationships. She suggests that a woman loving another woman can open up a whole new world of sexual intimacy.

It is often the case that those engaged in the debate of the relative merits of homosexuality and heterosexuality do not base their arguments on scientific knowledge. The issue is a value-laden one, and everyone's opinion of homosexuality is influenced to some degree by his or her emotional reaction to the subject. However, an understanding of the biological, psychological, and sociological forces that shape our sexual behavior can help us to arrive at a more rational view of homosexuality. This chapter will explore these issues.

Homosexual Behavior

Homosexuality can be defined as having an erotic attraction to, and engaging in sexual behavior with, a member of the same sex. The term homosexual, however, tends to be misleading because it implies that people can be placed into nice, neat categories when in fact these categories apply only to a relatively small segment of the population. The terms homosexual and heterosexual suggest an all-or-none phenomenon. That is, a person must be one or the other. The evidence strongly suggests that this view is not justified.

Kinsey was one of the first researchers to document the fact that human sexuality is not an all-or-none phenomenon. His findings suggested that homosexuality could be viewed on a seven-point continuum with exclusive heterosexuals at one end and exclusive homosexuals at the other end. Individuals who engaged in both homosexual and heterosexual behavior would fall somewhere between the extremes depending upon the relative degree of each type of behavior.

Psychiatrist Judd Marmor (1976) has also addressed the problem of defining homosexuality. He has argued that any simple definition fails to do justice to the variety of motivations that are associated with such behavior. It is misleading to apply the same label to the person who is exclusively homosexual by choice and the person who engages in homosexual behavior because members of the opposite sex are not available. Other people may have occasional homosexual relations out of loneliness, boredom, or curiosity. Certainly the differences between these three types of individuals are every bit as important as the similarities. These important differences are obscured if the term homosexual is applied in every case. The diversity of the homosexual experience has led to the suggestion that the terms homosexual and homosexuality be applied only to the behavior of an individual at one particular moment (Bell, 1976).

Incidence of Homosexuality

The first serious data presented regarding the incidence of homosexuality were those of Alfred Kinsey. He reported that 37 percent of all men, 3 percent of married women, and 26 percent of single women had at least one homosexual experience. These figures, particularly those for males, were among the most shocking to the American public of all of his findings. People interpreted this to mean that more than one-third of all males had homosexual tendencies. It did not, however, mean this at all. Many of the homosexual experiences were isolated events that had occurred during childhood. In fact, if only those experiences that had occurred beyond the age of fifteen were included, the 37 percent figure drops to 25 percent. Thus, Kinsey included in his homosexual category numerous men who had one childhood experience and were subsequently exclusively heterosexual. The 25 percent figure is also misleading because it includes those men who had "definite responses" to homosexual stimuli but no overt homosexual activity. In fact, only about 10 percent of Kinsey's males were "more or less exclusively homosexual" for a period of at least threee years.

Current data regarding the incidence of homosexuality are difficult to come by because of the problems associated with sampling. Based upon several sources, the best estimates seem to be that from 1 to 3 percent of males are "more or less" exclusive homosexuals and another 3 to 7 percent of men have at least occasional homosexual experiences (Bieber et al., 1962; Hunt, 1974). Data for women are even more obscure because considerably less research has been done with female homosexuality. Hunt did report that 3 percent of single women and slightly less than 1 percent of married women had had at least one homosexual encounter one year prior to the survey. These figures may be one to two percentage points low because no attempt was made to include homosexual organizations or the homosexual underground. It is of significance, however, that unlike increases in other forms of sexual behavior (for example, premarital sex), no researchers have reported an increase in homosexuality since the publication of Kinsey's data.

Homosexual Practices

Homosexual men and women engage in virtually the same sexual activities that heterosexual couples do with the obvious exception of penile-vaginal intercourse. Kissing, open-mouth kissing, petting, mutual masturbation, and oral-genital stimulation are all common male and female homosexual activities. Anal intercourse among men and breast stimulation among women are additional practices that afford pleasure. In short, the range of homosexual practices is just as diverse as heterosexual practices within the limitations imposed by anatomy.

There are a number of misconceptions regarding homosexuality that deserve attention. The first concerns the popular belief that homosexuals can be readily identified by their mannerisms and dress. The stereotype of the man who is "effeminate" or "swishy" and the woman who is described as a "dyke" or "butch" simply do not apply to the majority of homosexuals. Of course, these terms are accurate for a small proportion of gays, but these individuals are often as unappreciated by other homosexuals as they are by the general population. Most homosexuals look and behave no differently from heterosexual people.

Terms such as "queen" and "butch" suggest that homosexuals adopt sex roles within a relationship. That is, it is commonly believed that within a homosexual relationship one person prefers the passive, feminine role and the other adopts a more active masculine role. Again, although this may be true of a minority of cases, most homosexuals enjoy a variety of sexual activities and do not restrict themselves to behaviors characteristic of one sex or the other (Marmor, 1976).

One important difference between males and females who engage in homosexuality is that men tend to have more sexual partners than women. Men are much more likely to have numerous homosexual contacts; women are more likely to engage in homosexuality within the context of a long-term relationship. In a research study funded by the Kinsey Institute, it was found that 40 percent of gay men had more than five hundred partners. The majority of women had fewer than ten partners over a lifetime (Bell and Weinberg, 1978). This difference between the sexes is reflected in the much broader opportunities for men for making homosexual contacts in public places. Virtually every large city has gay bars, certain public baths, public restrooms, streets, and parks that are frequented by men who are interested in making a homosexual contact. The available meeting places for female homosexuals are much more limited.

This difference between male and female homosexual patterns may simply reflect a general difference regarding views of sex and relationships. Men are thought to feel that "sex for sex's sake" is an acceptable option whereas women are thought to believe that sex should be only one aspect of a deeper relationship. These values influence the nature of men's and women's homosexual, as well as heterosexual relationships (Freedman, 1971). After all, people are men and women first, and homosexuals second.

Theories of Homosexuality

In some respects it is misleading to discuss "theories of homosexuality." By asking what causes homosexuality, one is accepting the implication that homosexuality is somehow qualitatively different from heterosexuality. Although this may be so, many theorists, beginning with Freud, have argued that all human beings are born with the potential to be homosexual or heterosexual. At least one writer has suggested that every sexually responsive individual has the capacity to respond erotically to every other sexually responsive individual (Tripp, 1976). This view of humans as pansexual creatures suggests that the exclusive homosexual and the exclusive heterosexual are on different ends of the same continuum. Thus, rather than asking what causes homosexuality, it might be more

productive to identify those factors responsible for sexual behavior in general. With this caveat in mind, let us review the available evidence.

Virtually all of the evidence to be discussed in this section concerns homosexuality in men. Although the issue of homosexual behavior in women is certainly as important, there is very little in the literature concerning women. This bias began with Freud who explored male homosexuality in detail and paid relatively little attention to women. The bias continues today. Perhaps future researchers will attend to the issue of sexual orientation in women in greater detail.

Biological Theories

One view of homosexuality is that such individuals differ from heterosexuals either genetically or physiologically. The genetic theory has received support from Kallman (1952) who found that the concordance rate for homosexuality in identical twins was 100 percent whereas for fraternal twins the corresponding figure was only 8 percent. These figures would seem to offer strong support for a genetic basis for homosexuality, but serious questions have been raised regarding Kallman's methodology. Kallman is best known for his data suggesting that there is a genetic component to schizophrenia. However, data collected with modern research methods have indicated that Kallman grossly overestimated the importance of genetics. If recent data were available for homosexuality, it is likely that the same conclusion would be reached; namely, that Kallman's results cannot be accepted uncritically. In fact, other investigators have reported cases in which only one monozygotic twin was homosexual (Kolb, 1963).

Two other considerations make the genetic view unlikely. If homosexuality were transmitted by a recessive gene, it should have died out long ago since it seems safe to assume homosexuals marry and reproduce at a lower rate than heterosexuals. Additionally, most hereditary diseases have a prevalence rate in the neighborhood of 1 in 10,000. The prevalence rate for exclusive homosexual males is at least 200 in 10,000.

A second group of biological theories suggests that hormonal imbalances are an important factor in determining homosexuality. At least two studies have found hormonal differences between homosexuals and heterosexuals (Margolese, 1970; Kolodny et al., 1971). However, at least six others have failed to find such a difference (c.f. Meyer-Bahlburg, 1977). If hormones do play a role, their mechanisms are quite complex and far from understood. It has been found, for example, that administering androgens to male homosexuals does increase their sex drive but has no effect on their sexual orientation (Ford and Beach, 1951). Also, illness and physical and emotional stress can result in hormonal imbalances (Rose et al., 1969). So it is impossible to conclude which comes first, the hormonal imbalance or the homosexual behavior.

The most intriguing biological theory is that prenatal hormones can influence one's sexual orientation. This point of view has been summarized by John Money (1977) who argues that the fetal brain is either masculinized or feminized, depending on the hormones to which it is exposed. Thus, hormonal imbalances in the mother in the early months of pregnancy may play a role in sexual orientation. This hypothesis has received some support in animal studies (Clemens, 1974; Ward, 1972), but it is always impossible to know to what extent we can generalize from animal research to human behavior. It must be pointed out that although Money suspects that prenatal hormones may predispose individuals to certain sexual orientations, he believes that environmental factors play the major role.

The evidence regarding biological theories of homosexuality is tenuous at best. The most logical conclusion is that the evidence is sufficient to warrant further investigation, but it by no means conclusively demonstrates a relationship between biological factors and sexual orientation. The notion of hormones and the prenatal brain is particularly intriguing, but even if this hypothesis were to receive further support, it seems extremely unlikely that it could account for all homosexual behavior. Perhaps future research will demonstrate that biological factors are important in some small percentage of cases of homosexuality.

Psychological Theories

The focus of most psychological theories is the relationship between the parents and the child. Freud was among the first to report that homosexual males tend to have weak, ineffectual, or absent fathers and frustrating mothers. In an intensive study of males, psychoanalyst Irving Bieber and his colleagues came to much the same conclusion (Bieber et al., 1962). They reported that the most significant factor in the backgrounds of homosexuals was a constellation of a detached, hostile father and a seductive mother who dominates and minimizes her husband. They did conclude, however, that a truly loving father will preclude the development of homosexuality regardless of the mother's characteristics. Although most psychological theorists recognize the importance of parental characteristics, the mechanism by which these factors operate is open to question. We shall explore the alternative explanations offered by social-learning theory and psychoanalysis shortly.

The notion of a weak father and seductive mother as a determinant of sexual orientation cannot be accepted uncritically. First, this finding is based mostly on the reports of homosexuals seen in therapy. These individuals may not be representative of homo-

SEXUAL BEHAVIOR AND RELATIONSHIPS

Figure 16.1
Some theorists believe that a close affectionate relationship between father and son precludes the possibility of the son developing a homosexual orientation. (Freedman)

sexuals in general and one cannot be sure if their recollections of their parents' behavior are accurate. Second, many heterosexual men come from families with the homosexual constellation. In fact, the strong mother/absent father pattern is characteristic of urban black families and there is no evidence that the incidence of homosexuality is greater for black males than for whites. This would suggest that this particular family constellation may contribute to, but is not sufficient in itself to cause, homosexuality.

Psychoanalytic View. Psychoanalytic theorists suggest that the origins of homosexuality lie in the Oedipal conflict (see Chap-

ter 4). The failure to resolve this psychosexual conflict results in castration anxiety. Otto Fenichel (1945), a widely respected psychoanalyst, has suggested that the sight of female genitals elicits anxiety in homosexuals for two reasons. First, the sight of a person without a penis activates repressed fears of castration. Second, castration anxiety may cause the vagina to be perceived as an instrument capable of biting or tearing off the penis.

Fenichel also believes that homosexuals continue to be influenced by their "normal biological longing for women." But since they cannot tolerate creatures without a penis, they settle for "phallic women." That is, boys with feminine and girlish traits.

The notion that male homosexuals prefer effeminate partners has been described as patently false by several experts in the field (Freedman, 1971; Hoffman, 1977). A majority of homosexuals prefer masculine-appearing partners. Effeminate men are often viewed with disdain. Hoffman has concluded that there are a number of kinds of homosexuality and although psychoanalytic explanations may apply in some cases, there are many individuals to whom their principles simply do not apply.

Social Learning View. Social learning theorists also recognize the importance of the parent-child relationship but offer a quite different explanation for its contribution to homosexuality. The crucial element is that the weak, ineffectual father or the absence of the father fails to provide an appropriate model for the young boy. If an inadequate male model is coupled with a domineering, seductive mother who encourages and reinforces effeminate behavior in her son, then a homosexual orientation may result (Bandura, 1969).

A second learning explanation involves masturbatory conditioning (McGuire, Carlisle, and Young, 1965). There are three crucial elements to this hypothesis. First, as a result of unpleasant heterosexual experiences or feelings of inadequacy, the individual comes to believe that he or she cannot achieve a "normal" sexual life. Second, the individual has some sexual experience, that although not sufficient to produce a sexual variation in itself, does suggest fantasy material for masturbation. Third, and most crucial, as the person repeatedly masturbates to this fantasy material, the erotic value of the material gradually increases.

To illustrate how this process may operate, imagine an adolescent boy who tends to be rejected by girls his own age. Such a boy may have a homosexual encounter with one of his peers. Because he experienced pleasure from the encounter, and because he has had no comparable experience with girls, he may begin to fantasize about his male partner during masturbation. After several months or years of such activity, he may have developed a definite preference for homosexual relations. This scenario is highly speculative, but it certainly merits research attention.

The social learning theories appear highly plausible, but for the most part they remain to be confirmed by objective studies. It would seem, too, that there are many phenomena that are difficult if not impossible to understand in learning terms. If it is true that the longer the pleasure afforded by orgasm is associated with certain stimuli the more important those stimuli become, then we could expect that one's sexual preferences would be relatively stable. However, there are many examples in the literature of people who identify themselves as homosexuals for a long period of time and then, abruptly, develop a preference for heterosexual relations. The reverse situation can also occur. Considerations such as these would seem to suggest that other factors must be operating.

Cross-Cultural Views

Evidence gathered by sociologists and cultural anthropologists does not really suggest causes of homosexuality, but it does indicate that the prevalence and practice of homosexuality are influenced by the norms of a particular group. The first important observation to be made is that there are no known cases of societies in which heterosexuality is not the norm (Beach, 1977). In all societies that have been studied, heterosexuality is the preferred pattern for most people most of the time. Nonetheless, there are wide variations in views and practices regarding homosexuality.

In their survey of numerous societies, Ford and Beach (1951) found that of seventy-six societies, 36 percent disapproved of homosexuality and reported such activity to be rare or nonexistent. The remaining 64 percent sanctioned some forms of homosexuality. As just one example, the East Bay people of Papua-New Guinea encourage adolescent boys to engage in homosexual activities such as mutual masturbation and anal intercourse. Once they marry, they are expected to be exclusively heterosexual. However, there are cultural traditions that require occasional extended separations from their wives. During these periods it is considered acceptable to have a sexual relationship with a young boy. Such a liaison can be formed only if the boy's father gives his permission, and the boy expects to receive small presents from time to time (Davenport, 1977).

Sociological research has suggested that the preferences for certain types of activities may differ from group to group. For example, in one study it was found that 90 percent of Mexican homosexuals preferred anal intercourse over other activities. This percentage is much higher than is found in American homosexuals (Carrier, 1971). A study of an English homosexual community revealed that a preferred method of achieving ejaculation was for one partner to rub his penis against his partner's body without penetrating a body orifice (Schofield, 1965). In contrast, American homosexuals consider this practice to be somewhat immature (Hoffman, 1977). No one has attempted to explain why these national differences exist, but they illustrate that cultural norms can influence sexual practices.

The importance of the cross-cultural research lies in demonstrating that our attitudes and beliefs regarding homosexuality are shaped by the society in which we live. The prevailing view in the United States of homosexuality as indicating moral degeneracy, sexual deviation or mental illness actually places us in the minority. The cross-cultural data would seem to demonstrate that the view that exclusive heterosexuality is the only "normal" or "healthy" form of sexual activity is not valid.

Conclusion

Perhaps the best way to summarize our knowledge regarding the causes of homosexuality is to quote psychologist Martin Hoffman (1977) who has stated, ". . . we do not know its etiology" (p. 175). It is probable that a variety of forces must act together if a person is to develop a homosexual orientation. These forces are, to some extent known, but it is not known how they interact with one another. We have not reached the point where one, with any certainty, could design an environment that resulted in a specific sexual orientation.

Homosexuality and Adjustment

There are two primary issues concerning homosexuality and adjustment. The first concerns whether homosexual behavior itself is a form of psychological disturbance or whether it falls within the normal range of the human sexual experience. The illness or psychological disturbance theory has traditionally been a popular view in our society. Two major

arguments for this position are based on psychoanalytic theory and the notion that homosexuality is biologically abnormal.

The evidence discussed above should be sufficient to discount the biologically abnormal argument. Many societies sanction homosexuality and their members engage in it with no apparent conflict. In the animal world, virtually all species display homosexual patterns on occasion. Judd Marmor (1976) has pointed out that all civilized human behavior, from the cutting of hair to the cooking of food, is a departure from the strictly natural. One certainly does not label religious figures as mentally ill because their celibacy is not biologically normal. Marmor contends that the biological argument is simply a rationalization for our society's moral disapproval of homosexuality.

Interestingly, Freud (1951) did not consider homosexuality to be a form of mental illness. In a letter written to a mother of a homosexual he stated:

> Homosexuality is assuredly no advantage, but is nothing to be ashamed of, no vice, no degradation; it cannot be classified as an illness.

Nonetheless, most psychoanalytic theorists do view it as an illness. This view is based on the assumption that while the "normal" heterosexual progresses through the various psychosexual stages and arrives at the genital stage, the psychological development of the homosexual is arrested in one of the early developmental periods. The view of homosexuality as an illness was reflected in the official classification system published by the American Psychiatric Association (APA) until 1973. At that time the membership of the APA voted to remove homosexuality per se from the classification system and to include it under the category of sexual orientation disturbance. This category includes those homosexuals who have conflicts regarding their sexuality. Thus, homosexuals who are satisfied with their orientation and have no conflicts about it no longer have a place in the classification system.

The issue is by no means settled,however. Irvin Bieber, who has conducted extensive research on homosexuality, maintains that homosexuality does belong in psychiatric manuals. He is strongly supportive of guaranteeing homosexuals their civil rights, and feels that homosexual acts between consenting adults should be legalized. However, he does argue that homosexuality is a variation that results from a disturbance in heterosexual development. That is, he does not accept the view that homosexuality is at one end of a continuum of "normal" sexual behavior.

The issue comes down to a matter of values. There is really no way of proving or disproving whether homosexuality reflects a psychological disturbance. The point that many gay activists and mental health professionals make is that if homosexuality is labeled as a psychiatric disturbance, justification is provided for discriminating against homosexuals. It is our opinion that behavioral scientists should not provide that justification in the absence of conclusive evidence.

Psychological Adjustment of Homosexuals

An issue related to the subject of whether homosexuality per se is a psychological disturbance is whether homosexuals are more disturbed in general than heterosexuals. Once again, conventional wisdom has suggested that the answer is yes. Although views have been changing in recent years, most mental health professionals have maintained that homosexuals are more poorly adjusted in a variety of ways than are heterosexuals. This view came about because opinions regarding the mental health of homosexuals were based largely on therapists' observa-

tions of their homosexual clients, and a homosexual who seeks psychotherapy is likely to have psychological problems. Just as it is unfair to make statements about the mental health of heterosexuals based on heterosexuals seen in psychotherapy, it is unfair to generalize from homosexuals in therapy to the general homosexual population.

There is a fair amount of objective research that has compared psychological adjustment of homosexuals and heterosexuals. Unfortunately, much of the evidence is contradictory and hence it is difficult to arrive at any definite conclusions. If one is to look for trends, however, it would seem that male homosexuals may tend to have more problems of adjustment than male heterosexuals. It must be pointed out that several studies fail to find any differences in overall adjustment (Hooker, 1957; Dean and Richardson, 1964). Additionally, most studies conclude that male homosexuals are a very heterogeneous group. It includes both extremely well adjusted and extremely poorly adusted individuals. The Kinsey Institute survey concluded that relatively large numbers of homosexual males are as well adjusted as heterosexuals. Some 40 percent of their sample accounted for much of the psychological disturbance found in the homosexual sample (Bell and Weinberg, 1978). This survey also found that those male homosexuals who were in stable relationships were significantly better adjusted than gays without such a relationship.

The pattern of results concerning female homosexuals is noticeably different. In a review of this topic, psychologist David Lester (1975) concluded that "female homosexuals do not appear to be any more psychologically disturbed than female heterosexuals" (p. 121). In fact, several studies have found just the opposite. Freedman (1971) reported that although there were no differences in psychological adjustment between homosexual and heterosexual women, the homosexual women were functioning significantly better in such areas as work adjustment and self-acceptance. A second study reported that the only difference between the two groups was that the homosexual women were somewhat more self-confident than their heterosexual counterparts (Thompson, McCandless, and Strickland, 1971). The Kinsey data indicated that although the two groups of women were highly similar in overall adjustment, the gay women were somewhat more prone to thoughts of suicide.

It should not be surprising to learn that homosexuality in males may be associated with psychological disturbance. While one cannot be certain as to which comes first, the homosexual behavior or the psychological disturbance, it seems safe to assume that society places tremendous pressures on homosexuals. It may be these pressures that produce the psychological disturbances rather than homosexuality per se. Several theorists have suggested that homosexuals, particularly males, are similar to other minority groups (Hoffman, 1977; Hooker, 1957). They are the victims of prejudice. It is difficult indeed for the male homosexual to feel good about himself when society continually tells him he is immoral, a degenerate, or mentally ill.

The loneliness and apparent inability to form lasting, intimate relationships among many male homosexuals may be a result of the pressures generated by societal standards. Martin Hoffman argues that a social prohibition operates to prevent feelings of closeness between men. Sexual arousal may be sufficient to overcome the prohibitions against genital contact, but the arousal is not sufficient to overcome the prohibitions against intimacy. Because of these social prohibitions, many homosexuals cannot escape feelings of guilt—either conscious or unconscious—about their sexual behavior. These guilt feelings are bound to interfere with and contaminate a long-term relation-

ship. Thus, Hoffman argues that male homosexuals are promiscuous because society forces them into this type of behavior.

It is significant to note that society does not have the same prohibitions against intimacy between women, and gay women appear to have little difficulty in establishing stable, long-term relationships. Living together, sharing personal feelings, and physical displays of affection in public in women are all considered acceptable. Thus, gay women are not subjected to the same pressures that gay men are. This difference is reflected in the data presented above that indicated that gay women are as well adjusted as heterosexual women and perhaps more so in some areas.

In summary, there is no evidence that having sexual relations with members of one's own sex will result in psychological disturbance. Many homosexual individuals function at very high levels. A list of politicians, scientists, artists, authors, athletes, and the like, who are homosexual would be enough to convince even the most skeptical that engaging in homosexual behavior does not prevent outstanding personal achievement. It may be society's attitudes toward homosexuals that lead them to have psychological disturbances.

Coming Out

Individuals who think of themselves as homosexuals must decide if they will keep their sexual orientation secret or if they will openly present themselves as homosexual. The process of doing the latter is referred to as "coming out"—of the closet. This decision has important implications for the psychological well-being of the individual. The advantages are that one can receive much psychological support from the gay community and need no longer face the fear of discovery. The disadvantage is that there is the very real possibility of rejection and discrimination. Many parents are unable to accept their

Figure 16.2
Homosexuals are becoming more assertive in demanding their rights.
(Mimi Forsyth, Monkmeyer Press Photo Service)

child's homosexuality. Former friends are apt to react differently toward the individual who announced that he or she is gay. And there still is the chance that gays will lose their jobs once their sexual orientation is known. These factors make the decision to come out a difficult one indeed.

At present there is little scientific evidence available to help the homosexual make a decision. There is a fair amount of anecdotal evidence that implies that coming out can be a vehicle for personal growth (Jay and Young, 1975); however, objective information is badly needed in this area. It is hoped that society will become more accepting so that homosexuals need not pay such a high price for making their self-identity known.

Bisexuality

The concept of bisexuality has been brought to the attention of the layperson and

scientist alike only recently. Although Freud wrote around the turn of the century, that humans are bisexual creatures and Kinsey presented data in the late 1940s warning against the tendency to categorize individuals as either homosexual or heterosexual, it was not until the 1970s that bisexuality began to receive serious attention. James McCary, who published the first widely used college textbook on human sexuality in 1967, made no mention whatsoever of bisexuality.

The neglect of this phenomenon seems to be a result of the popular belief that people are in fact either homosexual or heterosexual. The individual who engages in both types of behavior is often thought to be denying his or her "true nature." Many people just cannot believe that a person can find pleasure in both kinds of relationships. Among the disbelievers are mental health professionals. Psychoanalyst Irving Bieber (1976) has stated that homosexuality and heterosexuality are two distinct categories and do not belong on the same continuum. According to this view, it is not possible to fall somewhere in the middle. Nonetheless, a considerable number of people do engage in sexual relations with members of both sexes. Categorizing sexual orientation as an either/or phenomenon is misleading.

The term bisexual is misleading as well. It suggests that individuals divide their attentions to homosexual and heterosexual relationships about equally and derive approximately equal levels of pleasure from both. Although this may be true of some individuals, it does not apply to most. Some individuals may behave in an exclusively homosexual fashion for several years and then shift to heterosexual patterns; many others may show the opposite pattern. Others who label themselves bisexual may be involved in a stable heterosexual marriage, but will have occasional, brief homosexual affairs. The variations in bisexual behavior are infinite.

It is also likely that the person who experiences sex with both men and women has quite different perceptions and reactions to the different experiences. For example, many of the men in Laud Humphrey's study who were observed having sex with other men in public restrooms were married. It would be simplistic to believe that because sexual arousal and orgasm were involved in both situations that the nature of the experience was the same. To the bisexual, comparing homosexual relations with heterosexual relations may be like trying to compare apples and oranges. This difference is reflected in the following quotation:

> I'm straight, but I need outlets when I'm away from home and times like that. And its easier to get with men than women. So I go into the park, or a rest station on the highway and get a man to blow me. I would never stay the night with one of them, or get to know them. It's just a release. It's not like sex with my wife. It's just a way to get what you need without making it a big deal.

And it feels less like cheating (Blumstein and Schwartz, 1977, p. 39).

The nature of bisexuality is made even more complex by the fact that often there is not always a close correspondence between one's self-identity and one's behavior. In a study of 156 men and women who had sexual experiences with members of both sexes, sociologists Philip Blumstein and Pepper Schwartz (1976, 1977) identified many instances of this inconsistency. One woman who was mainly heterosexual in her behavior labeled herself as a bisexual even though she had only two brief homosexual experiences and these had occurred ten years earlier. A second woman who had extremely limited heterosexual experiences and was in love with and living with another woman labeled herself as bisexual.

Another group of individuals think of themselves as either homosexual or heterosexual even though their behavior is best described as bisexual. For instance, the man quoted above was married and had frequent homosexual contacts and he thought of himself as heterosexual. Several women who labeled themselves as lesbians would occasionally have sex with a man with whom they felt an emotional rapport.

Blumstein and Schwartz also pointed out that a person's self-identity is not always predictive of his or her future behavior. One of their most dramatic examples involved a young professional woman who referred to herself as "purely and simply gay." As a child she routinely initiated sex play with her girlfriends. In adolescence she experienced a brutal sexual assault by a group of boys. She claimed that these two experiences led her to become a lesbian ten years prior to the interview. A year later the authors received a letter from this woman. She reported that she was in love with a man and intended to marry him. There were many other cases where reversals occurred. People might be exclusively homosexual for a number of years, then marry, and, then, perhaps ten to fifteen years later, obtain a divorce and enter into a homosexual relationship. These examples are of interest not only because they illustrate the nature of bisexuality but they also illustrate the nature of sexuality in general. One's sexual orientation is simply not the stable characteristic we once thought it was.

One finding of Blumstein and Schwartz that was of particular interest was that many individuals who were exclusively homosexual could not accept the concept of bisexuality. Especially in the case of gay women, bisexuals tended to be viewed as "fence-sitters." They were seen as denying and failing to come to terms with their homosexual natures. This places bisexuals in a particularly difficult situation. Although a small segment

---

The Problem of Gay Rights

While behavioral scientists are debating about the nature and causes of homosexuality, in recent years society has had to face the issue of the rights of homosexuals. The controversy associated with this issue is clearly illustrated in two recent referenda held at opposite ends of the country.

In mid-1977, voters in the Miami area of Florida were faced with the decision whether to repeal a law prohibiting discrimination on the basis of sexual orientation. Earlier in the year an ordinance was passed that prohibited discrimination against homosexuals in housing, employment, and public accommodations. Anita Bryant, entertainer and orange juice representative, was a prime force in initiating the referendum. While she reported that she was tolerant of homosexuality, she expressed concern that the ordinance made it possible for admitted homosexuals to teach in the school systems. She believed that since teachers serve as models for children, gay teachers could make the homosexual lifestyle seem appealing. Gay rights activists countered with the argument that sexual orientation was determined by the age of three to five (a belief that not all behavioral scientists hold) and so it was unlikely that homosexual teachers could influence children in school to adopt a homosexual orientation. They also pointed out, with justification, that heterosexual teachers were much more likely to molest children than were homosexual teachers.

On the West Coast, California voters were faced with Proposition 6 entitled the "School Employees. Homosexuality. Initiative Statute." If passed, this initiative would make it possible to dismiss any teacher who engaged in "public homosexuality" or "public homosexual conduct" which included encouraging private or public homosexual activity "directed at, or likely to come to the attention of school children and/or other employees." This was of particular concern to gay rights advocates because it meant that homosexual teachers would have to live in fear that their sexual orientation would be discovered.

Both campaigns were highly emotional and violence was not uncommon. But they did not do much to clarify society's position on gay rights. The gay rights advocates won in California but lost in Florida. It is difficult to assess what these results mean, but it would seem safe to say that they indicate that many people are confused about the nature and meaning of homosexuality.

of the general population may be tolerant and accepting of bisexuality, the majority of heterosexuals and many homosexuals view the bisexuals with disdain. The gay community and gay organizations are able to provide support for homosexual individuals so that they will have a means for maintaining their self-esteem. Unfortunately, such support systems for the bisexual do not for the most part exist.

Treatment of the Homosexual

The treatment of homosexuality is an extremely controversial topic. It implies that homosexuality is abnormal and thus requires treatment. As we have discussed earlier, many experts feel that homosexuality falls within the range of normal sexual behavior. This position would suggest that it is no more appropriate to discuss treatment programs for homosexuality than it would be for heterosexuality.

This point of view is well summarized by behavior therapist Gerald Davison (1976, 1978). Davison has stated that he would not agree to attempt to change a homosexual man's or homosexual woman's sexual orientation even if the individual voluntarily sought such help. His point is that homosexual individuals who profess an interest in changing their sexual orientation are probably motivated by the pressures brought to bear by a prejudiced and ignorant society. He asks whether a homosexual's request for therapy can ever be "voluntary" when that individual has been called "queer" and "faggot" by peers, a "sinner" by religious authorities, and "mentally ill" by college instructors. Even if a therapist assures such an individual that he or she is not "sick," the reassurances are not likely to be convincing if the therapist subsequently outlines an array of techniques that can be used in eliminating homosexual feelings and behavior. In sum, Davison suggests

that if therapists really believe that homosexual behavior is not pathological as many profess they do, then they should refuse to treat such behavior. The biases of therapists are made obvious by the fact that no one has devised treatment programs designed to help the heterosexual person become either bisexual or homosexual.

The opposite point of view is expressed by Bieber (1976). As stated earlier in the chapter, Bieber believes that homosexuality is a form of pathology and thus requires treatment. He does recognize that many homosexuals have no desire to change and he would not impose therapy on them, but he does feel that those who do voluntarily seek treatment deserve to receive it. Bieber agrees that societal prejudices provide some of the impetus for homosexuals to seek treatment; however, he argues that society merely reinforces what is already there. According to Bieber, the very nature of homosexuality creates in gay individuals a desire, whether conscious or unconscious, to become heterosexual. These desires would exist even if societal pressures were absent.

Along with providing treatment for homosexuals, Bieber argues for the establishment of strategies aimed at the prevention of homosexuality. Bieber believes that our knowledge is sufficient so that we could intervene in the case of prehomosexual boys to prevent them from developing homosexual patterns. By identifying these boys at an early stage, and providing treatment for them and their families, these boys could eventually develop heterosexual orientations.

A third position, falling somewhere between these two extremes, is represented by psychotherapists Seymour Halleck (1976) and Martin Hoffman (1977). These individuals, as well as numerous others, suggest that the therapist treat the entire individual and not just the homosexual behavior. A first step would be to help clients clarify their feelings and their goals. Some homosexuals may seek therapy because of societal pressures and not because they are really dissatisfied with their sexual behavior. By discussing these issues, some clients may decide that what they really want is to deal with feelings of guilt or shame, or to improve the quality of their interpersonal relationships whether they are homosexual or otherwise. Other clients may decide that they really want to develop the capacity to form heterosexual relationships. In either case, the therapist would attempt to help clients achieve their goals but only after thoroughly discussing these issues with them.

We shall now briefly review two approaches to modifying a homosexual orientation, but the reader should keep in mind that there is some question as to whether these procedures should ever be utilized. However, most psychotherapists would be willing to help clients modify a homosexual orientation as long as the clients had a full understanding of their own feelings and motives.

Psychotherapy

The assumptions and techniques associated with psychotherapy with homosexuals are similar to those presented in Chapter 14 regarding psychotherapy with sexual dysfunctions. The psychotherapist assumes that the homosexual behavior is symptomatic of an underlying and more pervasive disturbance. The therapist fosters transference and makes interpretations in an attempt to help clients understand the nature of these underlying conflicts. Once insight is achieved it is thought that clients are free to adopt more adaptive patterns of behavior.

The nature of the hypothetical underlying conflicts were discussed earlier in the chapter. These include, but are not limited to, a failure to identify with the same-sexed parent, intense fears of the vagina and castration anxiety in men, penis envy in women, and a failure to move beyond a narcissistic stage of psychosexual development. The psy-

chotherapist would attempt to identify which factor or combination of factors are operating and to help the client become aware of these conflicts.

There is a paucity of data regarding the effectiveness of psychotherapy in modifying homosexual orientation. Most psychotherapists do acknowledge that it is a very difficult condition to treat, if, for no other reason than because it is difficult to get anyone to give up behaviors that provide pleasure. The estimates of success rates appear to fall in the range of one-fifth to one-third (Bieber, 1962, 1976). These figures are only for those clients who are highly motivated to change. Most experts agree that it would be virtually impossible (and highly unethical) to modify the sexual orientation of clients who are coerced into therapy by the legal system or by family or friends.

Behavior Therapy

Many behavioral attempts to modify homosexual orientation involve the use of aversion therapy. This involves the pairing of some unpleasant stimulus, such as electric shock, with stimuli associated with homosexual behavior. After these stimuli are paired a number of times, the client will begin to lose interest in and fail to become aroused by the homosexual stimuli.

An example of this approach is provided by MacCulloch and Feldman (1967). They devised a technique called anticipatory avoidance learning to treat homosexuality in males. The clients were asked to view a slide of a male for as long as they found it attractive. They had the option of pushing a button which removed the slide of the male and replaced it with a slide of a female. If they did not push the button within eight seconds after the presentation of the male slide, they would receive a strong electric shock. There were several variations of this basic procedure which were intended to increase generalization from the consulting room to real-life situations. At the end of a one-year follow-up period, the researchers reported that of their forty-three clients twenty-five had no recurrence of overt homosexual activity.

In recent years, behavior therapists have been coming to recognize that it is not sufficient to eliminate homosexual tendencies. They must be ready to provide their clients with viable alternatives for sexual satisfaction. The gay man or woman who is no longer aroused by homosexual stimuli after a course of aversion therapy will not automatically become heterosexual. After many years of homosexual activity, clients may not feel confident in their abilities to initiate heterosexual relationships. Or they may be so anxious about such relationships that they would be dysfunctional if they were to attempt to have sex with someone of the opposite sex. In recognition of these problems several attempts have been made to devise techniques intended to increase heterosexual arousal and interpersonal skills.

Psychologists Joseph Blitch and Stephen Haynes (1972) reported the treatment of a twenty-two-year-old female homosexual in which they focused on increasing heterosexual behavior rather than decreasing homosexual behavior. The first phase of the treatment program involved systematic desensitization (see Chapter 18) to reduce her anxieties about touching and being touched by men. Second, the woman was taught to interact more effectively with men via role-playing procedures. After practicing interactions with men in the therapist's office she became more proficient and comfortable about such interactions in real-life situations. The third step involved orgasmic reconditioning. The client was instructed to gradually replace her fantasies of women with fantasies of men during masturbation. Two months after treatment, the client reported that she was having several satisfying relationships with males, had no homosexual contacts, and was using fantasies of men exclusively during masturbation.

While the behavior therapy literature offers many examples of successful attempts to modify sexual orientation, research is still in the preliminary stages. Most of the research is of the case history variety in which one individual or a group of individuals are treated. Without the use of appropriate control groups, it is not possible to conclude that the behavioral techniques per se are responsible for the results. Factors such as expectancy and client motivation may have played an important role. Nonetheless, the early results do provide justification for pursuing the behavioral approaches further.

Summary

Attitudes regarding homosexuality are extremely diverse. While the prevailing attitude in our society is that homosexual behavior is immoral or a sign of mental illness, there are many individuals who believe that taboos regarding homosexuality are illogical and truly liberated individuals are able to find sexual gratification in a variety of relationships.

Biological, psychological, and sociological factors have all been suspected of playing a role in the development of a homosexual orientation. The most plausible biological hypothesis is that prenatal hormonal anomalies may predispose one toward developing a homosexual orientation. The evidence, however, is far from conclusive. Furthermore, if this hypothesis is confirmed by future research, it probably will apply to a relatively small percentage of cases. Most psychological theories hold that the relationship between the child and the parents is the crucial element. Psychoanalytic theory suggests that disturbed parent-child relationships result in a failure to resolve the important Oedipal conflict. This can result in castration anxiety in males and penis envy in women, which in turn encourages a homosexual orientation. Social learning theorists suggest that the disturbed parent-child relationship results in an inadequate sex role model and reinforcement for sex role inappropriate behaviors by the parent of the opposite sex. Sociological and cross-cultural research demonstrates that sexual orientation and sexual practices are influenced by the prevailing attitudes of one's society.

The evidence concerning the etiology of a homosexual orientation in no way supports the notion that homosexual behavior is biologically abnormal. Such judgments are value-laden and are virtually impossible to prove scientifically. The evidence does suggest that male homosexuals are more likely to be psychologically disturbed than their heterosexual counterparts. The disturbances, however, may result from the pressures generated by a prejudiced society rather than the homosexual behavior. With regard to women, the evidence suggests that there are no significant differences in adjustment between homosexuals and heterosexuals.

The term bisexual includes those individuals who are aroused by, and have sex with, both men and women. The behavior of bisexuals is extremely diverse. Some may be predominately heterosexual and have only occasional homosexual contacts. Others may be exclusively homosexual for a period of time and then be exclusively heterosexual. Also, one's self-identity is not necessarily consistent with either current behavior or future behavior.

Some mental health professionals have argued that it is unethical to attempt to modify a homosexual orientation because there is no evidence that such behavior is abnormal. Others argue that the therapist should be prepared to help overcome feelings of guilt or shame that homosexuals may have about their behavior. A majority of therapists would be willing to attempt to modify a homosexual orientation but only after thoroughly discussing all relevant issues with the client. Two methods for doing so are psychotherapy and behavior therapy. Psychotherapy attempts to help clients become aware of, and resolve, the hypothetical underlying conflicts that are responsible for the homosexual orientation. Behavior therapy attempts to decrease sexual attraction to members of one's own sex and to increase attraction to members of the opposite sex with conditioning techniques.

References

Bandura, A. *Principles of behavior modification*. New York: Holt, Rinehart & Winston, 1969.

Beach, F. A. *Human sexuality in four perspectives*. Baltimore: Johns Hopkins University Press, 1977.

Bell, A. P. "The homosexual as patient." In M. S. Weinberg (ed.), *Sex research: Studies from the Kinsey Institute*. New York: Oxford University Press, 1976.

Bell, A. P. and Weinberg, M. S. *Homosexualities*. New York: Simon & Schuster, 1978.

Bieber, I. et al. *Homosexuality: A psychoanalytic study*. New York: Basic Books, 1962.

Bieber, I. "A discussion of 'homosexuality: The ethical challenge.'" *Journal of Consulting and Clinical Psychology*, 1976, 44, 163-166.

Blitch, J. W. and Haynes, S. N. "Multiple behavior techniques in a case of female homosexuality." *Journal of Behavior Therapy and Experimental Psychiatry*, 1972, 3, 319-322.

Blumstein, P. W. and Schwartz, P. "Lesbianism and bisexuality." In S. Gordon and R. W. Libby (eds.), *Sexuality today and tomorrow*. North Scituate, Mass.: Duxbury, 1976.

Blumstein, P. W. and Schwartz, P. "Bisexuality: Some social psychological issues." *Journal of Social Issues*, 1977, 33, 30-45.

Carrier, J. "Participants in urban Mexican male homosexual encounters." *Archives of Sexual Behavior*, 1971, 1, 279-291.

Clemens, L. G. "Neurohormonal control of male sexual behavior." In W. Montagna and W. A. Sadler (eds.), *Reproductive behavior*. New York: Plenum, 1974.

Davenport, W. H. "Sex in cross-cultural perspective." In F. A. Beach (ed.), *Human sexuality in four perspectives*. Baltimore: The Johns Hopkins University Press, 1977.

Davison, G. C. "Homosexuality: The ethical challenge." *Journal of Consulting and Clinical Psychology*, 1976, 44, 157–162.

Davison, G. C. "Not can but ought: The treatment of homosexuality." *Journal of Consulting and Clinical Psychology*, 1978, 46, 170–172.
28, 483.

Fenichel, O. *The Psychoanalytic theory of neurosis*. New York: W. W. Norton, 1945.

Ford, C. S. and Beach, F. A. *Patterns of sexual behavior*. New York: Harper & Row, 1951.

Freedman, M. *Homosexuality and psychological functioning*. Belmont, Calif.: Brooks/Cole, 1971.

Freud, S. "Letter to an American mother." *American Journal of Psychiatry*, 1951, 102, 786.

Halleck, S. L. "Another response to 'Homosexuality: The ethical challenge.'" *Journal of Consulting and Clinical Psychology*, 1976, 44, 167-170.

Hoffman, M. "Homosexuality," In F. A. Beach (ed.), *Human sexuality in four perspectives*. Baltimore: Johns Hopkins University Press, 1977.

Hooker, E. "The adjustment of the male overt homosexual." *Journal of Projective Techniques*, 1957, 21, 18-31.

Hunt, M. *Sexual behavior in the 1970s*. New York: Dell, 1974.

Jay, K. and Young, A. *After you're out: Personal experiences of gay men and lesbian women*. New York: Links Books, 1975.

Kallman, F. J. "A comparative twin study on the genetic aspects of male homosexuality." *Journal of Nervous and Mental Diseases*, 1952, 115, 283.

Kerr, C. *Sex for women*. New York: Grove, 1977.

Kinsey, A. C., Pomeroy, W. B., and Martin, C. E. *Sexual behavior in the human male*. Philadelphia: W. B. Saunders, 1948.

Kolb, L. S. "Therapy of homosexuality." In J. Masserman (ed.), *Current psychiatric therapies*, Vol. 3. New York: Grune & Stratton, 1963.

Kolodny, R. C., Masters, W. H., Hendry, J., and Toro, G. "Plasma testosterone and semen analysis in male homosexuals." *New England Journal of Medicine*, 1971, 285, 1170-1174.

Lester, D. *Unusual sexual behavior*. Springfield, Ill.: Charles C. Thomas, 1975.

MacCulloch, M. J., Feldman, M. P., and Pinshoff, J. M. "The application of anticipatory avoidance learning to the treatment of homosexuality. II. Avoidance response latencies and pulse rate changes." *Behaviour Research and Therapy*, 1965, 3, 21-43.

Margolise, M. E. "Homosexuality: A new endocrine correlate." *Hormones and Behavior*, 1970, 1, 151.

Marmor, J. "Homosexuality and sexual orientation disturbances." In B. J. Sadock, H. I. Kaplan, and A. M. Freedman (eds.), *The sexual experience*. Baltimore: Williams and Wilkins, 1976.

McCary, J. L. *Human sexuality*, 1st ed. New York: D. Van Nostrand, 1967.

McGuire, R. J., Carlisle, J. M., and Young, B. G. "Sexual deviations as conditioned behavior: A hypothesis." *Behaviour Research and Therapy*, 1965, 2, 185-190.

Meyer-Bahlburg, H. F. L. "Sex hormones and male homosexuality in comparative perspective." *Archives of Sexual Behavior*, 1977, 6, 297-325.

Money, J. "Human hermaphroditism." In F. A. Beach (ed.), *Human sexuality in four perspectives*. Baltimore: Johns Hopkins University Press, 1977.

Rose, R. M., Bourne, P. G., Poe, R. O., Mougey, E. M., Collins, D. K., and Mason, J. W. "Androgen responses to stress." *Psychosomatic Medicine*, 1969, 31, 418.

Schofield, M. *Sociological aspects of homosexuality*. London: Longmans, 1965.

Thompson, M., McCandless, B., and Strickland, B. "Personal adjustment of male and female homosexuals and heterosexuals." *Journal of Abnormal Psychology*, 1971, 78, 237-240.

Tripp, C. A. "Who is a homosexual?" In S. Gordon and R. W. Libby (eds.), *Sexuality today and tomorrow*. North Scituate, Mass.: Duxbury, 1976.

Ward, I. "Prenatal stress feminizes and demasculinizes the behavior of males." *Science*, 1972, 175, 82-84.

Weinberg M.S., and Williams C. *Male Homosexuals: Their Problems and Adaptations*. Oxford University Press, 1974.

Part Three

Topics in Human Sexuality

Chapter 17
Sex Differences and Sex Roles

Most of us have stereotypes regarding men and women and knowledge of a person's gender will tend to elicit certain expectations about that individual. We tend to expect young boys to be interested in playing baseball or football; young girls are expected to be interested in playing with dolls or in taking ballet lessons. Men are expected to have their career as their primary concern; women are thought to be interested in maintaining a house and caring for children. While such stereotypes may be undergoing some change at the present time, even the most liberated parent would probably feel some concern about a son whose main interest is his doll house or a daughter who spends countless hours playing with trucks.

Research in the area of sex differences has been going on for several decades; however, in the past ten years or so, interest in this area has increased dramatically. We are now just beginning to understand the nature and origin of sex differences. In times past it was simply assumed that men and women were fundamentally different and most people did not question why. That men and women had different values, interests, attitudes, and abilities was accepted as a fact of life. This view was reinforced by Sigmund Freud, who argued that anatomy was destiny. In recent years, however, accumulated scientific evidence has shown that the similarities between men and women far outweigh the differences. And most of the differences that do exist result from sociological and cultural forces rather than from anatomy or physiology. In this chapter we will explore theories of sex differences, the myths and facts about sex differences, and sex role socialization.

Theories of Sex Differences

In recent years, the issue of why men and women are different in behavior, beliefs, and interests has become controversial and even political. At the one extreme are those who argue that the differences are biological in origin. Such a view suggests that differences in anatomy and hormones between men and women lead to psychological and behavioral differences. At the other extreme are those who argue that biological differences play a trivial role in creating sex differences. These theorists believe that the differences result from differential sex-role-training experiences. That is, parents have different expectations for sons than they do for daughters and they treat them accordingly. Thus, boys learn to be boys and girls learn to be girls.

An "either-or" approach to the issue of sex differences is overly simplistic. The evidence suggests that both biological and social-learning factors are important. Although research in this area is just beginning, it is likely that a combination or interaction of these factors is responsible for at least some observed sex differences. Let us review the theories and examples of research findings in this area.

Biological Theories

The sex hormones, estrogen and androgen, have received the most attention with regard to biological factors that influence sex differences. The role that these hormones play has been investigated by psychologist John Money and his colleagues who have spent the past two decades studying cases of sex errors of the body at Johns Hopkins University. His research has documented that the sex hormones can have a profound effect upon physiological development (see Chapter 7) and has hinted that they may influence psychological development as well.

As one example, Money has studied androgenized females. These are women who, as a result of a genetic error or drugs administered to their mothers during pregnancy, were exposed to an excess of androgen during fetal development (Money and Ehrhardt, 1972). Although genetically female the external genitals of these infants take on a masculine appearance. The degree of masculinization can range from an enlarged clitoris to an underdeveloped penis. Shortly after birth, the infant's genitals are feminized surgically, and if necessary, cortisone is administered to suppress excess androgen production.

As adolescents and adults, these women are physically indistinguishable from typical women. Money, however, has reported that differences in behavior and interests between androgenized and typical girls exist. As adolescents, the androgenized girls showed a preference for boy's toys and activities and they preferred slacks over dresses. In comparison, the typical girls, who were of the same age, race, social class, and intelligence, tended to prefer dolls, indoor play, dresses, and jewelry. The androgenized girls also seemed less interested in a stereotypical feminine role. While they were as interested in marriage as the typical girls, they were less interested in caring for children and were more likely to give priority to a career over marriage.

Because this research is not experimental research, it does not conclusively demonstrate that the sex hormones are responsible for masculine and feminine interests and behaviors. Any number of factors could have contributed to the "tomboyism" of the androgenized girls. Perhaps their parents treated them differently because of the ambiguity of their gender at birth. But Money does believe that his research strongly suggests that male-female differences do have a hormonal component. He does state, however, that social learning plays a much larger role in the process of gender identity and sex role development.

Physiologist Milton Diamond (1977) agrees with Money (1977) that hormones are a factor in generating sex differences. And along with Money, he believes that hormones have their effect by masculinizing or feminizing the brain during the early months of gestation. That is, psychological differences between men and women can be traced back to four to five weeks after conception. However, Diamond believes that the biological foundations are much more important, relative to social learning factors, than Money does. Diamond does recognize the importance of environmental events, but he sees them as evoking the expression of behavioral characteristics that were "biologically programmed" much earlier in the child's development. Needless to say, many theorists disagree with Diamond, but it is important to recognize that there are those who argue that biology can play a major role in the development of psychological differences between men and women.

Money's theory that hormones have their effect by programming the brain in early development is consistent with a growing body of research that reports differences in the brains of men and women. We have known for a number of years that the human brain consists of two relatively distinct halves and that each half is associated with certain functions and abilities. In most adults, the left hemisphere of the brain is associated with language ability and referred to as the dominant hemisphere, and the right hemisphere is associated with nonverbal, spatial abilities. It has only been in recent years that researchers have discovered that men's and women's brain organization may be different.

In a review of this literature, psychologist Daniel Goleman (1978) has reported a variety of studies that suggest the existence of sex differences in brain organization. One finding that has received support in several investigations is that the two halves of the brain are more specialized for men than they are for women. For example, in a study of brain damaged adults, it was found that only men had specifically verbal deficits after left-hemisphere brain damage or nonverbal spatial deficits after right-hemisphere damage. The women showed less severe impairment in both verbal and spatial ability regardless of which hemisphere was damaged. Additional research seems to support the theory that such differences in hemisphere dominance are biological and not developed on the basis of differential socialization.

There are many implications of such findings. As one example, men and women can be expected to perform differently on a variety of tasks. Because women's hemispheres are less specialized for spatial and linguistic functions, it should be easier for women to perform tasks that combine the two skills, such as reading. The greater specialization of men should allow them to perform better in different activities at the same time, such as operating a piece of machinery while talking.

One concern that has been expressed regarding the type of research discussed above is that it may be used to justify sexism. If it can be scientifically demonstrated that men perform better on some tasks and women perform better on others, and that these differences are biological in nature, then certain occupations and activities may be closed to one sex or the other. While some people may wish to discriminate on the basis of sex, there is no scientific justification for doing so.

All of the research done in this area deals with groups of people and compares the average performance of a group of men with the average performance of a group of women. There is however, always a great deal of overlap in the performance of the two sexes. For example, perhaps it could be shown that *on the average* women make better editors because the job requires both linguistic and spatial skills. However, it would also be true that many men would have more editorial ability than the average woman. Thus, while a difference between groups may exist it tells us little about the performance of a particular woman or a particular man. Therefore, it would be absurd to select an editor on the basis of gender alone.

A related point is that people have the unfortunate tendency to view differences as indications of superiority and inferiority. Even if research had clearly documented substantial differences in abilities between the sexes (which it has not), it should not be used as justification for concluding that one sex is superior to the other. The research that has been done seems to suggest that men or women *may* have a slight advantage on some particular tasks, and not that one sex is superior to the other across the board. As neurophysiologists Diane McGuiness and Karl Pribram (in press) have observed, men and women are indeed different. What we need to make equal is the value we place upon these differences.

Social Learning Theories

Social learning theorists argue that male-female differences result from differences in socialization. That is, boys are taught to be boys and girls are taught to be girls. Our culture has developed certain expectations about what interests, values, and abilities boys and girls should have, and parents as well as peers and other adults influence the child in ways that fulfill these expectations. These expectations, which can be called sex roles, typically require boys to be independent, aggressive, athletic, unemotional, and so on. Sex roles for girls suggest that traits such as passivity, emotional lability, and nurturance are desirable.

Sex role stereotyping appears to occur very early in one's life. In fact, parents are likely to have different expectations of an unborn child depending on whether they expect a boy or a girl. A recent study also found that parents' perceptions of a newborn child depended on the sex of the child (Rubin, Provenzano, and Luria, 1974). Mothers and fathers were asked to rate their infants with regard to a number of characteristics within twenty-four hours of birth. While hospital records showed no differences between male and female infants in weight, length, muscle tonicity, or reflex irritability, parents perceived a number of differences between sons and daughters. Daughters were rated as softer, finer featured, smaller, and more inattentive. On a number of other characteristics, fathers showed greater differences in perceptions of sons and daughters than did the mothers. The differences, however, were always in accord with sex role stereotypes. For example, fathers perceived their sons as stronger and better coordinated whereas daughters were perceived as being more awkward and delicate.

Social learning theorists point out that differential treatment of boys and girls is likely to begin the moment they are brought home from the hospital. Mothers are more likely to tickle and engage in rough and tumble play with their male infants. On the other hand, they are more likely to respond in quiet play and face to face talking with their female infants (Moss, 1967). One investigator interested in sex differences in infants complained of parents' unwillingness to disguise the sex of their infants. Little girls were brought into the laboratory with pink ribbons taped to their little bald heads. When the mothers were asked to dress their daughters in overalls to disguise their sex, the experimenter was surprised to discover overalls with ruffles (Bandura, 1969). As children become toddlers, boys and girls are likely to receive different kinds of toys. Boys are likely to receive such toys as trucks and trains; girls may be given dolls. Through the process of reinforcement, children's attachment and interest in sex-typed toys is likely to be strengthened.

Children themselves are responsible for acquiring sex roles. By the age of eighteen months most children are beginning to develop a firm sense of being a girl or a boy. Subsequently, they seem to have a strong sense of motivation to adopt their sex appropriate role (Kohlberg, 1966). They will seek out information about their role and try to behave in ways that they believe they should behave. Part of this process will involve imitating the parent of the same sex. Boys are likely to want to grow up to be like their fathers and girls will want to be like their mothers.

Schools are also influential in the development and perpetuation of sex roles (Dweck, 1975; Etaugh, Collins, and Gerson, 1975). Girls are expected to be more proficient in

Figure 17.1
Children acquire many sex-related behaviors by imitating the same-sexed parent. (Dwyer and Zinkl)

subjects such as English and boys are expected to excel in math and science. Educational institutions may also shape career goals. Boys are encouraged to enter professions such as law, medicine, or science. If girls have aspirations along these lines, they may be encouraged to assume a helping role—such as being a legal secretary, a nurse, or a lab technician.

Finally the media serves to reinforce sex roles. Movies, television, popular songs, and books all convey what men and women are supposed to be like. In an analysis of children's textbooks it was found that women and girls were likely to be portrayed as being boring, passive, supportive, and even stupid. Boys and men were likely to be portrayed as brave, independent, active, and intelligent (Weitzman et al., 1972).

In short, social learning theorists can point to an impressive variety of factors that suggest that sex differences are environmentally acquired. To illustrate how potent the effects of environment can be, Money has discussed a case of normal twin boys (Money and Erhardt, 1972). At the age of seven months, one of the boys was circumsized with an electrical apparatus. Tragically, the current used was too strong and the penis was completely ablated. Several months later surgery was performed to reassign the child to the female sex. The mother of the twins was quite perceptive and reported that she behaved differently toward the children following the surgery without consciously attempting to do so. For instance, she allowed her son to be somewhat more messy and active, whereas the daughter was encouraged to be neat and curb her activities. By the age of six, there were clear differences between the children. One was definitely a little boy and the other was clearly a little girl.

It would be misleading to think that either biological or social learning theories must account for male-female psychological differences. All knowledgeable theorists, regardless of their orientation, recognize that biology and learning interact to influence such differences. Unresolved questions concern the relative importance of each group of factors. The extent to which biological and learning factors are important will depend on the specific difference being considered. To use an extreme example, the profession of nursing is predominately female, whereas the majority of physicians are male in the United States. There is no evidence to suggest that this difference reflects biological sex differences in abilities. In fact, in the USSR the majority of physicians are women. Learning or environmental factors play a major role in influencing women to choose nursing as a career and men to choose medicine in this country. On the other hand, the obvious physical difference in physical strength between the sexes does allow men to be more proficient at such occupations as hod carrier. Future research should allow us to learn more about the factors involved in more subtle varieties of sex differences.

The Differences Between Men and Women

As we mentioned earlier, many people assume that men and women are completely different. They are thought to have different interests, attitudes, values, personality traits, and abilities. With the recent interest in sex roles, however, we are beginning to realize that many of these "assumed" differences are not meaningful. Research in this area has become more sophisticated and in the past ten years we have gained an appreciation of how men and women differ and how they are similar. Let us review some of the major findings.

Sexual Behavior

As you recall from earlier chapters, men and women around the turn of the century were thought to be completely different with regard to their sexuality. Men were thought to have strong animalistic urges that demanded gratification whereas women supposedly had little interest in sex and submitted to intercourse only to satisfy their husbands. Of course, we now realize that women are indeed interested in sex, but the issue of possible differences between men and women has not been resolved.

Clearly, most men have more sexual experiences than women. They are more likely to masturbate, more likely to have premarital intercourse, and more likely to have extramarital intercourse. But the gap between men and women is closing rapidly. For example, in Hunt's (1974) survey, 84 percent of men and 31 percent of women fifty-five and older reported having premarital intercourse. For those between the ages of eighteen and twenty-four, 95 percent of men and 81 percent of women had premarital experience. The differences between men and women in other categories of sexual behavior are decreasing as well.

The relaxation of the double standard has generally been credited with an increase in women's sexual activity. As women learned that it was acceptable for "nice girls" to express their sexuality, they have done so—both verbally and behaviorally. This line of reasoning would suggest that the differences in sexual activity between men and women will continue to decrease as the double standard disappears from our society.

An argument could be made that hormonal differences between men and women are responsible for men's greater sexual activity. It has been found that androgen is related to sex drive in both men and women. And since the androgen levels in men are considerably higher than in women, one might expect men to have a greater sex drive.

This hypothesis seems unlikely for several reasons. First, there is not a one-to-one correspondence between androgen level and sex drive. People deficient in androgen may (but not always) experience an increase in sex drive after this hormone is administered. But additional dosages of the drug are unlikely to result in a corresponding increase in sex drive. Second, much of the research that has established a relation between sex drive and androgen has been with animals. In humans, the effects of hormones are highly variable. For example, Ford and Beach (1951) reported cases of castrated men who reported both sexual desire and potency for up to thirty years following castration. Their conclusion, and probably the most reasonable one, is that learning factors play a major role in determining sexual interest and activity for both men and women. There is no evidence at present that differences in sexual activity are biological in nature.

A related issue concerns the type of stimuli that men and women find sexually arousing. Kinsey and his colleagues (Kinsey et al., 1953) were among the first to collect data that suggested that men differed from women in what they found erotically stimulating. They reported that men were much more likely to be aroused by erotic materials, such as films, stories, or pictures. Also, men were thought to find depictions of "raw" or casual sex the most stimulating whereas women preferred stimuli containing romantic or love themes. An additional difference reported was that men, more than women, were aroused by visual stimuli; women found written and tactile stimulation more exciting.

These conclusions were based on survey research. That is, men and women were asked if they became sexually aroused in response to various stimuli. Two factors were probably operating to produce the difference in reports between the men and women. First, women generally have less experience with erotic materials than do men. They are not as likely to frequent pornographic movies or bookstores so they may not be aware of the extent to which these materials may be arousing to them. Second, it is less socially acceptable (at least it was in Kinsey's time) for women to be interested in erotic materials. Thus, they may have been reluctant to admit to a researcher that they were aroused by such material.

Recent laboratory research strongly suggests that men and women are not very different in what they find sexually stimulating. As one example, psychologist Julia Heiman (1975) asked sexually experienced men and women to listen to four audio tapes. The first tape was erotic, it depicted explicit heterosexual activity without any affection between the partners. The second tape, labeled romantic, portrayed a couple expressing their love and affection for one another, but with no sexual activity. A third tape, erotic-romantic, depicted both sexual activity and expressions of love and romance. The fourth tape was used as a control condition in which a couple had a conversation about a nonsexual topic. The results indicated that both men and women found the erotic and erotic-romantic tapes the most arousing. Neither group was aroused by the romantic or control tape.

A similar study compared the responses of men and women to filmed portrayals of casual sex, marital sex, and commercial sex (a man and a prostitute). In all three cases the films were identical and only the experimenter's introduction to the film was varied. Once again men and women responded similarly. They both were most aroused by the casual sex film. There were no differences in arousal between men and women for any of the films (Fisher and Byrne, 1978).

These studies call into question many of Kinsey's findings. There are no apparent differences to the extent to which men and women find erotic stimuli sexually arousing. Men and women appear to find visual and verbal depictions of sexual encounters equally arousing, and both sexes seem to find depictions of casual sex the most exciting. The last point made by Kinsey, concerning possible sex differences in response to visual and tactile stimulation remains to be tested. It may be some time before a researcher is brave enough (or foolhardy enough) to conduct laboratory research to test this hypothesis.

Sexual variations are one form of behavior for which meaningful sex differences are likely to exist. It is extremely rare for a woman to come to the attention of legal or medical authorities for engaging in behaviors such as pedophilia, voyeurism, fetishism, and the like. One explanation is that it is easier for women to express unusual forms of sexual behavior in socially appropriate ways. For example, a woman with exhibitionistic desires can obtain gratification from erotic dancing. Women who dress in men's clothing are not considered unusual whereas men who dress in women's clothing must be circumspect lest they be arrested. While such a social acceptability hypothesis may have some validity, it seems unlikely that it accounts for all of the differences between men and women. After all, it is no more acceptable for women to molest young children than it is for men, yet such behavior, or even desire, is extremely rare in women.

A more reasonable explanation involves the theory of sexual arousal discussed in Chapter 10. It suggested that men become aroused to a wider variety of stimuli than do women because they have immediate and obvious feedback about their arousal—namely, an erection. It may be more difficult for women to learn such associations because even sexually experienced women are not always accurate in recognizing physiological arousal.

It is also possible that men's greater likelihood of engaging in sexually variant behavior has a biological basis. As you recall from Chapter 5, the "something added" hypothesis suggests that all human life is initially female and something (a Y-chromosome and testosterone) must be added to make the structure male. Perhaps this makes it easier for something to "go wrong" in the development of males. Also discussed in Chapter 5 was the notion that the second "X"-chromosome in women serves a protective function. This protective function is relatively clear in regard to biological disorders and may also operate with psychological disorders (Lyon, 1962).

The biological basis for men's greater tendency to engage in sexually variant behavior is highly speculative. There has been little research that directly addresses this issue. However, there is little doubt that men are biologically more fragile than women and it is possible that this fragility contributes to the greater variability in sexual expression of men.

Intellectual and Personality Differences

As we mentioned earlier, many people believe that men and women differ on a wide variety of intellectual and personality characteristics. Many of these differences that are assumed to exist, however, arise from sex role stereotypes rather than scientific evidence. For instance, women are thought to be the talkative sex. Many jokes and cartoons depict women as spending endless hours gossiping with their friends or talking endlessly at men. A number of studies, however, have found just the opposite to be true. Men spend much more time talking than women

do and men are more likely to initiate topics and are more likely to interrupt others while they are talking (Kramer, 1974; Soskin and John, 1963). Perhaps more women should be creating jokes and cartoons about the sexes.

In an extensive and scholarly review of the literature on the differences between men and women, psychologists Eleanor Maccoby and Carol Jacklin (1974) concluded that there is solid evidence for only four differences between men and women. Let us review their findings.

There is strong evidence that males are more aggressive than females. This difference becomes apparent by the age of two to two and a half, and is observed in virtually all cultures. It is unlikely that this difference is learned, since observations of parent-child interactions have found that parents are no more likely to encourage boys to be aggressive than girls. In fact, boys are more likely to be punished for their aggressive behavior.

The evidence does point to a biological basis for this difference. Animal studies have shown that young animals injected with the male sex hormones are more likely to display aggressive behaviors as adults than control animals. Of course, one must be cautious in generalizing from animals to humans, but this research taken together with cross-cultural observations and observations of parent-child interactions strongly suggests that male-female differences in aggression have a biological basis.

Male sex hormones may provide a basis for aggression, but learning factors still operate in the acquisition of aggressive behavior in both men and women. For instance, men and women seem to learn to express their aggression in different ways. While men are likely to express it directly, women tend to use more subtle methods such as rejecting or ignoring someone (Feshbach and Feshbach, 1973). Also, while men may be more aggressive generally, when there is provocation women can be just as aggressive as men (Taylor and Epstein, 1967).

The second sex difference is that boys have more visual spatial ability than girls. This involves tasks such as the visual perception of figures or objects in space and may have implications for occupations such as architect or engineer. This difference is not found during childhood and becomes apparent in early adolescence. The evidence points to a genetic basis for this difference. Spatial ability is thought to be influenced by a recessive sex-linked gene that occurs among men more often than women. Of course, this does not mean that all men are superior to all women in spatial ability. There are many women with very high levels of this ability.

Two differences for which there is no apparent biological basis, but do seem to exist, are mathematic and verbal ability. Boys tend to perform better on mathematics whereas girls have the greater skills in verbal tasks. When young, boys and girls show equal ability on both of these tasks. The differences

do not become apparent until around the age of twelve or thirteen. The difference in mathematic ability may occur because it is related to spatial ability. But sex role stereotypes are also likely to play a role. Boys are *supposed* to be good at math, and they take more math courses than girls do. As discussed above, girls' superiority in verbal ability may result from sex differences in brain organization. At present, however, such an explanation is highly speculative.

Maccoby and Jacklin also dispel several myths concerning sex differences. For instance, girls are not more social or suggestible than are boys. Nor are boys better at tasks that require analytic ability. While there is no overall difference in the self-esteem of boys or girls, they do differ in areas in which they report the greatest self-confidence. Girls view themselves as more adept at social interactions whereas boys tend to see themselves as strong, powerful, and dominant. In other words, both sexes tend to have confidence in their sex role "appropriate" behavior.

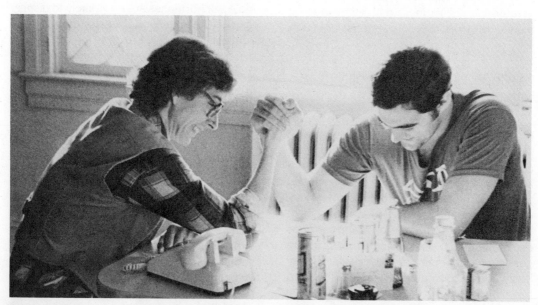

Figure 17.2
Men are usually expected to be more competitive than women. (Dwyer and Zinkl)

Fear of Success

One possible sex difference that has received much attention in the past decade concerns fear of success. In 1968 psychologist Matina Horner reported the startling result that 65 percent of her women subjects expressed a fear of success while only 10 percent of college men in her study had similar concerns. Horner tested for fear of success by asking men and women to write short stories in response to the cue: "After first

Sexual Harassment of Women	Among the many problems that working women must deal with is sexual harassment. A *Redbook* survey found that of 9,000 female respondents, 92 percent felt that sexual harassment was a problem on their job (Safran, 1976). The harassment can range from leering and ogling to threats regarding promotions, raises, and even termination if sexual favors are not forthcoming. The *Redbook* survey did not consist of a random sample, but it does present clear evidence that sexual harassment is a serious issue for many working women.

To the extent to which the survey is generalizable, it appears that sexual harassment is an everyday, everywhere occurrence. Women working in factories and on the Alaska pipeline complained of vulgar propositions from coworkers. Secretaries have described the area behind the file cabinet as "grope alley." College students have complained of professors who use the threat of lowered grades to induce sexual compliance. A woman who worked at a bank reported that the vice president would whisper vulgar "ditties" to virtually all of the women who worked there. Even women in supervisory positions were not immune. A woman who owned a real estate company had her best salesman quit because she declined to have a sexual relationship with him.

Because many women lose their jobs because they refuse to go along, or are forced to quit jobs they need or want, the financial effect of sexual harassment is obvious. But many women found it even more difficult to deal with the emotional effect. A typical story involves a woman who, after having had a coworker pat her on the behind, rest his hand on her thigh, and the like, finally complained. The coworker claimed that the woman simply misinterpreted his "friendly, affectionate" nature. If she complained to a supervisor, the problem was often treated as a joke. Faced with similar situations, many women reported that they began to believe there was something wrong with them. They wondered what they could be doing wrong to find themselves in such a situation.

Because sexual harassment is a form of sexual discrimination, it is illegal. In cases where women cannot obtain satisfaction when they confront the man involved, supervisors, or personnel departments, they can file a complaint with the city or state Commission on Human Rights or Fair Employment Practices Agency (the name varies from place to place). Or they can contact the Equal Employment Opportunity Commission of the Federal Government. These agencies have the power to set guidelines to prohibit sexual harassment and reinstate and award monetary damages to women who are victims. Unfortunately, these procedures can take several months or even years.

term finals John (Anne) finds himself (herself) at the top of his (her) medical school class." Men were given the John sentence and women were given the Anne version. In response to the cue, many women wrote stories that reflected concerns about such a high level of achievement. Some told stories in which Anne quit medical school and became a nurse so that her boyfriend could be the first in the class. One woman even wrote that Anne's classmates took turns jumping up and down on her body. The thrust of many of the stories was that Anne was less feminine, and hence liked less by her peers, for achieving success.

Horner's idea hit a responsive chord with psychologists and the public alike, and before long dozens of scientific studies and popular articles appeared in print about women's fears of success. But more recent research suggests that fear of success is not unique to women. For example, one study investigated the possibility that Horner's women expressed so much concern because they were dealing with an occupation that was dominated by males (Janda, O'Grady, and Capps, 1978). In this study, men and women were asked to respond to three cues in which a student was at the top of his or her class in engineering, child psychology and nursing. These three occupations were used because they were roughly equivalent in terms of status, but differed sharply in the degree to which they were male or female dominated. As predicted, women exhibited the most fear of success in response to the engineering cue; men had the most fear in response to the nursing cue. Interestingly, the men exhibited more fear of success overall than did the women. The results of the experiment suggested that both men and women have fear of success in relation to occupations that are not consistent with sex-role stereotypes.

The research dealing with personality differences could easily fill several large vol-

umes. It is difficult to reduce this work to a few simple conclusions, but two points deserve to be made. First, while there are clearly many differences between the personalities and behaviors of men and women, the differences are not as great as sex role stereotypes would suggest. (Recall that men are actually the more talkative sex.) Second, the extent to which differences are observed depends on the context or situation in which the behavior is observed. To use the topic of aggression as an example, men are more likely than women to express aggression toward a passive victim, but when provoked women are just as aggressive as men. Thus, it is quite possible, if not likely, that many of the differences that exist result from the divergent sex roles of men and women. If the trend of the last decade continues, and sex roles continue to blur, perhaps many personality differences will fade away.

Effects of Sex Roles

As we discussed earlier, boys and girls are taught to fill quite different roles. Little boys are encouraged to be independent, assertive, active, and in control of their emotions and to plan for a career. Girls are taught to be dependent, passive, emotional, and to expect to fill the role of homemaker and mother. Many behavioral scientists and men and women who support women's liberation argue that these sex roles place women in a subordinate or inferior position to men.

There is little doubt that personality characteristics that are considered masculine tend to be valued more than feminine traits. A dramatic illustration of this was provided by Inge Broverman (1970) and her colleagues who asked psychotherapists to describe either a psychologically healthy man, woman, or person. The professionals described the healthy man and healthy person in very similar terms. They were thought to possess traits such as competence, independence, and objectivity. The description of the healthy woman, however, was strikingly different. She was thought to have the traits of emotionality, conceit, and submissiveness. It is ironic that for a woman to be considered healthy, she must possess undesirable personality traits. The final irony was that there was substantial agreement between the judgments of men and women psychotherapists.

Two important implications of this rather disparaging view of women lie in the areas of psychological adjustment and occupational success. With regard to adjustment, the difference between the sexes is apparent during childhood. More boys than girls are referred for child therapy. This situation, however, is reversed for adults when more women than men are referred for psychological treatment. One explanation for this finding does involve sex roles. It has been argued that the range of behaviors considered appropriate for boys is much narrower than for girls, whereas the situation is reversed for adults (Nathan and Harris, 1975). To illustrate, consider the trait of aggression. Boys who are overly aggressive are considered bullies whereas a passive boy might be labeled a sissy. An aggressive girl, on the other hand, might be called a tomboy whereas a passive girl may be thought of as a little lady. Once boys become men the diversity of sex-role-appropriate behavior increases while it becomes more restricted for women. For example, it is perfectly acceptable for a man to be a chef even though cooking is an activity that is thought of as "women's work." But a woman who is an engineer or architect is likely to be thought of as masculine.

Sex roles may interact with marriage in contributing to psychological disturbances in women. In a large survey of the mental health of residents of midtown Manhattan, it was found that married women were somewhat more likely to have psychological problems than married men and single men were significantly more likely to be disturbed than single women (Srole et al., 1962). While many possible explanations for this finding exist, one reasonable hypothesis is that sex roles within marriage place greater stress on women than men. Even though changes are gradually occurring, the husband is assumed to have the responsibility of being the breadwinner and the wife's duties center on care of the home and children in most American families. Many women may find this role satisfying, but many others may feel trapped by the routine of housework, the isolation from adult contact, or the inability to pursue career goals.

Many college men voice opinions that suggest that they do not plan to abide by sex roles once they are married (Parelius, 1975; Komarovsky, 1973). A common attitude is that they would not find a woman very interesting if her only goal was to be a homemaker. However, it was also common that the men expected their wives to take primary responsibility for care of the children when the time came. Men seem to perceive equality in marriage as meaning that women should work, then withdraw to care for the children, and then return to work once the children are old enough. It is likely to be some time before the majority of men and women are truly equal partners in a marriage relationship.

Men are not immune from negative consequences of traditional sex roles, however. For instance, the stereotype that makes some men feel that they must be strong, independent, unemotional, and the like may prevent them from developing emotionally satisfying relationships. Their need to be perceived as "strong" makes it difficult for them to express their doubts, fears, anxieties, and so on. It is difficult to be close to another human being if one is concerned with concealing one's self (Jourard, 1971).

The Androgynous Person

A concept that has received much attention in recent years is that of *androgyny*. Psychologist Sandra Bem (1975) has argued that in order to be functioning fully one should possess characteristics that are traditionally associated with both men and women. That is, well-adjusted members of both sexes will have traits such as independence, assertiveness, tenderness, and sensitivity and will be able to express these traits in appropriate situations.

Bem conducted a series of studies to illustrate that sex roles can be restricting. For example in a laboratory situation, highly "masculine" men feel uncomfortable if asked to perform a "feminine" activity such as preparing a baby bottle. Similarly, highly "feminine" women experience feelings of discomfort if asked to perform a "masculine" activity such as oiling squeaky hinges. Bem's hypotheses suggest that adherence to rigid sex roles can be limiting in real-life situations, and androgynous people will be effective in a wider variety of situations. For instance, the androgynous man will not feel reluctant to participate in the care of young children and hence will be able to experience the associated rewards. The androgynous woman will be able to be forceful and assertive in situations in which such behavior is adaptive.

Because the concept of androgyny is just beginning to be investigated, much remains to be learned. There is, for example, some controversy as to how androgyny should be defined and measured (Spence and Helmreich, 1978). Also, one should not assume that the androgynous person is free from sex role stereotypes. Androgyny refers to personality traits and it is quite possible for an individual to be androgynous and still subscribe to traditional sex roles. For example, a man may possess both masculine and feminine traits (e.g., independence and gentleness) and yet believe that his wife should remain in the home to care for the children.

Prejudice Against Women

In our society, we have been aware for some time that blacks and other ethnic minorities are discriminated against. But it has only been in recent years that we have begun to realize the extent to which women are victims of prejudice. The problems of women provide an example of what has been called nonconscious ideology. This term refers to beliefs and attitudes that a person accepts because it is virtually inconceivable that things could be any other way. Thus, for many years our society simply accepted the fact that men were the executives, physicians, and college professors and women were the secretaries, nurses, and elementary school teachers. Many people did (and still do) believe that these occupational differences reflect inherent differences in abilities or interests. It simply never occurred to them that a woman's career might be influenced by prejudice and negative stereotypes.

A large segment of our society is becoming aware of the discrimination that women face in the job market, but things are slow to change. Many discrepancies still exist both in terms of occupational level and salaries. For example, while women make up 40 percent of the labor force, they make up only 5 percent of workers who earn $15,000 or more. Even female physicians, lawyers, and scientists receive salaries that are about 73 percent of that received by their male counterparts (Associated Press, 1979).

Laws prohibiting discrimination on the basis of sex and increased awareness on the part of the business community are producing change. Some companies now actively recruit or train women for higher level positions, but women in these positions are likely to have a special set of problems. They must deal with subordinates, both male and female, who may resent taking orders from a woman. Or they may have to deal with superiors who remain skeptical about women's ability to succeed at the higher occupational levels.

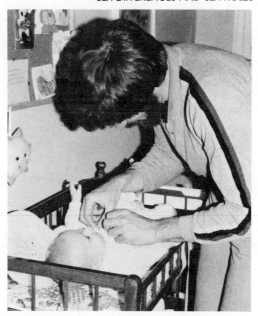

Figure 17.3
The relaxation of the double standard has made it possible for both men and women to enjoy activities that were formerly closed to them. (From left to right, Dwyer and Zinkl, Falk, and Freedman)

Much of the discrimination against women probably results from several misconceptions. For example, one often hears that women work for extras such as vacations or furniture and men work to support the family. Or that a woman is likely to leave a job for which she has received extensive training as soon as she becomes pregnant. But the prejudice seems to go deeper than that. The fact is that many people in our society are convinced that women are not as capable as men.

To illustrate this prejudice, psychologist Phillip Goldberg (1968) asked college men and women to rate a number of articles that had appeared in professional journals. Some of the articles came from disciplines that are traditionally feminine, such as elementary education and nursing, and some from those that are traditionally masculine, such as architecture or city planning. Two sets of articles were given to the students to be rated for competency of the author. One set was presented as having been written by a male and the other set was presented as having a female author. Goldberg was somewhat surprised by the results. For the masculine disciplines, both the men and women students rated the articles as being clearly superior when they thought the author was male. What was surprising was that the students, both male and female, also rated the articles in the feminine disciplines as superior when the author was male. Goldberg's conclusion was that even women are prejudiced against women. It would seem that another obstacle women must overcome is their own lack of confidence in their ability.

Both men and women have a stake in discarding inappropriate sex-role stereotypes. Women, of course, have the most to gain. Their ability to choose freely among alternative lifestyles and to pursue career goals has been severely limited in the past and, to some extent, remains limited today. Men, too, have much to gain. By rejecting traditional notions of masculinity, they can be more open to a wider range of human experiences. And, finally, relationships between men and women would certainly benefit if men and women could approach each other without preconceived ideas about what the other person is like.

Summary

Although research in the area of sex differences has been going on for several decades, behavioral scientists have only begun to explore the extent and nature of such differences. Both biological and environmental factors are important in generating sex differences. Differences in chromosomes, hormones, and brain organization may all contribute to sex differences in regard to a variety of behaviors. Environmental factors, such as sex-role-related expectations of parents, teachers, and peers also are important. Theorists may disagree about the relative importance of biological and environmental factors, but there is wide agreement that both categories of influence do play a role in generating differences between the sexes.

Recent research indicates that men and women are much more similar than was once thought. Men are more sexually active than women, but women are rapidly catching up in terms of behaviors such as premarital sex. Contrary to previous belief, laboratory research indicates that men and women find the same types of stimuli to be sexually arousing. One meaningful difference concerns variations of sexual expression. Men are more likely to engage in activities such as exhibitionism, transvestism, and pedophilia. A social acceptability hypothesis may account for part of men's greater variability of sexual expression, but biological factors may be operating as well.

Three sex differences in ability and one personality difference have received strong documentation. Males have greater visual-spatial and mathematical ability and they are more aggressive, whereas women have greater verbal ability. The differences in visual-spatial ability and aggression do seem to have a biological component. The origin of the difference in mathematical and verbal abilities is less certain. Sex roles also contribute to many of the observed differences between the sexes.

Sex roles can influence psychological adjustment and occupational success. It has been found that boys are more likely to be referred for psychotherapy than girls whereas for adults, more women than men are referred for therapy. Sex roles within marriage may also contribute to maladjust-ment in women. The concept of androgyny has been suggested as a possible ideal. The androgynous man or woman is not bound by sex role stereotypes and is thus free to behave adaptively across a variety of situations.

Women, unquestionably, are discriminated against in their attempts to pursue occupational goals. They are underrepresented at higher occupational levels and their salaries are lower than those of men within the same occupation. This pattern of discrimination may represent an example of nonconscious ideology—the inability to believe that things could, or should, be any different. As one example, women, as well as men, are likely to believe that women are less capable than men across a variety of occupations.

References

Associated Press. "Report finds no job gains for women." *Virginian Pilot*, January 21, 1979, A-4.

Bandura, A. "Social learning theory and identificatory processes." In D. Goslin (ed.), *Handbook of socialization theory and research.* Chicago: Rand McNally, 1969.

Bem, S. L. "Androgeny vs. the tight little lives of fluffy women and chesty men." *Psychology Today*, September 1975, 58-62.

Bem, L. S. and Lenney, E. "Sex typing and the avoidance of cross-sexed behavior." *Journal of Personality and Social Psychology*, 1976, 33, 48-54.

Broverman, I. K., Broverman, D. M., Clarkson, F. E., Rosenkrantz, P. S., and Vogel, S. R. "Sex role stereotypes and clinical judgments of mental health." *Journal of Consulting and Clinical Psychology*, 1970, 34, 1-7.

Diamond, M. "Human sexual development: Biological foundations for social development." In F. A. Beach (ed.), *Human sexuality in four perspectives.* Baltimore: Johns Hopkins University Press, 1977.

Dweck, C. S. "Sex differences in the meaning of negative evaluation in achievement situations: Determinants and consequences." Paper presented at the meeting of the Society for Research in Child Development, Denver, April 1975.

Etaugh, C., Collins, G., and Gerson, A. "Reinforcement of sex-typed behaviors of two year old children in a nursery school setting." *Developmental Psychology*, 1975, 11, 255.

Feshbach, S. and Feshbach, W. "The young aggressors." *Psychology Today*, April 1973, 90-95.

Fisher, W. A. and Byrne, D. "Sex differences in response to erotica? Lover versus lust." *Journal of Personality and Social Psychology*, 1978, 36, 117-125.

Ford, C. S. and Beach, F. A. *Patterns of sexual behavior*. New York: Harper & Row, 1951.

Goldberg, P. "Are women prejudiced against women?" *Transaction*, 1968, 5, 28-, 30.

Goleman, D. "Special abilities of the sexes: Do they begin in the brain?" *Psychology Today*, November 1978, 48-120.

Heiman, J. R. "The physiology of erotica: Women's sexual arousal." *Psychology Today*, 1975, 8, 90-94.

Horner, M. Sex differences in achievement motivation and performance in competitive and non-competitive situations. Unpublished doctoral dissertation, University of Michigan, 1968.

Hunt, M. *Sexual behavior in the 1970s*. New York: Dell, 1974.

Janda, L. H., O'Grady, E. E., and Capps, C. F. "Fear of success in males and females in sex-linked occupations." *Sex Roles*, 1978, 4, 43-50.

Jourard, S. *The transparent self*. Rev. ed. New York: D. Van Nostrand, 1971.

Kinsey, A., Pomeroy, W. B., Martin, C., and Gebhard, P. *Sexual behavior in the human female*. Philadelphia: W. B. Saunders, 1953.

Kohlberg, L. "A cognitive-developmental analysis of children's sex-role concepts and attitudes." In E. E. Maccoby (ed.), *The development of sex differences*. Stanford: Stanford University Press, 1966.

Komarovsky, M. "Cultural contradictions and sex roles: The masculine case." *American Journal of Sociology*, 1973, 78, 873-884.

Kramer, C. "Women's speech: Separate but unequal?" *Quarterly Journal of Speech*, February 1974, 14-24.

Lyon, M. F. "Sex chromatin and gene action in the mammalian X-chromosome." *American Journal of Human Genetics*, 1962, 14, 135-148.

Maccoby, E. E. and Jacklin, C. N. *The psychology of sex differences*. Stanford: Stanford University Press, 1974.

McGuiness, D. and Pribram, K. "The origins of sensory bias in the development of gender differences in perception and cognition." In M. Bortner (ed.), *Cognitive growth and development—Essays in honor of Herbert G. Birch*. New York: Brunner/Mazel, in press.

Money, J. "Human hermaphroditism." In F. A. Beach (ed.), *Human sexuality in four perspectives*. Baltimore: Johns Hopkins University Press, 1977.

Money, J. and Ehrhardt, A. A. *Man, woman, boy and girl.* Baltimore: Johns Hopkins University Press, 1972.

Moss, H. A. "Sex age and state as determinants of mother-infant interaction." *Merrill-Palmer Quarterly,* 1967, 13, 19-36.

Nathan, P. E. and Harris, S. L. *Psychopathology and Society.* New York: McGraw-Hill, 1975.

Parelius, A. P. "Emerging sex role attitudes, expectations, and strains, among college women." *Journal of Marriage and the Family,* 1975, 37, 146-153.

Rubin, J. E., Provenzano, F. J., and Luria, Z. "The eye of the beholder: Parent's views on sex of newborns." *American Journal of Orthopsychiatry,* 1974, 44, 512-519.

Safran, C. "What men do to women on the job." *Redbook,* November 1976, pp. 149 ff.

Soskin, W. F. and John, V. P. "The study of spontaneous talk." In R. Barker (ed.), *The Stream of Behavior.* New York: Appleton-Century-Crofts, 1963.

Srole, L., Langer, T. S., Michael, S. T., Opler, M. K., and Rennice, T.A.C. *Mental health in the metropolis: The midtown Manhattan study.* Vol. 1. New York: McGraw-Hill, 1962.

Taylor, J. T. and Helmreich, R. L. *Masculinity and femininity: Their psychological dimensions, correlates, and antecedents.* Austin: University of Texas Press, 1978.

Taylor, S. P. and Epstein, S. "Aggression as a function of the interaction of the sex of the aggressor and the sex of the victim." *Journal of Personality,* 1967, 35, 473-486.

Weitzman, L. J., Eifler, D., Hokada, E., and Ross, C. "Sex-role socialization in picture books for pre-school children." *American Journal of Socialization,* 1972, 77, 1125-1150.

Chapter 18

Sexual Guilt and Anxiety

As we saw in Chapter 14, sexual guilt and anxiety are thought to be major causes of sexual dysfunctions. Men and women who are unable to engage in or to obtain satisfaction from sexual intercourse are thought to have high levels of guilt and anxiety. There are, however, millions of people who are able to have satisfactory sexual relations but who still experience feelings of sexual guilt and anxiety in some situations. Their sexual performance may not be affected by these feelings but other aspects of their lives are. In this chapter we will examine how these feelings develop, how they can influence one's life, and how they can be overcome.

Guilt and Anxiety: Some Definitions

The psychoanalytic and social learning theory definitions of guilt and anxiety are similar conceptually, even though the terms used are quite different. Freud (1936) described three forms of anxiety. The first of these is called *reality anxiety*, which refers to emotional arousal in situations of realistic, external danger. Reality anxiety may be thought of as fear—such as the feelings people might have if they saw a large dog that was foaming at the mouth, growling, and running toward them. The second form of anxiety is called *neurotic anxiety*. Freud believed that the source of neurotic anxiety was the id or the instincts (for example, sexual drives). People with neurotic anxiety are believed to be fearful that their instincts will get out of control and they may do something for which they might be punished. For example, a person with strong sexual urges may be fearful of being disapproved of if he or she attempts to gratify those urges.

Freud's third type of anxiety, which can be thought of as guilt, is called *moral anxiety*. This form of anxiety has its origins in the superego, or conscience. According to psy-

choanalytic theory, people will feel guilty if they do something, or even think of doing something, that they consider to be "bad" or that violates their moral code. Freud described people with guilt feelings as having harsh superegos.

Although psychoanalytic theory uses quite different terms, the social learning theory definitions of sexual guilt and anxiety are quite similar conceptually to moral anxiety and neurotic anxiety. Social learning theorists would define anxiety as an unrealistic or irrational fear of external consequences. A person with sexual anxiety may be reluctant to approach others with the intention of forming a sexual relationship because of an unrealistic concern with being laughed at or rebuffed. The person does not feel the behavior itself is inappropriate but rather he or she is concerned about the reactions of others.

Psychologist Donald Mosher (1965) is primarily responsible for the social learning theory conceptualization of guilt. Working within the framework of Julian Rotter's social learning theory, Mosher suggested that guilt can be thought of as a generalized expectancy for self-mediated punishment for the violation of internalized standards of proper behavior. Mosher suggested that guilty people have definite standards of right and wrong and they will suffer a loss of self-esteem if they violate or even consider violating those standards. Along with feeling guilty, such people will seek atonement—that is, they will act as though they want to be punished for their transgressions.

While both the psychoanalysts and the social learning theorists agree that there is a difference between sexual guilt and anxiety, it is very difficult to demonstrate this difference scientifically. First of all, guilt and anxiety have similar effects on behavior—namely, they prevent people from doing certain things. People who feel guilty do not develop sexual liaisons because they feel that to do so is morally wrong. People who are anxious are reluctant to form sexual relationships out of concern about the reactions of others. The effects are the same: sexual behavior is limited.

A second problem is that most people probably do not make a distinction between guilt and anxiety in their own minds. For example, it would be an unusual man who thought to himself "did I fail to introduce myself to that attractive women because I was feeling guilty or because I was feeling anxious"? It is likely that in many people guilt and anxiety can be present simultaneously. Thus, the man described above may feel both guilty and anxious about approaching an attractive woman. He may feel guilty because to do so might be seen as being disloyal to his girlfriend, and he may feel anxious because he is concerned that she may brush him off. However, he is probably aware only of his general feelings of discomfort. There have been relatively few scientific attempts to distinguish between the two and they have had contradictory findings. For example, Janda and O'Grady (1976) reported that the responses of college students to a word association test containing sexual double-entendre words could be understood best in terms of guilt. Klenke-Hamel and Janda (1979) found just the opposite. So, although most theorists make a distinction between sexual anxiety and guilt, for practical purposes, the terms may be used interchangeably until a distinction can be empirically demonstrated. At this point, we must conclude that although a theoretical difference between guilt and anxiety may exist, their effects on behavior are very similar.

To summarize, both the psychoanalyst and the social learning theorist agree that anxiety refers to an unrealistic concern with external consequences of behavior and that guilt refers to a process of self-evaluation against standards of right and wrong. There are differences between the two views in regard to the underlying mechanisms. The dynamic theorists speak of the id and the superego while the social learning theorists speak in terms of generalized expectancies. As we shall see later in the chapter, these differences hold important implications for how guilt and anxiety may influence behavior.

Development of Sexual Guilt and Anxiety

Virtually all of our knowledge concerning the development of sexual guilt and anxiety comes from case histories of those with sexual dysfunctions. This provides us with information about those factors in the backgrounds of people with severe sexual guilt and anxiety (see Chapter 14) but we know relatively little about the development of less debilitating forms of guilt and anxiety. There has, however, been some research about the development of nonspecific guilt and anxiety. This research, taken together with the case histories of sexually dysfunctional people, provides a basis for speculating about the development of sexual guilt and anxiety.

The foundation for feelings of guilt and anxiety is laid during early childhood. The nature of the interactions and relationships with the parents is of crucial importance. Psychologist Robert Sears and his colleagues examined the characteristics of parents and how these characteristics related to the development of a conscience in their children (Sears, Maccoby, and Levin, 1972). They suggested that parents who have a warm, affectionate relationship with their children and who use withdrawal of love as a punishment technique are most likely to initiate the development of a conscience in their offspring. Parents who use withdrawal of love communicate to their children, either implicitly or explicitly, that they will no longer love them if they commit some transgression. For example, a parent may say to a child "I would be very disappointed in you if you did that." To the young child, this may be interpreted as a withdrawal of love, and it sets the stage for the development of guilt feelings for anticipated or actual violations of the parents' standards of proper behavior. A close, affectionate relationship between the parent and child is crucial because unless it exists the withdrawal of love will have little impact.

The research of Masters and Johnson (1970) illustrates the role of parental training in the development of sexual guilt. They described several case histories in which parents discussed, quite explicitly, the evils of sex. Such parents were likely to make assertions such as "no good woman ever desires sexual intercourse." Or they were likely to state that television shows, magazine articles, or movies that were the least bit sexual in nature were "disgusting to decent people." It is not surprising that children from such families develop strong feelings of guilt about their sexuality.

Research regarding the antecedents of anxiety also stress the importance of parent-child relationships. One factor that has been found to be related to the development of anxiety is the standards of performance set by parents for their children (Stewart, 1958). In this study boys were asked to describe themselves and the boys' mothers were asked to describe the way they would like their sons to be. The results indicated that the greater the discrepancy between the boy's self-description and his mother's ideal description of him, the higher the boy's anxiety level. This suggests that children who feel that they are not living up to their parents' standards are likely to develop feelings of anxiety.,

Although the study cited above was not specifically concerned with sexual anxiety, it is likely that this situation would affect one's heterosexual relationships as an adult. If a person grows up with the feeling that he or she cannot live up to the parents' standards, then that person is likely to develop feelings of

inferiority. These individuals will be concerned that others might evaluate them negatively. Consequently, they may be reluctant to form new relationships or to shift from superficial relationships to more intimate ones. This type of fear has been called performance anxiety by psychologists. Masters and Johnson (1970) have provided anecdotal evidence to support this line of reasoning. They discussed a case of secondary impotence in which the man's dysfunction was traced to his feeling that he could never meet the standards his father had set for him.

Parents who use harsh, punitive, and restrictive techniques of discipline are also likely to instill anxiety in their children (Kessler, 1966). Child psychologist Paul Mussen and his colleagues have suggested that parents who react this way when their preschool children express their curiosity about sexual matters may be instilling sexual anxiety in them (Mussen, Conger, and Kagan, 1974). Most young children will ask questions about sex, fondle their genitals, and run around the house naked on occasion. If the parents react harshly to these behaviors, the children are likely to grow up to be adults who have a great deal of conflict and anxiety about sex.

Once again the differences between psychoanalytic theory and social learning theory lie primarily in terminology and the hypothetical constructs invoked to explain guilt and anxiety. Both theories emphasize the importance of parental discipline and children's desire to please their parents. Freud (1961) believed that guilt had its origins in fear of loss of love. Young children between the ages of three to five first learn to inhibit their behavior because they fear punishment from an external authority—namely, the parents. Freud equated fear of punishment with fear of loss of love since he reasoned that love provides protection against punitive aggression. As children pass through the phallic stage and begin to identify with their parents, they begin to develop a superego. The superego, which represents a substitution of an internal authority for an external authority, takes over control of moral behavior. At this point the child will feel guilty for "bad" intentions as well as "bad" behavior since nothing can be kept secret from the superego. Freud did point out that some people never go through this process and as adults their behavior is governed only by the fear of being found out. Such people would be described as anxious rather than guilty.

The social learning view of the development of guilt and anxiety is similar except that it does not invoke concepts such as the phallic stage and superego. It is apparent, for example, that Freud's theory of moral development is consistent with the results of the experiment conducted by social learning theorists Sears, Maccoby, and Levin (1972). Their findings—that warm, affectionate parents who use withdrawal of love as a punishment technique are likely to have children with well-developed consciences—support the notion that identification is a crucial process.

Social learning theorist Donald Mosher (1961, 1965) has suggested that whether one's emotional reactions in a conflict situation are dominated by guilt or anxiety depend upon the punishment techniques utilized by the parents. Parents who promise vague and delayed forms of punishment are likely to promote in their children the development of internalized standards of proper behavior. Parents who rely primarily on immediate physical punishment are more likely to have children whose behavior is inhibited by anxiety.

To illustrate, consider two parents who discover their children "playing doctor" with their friends. Suppose the first parent takes the child into the house and has a talk with the child in which it is explained that such behavior is unacceptable. The child is told that if such behavior should reoccur, the child will have to be punished for his or her own

good. Imagine that the second parent simply spanks the child and sends him or her into the house. In the future, it is likely that the first child's behavior will be influenced by considerations of right and wrong—that is, the child will feel guilty. The second child probably will be concerned primarily with the prospect of "getting caught."

To summarize, it appears that both sexual guilt and anxiety have their origins in the early childhood years. The psychoanalysts and the social learning theorists essentially agree that children who are exposed primarily to physical punishment are likely to develop sexual anxiety while children who have close relationships with their parents and who are disciplined with withdrawal of love are more likely to develop feelings of guilt. Needless to say, the degree of sexual guilt and anxiety can vary considerably depending on the amount and severity of the punishment.

Figure 18.1
Children whose parents accept their displays of sexual interest are not likely to develop feelings of guilt or anxiety. (Hamel)

Effects of Sexual Guilt and Anxiety

Psychoanalytic theory and social learning theory diverge in their views regarding the effects of sexual guilt and anxiety. The psychoanalysts believe that sexual guilt and anxiety can be the basis for conflict that can affect behavior in a variety of ways. They suggest that the bases of many adult neuroses can be traced back to sexual conflicts acquired during childhood. According to this view, then, childhood experiences are crucial in determining adult behavior and personality because these experiences may have produced an underlying psychological disturbance.

Social learning theorists, while not denying the importance of childhood experiences, argue that behavior tends to be situationally specific. This view suggests that to understand any form of behavior we must examine it in the context in which it occurs. They question the validity of the notion that childhood experiences provide the basis for personality traits that influence one's behavior in a variety of situations.

To illustrate the difference between the two approaches consider the case of a young man who feels very uncomfortable about approaching women for dates. The psychoanalyst might argue that such behavior results from the manner in which the man resolved his Oedipal conflict. His relationship with his parents during the crucial phallic stage provided the basis for a relatively stable personality characteristic that is currently influencing his relationships with women.

The social learning theorist would argue that this young man's reticence with women has nothing to do with his hypothetical childhood sexual desires for his mother. The social learning theorists would be interested in the more obvious and observable aspects of the man's interpersonal relationships. The mother may have played an important role in influencing the man's behavior but not in the same manner as the psychoanalyst would suggest. For example, the mother, and perhaps the father, may have discouraged the child's attempts to be outgoing and friendly. Thus, he may have been somewhat withdrawn around his peers and, consequently, somewhat unnoticed. After years of what he perceived as rejection by girls, it would not be surprising if as an adult, he felt uncomfortable around women. The crucial point is that the social learning theorist believes that the learning history must be considered to understand the behavior in question. Let us now examine examples of the effects of sexual guilt and anxiety from both the psychoanalytic and social learning perspective.

The Psychoanalytic Perspective

A crucial concept in psychoanalytic theory is that mental processes of which the individual is unaware can influence one's behavior. This concept, called the principle of the unconscious, was in part a result of Freud's attempt to understand neurotic symptoms that did not seem to serve any logical purpose. Many of Freud's patients were women whose symptoms included *hysterical conversion reactions*—conditions in which some bodily function is impaired without any apparent organic basis. Hysterical blindness, deafness, or paralysis of the limbs are examples of conversion reactions. In treating the patients Freud came to believe that in many cases the cause was unconscious sexual conflict. The patient was thought to "choose" the symptom, at an unconscious level, because the symptom helped to alleviate repressed feelings of sexual guilt and anxiety. For example, a woman could develop paralysis of the legs shortly before her wedding day. The paralysis would serve the purpose of reducing her guilt and anxiety about having a sexual relationship by postponing it.

The effects of unconscious sexual conflicts can have more subtle and pervasive effects as well. According to psychoanalytic theory,

TOPICS IN HUMAN SEXUALITY

hysterical neuroses in both men and women have their origins in the castration complex. For women, the castration complex takes the form of penis envy, which occurs around the age of three or four when they discover that boys have something they do not—a penis. The girl is thought to blame her mother for withholding this organ and turns to her father who has the highly desired organ. This process plays an important role in the girl's heterosexual relationships once she becomes an adult. The nature of any possible neurotic behavior depends upon the manner in which the parents deal with their daughter during this stage.

One form of hysterical neurosis in women has been called the vengeful type (Abraham, 1948). A woman, motivated by her unresolved penis envy, takes out her hostility on all men. She does this by using her feminine charms to dominate and render men helpless. Consider P. C. Kuiper's description:

This character type expresses itself in a repetitive maneuver: A man is seduced and made helplessly dependent, upon which there follows a characteristic behavior pattern. The woman makes even higher demands, she wants to be not only taken care of, but extravagantly indulged. When she has taken from the man all he has to give, she turns away from him in triumph, or finds other admirers to stir up his jealousy. Not infrequently men are driven to suicide out of utter despair, overwhelmed by paralyzing fears of abandonment. The feeling of being abandoned means not being able to function as a man; he is castrated. Men get into these dangerous situations in consequence of a typical behavioral maneuver. The woman constantly arouses the man's sexual desires, which she at first gratifies, but then abruptly thwarts. The use of the word vampire illustrates well the sucking and biting aspects of the behavior pattern of these patients. The female genital is used like a biting mouth; . . . The oral-sadistic attitude is one of the determinants of this form of the female

castration complex. The following fantasy of a patient of this type is very illuminating: She imagined that she deprived all the men she had or could have intercourse with of their penises, which she had strung on a line like trophies in her room. This type of woman is a rewarding subject in literature, on the stage and in films. As long as the partner, or better, the victim is in the process of being conquered, love is convincingly feigned (Kuiper, 1972, p. 133).

These behaviors almost ensure that such a woman will be unable to develop meaningful intimate relationships. It is not unusual for such a woman to experience suicidal depression when she is between affairs. She seems to need the excitement of yet another conquest. Often, after many years of neurotic patterns and as she begins to lose her ability to attract men, she becomes depressed by her lack of satisfying relationships.

The male counterpart of this disorder is popularly referred to as a *Don Juan*—a man who is plagued by his unconscious fears of castration, which develop from an unsatisfactory resolution of the Oedipal conflict. He, too, has an insatiable need to have one sexual conquest after another to prove to himself that he is sexually adequate. Like his female counterpart, he becomes dissatisfied with his relationships quickly and never seems to be able to form a lasting one.

Another characteristic of the hysterical man is his intense need for approval and admiration. He may become a "workaholic" to try to satisfy his striving for success. This behavior is considered neurotic because he finds little pleasure in the work itself. His only interest lies in accomplishment so that he can win the adulation of others. Any success is perceived as additional evidence of his virility.

Hysterical neurosis is just one way that unconscious sexual guilt and anxiety can be expressed. Another is agoraphobia, a fear of open places, which is thought to be caused by unconscious fears that one will be sexually promiscuous. Compulsive handwashing is often viewed as a symptom of guilt feelings about masturbation. The important point is that psychoanalysts believe that it is possible for sexual guilt and anxiety to result in disturbances that, on the surface, bear little relation to sexuality.

The Social Learning Perspective

The interest of social learning theorists in sexual anxiety and guilt was stimulated largely by the work of Donald Mosher. Mosher (1966) formulated a conceptualization of guilt in social learning terms and constructed a scale to measure sexual guilt. The Mosher Forced Choice Guilt Scale includes twenty-eight items pertaining to guilt about sex. Here are a few examples:

Sex relations before marriage—
A. ruin many a happy couple
B. are good in my opinion

When I have sexual desires—
A. I usually try to curb them
B. I generally satisfy them

For both items alternative A is indicative of sexual guilt. The construction of this scale allowed researchers to readily identify individuals who are high and low in guilt. This made it possible to conduct experiments to examine the effects of sexual guilt and anxiety.

A crucial hypothesis in Mosher's theory was that the behavior of individuals high in guilt is governed by internalized standards of proper behavior. This means that their behavior should be relatively consistent across sexual conflict situations. Low guilt individuals, on the other hand, are influenced by the external cues in a conflict situation. If they believe they will be approved of or reinforced in some way for making sexual responses, they will do so. If they anticipate that sexual responses will be met with disapproval or punishment, they will inhibit such behavior.

In one experiment designed to test this hypothesis, an experimenter conveyed to half of the subjects that he had very permissive, liberal attitudes about sex. To the other half he presented himself as having very conservative, restricted attitudes. Following this experimental manipulation, subjects were asked to respond to a Word Association Test containing numerous sexual double-entendres (for example, blow, screw). The findings were consistent with Mosher's hypothesis. It was found that low guilt subjects responded with many more sexual words in the permissive condition than in the conservative condition. High guilt subjects, however, gave about the same number of sexual responses in both conditions (Galbraith and Mosher, 1968).

This hypothesis is consistent with the clinical observations of Masters and Johnson (1970). They pointed out that many people with high levels of sexual guilt and anxiety have difficulty in making the transition from premarital standards of proper behavior to marital standards of right and wrong. As children they were taught, and they grew up to believe, that any expression of their sexuality was evil. The issuance of a marriage license is not sufficient to overcome a lifetime of moral training. The unfortunate result is that their sexual adjustment to marriage is often unsatisfactory. People who have little guilt and anxiety could be expected to adjust to such changes fairly easily.

Recently there has been some interest in how low guilt and high guilt people perceive women. In one series of studies, women experimenters played either a warm, friendly, approachable role or a cold, distant, unapproachable role with men (Janda, 1975; Janda, Witt, and Manahan, 1976). After interacting with the women for approximately one-half hour, the men were asked to complete a likeability rating scale of the women. Not surprisingly, it was found that the low guilt men liked the warm, friendly women considerably more than the cold distant women. High guilt men, however, liked the cold, distant women just as much as the warm, friendly women.

The explanation offered for this somewhat surprising finding was that high guilt men may have formed idealized stereotypes of women —they have placed women on a pedestal. We may speculate that when a high guilt man is faced with a cold, distant woman, he interprets her behavior as rejecting. He may say to himself, "She is a nice person; she is just not interested in me." A low guilt man, however, will perceive a cold, distant woman as being just that—cold and distant. He will be less inclined to make excuses for her behavior.

A recent experiment may have important practical as well as theoretical implications (Janda and O'Grady, 1979). This experiment examined differences between low guilt and high guilt men in the amount of pleasure they were willing to give to a woman. The subjects were told that the experiment was a test of their ability to teach a woman (actually a confederate of the experimenters') a series of number problems. They were to reward her by the administration of pleasure via a "Brock Pleasure Machine." The apparatus contained a number of levers, lights, and dials, and looked impressive. It did not actually deliver any pleasure, however. The results of the experiment indicated that low guilt men administered more pleasure, overall, than did high guilt men. Also, the high guilt men significantly reduced the amount of pleasure they administered when they were

Sex Guilt and Sexual Activity in Dating Couples

There have been numerous experiments that have documented the relationship between sexual guilt and sexual activity. For both men and women, low guilt is related to a greater variety of sexual experiences and a larger number of sexual partners. Perhaps a more interesting question and one that has received less attention concerns the role of sexual guilt in influencing the degree of sexual involvement in dating couples. If stereotypes can be trusted, one would expect the sex guilt level of the woman to play a larger role than the guilt level of the man because in our society women are thought to be responsible for setting limits on the extent of sexual involvement.

Psychologists Judith D'Augelli and Herbert Cross (1975) have addressed this issue. They tested and interviewed over seventy dating couples in an attempt to determine the factors that influenced the sexual aspects of each relationship. Surprisingly, they discovered that the two most important factors involve the man. The first of these was the level of sexual guilt. The higher the guilt level of the man, the less likely it was that the couple had had intercourse. The second most important factor was the level of moral reasoning of the man. Third was the level of sexual guilt of the woman. These results were surprising because, contrary to popular thought, they indicated that the man assumes the responsibility for determining the sexual involvement of a couple. It seriously questions the notion that most men will attempt to go as far as they can and the woman will indicate when he has gone far enough. It would appear that men, as well as women, are sensitive to moral and ethical issues that are associated with a sexual relationship.

led to believe that they would be required to meet with the confederate some time after the experiment. Low guilt men slightly increased their administration of pleasure when they had this expectation.

These results suggest that one of the effects of sexual guilt and anxiety is that it influences one's feelings about giving pleasure to others. High guilt people appear to have some conflicts about the appropriateness of giving pleasure. The clinical implications of this finding may be important. Perhaps one goal of treatment programs for sexually dysfunctional people should be to assure them that it is not only appropriate but highly desirable to provide their partner with as much pleasure as possible.

This is just a brief review of some of the social learning theory research regarding sexual anxiety and guilt. It is clear however, that this approach differs substantially from the psychoanalytic approach. Social learning theorists look for very specific effects and do not assume that the behavior of a person with sexual guilt and anxiety will be consistent in a variety of situations.

Reducing Sexual Guilt and Anxiety

A large variety of therapeutic techniques exist that can be useful in reducing sexual guilt and anxiety. In this section we will discuss two such techniques—rational-emotive therapy and the behavior therapy technique of desensitization.

Rational-Emotive Therapy

Rational-emotive therapy was developed by psychologist Albert Ellis (1973), a psychotherapist who has published numerous scientific and popular books and articles on human sexuality. Ellis's credentials would seem to make him particularly well qualified to discuss approaches to reducing sexual guilt and anxiety.

The basis of rational-emotive therapy is known as the A-B-C paradigm. The A refers to a situational event; the B refers to a person's thoughts and feelings about that event; and the C refers to the associated negative emotional consequences—for example, guilt and anxiety. Most people have the tendency to believe that their unpleasant emotional reactions are caused by A—the things that happen to them. Ellis claims, however, that it is actually B—what people tell themselves about what happens to them—that cause them to feel guilty or anxious. For example, a college student might report that he feels very anxious because his girlfriend has been acting rather cool toward him lately and he is concerned that she is rejecting him. He is blaming his girlfriend's unfriendly behavior for his feelings of discomfort. Ellis would tell the student that his girlfriend's behavior had nothing to do with his feelings of anxiety. The responsibility would lie with the things the student was telling himself about his girlfriend's behavior.

Ellis believes that people with psychological disturbances have a tendency to tell themselves irrational things about the things that happen to them. The college student, for example, might have had a number of such thoughts about his girlfriend's behavior. Perhaps he thought: "If she leaves me, I'll never be able to find someone else who will love me." Or perhaps: "If she leaves me, I will be so lonely I won't be able to stand it." Ellis would claim that these irrational thoughts were responsible for the student's feelings of anxiety.

The source of many irrational beliefs can be found in the unrealistically high expectations many people have of themselves. A woman may have the belief that she should be faithful to her husband in body and mind. If such a woman were even to feel sexually attracted to another man, she would be likely to feel guilty. A man may be extremely anxious about approaching women because he cannot think of himself as desirable or worthwhile unless every woman he meets is attracted to him. To a man with these beliefs, a rejection, regardless of how tactful it may be, can be devastating. If such people, Ellis believes, could have more realistic and rational expectations of themselves, they would be much less likely to feel guilty or anxious.

The task of the rational-emotive therapist is essentially to modify what clients say to themselves at B. That is, the clients have to be taught to replace their irrational thoughts about the things that happen to them with more logical and realistic reactions. Ellis sees the role of the therapist as being very similar to that of an educator. The therapist must teach the client a logical way of thinking.

To the casual observer, a rational-emotive therapy session may appear to be more like an argument than anything else. Ellis is a very forceful and dynamic man, and he has been known to tell clients their ideas are nothing but "bullshit." He believes it necessary to be direct because the client's thought patterns are likely to be deeply ingrained. If the therapist is to have any hope of changing old, unadaptive patterns of thought, he or she cannot afford to be subtle. The dialogue below provides a sense of rational-emotive therapy. The client, a thirty-four-year-old woman, was recently divorced and sought therapy for her feelings of loneliness and depression.

Therapist: How long have you had feelings of depression?

Client: Ever since my husband left me about a year ago.

T: Your husband's leaving has made you depressed?

C: Yes. We were married for ten years and he left me for someone else. I feel like such a failure.

T: So you seem to believe that because your husband left, you're a failure. You weren't interesting enough or desirable enough to keep a husband. Is that right?

C: That's right—that's true.

T: That doesn't sound very logical to me.

C: What do you mean? (*with irritation*).

T: Who said you were a failure? I'll tell you who said so—you said so. You told yourself that because your husband left you, you must be a failure as a woman. It's that kind of nutty thinking that's causing you to feel depressed.

C: But I feel like such a failure.

T: Well let's just suppose that you're right. You were a failure. Suppose your husband thought you were boring both as a companion and as a bed partner. What's so terrible about that?

C: That would be terrible!

T: No it wouldn't. It would be too bad. It would be unfortunate. But it wouldn't be terrible. It's not the end of the world. Besides, you seem to be telling yourself that if your husband thinks you're sexually and socially inadequate, then those things must be true.

C: You mean I shouldn't consider myself a failure just because my husband thinks so.

T: That's right. That's the basis of your problem. If at A I do poorly and my husband thinks I'm inadequate then at B I must agree with him, beat myself over the head and at C, get depressed.

The rational-emotive therapist also makes liberal use of homework assignments. Homework was given to the client above to help her overcome her feelings of loneliness. First she was instructed to read Ellis's book *The Intelligent Woman's Guide to Manhunting* to help change her belief that women must wait for men to approach them. Then she was given a series of assignments that were intended to increase her assertiveness gradually. This woman was attracted to a man she had never spoken to that worked in her office. An assignment early in the course of therapy required her to simply smile and say hello when she passed him. Several sessions later, she was instructed to suggest that they have lunch together. The assignments were successful in helping the woman get to know this particular man and in feeling more at ease in her relationships with men in general.

Systematic Desensitization

Systematic desensitization is a behavior therapy technique that was developed by psychiatrist Joseph Wolpe (1958, 1969). It has been successfully used in the treatment of a variety of anxiety related disorders, including sexual dysfunctions (Rimm and Masters, 1979). The technique essentially involves the pairing of deep muscle relaxation with imagined scenes depicting the anxiety arousing situations. It is thought that the anxiety that is initially elicited by the scenes will be gradually replaced with feelings of relaxation. The relaxation will then generalize to real life situations.* The three components to the process are training in deep muscle relaxation, construction of an anxiety hierarchy, and pairing the scenes with the relaxed state.

Deep muscle relaxation is achieved through a set of exercises that require the client to tense, and then relax, opposing sets of muscles throughout the body. For example, the client might be asked to make a fist and to

*There are, however, several different theories regarding the underlying mechanisms (Wilkins, 1971).

hold it as tight as possible for ten to fifteen seconds. After relaxing for forty-five to sixty seconds, the client is asked to extend the fingers as far as possible for ten to fifteen seconds. After this procedure is repeated for all the major muscle groups, the client has typically achieved a deep state of relaxation. Clients who have received several sessions of training in this technique often report significant reductions in their overall level of anxiety. Most behavior therapists believe that this procedure has therapeutic value itself.

After the client has mastered the relaxation techniques, the anxiety hierarchy is constructed. This is a list of scenes, related to the client's fears, that are arranged in increasing order in terms of how anxious they make the

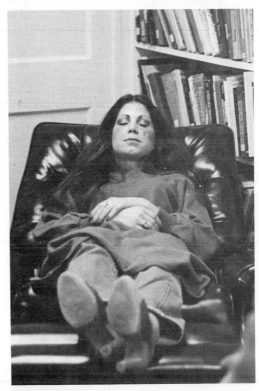

Figure 18.2
Desensitization is an effective technique for reducing sexual anxiety. (Dwyer and Zinkl)

client feel. Anywhere from ten to thirty such scenes are developed depending on the nature of the client's problem. The first scene typically represents a situation that makes the client feel only slightly uncomfortable. The last scene represents a situation that makes the client feel extremely anxious. Below are scenes from an anxiety hierarchy that was used in the treatment of a twenty-two-year-old college male who was anxious about relationships with women.

1. Saying "hello" to an attractive woman while waiting for an elevator.
2. Initiating a conversation with a woman after class.
3. Asking Susan who sits next to you in political science to have a cup of coffee after class.
4. Asking Susan for a date.
5. Picking up Susan for a date and meeting her roommates.
6. Sitting at dinner with Susan when there is a pause of two minutes in the conversation.
7. Going to a party where you meet several of Susan's friends.
8. Saying goodnight to Susan.
9. Telling Susan how you feel about her.
10. Talking to Susan about sex.

Once the hierarchy has been constructed, the client is asked to imagine each scene while in a deep state of relaxation. The client begins at the bottom of the hierarchy and works upward. Each scene is presented for five to twenty-five seconds until the client can imagine it without experiencing any anxiety. Some clients can complete this process in four to five sessions while others may take as many as twenty sessions. Once the client is able to imagine all of the scenes without feeling anxious, he or she will feel considerably more comfortable in real life situations.

These are just two examples of therapy approaches that can be useful in the treatment of sexual guilt and anxiety. While some therapists will rely primarily on one treatment technique, there appears to be a growing realization in the field of psychotherapy that a combination of techniques may be the most fruitful approach. For example, Arnold Lazarus (1976), a prominent clinical psychologist, has recommended what he calls a multimodal approach to therapy. Even psychoanalytically oriented therapists, such as Helen Singer Kaplan, recognize that no single technique is appropriate for all cases. The client who seeks therapy for a sex-related problem would be well advised to avoid therapists that rigidly adhere to a single approach.

Summary

Sexual anxiety generally refers to an unrealistic concern of incurring disapproval for one's sexual behavior. Sexual guilt refers to unpleasant feelings one has for violating or anticipating violating one's internalized standards of proper behavior. Although most theorists would agree that this distinction is a valid one, in real life situations it is very difficult to distinguish between the two concepts.

Psychoanalytic and social learning theorists agree that feelings of guilt and anxiety have their origins in childhood. Children who have close, affectionate relationships with their parents, and whose parents use withdrawal of love as a punishment technique, are likely to develop the potential for guilt. Children whose parents set unrealistically high standards for them and who use harsh, immediate forms of punishment are likely to develop the potential for anxiety. Psychoanalytic theorists believe that sexual guilt and anxiety can be unconscious and can be expressed in pervasive neurotic disturbances that may bear little relation to sexuality.

Social learning theorists, on the other hand, are more interested in situationally specific effects of guilt and anxiety.

Two methods of treatment for sexual guilt and anxiety are rational-emotive therapy and systematic desensitization. Rational-emotive therapy is intended to help clients think in rational, logical and scientific ways. Systematic desensitization is aimed at replacing feelings of anxiety with feelings of calmness and relaxation.

References

Abraham, K. "Manifestations of the female castration complex." In *Selected Papers*. London: Hogarth Press, 1948 (originally published in 1920).

D'Augelli, J. F. and Cross, H. J. "Relationship of sex guilt and moral reasoning to premarital sex in college women and in couples." *Journal of Consulting and Clinical Psychology*, 1975, 43, 40-47.

Ellis, A. "Rational-emotive therapy." In R. Corsini (ed.), *Current psychotherapies*. Itasca, Ill.: F. E. Peacock, 1973.

Freud, S. *Inhibitions, symptoms, and anxiety*. London: Hogarth Press, 1936 (first German edition, 1926).

Freud, S. "Civilization and its discontents." In J. Strachey (trans. and ed.), *The standard edition of the complete psychological works of Sigmund Freud*, Vol. XXI. London: Hogarth Press, 1961.

Galbraith, G. G. and Mosher, D. L. "Associative sexual responses in relation to sexual arousal, guilt, and external approval contingencies." *Journal of Personality and Social Psychology*, 1968, 10, 142-147.

Janda, L. H. "Effects of guilt, approachability of examiner and stimulus relevance upon thematic apperception responses." *Journal of Consulting and Clinical Psychology*, 1975, 43, 369-374.

Janda, L. H. and O'Grady, K. E. "Effects of guilt and response modality upon associative sexual responses." *Journal of Research in Personality*, 1976, 10, 457-462.

Janda, L. H. and O'Grady, K. E. "Effects of guilt on interpersonal pleasuring." Unpublished Manuscript, Old Dominion University, 1979.

Janda, L. H., Witt, C., and Manahan, C. "Effects of guilt and approachability of examiner upon associative sexual responses." *Journal of Consulting and Clinical Psychology*, 1976, 44, 986-990.

Kaplan, H. S. *The new sex therapy*. New York: Bruner/Mazel, 1974.

Kessler, J. W. *Psychopathology of childhood*. Englewood Cliffs, N.J.: Prentice-Hall, 1966.

Klenke-Hamel, K. E. and Janda, L. H. "Effects of guilt and modeling upon associative sexual responses." *Journal of Personality Assessment*, 1979, 43, 150–154.

Kuiper, P. C. *The neuroses: A psychoanalytic survey.* New York: International Universities Press, 1972.

Lazarus, A. A. *Multimodal behavior therapy.* New York: Springer, 1976.

Masters, W. and Johnson, V. *Human sexual inadequacy.* Boston: Little, Brown, 1970.

Mosher, D. L. The development and validation of a sentence completion measure of guilt. Unpublished doctoral dissertation. Ohio State University, 1961.

Mosher, D. L. "Interaction of fear and guilt in inhibiting unacceptable behavior." *Journal of Consulting Psychology,* 1965, 29, 161-167.

Mosher, D. L. "The development and multitrait-multimethod matrix analysis of three measures of three aspects of guilt." *Journal of Consulting Psychology,* 1966, 30, 25-29.

Mussen, P. H., Conger, J. J., and Kagan, J. *Child development and personality.* New York: Harper & Row, 1974.

Ottenheimer, L. "Unconscious factors in choice of a mate." *Medical Aspects of Human Sexuality,* March 1971, 130-143.

Rimm, D. C. and Masters, J. C. *Behavior therapy: Techniques and empirical findings.* New York: Academic Press, 1979.

Sears, R. R., Maccoby, E. E., and Levin, A. "Signs and sources of conscious." In R. C. Johnson, P. R. Dokecki, and O. H. Mowrer (eds.), *Conscience, contract, and social reality.* New York: Holt, Rinehart & Winston, 1972.

Stewart, L. H. "Manifest anxiety and mother-son identification." *Journal of Clinical Psychology,* 1958, 14, 382-384.

Wilkins, W. "Desensitization: Social and cognitive factors underlying the effectiveness of Wolpe's procedure." *Psychological Bulletin,* 1971, 76, 311-317.

Wolpe, J. *Psychotherapy by reciprocal inhibition.* Stanford: Stanford University Press, 1958.

Wolpe, J. *The practice of behavior therapy.* New York: Pergamon Press, 1969.

Chapter 19

Human Sexuality: Moral and Legal Considerations

The fact that human beings have a sexual nature requires them to make decisions about their sexual behavior. A person must decide with whom it is appropriate to have sex, under what conditions it is appropriate to have sex, or which sexual behaviors and techniques are appropriate. Societies and cultures must make decisions about a variety of sex-related issues. For instance, they must decide how to deal with sexual variations, abortion, sex education, and a host of related issues.Up to this point we have discussed a number of factors that influence the choices people make about their sexual behavior; namely, biological, psychological, and cultural factors. In reviewing this material it would not be difficult to form the impression that we are victims of our biology and environment—that we do not really have much freedom to choose how we will behave sexually. But even though behavioral scientists interested in human sexuality have a tendency to focus on the factors that influence sexual behavior, few would deny that human beings are rational creatures and have the ability to make decisions about what is right, wrong, proper, or improper sexual behavior.

Disciplines that do focus on the decision-making process include philosophy, theology, and law. All assume that people are capable of making rational decisions, and all three disciplines have attempted to provide guidelines and systems to aid people in the decision-making process. They have provided us with standards of morality, systems of ethics, and legal statutes that we can use (or not use) in making our decisions about how to behave sexually. Of course, things are never simple, and the standards, systems, and laws are not necessarily in agreement. Indeed, they are often contradictory. But a knowledge of theological, ethical, and legal systems can provide people with guidelines designed to facilitate the decision-making process. In the first part of the chapter, approaches to moral decision-making and

the relationship between morality and the law will be reviewed. Later, we will focus on the ethical and legal issues associated with a few sexual concerns that our society is currently struggling with.

Systems of Ethics

As was discussed in earlier chapters, our society's views of morality or ethics regarding sexual matters were derived largely from the Judeo-Christian tradition (see Chapter 2). This tradition is an example of one type of system of ethics called the *legalistic* or *code* approach. A second system that has been around since Aristotle but is currently being touted as the new morality is referred to as *situation ethics*. A third system, most closely identified with existentialism, is known as the *antinomian* approach. Let us review the assumptions of and problems associated with each approach.

The Code Approach

People who subscribe to a code or legalistic approach to ethics believe that moral decisions should be made in accord with some set of rules and regulations. For such people, solutions to moral dilemma are predetermined and can be "looked up" in the Bible, Talmud, law books, or any other accepted authoritative source. All major Western religious traditions have been legalistic or code systems and hence theology has played a major role in setting standards of sexual morality.

Advocates of a code approach have also been called absolutists because they believe the particular code they subscribe to represents absolute moral law—that is, there are to be no exceptions. They believe that there are indeed certain moral principles, usually derived from religious writings or Natural Law (which is often interpreted by religious authorities), that are universally applicable and should never be violated. One example of such moral absolutes can be found in the Ten Commandments.

The problem with code ethics, as pointed out by a number of philosophers, is that there are many situations in which following a code may not provide simple, easily identifiable solutions. As an example, Bishop James Pike (1967) posed the dilemma of a CIA agent who had been arrested in a foreign country for espionage. The evidence against him was strong enough so that there was little point in his lying in an attempt to save himself. But if he were to tell the truth it would endanger his nation and the lives of other agents who continued to operate covertly. Is this sufficient basis to ignore the commandment "Thou shalt not bear false witness against thy neighbor"?

Philosopher and theologian Joseph Fletcher (1966) cited an incident in which the forces of "secular law and legalistic puritanism" resulted in what many people would perceive to be an "immoral" decision. The case involved a woman who was convicted (later overturned in a higher court) of contributing to the delinquency of her minor daughter. She advised her daughter, who had the first of three unwanted, neglected babies at the age of thirteen, to use birth control if she was going to persist in such behavior. Perhaps legalists who do subscribe to proscriptions against birth control can sympathize with the lower court's decision, but many people would have difficulty in seeing this case in black and white terms.

Both Pike and Fletcher have discussed other problems with code ethics. Pike points out that many theologians argue that the code provided by the Ten Commandments and other Biblical injunctions should not be taken literally but viewed as providing principles that can be applied to contemporary situations. Such a view requires that interpretations of scripture be made and interpreta-

tions have a tendency to shift over time and to vary according to who is doing the interpreting. Pike raises the question of how absolute a moral principle can be if it changes from year to year or if it varies from parish to parish.

Fletcher points out that the complexities of life and the demands of justice and compassion will inevitably combine to generate more and more rulings. What is destined to evolve is an elaborate system that provides for exceptions and compromises—in other words, rules for breaking the rules. Fletcher comments: "Any web thus woven sooner or later chokes its weavers" (p. 19).

In spite of those liabilities, many people, whether they are aware of it or not, subscribe to a code or legalism approach to ethics. Some may support a code as a result of their belief in a selected authority; others may support it simply because that is what they have been taught. After all, parents typically discipline their children in accord with absolute standards (for example, "*Never* lie to me," or "I don't want you to *ever* bite your little brother"). Comforting as it may be to have a code of absolutes, a proponent of such a system must be prepared to provide unambiguous answers to issues such as premarital sex, abortion, and contraception. Many people would question whether there can be absolutes that can apply to every case.

Situation Ethics

As the term implies, a situation ethics approach suggests that decisions involving issues of ethics or morality must be evaluated on a case-by-case basis. The situation ethicist believes that absolute rules or codes do not exist and ethical judgments can be made only in the context of a particular situation. Situation ethics have also been called special ethics (Pike, 1967). They are special in the sense that they require taking into account the particular situation, the distinctiveness of each human relationship and the uniqueness of every individual.

The term situation ethics has often been used synonymously with the term the new morality. Actually, neither situation ethics nor the new morality is very new. The approach of current advocates of situation ethics has a parallel in the work of Aristotle, who emphasized the importance of equity above specific laws. He is quoted as saying, "Equity makes allowance for human weakness, looking not to the law but to the meaning of the lawgiver, not to the act but to the intention, not the part, but to the whole" (Davis, 1935, p. 187). Jesus, according to some theologians (Fletcher, 1966), was also sympathetic to situation ethics. He was prepared to reject formal laws if it served the best interests of others to do so. Jesus was willing, according to Fletcher, to ignore observation of the Sabbath to do forbidden work (Mark 2:27-28).

The term the new morality has also been around for a number of years. Shortly after the turn of the century, books began to appear with this term as their title (Long, 1967). Most of these books focused on the liberalization of sexual attitudes and increasing permissiveness of sexual behavior—with some authors approving and others disapproving. Many of these books were written by Christian theologians, which illustrates the controversy within the Christian religion as to what is appropriate and inappropriate sexual behavior.

Although the concept of situation ethics and the new morality have existed for some time, they did not have a major impact until theologian Joseph Fletcher published his book entitled *Situation Ethics: The New Morality* in 1966. Apparently, it was an idea whose time had come, and Fletcher's eloquent presentation of this system of ethics stimulated much debate. It hit a responsive chord in many people, including Christians who doubted that any system of rules and

laws could be applied universally in our complex society. Others were not so sympathetic and one theologian has described Fletcher's work as a symptom of the "sickness of Protestantism" (Fitch, 1968). Fletcher's approach to situation ethics will be presented here because he is one of its most influential proponents.

According to Fletcher, there is only one "thing" that is intrinsically good and that is love. Love is the only norm against which decisions or acts should be judged. And so, in any particular situation, the right or moral or ethical thing to do will be that which is the most loving.

The kind of loving that Fletcher is talking about is the Greek *agape*. This is not the sentimental, emotional love that might exist between a man and a woman or between a parent and a child. Rather, it is a spiritual concern for the welfare for others, regardless of whether any emotional bond exists. Pike (1967) described agape as the love of the unloveable.

Perhaps the most important point that Fletcher makes is that situation ethics provides only a method; it does not provide solutions. It can be applied to situations in order to determine the moral or ethical course of action, but it cannot provide guidelines that can be applied across a variety of situations. If one were to ask Fletcher if premarital sex, extramarital sex, abortion, or any other course of action was right or wrong, he would ask for specifics. Right or wrong can be determined only on a case-by-case basis.

Fletcher does not reject laws or codes of moral behavior completely. He does recognize that there is much of value in the Ten Commandments and other Biblical scriptures. Such writings, however, should be viewed as principles and may be disregarded if in any concrete case they conflict with love.

A number of criticisms of situation ethics have been made. One objection is that such an approach calls for more critical intelligence, more factual information, and a stronger committment to doing the right thing than most people are capable of. Critics of situationists have claimed that the reality of human sin necessitates laws to control us. People may not be able to cope with the freedom inherent in situation ethics.

A related criticism is that the situational method of decision making is too susceptible to conscious or unconscious rationalization of selfish motives. To illustrate, suppose a woman has been separated from her husband for a number of months and is feeling lonely as well as sexually deprived. If she were to meet a man to whom she was sexually attracted, would it really be possible for her to make a rational and objective assessment of all the factors involved in having an affair? It seems likely that her feelings of loneliness and sexual desire would influence her reasoning about the "rightness" of such an affair.

Bishop Pike has made the point that some situations do not provide a time period for conscious deliberation. Imagine a man and woman, each of whom for one reason or another feel a deep need for a human relationship. Suppose they meet at a party and a strong mutual attraction develops, and after several hours of talking and drinking they find themselves in bed, without either of them having made a conscious decision to have sex. Pike has stated that in cases such as this it would be impossible to provide an absolute answer even with fuller facts. He does recognize that such situations are not common and it may well be unethical to turn such a moment into a calculated decision. He commented: "To love and be loved, to want and know one is wanted—and precisely at the right time—is not the most common thing in the world. There are times for spontaneous action, as well as times for lengthy deliberation" (p. 97). Of course, code ethicists would be extremely likely to conclude such spontaneous sexual behavior is morally wrong.

In fact, they would argue that the fact that people have difficulty in arriving at rational decisions in moments of passion or other strong emotion is a good reason for having a code. In this regard theologian Elton Eenigenberg (1968) has written:

> The new morality is incredibly naive. It takes a fellow and a girl at the lake shore—and demands of them a miracle of objective evaluation of a deeply passional situation, and with that, decision-making at a rational level the UN would be proud of. People aren't made like that, and so God had to make a lot of things pretty clear beforehand (p. 223).

Antinomianism

Antinomianism can be thought of as the polar opposite of legalism. The term means "against laws" and advocates of this approach claim that people must enter a decision-making situation with no principles, guidelines, rules, or laws. Consequently, there is no way of knowing or predicting what antinomianists might do in a particular situation. Their choices are random, and erratic; they are spontaneous rather than deliberate.

There are several varieties of antinomianism. One form is libertinism, an approach followed by some early Christians. They believed that since salvation was a question of faith, it did not matter what they did (Fletcher, 1966). A second form was represented by the Gnostic claim to special knowledge. Gnostics believed they had a superconscience that made rules and guidelines unnecessary. They would just *know* what was right or wrong when a situation presented itself.

A third variant of antinomianism, and perhaps the most sophisticated, is the ethics of existentialism. Existential philosophers, such as Jean-Paul Sartre (1956), emphasize the importance of immediate experience. Their view of reality suggests that there is no connection between one moment of experience and another. This radical discontinuity view, as it has been called, leads to the conclusion that there can be no generalizing moral principles or laws since every situation has only its own particularity. In other words, one does what he or she does, and that's that.

Existential philosophy and the antinomianism approach to moral decision making has not had much impact on American philosophy and theology. In fact, one of the few areas in which situationists and legalists are in agreement is in their view of antinomianism as an unworkable approach to decision making. Existentialists, however, view reality in a quite different way than do the majority of American philosophers, and, if one can accept their view of reality, then antinomianism becomes an acceptable approach.

The Law and Morality

In our society, many aspects of human sexuality are regulated by law. There are laws about who can have sex with whom and what sexual techniques can and cannot be used. Other laws, such as those that regulate abortion and sterilization, impose control over our bodies, particularly in the case of women. While virtually no one would deny that laws regulating some forms of sexual behavior (for example, rape and sexual exploitation of children) are justified, many people have questioned the appropriateness of laws that appear to be attempts to regulate morality. Is it appropriate for laws to regulate the sexual behavior of consenting adults? Are laws against so-called victimless crimes such as prostitution, adultery, homosexuality, and bestiality justified? The answer, of course, depends upon your point of view. Let us summarize the rationale for attempts to legislate morality and the arguments that have been made to abolish laws pertaining to victimless crimes.

John Stuart Mill and the Wolfenden Report

In 1859 John Stuart Mill published a monograph entitled *On Liberty*. It has been cited by many legal philosophers as the basis for rejecting laws that attempt to regulate morality. In his essay, Mill explored the issue of social control over the individual morality. His views are summarized below:

> . . . The sole end for which mankind are warranted, individually or collectively, in interfering with the liberty of action of any of their number, is self-protection. That the only purpose for which power can be rightfully exercised over any member of a civilized community, against his will, is to prevent harm to others. His own good, either physical or moral, is not a sufficient warrant. He cannot rightfully be compelled to do or forbear because it will be better for him to do so, because it will make him happier, because in the opinion of others, to do so would be wise, or even right.

Mill's attempt to formulate an ethical principle to restrict social control of private morality has been widely disputed. It did, however, provide a foundation for a report produced in England by the Wolfenden Committee. In 1954 the committee was established in response to complaints that laws dealing with prostitution and homosexuality were unjust. Three years later the committee issued a report that, in many ways, was an application of Mill's principle and has become a classic case for those advocating the abolition of laws regulating victimless crimes.

The committee suggested that distinctions need to be made between crime and sin and between public decency and private morality. The report argued that the function of criminal law is "to preserve public order and decency, to protect the citizen from what is offensive or injurious, and to provide sufficient safeguards against exploitation and corruption of others." While maintenance of public decency did require laws, private morality was not a matter to be legislated. The committee concluded that unless it could be shown that issues of public decency or personal exploitation were involved, laws should not prohibit activities such as prostitution and homosexuality.

The views expressed by Mill and the Wolfenden Report have received much support. As one example, all laws pertaining to sexual activities performed by consenting adults in private were dropped from the Model Penal Code formulated by the American Law Institute. The Code questioned the constitutionality and appropriateness of laws that attempt to enforce purely moral or religious standards. Since the foundation of the code, several states, including Illinois, Connecticut, Colorado, Oregon and Hawaii, have revised their penal codes to conform to the Model Penal Code.

Perhaps more states would follow suit if it were not for the political realities involved in changing the morality laws. In the early 1970s, the Pennsylvania legislature abolished laws against fornication and adultery. Shortly afterward, newspaper headlines proclaimed that the state house of representatives had voted to "legalize premarital and extramarital sex." The politician who advocates reform of sex laws must be prepared to face charges that he or she is encouraging immorality regardless of how ridiculous such charges may be.

Democratic Rule and Social Necessity

There are two primary arguments that have been used to justify the legislation of morality. These are the principle of demo-

cratic rule and the social necessity of morality (Devlin, 1975). The principle of democratic rule suggests that any activity that is considered immoral by the majority of citizens of a society can be made illegal by the very fact that it is the majority opinion. In a democracy, all laws are made in accord with the preferences of the majority (or at least a majority of legislators) and, according to this view, the majority has a right to enforce its views of morality even at the expense of individual liberty. There is, in fact, no tradition in Western democracies that prohibits the legislation of morality. In accord with this line of reasoning Lord Patrick Devlin (1975), a prominent proponent for the enforcement of morals, has suggested that if society believes certain activities, such as homosexuality, are "a vice so abominable that its mere presence is an offence—I do not see how society can be denied the right to eradicate it" (p. 250).

The social necessity of morality argument suggests that the legislation of morality is justified whenever threats to moral standards challenge the very order of society itself. Devlin is also sympathetic to this view and argues that society has the right to use the law to preserve its standards of morality in the same way it uses the law to protect anything else that is essential to its existence. Devlin believes, for example, that laws prohibiting adultery are justified because they preserve the institution of marriage which is critical to the survival of our society. Other writers have questioned whether sexual immorality is really sufficient to threaten a society's common sense of morality, much less its very existence (Hart, 1975).

The Legislation of Morals

One consideration that theorists such as Devlin tend to neglect is whether or not it is possible to legislate morals. The research of

Alfred Kinsey and his associates casts serious doubts about this assumption. Kinsey estimated that 95 percent of all males could be legally classified as sexual offenders. One cannot help but wonder about the justice, to say nothing of effectiveness, of laws that are so thoroughly ignored.

Advocates of legislation of morality argue that the law should provide an example. That is, people tend to view the law as legitimate authority and if they know of the existence of certain laws, their personal values and attitudes will shift accordingly. This hypothesis was tested by asking college students to indicate the extent of their agreement with a number of statements involving moral judgments. Following this, one group of students was given the results of a survey that purportedly showed that 80 percent of college students strongly agreed or disagreed with several of the moral judgments. A second group of students was given information about recent legislation that was relevant to the moral judgments. After reviewing this information, all the students were asked to repeat their evaluations of the moral judgments. The results indicated that knowledge of peer opinions led to much more attitude change than knowledge of legislation (Berkowitz and Walker, 1975).

An argument related to the notion that the law should serve as an example of morality is that regardless of whether a law serves as a deterrent it should not be repealed. To do so would imply that the behavior in question is no longer morally wrong. For example, if laws against fornication are repealed, people may believe that society condones such behavior. This argument, too, has failed to receive empirical support. Students' judgments of moral issues were found to be unrelated to their knowledge of existing relevant laws (Walker and Argyle, 1964). The bulk of the evidence would seem to suggest that it is futile to attempt to legislate standards of sexual propriety.

Philosophical objections aside, several other arguments have been made against the legislation of morality (Packer, 1968). First, because such laws are violated by such a large segment of our population, the laws will be rarely enforced. We cannot, after all, incarcerate 95 percent of a population. This can result in arbitrary and capricious enforcement of the laws by police and the courts. Also, because many crimes of morality are difficult to detect, the police may be tempted to use undesirable methods in their attempt to do so. Should society be spending a portion of its resources to have police pose as homosexuals in restrooms or as customers in search of a prostitute? A third point is that the existence of laws that are so widely violated can lead to a decline in respect for the law in general. Many people feel this happened during Prohibition and continues to occur today with the morals laws.

Regardless of whether one believes that laws regulating sexual behavior are appropriate or inappropriate, one cannot help but be distressed by the state of such laws in our society. Rather than developing from a well-articulated philosophy, the morals laws have been instituted in a patchwork fashion. Some behaviors, such as homosexuality, are legal in a few states but can result in long prison terms in others. The absence of any sense of coherence in the laws can also result in situations that seem grossly unfair. For instance, in Tennessee the legal age of consent for women is twenty-one, but they can obtain a marriage license at age sixteen. So, if a married woman under the age of twenty-one has an extramarital affair, the man involved can be prosecuted for rape.

A Few Selected Issues

There is probably no aspect of human sexual behavior for which there is a clear consensus concerning appropriate standards of morality, but there are some issues that are more controversial than others. Currently, our society is grappling with several issues such as abortion, pornography, *in vitro* fertilization, and rape that are generating a great deal of controversy. Let us examine the basis for these controversies beginning with what is probably the most emotionally charged issue—abortion.

Abortion

The controversy surrounding the issue of abortion has been with us some time, but it reached a peak in 1973 when the United States Supreme Court ruled that individual states cannot prevent a woman from obtaining an abortion from a licensed physician if she is in the first trimester of pregnancy. Furthermore, abortion during the second trimester should be regulated only so far as the regulations relate to medical practice and the preservation and protection of the woman's health. The Court did leave the regulation of abortion during the third trimester to indi-vidual states, except in cases in which a woman's life is in danger.

This decision did not settle the controversy but added fuel to it. Since that time, Right to Life groups have become increasingly active in promoting their anti-abortion views, and in supporting political candidates who favor legal restrictions on abortion. There have even been attempts to generate support for a constitutional convention so that an amendment can be added to prohibit abortion. Pro-choice groups are not completely satisfied either. As one example of a difficult issue, in 1977 the Supreme Court ruled that states are not required to pay for elective abortions even when matching federal funds are available. The concern that many people felt about this decision was expressed by dissenting Justice Harry Blackmun who suggested that the ruling allowed states to do what they could not do after the 1973 decision. That is, they were free to deny abortions to women who could not afford to pay for them.

The issues surrounding abortion are many and complex, but perhaps the most basic

In Vitro Fertilization: A Moral and Legal Dilemma

Moral and legal considerations involving human sexuality are difficult but recent and potential scientific advances will only make such issues even more complex. As one example, consider the case of children that are conceived *in vitro*. The technique involves removing ova from the mother and mixing them with sperm from the father. The embryo is implanted in the mother's uterus. The first such child was born in 1978 and many more are likely to come. The *in vitro* fertilization procedure raises many moral and legal questions that we did not even have to think about a few decades ago.

Opinions regarding the morality of such procedures covers the full spectrum (*Time*, 1978). Ethics professor Rabbi Seymour Siegal sees no problem with the technique. He believes that couples who use the procedure are following the commandment to have children. According to Siegal, it is desirable to use modern technology when nature does not permit conception. God wants to have man's cooperation.

The other end of the spectrum is represented by Roman Catholic Priest William B. Smith. He argues that interference with nature in any form is not acceptable. Thus, the Church's reasons for opposing birth control and artificial insemination would apply to *in vitro* fertilization.

In vitro fertilization has the potential to create a legal quagmire. Suppose a woman wanted to have a child but did not want to go through pregnancy. It would be possible for her to have ova removed, have them fertilized *in vitro*, and have the embryo implanted into another woman who would serve as a surrogate mother and would carry the child to birth (presumably for a fee). But what happens if the host mother refuses to relinquish the child at birth? Who is responsible for the child if the host mother takes drugs or contracts an illness that results in a birth defect? If the host mother has intercourse after the implantation and bears fraternal twins, must she give up one of the children? Both children? Anyone with an active imagination could probably think of several additional situations for which there are no legal precedents.

As always, there are no easy moral or legal answers for the potential problems associated with *in vitro* fertilization. There are those who believe that the procedure should be prohibited. Others who favor the procedure point to the joy of couples who, after years of believing that they could not have children, have renewed hope. *In vitro* fertilization will probably take a place with issues such as abortion and victimless crimes that remain to be resolved by future generations.

---

point of disagreement concerns views of the status of the fetus—that is, when does one draw the line between human and nonhuman existence? Is the fetus essentially a human being with the same rights as other humans, or is it merely a bit of tissue that is qualitatively different from those of us that have been born?

Philosopher Tom Beauchamp (1975) has outlined four categories that serve as a summary of the various views. The first of these is called *strong continuity theories*. These theories, generally held by Roman Catholics and the Right to Life groups, hold that human existence begins the moment the ovum is fertilized by the sperm. What follows is a process of functional maturation only, and not increasing humanness. This view holds that abortion is destruction of human life and, consequently, is morally indistinguishable from murder.

The second category can be called *weak continuity theories*. These theories suggest that the fetus does have a special status, but it is not fully human until some time later in

pregnancy, rather than at conception. The point varies from theory to theory but might be the end of the first trimester, quickening, or viability. Abortions after this point are considered to be destruction of human life and are morally permissible only if some greater evil, such as the death of the mother, is averted. The 1973 Supreme Court decision reflects a position that seems to fit in this category.

The third category, *weak discontinuity theories*, takes the position that the fetus does have a special status that morally prohibits a woman from taking any course of action she desires. However, advocates of this position maintain that at no point is the fetus fully equivalent to human life. Thus, there are many circumstances that justify abortion. These may include deformity of the fetus, the health of the mother, and pregnancy as a result of rape.

Strong discontinuity theories, the fourth category, hold that a fetus does not have an ethically significant status. According to these theories the fetus is little more than a bit of tissue and if unwanted, the woman should have an unrestricted right to have it removed. According to this view, an abortion is no different, morally, from an appendectomy.

One's view of the status of the fetus is an important starting point regarding the morality of abortion, but both sides have made several additional arguments. Pro-choice advocates have raised questions about the morality of bringing unwanted and potentially neglected children into an overpopulated world. The cost to society of providing for such children makes it difficult to deal with any number of existing social ills. Those with anti-abortion views might respond to such arguments with the question of whether social utility should be used as justification for destroying a potential human being.

Another point made by pro-choice advocates is that views on abortion are related to one's religious and moral values. Consequently, abortion should be a matter of choice—no one should be forced to have an abortion nor should anyone be denied the right to have one. The decision should be based on the individual's values and not imposed by society. The response to this line of reasoning might be based on a point of view discussed in the previous section. That is, many people believe that the majority in any society do have the right to impose standards of morality on everyone else in that society. After all, if one truly believed that abortion was murder, would that person be behaving in a moral fashion if he or she condoned the procedure?

The arguments could go on almost indefinitely, but it should be obvious that there are no easy solutions when it comes to the problem of abortion. In many cases the issue seems to come down to trying to balance the sanctity of human life against the right of the individual to control her own destiny and body. Because these are both points of view with which most people are sympathetic, it may be impossible to ever arrive at solutions that are satisfactory to all.

Figure 19.1
Emotion is apt to run high when it comes to abortion. (Dwyer and Zinkl)

Prostitution

Clearly, the prevailing view in our society is that prostitution is immoral and should be illegal. In fact, it is illegal everywhere in the United States with the exception of a few rural counties in Nevada. The arguments against prostitution center on traditional religious and moral views of prostitution as sinful and/or immoral, the notion that prostitution supports Organized Crime and encourages ancillary crimes (robbery and assault, for example), its role in the rising incidence of venereal diseases, and its contribution to the moral decline of a community.

In recent years, a movement to change the prostitution laws has been gaining momentum. The American Civil Liberties Union and the National Organization of Women have both advocated the decriminalization of prostitution. They argue that prostitution is a victimless crime (although not everyone agrees with this assessment) and that the relationship between a prostitute and her customer is no different than other sexual relationships between consenting adults conducted in private.

A more interesting group is called COYOTE—an acronym for Call Off Your Old Tired Ethics. It represents the attempt of an ex-madam/prostitute to form a union for prostitutes with the goal of changing the image of prostitutes and the relevant laws. The group has a knack for publicity. At their national convention they declared 1974 as "The Year of the Whore" and adopted "My Ass Is Mine" as their theme song. They have also held a "Hookers Ball" and staged a "Hug-a-Hooker" booth at political conventions. It has been suggested that if they can become avant-garde in high social circles, then general attitudes, and hence laws, will begin to change (James, 1976).

Most countries have legalized prostitution and many writers have suggested that the United States should too. By decriminalizing prostitution and retaining laws regulating overt solicitation, the "public nuisance" factor could be dealt with. Hygiene and minimum age requirements could be dealt with by requiring frequent medical exams and licensing prostitutes. These measures probably would not eliminate all of the problems associated with prostitution, but many people feel that decriminalization would produce results that are to be preferred over the current situation.

It is unlikely that many people, if anyone, would agree that prostitution in itself is desirable. But many people do believe that it may be necessary in our less than perfect society. Those that do support decriminalization see it as a temporary measure until more desirable solutions can be achieved.

Pornography

As with abortion, there is much ambivalence about pornography. There are those who believe that pornography is an evil without peer and corrupts our youth and destroys the moral fabric of our society. On the other hand, many believe that there is no evidence that pornography causes harmful effects and that laws controlling it are a violation of individual freedom. The ambivalence in views has produced widely disparate treatment of sexually oriented material. On and around 42nd Street in New York City, a wide variety of pornographic movies, books, and magazines is freely available. In other communities, even relatively innocuous materials, such as *Playboy* magazine, cannot be publically displayed.

The ambivalence is also apparent in court decisions. In a landmark decision, the United States Supreme Court ruled in 1957 that to be considered obscene a work had to meet three criteria. The dominant theme of the work had to appeal to prurient interests, the work must be offensive to community standards, and the work had to be utterly without redeeming social value. In 1969 the Court ruled that possession of pornographic materials was protected by the Constitution but the sale and distribution of such materials was not. The vagueness of the pornography guidelines is perhaps best expressed by Justice Potter Stewart, who declared that although he may not be able to define pornography he knew it when he saw it. Of course, it is difficult to translate intuition into any kind of meaningful law.

Pornography is generally considered to be a victimless crime and the points discussed earlier regarding the legislation of morality apply here. One additional point that deserves discussion concerns the potential effects of pornography. Does it, as has been claimed, stimulate "perverse" behaviors and contribute to sex crimes? Although this has been an assumption that has been held for some time, it has only been in the last decade

or so that research has provided any meaningful answers.

There have been several studies that have exposed subjects to pornography in order to examine its effects. In one, married couples were exposed to erotic films once a week over a four-week period (Mann et al., 1973). The couples reported a slight increase in sexual activity that was generally limited to the night that they viewed the film. There was no increase in unusual sexual behaviors. Interestingly, the results of the study seemed to indicate that the anticipation of viewing pornography stimulated more sexual behavior than the actual viewing!

In a second example of research, college males were exposed to a variety of sexually explicit stimuli for ninety minutes a day, five days a week, for three weeks. There was an increase in sexual thoughts in the early stages of the experiment, but as the experiment pro-

Figure 19.2
Many people believe that prostitution is a victimless crime that should be decriminalized. (Dwyer and Zinkl)

gressed there was a steady decline in interest in sex. In other words, massive exposure to pornography became boring (Howard et al., 1973).

A study of sex offenders fails to provide a link between sex crimes and pornography (Gebhard et al., 1965). In this study, sponsored by the Kinsey Institute, it was found that a vast majority of sex offenders did have experience with pornographic materials. However, control prisoners had just as much exposure and, in fact, tended to become more sexually aroused from viewing pornography than the sex offenders did.

The results of research of this nature, while posing serious questions about the link between pornography, sex crimes, and immorality, do not prove that pornography is completely harmless. It is possible that the sexual attitudes and behaviors of children and adolescents could be influenced by certain types of pornography. There is, however, no evidence that pornography has any profound effects on adults.

Even the staunchest of civil libertarians who argue that laws against pornography are a violation of individual rights recognize that some regulation is necessary. For instance, children should be protected from exposure to certain forms of sexual stimuli for the same reasons many individuals and groups want televised violence reduced. Also, no one would condone the exploitation of children in the production of pornographic materials. It is inconceivable that anyone could defend "kiddie porn" on moral grounds because children are incapable of giving their informed consent to participate.

Rape

No one, of course, would question the immorality of rape or the laws prohibiting it, but controversy does exist about several aspects of this act. For instance, what standards of proof should exist to convict rapists? What types of sentences are appropriate for convicted rapists? What role, if any, does the

Figure 19.3
Pornography is viewed by many as a social evil. (Anderson, Monkmeyer Press Photo Service)

victim play in an act of rape? Should rapists be treated as criminals or as mentally ill? So, even an issue that, on the surface, is as straightforward as rape allows for a variety of interpretations of moral and legal issues.

The wording of the laws against rape vary from state to state, but virtually all of them contain certain elements. First, penetration must occur. Second, violence or threats of violence must occur. Third, the woman must make her wish not to have intercourse explicitly known. Fourth, any act of sexual intercourse is rape if the woman is incapable of giving her informed consent.

Using these guidelines many cases of rape are clearcut. The man who breaks into a woman's apartment and forces her to have intercourse on threat of her life is clearly guilty of rape. But many cases are not so straightforward. It has been estimated that nearly half of all rape victims are acquainted with the rapists (Amir, 1974), so the line between rape and consensual intercourse is not always clear. Suppose a man and a woman meet at a party and spend several hours drinking together. If they have intercourse later in the evening, should the woman be able to prove rape on the ground that her inebriated state made it impossible for her to give her informed consent?

A more controversial aspect concerns perceptions of the victim's role in an act of rape. It is not unusual for rape victims to report that events following the rape were more traumatic than the rape itself. Many people, women as well as men, have the belief that rape victims were "asking for it" by dressing or acting in sexually provocative ways. Those beliefs are often reflected in the treatment victims receive by the police and the courts. As an example, in 1977 a Wisconsin judge made the following remark concerning the scanty clothing worn by many girls while sentencing a fifteen-year-old boy for raping a high school girl: "Are we supposed to take an

impressionable person 15 or 16 years of age, who can respond to something like that, and punish that person severely because he reacts to it normally?"

If the victim does survive questioning by the police and the case goes to court, she may find the trial more traumatic than the accused may find it. She may find herself undergoing a thorough examination of her sexual history and if she has ever had intercourse outside of marriage, the defense attorney is likely to portray her as immoral and promiscuous and attempt to lead the jury to believe this reflects on her ability to withhold consent. That her sexual history may be fair game is ironic, because any previous arrests for rape on the part of the accused would be inadmissible.

There do seem to have been significant changes in attitudes over the past decade. Many police departments now have specially trained officers, usually women, to counsel as well as question the rape victim. Many states have adopted laws, following recommendations made by the National Organization for Women, that excludes the victim's prior sexual activities, except with the accused, as admissible evidence in court. And the Wisconsin judge was defeated in a recall election. Perhaps the more humane treatment of rape victims will lead to a higher percentage of them reporting the rape to the police and a higher conviction rate. Estimates of the percentage of rapes that reach the courtroom range from 10 to 50 percent. Many rapists have terrorized women with impunity.

A case of rape in late 1978 received national attention and may be an additional signal of changes in attitudes. This involved a case in Oregon of a husband who was arrested and tried for raping his wife. Until 1978, the definition of rape in all state laws limited it to men and women who were not married to each other. Oregon was the first state to change its law so that a husband could be charged with raping his wife. The traditional rape laws were irksome to those sympathetic to feminism because they reflected a view of women as being the property of men. That is, a man has "sexual rights" so long as he is married to the woman; that is, she "belongs" to him. The Oregon case, even though the husband was acquitted, may be viewed as indicating that women need not relinquish control over their bodies when they get married.

These few paragraphs have only lightly touched on just a few of the issues of rape. Several volumes could be written to explore the issues more fully. For instance, the age of consent and the sexist and racist aspects of rape are a few of the issues that deserve some attention. The point we do wish to make is that even sexual issues such as rape that appear to be straightforward are extremely complex from moral and legal points of view. It is rarely, if ever, sufficient merely to approve or disapprove of certain sexual behaviors or to be for or against certain laws regulating sexual behavior. The relation between sex and society is too complex to allow for any simple answers.

Summary

It is necessary for individuals to make decisions as to how they are going to behave sexually and in order to make rational and meaningful decisions, it is helpful to have a framework to work within. Three such frameworks, or systems of ethics are code ethics, situation ethics and antinomianism. Code ethics or legalism involves a set of rules and laws that are usually derived from religious writings or natural law. These rules and laws are viewed a absolutes that apply across a variety of situations. Situation ethics suggests that every situation must be evaluated on its own merits. No rules or laws can be universally valid, but only serve as principles.

Fletcher's situation ethics suggests that in any particular situation the right thing to do is that which is most loving. Antinomianism, which means against laws, reflects the view that both moral laws and moral principles are unnecessary. Existential philosophers, such as Sartre, have suggested that the reality of each moment is unique and hence no guidelines that are generalizable across time or situations can exist.

The second section in this chapter addressed the relation between law and morality. While virtually everyone recognizes that legal restrictions of some forms of sexual behavior are necessary, there is much disagreement regarding the extent to which society should attempt to legislate sexual morality. John Stuart Mill's essay *On Liberty* has served as a foundation for those who believe that laws dealing with victimless crimes are inappropriate because they limit individual liberty needlessly. A second view is that in a democracy the majority has the right to regulate by law any behavior it finds morally unacceptable. A third argument is that society has the right to make illegal any behavior it believes to threaten the very order of society itself.

The last section of the chapter explored some of the moral and legal aspects of four controversial sexual issues. These were abortion, prostitution, pornography, and rape. All of these issues are controversial, but the nature of the controversy is different in each case. There is much disagreement about the conditions, if any, under which abortion is morally permissible and should be legal. Most people would agree that prostitution is undesirable, but disagreement exists as to whether it should be permitted in our less than perfect society. With regard to pornography, some people view it as an evil with the potential to destroy the fabric of our society, others view it as relatively harmless. No one would deny that rape should be illegal, but there is much debate about rape-related issues such as its definition, the victim's role, and appropriate sentences for convicted rapists. The diversity of views of human sexuality that exists in our society makes it impossible to arrive at any simple moral or legal resolutions of sexual issues.

References

American Law Institute, *Model penal code.* Proposed official draft. Philadelphia, 1962.

Amir, M. "Sociocultural factors in forcible rape." In L. Gross (ed.), *Sexual behavior: Current issues.* Flushing, N.Y.: Spectrum Publications, 1974.

Beauchamp, T. L. *Ethics and public policy.* Englewood Cliffs, N.J.: Prentice-Hall, 1975.

Berkowitz, L. and Walker, N. "Laws and moral judgments." In R. L. Akers and R. Hawkins (eds.), *Law and control in society.* Englewood Cliffs, N.J.: Prentice-Hall, 1975.

Davis, H. *Moral and pastoral theology.* Vol. I. New York: Sheed & Ward, 1935.

Devlin, P. "Morals and the criminal law." In T. Beauchamp (ed.), *Ethics and public policy.* Englewood Cliffs, N.J.: Prentice-Hall, 1975.

Eenigenberg, E. M. "How new is the new morality?" In H. Cox (ed.), *The situation ethics debate.* Philadelphia: Westminster Press, 1968.

Fitch, R. E. "The protestant sickness." In H. Cox (ed.), *The situation ethics debate.* Philadelphia: Westminster Press, 1968.

Fletcher, J. *Situation ethics: The new morality.* Philadelphia: Westminster Press, 1966.

Gebhard, P. H., Gagnon, J. H., Pomeroy, W. B., and Christenson, C. V. *Sex Offenders: An analysis of types.* New York: Harper & Row, 1965.

Hart, H. L. A. "Social solidarity and the enforcement of morality." In T. C. Beauchamp (ed.), *Ethics and public policy.* Englewood Cliffs, N.J.: Prentice-Hall, 1975.

Howard, J. L., Liptzin, M. B., and Reifler, C. B. "Is pornography a problem?" *Journal of Social Issues,* 1973, 29, 133-145.

James, J. "Prostitution: Arguments for change." In S. Gordon and R. W. Libby (eds.), *Sexuality today and tomorrow.* North Scituate, Mass.: Duxbury, 1976.

Long, E. L. "The history and literature of the new morality." In H. Cox (ed.), *The situation ethics debate.* Philadelphia: Westminster Press, 1967.

Mann, J., Sidman, J., and Starr, S. "Evaluating social consequences of erotic films: An experimental approach." *Journal of Social Issues,* 1973, 29, 113-131.

Mill, J. S., *On liberty.* London, 1859.

Packer, H. L. *The limits of the criminal sanction.* Stanford: Stanford University Press, 1968.

Pike, J. A. *You and the new morality.* New York: Harper & Row, 1967.

Sartre, Jean-Paul, *Being and nothingness.* New York: Philosophical Library, 1956.

"To fool (or not) with Mother Nature." *Time,* July 31, 1978, p. 69.

Walker, N. and Argyle, M. "Does the law affect moral judgments?" *British Journal of Criminology,* 1964, 570-581.

The Wolfenden Report. New York: Stein & Day, 1963.

Chapter 20

Sexual Rights
and Responsibilities

A Position Statement

Toward Responsibility

References

The goal of virtually all sex educators, the authors of this volume included, is to contribute to the development of a society in which human sexuality is valued; a society in which people are free to engage in responsible sexual relationships with a maximum of satisfaction and a minimum of conflict, guilt, and anxiety. To this end, several writers have proposed their version of a "sexual bill of rights" (Kirkendall, 1976; Ramer, 1973). One such set of guidelines, with which the authors are sympathetic, has been developed by the Sex Information and Education Council of the United States (SIECUS, 1974). These guidelines are presented below:

A Position Statement

The philosophy of SIECUS rests upon three beliefs. They believe that: "(1) freedom to exercise personal sexual choice is a fundamental human right; (2) such freedom of sexual choice carries responsibilities to self and others; and (3) these responsibilities call for acquiring knowledge and developing a personal ethical code, in order to provide a rational basis for decision-making in all human relationships." In support of these beliefs, SIECUS is committed to efforts to generate acceptance of ten points. These are as follows:

1. Sex Education. Everyone—children and adults—has a basic right to free access to complete and factual information on all aspects of human sexuality.

2. Sexual Orientation. All people have the right to engage in sexual relationships with others of either gender so long as such relationships are nonexploitive. It is a violation of this right to discriminate against an individual on the basis of his or her sexual orientation.

3. Masturbation. Masturbation, and the fantasies that accompany it, is a natural form of sexual expression for people of all ages. In many cases it can serve to promote personal growth.

4. Contraceptive Care for Minors. Minors have the same rights as others of free and independent access to medical contraceptive care.

5. Explicit Sexual Materials. SIECUS agrees with the Majority Report of the President's Commission on Obscenity and Pornography. Such materials can serve useful functions and adults who so desire should have access to them.

6. Sex and Aging. Society has a responsibility to create conditions so that aging people can fulfill their needs for sexual companionship and expression. Contrary to popular stereotypes, older people do have such needs.

7. Sex and Racism. Efforts must be made to dispel the distorted views many people have of the sexuality of other ethnic groups. Such stereotypes can contribute to racism and distort the sexual self-concepts of both the racist and victim.

8. Sex and the Handicapped. The sexual relationship needs of the physically and mentally handicapped need to be recognized. Society has the responsibility to make it possible for handicapped people to fulfill these needs in accord with their capacities.

9. Sex: The Law and the Citizen. The law should not be concerned with the sexual behavior engaged in by consenting adults in private.

10. Sexual Health Care. Everyone is entitled to sexual health care and provision for such care must be made in health care planning.

Toward Responsibility

There is little question that our society has been moving in the direction toward accepting these guidelines. Sex education programs are no longer uncommon. Masturbation, homosexuality, and other sexual behaviors are now considered to be nonpathological by many people. Several states have repealed their laws concerning the sexual behavior of consenting adults. In the past two decades Supreme Court decisions have affirmed individual's rights to contraceptive care and to possess sexually explicit materials and have prohibited miscegenation laws. And society has begun to recognize that older people and the handicapped are not asexual. Of course, the views of SIECUS are not accepted by everyone, but there can be little doubt that they are much more accepted now than they were a decade or two ago.

In order for individuals to be truly comfortable with their sexuality, they must accept these guidelines, or whatever guidelines they find acceptable, at an emotional level as well as an intellectual level. It is one thing to support sex education but quite another to have frank, open, and honest discussions with one's children. Many young men profess a desire to have their wives be equal partners in the marriage and support their wives' decision to have a career. But it takes more than an intellectual commitment to the equality of women when it comes to dealing with issues such as child care and promotions that require a move to a distant city.

It is often this inability to both intellectually and emotionally accept sexual guidelines that leads to irresponsible behavior. For example, it has been found a number of times that a substantial portion of sexually active teenage girls do not use regular and reliable methods of birth control. Reasons cited include the notion that it would "cheapen" the sexual act to use birth control or they are fearful of seeking advice and/or medical help. Obviously a conflict exists. Such girls may believe that premarital sex is acceptable, but they do not feel comfortable enough with their decision to accept the responsibility that accompanies it. Needless to say, the boys these girls are having sex with should share this responsibility. It is ironic, and sad, that many people are more rational and responsible about trivial decisions than they are about sexual decisions. Many people give more thought to buying a car than they do to entering a sexual relationship.

It is likely to take several decades and a generation or two before people can feel comfortable with the sexual guidelines that are currently under discussion. It must be remembered that the parents of 1980 grew up in a time in which Kinsey was widely condemned for simply asking people about their sexual behavior. Changes have been rapid, but it is hoped that future generations will look back in puzzlement at the conflicts we are experiencing today. Perhaps our children will grow up in an atmosphere that will enable them to make responsible and gratifying sexual decisions.

References

Kirkendall, L. A. "A new bill of sexual rights and responsibilities." In S. Gordon and R. W. Libby (eds.), *Sexuality today and tomorrow.* North Scituate, Mass.: Duxbury, 1976.

Ramer, L. V. *Your sexual bill of rights.* New York: Exposition Press, 1973.

SIECUS Position Statements. *Siecus Report.* May 1974.

Further Readings

Athanasiou, R. "French and American sexuality." *Psychology Today,* 1972, 6, 2, 54–57.
The author dispels the myth of the authority of the French in sexual matters. This comparison of French and American sexuality revealed no differences between the two cultures in a variety of sexual activities.

Bart, P. "Depression in middle-aged women." In V. Gornick and B. Moran (eds.), *Women in sexist society.* New York: Basic Books, 1971.
A very good discussion of the emotional problems of middle aged women who are faced with the empty nest syndrome with emphasis on the cultural sources of these problems.

Belliveau, F. and Richter, L. *Understanding human sexual inadequacy.* New York: Bantam Books, 1970.
This paperback book condenses and reduces the technical jargon to make Masters and Johnson's *Human Sexual Inadequacy* comprehensible to those without a medical or scientific background.

Bem, S. L. "Androgeny vs. the tight little lines of fluffy women and chesty men." *Psychology Today,* September, 1975, 58-62.
Bem describes her research with sex roles and concludes that androgynous individuals are adaptable to a wider variety of situations than those bound by sex roles.

Bermant, G. and Davidson, J. *Biological basis of sexual behavior.* New York: Harper & Row, 1974.
A comprehensive analysis of biological influences on sexual behavior based on animal research mostly.

Berscheid, E. and Walster, E. *Interpersonal Attraction,* 2nd edition. Reading, Mass.: Addison-Wesley, 1978.
This is a relatively small paperback book, but it is as informative as it is fun to read.

Blumstein, P. W. and Schwartz, P. "Lesbianism and bisexuality." In S. Gordon and R. W. Libby (eds.), *Sexuality today and tomorrow.* North Scituate, Mass.: Duxbury, 1976.
This chapter discusses the results of one of the few scientific surveys of the bisexual experience. Perhaps its most important point is that one's sexual orientation can be quite flexible.

The Boston Women's Health Book Collection. *Our bodies, ourselves.* New York: Simon and Schuster, 1976.
An easy to read description of female biology and sexuality that includes many subjective descriptions of how women feel about themselves.

Brecher, E. *The sex researchers.* Boston: Little, Brown, 1969.
This paperback book provides insight into the work and personalities of some of the well known sex researchers.

Coleman, D. "Special abilities of the sexes: Do they begin in the brain?" *Psychology Today,* November, 1978, pp 48ff.
Coleman presents research findings that point to differences between men and women in their brain organization that may account for some differences in their special abilities.

Coleman, T. F. "Sex and the law." *The Humanist.* March/April, 1978, 38–41.
Coleman, an attorney and sex-law specialist describes recent developments in the laws

concerning rape, prostitution, transsexualism, homosexuality and private sexual behavior.

Comfort, A. *The joy of sex.* New York: Crown, 1972.

For those who would like more information about sexual techniques, this book presents advice in a sophisticated and tasteful manner.

Comfort, A. "Sexuality in a zero growth society." In S. Gordon and R. W. Libby (eds.), *Sexuality today and tomorrow.* North Scituate, Mass.: Duxbury, 1976.

Comfort discusses his notions of what changes may occur over the next few decades in sex and sexual relationships.

Crew, L. "Thriving decloseted in rural academe." In E. S. Morrison and V. Borosage (eds.), *Human sexuality: Contemporary perspectives.* Palo Alto, Ca.: Mayfield, 1977.

This chapter relates this gay college professor's decision to come out of the closet and his experiences that followed.

De Burger, J. *Marriage today.* New York: John Wiley and Sons, 1977.

An analysis of problems, issues and alternatives in modern marriage and a discussion of common patterns of American family life including nontraditional marital modes.

Dick-Read, G. *Childbirth without fear.* New York: Harper and Row, 1953.

A modern classic describing natural methods of childbirth.

Driscoll, J. "Transsexuals." In C. Gordon and G. Johnson (eds.), *Readings in human sexuality: Contemporary perspectives.* New York: Harper and Row, 1976.

The author's account of his time spent among transsexuals in San Francisco containing many early recollections of transsexuals who went through different stages before seeking sex alteration surgery.

Ellis, A. *The sensuous person.* New York: Lyle Stuart and New Library, 1972.

In this book Ellis points out errors and fallacies in several popular "how to" books. He argues that many people have the unfortunate tendency to view such books as standards which, at best, are difficult to achieve.

Ellis, A. *Sex without guilt.* New York: Lyle Stuart, 1958.

Ellis describes how his philosophy can help individuals with sexual inhibitions.

Fletcher, J. *Situation ethics: The new morality.* Philadelphia: Westminster Press, 1966.

This is one of the most informative and readable books that discusses situation ethics.

Freedman, M. *Homosexuality and psychological functioning.* Belmont, Ca.: Brooks/Cole, 1971.

This relatively brief book presents an overview of the research regarding the causes of homosexuality and discusses the overall adjustments of homosexuals.

Gebhard, P., Gagnon, J., Pomeroy, W. and Christenson, C. *Sex offenders.* New York: Harper and Row, 1965.

This is the largest Kinsey-style study of convicted sex offenders.

Gordon, S. "Freedom for sex education and sexual education and sexual expression." In S. Gordon and R. W. Libby (eds.), *Sexuality today and tomorrow.* North Scituate, Mass.: Duxbury, 1976.

In this chapter Gordon makes the point that both parents and educators have the responsibility to provide children and adolescents with factual and relevant information about sex.

Hariton, B. E., "The sexual fantasies of women." *Psychology Today,* November, 1973, pp 39–44.

Harriton presents data that indicates that sexual fantasies, even unusual ones, are a normal part of the sexual experience of many women.

Hatcher, R. *Contraceptive technology 1978–1979.* New York: Irvington Publishers, Inc., 1979.

The authors provide up-to-date information about birth control and family planning as well as medical concerns related to contraception.

Heiman, J. R. "The physiology of erotica: Women's sexual arousal." *Psychology Today,* August, 1975, 90–94.

Heiman discusses her research in which women were exposed to erotic films and physiological measures of their level of arousal were taken.

Hennigson, G. *The European witch persecution.* Danish Folklore Archives, Copenhagen, 1973.

Interesting description of witchcraft and the distorted theology of the Middle Ages during which thousands of women were burnt at the stake because of sex acts they presumably committed with the devil.

Hite, S. *The Hite report.* New York: Dell Publication, Inc., 1976.

A study of female sexuality based on interviews of more than 3,000 women giving subjective responses of their sexual experiences. This report is not a truly representative survey of female sexuality but a sharing of personal experiences.

Hunt, M. *Sexual behavior in the 1970's.* Chicago: Playboy Press, 1974.

A comprehensive study of the changes in sexual attitudes and behavior of American men and women. The authors describe how men and women feel in areas such as premarital sex, marital sex, extramarital sex and homosexuality. This is the most comprehensive survey of its kind since Kinsey.

Kallman, F. "Genetic aspects of sex determination and sexual maturation potential in men." In G. Winokur (Ed.), *Determinants of human sexual behavior.* Springfield, Ill.: Charles C. Thomas, 1963.

A good description of male and female chromosome compliments and various chromosomal abberrations. Technical but readable.

Kaplan, H. S. *The illustrated manual of sex therapy.* New York: Quadrangle/New York Times, 1975.

The illustrations and readable text present methods for dealing with sexual dysfunctions.

Kerr, C. *Sex for women.* New York: Grove Press, 1977.

Written for women who have sexual concerns though men may find it helpful in understanding their sexual partners.

Kinsey, A., Pomeroy, W., and Martin, C. *Sexual behavior in the human male.* Philadelphia: W. B. Saunders, 1948.

The now classic study of male sexual behavior includes detailed frequencies of various types of sexual activities including petting, masturbation, marital sex, prostitution and homosexuality.

Kinsey, A., Pomeroy, W., Martin, C. and Gebhard, P. *Sexual behavior in the human female.* Philadelphia: W. B. Saunders, 1953.

This is the most comprehensive survey of female sexuality which is still of great value today in spite of many methodological flaws.

Kirkendall, L. A. "A new bill of sexual rights and responsibilities." *The Humanist,* January/February, 1976, 4-6.

This bill of rights is similar to the one presented in the text but tends to be somewhat broader in scope.

Layman, W. A. "The 'saint or sinner' syndrome: Separation of love and sex by women." *Medical Aspects of Human Sexuality,* August, 1976, 46–53.

Layman describes a condition that can result from sex guilt in women.

Malinowski, B. *The sexual life of savages in North-Western Melanesia.* New York: Halycon House, 1929.

A detailed anthropological study of the sexual customs of a small society in the South Pacific.

Marshall, D. and Suggs, R. *Human sexual behavior in the ethnographic spectrum.* Englewood Cliffs, N.J.: Prentice Hall, 1972.

An excellent collection of anthropological and sociological studies of many societies in the East and West.

Mathis, J. "The madonna-prostitute syndrome." *Medical Aspects of Human Sexuality,* January, 1971, pp 202ff.

Mathis describes one rather dramatic condition that can result from sex guilt in men.

Mittwoch, U. *Genetics of sex differentiation.* New York: Academic Press, 1973.

Basic introduction into genetics with emphasis on male and female chromosomes; sex differentiation and chromosomal sex errors.

Morris, J. *Conundrum.* New York: Harcourt Brace Jovanovitch, 1974.

A sensitive account of a transsexual journalist who after a successful marriage decided to undergo sex reassignment surgery.

Murstein, B. *Love, sex and marriage through the ages.* New York: Springer, 1974.

A good description of the sexual customs and attitudes from the time of the Old Testament through the Middle Ages, Renaissance, Age of Reason and Victorian times to the present.

Myers, L. "The high cost of MDeity's prudery." In S. Gordon and R. W. Libby (eds.), *Sexuality Today and Tomorrow.* North Scituate, Mass.: Duxbury, 1976.

Myers points out that physicians, the experts many people turn to for advice, can be ignorant and judgmental about sexual issues.

Nerebeck, G. "The myriad motives for sex." In L. Gross (ed.), *Sexual behavior: Current issues.* Flushing, N.Y.: Spectrum, 1974.

This chapter and the commentaries that follow it may help readers explore their own motives for having sex.

Nilsson, L. *A child is born.* New York: Delacorte Press, 1977.

A Scandinavian photographer captures the mystery of birth. The book contains excellent photographs of human reproduction from conception to birth.

O'Neill, V. and O'Neill, G. *Open marriage.* New York: M. Evans Co., 1972.

The authors argue that open marriage provides marital partners with opportunities to develop intimate relationships with other people outside the marital relationship and thereby allows marriage partners to realize more of their potential.

Ottenheimer, L. "Unconscious factors in choice of a mate." *Medical Aspects of Human Sexuality,* March, 1971.

This readable article illustrates the psychoanalytic notion that unconscious personality factors can exert an influence over overt behavior.

Pike, J. A. *You and the new morality.* New York: Harper & Row, 1967.

Pike uses numerous case histories to illustrate the principles of situation ethics.

Placeliere, R. *Love in ancient Greece.* New York: Crown Publishers, Inc., 1962.

An authentic account of the sexual mores and customs of the ancient Greeks from Homer to the Hellenistic time.

Rainwater, L. "Some aspects of lower class sexuality." *Journal of Social Issues,* 1966, 2, 96–107.

A study examining the effects of poverty and lower social class status upon sexual behavior. The author noted that lower class couples are less likely to find their sexual relations gratifying than members of higher social classes.

Ramey, E. "Men's cycles (They have them too, you know)." *Ms. Magazine,* Spring 1972, 8-14.

A discussion of the hormonal fluctuations in men. In a longitudinal study the author discovered a 30 day ebb and flow of testosterone in men that is accompanied by mood changes.

Reiss, I. "Social class and premarital permissiveness among Negroes and whites." *American Sociological Review*, 1964, *29*, 688-698.

A discussion of premarital sex by a prominent sociologist which shows that blacks are generally more inclined to accept premarital permissiveness than whites.

Rubin, I. *Sexual life after sixty*. New York: Basic Books, 1965.

An authoritative book discussing the sex lives of elderly people. Many examples are provided to show that the later years are not sexless and that sexual responsiveness does not fade with age.

Rubin, Z. *Liking and loving: An invitation to social psychology*. New York: Holt, Rinehart & Winston, 1973.

This paperback book contains a great deal of information about interpersonal relationships and is as enjoyable to read as any novel.

Ryckman, R. *Theories of personality*. New York: D. Van Nostrand, 1978.

This undergraduate text will provide the reader with some more detailed information about the psychoanalytic and social learning theories.

Safran, C. "What men do to women on the job." *Redbook*, November, 1976. 149ff.

Several women who have experienced sexual harassment describe their experiences and the author offers suggestions about what can be done about it.

Skinner, B. F. *Walden Two*. New York: MacMillan, 1969.

A fictional outline of a utopian society in which sexuality is practiced on a communal basis.

Weinman Lear, M. "Is there a male menopause?" *New York Times Magazine,* January 28, 1973.

A survey of studies which show that divorces, extramarital affairs, male personality disturbances and sex problems peak sharply between the ages of 40 and 60 creating a male midlife crisis.

Glossary

afterbirth The placenta and fetal membranes expelled from the uterus after childbirth.

amnion The membrane which surrounds the developing fetus; also called bag of waters because it contains the amniotic fluid.

amniocentesis A procedure in which amniotic fluid is withdrawn from the amnion to test for genetic abnormalities prior to birth.

anal stage In psychoanalytic theory, the second stage of psychosexual development during which the primary erogenous zone is the anus.

androgen Collective term for male sex hormone; *see testosterone.*

androgen insensitivity syndrome A clinical condition in which genetic males develop female sex characteristics becase of the lack of responsiveness to androgen; *see testicular feminization.*

androgenital syndrome A clinical condition in females in which excessive androgen production leads to the masculinization of the external genitalia; can be treated with hormone therapy if the condition is recognized early.

androgyny Having both masculine and feminine personality characteristics.

androsperm Sperm that carries the Y chromosome; produces male offspring.

anima According to Carl Jung, men's ability to experience and understand women; feminine aspect in a man's personality.

antinomianism An approach to ethics that states that no rules or principles can be applied to moral decisions. Closely identified with existentialism.

aphrodisiac A substance thought to increase sexual arousal, desire, and/or potency.

apotemnophilia Erotic attraction or obsession for persons whose legs have been amputated.

autoeroticism Self-stimulation of the genitals to the point of sexual arousal; *see masturbation.*

bestiality An unconventional sexual variation in which a person engages in sexual contact with animals; *see also zoophilia.*

blastocyst Cluster of cells after fertilization.

bondage Use of physical restraints, such as ropes and chains, for sexual arousal.

case study method Intensive investigation of an individual, group of individuals, or a society.

castration Surgical removal of the testes.

cervix Lower bottle shaped portion of the uterus.

chancre Skin lesion symptomatic of syphilis.

chancroid Venereal disease characterized by ulceration at the points of physical contact.

chorion The outer envelope of the fertilized egg from which the placenta develops.

chorionic gonadotrophins Hormones secreted by the placenta that maintains the corpus luteum; can be detected in the urine of pregnant women two weeks after conception.

circumcision Surgical removal of the foreskin from the penis.

classical conditioning A form of learning, first identified by Pavlov, in which behavior comes to be elicited by a formerly neutral stimulus.

climacteric Physical and psychological changes that occur at the termination of menstruation in women and reduction in sex-steroid production in both sexes; also called *menopause* or *change of life.*

clitoris Organ which is the center of female erotic arousal. It is found at the upper apex of the labia minora, the organ in the female that acts as the receptor and transmitter of sexual stimuli.

code ethics *See legalism.*

cognitive events In social learning theory, thoughts, beliefs, or values that influence behavior.

coitus Sexual intercourse.

coitus interruptus A method of birth control in which the male withdraws the penis from the vagina prior to ejaculation; *see withdrawal.*

colostrum   Yellow substance secreted from the nipples during late pregnancy and immediately after birth which contains nutritious substances and anti-bodies that protect an infant from certain diseases.

co-marital sex   Sexual relations of a married couple with at least one other person; also called *swinging*.

coming out   A term to indicate the act of making one's homosexual orientation public.

companionate love   Feelings of affection and liking that couples of longstanding have for one another.

condom   A contraceptive device for males which consists of a rubber or animal membrane sheath that is pulled over the erect penis before intercourse begins.

contraception   Birth control device that interferes with the fertilization of the ovum by the sperm.

corpus luteum   A yellow mass (yellow body) which develops in the ovarian follicle and secretes progesterone.

correlational research   Research techniques that identify the degree of association between two sets of variables.

cunnilingus   Oral stimulation of female genitalia, usually the labia and clitoris.

diaphragm   A rubber or latex contraceptive device consisting of a dome-shaped cap held by a metal spring that is placed in the back of the vagina to the back of the cervix.

dilation and curretage (D & C)   Abortion technique in which the content of the uterus is scraped out.

Don Juan   In psychoanalytic theory, a man who is driven to make numerous sexual conquests in an attempt to reduce castration anxiety.

ectopic pregnancy   Pregnancy in which the fetus develops outside the uterus, usually in the Fallopian tube or abdominal cavity.

edema   Water retention; common problem during pregnancy.

ego   In psychoanalytic theory, the psychological mechanism that mediates the demands of the id and the constraints of the external world.

ejaculation   Expulsion of semen and sperm during male orgasm.

ejaculatory incompetence   An inability of the man to ejaculate within the vagina.

Electra complex   In psychoanalytic theory, the counterpart for girls of the Oedipus complex.

embryo   Human organism at the earliest stage of prenatal development; the period of the embryo lasts for two months following conception.

endometrium   Lining of the uterus.

epididymis   Network of highly coiled tubes which adhere to the testicles; site of sperm maturation.

episiotomy   Surgical incision made from the vagina toward the anus to avoid the tearing of vaginal tissues during childbirth.

equity theory   In social psychology, a theory that two people enter a relationship when it is profitable for both of them.

erectile failure   The inability of the man to achieve or maintain an erection.

erection   Elevation of the penis and hardening or stiffening activity during sexual arousal.

estrogen   Any of several femal sex hormones produced chiefly in the ovaries.

estrogen replacement therapy (ERT)   Hormone treatment which substitutes synthetic estrogen to overcome the loss of estrogen after menopause.

excitement phase   In the Masters and Johnson scheme of the sexual response cycle, the phase during which male and female sex organs show physiological changes as a function of sexual arousal.

experimental research   Research techniques that manipulate one variable to determine its effects upon a second variable.

Fallopian tubes   Tubes connecting the ovaries with the uterus that channel the ovum from the ovaries to the uterus.

fellatio   Oral stimulation of the penis.

fetish   Object needed for sexual arousal, such as leather, boots, lingerie.

fetus   Human organism in later phase of prenatal development; the period of the fetus lasts from the ninth week after conception until birth.

filtering model   A theory of mate selection in which couples pass through stages in the development of their relationship.

flagellation   Whip-like movement of the sperm. *See also sadism*, that is, whipping partner for erotic gratification.

flagellum   Tail of the sperm.

flapper   In the 1920s, a young woman considered bold and unconventional.

follicle A microscopic sac on the surface of an ovary which contains the developing ovum.

follicle-stimulating hormone (FSH) A hormone secreted by the pituitary which stimulates follicle development in females and sperm production in males.

frenum Delicate fold of skin connecting the skin of the shaft of the penis with the head of the penis.

gain-loss theory In social psychology, a theory that gains or losses are more potent than consistent rewards or punishments.

genitals Sex organs.

genital warts A type of venereal virus disease that is characterized by warts on and/or proximal to the genitals.

glans penis Head of the penis.

gonad Male and female sex gland; testicle (male), and ovary (female).

gonadotropins Male and female sex hormones.

gonorrhea Venereal disease caused by the virus *Neisseria gonorrhea*.

gynosperm Sperm that carries X chromosome; produces female offspring.

hetaerae Pleasure girls in ancient Greece who served their masters aesthetically, sensually, intellectually and sexually.

hermaphroditism A clinical condition in which a person has both male and female physical sex characteristics, usually with one sex dominating.

herpes Venereal virus disease characterized by painful blisters or bumps on the genitals.

Herpes simplex virus Virus causing herpes; occurs as type I and II.

homogamy Sociological concept according to which people have a tendency to select marriage partners who resemble them in certain ways such as age, religious and social class background.

homosexuality Sexual relations with or sexual attraction to members of one's own sex; opposite of heterosexuality.

hot flash Common symptom of menopause, referring to sudden heat sensation.

hymen The membrane partially covering the vaginal opening, also called the *maidenhead*.

hysterical conversion reaction A psychological disorder in which anxiety is expressed in a physical symptom.

hysterical neurosis In psychoanalytic theory, a psychological disorder characterized by penis envy in women and castration anxiety in men.

id In psychoanalytic theory, the innate, biological drives comprised of the libido and the death instinct.

identification In psychoanalytic theory, the process by which children resolve the Oedipal conflict; they attempt to behave similarly to the same-sexed parent.

implantation The burrowing of the fertilized egg into the lining of the uterus.

incest Sexual relations among family members.

infibulation Body piercing involving mutilation of genitalia.

interstitial cell-stimulating hormone (ICSH) A hormone secreted by the pituitary which stimulates the maturation of sperm cells in males; corresponds to the luteinizing hormone (LH) in females.

intrauterine device (IUD) Contraceptive device made of metal or plastic inserted into the uterus by a physician.

in vitro fertilization A procedure by which an ovum is removed from the woman and fertilized in the laboratory. The embryo is then implanted in the uterus.

in vivo desensitization A treatment technique in which sexual anxiety is reduced by gradually exposing the individual to anxiety eliciting situations.

keloid markings Body decorations popular among the Bala women of the Congo.

Klinefelter's syndrome (XXY) A chromosomal abnormality in males associated with underdeveloped sex organs, sterility, and often mental retardation.

labia majora Outer folds of skin surrounding the vaginal opening.

labia minora Inner folds of skin surrounding the vaginal opening.

laboratory research Research that is conducted under highly structured and controlled conditions.

lactation Production of milk by the breasts; usually begins within three days after childbirth.

lactogenic hormone (LH) A hormone secreted by the pituitary which stimulates milk production in the breasts.

laparoscopy Method of sterilization in which the fallopian tubes are cut and cauterized through abdominal incision.

legalism An approach to ethics in which moral standards are prescribed by an authoritative (usually religious) source. Also referred to as code ethics.

lesbianism Female homosexuality.

libido In psychoanalytic theory, the instinctual sexual drive.

lightening Descent of the fetus' head into the cervix during late pregnancy.

luteinizing hormone (LH) A hormone secreted by the pituitary which stimulates ovulation and the formation of the corpus luteum.

mammary glands Female breasts.

masochism Obtaining sexual gratification from receiving pain.

masturbation Self stimulation of genitals to sexual arousal; auto-eroticism.

mating gradient Tendency of men to marry downward in age, education, or social class, or tendency for women to marry upward along the same dimensions.

menarche First menstrual period.

menopause Cessation of the menstrual cycle.

menstruation Periodic shedding of the endometrium if pregnancy does not occur.

mental apparatus In psychoanalytic theory, it consists of the three psychological mechanisms: id, ego, and superego.

missionary position In sexual intercourse, both partners are lying down with the man on top.

monogamy Marriage of one man to one woman.

mons pubis A mound of fatty tissue in women under the pubic hair; also called *mons* or *mons veneris*.

moral anxiety In psychoanalytic theory, emotional arousal in response to violations of the standards of the superego.

motoro Sleep crawling tradition in Polynesia in which young men slip into the family sleeping room and have intercourse with the young girl amid her parents and relatives.

Muellerian duct A pair of ducts found in the embryo from which the female reproductive system develops.

multilateral marriage Group marriage.

myotonia Tightening of the muscles of the pelvic floor during sexual arousal.

necrophilia Sexual attraction to or intercourse with corpses.

Neisseria gonorrhea Virus causing gonorrhea.

neurotic anxiety In psychoanalytic theory, a fear that one will lose control of the instincts which may result in punishment.

nonspecific urethritis (NSU) A venereal disease involving frequent and/or painful irritation.

observational learning A form of learning in which behaviors are acquired via observation of models.

Oedipal conflict In psychoanalytic theory, the development of feelings of sexual attraction toward the opposite-sexed parent and feelings of jealousy and hostility of the same-sexed parent.

operant conditioning A form of learning in which behaviors are acquired via reinforcement.

onanism Withdrawal of the penis from the vagina before orgasm, *coitus interruptus*; sometimes used to refer to *masturbation*.

oral stage In psychoanalytic theory, the first stage of psycho-sexual development. During this stage, the erogenous zone is the mouth and gums.

orgasm Climax and release of sexual tension.

orgasmic dysfunction An inability of the woman to reach orgasm.

orgasmic phase In the Masters and Johnson scheme of the sexual response cycle phase during which orgasm takes place.

ovarian dysgenesis Chromosomal abnormality in women in which an X chromosome is missing; *see Turner's syndrome.*

ovary Paired sex glands in females that house eggs and produce sex hormones.

oviduct Tube connecting the ovary with the uterus; *see Fallopian tube.*

ovulation Release of a mature egg from the ovary.

ovum Female reproductive cell (egg); pl. ova.

partialism Obtaining sexual gratification by looking at specific body parts such as breasts or buttocks.

parturition Childbirth.

pause technique Used in the treatment of premature ejaculation whereby the man is instructed to cease coital movements when he feels the urge to ejaculate.

pederasty Sexual relations between a man and adolescent boy, prevalent tradition in ancient Greece.

pedophilia Sexual attraction to or intercourse with children.

penile plethysmograph A clinical device to measure sexual arousal in men by detecting changes in penile volume.

penile strain gauge A clinical device to measure sexual arousal in men by detecting changes in penile circumference.

penis envy Concept in psychoanalytic theory suggesting that the woman envies the man for his possession of a penis.

phallic stage In psychoanalytic theory, the third stage of psychosexual development during which the primary erogenous zone is the genitals.

phallus Penis, usually erect.

phimosis Tight fitting foreskin that cannot be drawn back over the head of the penis.

placenta Organ of fetal and maternal exchange of oxygen, nutritional materials and waste products.

plateau phase A phase characterized by the excitement phase going no higher while the body prepares to move into the orgasmic phase.

Plissit model A conceptual approach to the treatment of sexual dysfunctions that provides four levels of therapeutic intervention.

polyandry Marriage of one woman to several men at the same time.

polygyny Marriage of one man to several women at the same time.

postpartum blues Feelings of depression, irritability and fatigue sometimes experienced after childbirth.

premature ejaculation Ejaculation before you want to.

prepuce Foreskin of the penis.

primary impotence A condition in which the man has never had an erection sufficient to complete coitus.

primary orgasmic dysfunction A condition in which a woman has never experienced orgasm under any circumstance.

progesterone Female hormone produced by the *corpus luteum* in the ovaries.

prolactin A hormone secreted by the pituitary which induces lactation.

prostate The gland in the male that secretes a fluid that is a component of semen.

prostitution Indiscriminate sexual relationships for payment.

pseudohermaphroditism A clinical condition in which a person has a mixture of female and male reproductive structures but has the sex glands (testes or ovaries) of one sex.

psychic determinism In psychoanalytic theory, the principle that behavior is determined by unconscious material.

pudendum External female sex organs (pl. pudenda).

quickening First fetal movements perceived by the mother.

rape Violent, forcible sexual act committed on an unwilling victim.

reality anxiety In psychoanalytic theory, emotional arousal in situations of realistic external danger.

refractory phase In the Masters and Johnson scheme of the sexual response cycle, the phase following orgasm where the male is temporarily not responsive to sexual stimulation.

repression A psychological mechanism whereby conscious thoughts, feelings and fantasies are displaced to the unconscious.

resolution phase In the Masters and Johnson scheme of the sexual response cycle the phase during which male and female sex organs return to their non-aroused state.

rhythm method Method of birth control in which a woman abstains from intercourse for several days before and after ovulation.

romantic love A state of intense affectionate absorption in another person.

sadism Infliction of pain on a partner for sexual gratification.

saline injection Abortion technique in which amniotic fluid is withdrawn and replaced by saline solution to induce labor.

scoptophilia A form of voyeurism which focuses on the observation of sexual acts or the genitals.

scrotum The pouch of skin which contains the male testes and their accessory organs.

secondary impotence A condition in which the man has at least some history of successful sexual functioning but currently suffers from erectile failure.

secondary orgasmic dysfunction A condition in which the woman has had at least some history of successful sexual functioning, but is unable to reach orgasm at present.

semen Fluid comprised of secretions from the prostate gland and seminal vesicles that is ejaculated from the penis during orgasm and contains sperm.

seminal vesicles Two pouches behind the bladder that secrete a fluid comprising semen.

seminiferous tubules Highly coiled tubes in the male testes which produce sperm.

sensate-focus Exercises used in treatment of sexual dysfunctions in which partners are instructed to give each other nongenital pleasure.

serial monogamy Pattern of marriage, divorce, remarriage, and subsequent divorce.

sex chromatin Dark staining spot found in the cells of females; also called Barr body.

sexual dysfunction An inability to engage in, or derive satisfaction from sexual intercourse.

sperm Male reproductive cell; also called spermatozoon, pl. spermatozoa.

spermatogenesis Sperm production.

spermicides Contraceptive foams, jellies, creams, or suppositories that contain chemicals that kill the sperm.

squeeze technique Used in treatment of premature ejaculation whereby the woman applies digital pressure to the penis when her partner feels the urge to ejaculate.

stimulus-value-role theory A filtering model of mate selection.

strong continuity theories With regard to abortion, the position that states that human existence begins at the moment of conception.

strong discontinuity theories With regard to abortion, the position that the fetus has no ethically significant status.

superego In psychoanalytic theory, the psychological mechanism that represents internalized societal standards; sometimes referred to as the internalized parents or conscience.

superincision Extreme version of circumcision practiced by a number of societies in the South Pacific.

survey method Research that collects a limited amount of information from a large number of individuals.

swinging Sexual relations of a couple with at least one other person; *see also co-marital sex.*

syphilis A venereal disease caused by the virus *Treponema pallidum.*

systematic desensitization A behavior therapy technique whereby sexual anxieties are gradually reduced.

testicular feminization A clinical condition in genetic males who develop female sex characteristics because of lack of responsiveness to androgen; *see androgen insensitivity syndrome.*

testes Male reproductive glands located in the scrotum that manufacture sperm and sex hormones.

testosterone Male sex hormone produced in the interstitial cells of the testes.

toxemia Retention of toxic body wastes during pregnancy.

transsexualism A sexual variation in which a person feels he or she is of one sex, but is trapped in the body of the opposite sex.

transvestism Sexual behavior in which a person dresses in the clothing of the opposite sex for sexual gratification.

Treponema pallidum Virus causing syphilis.

trimester Period of three consecutive months during pregnancy.

triple X syndrome (XXX) Chromosomal abnormality in women caused by the presence of an additional X chromosome.

tubal ligation Method of sterilization in which the Fallopian tubes are tied to prevent the passage of ovum.

Turner's syndrome (Xo) Chromosomal abnormality in females associated with underdeveloped sex organs, short stature, infertility and sometimes mental retardation; also called *ovarian dysgenesis.*

unconscious In psychoanalytic theory, feelings, thoughts, and fantasies of which the individual is unaware.

uterus Female organ in which the fetus develops.

vacuum extraction Abortion technique in which the content of the uterus is sucked out; also called vacuum aspiration.

vagina Barrel-shaped genital organ in females which receives the penis during intercourse.

vaginal douche Washing out the vagina after intercourse or for hygienic purposes.

vaginal photoplethysmograph A device to measure sexual arousal in women by detecting changes in vaginal vasocongestion.

vaginismus An involuntary contraction of the vaginal muscles that prevents the insertion of the penis.

value consensus Agreement between couples on issues such as religion, child rearing, sex roles, etc.

vasectomy Surgical method of birth control for males in which a small section of the vas deferens is cut out then tied so that the ejaculate is free of sperm.

vasocongestion Swelling of male and female sex organs during sexual excitement.

vas (ductus) deferens Duct in the male reproductive system which conveys sperm from the testes to the urethra.

venereal disease Any contagious sexually transmitted disease.

voyeurism Obtaining sexual gratification from viewing members of the opposite sex in partial undress, total undress, or in some sexual activity.

vulva External female sex organs including the labia majora, the labia minora, the clitoris, and the vaginal opening.

weak continuity theories With regard to abortion, the position that human existence begins some time after conception; usually at end of first trimester or quickening.

weak discontinuity theories With regard to abortion, the position that the fetus does have a special status but is not fully equivalent to human life.

withdrawal method A method of birth control in which the male withdraws the penis from the vagina prior to ejaculation; *see coitus interruptus.*

Wolffian duct Duct system found in the embryo from which the male reproductive system develops.

XYY syndrome Chromosomal abnormality in males caused by the presence of an extra Y chromosome.

zoophilia Sexual contact with animals; *see bestiality.*

zygote Fertilized egg.

Name Index

A

Abarnabel, A. 21, 27, 37
Abraham, K. 417, 425
Abrahams, D. 249
Abrahamsen, D. 301, 312
Acton, W. 36
Agras, S. 366, 367
Almeda, J. 135
Alsikam, M. 190, 193
American Law Institute 432, 443
American Medical Association 10
American Psychiatric Association 63, 341, 342, 367, 378
Amir, M. 355, 356, 357, 367, 441, 443
Anderson, V. E. 248, 261
Annon, J. 334, 337
Aquinas, Thomas 29
Argyle, M. 434, 444
Aron, A. 223, 241, 253, 261
Aronson, E. 246, 249, 260
Aronson, V. 263
Ascher, L. M. 333, 337
Associated Press 406, 409
Athanasiou, R. 225, 241
Ausubel, D. 305, 313

B

Baker, D. 121, 137
Baker, L. D. 337
Bandura, A. 75, 76, 83, 376, 387, 397, 409
Barlow, D. 366, 367
Barmack, J. 65
Barnhart, S. A. 249, 261
Barr, M. L. 118, 134
Bar-Tal, D. 250, 260
Bartel, G. 278, 279, 280, 289
Beach, F. A. 112, 115, 121, 134, 196, 197, 214, 223, 241, 375, 377, 387, 388, 389, 410
Beauchamp, T. L. 436, 443
Beigel, H. 225, 241
Bell, A. P. 372, 374, 379, 387
Bell, R. 209, 269, 289
Bell, R. R. 271, 289
Bem, S. 207, 214, 406, 409
Benjamin, H. 357, 361, 367
Bennett, W. 190, 193
Bentler, P. 357, 369

Bergler, E. 56, 64
Berkowitz, L. 434, 443
Berlin, H. 305, 313
Berman, E. 294, 313
Bernard, J. 43, 64, 267, 289
Bersheid, E. 245, 248, 249, 251, 254, 255, 257, 258, 260, 261, 263
Bertram, E. G. 118, 134
Bibring, G. 139, 140, 174
Bieber, I. 83, 373, 375, 381, 384, 385, 387
Blank, D. 122, 135
Blaylock, B. 248, 260
Blitch, J. W. 385, 388
Blos, P. 347, 369
Blum, G. S. 72, 73
Blumer, D. 114, 115
Blumstein, P. W. 382, 383, 388
Bond, J. 352, 353, 367
Borgaonkar, D. 121, 131
Bornstein, B. 311, 313
Bourne, P. G. 375, 389
Bowman, K. 301, 313
Brady, J. P. 334, 337
Brandon, S. 20, 38
Brandsma, J. 364, 368
Brazelton, T. 150, 174
Brecher, E. M. 45, 64, 133, 134, 281, 289
Bregman, S. 112, 115
Brenton, M. 121, 136
Briddell, D. W. 76, 77, 83, 226, 241
Briggs, J. 120, 135
Brittain, R. 121, 136
Broderick, C. 190, 193
Brothen, T. 245, 260
Broverman, D. M. 48, 64, 409
Broverman, I. K. 48, 64, 404, 409
Browning, E. B. 54
Brownmiller, S. 357, 367
Bryant, C. 367
Buchan, W. 134, 135
Buck, C. 346, 347, 368
Bucy, P. 113, 116
Bullough, V. 19, 29, 38
Burgess, J. 248, 258, 260
Burton, R. 206
Bustos, A. A. 250, 262
Butler, J. 153, 154, 175
Butler, R. 301, 303, 313

Byrne, D. 237, 241, 247, 248, 260, 400, 410

C

Caddy, G. R. 77, 83, 225, 241
Caird, W. K. 334, 337
Calderone, N. 27, 39
Calmas, W. 344, 367
Cantor, N. 27, 39
Capellanus, A. 31, 39
Capps, C. F. 404
Carlisle, J. M. 74, 83, 354, 369, 376
Carnegie, D. 246, 261
Carrier, J. 377, 388
Cary, M. S. 250, 261
Casey, M. 122, 135
Chang, J. 206, 207, 214
Chesser, E. 35, 39
Chiappa, J. 131, 135
Christenson, C. V. 225, 241, 344, 351, 355, 356, 368, 440, 443
Clanton, G. 275, 283, 289, 290
Clark, A. 271
Clark, G. 121, 137
Clarkson, F. E. 48, 409
Clayton, P. 311, 313
Clemens, L. G. 375, 388
Cohen, M. 344, 367
Cole, C. 281, 290
Cole, T. 112, 113, 115
Coleman, J. C. 328, 337
Colles, J. S. 13
Collins, D. K. 375, 389
Collins, G. 397, 410
Colton, H. 4, 5, 13
Comar, A. 115
Comfort, A. 227, 241
Commission on Human Sexuality 296, 313
Commission on Population Growth 172, 174
Conan, P. 122, 135
Conger, J. C. 80, 84
Conger, J. J. 415, 426
Conover, P. 282, 290
Constantine, J. 282, 283, 290
Constantine, L. 282, 283, 290
Coyer, S. 49, 64
Croake, J. 61, 65
Cross, H. J. 420, 425

461

Subject Index

Photo Credits